The Concept
of the Social in Uniting
the Humanities and
Social Sciences

MICHAEL E. BROWN

The Concept
of the Social in Uniting
the Humanities and
Social Sciences

TEMPLE UNIVERSITY PRESS
PHILADELPHIA

TEMPLE UNIVERSITY PRESS
Philadelphia, Pennsylvania 19122
www.temple.edu/tempress

Library of Congress Cataloging-in-Publication Data

Brown, Michael E., 1935–
    The concept of the social in uniting the humanities and social
sciences / Michael E. Brown.
        pages cm
    Includes bibliographical references and index.
    ISBN 978-1-4399-1015-3 (hardback : alk. paper) —
ISBN 978-1-4399-1017-7 (e-book)   1. Social sciences.
2. Humanities.   I. Title.
    H61.B678 2014
    300.1—dc23
                                                        2014003998

ISBN 978-1-4399-1016-0 (paperback : alk. paper)

Printed in the United States of America

2 4 6 8 9 7 5 3 1

Contents

Introduction: *What Is Human about Human Affairs?*   1

I SOCIALITY: *THE PROBLEM OF DEFINITION*

1 The Urgency of Defining the Social   23

2 Society as a Basic Fact   33

3 Dependence and Autonomy   52

4 The Certainty of the Social as the Basic Fact   76

5 The Sociality of Agency   101

6 Models, Theory, and Theorizing   114

7 Theorizing   131

8 Historicism and Its Alternative   150

9 Social Facts, Situations, and Moral Stakes   163

II SOCIAL ACTION

10 Can "the Social" Be a Proper Object of Theory?   183

11 Further Problems in Theorizing the Social   196

12 Social Action as Action   208

13 The Self of the Actor   223

14 Self and Situation   233

15 Self and Agency   252

16 Social Action Reconsidered   269

III SUBJECTS AND SITUATIONS

17 Overview   287

18 Causes of Failure in the Social Sciences   302

19 Objects and Their Subjects   323

20 The Positive Sense of "Situation"   343

21 Practices, Situations, and Inter-subjectivity   352

22 Criticism, Inter-subjectivity, and Collective Enunciation   377

23 Criticism and Human Affairs   384

24 Collective Enunciation   399

25 Subjectivity and Objectivity   413

26 Summary, Reprise, and Transition   432

Acknowledgments   439

Notes   441

References   495

Index   509

The Concept
of the Social in Uniting
the Humanities and
Social Sciences

Introduction

What Is Human about Human Affairs?

Humans are individuals through and through: they are born alone; they live and decide alone; they die alone, and much of their labor is spent in a never completely successful effort to close down the gap of their separation from their neighbors and God. Humans are social through and through: the conception that gives them existence and the childbirth that brings them into the world . . . are social acts; the food that becomes their physical substance, the language with which they think, decide, and perhaps rebel, are socially given. The relations between these counter-truths are deep and complex. As long as this is true, there can be no adequate theory of the relation of the individual to society, and hence no adequate statement of the relation of the poet to society. —PAUL RAMSEY, "Society and Poetry"

The most common denominator of most uses of the word society is the fact of sociation, animal or human. . . . In the social thought of the twentieth century two uses of the word are distinctive. In one, society has a negative, even pejorative cast; in the other, laudatory. In the first, society is contrasted deprecatingly with COMMUNITY. In the second, society is counterposed to the political state's sovereign power. —ROBERT NISBET, "Society"

And we have already established that a society is not a group, nor a grouping of groups, nor even struggling groupings of groups. *Collectives* are both the matrix of groups and their grave; they remain as the indefinite sociality of the practico-inert, nourishing groups, maintaining them and transcending them everywhere by their indefinite multiplicity. Where there are several groups, the collective is either a mediation or battlefield. —JEAN-PAUL SARTRE, *Critique of Dialectical Reason*

Individuals, not groups, are the ultimate moral claimants in a democracy, but this is consistent with taking cultures into account in considering the moral claims of individuals and groups that speak on their behalf.
—AMY GUTMANN, *Identity in Democracy*

It is widely agreed that the individual is, as Amy Gutmann puts it, "the ulti-mate moral claimants in a democracy" (2003, 57). I interpret this to mean that individual persons are the ultimate *referents of* moral discourse. While it is difficult to disagree with this statement, it poses familiar and apparently intractable problems for those disciplines in the social sciences and humanities

for which the ontological priority of society is fundamental to their understanding of human affairs. In this and other respects, the claim itself is fatefully
ambiguous. The ambiguity arises in part because of a failure to clarify the idea
of the social in a way that brings the idea of individuality into correspondence
with it without relying on a metaphysical foundation for the distinction. The
problem has to do with the coherence of our general notion of human affairs,
which I discuss in regard to two related theses: first, *as things stand*, the human sciences share a common object, and second, this unifies them theoretically as a single field. I try to show that this shared object is an irreducible
and irrepressible sociality and that these qualities are evident when the social
is identified as a course of activity and described according to conditions of
agency-dependent objectivity. This involves showing, first, that sociality, so understood, is taken for granted as logically prior to prevailing theories and as the
ultimate object of theoretical concern; second, that it is radically transformed
by its standard representations into something altogether foreign to its logically
prior conception; and third, that there are significant consequences of returning to that sub-theoretical conception for our very notion of theory no less than
for formulating and evaluating specific theories.

The idea that the human sciences form a single field raises a number of
interrelated issues. For one, it is necessary to explain how it is that the common object is always presupposed but virtually never formulated as a concept.
Moreover, if it turns out to be true that the language of individuality, which
necessarily takes the skin as a natural boundary, and the language of agency
in action, which does not require that assumption, are significantly distinct, as
I suggest in Part I, then the theoretical relationship between individuality and
sociality will be dramatically different from its familiar representations and
can be expected to have different consequences for our notions of moral discourse, critical thought, and practical deliberation. Finally, if one can agree that
theory in the human sciences is under a logical as well as a moral obligation to
find itself in its object and its object in itself—that is, to recognize the capacity
to theorize in the very life that it attributes to its object and to acknowledge that
same form of life as immanent to theorizing itself—then theory, as defined,
must be understood in relation to its fundamental condition, which is the activity of theorizing. In that case, it is a mistake, as I try to show in Parts II and III,
to assume that the familiar distinction between the order of presentation and
the order of justification is valid for setting criteria for evaluating theoretical
works. However, the philosophical and moral appeal of Gutmann's proposition
and its virtually axiomatic status in all studies of human affairs have made it
difficult if not impossible to theorize the sub-theoretical idea of the social and,
perhaps more controversially, for the human sciences to be able to resolve or at
least negotiate the ontological ambiguities of the proposition itself in order to
reclaim the social as their common object. A brief discussion may help clarify
the significance of this problem.

Gutmann's proposition assumes, first, that the concept of democracy is independent of the concept of society in the modern sense of the term and, second, that the individual is a distinct and complete entity prior to its reference in moral discourse. It is necessary to my argument that both assumptions are legitimately subject to doubt. It may be obvious that democracy is possible only within society, but it would be premature and possibly wrong to say that society is possible without its being *in some sense* democratic. Neither term is clearly enough defined in current social, political, and philosophical thought to preclude the possibility of an essential connection between them, or even the possibility of their identity, or to allow each to be conceptualized independently of the other. On the one hand, a narrow technical definition of both terms might preclude the possibility of an essential connection, but at the sacrifice of what they are ordinarily intended to bring to notice. On the other hand, broad definitions are likely to trivialize the question or leave it undecidable.

Beyond the question of how to define "society," "democracy," and "individuality," to be able to say that the individual is a distinct and complete entity such that she can become the moral referent of last resort depends on a particular conception of moral discourse and, therefore, on a corresponding sense of what is meant by "discourse." Whatever else might be said about the more general idea, it seems clear that moral discourse cannot be conceived of within and according to the boundaries of one or another specialized discipline. Therefore it must be conceived of at some other level of knowledge. If individuality, as the index of moral discourse, takes its meaning within and draws its significance from a supra-disciplinary discourse, and if the concept of the individual is constituted as a referent within it rather than within any particular specialized discipline, then two related questions must be addressed before deciding what is required of an ultimate referent of moral discourse. The first is "What is moral discourse?" and the second is "What makes it supra-disciplinary?" These questions presuppose something of an answer to a yet more fundamental question that is unavoidable in all the human sciences: What is distinctively human about human affairs such that one can speak intelligibly about moral discourse and its ultimate referent and can reasonably consider its value in and significance to whatever greater discourse might represent a possible unity of the human sciences? The answer I propose suggests that moral discourse may be our most general and inclusive discourse on human affairs, insofar as it is organized according to the idea that each person has an obligation to every other in her capacity as an exemplary instance of human existence. In that case, it may not be the individual as such that is the ultimate referent of moral discourse but *human* life itself.

Such a discourse would be guided by an idea of society quite different from and more general than can be specified by demographic, territorial, or juridical determinations; by reference to a tradition, a common history, or an institutional formation; or by identifying relations of sovereignty. In this respect it would be both humanistic and self-critical, given a well-founded clarification of those terms. The individual can then be taken as an ultimate referent but only by virtue of its social being and the immanence of sociality to individuality. Indeed, the latter claim is no less compelling than Gutmann's and the problem remains how to reconcile them. They cannot be reconciled on the basis of standard definitions of "society" and on the standard conception of the individual as an independent, skin-bounded agent but for circumstances that compromise that essential independence. The problem is to try and ascertain the logical conditions of a moral individuality that is irreducibly social in its being and therefore cannot be conceived of according to the familiar idealization of independent subjectivities. Possible solutions will, of course, depend on what can be said, theoretically, about sociality as such.

It is partly in this regard that this book attempts to clarify what I take to be a prevailing but still mysterious idea about the nature of human affairs generally thought to be fundamental to those fields that claim to provide knowledge of such affairs: the humanities, the arts, philosophy, and the social sciences—what I mean when I refer to the human sciences. The idea is that human life is social in a certain way and in all conceivable respects before it is anything else—when thought of in regard to its essential reflexivity and according to the work we require such a conception to perform *as things stand*. It is a fundamental idea to the extent to which it promises to bring those disciplines into a coherent non-synthetic unity in their own terms, beyond what is typically meant by interdisciplinary cooperation, and to do so without sacrificing respect for what the various disciplines offer by way of theory and methodology. I argue that this promise can be fulfilled within certain limits but only by working through the implicit logic by which each discipline establishes the referential force of its language, thereby identifying its own distinct and proper object domain, and demonstrates the significance of that objectivity to the most conceptually inclusive and morally compelling concerns of the study of human affairs.

In this respect, my investigation is an immanent one, aiming only to clarify the common object as it is indicated by the various disciplines despite differences among them. Accordingly, I initially address that object under the aspect of its possible latency, as *sub-theoretical* in contrast with *pre-theoretical*. This means, first, that it is epistemically prior to the sorts of explicit theory on which those disciplines typically rely and, second, that its signifiers are internal to what is often referred to as pre-philosophical discourse—though this is typically neglected for plausible but insufficient reasons that will be discussed in some detail.

The idea at issue has two parts. The first says that a notion of the social dimension of life as irreducible underwrites and is the ultimate referent of all attempts to theorize human affairs *insofar as those attempts have to do with what is recognizably human about those affairs*. The second says that this notion is not adequately represented by the concepts ordinarily taken to define or guide us toward it—for example, interaction, cooperation, solidarity, exchange, interpersonal relations, social fact, social action, group, organization, institution, society, social structure, and social system.

———

The first problem that arises in an attempt to substantiate the idea that a common object unites the human sciences has to do with a disturbing fact about the relevant literatures. The disciplines in greatest need of clarification about the meaning of "social," those which cannot avoid appealing to other discourses or fields, including the arts, psychology, and anthropology, systematically rely on an unstated but profound intuition of the irreducibility and irrepressibility of the social aspect of life. Unfortunately, there is nothing even approaching clarity about the content of that intuition. None of the disciplines provide the requisite sense of what is logically required of a conception of the social in order for it to be compatible with their disciplinary claims, including justifications of their claims to specialized knowledge.

This is particularly poignant in P. F. Strawson's comment on a problem facing the tendency of the "philosophical tradition to work through epistemological and ontological questions in abstraction from the great fact of the concept-user's role as social being":

> For it is not as if each one of us builds up his cognitive picture of the world, acquires his concepts, develops his techniques and habits of action in isolation; and then, as it were, at a certain point, enters into relation with other human beings and confronts a new set of questions and problems. On the contrary, all this cognitive, conceptual, and behavioural development takes place in a social context; and, in particular, the acquisition of language, without which developed thinking is inconceivable, depends on interpersonal contact and communication. . . . One might well think it strange to use that human plural, "our," without adding, and regarding as an equally basic feature of *our* scheme, that each must see himself in some social relation to others whose purposes interact with his. If our subject is man in his world, it seems necessary to admit that this world is essentially a social world. (1992, 80–81)

I refer to this twofold lapse, of which Strawson is no less guilty than most other analytic philosophers, as an elision, in the sense of a tendency to slur or gloss over what is tacitly taken to be essential to the disciplinary intelligibility of a knowledge-constituting discourse.[1]

The exceptions to this lack of clarity are few and, for the most part, relatively obscure.[2] But it would be noticeable in any case, since, as I try to show, it paralyzes the theoretical imagination at the very point at which that imagination confronts its most difficult and fundamental conceptual problems. This is especially evident to the extent to which (1) references to sociality are systematically unavoidable, (2) every discussion of the rationality of human action that aims to be at all comprehensive relies on the possibility of such references, and (3) the lack of clarity is not simply a defect that can be cured by a reasonable deployment of available concepts but rather indicates a crucial feature of the social itself and a fact about the relationship between the social and the possibility of its being theorized.

With these observations in mind I proceed along both negative and positive lines. On the one hand, I consider the most likely temptations to ignore the elision, including the appeal of standard theoretical models whose elegance and prior successes may seem to justify begging the question. These temptations may arise in connection with three philosophical concerns: (1) the need for any theory to present a simple enough concept of its object for it to be possible to refer to its instances with confidence and with a reasonable degree of reliability, (2) the need to limit the scope of such a concept to the point at which the possibility of its logical extension is fairly obvious, and (3) the need for a convenient way to compare theoretical options according to the relative validity of their central propositions. Temptations to beg the question may also arise from pragmatic considerations about the need to place limits on criticism when it threatens to overwhelm coming to conclusions, especially in regard to interpreting, translating, teaching, and applying theories.

These and other such issues are undoubtedly connected to ideas about the status of theory in the human sciences and, therefore, about the character of the knowledge typically claimed by those disciplines: In what sense can such theories be sustained, confirmed, or refuted? In what sense can they be said to represent a reality? If what are claimed to be instances of knowledge in those fields are always contestable and always in the process of being revised, in what sense can they be considered knowledge? Is cumulative knowledge in the human sciences possible? If not, what distinguishes what they produce from opinion, taste, and ideology? If prediction and generalization are not central aims of those disciplines, what does it mean to say that they provide knowledge over and above mere description and the expression of values?

On the other hand, key sections of this book have to do with what is positively involved in coming to terms with the idea of the social when it is important to maintain a rational connection between theory and the sub-theoretical ontological commitments entailed by taking account of what is human about human affairs. I eventually distinguish what is *sub*-theoretical *to the activity of theorizing* from what is *pre-theoretical to a given theory*. The latter has to do with what is taken for granted but can be made explicit and the former with the sense of an indeterminate referent in regard to which the adequacy of any theory must always be subject to question. In effect, what is sub-theoretical is always and incurably latent to the activity of theorizing. In that sense, it is an ultimate referent, a source of theoretically motivating tension, and the stimulus of an intuition crucial to the theoretical enterprise.

———

Despite appearances to the contrary, I do not defend a particular metaphysics. Rather, I describe something that is almost but not quite a concept and that I believe authorizes the unity of the human sciences in regard to the possibility of an object in common—that is, as far as the questions with which they are bound to deal, *as things stand*, entail the existence of just such a reality. Clarifying this quasi-concept involves eliciting what is presupposed in asking those questions as they are typically asked or even in taking their interrogatory force for granted. It will appear that its very nature makes those presuppositions obscure, so that attempting to make them explicit will change the relationship between a given theory and the sub-theoretical notion it is supposed to illuminate. It will further appear that this apparently self-defeating movement from the sub-theoretical to explication is nevertheless an internal and logically necessary feature of any realization of the concept of the social that is at once theoretical and practical.

Among the unavoidable questions are the usual ones about the good, the true, and the beautiful; what is right and reasonable; the rational conditions of prudence and altruism; how justice is to be reconciled with self-interest; the relationship between self and other; the possibility of freedom; the difference between knowledge and opinion; and how morally significant practices can be reconciled with the somewhat different moral demands of their instances. It is a matter of principle in the human sciences that nothing said about human affairs should be construed in a way that is inconsistent with being able to ask just such questions and expect reasonable discussion and the possibility of answers that can and must be taken seriously. Nevertheless, the principle is typically betrayed by the very constraints that seem essential to the special rationality and reflexivity of theoretical work. I try to show that it has no hope of being realized unless we begin from the perspective of people living together, and sustain that critically, as the basic fact underlying the work of theorizing human affairs. It is in this sense that the vitality of human life must be conceived of as fundamentally social rather than psychological.

It is, then, necessary first of all to conceive of subjectivity without a subject or subjects, and only then and in that regard to consider how to theorize effective individuality: such a conception points to the theoretical indispensability of the social in a way that strongly suggests that what is distinctively human about human affairs is the immanence of sociality. If so, the individual should be the last rather than the first referent of the philosophy of mind, action, and knowledge, and of the human sciences in general. This does not contradict the proposition that the individual is the ultimate referent of moral discourse; nor does it imply that the individual psyche is an effect of the positive causal elements of social reality, which Émile Durkheim referred to as thing-like "social facts" (1982, 50). I try to show that it is only from the point of view of sociality, constrained by the obligation to consider what is human about human affairs, that theoretical problems having to do with freedom and moral obligation, and, concomitantly, utility and justice, can be addressed without having to rely on causal models that appear inconsistent with the foundational idea of freedom in society or without having to depend, tautologically, on the sufficiency of moral intuition in order to argue against moral indifference.

From this point of view, the history of theoretical controversy in the human sciences can be written in terms of the degree to which the immanence of the social is considered problematic within historically specific discourses and, in any case, according to how it is represented. I try to show in what ways the reality *attributed to* human affairs under the aspect of their being human differs significantly from what is generally *represented to be real* in the relevant disciplines, specifically in regard to descriptions and accounts of social entities, institutions, cultures, events, intentions, and joint or collective actions of individuals when these are not described under that aspect. If the argument succeeds, it should influence the disposition of a number of philosophical issues insofar as they bear on theoretical work in the human sciences. These include the relationship between criticism and knowledge; the status of the distinction between subjectivity and objectivity; what it is to think historically in contrast with thinking ahistorically; the relation of language to inter-subjectivity; the relations among ideology, interest, and practice; and the ways in which we might define discourse, mind, action, society, culture, and individuality such that we can understand how they are related.

To this end, I rely on two crucial distinctions—on the one hand, between *agency-dependent* and *agency-independent* objectivity and, on the other, between *action*, which is an event, and a *course of activity*, which is not. While I try to justify these distinctions, they are, in effect, the organizing principles of this book. My account of the ontological presuppositions of the human sciences is intended to clarify some of their most surprising implications for our most general ideas of theory, knowledge, and criticism, and to examine several interrelated theses in regard to those implications. Among these are, first, that reference to human affairs has to do with relations among objects, which are essentially agency-dependent; second, that a logically defensible sense of such objects requires conceiving of human affairs as courses of activity in contrast with action; and third, that this depends on the validity of inferring a noninteractive—noninterpersonal—sense of inter-subjectivity from the logical requirements of the concept of agency-dependent objectivity. To the extent to which the grounds that validate the overall perspective become clear, including the meaning of "what is human about human affairs" and the reasons why it is necessary to think of sociality as intrinsically critical, the task of self-conscious criticism will be less a matter of specialized judgment than one of demonstrating in detail and without exception what is distinctively human about every case at hand—that is, in what respect it is an instance of such affairs. I try to show that this implies that criticism, no less than sociality, is immanent to those affairs and that the two are internally related in that each can only be conceived of in terms of the other.

I use the expression "as things stand" non-ironically. It indicates that the rationality of our discourses on human affairs commits us to specific dispositions that influence what we take to be legitimate topics of dispute, the proper jurisdiction of doubt, if and when it is appropriate to ignore uncertainty and what it means to confront it, the sort of unit of meaning that can be evaluated as a whole, whether meaning can be thought of generally in terms of continuity across situations or as strictly situated, how one might decide that a proposition is true for all practical purposes, and the like. To think or write according to how things stand is to operate within those discourses, though it remains to be seen how they are organized in their own terms and how they transpire as instances of human affairs in their own right. But to speak of operating from within them suggests that one might choose a different point of view and that there is a transcendental position from which such choices can be evaluated. I try to show that it is not necessary to accept either option and that even the most rudimentary reflection on human affairs reveals a systematic elision of something that nevertheless serves as a sub-theoretical basis of our knowledge of those affairs—namely, that they are immanently social. It is not so much that the idea of what is absent in writing (or in theory) but necessary in thought (or in theorizing) can be made explicit as that the systematic character of the elision points to a region of being inconsistent with the line typically drawn between the proper subject matter of the humanities and the proper subject matter of science. This book is, in effect, about that region and, therefore, about the sort of knowledge that corresponds to it and the significance of that knowledge to understanding the connection between the humanities and the social sciences.

We have more or less abstract names for the basic fact of sociality. Examples are solidarity, association, group, ensemble, collectivity, sharing, agreeing, cooperating, discourse, communication, common interest, the public sphere, the social contract, the general will, the body politic, revolution, language, culture, community, and society. Sociology can be thought of as a discipline aimed at regulating the use of such terms according to a highly flexible language in which they circulate as "non-rigid signifiers." The use of any one is typically situational or occasional but, within those limits, it is not responsive to or governed by a stable referent. There is no accountable connection *within their circulation* between the ostensible signifying agent (the word) and what is both signified and capable of being signified. Discourses that deploy these terms are not intended to come to a resting point; rather they are intended to leave reference, and themselves, endlessly open. This is not because the terms have not yet been defined. It is because they cannot sustain their meaning-fulness without circulating. While the movements of signifiers are typically thought of as comprising a process of the exchange of information about a definite object, the circulation of constitutionally indefinite words demands referents that can never be forthcoming.

Such a movement cannot be imagined within the contours of the meta-phor of exchange. The words we are most likely to use when discussing human affairs are signifiers that by their very restless nature demand to circulate; in doing so, they are bound to resist their ostensible linguistic and epistemic functions. Their very use effectively begs the question of what they or their various uses might have in common. As a result, our discourses about human affairs seem to predicate conditions or entities that, constitutionally, cannot be instantiated sufficiently for predication to be conclusively informative: *then the fact that the referent of propositions about human affairs is indefinite suggests that such propositions are not subject to the standard logic of belief.* This does not mean that it is impossible to improve how we speak about and theorize the social aspect of life or to form better ideas about it. It does mean that whatever we say *about* human life will never satisfy what we require as long as coming to a solution is thought to entail nothing more than improving the explicitness and precision of our definitions. Such rigor envisions a definition capable of representing something (the social) as fixed despite the fact that it must also represent the very unfixable activity involved in *coming to* a definition. The definition would therefore exclude a key instance and to that extent leave the problem, which had been taken to be one of representation, without a solu-tion. How, then, can the latent sub-theoretical "referent" of the term "social" be brought into theoretical play without undoing what is significant about it to our understanding of what is human about human affairs? It appears that it cannot if the problem is merely one of referents and representations. Therefore it must be a different problem.

In any case, the sheer amount of time and energy that has already gone into trying to rationalize the language of the social dimension of life shows that one cannot take for granted the possibility of a reasonably settled sense of that reality. This means that the elision of the concept of the social should not be ignored for at least two reasons. First, ignoring it diminishes the pros-pect of grounding discourse in a discursively verifiable reality. Second, doing so makes obscure what needs to be confronted directly—namely, the fact that theories of the social aspect of life invariably contradict the plausible intuition that there is more and other to that aspect than meets the eye. Indeed, at the risk of seeming contradictory, one might argue that such a reality is partially realized in the proliferation of aporias, paradoxes, and problems that typically erupt in discourse when something pertaining to the idea of the social (includ-ing discourse itself) becomes an issue. For example, let us suspend, for the mo-ment, the convenient temptation to treat such a "problem without resolution" as one that might be solved by an application of intelligence or one that signals irreconcilable differences in values. Instead, let us consider the possibility that aporias connected with the idea of the social expose an ambiguity inherent in the phenomenon itself. It is then possible to entertain the following hypothesis: ambiguity, in the broad sense of the word, is a necessary feature of our discourse on the social aspect of life and a necessary feature of that very life; it provides the immanent prospect of continuous self-transformation discussed by Mikhail Bakhtin according to his influential conception of "dialogue," and by Harold Garfinkel in his comments about the "essentially reflexive" character of living and doing together (Bakhtin 1968; Garfinkel 1967).

In other words, if sociality as such is understood to be intentional in the sense of always moving beyond what it momentarily seems to be, that is, as an instance of *intentionality*, we must say that it intends, is intentional to, that very movement throughout its course; and this movement, or so I argue, is sociality itself. If this is a basic fact about human affairs, then it must be respected within the course of activity of every instance of discourse and in regard to how it makes itself evident in each and every assertion. Otherwise, a discourse is bound to be overwhelmed by what it cannot avoid but cannot assert, the sub-theoretical ground of its founding intuition; and it must not be overwhelmed if it is to remain motivated and therefore to exist as discourse.

The problem is that, given the lack of clarity about the meaning and possible sense of the word "social" and given the possibility that there is something about its referent that resists clarification, it is reasonable to suppose that topical discourse, including the theories about the topics that it warrants, cannot avoid the regressive repetition and apparent disorder rooted in uncertainty, in contrast with ambiguities that involve clear and equally plausible representations. But might not that be indicative of the nature of the principle object itself, possibly an inherent ambiguousness? Furthermore, might it not also indicate something about the object that reflects a crucial limitation of any theory that purports to identify its immediate and most general referent as an instance of human affairs? If it is reasonable to answer both questions in the affirmative, then we are led to consider the discourses themselves, including theories, as instances of what is distinctively human about human affairs, and therefore as caught up in an uncertainty that cannot be reduced or eliminated by the standard methods of self-critical reflection, in particular rational detachment and analysis. I address this in Chapter 7 and in Part II according to a distinction between theory and the activity of theorizing that expresses the more general distinction between action and "the course of activity." The inherent ambiguousness of topics having to do with human affairs lies, then, in the fact that the idea that sociality marks them as distinctively human only clarifies its own object by being an instance of it. Since their topicality within discourse has to do significantly with their being oriented to what is distinctively human (and therefore essentially social), their realization as topics must show itself to be of the same order as the discourse in which they are constituted as realizable, therefore, to be instances of the same reflexively incessant movement. This can be so only if ambiguousness is an internal feature of topical discourse and therefore of all possible topics.

Perhaps it is sufficient to say at this point that the apparently incurable ambiguousness of topics having to do with human affairs lies in the logical fact that no discourse can express a final and decisive version of what is human about them. Or, it can at the cost of undoing itself as discourse: discursivity comes to an end with any assertion of finality. In the alternative, it would have to exempt itself from what it purports to make decisively explicit as the humanness of human affairs. This would fail because a discourse on the finality of discourse is contradictory. What may be most generally confirmed in the course of topical deliberations is not so much a discursively valid conclusion but a sense that it is the principle of discourse, of discursivity, that it is interminable from within, though it may always be disrupted or otherwise fail. However, when the recognition of the principle is associated with a failure to be able to continue, parties may be tempted, regressively, to conclude that it was futile even to have begun, and observers may be tempted, progressively, to counsel them to patience. Both temptations are misleading.

It is, then, in regard to the *inevitability* of ambiguity, what I call ambiguousness, that sociality can be thought of as virtual and human affairs can be thought of as affairs. The former neither makes itself explicit in a theoretically satisfying way nor expresses, in any ordinary sense of expression, the history of its struggle to be heard beneath discourses that make such a hearing all but impossible. Sociality is, then, not something that can be rendered positively, as a notion ready to be conceptualized and prescribed as the proper object of a belief. I try to show that it is also neither irrelevant nor unfelt. Its way of being virtual is *active* even though it cannot be registered in the explicit terms and strategies of a language of topics (a language of topicality). There is an analogy to be drawn in this respect to the moment at which "reason" originally appears in the course of the mind's self-expression and, as Hegel reminds us, does not yet know (intend) its own history—its own possibility and the struggles that define that possibility—and therefore "cannot teach." Similarly, the simple and immediate intuition of a sociality tied to what has become explicit in topical discussions can neither teach itself nor remember, and therefore reflect on, the struggles that were involved in its having come to itself (as the realization of the movement or development of an intuition). This is so whether the parties are laypersons, philosophers, or specialists; and it may be one reason why discussions that presuppose the social are rarely if ever satisfying and why the lack of satisfaction seems incurable.

Incurable dissatisfaction may indicate that such discussions cannot admit the possibility of being decisively complete without undermining the fact on which their discursivity, which is to say their spontaneity, momentum, and reflexivity, depends—namely, that they are social through and through and do not consist merely of alternating or competing monologues, as in standard models of communication constructed on the analogy of exchange and in regard to the

impossible criterion of a meeting of minds. This suggests that alongside the uncertainties of the discourses is the certainty of their ineffectiveness: they cannot
constitute the unity of topic and idea that appears, from outside, to be their
purpose. Recognition of this as a fact is the moment at which criticism engages
the most general conditions of its own possibility, by treating what seems to be
a defect of topical discourse, its endlessness—and, consequently, its seeming
tendency to degenerate into disorder, silence, or repetitiousness—as an indication of what is covertly but actively substantive in it, what it actually can realize.

The key idea is that, in a certain sense, the endlessness signifies itself: it is
self-referring, or reflexive, insofar as it expresses a necessary feature of sociality. That is, the endlessness, in its own terms, reveals the one certainty that
abides within any discourse (not necessarily in its parties taken one by one):
that something essential is missing. This unsatisfiable desire for finality, immanent to discourse, displays itself in the form of resistance to any possibility
of stabilizing topics and thereby guaranteeing the reliability of their distributive effects. It is in this regard that we can understand why discourses rarely
end with the finality of a self-sufficient representation or a definitive theory.
This is indicated by reactions to anti-discursive challenges to stay on point or
get to the point and by increasingly individualized demoralizing demands for
agendas, summaries or recapitulations, examples, and simplifications designed
to impose finality on a history, a self-movement, that is, from both theoretical
and phenomenological points of view, bound to resist it. This apparent paradox
reveals one part of what is distinctively human about human affairs: the possibility of their being self-reflective—and therefore the possibility of what John
Searle (2001) calls, and then leaves behind, "rationality in action"—relies on a
notion of a sociality that cannot be acknowledged by means of the standard
theoretical language available for acknowledging.

If self-reflection somehow requires overcoming the force of the elision of
sociality, or avoiding its effects, then it must involve something altogether different from whatever can be described as a mental state, an argument, or even
a self. None of these overcomes that force; rather, their theoretical significance
seems to depend on suppressing the fact of sociality, and on suppressing the
fact of the suppression. While sociality has yet to be adequately characterized,
it is fairly clear that any characterization must take account of it as *a reflexive movement without the prospect of completion*; and I try to show that these
aspects are what brings together criticism and the human affairs that are its
object, constituting each as an instance of the other.[3]

I use the word "discourse" loosely to refer to a certain idea of a course of activity often associated with Ferdinand de Saussure's (1986) concept of speech in
contrast with language. For Saussure, speech is an operation on language considered as a system the elements of which are "values," or relations of difference.
It is spontaneous in the sense of being individuated in certain ways yet partially
rule-governed by virtue of a relation to the linguistic system mediated by community norms. As a course of activity, it has, from a standpoint theoretically

attributable to any of its parties, its own momentum by virtue of which it constantly generates sufficient reasons for anyone to do something that might bear on that momentum. The latter is, then, the source of spontaneity experienced more as a "fitting in" than as the socially indifferent freedom of independent subjects associated with solitary deliberation and the performance of speech acts. Later sections take up the problems of defining "discourse," including examining its connections with other key terms, in regard to the question of what is human about human affairs as things stand. Initially, I focus on the point of view of observation, which can be understood for present purposes to be similar to the point of view of momentarily detached or alienated parties. In doing so, I raise some questions about the distinction between external and internal perspectives when what is at issue is a course of activity in contrast with mutually regarding actions.

––––––––

Considered from an externalized point of view that addresses a discourse as a particular describable event, the elision of its social grounds may make the activity itself appear futile. The absence of so essential a referent leaves every discussion fundamentally ungrounded and without an immanent prospect of discursive continuity. The activity that follows among parties can be thought of by observers or the disaffected as oriented by the possible or anticipated effects of futility: either toward managing the tension engendered by an evident absence without remedy or attempting to instate an extra-discursive principle that can provide the semblance of an agreement regardless of the lack of adequate grounds for one. Apart from a straightforward imposition, these might appear to include what Ralph Turner referred to as "emergent norms" (1964, 394), which are thought to be regulatory effects of interaction under conditions of uncertainty. The standard notion of communicative action assumes a collectively internal self-ordering capability. Therefore, some sort of mechanism seems to be social psychologically required in extraordinary instances of interaction to the extent to which it offers an external ordering function to a discourse apparently unable to order itself.

One might argue that the need for such a supplement arises from the essentially contested character of certain privileged concepts that appear or might appear in the course of discussion, perhaps because they incorporate value judgments or represent cognitively dissonant meanings. But from what has been said so far it seems preferable to say that it is because addressing topics without regard to the conditions of their being topical (having distributive effects) may threaten the ability to continue addressing them in a way that preserves their topicality—for example, by not putting their distributive relevance or authority into question. In either case, discourse would appear in danger of losing its motive force. This reinforces confidence in the hypothesis that incompleteness is a feature of discourse itself and not something that happens to it. But it suggests that this frailty of the collective is overcome, if at all, by individual initiative or by a different collective process, perhaps one associated with confluent responses to deviance. In other words, if we assume for the moment that topical discourse operates as a medium of communication among discrete interacting individuals, then it may be the controversial nature of what is discussed that makes it incomplete. Or it may be a result of a premature decision by a plurality of the parties about what is at stake in their discussion. In any case, it might seem that the elision of the social is not responsible for the momentary unreliability of communicative gestures. Alternatively, communication cannot appear reliable and therefore repeatable when there is no way of expressing, in a nontheoretical communicative way, a basis for such reliability. What matters then is clarifying meaning, perhaps through a succession of negotiations.

But is reliability the crucial issue? It would be for individuals exclusively interested in the effects their utterances have on others, which is the thesis momentarily under consideration. If, however, discourse already instantiates the social, and is not just an epiphenomenon of a plurality of individually motivated acts, perhaps in the form of exchange, the problem of its incompleteness must lie in what about sociality itself is *essentially* incomplete and *therefore* resistant to the prospect of completion. That is, it may be that the model of discourse is at fault rather than that the elision of sociality indicates a possibly tragic contradiction and therefore an opening for a different model based on a principle altogether different from exchange. So far, however, the method of modeling is not itself in jeopardy. So the elision of the social does not yet appear to be the crucial problem.

We are operating for the moment within a perspective that cannot include such a notion, so the incompleteness of discourse still seems due either to the controversial character of its topics or to the possibility that something about the continuity of topical discourse excludes referring to its own grounds, not merely to what it is for it to be topical but to what it is for it to be discourse. It seems, then, that the latter is the better explanation, but only within that perspective. This is so if one wishes to understand discourse in the way required by that perspective, as a collective phenomenon that expresses mutually oriented individuated intentions. To the extent to which the idea of the social remains opaque, it is necessary to consider the effects of its elision on the ostensibly separable individuals engaged in discourse such that what is said by each on the basis of the elision (not on the basis of what is elided) never quite seems to get to the point; or it only seems to get to the point as an effect of an extra-discursive clarifying operation or intervention. This is one source of the analogy between conversation as posing a problem of reconciliation and a certain conception of work as technique, in the sense of an independent process indifferent to its materials.

———

Suppose, however, that the problem is not merely to clarify the idea of sociality but to come to terms with the possibility that it is not the sort of thing that can make itself clear according to the information exchange model of communicative language that informs most theories of discourse. If so, we can assume that those theories are inadequate to what makes discourse conceivable (as discursive and as an instance of sociality). What then appears at stake is not the relationship between discourse and its grounds, as if the two are distinct, but the constitution of discourse as something quite different from interactions among distinct individuals in which what they *do* together (e.g., exchange messages) is internally related to what constitutes *being together* in the sense of a togetherness for which individuality can only be ostensible.

Nevertheless, even without going beyond the idea of communication as object-oriented exchanges that cannot intend their own grounds, we can find instances that fail to conform to the exchange model, suggesting again that sociality is immanent to what is being done over and above what might be attributed to parties taken one by one. For example, that discourse is essentially incomplete might account for the fact that it often finds itself falling into extremes—either an indecisiveness related to what I refer to as an attitude of waiting, which I try to show is necessary to the idea of discursive speech (speaking), or a decisiveness that cannot guarantee consensus by any appeal whatsoever to logic or fact, *since what is ultimately at stake in every instance of discourse is the subjectivity on which the factuality of a fact or the reasonableness of a reason depends.* I argue that such a subjectivity cannot be individualized (or reductively composed of individuals) and that it corresponds to what Rousseau thought of in terms of the most basic premise of all that can be said to transpire among people living together—namely, an irrevocable equality of dependence among them that makes itself evident as something that can be named but for which sufficient acceptable predicates have yet to be found. For Rousseau, this was the "general will," in which generality cannot be defined by a number or ratio (1978b, 53–54).

My aim is not, however, to form a concept of sociality in the usual sense of concept formation. Such a solution would appear to be no less incomplete than the discourses in which the notion is elided in the first place. It is, rather, to consider what sort of ontology is presupposed by the illegibility of the referent and how it nevertheless works its way into discourses that otherwise appear to exclude it. The important issues have to do with the difference it might make to theory and to the philosophy of the human sciences. Above all, it should be possible to clarify the sub-theoretical ontological basis of the idea of the social that is, as things stand, key to understanding what is human about human affairs and to understanding the immanence of criticism to those affairs such that it might be possible to appreciate the internal character of the relation between the object of inquiry and the theory and methods by which that object makes itself known. To the extent to which this succeeds, it should appear that the ontology that determines the idea of the social yields a critique of its own foundation, which is to say of "*the way things stand.*" It is only then that the phenomenology of criticism, the relationship between the sense of "being" and the sense of "knowing," becomes criticism's own object.

————————

If one problem in the study of our knowledge of human affairs has to do with how theory can be an instance of its object, how a theory of human affairs shows itself to be an instance of such affairs, then an inquiry into the notion of the social should put it on a new footing. The more general problem is how to make legible an ontology of which we only have indications and the sense of prospective endlessness, and to make it legible without reproducing the very conditions that make legibility impossible. In any case, it would be misleading to try to summarize in an introduction what can only be intelligibly presented in the *course* of an inquiry in which it is neither possible nor desirable to sustain a distinction between the order of discovery (the "memory" of struggle) and the order of justification (the evaluation of reasons). It is nevertheless possible to list some of the main points, though it must be kept in mind that this reduces what can only transpire in the course of reading to a formal structure, as if it were sufficient to describe a piece of music in terms of the formal properties that articulate only its most abstract identifiable movement (see Raffman 1993).

This book addresses three overriding questions. First, how does identifying the endlessness of discourse with what that endlessness seems to presuppose, which is sociality, allow us to determine what is human about human affairs? Second, if it does, is this sufficient to identify a common object for the human sciences, and a common mode of inquiry? Third, in what sense is such a mode reflexive and therefore self-transcending, and therefore capable of moving us beyond the ways in which we ordinarily think about human affairs? Addressing these questions implicates several more or less speculative propositions:

1. The objective field of the human sciences is human life. This is meaningful if there is something distinctively human about human affairs that can only be recognized by a science, or knowledge-constituting discipline, that corresponds to that idea.
2. Human life can only be understood in terms of what is distinctively human about it. I refer to this generally as involving a course of activity, which is different from action, practice, activity as such, process, and the like, which cannot be reduced to the effects of individual intentions, originary events, conditions and consequences, or states of mind, and which cannot be registered according to an ontology of spatiotemporally distinct entities (or, at least, there is no subject position that can be imagined as both inside of and competent to observe such entities).
3. A course of activity cannot be treated as a distinct whole, and no absolute particulars can be found within it except as moments—in

which case the distinction between within and without is at least dubious. Thus, it is not composed of and is not epiphenomenal to what individuals do; nor can it be considered a collective expression of or solution to statistically common or overlapping intentions of individuals.

4. The normal expression of a course of activity, in the face of anything that purports to impose a repeatable order on it, is, from an external point of view, resistance. Therefore, activity tends to reproduce its own principle, though never by repetition. In conventional terms, this suggests that a course of activity lies on the side of production or generativity, in contrast with particular realizations of productive action (products) or the establishment of reasonable limits (e.g., value-based norms) to what can be done sensibly by particular, presumably intending, agents. Resistance to articulation and the order of repetition is to be understood in terms of the idea of a course of activity—which involves a momentum of constant self-transformation that does not exist as such under the logic of repetition. In this sense, resistance is a matter of life against death as in nonlife; and this is what may account most generally for why policy debates, for example, are essentially inconclusive. In other words, they *must* remain discursively open if participation is to be possible in the future, which is a necessary feature of every participatory gesture, if participation is to envision a future that is, after all, its own possibility as a course of activity. From this point of view, resistance is not a matter of certain concepts being "essentially contested" because they represent and then make obscure intractable differences among distinct parties. It is simply how sociality appears under the aspect of the elision of its idea.

5. To realize the project of establishing the social as an irreducible course of activity, individuality must be thought of as merely ostensible and as momentary rather than as indicating ultimate units of analysis. If individuals are moments, so are objects insofar as they are agency-dependent objects. Thus, I usually refer to individuals and objects as ostensible from a point of view internal to a course of activity, and as moments from an external, or theoretical, point of view. This has implications for the meaning of the terms "subjective" and "objective," given the requirement that the human sciences address what their object (human life) addresses—namely, agency-dependent objectivity. In other words, *the object of the human sciences must be logically identical with the object of their object.* Therefore, to clarify and gauge the scope of the ontology of the social, it is necessary to imagine a universe composed only of agency-dependent objects. It will turn out that this entails that what are ordinarily thought of as radically different, objects (things) and subjects (persons or consciousnesses), are

both instances of subjectivity. "Subject" and "object" are, then, logical terms with no specifically referential value. This, in effect, purifies the notion of agency-dependence, establishing it as an idea in the greater sense of a conception that has a life that can be followed in the course of another instance of life—in other words, the activity of criticism.

———————

I have written this book in a way that may occasionally seem overly redundant, but that is designed, whether or not it succeeds, to preserve the state of the argument at each moment in which there appears to be an important turn or a new point of departure. That is, I have tried to build into the text something on the order of a memory so that the inter-dependence and overall significance of its various claims are evident throughout. Nevertheless, or perhaps because of this, readers may find it helpful to begin by reading the last section of Chapter 17 for a concise summary of the logic of the argument of the book.

I
Sociality

The Problem of Definition

1

The Urgency of Defining the Social

W hile it is now taken virtually for granted that humans are essentially social beings, an important implication that is less likely to be acknowledged is that sociality is immanent to every instance of human affairs. The idea of the general will, a subjectivity beyond subjects, remains confusing and has been only rarely submitted to conceptual analysis. It is nevertheless presupposed whenever we consider people living among people and therefore whenever language and self-reflection are issues. The confusion engendered by this presupposition is evident in the persistence of cognates of interpersonal behavior (sharing, communicating, etc.) in accounts of collective happenings that nevertheless appear to resist application of those terms because of their scale or reach, an incurable indefiniteness of context, or an intransigent lack of clarity in the connection between agency and subjectivity. Examples are formal transactions and practices that assume a plurality of actors beyond those immediately present; economic actions that are context-dependent but essentially individuated and, in that regard, unsituated, a politics that can be expressed only within an ongoing and intrinsically volatile public medium; and discourses that take form as ongoing accomplishments in which every discursive moment mediates every other such moment, operating across and not by way of individuals. Thus, the language available for speaking generally about what people do together is inadequate to most of the examples typically given.

The fact that the word "social" remains vague explains why it has proven difficult to clarify the meanings of many of the terms associated with it without appearing to violate the sense that they have something in common. Examples are community, reciprocity, mutuality, exchange, social order, civil society, cooperation, and culture. The meaning typically attributed to each term excludes at least one of the others. Social order and community have altogether different referents. Similarly, mutuality is typically imagined in opposition to the impersonality of exchange, and culture specifies an independent domain of normative facts for which sociality is nothing more than background.

Little can be found in the North American literature that comes close to discussing its meaning beyond what is offered by the *Oxford English Dictionary*'s references to "social" as the ability "to be associated or united *to* others," and as a condition of being "associated, allied, or combined." Monographs as well as introductory texts familiarly refer to "relations among individuals" as sufficient to indicate the meaning of the term without any need for a formal definition. Standard usage generally assumes that sociality is a variable property of human affairs having something to do with the copresence or coming together of persons (such that they are momentarily social in the limited sense of taking account of others). Associated, related, or interacting persons are then conceived of as distinctly abiding individuals who may or may not act socially and for whom, in any case, sociality is not a necessary condition of their being human.[1]

————

The problem of definition arises fundamentally in regard to two different but not necessarily incompatible points of view. The first identifies the knowledge people have of others in general as a function of their inescapable inter-dependence and the corresponding abstract and inclusive sense of a "Law" engendered by an irresistible mutuality that is experienced as both immutable and evidence of freedom. The hypothesis that knowledge of one's self is a function of one's knowledge of nonspecific others suggests that it is through self-knowledge that each individual experiences something of a reconciliation of utility (which separates people as means relative to each other's ends) and justice (which brings them together as ends in regard to which no other is merely a means). The immediacy of this experience, its relation to action, need not be explicitly conscious. It lies in each person's sense that her freedom cannot be imagined outside of the realm of freedom constituted as the rule of law, Rousseau's evidence for the existence of the social contract distinct from the form of government. How, then, is reconciliation possible and what sort of experience confirms it? Is the sense of a connection between justice and utility a matter of evaluation and judgment and therefore contingent, or is it necessary, intuitive, and immediate? What preexisting relations are assumed by the idea of law consistent with the idea of freedom? What sort of freedom requires acceptance of the rule of law? Can freedom be imagined without such an idea? What sort of creatures must people be if they are to be free under the rule of law? To address these questions, we have to consider the uniqueness of human society and the kind of knowledge that corresponds to it in its uniqueness. The uniqueness of society has been traditionally understood in contrast with "the state of nature," and the relation of knowledge to society has to do with how sociality can be a basic fact that grounds knowledge and, if so, in what sense it is "basic."

The second point of view has to do with considerations of agency and the conditions under which it is possible to form a general idea of agency commensurate with the idea of "all practical purposes" (in contrast with the specifiable intentionality of separable acts directed by particular purposes). In its secular form, and at a minimum, the internal relation of sociality and agency supports the proposition that the actions of each person, by their very nature, take account of and are not merely responsive to the actions of both specific and nonspecific others. At a maximum, it supports the idea that sociality is an activity and not a state of affairs, and, therefore, that it must be *constitutionally* motivated—where motivation has to do with immanent tensions associated with contradiction, lack, aporia, or paradox, depending on the context of inquiry.

I identify the first point of view with Rousseau's account of the social contract, in which a positive disposition of the one toward the many (whether or not the many is taken to reside in the one) is a necessary condition of law. As such, it is the basis of the crucial modernist distinction between authority and power. I identify the second with Karl Marx's (1978) account of the historically specific socialization of labor characteristic of capitalist production, his notion of an ensemble of social relations in which "action" always refers to an intentionally constituted momentary event inter-dependent with other such moments, and his account of value as the meaning something socially constituted has in regard to the most general feature of all that is socially meaningful—the difference it makes among things that make a difference. I take it that both points of view preclude a reductive sociology.

In what follows, I use "sociality" and "society" interchangeably, depending on whether the emphasis is on the ongoing character of the social or on social life in contrast with its negation, though the first is the more general term. My account of Rousseau addresses how he conceives of sociality in *The Social Contract*. Thus, I do not rely on hypotheses about whether there is an overall unity to his thought, and I do not deal with writings that are said to qualify or compromise his concept of the social. Therefore, I do not consider the text from the point of view of the philosophy of politics (see Rawls 2007, 191–250). In effect, I treat it as an essay in the construction of a specific idea, which is a far more limited purpose than that of most commentators. When I enlarge on his ideas, it is from this narrow point of view and not, for example, with the aim of integrating his notion of "pity," one of his "two principles prior to reason," with the notions of a "first convention," an ambiguous expression that invokes both a norm and a coming together, and a "general will."[2] I consider the issue irrelevant to Rousseau's account of the sort of sociality that uniquely mediates the relationship between utility and justice.[3]

On the surface, Rousseau's account of the social contract appears to rely on a radical distinction between society and the state of nature distinct from the idea of human nature with which it is often conflated (see Starobinski 1988,

147).[4] Each is described as a totality such that the line between them seems perfectly clear. The difference is, then, unambiguous to any sentient creature capable of reason; and it must be if, as Rousseau seems to say, society is *chosen* over nature in a self-transforming "passage" from the one condition to the other:

> I assume that men have reached a point where obstacles to their self-preservation in the state of nature prevail by their resistance over the forces that each individual can use to maintain himself in that state; Then that primitive state can no longer subsist, and the human race would perish if it did not change its way of life. . . .
>
> This passage from the state of nature to the civil state produces a remarkable change in man, by substituting justice for instinct in his behavior and giving his actions the morality they previously lacked. Only then, when the voice of duty replaces physical impulse and right replaces appetite, does man, who until that time only considered himself, find himself forced to act upon other principles and to consult his reason before heeding his inclinations. (Rousseau 1978b, 53, 55–56)

Rousseau concludes that, given what man gains from the passage from nature to society, "if the abuses of this new condition did not often degrade him below that from which he has left, he ought to bless ceaselessly the happy moment that tore him from it forever, and, from a stupid, limited animal made an intelligent being and a man" (55–56).

I take it that the "abuses of this new condition" apply neither to the social contract nor to the "primitive act of confederation" but to forms of society as achieved over time.[5] They apply to the historically articulated society alluded to by Rousseau in his essay on inequality, which depends on the exercise of particular wills and is bound to compromise or undermine the most general condition under which each person cannot but recognize the equality of all, a condition on which even the most burdensome of non-despotic states depends. In other words, the social dimension of the civil state provides all that is essentially human in the general will and the body politic, regardless of whatever happens in the course of the development of its institutions. To the extent to which this contradiction cannot be avoided, Rousseau provides something of a historical conception in which human affairs are realized only by way of a constant working through of the fundamental opposition between the particular and the general wills (in each and among all). But what matter most in these passages for my account are the contrast Rousseau draws between a basic sociality and a state of nature, the relation between the two, and the way in which the former achieves its status as a concept by its opposition to the latter. What is theoretically problematic in this is that the state of nature is explicitly identified as the absolute negation of society: the point of view of each precludes the intelligibility of the other as a condition of human life. Thus, justice, duty, right, principle, reason, intelligence, and humanness are opposed by what they logically exclude: instinct, impulse, appetite, separate existence, inclination, stupidity, ignorance, and animality. It follows that the question of society can be raised only within society and that society provides no perspective from which nature can be understood as a totalizing condition of human life or that the mere capacity to be social (e.g., "pity") can be conceived of as a distinctively human tendency. This means that nature is not, strictly speaking, "other" to society: the latter cannot be conceived of as a solution to problems posed by the former.

This version of Rousseau's account of the social contract, as a morally significant choice motivated by insecurity, or even as one term of the "useful fiction" of society versus nature (Sherover 1974, xxi), seems to be undermined by its own presupposition. I attempt to show that the theoretically important question is not whether the relevant passages should be read literally or, what amounts to the same thing, as providing merely a useful fiction. It is not whether the narrative means what its sentences say and what its form implies but what it establishes for the phenomenology of human affairs and the theory of what is human about them, at least in regard to what it shows to be fatefully *inconceivable*. I argue that it presents a basic fact that is irrefutable from the standpoint of the reader, which, it turns out, is the standpoint of everyone, every being one is committed to describing as human.

Few commentators today hold Rousseau to the strictly literal meaning of his account, which is that at a particular time, humans in a state of nature came together in a "first convention" that performs the norm on which it depends, choosing to enter into association with others whom they could not have known in advance or learned to trust, and with whom there was no nontrivial motivational basis for active identification. It might be argued that the propensity of human beings to pity instances of their kind provides such a basis, but whether or not it does is not crucial to my project. In any case, I am not convinced that the argument is valid. Rousseau does not form a *concept* of pity in the *Second Discourse* in the same way that he forms a concept of sociality in *The Social Contract*, though he includes it as one of the two principles prior to reason (Rousseau 1997, 152–153). Unlike the other principle, that of concern for oneself ("well-being and self-preservation"), pity *disposes* man in a state of nature only in the negative sense of inspiring a natural repugnance in us "to see his kind suffer" (152). It does not otherwise initiate active concern. One purpose of Rousseau's discussion in the *Second Discourse* is to provide a sufficient reason to reject a negative view of humans in their "natural state" and the consequences of that view. It is in that respect a part of the argument of *The Social Contract*. But it seems to me that his concept of sociality is formed no less independently of what he says about pity than of what one might say about opposable thumbs or any other species-specific property that is not in itself positively motivating.

This basis of sociability (plus concern for oneself) may appear to be part of both the substance and limit of natural law. However, it does not describe the positive inclination required by sociality—that is, by an active relation with others in contrast with the mere capacity to participate in or to be drawn into such a relation. It does not show how indifference gives way to concern and anticipation. From this point of view, "pity" effectively stands for Rousseau's denial that humans are naturally hostile and cruel and, therefore, that they can live together only under an absolute ruler or a tyrant. If it signifies anything more, it is the capacity of humans to identify at a pre-social level with others of their kind, though it might be difficult for them to determine what is and is not their kind. Since there is no way to specify what this capacity would look like in nature, and there is every reason to accept Rousseau's claim that indifference is more characteristic of one toward another in that state, it seems that pity is not theoretically relevant to his concept of society. Again, as I read the *Second Discourse*, pity is not the sort of concept one would need if it were to signify more than a capacity (against the view Rousseau attributes to Thomas Hobbes)—namely, a disposition. If it is a disposition, it can show itself as relevant to the formation of society only if other conditions give it motivational focus or connect it to some socially necessary disposition. It seems to me that these conditions are outlined in the argument of *The Social Contract* and nowhere else.

In any case, the interpretation that characterizes the narrative of transition to the first convention as a useful fiction begs the question of why the narrative is there in the first place. Why might such a fiction be necessary to Rousseau's theory? Perhaps it is what the narrative does to the reader in the course of reading that allows us to appreciate its significance; and what it does is prove something basic to the possibility of being certain about what is human about human affairs and therefore of knowing those affairs under that aspect. I try to show that the use of the narrative becomes intelligible and effective when read as an allegory intended to demonstrate the "truth" of society beyond a reasonable doubt, which is to say the truth of the claim that society is founded on an equality among people that cannot be compromised (for any practical matter). It turns out that this, and not the fact or fiction of an agreement, accounts for the continuity of society across circumstances and generations. It is in this regard, and not in regard to what is ostensibly gained by individuals in forming society, that defining sociality takes on its theoretical urgency for proponents of the Rousseauian point of view.

———

The idea of an asocial state of nature cannot provide for imaginable conditions of human life. It follows that everyone capable of reading Rousseau's text, everyone able to consider the social aspect of life, is already implicated in a relation of some sort with a virtually unlimited plurality of unnameable others—that is, with others in general. To be societal in this way, to be *of* society through and through, is to be able to imagine that whatever can be said about society can be denied *but to be unable to imagine how the completion of that negation could support human life*. The negation would certainly include the denial of language and, therefore, its own possibility. As a result, what it signifies, if it signifies at all, can be imagined substantively only if it does not correspond to a negation. Therefore, it does not signify.

To negate the idea of a universe in which every instance of intentionality is social, to deny all that it could possibly be and not just to deny what has been said about it, is to suggest that there is a referent but, at the same time, to make it impossible to conceive of one. If language is a systemic feature of that universe and its meaningfulness, it alone provides for the possibility of referring, naming, describing, and negating and, therefore, for the sort of positive imagination that intends things that might or might not exist (the sorts of things about which beliefs can be judged plausible or not, or true or false). This implies that the negation of society cannot be imagined positively either *through* language or as *supporting* language and that the sort of imagination necessary to entertain a notion of society plus its negation is impossible without a language in which speaking is spontaneous and meaningful—that is, without society. To claim otherwise would amount to saying that there is a world that must but cannot be conceived of as humanly livable. It would be to say that the life world in which the relevant sort of imagination is inconceivable can be imagined from within a life world in which the *absence* of such imagination is inconceivable. At issue is whether a belief that human life can exist as human without society can be sensibly formulated and, therefore, whether society can be defined intelligibly according to such a condition. The problem is that the lack of a definition of sociality makes it difficult to resist the temptation to identify society as the complete negation of its complete negation, as when *it* is said to account for law and order, rights, obligations, and so forth, in contrast with the putative effects of its total absence. Society as the negation of its negation appears substantively as the negation of chaos, and as protection against that possibility. But since such a capacity cannot arise from within the chaos of indifference, the characterization begs the question of how society should be defined as something that can provide a solution to a chaos that does not allow for even a hint of society.

To claim that society presents a solution to the possibility of no society is to presuppose what cannot be presupposed. One might then say that to believe in the possibility of human life in a state of nature without language and mutual recognition is not to *believe* in the usual sense of the term. If I were to *say* that the lion has beliefs about the state of nature, I surely do not *mean* that it believes the truth of certain propositions. Nor do I mean that what the lion "believes" is part of a structure of beliefs and other such facts. Indeed, I cannot mean that the lion, *qua* lion, has *beliefs*, unless I also believe that lions are humans disguised as animals. To say that believing is a function of language means, among other things, that it reflects a capacity to compare and classify at the same level of abstraction as the putative object of belief. Society, understood as a universe or realm of being, can be a term of comparison only in the company of many concepts and beliefs, and in regard to the state of nature, if it is possible to imagine two absolutely opposed ways of living as a human being. One might argue that it is possible to project a conception of the negation of society from within society because the very capacity to use language allows its parties to conceive of not having anything of what they have even if they cannot name each thing. The questions are, first, does imagining not having what one has, including language, constitute a negation, or does it merely involve a series of specific denials or an improperly qualified rather than total view of the language being denied? Second, can one use language to conceive of a humanity without language?

First, it is not at all clear how a societal creature can dissociate itself from the very conditions that allow it to represent any condition as *total*. It would have to do this in order to imagine a *negation* of society from within, and it is this possibility that we are considering. In that case, the claimed negation will be something different from what is intended by the word "negation." The idea of a being in a state of nature precludes the capacity to represent, which stands as the most compelling presence of society itself. This is not to claim that there is no imagination beyond language. It merely says that where imagination requires language, as is obvious in the case of imagining society and its negation, what cannot be linguistically represented cannot be imagined in any useful sense of the term. Whatever critical point of view is adopted from within society cannot be inconsistent with the fact of language and it cannot be total in the way a negation of a totality would have to be. What is important in this is that the lack of a definition of sociality, or at least a reasonably clear conception, forces us to consider what cannot reasonably be considered: when we think of events, acts, or things as social without a comprehensible sense of the idea, we are likely to take recourse to a convenient default entity, which is to say a conventionally named semblance of sociality. This is typically an aggregate or categorical collection, like a nation, whose boundaries, distributions, and central tendencies are considered its most telling facts. What those facts are about is at best taken for granted. At worst, they confuse substance with what is determined by method. Whatever negation they make conceivable (of the sort of passive aggregation presupposed by such analyses), it cannot be a negation of society.

The question remains as to what is it about social life that supports the common characterization of it as having boundaries, distributions, and tendencies, and suggests that those characteristics might be denied. To the extent to which reference to an aggregate, or any received category, is adequate to describe it, individuals are likely to be posited as constituent units, elemental referents of a general account of human affairs. This raises the further question of how they can be conceived of as independent of something that encompasses them and gives them whatever unitary form is possible. The question can, of course, be begged, but what generates it, the irrepressibility of a sub-theoretical notion of an irreducible sociality, is bound to remain troubling for any attempt to theorize society according to a default "entity" constructed within limits convenient to prevailing methodological dispositions, techniques, and discourses. One immediate consequence is the temptation to think in terms of origins and, therefore, a pre-social state of being or, as in recent discussions of societal evolution, a notion of sociality so primitive in its lack of articulation that it cannot be treated, even on an extended evolutionary scale, as a precursor to what are familiarly taken to be exemplary instances of society.[6] In either case, a negation of society is the *logical* basis of whatever concepts are used to describe pre-social conditions, and, as we have seen, it is impossible to form such concepts. We are then forced to confront directly the problem of substantiating what has been seen since the eighteenth century, especially by Rousseau, as unavoidable, irreducible, and virtually beyond definition or clarification—namely, sociality as such.

In what follows, I do not argue for a metaphysics of social entities or that society can be defined in standard sociological language without appealing to the idea of a state of nature. I claim that it is impossible, from the Rousseauian point of view, to think about human affairs without appealing to some notion of sociality as a sub-theoretical basic fact. In that case, much of what is problematic about those affairs has to do with the elision of what makes such thought possible in the first instance. To the extent to which we find ourselves unable to avoid dealing with the human aspect of human affairs, either we come to terms with the elision or our attempts to account for those affairs will be tragically contestable or beside the point. I argue that coming to terms with the elision from the first point of view for which sociality is particularly problematic requires acknowledging the immediate effect of Rousseau's narrative of the social contract on its reader. On the one hand, if the narrative is just a "useful fiction" that can have no such effect, the reader is free to concentrate on an idealized notion of society as an extension of a "first convention" that culminates in "the total alienation of each associate, with all his rights, to the whole community" (1978b, 53). On the other hand, if it presents society as the negation of nature, it tends to promote the idea of a system of mutually determining operations the relative autonomy of which is always dependent on a totalizing motive, presumably shared by all members, to create and preserve systemic conditions of rational action over and above whatever might express local and possibly opposing interests. If the problem with the first is that it lends itself to an untenable idealism, the problem with the second is that it requires a negation the reality of which is inconceivable. In that case, it begs the question of the meaning of society it was intended to answer. If the presence of the narrative in *The Social Contract* is to be understood despite the well-established criticisms of its literal meaning, it must be considered for its effect on the reader in the course of reading and the theoretical significance of that effect. While not directly theoretical, the effect is crucial for Rousseau's way of proving that what is distinctively human about human affairs is their social dimension. For this, it is essential that Rousseau's readers be *possible* readers—beings in society who are, as such, unable to imagine the negation of society, though able to deny all that it appears to be.

Given information, time, and other material conditions of deliberation, any creature capable of the speech of reason is open to hearing and responding to different sides of a question at any level of abstraction at which it is posed. Being able to hear different sides requires at least an ability to grasp the difference between intelligible and unintelligible expressions, regardless of what otherwise might be said about their content; a sense of what it is for one side of an issue to be different from another side; a sense of what it is for a difference to be significant; and an ability to tolerate significant differences that might arise and that cannot be anticipated—and, of course, to appreciate the vagueness of the idea of a side. A creature able to do all this, and more, must be said to share society (and humanity) with Rousseau's readers and, therefore, to be unable to imagine its negation.[7] Furthermore, given the Rousseauian claim that the way in which humans fit the fact of society is by being *essentially* social rather than by being accidentally and/or partially so, the problem cannot be resolved simply by saying that association with others, in contrast with isolation or solitude, impairs the imagination—making it difficult but *not* impossible to imagine a referent of the negation. Rather, being social is all that can be imagined as what is generally human about human affairs—a fact that thereby qualifies even the senses of isolation and solitude. This last proposition poses a difficulty, since it implies that sociality can be imagined only from within sociality. How then can a "first convention" occur? For now, it appears that whether it is worthwhile to live in society is a question to which there can be no answer—because it is impossible to conceive of, to imagine positively, an alternative to society.

2

Society as a Basic Fact

There is no doubt that human beings can imagine a humanly livable state of nature. But it cannot be the sort of nature that is the negative of society. Rousseau's characterization of the state of nature as a realm of necessity that excludes all that being human requires envisions only nonhuman creatures—"stupid and limited" (1978b, 56)—unable to reach beyond their biological urges and incapable of forming ideas about their own situation and about the possibility of society that can support an intention to enter into a self-transforming association with other such creatures. Indeed, there could be an issue only for social beings able to imagine a substantial existence associated with their own negation. Since that is beyond their capacity, the notion of such an existence cannot be intelligible to them. If the claim that the social contract arises from within a state of nature is crucial to Rousseau's argument, it is difficult to see how the argument can be sustained. It seems that questions about the existence and value of society, like those about the existence and value of the universe, cannot be answered, which suggests that they are questions only in the purely grammatical sense of the term.

We might conclude, then, that the narrative of the social contract, which begins with what society cannot be, can persuade but cannot convince. In this sense, it may be a rhetorically "useful fiction," but that is not enough to show why it might have been a necessary part of Rousseau's argument. If its usefulness is aimed at doing no more than persuading readers that the hypothesis of the social contract is true even though they are given no logical or fact-based account of its possibility, then we can dismiss *The Social Contract* as ideological or merely one point of view among others. I believe that those who think of the narrative as a "useful fiction" miss what is overwhelming about this crucial

part of the text, what it does to the reader—namely by way of producing an irresistible sense of a social reality that knows no exception. Because of this, they
are liable to fall victim to the fallacy of interpreting the idea of the general will
as essentially totalitarian. I try to show that it is through the exercise of reason,
and not merely by the use of persuasive language, that Rousseau produces a
sense of the absolute certainty of the social contract and the general will: but he
does this through that aspect of practical reason that is necessarily allegorical
in a way that I describe in Chapter 4. The idea is that Rousseau's account of the
state of nature as the negation of society is designed to show that the former is
inconceivable from the human point of view and that, therefore, when we think
of human affairs, including our personal affairs, we are already thinking, as it
were, sociologically. To demonstrate this requires further work on how he proceeds and how we might read him, as it were, proceeding.

Let us go back to the problem posed by the fact that the narrative cannot be
true; and let us dismiss the idea that it is a fiction merely intended to persuade.
Why, then, should we take seriously the questions Rousseau addresses about
the origin and moral significance of society? Perhaps his theory can be saved by
simply dismissing the narrative altogether. In that case, we might treat the book
as a standard instance of political/social theory and summarize his descriptions of the social contract in relation to other concepts, such as the body politic
and the general will. We might then conclude (1) that *The Social Contract* re-
states an ancient and still valued republican idea—namely, that a peaceful and
just society is one in which people understand their obligations to one another
and are able to suppress their self-interest sufficiently to guarantee the rule of
law—and (2) that it presents a plausible brief for the superiority of Rousseau's
version of the social contract to what he takes to be Hobbes's solution to the
problem of social order. However, this version of the republican idea supposes
that society can be organized in the same way in which individuals organize
their domestic and local affairs, engaging in projects that require others to be
taken into account. In that case, the idea of a social contract falls under the limitations of the juridical concept of a contract. This has the virtue of respecting
both freedom and the necessity of restraint under conditions of an agreement.
But this is far too little and it presupposes too much. For one thing, one cannot justify extending a model of mutuality among familiar parties to a specific
agreement to the limitless affairs of a community of strangers and its future
generations. Rousseau discusses this at some length in order to show that behind all particular agreements there is something that underlies the very possibility of agreement, and this cannot be the same sort of thing as a particular
contract among specific individuals.

It seems that if we eliminate the narrative and reject the principle that
"might makes right," we are likely to rely on an idea of a contract that cannot
provide an adequate model of a social order in which utility and justice are reconciled. So we must return to the narrative, since it appears to be a necessary
part of Rousseau's argument. But if we accept it as something other than a true

story, which it is not, or as a useful fiction, with the problems just discussed, then we have to discover how it might contribute, first, to the reasonableness of his claim to have reconciled justice and utility, second, to our understanding of how a society can exist beyond its membership at a particular time, and third, to our sense that the social contract is true beyond a shadow of a doubt. It is important to remember that the text in which the narrative has its significance is intended not only to establish the truth of the social contract but to provide a foundation for one of the most influential sociopolitical theories in modern thought.

W hy would a great philosopher feel the need to defend the very idea of society, much less try to give it substance as something absolutely different from the state of nature, and why would he offer a narrative account of a founding event that cannot possibly have occurred? Why would Rousseau even spend time on the idea of society when what he wants to show is how justice and utility can be reconciled even though "utility" appeals to self-interest and "justice" to a sense of a common interest? In other words, why is a narrative of the origin of society necessary for establishing a relationship between law and freedom, and, if so, why is it necessary, first, to set the stage for the emergence of society from a state of nature and, second, to explain the continuation of society by conditions that could not have existed in a state of nature? If law is prior to society, then an explanation of legitimacy and a general sense of an obligation to give the benefit of doubt to authority will be different from what is required if law is immanent to society. Rousseau arrives at the latter position, partly because he believes the former is easily refuted and partly because he recognizes that a secular solution is necessary if there is to be a body politic in which particular wills find a basic principle of unity. Theories that correspond to the first position are likely to emphasize force, which fails to explain "right," and ideas about human nature that confuse effect with cause. Rousseau's position requires a distinction, foundational to modern sociopolitical theory, between power and authority. Power is essentially external to society while authority expresses a sense of right already implicit in society. He considers the immanence of the law to be demonstrated initially by the logical failure and inaccuracies of theories that emphasize the necessary imposition of law by force or in response to the moral limitations of human nature. The social contract is the default position left after his criticisms have done their work. He proceeds to formulate a positive concept of a social contract that not only satisfies the liberal requirements of a republican ideal in which justice and utility are reconciled but establishes the possibility of a durable community of volunteers, strangers who accept, as a matter of right and a gift of freedom, the rule of law. But, as we have seen, a literal reading finds weaknesses in Rousseau's account of the emergence of the social contract from the state of nature. My response is that that is the wrong literal reading: the narrative is not about a chronological

sequence, though it describes one. It is about the incompatibility of two conditions of life (nature and society), only one of which can support anything that
it is reasonable to say is human about human life. From that point of view, it
appears that the chronology is a kind of method, not the content of a claim.

If society is a basic fact, as Rousseau says, then we need to see how he has
demonstrated this beyond a reasonable doubt. His history of the social contract
as a movement from nature to society cannot do this; and characterizing his
use of language as literary is beside the point. There are, then, two questions
that must be answered before addressing the significance of Rousseau's idea
of the social contract to our understanding of what is human about human affairs. (1) Why is it necessary to defend the idea of society at all, and (2) how does
Rousseau's narrative uniquely demonstrate a truth about society independent
of the historical account? How can a narrative that cannot be true to the event
it purports to describe, which is the moment of society, nevertheless be able to
establish that moment as a basic and irrepressible fact? And how might it be the
case *that society cannot otherwise be shown to be basic and irrepressible*?

One reason why it is necessary to define and defend the idea of society
might be that there are serious issues about human affairs that can be discussed only on the presupposition of a holistic sub-theoretical notion of being together such that differences among parties are to some extent overcome
beyond what rationality, pure cognition, allows. As is often the case, where a
discussion engages differences in moral perspectives, interests, or ideas about
what is and is not relevant, it is not easy to separate content, which is what
rationality manages, from questions about the sincerity and trustworthiness
of the parties and whether there are unstated agendas that make it difficult
to anticipate the consequences of a deliberative settlement. Such questions are
pragmatically and logically prior to considerations of content; and the tension they express is bound to persist throughout every discussion that bears
on human affairs. This is not only because intended meanings are subject to
interpretation or may appear at odds according to the differing moral, political,
cultural, or social values of the parties but *because such discussions are necessarily about their own possibility as well as about their immediately intentional
content*. Whatever agreement occurs during a serious discussion must reflect
on conditions of trust, which presumably are conditions of mutuality, as well as
on the sufficiency of the argument aimed at deciding content. As I try to show,
the first, by its very nature, can never be sufficiently settled to bring reflection
on the discussion itself to an end.

If there are no reliable signifiers available for such an underlying sociality,
or there is no shareable access to even a bare sense of the latter, reasons may be
invoked in the course of discussion that refer to substitute objects that can be
conveniently signified, like nameable entities, occasions, and states of affairs.
Such reasons will not be sufficient to a conclusion when the discussion leading
up to it systematically presupposes something about the conditions of settling
disagreement that cannot easily be made accessible to reflection. On the one

hand, such conditions can be brought to notice only in ways bound to disrupt the fluidity and momentum of discussion. On the other, any attempt to bring them to notice will be inadequate to the problem of representing them. If discussions about human affairs presuppose a sociality that they cannot register and therefore effectively omit, no conclusion can be satisfactory. This would be so in regard both to content and to a sense parties might have of having participated in the sort of process in which even the losers should feel obliged to accept the result. Unless it is possible to imagine a discussion in which parties have no reason whatsoever to doubt one another, the result will always be somewhat unsatisfactory. I try to show that this condition can be met only if human activity, including "discussing," is understood according to principles quite different from the notion of communication as exchanges among individuals and different from characterizations of courses of activity as particular events or particular actions. For now, I proceed as if discussion does involve exchanges among persons according to meanings they intend to convey. In that case, any mention I make of sociality should be taken partly as a promise of something yet to come and partly as a convenience. Even if we accept the exchange model just for this moment of inquiry, if Rousseau is correct it should be possible to demonstrate that society is the basic fact beyond the shadow of a doubt. This requires demonstrating how trust is prior to any discussion, whether the latter is conceived of as a series of exchanges or something else.

From this point of view, we might say that for a discussion or debate to succeed in producing consensus among divided parties (either about a content or about whether the issue should be considered settled), something like an "original position" is presupposed, in which trust is predicated on something other than the status or perceived traits of the parties: that is, parties have nothing to prove prior to their discussion. The fact of sociality is prior to dispute, deliberation, and the settling of accounts; and it is precisely this mediation that is crucial though inaccessible to the discursive process (see Blum and McHugh 1984). It is not adequately described by reference to shared values, shared meanings, and commonly accepted norms. These presuppose the very solidarity they are said to explain. So we are left with the idea of a crucial referent that is generally missing from discussions in which it is implicit. Parenthetically, this critical absence may help explain why it has proven so difficult to establish a credible idea of a progressive democratic polity in which policies are predicated on prior policies and on reasons that accumulate as mutually referring principles of legitimate decision making that even those on the losing side of a debate feel constrained to accept.[1] Without something like solidarity, continuity might be imagined but not a continuity accompanied by a sense of legitimacy grounded in an understanding of law in relation to freedom.

What must be demonstrated is that it is not possible for debating parties to imagine what is essential for issues to be worked through when *the social is represented as an entity or state of affairs contingent in content and self-identical in form over time.* To know the essentially social is not something one can choose to do: it is not a result of the deliberative cognitive activity Daniel Kahneman identifies, somewhat playfully, as mental "system 2" (2011, 20). It involves an *immediate* recognition of the necessity of the social, a recognition beyond verbal control but essential to discourse; and this state of being, which is more than what is usually considered to be knowledge, is what Rousseau's account must provide for if there is to be a basic fact about human affairs and therefore a sense of what is human about them. I want to show that the only way this could have been done is through the use of the very narrative that appears to be historically false and logically flawed—but only if it is read against the grain of a literal reading, and if that is supported in other respects by Rousseau's text. In what follows, I try to prepare the ground for this interpretation.

Political theory has tended either to reject or ignore the immanence of the social, most often in favor of individually reductive theories of agency in which social facts are taken as causal conditions of what individuals do. As such, social facts are different from the sorts of fact that people are said expressly to take into account in forming reasons for deciding to act one way or another. While the distinction between reasons and causes is no longer philosophically secure, it remains important to theories that explain action as a particular event that is a resultant of objective constraints mediated by beliefs and subjective considerations mediated by desires (Davidson 2001d, chap. 1; compare Schutz 1967; Taylor 1985b). Theories of this sort take the individual to be the origin of an "action in its course" and to remain the same throughout that course (see Weber 1947, 88). The individual is at any moment precisely what she was at any other moment; and whether she is alone or with others has no more bearing on what sort of person she is than whether she is described before or after she decides to act and then acts. Acting and being social are thought of from this point of view as altogether different, and politics is correspondingly conceived of without regard to what is human about human affairs. This separates politics from a theory of justice aimed at reconciling the particular and general wills on the basis of a prior solidarity in which the individual cannot be an origin in the sense required by standard accounts of action.

Attempting to combine politics and justice while maintaining the idea that individuals are origins and individuals and groups are distinct particulars (e.g., entities, agents, states of affairs) threatens one or both of two indispensable propositions. The first is that the individual is the ultimate referent of moral discourse, as I suggest in the Introduction, so I assume that no political theory is valid that fails systematically to include a concept of moral discourse.[2] The second has an even stronger claim to universality. It says that humans are social beings. This implies that individualism cannot provide a foundation for a theory of politics when such a theory includes a concept of moral discourse in which the first proposition is true. The failure to register the immanence and irrepressibility of the social favors the individualistic ideal of the first proposition, providing a view of society as either separable individuals momentarily living together or speakers/doers who grant substance and confer form on the social through their speech and conduct. The moral principle gives priority to individuals but rejects what defines and thereby essentially limits their individuality, effectively sacrificing the theoretically necessary principle that humans are social through and through. In a normal discussion having to do with human affairs, the first principle is easier to sustain than the second, and my point is that this may raise inexpressible doubts about the legitimacy of any process of coming to a conclusion and the rightness or fairness of the conclusion itself. There is an additional theoretical bias that is a likely result of the silence of the social—namely, a tendency to model discussion on the interaction of individuals. It says that the aim of a discussion is a meeting of minds and that this comes about through exchanges of information, acts that represent an intention to make a substantive difference. But since reading minds is impossible and inferences from gestures, inflections, and the like are uncertain, it is difficult for each party to feel sufficiently understood to guarantee that if there is a meeting of minds she will know it.

The problem of representation is twofold. It has to do with acts said to express intentions and a process the result of which may represent but not please all the parties. If the social is irreducible, it can be experienced only holistically and, therefore, sub-conceptually. The experience is, presumably, internal to social activity, not something that arises or is brought to it. In speaking with others, we experience a connection that *words themselves cannot constitute though their usage requires.* That connection may be elided or it may be suppressed. It is normally elided but not always actively suppressed. That is, in the midst of a discussion we are unlikely to point to the social conditions of its continuity and momentum, though something untoward may bring them close to the surface; but there are times when the course of a discussion turns on a totalizing frame that is inconsistent with the immanence of the social. For example, questions like "Why do you say that?" and "What do you suppose she really meant?" and statements like "You should think before you speak" provide a frame that is definitively asocial. Each identifies agency with ideal individuality, assumes more about representation than should be assumed, and takes the individual as an origin (as in the required type of answer to the first question). It can be hypothesized that parties to such a discourse are likely to be more tense throughout and less comfortable with the result than parties to a discourse that is compatible with a social frame in which responsibility is seen as distributed and the settlement of an issue requires more than justifications; it requires parties to become engaged such that recognizing a truth amounts to recognizing and living the sociality that sustains it. However, while suppression can be expected to lead to a sense of dissatisfaction, so should elision. The former actively eliminates something necessary while the latter merely leaves the situation uncertain.

It appears to be the case, then, that what we say and hear typically contradicts the experience of solidarity. Since this abiding contradiction is not likely to come explicitly to notice in the course of a discussion, it leaves a vague impression on all parties that their discourse is somehow incomplete in ways it should not be, regardless of what they think about the conclusion itself. The problem has something to do with the uncertainties and ambiguities of representation where solidarity is indefinite, as it can only be. There are, however, many instances in which parties who disagree over an issue nevertheless agree that it has been settled and that the process is satisfactory. The question is why? If there is something about the social that entails its silence in discourse, if the legitimacy of a process of discussion is predicated on a shared sense of solidarity, and if discourse cannot take itself as its object, there seems to be no index of solidarity available that can explain why the losers of a debate might accept the legitimacy of the result. Once we recognize that the problem is unavoidable, we can try to understand situations in which it seems to have been resolved. We will see that this requires shifting from an individualistic frame of reference to a social frame—and from one view of the social (as entity, state of affairs, predicate) to a view that is radically different and implicit in the idea that human affairs are essentially and irreducibly social.

The following example, involving Bert and Ernie, is intended to remind us that a justified belief is not sufficient to an undertaking motivated by a sense of obligation (or commitment) and that when parties to a discussion come to share the same sense of obligation, the standard models of communication and rationality are not helpful in understanding why. It turns out that the idea of solidarity, on which so much seems to depend, is part of the problem.

Let us suppose that Ernie has been able, by appealing to certain reasons, to convince Bert that a claim, X, is true in the sense of worthy of being believed. Assume that their discussion does not support reference to their being together and possibly sharing a background of interrelated values and meanings. This poses a problem of representation, since whatever might be traced to their sense of togetherness (e.g., appreciative or egalitarian gestures) cannot become a topic without doing violence to the discussion itself. Therefore, both Bert and Ernie have good reason to wonder if they have understood each other enough to warrant ignoring the possibility that they might not have understood each other as much as they would have liked to. For Bert, there is nothing about the conclusiveness of the discussion to suggest a cause of or reason for moving from the shared explicit conclusion to a sense of obligation to follow its implications or act on them (see Keen 2007). Let us nevertheless imagine that Bert does become committed to the justified claim and feels obliged to act on it. This cannot be explained by the justification, since that only provided reasons to believe. The feeling of commitment may be influenced by the justification, but it is independent of the logic of justification and, in any case, is external to the discussion itself. Indeed, no matter how plausible the reasons for believing X might seem, they entail no obligation; and no matter how strong the sense of an obligation, it cannot be explained by reference to citable reasons for holding the belief. Looking at this from Bert's point of view, we might ask how he would go about convincing his other friend, Maria, to share his sense of obligation. Clearly it would help if he reviewed the reasons for holding the belief in the first place; but, as we have seen, that cannot help explain a sense of obligation to go further. Since Bert cannot justify the sense of obligation simply by an appeal to the same reasons for the belief, he might provide further information. But that introduces facts outside of what justifies the belief and, in any case, will have some of the same problems involved in relating belief to a readiness on the part of the believer to go further.

From what was said earlier, a shared sense of solidarity might be enough to explain how Bert can convince Maria to accept the obligation in fact and not just as a matter of form, perhaps by the ways in which reasons are enunciated or intimacy enacted. But even if this were possible for two, it is hard to see how it would work for a larger number. One reason is that discussion among many parties is likely to be governed by the circulation of belief-related reasons independent of any suggestion of obligation. But regardless of the size of the group, there is still the question of how a sense of solidarity can be shared. For Rousseau, there are two parts to it: How can a sense of solidarity or unity be shared? What about solidarity can create a common sense of obligation? There is no issue of representation in this, as there is in the justification of a belief. That is, in justifying a belief, reasons must be reasons anyone might accept, and what counts is whether "anyone" includes all those present (or possibly present) to the discussion (Nagel 1970, 96). Commitment does not rely on reasons, though they may be relevant to a pre-justification desire to go "beyond belief." It relies on a sense of connection to the others or to one or another possible outcome that is not about reasons and that either presupposes representation or is somehow identical with it.

Another way of getting at this problem is to ask what sort of experience accompanies a sense of commitment when it follows the justification of a belief. What was at stake for Bert in Ernie's justification was not something *about* one or another fact pertaining to the object of the belief, though that may have been what was at stake for Ernie. It was about the totality to which the facts were pertinent. That is, it somehow included a principle of relevance that could not have been satisfactorily demonstrated in the course of the justification and that, therefore, must be thought of as relatively independent of it. The experience at stake for Bert is holistic and not particular. It is the experience of something that can only be known as shared. To that extent, it is an experience of the society in which it is possible to conceive of the significance of the facts.

As long as people are ironical enough about their beliefs to act as if they are satisfied with convincing arguments based on reasons, thereby forestalling commitment and the social recognition it entails, it is not difficult to maintain the façade of a meeting of minds. Once parties find themselves engaged or committed, they can never be sure that there has been a meeting of minds, but it may not seem to matter. This does not necessarily lead to unhappiness since the irony that precludes commitment—as a non-ironic matter of principle—also softens the blow of losing what openness to being committed brings to discourse—namely, a prior commitment to society, and, of course, the momentary satisfaction of realizing the immanence of the social in what is otherwise merely an assertion, justified or not. There is a yet more general conclusion: when individualism prevails, the result of a discussion aimed at justifying a belief that many can share is likely to leave sore losers and a general sense of incompleteness, or an ironic sense of such discussions as, by their nature, morally insignificant.

———————

Two hypotheses can be defended on the basis of the discussion so far. At the least, they dramatize the importance of the idea of an irreducible sociality and the political significance of the general will that corresponds to it. The first says that the reasons given to justify a belief are unlikely to be sufficient to its making a difference, whatever else might make it convincing. This is not only because there is no rational limit to possible reasons. Certainly there is no limit if the discussion is not otherwise constrained, and it always is. However, there is one cause of insufficiency that surpasses all constraints: the irreducible irrepressibly social aspect of life. It is an indispensable reason that all parties share and can know that they share beyond their particular interests; but it defies thematization and explication. It is suppressed when referred to as an entity, a type of action, a predicate, or a state of affairs, to the extent to which they effectively omit any implication of an irreducible and irrepressible socially reflexive general will. I characterize the social as a *course of activity* in contrast with an entity and a state of affairs. I take this to be consistent with Rousseau's idea of the social contract and what is actually presupposed by the human sciences. As such, it appears as systematic resistance to theory (in the usual sense of theory as bringing a propositional argument to a conclusion). The second hypothesis is that the necessity of this reason overrides differences of values, preferences, or beliefs regardless of whether they are negotiable and whether they have been negotiated to the point of apparent agreement. If there is such a reason, and if it is inexpressible (or is otherwise missing), then it is likely that the losers in a debate will be unsatisfied with the final decision—that is, its justice. This is so even if their voices have been heard and proper procedures have been followed, thereby meeting Stuart Hampshire's criteria for judging whether a decision is just (2000). It is also likely that those who prevail will, for the same reason, evaluate their victory in terms other than the reasons initially given in justification—as when the result is attributed to good strategy or the realization of political capital, or right because it is supported by a majority.

A belief justified in the course of a discussion might be convincing even though it lacks an appeal to the prior sociality that is the fundamental condition of its being formed as a belief and received as justified. But it is unlikely that it will be felt by all the parties to be binding in the sense of imposing an obligation to act in a way that either treats the belief as having normative force or finds a norm within it. If it is binding, what follows should be seen as reflexive to the mutuality and reciprocity compatible with a general will that reflects the equality of each member of society in her dependence on all the others taken as a whole. Otherwise, acceptance of the belief would be merely formal and, therefore, unreliable as far as allowing parties to anticipate what might come next. Parenthetically, we see how an obligation that comes to be attached to a justified belief can lead either to further intellectual activity (more discussion) or to an engagement with the world and, therefore, to a different situation, just as we have seen how justification and commitment are two different sorts of condition. Each cannot be inferred from the other, and there is nothing in either that is necessary to the other.

It seems to follow, contrary to Hampshire's expectation (2000), that the more an adversary procedure involves "hearing all sides" beyond some threshold, as in courts and legislatures, the more the result is likely to be suspect, leaving the original conflict intact, though shifting its register.[3] Adding reasons, or allowing for a plurality of reasons, does not address the effects of the lack of the most essential reason for attributing rationality, and, as Hampshire sees it, legitimacy to the process. One important effect is the belief on the part of losers as well as winners that it is both sensible and morally obligatory to accept the result. To this extent at least, content counts and not merely words, procedure, or form; and it seems that reference to "sides" is, under the circumstances, too vague to provide a sense of justice beyond the merely contingent and relative fairness of established procedures (no matter how open they might be to all manners of expression and opinion).

While it is not possible without further work to say what might be expected if the basic fact of sociality were somehow to become explicit, it is possible to anticipate some overall effects of its elision. For one thing, it is unlikely that political discourse, of the dialogical sort often described by theorists of civil society as the substance of the public sphere, can provide a basis for a cumulative, progressive, reliable, and self-corrective polity. Rather, it is unlikely precisely in regard to the fact that the elision compromises dialogue. It deprives it of an essential referent and reasons that depend on that referent. In that respect, what appears dialogical is self-defeating and bound to breed suspicion among all parties that whatever rational continuity seems momentarily to exist is a cover for hidden agendas and covert exercises of power, precisely what the concepts of the public sphere and civil society were designed to overcome. In other words, civil society predicated on dialogue without reference to the sort of extra-civil equality that is a necessary condition of dialogue ultimately shows itself to be founded in the play of particular wills.[4]

The discussion so far suggests that, on the one side, the endlessness of political debates and the dissatisfaction, ill will, and resentment that often accompany them disguise what is at stake when dissatisfaction is attributed to facts external to the discourse itself—for example, correctable errors such as failures of process or representation, the incompatibility of values, and a failure of the parties to understand the issues under consideration. On the other side, what is at stake in the endlessness and ill will that accompany a sense of premature closure is that the rationality of all such discourses is fatally compromised when something is missing that is crucial if there is to be a genuine meeting of minds: whatever conclusion seems to have been arrived at will appear to be merely formal and therefore legitimately subject to challenge. The sense of closure as premature is on the order of a belief, perhaps inarticulate but no less active, that a conclusion is valid only if it is not incompatible with the basic fact of equality among parties each of whom depends on all and is therefore obligated by that condition in common—which is the decisive fact on which the moral grounds of dialogue and justice depend.

The requirement that there be no violation of the basic fact cannot be tested as long as the question of trust, which depends on that fact, is elided or suppressed. Without such a test, the rationality of a discussion, the justice of its process, and the reasonableness of its conclusion cannot be satisfactorily decided and, therefore, momentarily laid to rest. But regardless of whether parties express dissatisfaction, whatever has been *justified* in the course of the discussion, by appeals to reasons other than those that correspond to the basic fact, is unlikely to support the sort of commitment that allows the parties to settle on a reasonable end to discussion. That depends on the confirmation of a preexisting solidarity. Note that as yet nothing in this implies that a commitment to act necessarily leads to a particular action or that it is a particular autonomous state of mind.

Without an evident connection to that fact, it is understandable that at least some parties would be tempted to see the final result as little more than the result of power and interest or the expression of a hidden agenda. This is possible in any case because sociality, society, is always presupposed in ways that make it difficult to acknowledge it as a basic fact and because issue-oriented discussions such as debates are always incomplete without some sort of evidence that sociality is the ultimate referent of discourse on human affairs and the final reason for any justifiable conclusion. The absence of such an acknowledgment effectively denies the basis of mutual trust, of a sense of inhabiting the same worlds, resulting in a sense of the discussion as merely the play of particular wills. If the hypothesis about the significance of the absence of a social referent is plausible, it provides another reason to try to formulate an idea of society despite the difficulties of doing so. In this regard, the Rawlsian original position, from the standpoint of which it is possible to imagine a rational discussion about what is constitutionally just, relies on the possibility of recognizing the equal dependence of each on all: the ability to see one's own basic interest (equality under a "veil of ignorance" in which nonbasic particular interests are momentarily suspended) as a function of one's dependence on all (Rawls 1971, 17–22, 118–192). It also provides another explanation of why it is difficult if not impossible to demonstrate the basic fact in the course of political debate—because the terms of any such debate and the procedures designed to ensure its legitimacy exclude, as a matter of their justificatory language and its level of abstraction, reference to society as an association of equals—though they allow for statistical generalities and distributions that pertain to people taken as scattered or as independent and unsocial, Rousseau's "multitude" (1978b). Moreover, even if this were not true, to the extent to which, say, a political debate runs its course on the basis of the elision, one would somehow have to remove oneself from it in order to demonstrate the basic fact on which it depends—and even then it would not be possible to communicate that result to parties still caught up in the debate.

The model of rational action often taken as the ideal type and therefore natural tendency of topical discourse, and of dialogue, poses the central logical problem inasmuch as it tends to exclude all but expedient action (of which prudential action is usually, though with difficulty, considered an instance) and includes other considerations only to the extent to which they can be translated in just such terms. That is, the model that provides the most general defense of procedural justice, essential to traditional conceptions of democracy, fails to include the one indispensable nonexpedient reason to which every resolution of differences must in some way appeal, and which rational actors should be expected to endorse. That it is both necessary to and virtually inadmissible in discourse suggests one of two things: either something fundamental about the model and its way of understanding discourse is at fault, or the model can be saved by re-presenting the social in a way that completes what is otherwise an incomplete account of rationality. I eventually argue that this latter option is not available because of what the model itself requires of its referents and because any explicit representation of the social would violate the original position, which requires a cross-sectional appraisal and, therefore, a static conception of society, and the obligation implicit in the idea of a veil of ignorance, which is an obligation that memory cannot honor.

But regardless of whether this is correct, it should be clear that a model of rationality that fails to include the social as immanent to every one of its terms and conditions cannot support an expansive idea of justice or, indeed, any conclusion about human affairs. It provides, instead, an account of the willingness of the parties to play a game in which they must agree not to take seriously what they normally believe or care about, in the interest of somehow being serious together. But what they are supposed to be serious about together cannot be clear as long as there is a systematic omission of an indispensable referent from the deliberations, the very one on which the ideas of an original position and a veil of ignorance depend. As far as the possibility of the *continued* legitimacy of a decision in which justice might be an issue, memory of the course of a deliberation, which is to say the struggles that produce reasons out of uncertainty and ambiguity, is no less important than the deliberation itself. But memory is unlikely to recover that history, in which case the conclusion may appear, at least to some, as little more than a game-defined solution. This would be a form of justice but not a matter of its substance, which is its ratification of the basic fact.

Memory cannot easily be detached from interest and cannot reproduce a version of the original position necessary for the result to be just in the long run required by the idea of justice. Memory reconstructs what happened in light of what is revealed after the veil of ignorance is dropped. Game-related satisfaction (e.g., that justice has been achieved) has to be evaluated against what might appear retrospectively as the costs of having excluded knowledge that ought to have been included in the original deliberation, in particular one's knowledge that one is of society and one's hope, which must somehow find validation in advance of deliberation, that the others acknowledge this same fact and its importance to the rationality of the final decision. Memory might be able to sustain the continual sense of the legitimacy of an arrangement required by an applicable theory of justice but only if it recollects the element of trust that guaranteed the absence of hidden agendas and power among the parties during the course of their deliberation and their corresponding submission to the general will. Parenthetically, I assume that the standard view of rationality would take the endlessness of discourse as an aberration in reasoning rather than as a symptom of something missing from the model of rationality. I have been suggesting that this missing element is the social aspect of what humans think and do, though as yet I have been able only to hint at what makes it difficult to enter that aspect into discourse and to take it theoretically into account.

In further support of the thesis that evident recognition of the basic social fact is necessary to the rationality of any decision about law or policy no less than its reasonableness (Rawls 1999a, 11–12, 131–140), we can observe that a number of questions are again being asked about how the lives of the citizens and peoples of a modern nation should be ordered; the attitudes appropriate for evaluating policy proposals in regard to the idea of law and the rights and obligations of citizens; how to define citizenship where territorial boundaries are permeable and in constant flux; the conditions under which resistance, rebellion, revolution, and war might be justified; the substance and limits of sovereignty; the conditions and limits of representation; and the proper sphere of government. One consideration adds to the urgency of these and other such issues. Decisions about them will have more or less desirable general, inclusive, and preemptive consequences. The anticipation and evaluation of these depend on assumptions about how *society* is possible and sustainable beyond the *national* juridical form in which power and authority are increasingly indistinguishable.[5] But, while formal reference to assumptions is always important, it is not the main problem for the rationality of discourse. The latter depends on pre-deliberative confidence among parties in the social validity of referring no less than in speaking meaningfully in the first place. The evaluation of the possible consequences of settling a debate prematurely also depends on the implication of all possible parties as inter-dependent equals before they express their differences.

In *The Social Contract*, Rousseau argued against the familiar claims that human nature and force are necessary and/or sufficient to explain social order—given a minimalist and morally neutral notion of what capacities are assumed by any possible conception of human society. In the process, he attempted to show that society constitutes a distinctively human kind of freedom regardless of its possible degradation in the course of the articulation and development of its institutions. He understood the latter as symptomatic of the conflict between the particular and the general wills but not as the only possible outcome. The crucial point is the tension and the constant movement it engenders, not the inevitability of degradation. It was on that basis that he was able to reconcile justice and utility—"what right permits" and "interest demands" (1978b, 46). He first showed that theories that rely on force and human nature are either self-contradictory or otherwise confused and cannot support the concept of society presupposed in any discussion of "right" and "interest."

There are two main parts of his argument. One demonstrates that certain familiar assumptions are inconsistent with another more fundamental but ignored assumption (the basic fact of inter-dependence) *the truth of which can be demonstrated for all practical purposes and without reasonable theoretical exception or qualification.* It follows that no theory of society can ignore that truth and still be free of paradox. Recognition of the sociality identified with the social contract (equal dependence of each on all) and embodied in the general will (a nonpsychological, noncultural subjectivity that subsumes, and does not merely bring into alignment, all others) is a necessary condition of being clear about right, law, judgment, belief, rational action, desire, participation, agency, and justice as far as their concepts are consistent with what is human about human affairs.[6] The second part completes the first part by demonstrating that it is not possible to imagine an alternative to the basic fact, which he calls the "sacred right,"[7] and therefore to conceive of human affairs, including selfhood and individuality, apart from that fact, regardless of what reference to force and nature might add. This is the focus of what follows.

To the extent to which the assumptions that underlie political and social theory do not include the basic fact, there can be no reasonable expectation of their forming a reasonably complete and consistent basis for drawing valid conclusions. The burdens of Rousseau's narrative of the transformative emergence of humankind from an original state of nature, which I interpret as an allegory rather than a narrative account of origins,[8] are to show that society is both basic and irresistible and to establish that there is only one way of showing that it is true, by showing it as immediately accessible to and irrefutable by thought. This involves demonstrating that all conceivable practical purposes presuppose the immanence of the social and then completing the argument by providing the only evidence sufficient to confirm it as an irrefutable and ineluctable matter of fact—by showing that it is not possible sincerely to doubt it, though it may be possible to forget it.

Given that he has succeeded in showing that appeals to force and human nature cannot account for the meaning and determination of "right" and "legitimacy," and cannot explain how law can function without freedom and how the two are related, Rousseau proposes to demonstrate the following propositions by an appeal to experience. (1) It is impossible to think about anything having to do with human affairs without taking into account the idea of an irreducible, unqualifiable, and unlimited sociality. (2) Thinking about instances of those affairs, no less than considering them in general, cannot avoid at least an intimation of that idea—either directly or tacitly in the form of unease about any ostensibly final answers to questions about them. (3) If both propositions are true, then the claim that society is the basic fact is true for all practical purposes. That is, all that we call purposes are predicated on it in any but the most trivial sense of purpose. It follows from the third proposition that a non-mechanistic idea of practicality refers us to a virtually unlimited number of practicalities and to the impossibility of setting fixed boundaries among them. To refer to a practice is, then, to refer to something like a relatively coherent field of practices. To omit the latter is to trivialize the former. The evidence offered by Rousseau for the basic fact is that the state of nature is *unthinkable*. That is, it is unthinkable insofar as it refers to a condition in which every activity is singular and distinct from every other activity except in the limited external, asocial, and abject sense of connectedness implied by standard individualistic theories of action and the Hobbesian notion of the state of nature. For those theories, action is intensively and determinatively situated: it is involutional in its rationality—as in panic or the progressive tendency toward mechanistic approaches to problem solving by an isolated problem solver.

Individualistic theories are occasionally bolstered by a mischievous analogy between how humans live and act together and what nonhumans (understood as instinctive creatures) do that resembles what humans do. What is mischievous is the suggestion that the motivation of nonhuman sociality in its particular forms, presumably either instinctual or otherwise encoded in the course of evolution, is evidence for the fact that human sociality in its particular forms is also biological in the same sense.[9] On the contrary, Rousseau's demonstration that the state of nature is unthinkable for humans confirms the idea that society is the basic fact and makes it irresistible and, in that sense, axiomatic—whether or not it can be made otherwise explicit. Before proceeding, we need to consider the possibility that the assumption is not axiomatic. For if it is not, a prima facie case might be made for the significance of the social without having to claim that human affairs are *essentially* social, in which case there may be human affairs, including actions, that are not social. But this leaves open the possibility of believing what, for Rousseau, is not believable—that humans can be human without being social and that being social is not a distinctively human way of being.

To say that sociality is contingent is to say that there are occasions on which what human beings do together should be accounted for by reference to points of agreement among sovereign subjects rather than to something that precedes individuality and therefore agreement. The difference made by being together may then be explained by the pressure on each subject of social facts. For Durkheim, such a fact is indicated by the prevalence of a type of behavior or representation. Prevalence may lend confidence to a belief that something observed and then counted indicates or even constitutes a social fact. But it is logically different from such a fact. Prevalence is a matter of counting instances. It cannot describe the connections that must exist among such facts if they are to be social facts. Nor, for the same reason, should one be confident that prevalence is even an indication of a social fact, since, before there can be a conceivable indication, a representation, there must be at least a rough theory of how the one fact (prevalence) can represent or indicate another when that other is defined in a way that is inconsistent with the principle of the ostensible index. To my knowledge, there is no such theory, and Durkheim's (1982) discussion does not provide for one.

What makes a fact social for Durkheim is its structural value to the irreducible collectivity of social facts of which it is a part, the difference it makes among things that make a difference; and this has no necessary connection to prevalence. To know S as a social fact is to locate S in a network of social facts each of which bears on all the others. It is the fact itself and not prevalence that gives it normative force. There is no way of going from a record of "behaviors," which are somehow selected in the first place, to a social fact. Indeed, Durkheim understood quite well that the very selection of the objects to be counted cannot be free of the world of social facts in which it takes place. One might say, then, that it is not that a regularity is or indicates a social fact but that a regularity alerts the scientist to the possibility of such a fact and, therefore, to observations of a qualitative nature. But this will not do, since the best we can say is that when the scientist is put on the alert by a regularity, that may be a social fact about social science but it is not justified by any known methodology or rules of inference. Indeed, as Durkheim (1982) constantly reminds his readers, statistical regularities should be treated with suspicion, since nothing about them suggests that they will continue (other than as social facts themselves or the operation of socially external power) and social facts are presumed to be relatively constant through changes in society, topological features of social space, because of their participation in something like a structure of such facts.

To deny that sociality is fundamental assumes further that a reasonable judgment can be made about what belongs to the individual alone and what belongs to that individual under the aspect of being among others. But it is not clear how such a judgment could be verified or what sort of observer could be in a position to make such a judgment with the requisite confidence to apply it. The problem is exacerbated when one insists on the individual as the starting point for thinking about human affairs since there is no way to determine when it is appropriate to decide that the line between personal and social has been crossed; and, even if we grant the individualistic premise, the risks

of misunderstanding are probably greater for overpersonalizing than for over-
emphasizing the social. Beginning with the social, however, does not require
disavowing individuality and does not bring into doubt the possibility of doing
so; nor must it rely on an unacceptable metaphysics of social entities (compare
Ruben 1985). It depends, of course, on what is meant by "social," and I have assumed so far that it is better to avoid thinking of society as a particular kind of
entity or state of affairs, or of "social" just as a predicate. To the extent to which
sociality consists of courses of activity irreducible to units, beginning with it
opens the possibility of a default position momentarily in favor of individuality as long as it preserves the idea that humans are, as Jean-Paul Sartre (1992)
reminds us, beings in a situation, or constitutively situated beings. I interpret
Sartre to mean that humans are essentially social. That is, it may be possible to
salvage individualism without sacrificing the idea of the social as the basic fact
and without hypostatizing the idea of the individual.

Before considering that possibility, remember that, up to this point, Rousseau's argument in favor of the priority of society to law, social order, and republican morality is neither obviously false, which speaks in its favor, nor fully
convincing, which speaks to the need to demonstrate that the proposition "society is a basic fact" applies both at the level of history and at the level of experience. For this, we need more than the case Rousseau makes for convention as
the default position when we are forced to reject the idea that might makes
right. He argues that to invoke force as sufficient to establishing stable and legitimate authority is to face the logical implication that force is equally legitimate when used to overthrow those who originally employed it. It follows that
might, which requires coercive force, cannot explain right, which requires legitimacy.

Rousseau can only succeed in establishing the truth of the basic fact if he
persuades his readers that he is identifying and solving an urgent problem they
already share with one another and with him—namely, an underlying concern about how common life is possible when justice and utility seem at odds.[10]
Since no obvious solution based on force or human nature recommends itself,
it might be thought that, holding foibles constant, humans are always ready to
recognize a common interest and subordinate themselves to it. Yet to prove this
requires that he consider what his text actually does to its reader in the course
of reading—in contrast with standard notions of proof. That is, he must establish and not merely prove the truth of the basic fact, without further argument
and without any appeal to intuition—as when one says that something is taken
for granted. What he must make overwhelmingly evident is that it is not possible to think about human affairs without reference to the basic fact and it is
not possible *not* to think about them in some sense of "think."

———————

At the outset, Rousseau's account of the social contract presents itself as
preempting the distractions of false but otherwise appealing propositions

that run counter to what is basic about the basic social fact; and by the end of Book 1, it is fairly clear that reflections on personal identity are, in a crucial respect, irreducibly social. So there is no conceivable position regarding what is human that lies outside of society. What is needed is a demonstration, at once substantive and methodical, that exhausts the subjectivity of the reader leaving nothing of it that is exempt from what is demonstrated. Such an incontrovertible truth is grasped in a radically different way from the results of a formal or an empirical proof and the reasonable inclinations of intuition. In order to put ourselves in a position to appreciate the demonstration, we must first agree that the narrative of the transition of humanity from nature to society, the most cited part of *The Social Contract*, should not be interpreted literally or as a fiction, since that would involve him precisely in discourses incapable of demonstrating any incontrovertible truth: society can be the *basic* fact only if its truth is immediate and certain, which is beyond what mere argument can do. In that respect, his arguments with other thinkers would be distracting except that by eliminating their claims largely on logical grounds he makes a case for attempting to demonstrate the truth of the basic fact by other means than argument.

It turns out that the demonstration can appeal only to those for whom sociality is memorable (and therefore forgotten only momentarily, perhaps with a fleeting sense of shame), which, as suggested previously, includes all human beings. It is tempting to say that there are exceptions and that the demonstration will not appeal to two types: those who are able to reserve for themselves a different status or subject position essentially outside of human affairs (without somehow doing away with the intelligibility of all that is meaningfully associated with the use of expressions such as "themselves") and those radical utilitarians who attempt systematically but futilely to purge their memory of society and for whom all that people do is immediately, abjectly, and asocially practical and therefore subject essentially to the exigencies of a moment (which moment can itself be described only as an abstraction unrelated to other abstractions). Neither exception works, because there is no comprehensible subjectivity outside of what is human about human affairs and because the very insistence on characterizing people relies on some notion of social reality. Radical utilitarians can reject the idea of an irreducible sociality prior to individuality only in regard to others; they cannot avoid accepting it, in practice if not admittedly, for themselves.

3

Dependence and Autonomy

The appeal of Rousseau's arguments against received theories and in favor
of the idea that human affairs are essentially social before they are anything else depends on whether he successfully demonstrates that there
is an immediate sense shared by all human beings that everything about them
reflects, as an indisputable fact, that their being social is the essence of their being human. He first attempts to show why the standard theories of right should
be rejected. Only then does he show that human life cannot be conceived of in
the state of nature and, therefore, can be conceived of only in society in contrast
with a mere "multitude" or aggregate. It follows that to be human is not only to
be social but to be able to know oneself only as a social being.

That he begins by refuting the standard theories appears to indicate that
Rousseau intends to prove, as one does a theory, that the "act of association
produces a moral and collective body" in which "each member" is "an indivisible part of the whole" (1978b, 53). This involves showing in what ways received theories that explain legitimacy by reference to force, conquest, slavery,
human nature, and the priority of majority rule, are logically defective, or that
they presuppose precisely the conditions of unanimity and legitimacy that they
purport to explain. If the issue is proof, Rousseau's theory should be judged
according to the same criteria used to judge the others, which are, presumably,
the normal logical requirements of any argument. These include clear definitions, valid assumptions, well-formed and mutually coherent propositions free
of paradox, and conclusions compatible with what else is known about human
affairs. The problem is that, by itself, this would leave his position as vulnerable
as those he refutes. The failure of alternative theories may increase one's confidence in Rousseau's, but it does not imply that his is true, as he seems to claim

(1978b, 52–53). He has almost certainly oversimplified the rejected theories and may well have failed to exhaust the available possibilities, and he is required to exhaust them if his theory is to be justified by reference to the lack of acceptable alternatives.

There are other reasons to challenge the validity of the claim that "the social order is a sacred right that serves as a basis for all the others" and that, since that right comes neither from nature nor from force, "it is therefore based on conventions" (1978b, 47). The term "convention" is nowhere clearly defined in *The Social Contract*, and, in any case, the idea that society is "a sacred right" is not defended as it would have to be if the claim is intended as a theory. Nor does Rousseau clarify and explain the relationship between the ideas of an "association" and the "general will." Why should one lead to or be implicit in the other? It seems either that the theory is not true or that it is not a theory. If it is not a theory, does this mean that it is unintelligible or that it is false? Strawson (1992) explicitly endorses the idea that society is immanent to all that humans do as humans as well as the idea that this is both an article of knowledge and incontrovertibly true. I believe that a great deal of the literature of philosophical analysis assumes both and then curiously proceeds to ignore them. If the idea that society is the basic fact is not *false*, what is its status as knowledge? If it is not *falsifiable*, does this mean that its status cannot be decided, in which case the value of the idea for any reasonable purpose is impossible to ascertain? I show that when we turn to the narrative, not for its story but for the possibility of an unavoidable reader effect, we are immediately confronted with the truth of the basic fact as a certainty beyond what any theory can provide. How far does this take us? I argue that it goes quite far enough, since Rousseau's exploration of the implications of the social contract take his readers into issues that are undeniably important and that take that truth as axiomatic to any acceptable solution.

————

No matter how plausible Rousseau's conclusion about the dependence of right on convention is in comparison to its alternatives, it is incomplete because he has not yet demonstrated that society is the basic fact and basic right, and it is clear that this cannot be shown by argument alone. How, then, can we know that the following statements about the social contract are true, as they must be if society is the basic fact?

> Since each one gives his entire self, the condition is equal for everyone. (1978b, 53)

> As each gives himself to all, he gives himself to no one. (1978b, 53)

> *Each of us puts his person and all his power in common under the supreme direction of the general will; and in a body we receive each member as an indivisible part of the whole.* (1978b, 53; emphasis in original)

Moreover, what are we to make of the language and substance of the following summary?

> Instantly, in place of the private person of each contracting party, this act of association produces a moral and collective body, composed of as many members as there are voices in the assembly, which receives from this same act its unity, its common *self*, and its will. (1978b, 53–54; emphasis in original)

Why "instantly"? How does an act immediately perform a "moral and collective body"? In what sense is "the whole" a form of life? And in what capacity does its "will" lie? To know oneself as "an indivisible part of the whole" is to know society as the basic fact. But "know" cannot mean, in this context, having learned or come to know, having a justified belief, or drawing a conclusion from logical inference or the accumulation of evidence. For Rousseau, this "knowledge" is instantaneous and certain beyond possible doubt. Only when this is demonstrated is the argument in favor of a first convention and the necessity of a social contract complete. Only then can his readers both know without qualification that they are *of* society and not simply *in* it and know, equally without qualification, that they know it. It is at that moment that our knowledge of the truth of the basic fact makes us all theoreticians. This is what the narrative accomplishes but only when read against the superficiality of a "literal reading."[1] To the extent that Rousseau accomplishes this, his theory cannot be understood as one theory among others but as something altogether different: *it is the only knowledge about which it is impossible to be ironical and which has the power of an inerrant memory to command the imagination.*

The effectiveness of Rousseau's account of the social contract, which is to say the immediate certainty of the truth of the basic fact to anyone who reads or might read the text, requires a further step. This has to do with the evaluation of historical societies according to the consonance of their institutional arrangements with the general will and with what immanent sociality entails for the ideas of a general will, sovereignty, law-giving, the state, and what Michel Foucault calls "governmentality" (2007, 108–109). It involves showing how the trustworthiness and rationality of political discourse depends on the immanence of the social, so that all will feel the weight of its elision or suppression. But politics, which has to do with difference, is an aspect of sociality, and therefore is itself immanent to human affairs. It is misunderstood when abstracted from the social and then characterized as a distinctly articulated functional component of what is then named "society." It follows, first, that sociality is no less an aspect of theoretical and practical reason then it is of discourse per se, and, second, that its concept cannot be recovered by the usual methods of philosophical analysis. With these hypotheses in mind, I resume my account of the problems posed by dissatisfaction in discourse.

I have suggested that reading *The Social Contract* for what is unique and indispensable about it is to grasp the incontrovertible truth of the basic fact. It follows that Rousseau's criticisms of the standard theories are important insofar as they establish the most obvious consequences of two errors. The first is to define the state of nature as the negation of society, and the second is to confuse the former with the formative conditions of the latter. These disqualify the standard interpretation of the narrative of the first convention as a story with a plot (the coming together of human beings out of a common need that is not yet a need in common) and its resolution (the social contract). But they do not disqualify a reading that is faithful to what the narrative itself performs on its reader that is immediate to the senses of "nature" and "society" (see Brooks 1984, xi).

Rousseau's characterizations of the alternative theories are oversimplified and his criticisms do not envision even the possibility of reasonable responses.[2] Consequently, that part of his argument is insufficient to justify his claim that his position is all that remains when the others have failed. But this is not a weakness; rather, it sets the stage for what is original in the text, and setting the stage requires nothing more than a prima facie case to the effect that it is worth seeing whether there can be certainty beyond the probabilistic truths of historical arguments and the merely logical truths of claims whose assumptions are questionable. To complete this trope for its effect requires that we read the narrative against the grain of the standard interpretations. Rousseau's narrative is summarized in the following quotations:

> I assume that men have reached the point where obstacles to their self-preservation in the state of nature prevail by their resistance over the forces each individual can use to maintain himself in that state. Then that primitive state can no longer subsist and the human race would perish if it did not change its way of life. (1978b, 52–53)

The task is, then, to

> find a form of association that defends and protects the person and goods of each associate with all the common force, and by means of which each one, uniting with all, nevertheless obeys only himself and remains as free as before. This is the fundamental problem which is solved by the social contract. (1978b, 53)

The requirement that the act of association yield an immediate and self-reflective transformation of the associated individuals and a constitution of human affairs as distinctly human gives greatest importance to what the narrative does to the reader rather than to what it says to us about people, things, and events. This allows Rousseau to show, as he must, that an immediate recognition of the truth of the basic fact not only is possible for philosophers but imposes itself without recourse on all who might think about human affairs beyond their simplest inclinations, which is to say all human beings. If he succeeds, he will have provided support for two nonobvious but intuitively compelling conclusions. First, what is revealed by evident dissatisfaction with debates about policy and laws, *beyond what appears to be discontent with the effects of having to compromise,* is that participants are aware that no conclusions possible under prevailing assumptions can be noncontroversial and that, therefore, all are bound to be less than satisfactory from one point of view or another. Second, this is not merely a result of the use of a value- or interest-laden language or of incompatible goals, though these might be subordinate factors in a value-added account of dissatisfaction.

To suspect that no resolution of differences can be satisfactory, and to suspect that this is not merely because of competing values or preferences, is to open the possibility that *expressing* dissatisfaction insinuates the sub-theoretical idea that what people have in common cannot be expressed in the same terms that typically qualify discussions of human affairs. Rousseau's account of the social contract suggests that the rationality of all further decisions by people among people depends on a first convention, which is to say a moment of unanimity. Dissatisfaction in the course of such decisions indicates an awareness on the part of each individual that it is impossible to sustain a rationalizing self-concept without acknowledging the dependence of each on all and not merely specific others. To sustain a self-concept adequate to participating in rational decision making requires a sense of the equality that lies at the base of sociality. The coherence of the body politic as an ongoing expression of the general will gives the idea of a self-concept its meaning and, with that, the meaning of ideas associated with agency, such as value, judgment, and interest. This implies that a rationalizing self cannot be identical with or inferred from the sort of individuality presupposed by theories in which the social is either derived from nonsocial assumptions or epiphenomenal; and it implies a contradiction between sociality and the self-sufficient subjective continuity thought by many theorists of action as necessary for an act to be meaningful as well as expedient and prudential. That is, it implies that the reasonableness of reasons for an act, first and foremost, reflect the facts that one is human only among others and that each depends on all for whatever right and freedom are involved in action.

I conclude that the general uneasiness of political discourse expresses a shared sense that something is missing that is prior to any possibility of reasonable agreement, including agreeing to disagree, and that this missing referent—or the fact that it is missing, its positive absence—is an essential condition of discourse itself. This undoubtedly poses difficulties in conceptualizing "agreement" and "coherent organization," therefore the possibility of reconciling differences, which is considered necessary for conceiving of historically specific societies and what Rawls calls "the law of peoples" (1999a). But such difficulties become significant only when a theory begins with a particular society as its object of explanation rather than with the very possibility of theorizing under conditions that can be made apparent only in the course of theoretical work. From this point of view, uneasiness expresses a missing but essential sub-theoretical referent and, in that respect, is the immediate motive for theorizing as well as for imagining any reconciliation or management of differences. This suggests that a virtually ineffable holistic or totalizing notion of sociality underlies the meanings of discursive order, law, justice, utility, and the rationality of instrumental concerns. If so, then most philosophies of social, economic, and political action, collective-signifying language, and the possible reality of social entities are inadequate to their ostensible objects. This literature has, despite itself, brought us closer to recognizing the indispensability of the idea of the social and to understanding the limitations of standard formulations in the study of human affairs. In what follows, I am concerned with what can be meant by a prior sociality, the equality presupposed by the very idea of the social, and how this sits with the contemporary analysis of action and the attempt to apply it to altruism and, by inference, to the reconciliation of justice and utility.

If one agrees with Nagel (1970) that there may be "timeless reasons" for a given act—say, based on the expression of a need regardless of whose need it might be—and if we momentarily accept Rousseau's version of the idea that humans are essentially social, the most basic of these reasons, in the sense of mediating all others, has to do with an equality of inter-dependent beings that cannot be qualified. It is a reason for all who know themselves as social before they know themselves as individuals. By hypothesis, to know one's self in this way is to "know" in the midst of the activity of performing sociality, and this "knowing" cannot be a mental state distinct from the performance. My reading of Rousseau's narrative is intended to answer the question whether it is possible *not* to "know" oneself first as irreducibly social. If not, then this basic reason, on which the reasonableness of all other reasons depends, does not correspond to individualistic notions of agency or to the absolutely individuated continuity of a self that Nagel refers to in his defense of prudential or future-oriented reasons, and, by analogy, altruism (see 1970, 78).[3] In that case, individuality must be thought of as an ostensible product, a moment, or an ongoing accomplishment of association as such; and agency always transpires within a course of activity in which it is constituted as a social fact inexplicable by reference to individuated selves and their ostensible intentions or personal reasons.

Another way of putting this is to say that, absent the most fundamental condition of reasoning together—namely, an acknowledgment of the social and therefore of the middle to long run to which all policy and much philosophy are oriented—prudential considerations cannot motivate the very discussions to which they would seem most urgent and appropriate. The Rousseauian argument goes further. It also holds that the same is true for the short run. That is, no utilitarian undertaking can be rational in its course unless it is compatible with the basic fact of sociality. If it is, then it ceases to be specifically utilitarian and there are no purely instrumental acts, so that instances of the type of action typically featured in philosophies of action are either rare or nonexistent.

To support both parts of this thesis, its short- and the middle- to long-run aspects, requires showing that there is something essentially indecisive, not merely "essentially contestable" or even nonrational, about considering human affairs in a way that elides or suppresses what is nevertheless presupposed as the comprehensive and irreducible fact of sociality. When this is taken into account, priorities and substantive conclusions are likely to be different from when it is not. For example, reliance on demand-based distributional solutions to material inequality would no longer be consistent with what is human about human affairs and therefore with the collectively subjective dimension of "demand" and "satisfaction" (see Sen 2002, 681). Nor would it be adequate to substantiating the practical conditions under which sociality reveals itself as the basic fact about lives in common, about people living among people. This is the significance of Rousseau's use of "equality" in regard to the necessary but ambiguous relationship between the first convention and the social contract when the latter is understood as the upshot of a coming together that is, for each, a relinquishing of all coercive power—in other words, of all that is incompatible with the very notion of coming or being together in the form of an association. Moreover, when sociality is taken into account, what can be conceived of as individual reasoning crucially involves *being within* a self-reflecting (reflexive) course of activity. Within that course, the content, which includes the order of consideration and anything that seems to anticipate a conclusion, most immediately appears as an ongoing activity that insinuates itself as fundamental and irrepressible beyond ostensibly individual interventions. In addition, the practicality of any practical reasoning that operates from the point of view of a deliberator's rationally oriented "original position" of selfless impartiality must be understood as an internal feature of the collective and not as an attitude voluntarily assumed by each deliberator on the basis of a rationality external to the social dimension of what she does.

The originality of this position is neither voluntary nor individual. It is, rather, an immanent feature of the elementary experience of being social. *The possibility of there being rights and privileges enjoyed and then suspended in an original position should then be understood as a reflection of the dependence of each on all, so that justice is, in effect, society itself.*[4] This means, first, that those rights and privileges must be understood as constructs of society and, second, that their suspension must also be conceived of as such a construct. It follows that the moment prior to deliberation among equals is no more committed to equality than the moment prior to that moment, which, in turn, is the moment in which the assumption of the original position is itself determined. In other words, the original position of impartiality presupposes another original position. The one "prior" to deliberation appears to be vested in an individual, while the second can be vested only in the social. But if the social has that priority, it is an unacceptable abstraction to say that the position that appears to establish equality represents an individual. If we accept the social as the basic fact, then we must conclude that there is no originality to the "original position" and deliberating together cannot be conceived of as beginning with that as a fact.

Placing such a position at the beginning of a course of deliberation assumes what I believe is indefensible: that suspending one's status and sense of entitlement in the interest of reasoning together as equals is an exception to one's essential sociality rather than already continuous with it. In this respect, it confuses a historically specific society, presumably organized as a structure of rules and institutions, with the sociality that is fundamental to any cooperative activity whatsoever. Given the order that such a structure is said to impose on its members, it is difficult to imagine the degree of individual autonomy presupposed by the original position, and no less difficult to imagine how the veil of ignorance could *become* the norm it must be if it is to be distributed across prospective deliberating parties in a way that contributes to the rationality of the sort of mutually responsive deliberation for which it is assumed to be a prior condition.

Equality in deliberation is certainly imaginable as a socializing moment of a course of activity in which people are *already* committed to one another as equals. For this, the veil of ignorance can be said to operate as a mnemonic device that validates itself as such in the course of collective activity. One might say that equality can be recalled only *en ensemble*, as something validated only in a course of activity in which individuals are not primary agents, though each might then be said to assume it as a presupposition of their participation. This moment of collective recollection may appear as an event in which equality is actually constituted, but only when inequality becomes an issue in the course of discussion, threatening to bring the latter to an end—as when one party claims responsibility for equality by virtue of having explicitly declared it. Otherwise, a socially valid expression of equality, one for which no individual explicitly takes responsibility, brings the basic fact into play in whatever follows.

It is only from a hypothetical position outside of a course of activity that it is possible to identify particular results with individual intentions. To say that a group decision has occurred as a result of an agreement is misleading when "agreement" is taken to mean "a meeting of minds." The things we call minds do not meet. Given the concept of a course of activity, a settlement of an issue cannot be accounted for by reference to the various parties having come to a belief that the conclusion is justified by one or more of the reasons that had been circulating. This may appear to be so in retrospect, and therefore as an altogether questionable hypothesis, but not during the course of activity itself.[5] Once we grant the significance of the idea of a course of activity, the general course of decision making cannot be thought of on the model of a progressive rationalization of what was initially a problem for which there was no consensually prescribed algorithm. This would require each party to go through an identical process in coming to a decision and then joining the others in agreement. But this is possible, given the limits of the discussion so far, only if individuality is prior to its instantiation in a collective course of activity. In finding herself in the midst of such a course of activity, the individual is already *of* and not merely *in* the collective, where agency asserts itself over and above its ostensibly individual moments. In that sense, it might be better to say that the person is given to it, as in a calling, or is committed. Within the course of activity, what appeared to be a meeting of minds based on rational deliberation by each party must be thought of instead as a collective realization of agency by virtue of processes that are not described by individualistic models.

The idea of "being *of* society" is a resource for theoretical work, though when we consider the distinction between theory and theorizing, we see that this is more complex than might otherwise appear (see Chapter 7). For the moment, I take "theory" to mean a tendentiously consistent set of propositions, and "theorizing" to mean a course of activity that is logically prior to the constitution of a justifiable theory (see Chapter 7). Society is inconceivable if people are thought of as pre-social individuals who *acquire* social knowledge and social traits that are simply added to a preexisting nonsocial form of life. This clarifies the idea of what it is for someone to be *of* society. For one thing, it involves having immediate but not necessarily representational access to the fact that all are equal in the dependence of each on all. This is a *having in common*, or a sharing that is not reducible to individual subjectivities, though it is difficult, if at all possible, to register this in a formal theory. Having an immediate sense of one's equality with all others is not the same as having a belief. The latter is usually ascribed to an individual, but the former is supra-individual, as is illustrated in the common use of words like "sharing" to express an irreducible sociality. At most, it is at the outer edge of individuality and has little if any connection to a self as that is usually conceived. It is a sense of living within a common activity such that one is effectively one of many and the many of one, and this intuition, with its attendant pleasure, and possible dread, is unavoidable regardless of whatever else is in the mind of the person. Exceptional cases might appear possible, but they are exceptional only within sociality and not to it. For example, a party to a course of activity may try momentarily to imagine herself apart from all others, but doing so requires imagining an unimaginable condition, and she will be unable to avoid finding herself once again within that course. Even the intelligibility of simply leaving, and the constitution of the memory of doing so, expresses what is possible within the course of activity.

To know one's dependence on all others cannot mean to know in the sense of standing apart from the object of knowledge and being able (but not necessarily having) to instantiate it or form a proposition about it. Knowing the essential reflexivity of the social and the inter-dependence entailed by it cannot be separated from enacting that knowledge: enacted knowledge does not consist in the extraction of something extra to enacting, which is usually what is referred to by "knowledge." It is not "knowledge of," "knowledge about," or "knowledge how," all of which beg the question of what knowledge is when it lies in the doing as such. To beg this question is to assume that the only knowledge that counts is either prior or subsequent to an act and that what goes on between these points in time is of no account whatsoever, or that what goes on is merely execution and therefore might be done as well by a machine as by a human. A pedagogy that ignores the course of activity, and the knowledge that is immanent to it, teaches what has been done as if there had never been a doing of it (Blum and McHugh 1984, 64–65, 127; Derrida 1997, 8, 14, 16).

To know sociality is not just a matter of feeling or sensing the existence of connections. It is also not the same as knowing something of which one is not a part or from which one can separate oneself either in life or for the sake of scientific study, at least not if it is anything even approximating Strawson's (1992, 81) claim that sociality is immanent. Once we admit the related sub-theoretical ideas of inter-dependence, the course of activity as inclusive of but not determined by individual intentionality, and sociality as essentially reflexive, we have little choice but to say that the knowledge in question requires its own epistemology. It is not to be understood according to the familiar contrast between empirically based or logically derived knowledge and assertions that cannot be imaginably falsified or subject to the usual methods of verification. Instead, the contrast is between knowing the social from within it, no matter how we may come to characterize that knowledge, and attempting to deny what cannot be denied, to assert the possibility of a state of nature in a self-estranging desire to separate knowledge from its social foundations. This states the problem; it is not yet a theoretical claim. It is a result of the discussion so far and of where that discussion has taken us in regard to the relationship between the idea of the social and the idea of a socially correspondent knowledge.

———

It might appear that immediate and overwhelming certainty about one's dependence on unnameable others constitutes, for the special "other" we might call the theoretician who is determined to take this into account, an individuality inconsistent with the ideas that sociality is immanent to human affairs and that persons are social through and through. This might seem to justify reinstating an individually based cognitivist approach to social knowledge. Can one deny that such a feeling of certainty transpires within individual persons? If so, how can persons, at the moment of that feeling, be considered merely ostensibly individual? Isn't the very fact of this feeling inconsistent with the claim that the social is both prior and immanent and that humans are essentially social creatures?

This feeling of immediate certainty does not constitute the same sort of "individual" intended by those for whom individuality is logically and practically prior to sociality; and it is this sort that is at issue. It is radically opposed to the individuality intuited from what the person observed reports or the observer might claim to have seen. But it is this latter individuality that has consistently resisted incorporation into theories of the social except as a term of what has proven to be an unsustainable opposition between society and personality (or self). *How, then, can a properly conceptualized individuality, one that is always already social, be thought of as internal to the social aspect of life? I believe that the most promising answer, which will need a great deal of discussion, is that individuality is a momentarily distinguishable manifestation of the social to itself.* As an instance of the reflexivity of a course of activity, it is represented only superficially and misleadingly when described as an individuated act or the act of an individual person. It displays itself, over and above whatever can be said about distinct persons, as an unlimited mutuality that abides no exceptions and therefore supports no internally generated position of transcendence, including that assumed or required by theories of self-regard.

From this point of view, to know one's utter dependence on unnameable others, as in Rousseau's first convention, is to know mutuality in a noncognitive, extra-individually, overdetermined, and unalienated sense of *being* mutual above all—with others who cannot be conceived of as other in the sense of being alien. Mutuality is a condition of human activity and not a particular relationship, act, or attitude a person might choose over non-mutuality. It is to be and to know from within and not apart from sociality. In this regard it is useful to consider Nagel's account of altruism from the point of view of the priority of the social rather than as the product of an action-originating self the continuity of which is internal to the skin-bound person:

> There is such a thing as pure altruism (though it may never occur in isolation from all other motives). It is the direct influence of one person's interest on the actions of another, simply because in itself the interest of the former provides the latter with a reason to act. If any further internal factor can be said to interact with the external circumstances in such a case, it will be not a desire or an inclination but the structure represented by such a system of reasons. (1970, 80)

What follows is a reflection on what might be meant by a "structure represented by such a system of reasons" and where such a structure might be found if it is logically different, as is suggested by Nagel's proposal that the system represents the structure, from the "system of reasons" that presumably inheres in the individual. What counts for Nagel is that both the altruist and his or her beneficiary must be thought of as instances of what he terms "someone." A need that appears as potentially anyone's provides a "timeless reason" for acting, a reason that is sufficient for anyone to consider and that does not require for its immediate effect knowing more about the individual in need than the fact that he or she is "someone" in need. This means that the need of another motivates anyone who recognizes it to direct herself to that need and not to the person as such. Indeed, recognition of the need is already a movement toward whatever it requires. There is no distance, or gap, between the perception and the onset of action, at least none that resembles what is said by theoreticians of action to lie between a personal desire or intention and the undertaking of an appropriate action. Parenthetically, the actual experience of a "someone" on the action side of the equation cannot be confirmed by an argument about timeless reasons since such an experience concerns what one is doing when one is being altruistic and the character of one's conduct when one acts altruistically. The argument does not justify altruism; nor could it. If there is any experience associated with being a "someone" capable of appreciating another "someone's" need, it must instead be dramatic in the way sudden illuminations or conversions are dramatic. The perspective from which altruism is conceivable comes to the actor immediately, as part of what it is for her to be social. It must have existed prior to its ostensibly individuated manifestation as an apparent responsiveness to a need. To apprehend oneself and another as "someones" is already to be implicated in discourses and related activities in which "being someone" has the only theoretically realizable content it can have—a non-individuated object of a non-individuated subject, where subject and object are effectively interchangeable. Indeed, this whole complex of altruism is recognizable as such from that same perspective, where the observer is also a "someone" observing "someones"—as if the social is doubly acknowledging itself.

Nagel's analysis is intended to sustain the standard theory of action in which "action" refers to behavior with reasons sufficient to the undertaking. He offers a solution to a problem that otherwise seems to challenge the theory—namely, the existence of a gap between reasons and the undertaking presumably based on them, at least in the case of altruism. There is a qualification: it is assumed that the skin is a natural boundary of agency, ruling out any solution that goes beyond individuality. Within that limitation, the solution says that the gap does not exist for at least one type of action, and possibly for many if not most others, since there is a type of reason that is, by its very nature, sufficient to set a disposition into motion. This arises from the expression of a need, and it is timeless in that it is the need, and not the person who has the need, that sets the disposition in motion. The disposition itself must be lodged somewhere within the agent. Nagel elsewhere discusses the "impersonal" aspect of consciousness, which is presumably open to timeless reasons such as needs (Nagel 1991) and is tied, beyond the limitations of reflection and memory, to the continuity of the self. This notion of a self that authorizes an immediate response to timeless reasons places such reasons within the agent, motivating her regardless of differences among the situations in which she might be called on to act. Most important for the theory is the idea that such reasons are immediately connected to the corresponding action. There is no gap between the intention and the undertaking. The theory of action is, therefore, not invalidated by the possibility of altruistic action, which had seemed to be action in which another's reasons and one's undertaking are problematically separate in ways causes and effects should not be. Instead, timeless reasons uniquely fulfill the conditions of a causal analysis of action by providing an immediate connection between the disposition that operates like a cause (the timeless reason that immediately disposes) and the act that operates like an effect.

There is a different and, I try to show, equally plausible and less problematic solution. Its strength lies in its rejection of the assumption that agency resides exclusively within the skin-bound individual. It says that timeless reasons and presumably timeless "someones" (whose needs signify just such reasons) are essentially social. It is difficult to imagine what else can be meant by Nagel's reference to timelessness. Nagel seems on the verge of acknowledging just such a possibility and, as we will see, certainly speaks of sharing and other social cognates as if it is not unreasonable to do so; but he fails to give them theoretical weight. Absent a settled concept of the self, it is not unreasonable to suggest an alternative to the idea of a continuous ego from which acts are initiated by reasons, as long as that alternative, which in this case asserts the irreducibility of the social and denies the identification of agency with individuality, provides for the appearance of individuality.

There are several reasons why this conclusion can be a legitimate starting point for a different analysis of action, given that the expressed need requires more than what the needy individual can do for herself. First, Nagel's argument suggests that *someone* (as needful), and not a "this one" or "that one," is the properly central figure of a theory of altruism. This is so because the simple presentation of the need provides a sufficient reason for all others to respond. So, on the side of need, which is the content of the timeless reason, individuality is inconsequential to the tendency to respond. Second, it is not unreasonable to venture a conclusion that omits reference to an agentic self, based on the following propositions I derive from Nagel's analysis. (1) The expressed need is indifferent to the qualities of the person in whom it is presumably vested. In that sense, the reason it provides for another to act is timeless. From the point of view of the respondent, the needful one is merely a vehicle for the expression of the need. (2) A "structure of reasons" that is only *represented* by the individually held "system of reasons" must be different both in content and location from that very system. To conceive of a structure underlying an individually vested system of reasons does not require that the structure be individually vested; and it may be reasonable to doubt that such a system, even if it exists, is vested in an individual. (3) It may be supposed that the encounter is between one who needs timelessly and another who responds in a way that is therefore also timeless. The point at which a need is expressed is an encounter of at least two parties both of whom must be assumed to understand what it is to know that *anyone* might have a need requiring assistance and to know that such needs are by their nature individually vested but indifferent to any particularizing relationship that might exist between the one who is needful and the one who is responsive. Each, then, represents the universal category "someone"; and theirs is an encounter of "someones" in which each is no one in particular, in the sense of no one whose name or biography matters. In effect, the existence of timeless reasons is evidence of a subjectivity that transcends situations, and it is the most important evidence that the theory of action provides, despite itself, against the individuality of that subjectivity.

For both "someones," the need and the tendency to respond are paired, as they are for every instance of reasonableness. Their pairing is not, in the universe of such instances, contingent. If they are independent of other facts and are, instead, inseparable features of reasonableness, and if all persons are, as almost all theories of action claim, instances of tendentious reasonableness, then the contingency of the meeting of the two "someones" (need with disposition) can only lie beyond individuality. This is so whatever is added to suggest an idea of their meeting as an event. For the time being, the likely candidate is an irreducible sociality of the sort invoked by Strawson: "If our subject is man in his world, it seems necessary to admit that this world is essentially a social world" (1992, 81). I would add that it is a world in which the language of agency makes no *necessary* reference to individuality since being "in" such a world is nothing more than being *of* it.

It is possible, then, to consider sociality and not individuality as the determinate locus of timeless reasons and altruistic dispositions, though, as will become evident, this does not exclude something like individuality. A "someone" who immediately grasps another's need as "someone's," and in the grasping feels an obligation, must also know her own needs as "someone's": both needs qualify as timeless. However, this weakens any attempt to assimilate altruism to the standard theory of action as an effect-like consequence of desire and belief. The type of cause invoked by the standard theory is different from the relation of mutual entailment posited between a timeless reason and a timeless response tendency. That theory relies on external relations appropriate to strictly causal accounts and on causes that are virtually sufficient to their effects. To that extent, the gap exists as an artifact of the theory. This is why the theory cannot account for its closure and, therefore, the actual undertaking. Nagel offers timelessness as a solution, but the fact that this relies on something like internal relations is not compatible with a strictly causal account.[6] What is most important is not, as Nagel believes, that the idea of a timeless reason gives the undertaking an immediately prior sufficient condition. Rather, the very idea of timelessness envisions a universe in which reasons and acts are no longer separable, and action is predicated at least partially on reasons that are timeless: any *meaningful* action could therefore be anyone's. In such a world, that is how whatever is being done is intelligibly connected to whatever else is being done and how it sustains its presence throughout every course of activity in which it occurs. Timelessness must be relative to something, which is the problem for which I suggest a possible solution.

From the point of view of what is increasingly becoming a hypothetical individual (or ostensible individuality), it follows that to act in regard to timeless reasons is to be *of* the agency of the moment, whatever the moment is a moment of. It is to be constituted as the active side of those reasons; and their timelessness, which Nagel posits as an aspect of a "structure," resides outside of individuality. This implies that no meaningful undertaking *originates* within a person. It is already implicit in the needful expression, and therefore in the putative structure of which it is a part, and therefore in whatever accounts for that structure. Thus, an alternative theory of the relationship between agency and action would have to begin with something prior to individuality. The most likely candidate is the social conceived of as immanent, irreducible, and a course of activity in contrast with an event or a state of affairs.

Suppose there is still a desire to extend the standard individualistic theory of action to include altruism, which is otherwise analogous to action at an unbridgeable distance from its causes, rather than to entertain an alternative theory. It is difficult to imagine how a respondent to a need, who is "someone" set in motion by a timeless reason, can, *in the midst of confronting that need,* be thought of as a self in the usual sense of a spatially contained but practically horizon-less content of a personality whose continuity extends beyond any specific situation (see Searle 2001, 95–96). The difficulty arises because of the *immediacy* with which timeless needs must be apprehended if they are to define the object of an immediate obligation. Ironically, the obligation of "anyone" whose need to respond to the other's is also immediately apprehensible as "someone's" need. Subjectivity in the midst of confronting that need is radically different from that of a subject interpreting another's expression, evaluating reasons, and anticipating doing something in response. The former subsists within a field of needs presented among "someones" rather than the series of individually located needs to which another might or might not respond, relieved by periods of needlessness posited from the point of view of someone merely anticipating doing something. And we have seen that all action can be considered responsive to timeless reasons in one respect and to one degree or another if altruism is included in the theory of action and if the idea of social action as taking others into account generalizes to all instances of human action, as Strawson seems to have claimed.

How tangible, then, is the self that belongs to a universe of timeless reasons some of which are brought into play through expressions that effectively perform such reasons, presumably independently of whether a respondent is near or even hears or sees their expression? Of course a person may be doing something that obliges no one, but the question is whether a universe is conceivable in which such a person, who acts without any connection to another, might humanly live. That is, we may return to the possibility of a universe of distinct persons, but only after we exhaust what seems implicit to the contrary in a causal theory of action that includes altruism by ascribing timeless reasons to certain expressions, thereby bringing what otherwise appears to be another's reason (need) into alignment with the actor's own undertaking (response).

The standard theory of action, as a function of desire and belief, is intended to be general to a universe of agents; when it is modified it is general to *that universe* correspondingly modified. We have seen that timeless reasons are independent of individuated agents, both needy and responsive. They put actors in a condition analogous to the veil of ignorance, where the detachment of the person is assumed in the very idea of responding to a timeless reason—which is to say, committing themselves to a universe in which there is a timeless aspect to every expression that might be met by an appropriate response. If there are selves in this universe, they are separate from whatever is personal. Timeless needs and their respondents are, from the point of view of possible skin-bound persons, abstract, suggesting that something concrete has been left out. But if one thing that is at issue is this very point of view, then instead of deciding that the theory is vitiated by its excessive abstraction, we should say that what is at stake is precisely what is concrete, and I have already suggested that the social is the prime candidate. We are led to this point by the abstractive implications of Nagel's elaboration of the theory of action; but we stop too short when we fail to see what is implied by the impersonality of timeless reasons. It seems that "someone" indicates only that the location of a need to which there is an obligation, which is a new timeless need, is necessarily abstract relative to the ostensible concreteness and specificity of persons. It cannot be specified without undoing the possibility of altruism, by removing the necessity of the obligation a timeless reason imposes in favor of conceiving of the altruistic act as a decision based on a momentary coincidence of subjective desire and objective belief.

It is the sheer presence of the need, and not its location in any particular individual, that accounts for what now can be seen only as altruism by a *third party*. This is so if we take Nagel at his word and reject any ad hoc attempt to make the theory of altruism consistent with the individualism that it seems to refute. We have seen how Nagel's concept of timelessness reveals the underlying ontological presupposition of the social as irreducible, irrepressible, superordinate to individuality, and the locus of agency, where the latter is conceived of according to a *relationship between a needful intention that is someone's response to someone's presented need* and a *course of activity that subsumes both* and appears only momentarily and from outside of it as a distinct act.

––––––––––

There simply is no individuality worth mentioning when altruism, understood as emending the theory of action, is considered as exemplary of the moral disposition of practical reason. This is so even though the altruistic response, which is timelessly internally related to the expression of need, might appear as a performance by a specific person.[7] The obligation performed by the expression of need also constitutes a need in response to a need. Because this suggests a chain without clear demarcations, even the appearance of individuality begins to fade in theoretical significance. We might conclude that altruistic dispositions are expressed *in* activity (not *by* particular actions) in which ostensible altruistically inclined individuals are implicated and then appear as non-particular in relation to non-particular others who are themselves not apprehended, from the point of view of the obligation projected by the performance of a timeless reason, as separable individuals and therefore as distinct others. Such a disposition shows itself to be a feature of a course of activity keyed in by the performance of a need that "someone" might possess, such that whoever appears momentarily obliged to respond is actually another "someone" being drawn along within a course that he or she does not initiate and cannot control, because that "someone" cannot, by definition, be an instance of altruistic *agency*.

If one is tempted to say that this ongoing performativity of needs in regard to one another is initiated by a specific one and not merely "someone" who could be "anyone," it can only be by something particular that presents itself as *timefully* needful within the very course of activity through which timefulness is replaced by timelessness: "need" replaces the specific need in due course. This does away with the individualistic notion of a need, though it is still not clear how we can capture the idea of a movement, or circulation, in which needs are predicated on and predicate needs. Here, Rousseau might be helpful. For now, the idea of a course of activity is an adequate substitution for the idea of an expression of a timeless reason. We no longer have recourse to the notion that altruism involves a particular person acting individually to fulfill the particular need of another particular person, which is to say, doing something for a reason that belongs to another. Given these possible implications of Nagel's position, it seems that his accounts of prudence and altruism cannot sustain the theory of action to which they appeal and which they presumably emend. In fact, they pose a greater challenge than that posed by the gap between reasons and undertaking. They take us closer to the basic fact of sociality and further away from a prior individuality. It is in this regard that I discuss some further features of Nagel's theory.

Despite the relative indistinctness of both, it is the other "someone" toward whom the altruistic response is directed. However, "someones" cannot be particular in the sense required by the theory of action, and therefore cannot be objects of confident orientation. The important point is that altruism should not be thought of fundamentally as directed toward another in particular but *toward* as well as *by* the fact of sociality, including the sociality of needs-expression. Suppose Nagel is correct in saying that there must be some sense of identification with others if altruism is to be possible. And suppose I am correct in inferring that the self in which the agency of altruistic action is presumably vested (which is also an instance of "someone") cannot support an identity in the usual sense any more than the performance of a timeless reason depends on a particular personal identity. It follows that at no point is altruism individualized and at every point it is social. It must be seen as oriented by and toward the sheer fact of sociality. To the extent to which it is nevertheless necessary to speak of individuals, altruism refers to *parties to courses of activity* beyond any attributable individuality, not to individuated *agents* specifically disposed toward specific others. In being altruistic, we perform the fact that we are equal in our dependence on an unlimited multiplicity of unnameable others; it is in this sense that we can be said to identify with "someone" in need. *In that regard, all action, all that is done by social beings, must be considered in one way or another to be altruistic; and that is where any more extended theory of altruism must begin.* I take it that this was one part of the problem Rousseau set out to solve: "I shall try always to reconcile . . . what right permits with what interest prescribes, so that justice and utility are not at variance" (1978b, 46).

Nagel takes appropriate issue with egoistic theories of altruism and tries to show that the mere expression of a need is sufficient to create an obligation. This is because the reason to act on such an expression is timeless and in that respect objective. Thus, he has to think simultaneously of both the expression and the obligation, subjectivities logically distinct from particular persons. This undermines what is ordinarily said about agency, intention, satisfaction, and action. Moreover, it is the recognizable *articulation* of need and not a particular need that constitutes the practical reason of altruistic agency. Foreclosing embodied agency seems to suggest that, unless one posits, ad hoc, a temporally transcendent and trans-situational self behind the active self, *we can consider altruism as manifesting the social in regard to itself,* a reflexivity of sociality ostensibly performed by individuals but more easily understood as a collective performance in which the social expresses itself in the form of an individuality that is different from the specificity and particularity of separable persons.

This interpretation of Nagel's theory points to the possibility of accounting more generally for inclinations not exclusively traceable to egoism and set habits of judgment. This depends on a defensible conception of the social, and on a commitment to what is entailed by its being irreducible and irrepressible. Despite Nagel's disclaimer, reliance on a notion of the self resonates with egoism. It leaves traces of individualism inconsistent with what his theory requires, as it were, sub-theoretically, which is that there are "someones" on both sides of any needful expression that yields a timeless reason to act. Nagel's versions of altruistic and prudential action perform the same comprehensive and irreducible sociality that philosophers tacitly admit into theory when they use words like "sharing," "in common," "community," and the like. These are rarely analyzed and theorized, but it would be inaccurate to classify them as pre-theoretical. I have been using the term "sub-theoretical" to refer to notions that are latent in principle. By this I mean notions that are unavoidably, as it were, interpellated into discourse but can only be undermined by any semantically specific representation. Nagel seems to take Strawson's programmatic statement a step further toward challenging the individualistic foundations of the theory of action and therefore toward challenging established conceptions of the forms and conditions of agency. The challenge is insufficient unless it is extended to the received and convenient particularistic notions of social entities, situations, locations, events, and the like, all of which are intended to skirt the issue of what "social" does to terms that it may seem, at first glance, merely to modify. To this end, I later discuss agency-dependent objects in connection with more elaborate conceptions of a course of activity and the immanence of the social, both of which depend on a Rousseauian notion of equality. When these ideas are more or less in place, it will be possible to say when it is appropriate for the theoretician to reintroduce the idea of individuality and how this can reasonably be done.

In the interest of clarifying Rousseau's idea of how humans exist as such only together, I have argued that Nagel's account of altruistic agency reverses the relative priority of individual and social, fatefully challenging the theory of action on which it relies. However, there remains a problem for that interpretation that may restore the priority of individuality. In realizing that I am "someone" responding to "someone's" performance of a timeless reason to act, I *find* myself having an obligation. This finding can only be sudden and pre-reflective, so that the experience associated with it seems to be exclusively mine. Parenthetically, it will not do to identify the experience with an innate disposition to take account of others, as Nagel seems to have done in a later book (1991), in which case, the sudden, pre-reflective sense of obligation is vested pre-socially in individuals. That introduces an ad hoc construct that begs the question before it can be heard against what is already taken for granted. Even without bringing in an other-directed disposition, the immediacy of the experience of the obligation, which appears to be subjectively exclusive, seems to bring back the priority of individual subjectivity in a way that is inconsistent with the thesis that sociality is the basic fact and, therefore, essential for conceptualizing agency. Yet it is difficult if not impossible to deny the first part of this thesis even for those who deny the second part. In what follows, I try to show how the apparent individualization of the experience of timeless obligation looks when sociality is prior to individuality. For now, I take the priority of the social to be a reasonable hypothesis, in light of what has been discussed so far.

It should at least increase our confidence in the following proposition: that the sudden realization of an obligation based on a timeless reason itself is a self-evident manifestation of the basic social fact. The feeling of obligation is no less a performance of sociality than is the expression of a need (as "someone's"). That it might be self-evident to an individuated subject does not imply that such a subject is the foundation of agency or that the sudden sense of obligation comes with a sense of its "being mine." The existence of an intention or an experience is not sufficient to identify a particular subject as the agent of any particular act or activity. We should say instead that the experience of an obligation based on a timeless reason subsumes, for that moment, all instances of individuality, as if each instance is a moment of the social, and none is its instigator or effect.

To feel *suddenly* that I am someone *in the course of an activity (within the tension of an obligation)* is to be certain for the moment that I am nothing more or less than anyone, not that I am a privately feeling being. The individuality of my feeling registers the immediacy of being equal with all others such that "my" and "their" reasons can be timeless and therefore "anyone's." It is not a feeling of isolation or of being related to some others and to different degrees, both of which are results of reflecting on the feeling of obligation. To say that an obligation is felt is to say that there is an individuated moment of sociality accompanied by an appropriate feeling *anyone* might have. While this allows for an extra-theoretical individuality of feeling, it does not demonstrate the individuality of agency, or show that such a feeling is any more relevant to understanding agency than the fact that humans are physical creatures. It is one thing to use the term "individual" to indicate participation (being a party to something or being among others) and another to say that participating involves determining a collective course of activity. I discuss this later in connection with sociality conceived of as a course of activity. For now, the operative sentence in Nagel's account of altruism is that there is "an aspect of your attitude towards your own needs, desires, and interests which permits you to regard them as worthy of consideration simply as *someone's* needs, desires, and interests, rather than as yours" (1970, 83–84).[8]

If regarding something as worthy is to undertake an obligation, what is involved in considering such a thing as not just mine but as nevertheless compelling? "Considering" seems too detached to allow for the fact Nagel wants to highlight, that we ordinarily respond to needs that immediately obligate us regardless of whose needs are expressed. We certainly can make a judgment on the basis of which we might be so moved, but there is nothing in Nagel's account that requires the individual to be more than a vehicle of a disposition the content and momentum of which exists independently of that individual whatever else is going on in her mind. Nagel does not consider all dispositions to be internal to the individual, and that comes close to admitting that an individual may sincerely perform or present a disposition without being motivated by it or without its being his or hers. The immediacy with which an obligation is grasped suggests that it is socially constituted as a course of activity already under way—therefore something graspable; and, for Nagel, there is no ongoing activity within the individual that can explain the internal relation of "someone" who needs to "someone" who might respond.

One might still claim that the sudden realization of an obligation is inconsistent with the idea of immanent sociality, by distinguishing between the suddenness of a realization and what is suddenly realized. To respond to a timeless reason (e.g., a need) is to act as a member of society, as "someone" for others before being one. But the suddenness of the experience does not demonstrate the priority of the social. An obligation to a timeless reason is presumably prereflective. It is experienced as relentlessly imperative and can be relieved by what the respondent chooses to do. That seems to make it an experience that belongs to the individual, in which case we might conclude that, while the social only realizes itself in the individual, the individual is the agent of the responsive

act. It seems to follow that the idea of a suddenness with which the social realizes itself in the individual (as an obligation to "someone's" performance of a
timeless reason) is inconsistent with the general claim that sociality is prior to
individuality, suggesting that the former is not the basic fact. Suddenness is a
strictly individualized experience, and it is an essential condition of the obligation entailed by the expression of need: altruism, like all other types of action,
must have a reason, and reasons belong to the individual because they belong
to intentions.

One problem with this lies in the assumption that altruism requires that the
individual be personally motivated to act in regard to another's need. This may
occur when individuality seems to surpass the sociality that makes it possible.
My interpretation of Nagel's theory suggests that the general case is different.
We always take account of others' needs even when we appear to be acting self-
ishly: this is what it means to be social. To do so is not evidence of a personal
trait, a habit, an internalized norm, or a pro-social motive. If altruism were
contingent on the inclinations of self-willing individuals, it would be difficult
to imagine how society could survive. The mere fact of being *of* society involves
never failing to participate in and being subsumed by a course of activity. A
performance of need and its consequence constitute obvious instances of being
of society. What is crucial is not the timelessness of the reason but the fact that
the expression is a socially subsumed gesture, a performance completed only as
an obligation of "someone who might be anyone." This is consistent with the
idea that we always act within ongoing relations of mutuality, as socially constituted parties; and this is incompatible with the idea of individuality required by
the standard theory of action.

The outcome of any action is always partly to the benefit of another—that
is, to anyone taken into account by the simple fact that the behavior has a reason; and that is what is at issue. The one identified from a third-party point
of view as the agent of the behavior may be said to benefit from doing it or to
simply enjoy it. But this does not mean that the behavior was exclusively or
primarily initiated by anticipating gain or pleasure, though both might be part
of the experience of doing it (see Davidson 2001b, 9–19). Whether the person is
gratified by what she does is not the issue. Having reasons presupposes a course
of activity that does not belong to the individual, who only appears to be the
origin of the action; and that the standard theory of action focuses on "behavior with a reason" means that it fails to see the priority of the social in the very
having of reasons.

Using the word "altruism" typically suggests a virtue that individuals may
or may not choose to honor. It follows that what is crucial to the relief of a need
that is beyond the needful individual's capacity to satisfy is another individual's
state of mind. This may be true at the point of the actual satisfaction of a given
instance of need, but I have been concerned with the relationship between the
expression of a need and an obligation, where the expression performs a timeless reason and, in that sense, an obligation that also is a need. So far, the social

shows itself in the relationship between the two, and that relationship is social before individuality can enter analysis. We can, of course, use "altruism" moralistically to refer to a virtue, but only for the very few situations in which society appears to have been weakened or suspended, as in war. If we say that what has been weakened or suspended is sociality as such, it is difficult to imagine how one could speak meaningfully of universally recognizable virtues: to refer to something as such a virtue is already to be caught up in the social, though not necessarily in the particulars of a named society—that is, a nation. The confusion between the possibilities of altruism and agency that I believe haunts Nagel's account (1971, 15) can be resolved in favor of agency if it is conceived of as a performance rather than a condition of sociality. At best, the possibility of altruism would be derived from agency as a social fact rather than provide a test case for a theory of agency founded on individualistic theories of action and practical reason.

There are some residual issues about the experience of suddenness that have to do with belief and our knowledge of the social. For example, it is tempting to say that there must be a belief on the part of the potential altruist that someone is in need and a further belief that this constitutes a timeless reason that contributes to whether the altruistic potential is realized in action. But a belief is usually thought to be something arrived at; it does not appear suddenly in one's mind. In that case, it is separate from the sudden experience of certainty. This is so at least when we think of a justified belief or a belief that one holds only pending justification. Altruism seems to require just such a belief, since the altruist presumably cares about whether there is an actual need and what sort of reason it might constitute. But we have already established that the appearance or even hint of "someone's" need is sufficient to engage the altruist because it is immediately apprehended as a timeless reason and an obligation. That it is subject to review from a third-party perspective is irrelevant. There is, on the part of the potential altruist, as yet no question of a justified belief, and what we have is a sudden experience of certainty, the certainty of an obligation.

Perhaps the experience of something like certainty is a fact about beliefs in general. When we arrive at a belief and are able to justify holding it, there is still a moment in which we are certain beyond the limits of its justification. The *sense* of a belief's being true, without which we might be wary of referring to it as a belief, is always immediate and certain regardless of whatever argument provides the intellectual ground for, say, comparing it with other beliefs. To deny this would be to identify justification with experience, and a belief is an experience of truth with or without justification, though not necessarily without a sense of the struggle that it momentarily resolves (in a different way from the way in which justification resolves doubt). This does not, of course, deny that justification or its absence may come to be crucial to a change in belief, given a context in which the sense of truth is not enough.

Insofar as beliefs cannot be separated from the discourses in which they and their statements figure, there is one justification that seems indistinguishable from having a belief. But it does not take the form of an argument, so the word "justification" may not be appropriate. Believing, like speaking, is never a private affair. It is part of an immanently social course of activity. There is something about sociality that is key to the holding of any belief. It at least reinforces the belief. Certainty is nothing if it cannot, in principle, be shared. It is in this sense that sociality functions somewhat like a justification. It provides something that cannot be withheld without undoing the belief—namely, the immediate, overwhelming, and always sudden experience of one's dependence on all without qualification and unencumbered by any other experience. This is the equality with which Rousseau's social contract begins.

Of course this is not a reason in the sense of something deliberated on. Nor is it a reason in the sense of something we grasp intuitively or that has come to notice or that we are simply used to taking into account and that might or might not validate a particular action. It is, like Nagel's timeless reason, *a reason that it is impossible not to know.* From this point of view, some part of every belief has to do with the fact that it is "someone's" in relation to other "someones," timeless at the moment it is held because sociality is, in a way yet to be discussed, timeless. In later chapters, I try to clarify the idea of "an attitude of waiting," which is the primary mode of responsiveness within an immanently social course of activity. For now, an attitude of waiting resembles the altruist's awareness that there are timeless reasons such that "someone's" need is one and such that anyone might be needful. The altruist cannot know need without knowing obligation, the dependence of each on all, just as being within a course of activity includes a constant attitude of waiting that cannot be separated from any meaningful instances of behavior, including what are called speech acts. One might then say that speaking is by its very nature altruistic. This is because it invariably instantiates the basic social fact—not because it serves an ulterior purpose of communicating in the sense of attempting to bring about a meeting of minds. The suddenness with which speakers and actors realize that they depend on all others is the moment that taking those others into account—in the sense of knowing certainly that one should—is a noncontingent feature of being caught up in any course of activity. It follows that, on the very basis of the suddenness with which a person experiences the truth of her dependence on others in the given instance, individuality can be thought of only as momentary and not as basic, as far as concerns acting and agency.

The suddenness with which one apprehends one's connection with others based on equal dependence yields the certain truth of the social and, at the same time, the equally certain truth that one is only momentarily and ostensibly individual, that there can be no "one." This means that the moment in which individuals grasp their dependency on all is the moment of their being fully and irreversibly social. The suddenness of that experience is in common and cannot be accounted for in individualistic terms. The individual for which that experience is available is already a moment of something other than individuality. It can be said to be a realization of sociality but not to be an agency that makes sociality real or represents it. *The ostensible individual cannot be said to know sociality in the sense of having that knowledge as a particular mental fact that resides within the body of the mind but can be said only to know the social in the throes of being social.*

Suddenness is an eruption of "being in the throes of an activity," which is what I believe Sartre means when he says that the human is a "being in a situation." It is not a matter of stepping outside of it; therefore, it is not an exception to the irreducibility of the social. Chapter 4 completes my interpretation of Rousseau's narrative as leading to a critical conclusion: the immanence of the social is an apodictic truth uniquely demonstrated as such by an allegory in which a truth about human life is given by the abject failure of its negation.

4

The Certainty of the Social as the Basic Fact

S o far, I have discussed one idea that requires something like a definition of "sociality." It says that humans living together cannot imagine human existence in a state of nature defined by the negation of society and that any other definition of the state of nature assumes society. Since every person lives among people, no one can imagine herself outside of that encompassing fact, and therefore outside of a universe in which each depends on all and responds to every other as someone that could, in important respects, be anyone. Each of us is, then, social through and through and our conception of what it is to be human is essentially social: we are all, at bottom, "someones" and the way of being someone is not at all impersonal or detached. If we are essentially "someones," and if an instance of "someone" exists only in the form of the dependence of each on all, then we are inseparable from others in all that we are and do and this must register itself one way or another in personal experience. It is in this regard that we can refer to society as a basic fact—not only for human beings but for human affairs. An observer might claim that social beings sometimes act in ways that are not social. But such an observation cannot be made from within society, since no exception can be recognized from that position. Even if such an observation were possible, it is not possible to show how the line can be drawn between what is social and what is not, since drawing lines for the sake of a comparison is an irreducibly social activity. At the very least, given the plausibility of the hypothesis that human beings and their affairs are essentially social, observers and theoreticians are best advised to act on the assumption that every act is socially reflexive regardless of what else can be attributed to it (see Blum and McHugh 1984). This still says nothing about what people do as members of historical societies in the sense of a rule-governed institutional

order or territorialized system. That requires an investigation into the ontological aspect of universal inter-dependence in regard to the relationship between
objectivity and agency, which I undertake in later chapters. Note also that the
argument so far has been primarily conceptual and logical. It has not yet shown
how Rousseau's narrative uniquely demonstrates the truth of the basic fact as a
matter of immediate certainty, and this is necessary to any account of the continuity of historical societies.

It follows from the impossibility of conceiving of its negation that society,
understood for the moment as the necessary association of equals, cannot be
explained by the motivation alluded to in Rousseau's narrative of the "original compact"—namely, insecurity and a corresponding desire for peace, since
these are identified psychologically with pre-social individuality. This means
that it cannot be characterized as a negation of its negation—society as the antithesis of and remedy for the state of nature. It seems, then, that society and
nature can have nothing to do with one another in a theory of human affairs.
Rousseau avoids this dilemma to the extent to which the confirmation of society as the basic fact depends on the revelatory character of his narrative of the
social contract when it is read as an allegory.

The narrative that runs from insecurity to a willingness to associate with
an indefinite plurality of others whom one could not have known cannot explain either the onset of society or its continuity beyond the lives of those who
presumably formed it. To explain association by a prior insecurity requires
imagining so fateful an insecurity from within a situation imposed by a state
of nature. We have seen that this is not imaginable to essentially social beings.
A sense of insecurity arises only in contrast with a sense of security, as something lost, which assumes a social standard. Insecurity can explain a collective
willingness to associate only if it is distributed; and a distribution capable of
confirming individual decisions assumes the existence of society. To imagine
leaving a state of nature is to imagine leaving the "realm of necessity" that is
all one has ever known. It requires imagining leaving together, which is to say
leaving for something already socially established. In either case, it assumes
what is to be explained. Finally, to leave nature is not to go somewhere else,
for there is no other place imaginable from that state of affairs. If it is to go
toward its negation, which is society, that must exist and be known in advance
by a plurality of immigrants from nature who, in this sharing of knowledge,
must already have constituted themselves as a society. Insecurity cannot, then,
explain the beginning of what it assumes—namely, society.[1] If the social is, first
of all, the dependence of each on all, and if that is logically prior to form, body
politic, structure, or system, and if universal inter-dependence is realized only
in courses of activity, then the dialectical other to society is not nature but the
cessation of activity in its course, a condition that is, perhaps surprisingly, part
of activity itself and of the very experience of participation.

Even so, it is still not entirely clear whether sociality is the form human life
takes or a distributed sensibility. So far, it seems to be the former. But there is a

long history of the idea that individuals internalize sociality as part of the formation of the ego even before they internalize normatively constrained social relations, and this assumes that individuality is first and that sociality emerges in the course of the struggle, futile though it may be, to return to a primeval pre-social state. One interpretation of Rousseau seems to support the idea of a distributed sensibility. It says that humans, who are "born free," eventually come to share a sense of the necessity of living together, and that this is to be explained by reference to the individuals who can share it and not to something independently substantial about sharing. Sociality is, on this interpretation, a contingent property of individual subjects and not a prior quality of being human. It is, at most, a practical necessity in which individuals see one another in relations defined by their goals (e.g., as family members, competitors, or irrelevant to goal attainment) and not as "consociates" for whom the word "we" has a deep and abiding meaning beyond instrumentality (see Schutz 1967).

If this is true, then Susan Sontag is wrong when she says "no 'we' should be taken for granted when the subject is looking at other people's pain" (2003, 7). She is wrong from this point of view not because "we" *can* be taken for granted under those circumstances, but because no "we," in the intimate sense of "I and thou," can ever be taken for granted except as a pronoun most people learn to use predictably.[2] She is right if "we" is a first and not a learned sense of the relatedness of self and others: she is right if the self is already social and wrong if sociality is a learned and contingent disposition. In any case, learned sociality trivializes the idea of the social, since the evident presence of pain qualifies as a timeless reason that all, and not merely some, humans can recognize as such and in that respect know themselves as "someones." I do not believe that Sontag would dispute this. It is one thing to say, as she does, that one cannot appreciate the pain of another, in which case the use of a discursively intimate "we" would be untoward; it is another thing to say that one cannot appreciate that another is in pain (see Gilbert 1989, 167–203). That seems false, and there is, in appreciating that "someone" is in pain, a legitimate, virtually compulsory, implication of "we." Sontag's point does not require that we know another's mind and feelings. Nor does it requiring disagreeing with the idea that pain presents a timeless reason plus an obligation that logically implies sociality. The failure to consider the pain of certain others may then be understood, in part, as a result of taking (even accusing) them to have voluntarily placed themselves outside of the societally sustained dependence of each on all. This works by seeing their otherness as a property of each individual so distinguished. They can then be cast as instances of pure, asocial individuality classifiable metonymically (as in racism) as a type that excludes, by virtue of its own monstrous disposition and the incorrigible conviction of each instance, the social which would otherwise embrace them. The refusal to regard the pain of "others" is, from this point of view, based on regarding them as creatures of the very nature that society itself cannot abide, and not on an inclination simply to disregard what others might feel as a result of having been persuaded to do so (as in demonizing an "enemy" population) or of lacking the skills or knowledge to go beyond a selfish disposition to disregard those others. That the latter are in pain then appears to be nothing more than an expected reflection of the "realm of necessity," something familiar to hunters, torturers, exterminators, concentration camp guards, and those who advocate preemptive war and who speak glibly, as former secretary of defense Donald Rumsfeld famously did in a television interview, of being altogether indifferent to collateral damage ("I don't think about it"). The refusal of regard is in this sense a defense of society. It goes wrong by confusing society with a bounded entity—the nation, for example—rather than a course of activity that cannot be reflexive to boundaries.

It seems that a conception of the social as a distributed quality is at odds with Rousseau's account of the social contract, the general will, and society as the realm of morally relevant, recognizably human freedom. It takes the idea of the social contract to mean that society is the sum of distinct properties of distinct atomic constituents. Positing nothing but pre-social individuals who may or may not become social, such a theory cannot find its way back to an idea of society as a self-transforming totality different from a "multitude" or "all." This is a negative consequence of giving ontological priority to absolutely distinct individuals who may be able to share but are not essentially social beings. I want to show, beyond the arguments considered so far, that *The Social Contract* provides an immediate sense of the truth of the priority of the social. One part of this involves recognizing that an idea of society requires that its elements, whatever they turn out to be, are constituted within it as of the same order of fact as the social totality itself. Rousseau must be shown to demonstrate the truth of the basic fact beyond what can be proven about the virtually infinite declarations and claims in which it figures. This involves interpreting the familiar narrative in which the social contract appears as a meeting of otherwise separate individuals who have left the state of nature that they had independently found intolerable in order to enter into an association based on the subordination of each to the will of the "whole," from which all meaningful rights, freedoms, and protections derive. When the narrative is read as an allegory rather than as speculative history or a useful fiction, it demonstrates the truth of the basic fact beyond a shadow of a doubt by establishing that no alternative whatsoever is thinkable.

This requires reading the text for what it performs on Rousseau's reader—that is, on the very activity of reading. The problem is to show how the text brings the irreducibility, irrepressibility, and comprehensiveness of the social immediately to mind. While I am sympathetic with Rawls's attempt to establish conditions, by means of the "veil of ignorance," such that whatever an individual's "temporal position, each is forced to choose [a principle of distribution] for everyone,"[3] it seems better to approach the problem of being social, in order to imagine society and therefore justice, at the level at which it appears as the basic fact rather than at the level of individual consciousness at which it does not and apparently cannot. To get there involves reading against the grain of what Rousseau says:

> I suppose that men have reached that point at which the obstacles to their preservation in a state of nature . . . overwhelm the forces which each individual could employ to maintain himself in that state. Then that primitive state can no longer subsist, and humankind would perish if it did not change its way of being. (1992, bk. 1, chap. 6; my translation)

> However, since men cannot engender new forces, but can only unite and direct those that exist, they have no other means to preserve themselves than to form by aggregation a sum of forces which might triumph over the resistance, to put them in play in a single move and make them act in concert.
>
> This sum of forces can only be born out of the concourse of many; but the strength and freedom of each man being the first means of his conservation, how can he concede them without harming himself and without neglecting the care he owes himself? [The problem is] to find a form of association which defends and protects with all the common might the person and property of each associate and, by which, each uniting himself to all still obeys only himself and remains as free as before. This is the fundamental problem the solution of which is given by the social contract. . . .
>
> In short, each giving himself to all gives himself to none; and since there is no associate over whom one does not acquire precisely the same right that one cedes over oneself, one gains the equivalent of all that one loses, and more strength to conserve what one already has. (1992, bk. 2, chap. 6; my translation)

Parenthetically, the narrative form is more pronounced in the early draft of *The Social Contract*, known as the "Geneva Manuscript" (Rousseau 1978a, 153–159), and in the *Discourse on the Origin and the Foundations of Inequality among Men* (1964, esp. pt. 1). It is grammatically muted in *The Social Contract* itself, which, given additional internal evidence, suggests that something other than history is at issue in that text. For Rousseau, it is the very concept of the social and the source of its certainty as the most basic fact beyond any appeal to history. The preceding passages appear to explain the existence of society as a momentous event brought about by situated motivations shared by all humans. Roger Masters summarizes Rousseau's account as follows: "Given the impossibility of preserving human life in the last stages of the state of nature, men are forced to form civil societies. At that time, reasoning and independent men are faced with a 'difficulty' which Rousseau summarizes" as having to reconcile what appear contradictory—namely, to discover a form of association capable of providing the requisite security while retaining the capacity of those associated to act freely (1968, 314).

The difficulty of avoiding the narrative effect appears in literalist summaries of Rousseau's account of civil society that not only invoke motivational tendencies consistent with a decision to move from nature to society but mark them as central to a certain understanding of the logical structure of the account, as when Masters concludes that "the natural impulse to self-preservation forces reasoning men to seek their own security in the security of a legitimate political society" (1968, 349). The voluntarism of this makes it difficult to understand how subsequent generations might have come to accept the social contract; and it is clear that a prior degree of trust is necessary if individuals are to lay down their arms at the presumably unprecedented moment of the first convention, which implies, paradoxically, that society precedes its founding event. The difficulty lies in the nagging sense that the original convention and the formation of a social contract might not have occurred—but for the unaccountable convergence of unaccountably like-minded individuals. To appreciate the universality of the first convention, which is also the moment of the contract itself, it is necessary to continue the immanent critique of the *narrative* to the point at which an alternative reading becomes more persuasive than the putative literal one.

The narrative appears to say that the mere fact of being together means that each hopelessly insecure natural being, in the presence of others she knows to be of her kind, has no choice but to relinquish her own powers and depend on all for protection. This presumably reduces the *uncertainty* and consequent insecurity of individuals in nature, and it eliminates that insecurity from the society formed on the foundation of the first convention and from the social character of the distinctively human beings formed on that same basis. Uncertainty about consequences in nature is not the same as uncertainty in society. Whatever insecurity is felt by a member of society is for that person alone but only in a very limited sense, since it is not because of a sense of being unprotected. Each can be said to be alone *in* society only in the sense of being an occasion for the assertion of society itself in the performance of timeless reasons. Even if we were to decide that living in association with others according to the social contract inevitably generates insecurity, it would be incorrect to say that this can be traced to the state of society itself, for it could not be the totalizing insecurity imposed by the state of nature, and we have already seen that need, including a sense of insecurity, appears both as socially constituted and as a timeless reason that belongs to the very fact of society and to our being *of* society.

In other words, if an individual feels insecure *in* society as a private experience, that certainty is accompanied by and subordinated to the certainty that there is no general state of affairs outside of society that can be the cause. There is a radical difference between the general insecurity that invariably arises from conditions of life within the limitlessness of nature and the moments of insecurity that an associated person experiences under the altogether different conditions of society. The one generates suspicion, alertness, and a readiness either to flee or attack, while the other generates a suspicion turned inward, against the socialized individual herself *relative to* the basic fact of her dependence on all others *but not caused by that dependence*. The loneliness of someone *of* society belongs to society in the same way that pain or need belongs in an important way to society; and empathy, understood as responsiveness based on a generalized sense of obligation, is a feature of a form of life in which each is dependent on all. More needs to be said about emergent moments of individuality, but it is enough for now to see how what is typically ascribed to individual persons alone or one by one may have a distinctly and overwhelming social aspect.

In passing, it should be clear that Rousseau does not conceive of the "particular will" as identical with or even similar to the will of a creature in nature, to a "naturally selfish" will. Its particularity lies in its being "local" in the special sense of the intersection or overlapping of courses of activity. And this manifests the general will relative to what remains of social beings apart from their participation in the indivisibility of the general will—in special regard to the idea of "personal advantage," which for Rousseau expresses, by its very nature, social relations (in *The Social Contract*, book 3, chapter 2; book 2, chapters 2 and 4). That remainder is no less social for failing at any instant to be of the whole. Its way of being outside of the general will is to display in all respects the internality of its relationship to it. This relationship must then be seen as ambivalent insofar as anyone's recognition of dependence on others amounts to a recognition that though the needs guaranteed by association will be met, they will not necessarily be met in the same way and in the same time for every member.

It seems that the transformation of individuals in the move from nature to society is sufficiently comprehensive to erase from memory the very motivation that led them to join with previously unknown others. This makes it impossible for them to recall why it had been necessary to leave all that they "knew" and "had" when they were creatures in nature, and, therefore, impossible for them to communicate the necessity of association to subsequent generations. The narrative implies a loss of memory, and a loss of memory implies a temporal limit of the social contract that cannot account for the continuity of society and therefore the unity of justice and utility that allows for all rights and freedoms, the security provided by the rule of law, and all those qualities that define what is distinctively human.

How, then, can the social contract be both a contract and, at the same time, the origin of society as the basic fact about human affairs? What sort of knowledge can replace memory in accounting for the continuity of society? Answering these questions requires facing the difficulty of conceiving of people in nature agreeing to associate without there being some prior basis of trust, unless the mere presence of a large number is sufficient to explain the willingness of each to disarm and "give themselves to all." The difficulty is compounded by the fact that the presence of all (or even many) must have been either accidental, which cannot guarantee the history presumably rationalized by the social contract, or to have been founded on a prior association, *in which case there never was a "state of nature."* One might respond that humans are naturally capable of pity for their kind, but this cannot explain why each would rely on all others for protection.

We are left, then, with three theoretically crucial ideas. First, insecurity and pity cannot explain a decision to associate though they may contribute to the quality of an association already in being. Second, the act of assembling presupposes precisely what it is supposed to explain. Third, even if we say that insecurity explains association, people who have come to society from the wilderness and become *of* it will never again have to face the same conditions that motivated them in the first place, and therefore will be unable to take them into account in *reaffirming* the first convention; or, if they are somehow able to remember in a linguistically valid way, they will lack the continuing experience with insecure conditions that can confirm a belief in the necessity of a social contract. It follows that all that could bind future generations to the social contract would be the inability of society ever to overcome the state of nature, to negate its own negation. In that case, either the work of associating is never done, *or there is an imbedded principle in the narrative, hidden from its literal interpretation, that accounts for the necessity of society regardless of specific motivations, and that immediately appeals to every being capable of reason.*

If society is not sufficient in itself to overcome the state of nature, there would have to be a constant renewal of members' commitments, individual by individual (as Hampshire [2000] seems to believe in his account of "justice as conflict"). This envisions a perpetual crisis based on the ever-present possibility of regression to a state of nature or of an overly articulated society that can only undermine its own possibility. A crisis of that order cannot provide support for each to rely on all. At best, it can lend itself only to an extreme centrist form of sovereignty or, at worst, to despotism or fascism, with a corresponding degeneration of society to the absolutely dependent form of an aggregate. Given how crises are experienced, acquiescence in society seems no more likely than refusal and resistance. In that case, continued association is nothing more than an improbable possibility; society can neither dispel insecurity under such conditions nor find its justification in the idea of a social contract.

It is important to remember what is at stake in the idea of a social contract, regardless of what is problematic about the concept. To the extent to which reliance of each on all is undermined as the foundation of an embodied general will, there seems no default position left to account for the possibility of reconciling justice and utility and, therefore, for a general and continuing commitment to social order supported by the trust implicit in that reconciliation (Rousseau 1964, 197). This is reinforced by the familiar fact that most conjunctural accounts of social change use this diachronic language; and recourse to the ideas of "conjuncture" and "crisis" is a virtual staple in political discourse, political sociology, and history (see Brown 2009, 198–200). The possibility that society is insufficient to overcome insecurity and the possibility of a regression to a state of nature would be fatal to Rousseau's theory. But it would be simplistic to read these into his account of the problematic aspects of maintaining the general will. In any case, it is clear that he has more in mind when he says:

> The engagements which bind us to the social body are only obligatory because they are mutual, and their nature is such that in fulfilling them one cannot work for others without also working for oneself. Why is the general will always right, and why do we all constantly wish for the happiness of each, if not because there is no person who appropriates to himself that word "each" without having himself in mind while voting for all? This proves that equality of right and the notion of justice it produces derive from the preference that each person gives himself, and consequently from the nature of man; that the general will, to be such, must be general in its object as well as in its essence; that it must originate from all to apply to all, and that it loses its natural rectitude when it tends to some object which is individual and determinate, because then, judging what is foreign to us, we have no true principle of equity to guide us. (1992, bk. 2, chap. 4; my translation)

It is not the specter of the state of nature that haunts society and keeps us bound to it. It is clear that a different sort of principle is at work.
The literal interpretation of the narrative account of the social contract must be rejected, and with it the idea that society and our commitment to it are sustained against the constant threat of dissolution and the insecurity associated with the idea of a perpetual crisis of the social as such. What must not be rejected, however, are the phenomenological and epistemic effects of the narrative independent of the relations of origin and succession and the inevitable contest between the general will and the state. That is, the narrative must be understood, *first of all*, in terms of what it does within the act of reading and, thereby, to the reader. This is because its effect is immanent to the narrative itself, though it is typically ignored in favor of the impossible logic and secondary effect of the story as "literally" told.[4] The narrative inscribes a principle that, in itself, accounts for the continued commitment to the social contract by everyone regardless of the historical society in which they live, their generation, and how such a commitment might be justified. According to this, being *of* society is not something that can be motivated in the usual sense. We should agree with Rousseau in rejecting the idea that nothing about society threatens a return to a state of nature, and we should reject the motivational account of recommitment supported by what is, then, an illusory threat. However, to come closer to the principle, we need to reexamine the literal interpretation from a

somewhat different perspective to see if it yields the principle in its own terms and despite itself.

To the extent to which nature brings about a motivating state of insecurity on the part of all, and coming together satisfies it, there must be something about human association that erases the cause of insecurity—which is a generalized sense of threat without the prospect of relief. Unfortunately, there is no way to imagine any such prospect, since the sort of imagination that might know it is available only to those already socialized. It follows that there can be no pre-societal belief in the efficacy of association. However, being with others, in the sense of being *of* society, entails a special kind of belief that is immune to doubt and, therefore, skepticism. This suggests either that there never was or could have been a social contract in the literal sense of the narrative, which must be conceded, or *that the social contract is not the sort of thing that can have a history stemming from an origin but can only have happened if it is and had been already happening*. The latter seems correct, which makes it possible to answer what has been perhaps the most vexing sociological question about the social contract: How can the general will be an immanent feature of society? It can be immanent only if (1) there was never a *first*, pre-social, association, (2) there is something about association per se that constitutes *it* as an embodied general will, and (3) there is something about human activity that is already an instance of association. My reading of Nagel is intended to make a strong case for the third point. My critique of Rousseau's narrative is intended to make a case in favor of the first and second points.

Again, the narrative says that association fatefully re-situates insecure individuals whose individuality had to do with their physical survival alone. Their physical powers and cunning are not merely suspended; they vanish in a totalizing moment of vulnerability, to be replaced by the collective power of the "all" on whom each absolutely depends. This new power resides in the authority of a general will that is internally divided as both general and particular and never merely one or the other. This is, therefore, not a tragic contradiction but a fact about generality and particularity—namely, that they are internally related. It is a necessary feature of the general will that it is impossible to refer meaningfully to a state of nature, which is to say that such a state is inconceivable. This follows from the propositions that social beings cannot conceive of nonsocial existence, that social beings are inter-dependent, and that inter-dependence is irreducible and irrepressible. An exception to the general will would mean that it is no longer general. Associates would find themselves in the midst of doubt about the value or durability of their association, which means, in effect, that they are not associated except in the purely utilitarian sense that requires an untenable instrumentalist narrative in which there are only particular wills. Such doubt would amount to a breakdown of the rule of law and would be fatal to the trust required for an association in which individuals' powers are substantively and not merely formally erased. A failure of trust is analogous to the sense of insecurity associated with the state of nature insofar as each can only view all others with suspicion. Under the auspices of a general will, all are equal in the absolute dependence of each on all; and all benefit from that equality, though not necessarily equally in the course of events. To choose against this condition or to yearn for a return to nature would be to deny one's humanity and, paradoxically, to do so from within a humanity that cannot deny itself. The associated self is radically different from the isolated brute self whose powers of self-protection, while possibly adequate to some emergencies, are inevitably inadequate to a general condition of constant threat. A social being does not experience regret for nature lost or nostalgia for natural freedom, since the state of nature is inconceivable and the state of society is the condition of distinctively human experience. Law expresses human freedom, as Rousseau says, because it is by virtue of law that rights exist and each is enabled freely to act within the constraints of mutual respect imposed by the general will, chief of which is not to act in a way that undermines the sense of trust necessary for a durable association.

Since associates cannot imagine a human existence in a state of nature, they can have no positive image of it. Continued adherence to the collective must depend, then, on other causes than insecurity and a belief that only society can sustain human life. Such a belief cannot have arisen in a state of nature and therefore cannot be part of a decision to leave it. The continuity of membership across generations, as well as throughout any instance of life, cannot be a consequence of the sort of cause to which "motivation" refers and "decision" requires, so there must be another principle that explains the commitment to society across the *longue durée* and regardless of differences among particular wills, one that is true for all who are *of* society, and true without exception.

If human beings are essentially social, they cannot have decided to leave a state of nature and they cannot have a memory correspondent with such a state. Therefore, there is no original instance to explain. Similarly, since it is impossible for social beings to reject society, it is meaningless to try to explain why they remain members or why they might decide to leave. It follows again that either we must reject the literal interpretation of the narrative or conclude that Rousseau does not provide an intelligible concept of a social contract. As I read him, the text is designed to show, first, that humans are essentially social, second, that social beings necessarily act as if there is a social contract, and, third, that they do so because the society of the social contract is not the negation of nature. This is how I interpret the following passage, where Rousseau speaks of finding

> a form of association that defends and protects the person and goods of each associate with all the common force, and by means of which each one, uniting with all, nevertheless obeys only himself and remains as free as before. This is the fundamental problem which is solved by the social contract. The clauses of this contract are so completely

determined by the nature of the act that the slightest modification would render them null and void. So that *although they may never have been formally pronounced, they are everywhere the same, everywhere tacitly accepted and recognized.* (1978b, 53; emphasis added)

The problem is to determine what the "act" is that has a "nature" and that determines something that underlies the possibility of society. Since "the clauses" of the contract "may never have been formally pronounced," they must be known in some other way, and Rousseau's use of the word "act" merely indicates what needs to be explained. I have proposed that we consider the narrative as an allegory designed to do what allegories do, which is to remind us of a truth beyond doubt. I want to show that the narrative performs, as it were, the truth of two propositions as a matter of immediate experience: one cannot have chosen to be *of* society, and one cannot decide to leave or otherwise reject it. These are immediately true because of the impossibility of imagining conditions of either entrance or exit, which entails that one knows oneself only as *of* society and within it.

———

The same result follows from another perspective on the literal interpretation, one that focuses on the consequences of each individual ceding her powers of self-protection to the association of all, which, in turn, exercises a greater power on behalf of each than can be exercised by each alone. It follows that associated individuals who depend entirely on the association for their security and freedom are transformed in virtually all other respects. They gain what nature can neither allow nor provide for—namely, interests beyond the present, thoughts of self and other, identity, communicative capacity, relations, rights, freedoms, and self-reflecting attitudes that substantiate their association and make each immediately recognizable to every other as a human being whose personal issues are, fundamentally, common affairs.

The literal translation again ends by presupposing its antithesis. It does so to the extent to which it is true—as that interpretation is bound to recognize as a consequence of entering into association with others one cannot have known in advance—that the motivation that explains the continued willingness to associate must be as overwhelming as the original state of insecurity. Both exhaustively determine their different forms of individuality, though what appears as individuated must be radically different for each state of affairs: the first convention transforms the asocial and insecure creature of need into a social being whose freedom under law is substantiated in all respects by her self-knowledge as dependent on all and her inability to imagine a state of nature as the negation of society and, therefore, as an alternative to it. The anticipated consequences are, first, self-knowledge that depends on one's knowledge of others, nameable or not, and, second, a generalized sense of security afforded to each exclusively by the association. The unanticipated consequence is the total transformation of the subject, including the mediation of all her knowledge of herself and the world, and, correspondingly, the constitution of a subjectivity that cannot know nature as its history. It is unanticipated because the literal interpretation begins by considering only the most immediate correction society makes of the state of nature—namely, the elimination of insecurity. But that *entails* the inherency of the general will and its tension with a socially constituted particular will radically unlike whatever is constituted as will in a state of nature.

It is important not to misunderstand Rousseau's intention in using the word "gain" when he says that "one gains [in association] the equivalent of everything one loses, and more force to preserve what one has" (1978b, 53). "Gain" normally suggests an accumulation by addition. But all properties that can be ascribed to a social being must be understood as fundamentally socialized: they must therefore pertain to that form of life in its wholeness. A social being is, in that respect, no less indivisible as such than the general will. All else is, without any possibility of irony, irrelevant to what is human about human beings. Nothing about such a being accumulates in the form of gains. All that constitutes a social being is given beyond measure *in* the moment of the social contract: "Each of us puts his person and all his power in common under the supreme direction of the general will; and in a body we receive each member as an indivisible part of the whole" (53). The transformation is total; that one is a social being knows no exception. In other words, more than citizenship, therefore political theory, is at stake.

––––––––––

The difficulties involved in imagining any literal interpretation adequate to Rousseau's concept of the social are compounded by several points that bear on how the social contract can endure across time and generations. First, it is inconceivable that any pre-social being could imagine *society* as a result of simultaneous decisions by *all* based, as the literal reading must have it, on at least five necessary conditions: (1) the simultaneous formation of an irresistible desire on the part of all pre-social members of the species to escape the state of nature without being able to imagine anything beyond it; (2) beliefs that support the notion that insecurity can be overcome by associating with unknown creatures who belong to the very state of nature in which insecurity is relentless; (3) a belief that a total society is possible, as something greater than any collection available to individual experience, and can provide protection beyond what can be provided by any individual or aggregate of individuals; (4) a belief that all who need to will decide at the same instant can do so with identical results; and (5) a belief that all who need to decide not only share the appropriate desire and beliefs but know that all others do as well. On the contrary, living together in society must be possible for social beings who have never known a state of nature just as it must be for those hypothetical creatures said to have emerged somehow from it. The social contract necessarily binds everyone who cannot imagine an alternative; otherwise, Rousseau has not solved the problem of reconciling justice and utility. It binds everyone not because of its origin, and not because of a motive that might justify a first convention, but because it is impossible for social beings to imagine not being in and of society, and, therefore, it is possible for them to know their essential sociality only as an immediate experience beyond propositions, doubt, and argument—that is, as immanent.

To summarize, literal interpretations of the narrative of the first convention are, despite themselves, ultimately unable to avoid recourse to a nonliteral reading. It always appears that, without such a reading, the idea of a social contract is incomprehensible, and it is impossible to see how it can be identified as a durable foundation of society understood as a body politic. In other words, there appear to be no alternatives able to avoid three fatal problems. The first, which confuses society with an aggregate or a nation, relies on an idea of power that cannot be reconciled with the conception of a body politic and on an idea of territory that has no sociologically valid referent. The second relies on the unintelligible claim that society is constituted as a solution to a general problem posed to all individuals by the ever-present possibility of a state of nature. As such, it is conceived of as a perpetual state of emergency in which law is undermined by the dependence of internal order on the application of force by a state opposed to any possibility of a socially constituted body politic, and in which emphasis on the security of the population substitutes an aggregate for a society. The third involves relying on an overly convenient reductive individualism that begs the question of what is human about human affairs, often as a way of avoiding the philosophical and theoretical problems involved in justifying the simplification.

Parenthetically, an acceptable approach to a possible alternative would require reexamining the relationship between sociality and historicity and, in particular, the ontological presuppositions of the human sciences. This book is intended to reinforce this possibility by focusing on the implications and entailments of those presuppositions so that they might be addressed by an immanent critique respectful of their most powerful possible expression and therefore for what they might offer beyond themselves consistent with the idea that the human sciences constitute a unified field based on a common objectivity—namely, what is human about human affairs.

It follows further that the individualistic and literal interpretations of Rousseau's narrative are bound to appear superficial to his readers since the latter are social beings and, therefore, unable to imagine the state of nature as humanly livable. They can, of course, understand a story of an origin, but not as their own or how it might be true for any human being. This is because, imbued with language, they are already social beings and can have nothing of the state of nature about them or even the slightest degree of irony in their sense of being social. For now, it is important to remember why the five conditions of the narrative's being true listed above cannot be met and therefore why, in order to preserve the idea of a social contract, it is necessary to read it as something other than a historical account or a "useful fiction." While it may be true that there is an advantage to ceding one's power to all, there is no foundation for a creature living in a pre-social state of nature to imagine it as a possibility. There would be no basis for assuming that others in the state of nature and, therefore, untrustworthy because unsocial, would relinquish their own powers at the same moment, and no reason to think that, even if they did, the agreement of each to subject herself to all would not be merely expedient and therefore unreliable. It would then be reasonable for each to conclude that some others might have reserved their original power, thereby gaining an unacceptable advantage over those who had conceded their own. They might intuit the value of combined powers but not as a departure from nature and not as implying anything on the order of justice. They would have no reason to be respectful of others even if they could hope for respect from them.[5]

This is not to criticize Rousseau's or any other version of the social contract. It is to show that a literal interpretation of his account of the origin of society cannot be defended without betraying the text as a whole. At best, it leads to the paradox of both asserting and denying that people are motivated to form society from a position external to it. Either Rousseau's account of the social contract must be disregarded as false and in any case irrelevant to accounting for the persistence of society beyond a single contracting generation, both of which discredit all that follows in his text, or he must have had something other in mind than what appears in the literal interpretation. We have little choice but to ask what is accomplished by a narrative in which the principle of law appears to reconcile utility and justice by virtue of its emergence, as a principle, from a lawless and unprincipled state of affairs and as a concomitant of the subjective aspect of the social contract, which is the general will. We have eliminated recourse to the ideas that the narrative is intended as a historical explanation because the emergence itself is unthinkable, that it is a useful fiction because that leaves us with the same problem of interpretation, and that a general will can take form among nonsocial beings because the state of nature precludes that as a possibility. *If the theory of the social contract is at all valid, the claim that the narrative is intended as a description is false.*

Two conclusions can be accepted as working hypotheses. One is that the narrative demonstrates the truth of something altogether different from the idea that the social contract begins with a first meeting of minds. The second, which is more controversial, says that the very nature of that truth means that it cannot be demonstrated effectively by any means other than the one adopted by Rousseau. This requires reading the narrative as instating something altogether different from the story that is its literally attributable content. To know the truth of the social contract from this point of view is to experience the social as a basic fact, and this cannot be the same as having a justified belief. For one thing, the truth of the social contract does not carry the irony with which positive beliefs are registered as representational knowledge: it does not imagine a "knowing subject" behind and detached from what is known, though it implicates a reading subject who now reads the narrative for its antithesis—namely, an allegorical "sense" of human affairs that cannot otherwise be brought to mind. Reading the narrative for the allegory brings together, in a single luminous moment, the knowledge and the fact of knowing, which is also to say that it momentarily provides an unqualified truth that needs no further justification, repetition, elaboration, or rhetorical emphasis. Such a reading is indispensable to the theory as far as the latter bears on what is human about human affairs; and, at the same time, it shows itself to be an instance of those affairs. It demonstrates the necessity and inevitability of our commitment to society by appealing to something radically different from an origin. It makes our commitment knowable as an immediate and irrefutable fact: it does not rely on argument or persuasion so it is not vulnerable to criticisms that rely on positive methods of fixing belief.[6]

The allegory of the first convention—the moment of humanity—demonstrates in the way successful allegories do that we can imagine ourselves and, indeed, anything else having to do with human affairs, only as essentially social. We cannot imagine ourselves, or imagine "imagining," without spontaneously spoken language, without reliable others, without mutual regard, without the capacity to participate in the activity of forming concepts, without all that society makes of us, which is to say, without a sociality so basic that it cannot be adequately represented or summarized by a list of socially relevant individual traits. It demonstrates that life outside of society is inconceivable, that to conceive of human life is already to have conceived of society, not simply as an idea but as *consciousness conscious of itself.* This way of thinking about the reconciliation of utility and justice is far from the idea that a logically negative concept is defined by what it negates, and it does not depend on *deducing* the proposition that society constitutes the realm of freedom outside of which no freedom and nothing that can be called "knowledge" can be recognizably human. Certainly there is some truth to the former, and the latter is, in some sense, inferred by Rousseau from his critique of alternative theories. However, neither is sufficient to what he wants to accomplish for his readers, what he wants them to know pre-philosophically, extra-reflectively, and apodictically so that he can proceed to discuss the implications of such knowledge for understanding human affairs.

In what follows, I do not claim that one should avoid reading the language of a text as it is written, since that would be absurd and since the very idea of an allegory, like every other textual effect, depends on taking what is written seriously in as many respects as possible. Indeed, I rely on the familiar idea that a serious reading always goes beyond what is inscribed. At issue are the stakes in bringing a reading to fruition beyond what literality permits, and the insufficiency of literal re-inscription (reflecting rather than reflecting *on* what is written) to understanding the content or effectuality of any text. It seems clear that no attempt to read a text can complete it, and therefore all readings must be untrue. But every reading should make a difference to the reader in the course of reading and, at least, do so by virtue of the work of reading the text for what is immanently beyond it. The idea that a line can be drawn between literal and serious assumes a distinction that is practical only for the moment and that can be superseded only in the course of theorizing the activity of reading itself. In the case of *The Social Contract*, acknowledging the allegory saves the text as a whole from the trivializing result of reading the narrative as either a historical or deliberately fictional account.

The allegory will not be readable by those whose notion of freedom is defined by an adversary relationship among "particular wills" each of which is independent of all others. This implies indifference to the problem of reconciling justice and utility and, therefore, to the very possibility of what Foucault (2007) refers to as "governmentality." That is, it cannot be read by those determined at the outset to resist it dogmatically. Rousseau's reader must be able to address his text in a way that allows the basic fact to appear as an effect and not merely a conclusion of an argument. Literalists reject this without considering the stakes, one of which is the possibility of a self-regulating society. The theoreticians among them reject it insofar as their concept of reading conforms to a theory of reception in which the order of inscription and the architectonics of what is inscribed dictates the order of what the reader can be expected to know—so that literal reading, which particularizes the text, must precede interpretation and use. The latter are then constrained by the former, typically in the interest of preserving a certain objectivity of the text against expropriation and arbitrariness, which is to say the order of values and tradition versus the anomic chaos of the state of nature. Not to acknowledge the dependence of each on all others makes human freedom and therefore justice unintelligible (for a possible consequence, see Sartre 1988, 65–69). Rousseau's text addresses all who might be involved in discourses in which reference to the social is actively suppressed or elided and is, therefore, profoundly latent—which is to say all who share language in the sense of being able spontaneously to speak but not to speak spontaneously about speaking. His text anticipates a discourse that suppresses what most pertains to the fact and idea of discourse—one that is, to put it in Jürgen Habermas's (1970, 1971) terms, "distorted" by its paradoxical and therefore necessarily self-manipulative denial of the sociality on which it depends.

The specifics of Rousseau's demonstration are as follows. What is at stake is that the fact of "people among people" is systematically denied by canceling, characteristic by characteristic, anything that might allow for the necessity of the sub-theoretical notion of sociality. While this may not be deliberate, it is not disinterested. All that remains of what is human about human beings after the denial is the utilitarian, or expedient, aspect of their lives, which are then seen, with minor qualifications, as fundamentally driven by necessity, as in the state of nature. Ironically, this denial of the immanence of sociality relies on at least one exception to that idea—namely, the subjectivity entertaining it.[7] To conceive of a state of nature inhabited by such creatures is to assert that they are not human. In contrast, our being social seems to involve, as Nagel says in his critique of moral skepticism, "forms of thought and action which it may not be in our power to renounce," or, I would add, to imagine renouncing (1970, 144). We experience our humanity holistically, by virtue of the relation each has to all and by virtue of the constant incorporation of each into society as an internally indivisible member equal in that respect with all others.

What follows *philosophically* from the demonstration that the state of nature is unimaginable is that it is possible to conceive of human affairs only as essentially social. Since the social does not stand apart from those who are *of* it, it refers to activities that transpire across bodies—activities that cannot be understood as human by any theory that individualizes those bodies, as in the attempt to conceive of society as radically post-natural. Parenthetically, even the notion of a "state" of being derives from the attempt to characterize nature as a pre-social universe from which individuals find their way into a society of which they can, by definition, have no conception. Such a formulation constitutes a regression to the very anti-societal discourse that Rousseau's allegory is intended to unsettle. In that case, *it is also necessary to deny the validity of any state-descriptive view of sociality on the grounds that it would model sociality on precisely what it cannot imaginably be (namely, the effect of a state of nature).* Of course, it does not follow that the *desire* to deny society is overcome by the force of the allegory, no matter how successful it might otherwise be. All that Rousseau shows is that it is impossible to think or speak meaningfully about human affairs apart from its essential sociality.

What follows *phenomenologically* is our immediate certainty that a state of nature is inconceivable as a condition of human life. It is perhaps better to say that we cannot conceive of human life in its human aspect in nature conceived of as a realm of necessity. Even the attempt to do so diminishes our sense of what is human about human affairs. It also appears that a logically negative concept of nature, taken as the condition of a constant crisis of society, is not relevant to human affairs despite endlessly informing debates about those affairs. Society cannot be understood as protection of humanity against the threat of a return to a state of nature. Claims of this sort corrupt political discourse by positing an ideal problem—for example, a "war against terror" that can only be conceived of as interminable—that cannot be solved without undoing the very conditions of society. That is, while it might make some sense programmatically, the exclusive reliance on the metaphor of war increasingly incorporates a dependence on worst-case scenarios. Even now, this is defended not as an attempt to save society but to secure that declining portion of the statistical aggregate, the "population," that falls outside of the necessarily expanding category of "collateral damage." This is only one consequence of the systematic attempt, characteristic of contemporary conservatism, either to deny that society is a form of life or to encourage indifference toward its inclusiveness by exclusionist appeals to patriotism in the name of the nation, loyalty in the name of authority, and other self-contradictory moralisms based on sectarian aspirations, a desire to win a "war of civilizations," or a belief in the rightness of an adversarial conception of freedom in a world of necessarily inter-dependent subjectivities.

To say that the capacity of individuals to go beyond the basic fact is discursively mediated is to admit that the positivity of the social is only immediate from the point of view of the collective, which is necessarily the point of view of each in regard to her dependence on all. This is evidenced by the urgency, repetitiousness, and regressive character of political discourse when the question of sociality is systematically begged. To the extent to which the will to participate in the collective is spontaneous, its mediations are not identical for each instance of that will, though "each" remains a social being that, in regard to its sociality, can be thought of as a "singularity" that presupposes connectedness and therefore the immanence of its tendency to change. Such beings are inevitably drawn into a politics that can offer no personal satisfaction, since what is available to the collectivity becomes available to its singularities only within and through the courses of activity in which they are constituted as such and transformed; and it is the very idea of a course of activity that is theoretically most at stake in the idea of society as the basic fact and basic right.

Once one is confronted with the fact that the state of nature as a condition of society is unimaginable and the corresponding fact that one is *of* society and not just in it, one cannot find oneself or any of one's kind outside of the vast company of others, the unlimited community of strangers from whom one's obligation to all is returned multiply in the form of rights and the only freedom conceivable for a human being. We are, then, no longer tempted to address questions about the origin and worth of society. I argue later that this "finding of ourselves" is evident in an *attitude of waiting* that accompanies each moment of discourse—from the apparently simple gesture to the speech act and the argument. For now, it is enough to acknowledge the allegorical force of Rousseau's narrative, the certainty to which it gives rise, and some of what that entails. It is important to keep in mind that the object of that certainty cannot be the social contract as it literally appears in the narrative. Rather, it is the sense of an obligation to all inseparable from the freedom that is distinctively human: the utility and justice that Rousseau non-synthetically reconciles are not pre-social pleasure and the subordination of individuality to authoritative enactments: "interest" belongs to each in light of their dependence on all, as does "justice," though these reflect different perspectives each of which is immanent to what is distinctively human. *The social contract does not signify an event but an ontological condition.* This leaves open an important theoretical question that can be addressed only as part of a more developed account. Does the fact that each knows herself, immediately and certainly, to be dependent on all mean that she also knows that all others know that same basic fact in the same way? That is, what is the character of the "equality" implicit in the idea of the social?

There remains another problem that is less theoretically demanding. It has to do with the relevance of the social contract to political discourse. How does the dependence of each on all—which implies that everyone is, first of all, someone who could be someone else—bear on the rationality and reasonableness of political discussions? If it is acknowledged as a basic fact, then the range of policies available will be different from those that appear legitimate when it is not. However, more than the certainty of being *of* society is necessary. A positive conception is essential if sociality is to qualify as the feature of practical reason that involves "reasonableness" in contrast with a purely instrumental "rationality" (Rawls 1999a, 28, 177). We have seen that most topics having to do with human affairs cannot be addressed satisfactorily in their own terms. This is consistent with the claim that sociality is a basic fact on which reasoning across differences depends. It cannot be elided, distorted, or manipulated without undermining practical reason itself, which is the immanent reason of human affairs, and, at the same time, without bringing into play those self-defeating discriminatory and exclusionary practices in which reason becomes corrupt and appears to negate itself (see Butler 2000, 136–181; Horkheimer and Adorno 1972).

I began with a short description of two points of view from which it is crucial to grasp society as the basic fact and, therefore, to clarify that idea, at least by showing what it cannot mean. This chapter has continued the discussion from the point of view of the dependence of each on all; and it has explored some implications of the corresponding fact that human life in a state of nature is unthinkable. This does not mean that we are social by default, but that being social is what is meant by being human. One implication is the invalidity of any theory of society that assumes the possible existence of its negation. Another is that any discourse that ignores or suppresses the basic fact is bound to leave its parties dissatisfied beyond whatever practical or moral conflict might still exist among them. In the course of discussing the social contract and the consequences of being *of* society, it becomes clear that any definition would have to be consistent with the proposition that sociality as such has no determinate form beyond the simple dependence of each on all. That is its essential attribute, which makes its elision in discourse both understandable and difficult to avoid. This does not mean that the social is insubstantial, a construct, an ideal, or an illusion. Rather, theories in which "society" refers to a relatively fixed and structured formation define it in a way that excludes the very activities of trying to define and theorize it, which are themselves human affairs and therefore essentially social. The alternative to something fixed and structured is not chaos or formlessness, but it cannot satisfy a language devoted to particularities such as events and actions and to a radical but unrealizable distinction between subject and object. I have used the expression "course of activity," which is not a particular, in contrast with "action," which is, and will suggest a way of thinking about society that is anti-reductionist and that does not sacrifice the philosophically crucial internal relation of theory and its object to the self-deceiving irony of the theoretician who aspires in her every concept to register the radical externality of theory to its object.

Nevertheless, a common response to Rousseau has been to think of his concept of society as a state of affairs distinct from but present as such in every one of its individual manifestations. From this point of view, it is a form of life "for itself" that gives form to the lives of members who exist "for others" and only then "for themselves." This has led some to draw totalitarian implications from *The Social Contract*, on which I have already commented, and others to read it as unremittingly Romantic (see West 1995, 43; Babbitt 1928, 98). The latter invites an interpretation of Rousseau's criticisms of historical society as condemnatory of society as such (West 1995, 42). This can only, if at all, be said about *The Social Contract* if it is understood as part of a greater text that includes all his writings, including his reflections on them, as if whatever intention each might have had as a textual venture is subordinate to an inclusive intention in light of which each text must be understood. Whatever is gained by such a condensation, and regardless of Rousseau's accounts of his work in his autobiographical writings, this ignores the self-sufficient and positive character of *The Social Contract* when read for what is unique in it—namely, its conception of the social and the demonstration of it as the basic fact (see Starobinski 1988, ix, xiv, xv). It does not adequately represent the coherence of the greatest part of the text in which Rousseau conceives of sociality as the dependence of each on all,[8] in which he distinguishes power from authority in a way that inaugurates modern social science and modern theories of democracy, and in which he shows that the idea of a body politic presupposes a general will that is spontaneously acknowledged in the irreducible dependence of each on all and an internal and tense relationship between the general and particular wills.

To characterize *The Social Contract* as a typically Romantic work is to risk underestimating its theoretical originality. In that case, it is likely to appear either as little more than a footnote to the history of an idea or an expression of an ideology. Reading it for its originality, beyond Rousseau's demonstration of the truth of the basic fact, provides access to a cogent and powerful argument to the following effect, given the fundamental problem society must solve if it is to exist as such. Justice and utility are reconciled only under a rule of law that transcends particular enactments (legislation), is distinct from any attempt to exercise power, and expresses the freedom constantly conferred on individuals by a vast community of inter-dependent strangers each of whom is, as a necessary feature of the practice of such a community and its members, an end and not a means. It is in this respect that one can gauge Rousseau's influence beyond what is most often attributed to him in secondary and derivative accounts. Two related examples of reading for what is original in Rousseau are Durkheim's

(1965) summary interpretation of *The Social Contract* and interpretations by later writers of Durkheim's only theoretical work, *The Rules of Sociological Method* (1982).[9] Arguably, the most influential non-Rousseauian interpretation of *The Rules* favors the idea of a fully articulated social system for which the sub-institutional depths of society, in which sociality apparently takes the form of self-motivating courses of activity and "the individual is an infinity," is of little if any account (Parsons 1949; see Goffman's 1983 critique; compare Anne Warfield Rawls 2002). While Durkheim's (1965, 82–83) concept of the social as the interaction of social facts owes a great deal to Rousseau's demonstration that human affairs are only conceivably human if they are essentially social, this is not discussed in Parsons's influential account of Durkheim's work, in which Rousseau is indexed once, and then only in regard to the "paradox" that "as a Protestant a man is, in certain respects, forced to be free" (1949, 332; see also 350–365).

The analytical frame of reference of "system" is identified with Parsons and will be discussed in more detail later. It was partly based on recognizing the dependence of each on all as essential to any concept of society (Parsons 1951, 72), though this played no discernibly significant role in the theory itself. Most system theorists account for membership and agency in psychological terms, as products of learning and internalization, rather than as implicit in the very possibility of people living together and engaging in common or shared activities. Durkheim was not indifferent to the independent effects of sociality, but Parsons's emphasis on the intersection of personality (as resource) and social system (as source of control) left his theory insufficiently attentive to what later came to be referred to as "everyday life." In any case, the idea of a sub-institutional sociality cannot be included in his typology of levels of explanation (and "action"). Therefore, it has no logical connection to his meta-theory of action or his theory of society as a system of action. It follows that excluding from the theory what was admittedly necessary to the constitution of its object presents an incurable defect if the theory is taken as the only resource for explicating the idea of sociality as the basic fact (see Durkheim 1933; Parsons 1949, 1951, esp. chap. 1).

The difficulty of acknowledging the social as such also reflects the positivist turn in the academic culture of mid-century North America. With few exceptions, "human traits," such as "pro-social" inclinations, were seen as individual effects of learning rather, say, than ongoing collective accomplishments within fluid and unreliable circumstances (for two notable exceptions, see Goffman 1959 and Garfinkel 1967). It would have been difficult in any case to acknowledge the sub-theoretical notion of the social, though, as Floyd H. Allport (1924) showed in his research on "social facilitation," it was equally difficult to avoid it as a presupposition. It also was not formulated as a theoretical issue within the "action framework" or the version of system theory that Parsons derived from that framework. The result was not merely a diminished conception of agency but a diminished conception of society the operation of which depended on individuals as system resources, in other words, as members for whom the terms of membership are "latent"—allowing participation to be both spontaneous and unburdened by reflection on its history, its possibility, which is to say on its connection to the basic fact.

The weakness shows itself at the extremes of what the theory takes to be its object because of the low tolerance for strain built into the concept of a system and because of its limited resources for dealing with diversity (Brown and Goldin 1973). The theory begins with the idea of a pre-socialized individual in need of a socialization that can only be institutional (as in the ideal type specification of family and school as agencies of socialization). This makes a version of the negation of society virtually unavoidable if the theory is to provide any account of the reproduction of social order across cohorts and generations; and it is here that the concept's limitations are most obvious. Two types of pre-socialized individuals are imagined, newcomers entering from another society and presumably pre-social infants. Each case reveals a fundamental problem with the theory of the social system similar to the problem revealed by its explanation of "collective behavior" as institutionally deviant (Smelser 1963).

For collective behavior, the question is how a system can recover from a pervasive strain (incompatibilities among its functional subsystems—economy, polity, culture, and modes of coordination—understood as conditions of rational action) sufficient to set social forces in motion on a large enough scale to constitute a popularly generalized reaction. Given the assumptions of system theory, there are no specifically articulated functions (rational subsystems) available to reduce an abnormal degree of strain, to restore conditions prior to the onset of strain, or to reverse a generalized reaction to it. An abnormal strain is one that surpasses the normal self-equilibrating capacity of the system, and the normal capacity is the object posited by the theory. To restore normal conditions is not merely to eliminate a disturbing factor or correct a minor dysfunction; it is to add something that has its own effects, and these may or may not be compatible with the "normal" functioning of the system. In other words, attempting to restore a putative *status quo ante* imposes something new on the system and is therefore likely to be an independent cause of strain. Finally, the existence of a generalized reaction, the collective subjectivity of system strain in the reductive form of a distributed generalized belief at odds with normally socialized system-functional beliefs, is no less systematically disruptive than any social force, and because it is reactive and socially pervasive it exceeds, and therefore contradicts, the system imperative of coordinative integration (and therefore inclusiveness). This is why the term "collective behavior" was virtually defined, from both the system and member points of view, as informal or noninstitutional and therefore nonrational politics, or, as in Parsons's characterization of the student movement of the 1960s, a politics against reason (see Smelser 1963; Parsons 1968; compare Brown and Goldin 1973). *The problem is that system theory predicts both strain as a condition of the totality and an inability to reverse strain within the limits of the "conditions of rational action" that constitute the normal operation of the system*; or it requires a psychological solution to a social condition in the form of a change in a belief held by many though likely to have been carried into action by a relatively few.

The question about how individuals are converted to members functioning as system resources is different for those entering a society as adults and for those born into it. By hypothesis, entering adults have already been socialized to another system. Therefore, they are likely to experience enough ambiguity to make them self-reflective to a degree that undermines the latency of what entrants are supposed to have internalized when they become authentic members. By this reasoning, they are likely either to be less reliable members than those born into the society or to be merely formal members. In this respect, the theory generates an external "other" who is not likely to become "one of us." This is unexpected and may be because of a confusion of the nonterritorial concept of "society" with that of "nation," a confusion that reflects the theoretical elision or suppression of the sub-theoretical basic fact, which cannot be exclusionist or identified by reference to an intersection of space and time—that is, a place.

Parsons's account of the socialization of children assumes their emergence from a pre-social state of nature, so that their socialization is both initially determined by their parents and the family configuration (1951, 226–230; also 1954, 145). This implies that early socialization is fundamentally local and therefore likely to produce significantly diverse products. The theory says little about the degree of diversity likely to undermine the coherence and consistency of culture (shared values and meanings), which is, on the condition of boundary maintenance, the principle functional subsystem of society understood, in Parsons's terms, as a social system. It is also unclear how diversity can be limited and managed, and the theory requires that it must be (without reference to power).

To the extent to which Parsons's hypotheses about deviance emphasize variable and imperfect socialization and the localization of socializing practices, the system is vulnerable to degrees of inconsistency and incoherence greater than the reliability required to account for either "boundary maintenance" (latent shared values and meanings) or the integration (coordination) of effort and, therefore, for the degree of social order necessary for a system to function effectively. The problem is different from the one posed by adult aspirants for membership, who do not emerge from a state of nature but from a different regime of socialization and different and necessarily abiding latencies. If both newcomers and infants are considered as social beings in Rousseau's sense, the problem seems less devastating, since the explanation of latency shifts from socialization practices to the fact of simply being among others. In that case, one would need a theory that allows for dispositions to participate in situated and ongoing practices. But that would require a very different model from that of a system.

Given the problems posed by the inability to guarantee reliable socialization and the inability to determine conditions under which it is possible to manage and reverse the effects of strain, the question system theory needs to address is how to conceive of society as an institutional order without bringing in at the most basic level what is sub-theoretical to all such conceptions—that is, the basic social fact—and it appears that the latter defies state-descriptive, system-type accounts. However it is defined, "sociality" must refer to something more fluid than a fixed morality or a systematically reinforced rational division of labor and it must do so in a way that challenges any concept that can be reduced to considerations about individuals. I should add that there are purposes, ignoble or not, for which it is necessary to ignore the basic fact, as Rousseau noted in his accounts of war and rule over a "multitude" (simple aggregate) just as there are purposes for which it may appear necessary to ignore the categorical imperative, that human beings are ends or values rather than means, as in war, the use of force or threat to maintain conditions of discrimination, persecution, exploitation, or oppression, and under the warrant, legitimate or not, of declarations of a "state of exception" (Agamben 2005).

For now, it is enough to indicate what might be at stake in the Rousseauian point of view in which defining the term "social" is urgent. We apparently cannot do without a concept of the social that invokes the idea of a first convention and the general will. Yet the idea remains opaque when we try to bring it to notice as an idea among ideas. It is nevertheless illuminated by Rousseau's demonstration that it is possible to imagine human life only as social in the sense of an irreducible dependency of each on all. The debasement, corruption, or perversion of the social contract is conceivable; but while this can give rise to a multitude, it cannot lead to a state of nature from which the possibility of society, and therefore of humanity, might be imagined as a solution. Before moving to the second point of view, we can anticipate from what was initially said about it that the two positions will tend to converge on a notion of the social as essentially in motion rather than essentially at rest and on the idea that the problem of definition is, for theory, unavoidable but not solvable in the strict sense of "definition."

5

The Sociality of Agency

The second way of addressing the idea of the social also emphasizes its centrality to any theory that claims to represent or express what is human about human affairs. The key texts can be placed conveniently under two related theoretical registers, Marxism, by which I mean the critique of capital in regard to its intrinsic limitations, and post-structuralism, by which I mean the critique of the theory of the sign.[1]

Thesis I of Marx's "Theses on Feuerbach" states:

> The chief defect of all hitherto existing materialism . . . is that the thing, reality, sensuousness, is conceived only in the form of the object or of *contemplation*, but not as *human sensuous activity, practice*, not subjectively. Hence it happened that the *active* side, in contradistinction to materialism, was developed by idealism—but only abstractly, since, of course, idealism does not know real, sensuous activity as such. (1978, 143; emphasis in original)

This means that subjectivity, reduced either to individuated consciousness or magnified as culture, is lost to the idealist no less than it is to the vulgar materialist.

> Feuerbach resolves the religious essence into the human essence. But the human essence is no abstraction inherent in each single individual. In its reality it is the ensemble of the social relations. Feuerbach, who does not enter upon a criticism of this real essence, is consequently compelled: (1) To abstract from the historical process and to

fix the religious sentiment as something by itself and to presuppose an abstract—*isolated*—individual. (2) The human essence, therefore, can with him be comprehended only as "genus," as an internal, dumb generality which merely *naturally* unites the many individuals. (Marx 1978, 145; emphasis in original)

Thesis VII concludes:

Feuerbach, consequently, does not see that the "religious sentiment" is itself a social product, and that the abstract individual, whom he ana-lyzes, belongs in reality to a particular form of society [that predicates its intelligibility as such on] the standpoint of . . . socialised humanity. (1978, 145)

The theses are not intended to establish that individuals are effects of a fully formed society. Rather, they converge on the key proposition from *The German Ideology* that "the first premise of all human history is, of course, the existence of living human individuals" (Marx and Engels 1976, 31). What counts here is not the organism, the relation of humans with the rest of nature, but agency and therefore activity; and what counts about human beings is that what they do is "a definite form of expressing their life, a definite *mode of life* on their part" (31; emphasis in original). That "what individuals are depends on the ma-terial conditions determining their production" (32) means that individuality itself performs a social reality that cannot be understood as causally, mechani-cally, or structurally determinate.

To say that the assertion is a "first premise of all human history" only *ap-pears* to set the stage for formal derivations; it is not a primitive assumption in regard to which positive theories ultimately are to be evaluated. This is clear from both the content and the rhetorical features of Marx's prose. For example, the mitigating expression, "of course," indicates that the assertion lacks the sta-tus of a positive proposition within a formal argument. It signals that some-thing is being said about language itself. From that point of view, the assertion states a rule for forming meaningful statements about human affairs according to what is distinctively human about them independent of biology or classifica-tion by species. Marx's own references to "species being" reinforce this inter-pretation insofar as they identify what is human with what it is to be social. Otherwise, "human affairs" refers to nothing but formal "objects of contempla-tion" constituted as such by "dumb generality." That these references also rely on "the standpoint of . . . socialized humanity" in no way undermines the point.

To make affairs humanely intelligible is to account for them in terms of how they make themselves accountable. It follows that species specificity in any other sense cannot be a basis for theorizing, since that requires a compari-son among categories that effectively eliminates consideration of what is hu-man about those affairs. What is distinctively human must be understood as specifiable only *within* human affairs. It is only in this sense of a language-constituting rule that the claim can be a "first premise of all human history." This conclusion is reinforced by what Marx says about individuality. Under modern conditions, the intelligibility of the concept of the individual has to do with the overwhelming historical fact that production, which is to say production *insofar as it is conceivable in its generality,* "presupposes the *intercourse* of individuals with one another." The form of this is "again determined by production" (Marx and Engels 1976, 32; emphasis in original), where production has to do with the reproduction of human affairs no less than the creation of goods for sale.² Individuality must therefore be held to express irreducible social facts. The individual cannot be conceived of alone, "in isolation," but only as an abiding possibility among people caught up in their relations, and, given the dependence of each on all, conceived of in such a way that individuality is an extrusion, or moment, and not a logically prior concept or basic fact. It follows that *agency, which has to do with the nature of activity, cannot be understood in individualistic terms or by reference to pre-social individuality.*

This account implies that sociality has priority for critical theory, which is theory reflexive to the conditions of its possibility as an ongoing accomplishment within the activity of theorizing. This is because all assertions about human affairs return to the social in one way or another. To the extent to which such an assertion is "a premise" limits what can be taken as a valid statement about human affairs by establishing what would be invalid, it risks returning to the transcendental essences that Marx was at pains to criticize and denounce. Nevertheless, theory has little choice as things stand but to attempt to establish sociality as an idea among ideas, in effect to substantiate it according to its status as the basic fact. But about what is it the basic fact, individuals or the association? One is tempted to say both, but this cannot simply mean that each person, each psychological being, by her nature, seeks the company of others. This would preserve the idea that "the human essence" is an "abstraction inherent in each single individual."

———

To avoid this dilemma, it is necessary to reflect on the chasm opened up by Foucault's (1994) devastating critique of the presupposition of individuality in the human sciences. This has led some theoreticians to conclude that only politics is distinctively human, or, in the alternative, that the individual remains a free-floating subject in tragic contradiction with the conditions of life. Foucault seems to contribute to the force of these conclusions in his concluding section of *Madness and Civilization,* where he suggests that the dialectic of reason has led to a situation in which madness and art, as modern reason's absolute others, are, paradoxically, all that reason can acknowledge as giving voice to the distinctively human aspect of human affairs; that is, reason finally knows itself but only against society. But this can only be *personified* by abstracting it from the text's systematic renunciation of individualistic presuppositions:

By the madness which interrupts it, a work of art opens a void, a moment of silence, a question without answer, provokes a breach without reconciliation where the world is forced to question itself. What is necessarily a profanation in the work of art returns to that point, and, in the time of that work swamped in madness, the world is made aware of its guilt. Henceforth, and through the mediation of madness, it is the world that becomes culpable (for the first time in the Western world) in relation to the work of art; it is now arraigned by the work of art, obliged to order itself by its language, compelled by it to a task of recognition, of reparation, to the task of restoring reason *from* that unreason and *to* that unreason. (Foucault 1965, 288)

From the point of view of reason against society, madness and art remain tragically absorbed in negativity: tragically because they emerge as reason's excluded others and, nevertheless, as what reason must finally confront within itself but cannot within the modernist episteme—since the latter compromises its own foundational topics of "life, labor, and language" by appealing to an already failed individualism. Given Foucault's critique, the negativity of madness and art appears, like the implicit negativity of the social, as the immanence of critique and, one ought then to say, the activity of theorizing, throughout the seemingly endless project of purifying knowledge in the face of whatever momentarily threatens to corrupt it, and restoring the powers knowledge ratifies in the attempt to generalize pure reason as the only legitimate means of reflection. This self-protective project derives from reason's need to distinguish itself from what appears to be reason, and therefore its need, which finds itself increasingly externalized, ejected, to settle the issue by purifying the idea of the reasonable in the self-negating form of radically individuated rationality. Similarly, the constant presence of a threat to freedom, under conditions in which freedom is identified with thought, contemplation, rather than activity, requires a never-ending search for sites in which reason ought to prevail and a constant effort at clarifying the processes by which it makes itself known.

The effort to rationalize reason against its unavoidable self-negation, ironically, reflects an *unreasoned* reaction to an endless series of exceptions. Apart from art and madness, there are the fixed rules of tradition, the imponderable will of charismatic authority, the force of unreason in its more obvious political forms, and, as Gustave Le Bon (1952) made clear almost a century before Foucault, sociality itself. The tendency to see the last two exceptions as "merely" political places severe limits on understanding society, unless "politics" refers to something radically different from the norm-governed play of definite powers said to constitute the functionality of the state, and from the socializing functions performed by the ostensibly representative organizations once thought of as constituent elements of two putative entities that can only be conceived as radically opposed—namely, the state and civil society.

The play of power and the functions have always been contradictory in their necessary dependence on one another and in the impossibility of mutual regulation sufficiently stable to support both. For Foucault, what is new in postmodernity—which is also to say in the secret heart of modernity—and its reconfigurations of power, knowledge, and identity is the disappearance of the "figure of the individual," by which I understand him to mean individuality, in the last most blatantly self-promoting moment of a categorical and quantifying rationality incapable of acknowledging any limits. The latter's irrepressible excess shows it to be, within an episteme for which individuality has become an intolerable but unavoidable burden, a paradigm of irrationality. What remains positive about it is that its excessiveness conjures the spectral presence of a formless agency, neither grounded nor manageable, that makes itself felt as a corruption of the ordinary, like the sort of alien and indefinite presence uncannily known to believers at a séance or those who are "born-again." This stands in stark opposition to the order of reason that brings it into play by the refusal to acknowledge the basic fact of sociality. The refusal, in the interest of purifying reason, ultimately aims to excise the very social fact of theory from human affairs, consequently conceiving of those affairs as always tending toward irrationality. In this moment in which purity is corrupted of its own accord, reason excludes as a matter of principle what Gayatri Spivak (1987) identifies as a sub-alterity unintelligible to the self-generalizing anti-critical discourses of power, Homi Bhabha (1994) as "immigrant intelligence," and Michael Hardt and Antonio Negri (2004) as the democratically disposed "multitude" immanent to the logic of "Empire."

Foucault ends by showing that it is not possible under the circumstances to extract a conventional sense of the political from the modernist idea of rational action without undoing the very concept of action. It would then be impossible to decide what is and is not political as well as to identify agency with anything accountable as such in the individualistic terms of desire, belief, choice, and decision required, as Davidson reminds us, by most philosophies of action.[3] The notion of power as everywhere (or nowhere in particular, or where it had never seemed to be) seems to bring us back to Sartre's observation that "we were never so free as when the Nazis occupied Paris"—except that, while now everything appears to be fateful, in the sense of making a difference whose limit cannot be anticipated, it is no longer possible to tell what difference is being made; and if power is everywhere, there is nowhere for it to be: it follows that there is, in regard to such power, no denotable where, there, or here.[4]

But this is not necessarily all, given the contemporary analysis of immanent power as "bio-power," in which individuality becomes a pure abstraction, useful only for ideological purposes (Foucault 2008). The "pathos" of the theory of rational choice was originally expressed in the impossibility of theorizing individuality in a way that connects it to an idea of what is human about human affairs.[5] It now also lies in the impossibility of theorizing an abstract individuality without sacrificing the idea of society on which that abstraction depends. The best that individualism can do is to conceive of society as a consequence of interactions among private wills, which, as Rousseau showed and a century of social science has largely confirmed, does not take account of the dependence of each on all, when the latter refers to the irreducible form of life the Enlightenment referred to as "the people" and a "body politic." The will of "socialized individuals" is conceivable on condition of something like a general will (which cannot be general in the sense of distributed within a population). Domination arises in relations among particular wills indifferent to the general will. When it is a feature of a historical society, it consists of the play of power against itself—power only conceivable as a reflexive multiplicity (Butler, Laclau, and Žižek 2000; see also Williams 1977). In that case, control and not identity is the primary expression of the plurality of particular wills, and it is implied by what Marx referred to as the "real subsumption" of labor by capital.

Nevertheless, as is illustrated by Gutmann's (2003) account of identity politics, the idea of individually self-referring identity remains difficult to resist, especially in the face of what appears to be increasing intolerance in an era in which "the society of producers," and not merely individuals, is the projected object of exploitation. To salvage the concept, Habermas (1987) has claimed that the problem is modernity itself, insofar as it intensifies self-reflection beyond what a stable identity can endure. Because he sees this as independent of its "material" aspect, he concludes that a transition to an effective and emancipatory post-capitalist democracy requires a "working through" of this aspect of modernity rather than evasion or a premature instantiation of it as a political project. Underlying his discussion is a distinction between modernity, which specializes in reflection, and what he was then forced to conceive of as a virtually reflection-free pre-modernity. But it seems clear that the idea of a reflective-free humanity has no potential for over-reflection and the idea of an overly reflective humanity has no base, no standard, from which to work through what it apparently cannot avoid. Moreover, the distinction begins to look very much like the fallacy of assuming the negation of (modern) society as its very condition, in which case that condition remains potent so that the option of "working through" is confronted with the "natural," "pre-modern" option against change.

Among the many problems that haunt the discussion of modernity taken as a historical epoch without regard to its material situation and to what makes it possible to conceive of an *epoch* in the history of *society*, are, first, the inability to conceptualize a coherent relationship between individuality and sociality, second, the difficulty of imagining a history in which self-reflection emerges from its very absence, third, the difficulty of imagining a society of any epoch in which self-reflection has no place, and, fourth, a failure to develop a language suitable for addressing what is human about human affairs. Each of these has been addressed by Derrida (1997), who offers an opening to conceiving of the prospect of a self-reflective sociality, beyond but never indifferent to politics. The reflexivity of this prospect, its presence as mere prospect and as a condition of a form of life always about to be lost (and in that respect always being rediscovered), begins with the illusion of identity and the apparently separate and self-contained groups to which we are led by that illusion. It thereby becomes necessary to delineate the boundaries of friendship, consociation, and therefore the limits of compassion that, in an ideological re-moralization of the local, appears as a product of presence and familiarity, of what C. H. Cooley (1962) famously referred to as "primary groups."[6] The self-reflective quality of sociality appears at the outset, then, to be a matter of isolated consciousnesses paradoxically reflecting on what they cannot imagine. In that regard, sociality initially appears as the individual's loss, which is also a loss of memory and a sense of the significance of what has been and is being done. What is gained, since what is so completely lost could never have been owned, is the putting of ownership of the social into question, thereby yielding the same certainty that follows Rousseau's demonstration that the state of nature is unimaginable. However, in this case the *immediate* sense of certainty lies in the post hoc and contingent discovery that one was never alone. If the result is nothing more than regret, the demonstration will have failed. It will have produced nothing more than the self-satisfaction of a transcendental subject, one who can lose nothing and therefore can discover nothing; and the meaning of "alone" will have thereby been reduced to a regressive denial of everything but the mind of the individual before the discovery was made—from which the sense of a greater world, including anything that could be lost, would somehow have to be reconstituted. But regressive denial is not a true regression, since it stems from the discovery of what one cannot deny and does not return to a situation prior to one's helplessness to the reflexivity of sociality itself.

For Derrida, this is, then, merely a beginning, given the momentarily tragic realization that morality and self-reflection are intelligible only when they express the pathos of the deepest and therefore most extensive consociation. The pathos arises from the following compound fact. First, despite the appearance of individuality, the passage to self-reflection bears a sense of reflection as intrinsically collective, perhaps inextricably bound up with what is deconstructive about spoken and therefore spontaneous language. Second, consociation cannot be realized linguistically without bypassing its exemplary and demonstrable prospect, the equality it presupposes. It is in this respect that the death of a loved one constitutes, at a moment, the loss of a veritable universe; and grief is thereby articulated in each moment of grieving as an expression of a totality. The capacity to lend oneself to all—and thereby to receive what only all can give—at the moment of the death of another depends on apprehending that other as still "someone" and to re-cognize, remember dramatically, that one experiences the death of another in the same way one experiences a rediscovery of one's social being when trying and failing to imagine an alternative to society. It is, with its own obvious inflection, the experience of being equal with all under the warrant of a loss of a veritable universe. The drama of that re-cognition lies in the confirmation in experience, as it were suddenly, of what we already could not have but known—an experience that leaves in its wake the same ambivalent mix of helplessness and recovery within helplessness that accompanies every momentarily individuated instance of society's reflexivity to its own possibility. This is why grief knows itself only insofar as it is absorbed in an irreducible course of activity, beyond the moment of individuality and immediately specific others.

For Derrida, "It is *thanks* to death that friendship can be declared. . . . And when friendship is declared during the lifetime of friends, it avows, fundamentally, the same thing: it avows the death thanks to which the chance to declare itself comes at last, never failing to come" (1997, 302; emphasis in original). It is necessary to add that the very idea of friendship depends on the possibility of such an experience, such a reflection, and not merely hypothetically. This means that there is a generalized as well as a particularized aspect of the social, and it is difficult to avoid concluding that this gives at least some substance to the idea of a general will. Beyond that momentary experience of the loss of a universe in the particularizing death of someone, the reflexivity of consociation in which the social is its own object requires what spontaneous speaking puts beyond what otherwise might pass for an intensely rhetorical figuration. Here, there is no dispute over whether a literal interpretation of the poststructural texts is sufficient to understand them. Indeed, they are too elaborate and relentless to support such a simplification. The term "literal" has no application to theoretical work that respects the complexity of its subject matter, is expansively conceptual, intensively critical, and unremittingly self-critical. The problem is not, strictly speaking, one of interpretation but of reading a text as sincerely as it presents itself—in effect, *reading in the mood of writing.*

————

This version of post-structural criticism poses the problem of how the immanence of sociality is or can be registered, and by whom or what. Despite well-known disclaimers by a number of Marx scholars and theoreticians, it appears in the "Theses on Feuerbach," Marx's analysis of the concept of "capital," and to some degree in *The Communist Manifesto* and other works—if the latter are read in connection with his "critique of political economy."[7] Read that way, these texts concentrate on two overriding concepts: the constantly imposed simulations of the socialization of labor as a necessary feature of commodity production and the impossibility of rationalizing capitalist relations of production. The first has to do with conditions of reproducing the *social* "forces of production." This depends, most generally, on the possibility of diverting an increasing portion of the product (value) to the sociality of productive life that makes surplus value (deployable wealth) possible. It is well known that such a diversion cannot be reconciled with a political economy driven by the social relational aspect of capitalist production—that is, with the necessary prerogatives of private ownership (investment) vis-à-vis "the forces of production." The latter is social labor embodied in what Marx refers to as the "collective laborer" constituted at the moment of industrialization, which is already postindustrial, and that is itself implicit in the fullest expression of the capitalist mode of production as "the society of the producers."

The second concept, which has to do with the rational reproduction of the relations of production, is problematic because of the contradictory character of the abstracted relationship between price and value, between the product (surplus and therefore generally deployable value) and the financial conditions of producing it. While the two concepts are related, this one requires a different emphasis from what is immediately relevant to thinking about sociality. We have seen that, for Marx, sociality is a necessary feature of the production of commodities—what sociologists used to refer to as "everyday life" when it seemed impossible to acknowledge its connection to the historicizing concept of a "mode of production." The second concept emphasizes the conditions of universal exchange, which, among other things, authorizes "class" as an operative and critical construct in contrast with class as a sociological or political/economic category.[8] To the extent to which reference to sociality enters into the rationalization (self-critique) of exchange, it constitutes the priority of relations among things to relations among people and/or productive activities.

There is a possible reading of Marx's critique of "capital" from which one can draw the suggestion, short of a hypothesis, that the socialization of labor in commodity production constitutes an essential duality of mind, at the level at which mind is conceived of as irreducible, which can be realized theoretically.[9] One side has to do with *subjectivity within agency*, when the latter is conceived of according to socialized production, or value-related activity that operates across bodies.[10] This seems, in one respect, to be the sort of subjectivity that most easily fits the typical examples of "mentality" in the philosophy of mind when it is described apart from the assumption that the skin is a natural boundary. To the extent to which it is not divorced from its conditions, it cannot be described in individualistic terms, as existing exclusively within distinct bodies.[11] Rather, it must be described by appropriate sociological concepts, as transpiring across bodies—in other words, as irreducibly social. This is theoretically necessary to a conception of agency suited to the particular universe of collective conditions of rational action defined as "the capitalist mode of production."

The other side of this duality has to do with personal agency conceived of negatively, in regard to what is left out of or is otherwise a matter of indifference to socialized production—rationality without a significant object. The idea of such separable selves cannot be accounted for by the critique of capital or, I believe, by any known theory of the capitalist mode of production.[12] Marx's concept of alienation does not apply to individuals taken one by one (or as a population delineated categorically) but to the relationship between the constitution of labor as a force of production (relative to some index of value—e.g., a proportion of the money supply) and the overall effect of its application, and what that implies for a subjectivity that cannot be reduced to the distinct minds of distinct individuals. This interpretation is reinforced by Marx's comments on laborers "bearing their labour power" to the market (such that they must be understood as being social beyond the moment of exchange of labor power for a wage), social determinants of the minimum wage (such that there must be something intrinsically active in the domestic and expressive ensembles necessary to the combination of *labors* as a factor of production), and the inability of capital's own functionaries to rationalize what they do and what is done within the mode of production without, as Marx shows in the third volume of *Capital* (1990c), taking account of certain irrevocably generalized features of that mode (e.g., general, extra-local costs latently associated with production per se).

In passing, it would be misleading to read Marx as claiming, as a matter of theory, that persons are different sorts of actors in different sorts of contexts (e.g., within and external to production). This is because his critique merely indicates what capital's own political economy omits (and apprehends only through its apparently negative effects), and shows the consequences of doing so; but he attempts to prove that agency is *essentially* social specifically in its constitution within the capitalist mode of production and the history it makes possible—and in regard to the extension of the socialization of labor to the "society of the producers." That is, his references to concrete labor, the "bearing of labour power" to the market, domestic life, and the like, speak more to the postcapitalist aspect of the capitalist mode of production than to what is distinctively (idealistically) capitalistic about it. And they identify the limit of Max Weber's conception of money as a medium of universal rationalization (1947, 280–294), where Weber was unable to account for those conditions intrinsic to the relations of production, such as the contradictory relation between money and value, that make it impossible for capitalism to sustain the necessary conditions of rational policy in the accumulation of wealth based on the production of commodities.

My point is that Marx allows for the possibility of theorizing what is suppressed in standard accounts of capitalist production and exchange—namely, sociality. But that is not part of his critique of capital; nor does he attempt to formulate a theory of it. The critique focuses on what are constituted as conditions of rational action under the capitalist mode of production, *according to the latter's account of itself*, and how those conditions are transformed as their contradictory aspects are realized. It is only from that point of view that the idea of the social is exhaustively tied to the socialization of production, beginning analytically and not chronologically, as it might seem, with the abstraction of human labor as "labor power" and as a "factor" in production, and ending with what is presupposed, surprisingly, from the start—that is, "the society of the producers." The latter stands as both the most general condition of capitalist "production" and the rational obstacle to the free "circulation of fictitious capital" against the production of what is needed to preserve the socially reproductive capacity of the ensemble of human labor, in contrast with the summed labor of all, to produce an expanding surplus of real "value," which is, finally, the capacity to produce and reproduce the conditions of sociality.

In summary, I have discussed two paths by which the idea of the social emerges as a crucial topic requiring something on the order of a definition. My discussion of the Rousseauian version of the social contract suggests a line of possible convergence. However, the literatures remain distinct without a clear theoretical connection beyond an otherwise unaccountable agreement simply to divide intellectual labor between what it is to be together, as it were, abstractly, and what it is to be together under specific "historical" circumstances, in a way that is historical in itself. Much of modern philosophy in the United States remains indifferent to what these two positions disclose. As a result, the sense of what it is *to be* social is rarely discussed, though a few philosophers, most notably, John Searle and Margaret Gilbert, have attempted to clarify some of what is involved in our use of the term and its associated expressions, and others, notably Davidson, have formulated theories of meaning, belief, and desire that seem to presuppose such a concept.[13] When it is discussed, the ontological issue is glossed over, even in Frederic Schick's provocative suggestion "that we need to invoke a concept of 'sociality,' so defined that a person is 'behaving socially' if and only if he is choosing as he thinks some other person or group of people want him to choose, and choosing so because he thinks this *independently of any consideration of the consequences he foresees*" (quoted in Black 1990a, 124; emphasis in original).[14]

Curiously, this is also generally true of sociologists. Other than Durkheim's attempt to clarify the idea of social facts by speculating about how they make themselves known to individuals (essentially as relatively fixed, objective, and resistant to will), there is little in the sociological literature that bears directly on the ontological status of "society" and of the condition of being "of" society, though some proponents of Actor-Network-Theory have recently argued that the status of the social is, at most, merely epistemic or "political" (see Latour 2005). Sociology has a reputation, both positive and negative, for specializing in the constitution of a non-distributable consciousness conceived of as a relatively integrated and irreducible subjectivity across bodies (intentionality, effort, and reflexivity). This is often said to be a necessary condition of all concretely situated contexts of thought and action, though the lack of a developed conceptualization has made it difficult to convey this without recourse to individualistic accounts, thereby betraying what is entailed by the idea.

This is perhaps one reason the field has come to be emblematic of "relativism," even though its notion of the relativity of conditions of action has little to do with what is generally, and often invidiously, associated with the term. In assessing the justice of this attribution it is important to note that what is most often thought objectionable about relativism is that it appears to separate humans by object-dependent types or "traditions" that, when extended logically, particularizes and fixes subjectivity, leaving no room for common experience, mutual appreciation, sharing, joint action, or, indeed, consociation (and therefore sociality as such). The attribution is mistaken to the extent to which there is no necessary implication of reductionism in the sociologist's idea of the relation of subjectivity to context: "subjectivity," relative to the sociological problem of explaining either the constitution or conditions of agency, does not refer to individual minds and bodies.

In that case, at least theoretically, the most prominent sociological version of relativism refers either to a social conception of agency, in which "agency" is defined by conditions of rational action and "action" is not conceived of as the attempt to fulfill individual intentions in the observed event, or to causes that do not require a concept of agency at all (a hypothesis often attributed to structuralism). Despite the expedience of a reductive strategy (where facts about individuals are aggregated to *indicate* what theory can only identify as the antithesis of aggregation), the dependence of the idea of subjectivity on the idea of a context informs many of the standard models of social life that attempt to summarize "contexts of action" over both the long and the short run of sociality. The charge of invidious relativism may depend on confusing what is merely expedient with a matter of principle. It is valid only if "social" refers to the aggregation of individuals (as subjects) or something approximating an aggregation, such as composition according to a standard measure by which, under the warrant of methodological individualism, different "values" can be brought together (e.g., as overlapping or complementary). The standard models, discussed in Chapter 6, vary in how much weight they give individuality in comparison with sociality, and so, depending on their emphasis, they are more or less liable to the criticism. But they nevertheless share the purpose of establishing a theoretically defensible conception of sociality that applies to more than the specific cases used to illustrate it. It is important to keep in mind that virtually none directly responds to the two paths along which the problem of the definition of "sociality" arises in the first place—the one identified with Rousseau's version of the social contract and the other identified with post-structuralism and Marx's critique of capital. As a consequence, all ultimately beg the question, though in ways sufficiently compelling to make it appear reasonable to do so.

As far as the convergence of the two points of view is concerned, both seem to lead to sociality as a basic fact, but only the second describes this in terms of historical limits (but see Derrida 1994, 51, 68, 87, 102, 109, 117, 184n). In that case, the social appears fundamentally as a course of activity for which participation registers itself as an attitude of waiting, in contrast with an instance of action, a predicate, an event, or an entity. It is in this sense, on the one hand, that Marxism and post-structuralism make it possible to read Rousseau as a modernist thinker with postmodernist implications, though there is still a considerable distance between the basic fact of sociality and what might provisionally be called its manifestations. On the other hand, the Rousseauian idea of equality, qualified by Marx's idea of history as immanent to the social, and the obligation of every theory of human affairs to find itself in its object and its object in it, may be sufficient to move us forward. That is, they point toward the ontological considerations necessary to clarifying what is human *as things stand* and, therefore, to describing the human sciences in terms of a shared objectivity. My qualifying reference to the idea of "as things stand" should be taken as a deliberately phenomenological inflection, by which I mean an attempt to describe a reality from within the living of it or an activity from within its course. In what follows, I consider some models that attempt to clarify the idea of the social in terms of what might be called, after Sartre, the "practical ensemble," something that does not lend itself to the identification of units of analysis or to state descriptions. Each model shows itself as incapable of establishing a concept of the social to the extent to which it fails to find itself in its object and/or fails to account for that object's immanently historical character. By and large, losing the internal relation of theory and its object is exacerbated by a failure to come to terms with Rousseau's notion of the equality of mutually dependent subjectivities, where their inter-dependency is irreducible, while relying on static descriptions and types at the expense of historicity is a result of failing to come to terms with the idea that history must be conceived of as immanent to every instance of human affairs. How it can be immanent is discussed throughout this book.

6

Models, Theory, and Theorizing

The most prominent models used to represent the social aspect of human affairs are known by their key concepts: system, exchange, structure, rule-governed practices, networks, and rational agency. Each stands for a paradigm of what is and is not reasonable to claim about the nature of the activities, representations, and subjectivities of "people among people," and for each, units of analysis are conceived of, as far as possible, as relations. While they overlap in many respects, there are significant differences among them, though they all either elide or suppress the underlying idea essential to extending any model of social reality beyond the specific cases for which it is formulated in the first place. Extensions are valid to the extent to which they refer to an idea of the social inclusive enough to represent what is human about human affairs in all its instances and in every detail; that is, there are no valid non-human abstractions from what is human about human affairs. Before discussing particular models and the significance of this requirement, more needs to be said about the idea of a model, in particular about the ways in which sociologists use references to sociality as a discursive resource in contrast with a conception that captures what Cornelius Castoriadis refers to as the "social historical" (1987, 221–272).

Models are, by their nature as ideals, formal and in that sense "pure" (see Weber 1947, 88–118). They begin by simplifying their object in a way that cannot be understood as a representation, an analogy, or even a simulation of a reality—that is then apprehended as such within an altogether different language, or "imaginary," with its own tropes, associations, and discursive conventions. A model is designed to breathe life into the simplification by setting it in motion according to what is allowed by the ideal it constitutes. It must at least preserve the capacity to learn and to reproduce that capacity, and therefore to reconcile identity and change. This may involve specifying rules or norms relative to the functions that are the logical conditions of the model's integrity and its extension, as such, in time. But the life it constitutes belongs to the model as its own mode of self-realization. There is no theory or meta-theory presently available that accounts for the relationship between any such simplification and what it presumes to have simplified; so the model itself appears as the exemplary instance of the latter, which is then left untheorized, almost as an afterthought. In the human sciences, a model is, in effect, a theory of itself, its aim the perfection of a text, the textualization of an idea of life. Beyond that, its philosophical status is not clear.

Whatever else it might do, a model constitutes a novel reality, therefore one that might be imposed as a practical matter, or that might clarify an already imposed simplification, as in attempts to bring what had been thought of as non-economic instances of social life under the reductive logic of neoliberal models of economic rationality. That is, behind every model is an intention already in play and the assumption of an apparatus of power already in place. Its creativity lies in its presenting a project, not in describing something against which such a project might be conceived and even projected. Instead, one might think of human affairs as occasionally modeling themselves, so that one might say that certain models can indeed represent those affairs. This possibility has to be imagined, however, within a course of activity the momentum of which is necessarily incompatible with any such objectification, which suggests an immanent contradiction between the momentum of a course of activity and an unsettling objectifying aspect of its reflexivity. For now, the instantiation of a model within a course of activity might be thought of as a moment of self-reflection, but not as an exportable representation of the sociality of that course.

Interpretive applications of models always exceed their technical and empirical limits, but rarely if ever in the most generally desired direction, which is toward the social as the basic fact, since it is their function as ideal to *constitute* a radical departure from it. Since the radical departure lies in assuming that human affairs are repeatable, models are self-representing in a way that is incompatible with what is human about those affairs. Models that purport to *re-present* human affairs beg the question of what is meant by human affairs simply by ignoring them in favor of a project already imposed (or received) or in the process of being imposed. This is so regardless of how often a model is modified in light of what are called further observations of an object that, while it can be subjugated, cannot model itself and cannot recognize itself in a model. Attempting to identify the social with any structural or functional ideal presupposes that it is the sort of thing that can be described in terms that apply to a radically different thing, what the model uniquely constitutes as real. In other words, regardless of the differences among them, the available models effectively beg the crucial ontological question of what the social might be such that it can be modeled in the first place and such that a particular model might be taken as a more accurate simplification than the others. The few attempts by philosophers and social scientists to come to terms with that question and related issues are typically ignored or their work caricatured, largely on the grounds that they express an unacceptable worldview or are unscientific, literary, naïve, nihilistic, or deliberately obscure. Consequently, it is often taken for granted that whatever is referred to as an instance of the social can be described by properties appropriate to an entity the motions of which routinely transpire within fixed and narrow constraints. This is evident in cross-sectional analyses that assume the constancy of their object beyond its appearance at the moment of observation. I believe that it is also true of models that describe systems processually, as *tending toward* equilibrium, adaptation, self-generation, goal-attainment, or successive expressions of an identity.

The most prominent non-sociological literatures directly on point are identified with controversies in the humanities around issues associated with cultural studies, literary theory, and critical historiography. Among those issues are the following: (1) paradoxes in the theory of meaning associated with a concept of the sign as a unit of meaning composed of contradictory elements—that is, signifier and signified; (2) problems of how to read references to "reflexivity" and "immanence"; (3) disputes about the meaning and possibility of "translation"; (4) self-contradictory aspects of interpretation and textualization; (5) questions about the meanings of "intelligibility," "sense," and "truth" in regard to the possible immanence of metaphor to discursive language; (6) problems in reconciling temporality with the extra-temporal notion of immanent historicity; (7) controversies around the dialectics and internally historical character of textuality in relation to writing, reading, audience, reception, authorship, and criticism; (8) questions about the meanings of "subjectivity," "agency," and "voice" when individualistic assumptions about perception, cognition, deliberation, and expression are suspended; (9) problems having to do with the concept of friendship and, therefore, the general will, the commons, civility, justice, and democracy, and with the nature of theory itself when society is thought of as an ongoing accomplishment; (10) questions about the forms in which the subjectivities left out of a given theory or type of theory nevertheless show themselves to have been essential to but are incapable of being included in the theory; (11) difficulties involved in distinguishing between idea and expression and between text and context; and (12) the critical reemergence of the ages-old problems surrounding the relationships among, and therefore the meanings of, interest, belief, discourse, action, practice, theory, knowledge, power, and history. In one way or another, each problem, issue, debate, or question implicates the idea of the immanence of the social to human affairs; but the way the social is typically referred to omits or bypasses that implication.

Neglect of these literatures or the relegation of their chief concerns to the margins of the social sciences and philosophy, including those subfields influenced by critical theory, has contributed to the impression that there is no essential unity of the human sciences and, therefore, nothing distinctively human about human affairs beyond what is conventionally declared within the institutional limits of each discipline. This is often substantiated by the historiography of the late modernist attempt, always against considerable opposition, to dissociate social studies from the humanities as a way of establishing a secular sociology, including economics and politics, according to a naturalist conception of knowledge (see, for example, Gordon 1991). This relies, in part, on an idealized, unsustainable opposition between culture, thought of as what humans do for themselves, and nature, thought of as what is done for or to them by nonhuman reality.

Perhaps one of its most important institutional effects is a curriculum that presupposes a radical distinction between fields that constitute knowledge of an independent reality, in the naturalistic sense of science, and fields that are thought to specialize in values, symbols, expression, persuasion, the nonintentional aspects of desire, the practical uncertainties associated with collective memory, and the analogy-generating tropes of what Rawls calls "comprehensive doctrines." It is then tempting to conclude that the latter are logical residues, what remain at issue about human affairs after exact terms are set for comprehending the external, nonhuman, world. Their subject matter resides outside of the domain of authentic knowledge, and is thereby seen, much like folklore, as arbitrary, traditional, cultural, or willful in its determination. Nevertheless, there have been numerous attempts to reclaim the status of a knowledge-constituting field for human studies independent of the logic appropriate to nonhuman nature. I consider two that bear on my general thesis. One models itself on a particular stage of natural science inquiry. It attempts to reduce the impact of observer biases on the grounds that, even without the possibility of measurement, unbiased observation can approach what is objectively real about a practice, an attitude, or an event within the limitations of language and representation. Another models itself on a different stage. It devises a relatively unambiguous language capable of yielding reliable and rationally comparable propositions that can be considered valid according to other well-established positive criteria. When such a proposition is the object of appropriate attitudes, such as descriptive (believing) and evaluative, operating within the recognized range of the socially accepted types such that, for example, a descriptive account is plausible and therefore true prima facie, it can then be tested by additional information for whether its plausibility can be sustained. If so, it can enter the stock of public knowledge as valid and true for all practical purposes. The measure of truth, or even acceptability, lies in the difference the account makes to that domain, in other words, its value.

This second strategy does not require imposing the logic of the natural sciences on the sciences of human affairs. But it also begs the question of the validity of the distinction between knowledge-constituting and expressive or value-oriented fields. That is, it raises the issue of an alternative to the received concept of truth on which is predicated the claim that some radical versions of the humanities deny the possibility of truth and are thereby opposed to any and all realisms. It remains tied to an epistemological principle that subjective claims (in the sense of claims about the world that cannot be summarized by unambiguous sentences and that appear to be context- and therefore perspective-dependent) may lack the qualities of reliability, falsifiability, and verifiability; and it sides with objectivist methods and claims against whatever remains "merely expressive" or a disguised value judgment. But it does not deny in principle the possibility of expressive or value-related knowledge. That is, it exempts itself from the distinction by relying on it while expanding the standard notion of truth to include some of what had been excluded in the name of pure objectivity. Both strategies avoid challenging an idea that underlies a minimal version of the standard concept of truth—compatibility between the referents of certain propositional attitudes (e.g., beliefs) and the contents of statements issued (publicly) in a language that guarantees their intelligibility as claims to know (whether or not it is otherwise possible to demonstrate their specific truths). The second strategy assumes that truths in the human sciences involve an otherwise unmotivated consensus based on the application of logic to a total value-delimited field of information. The result is intelligibility plus the possibility of reiteration, translation, and summary without further question about content. It is the lack of further question that supports the claim of truthfulness, as this strategy has it, and this is why the difference between fictional and nonfictional texts is, from that point of view, not crucial to the applicability of the concept.

If a sentence is intelligible in that its meaning confirms the integrity of a language intended to support a total disciplinary field within the human sciences, in contrast with relatively unrestricted spontaneous discourse, then it can be said to be true for all practical purposes. This is so even though formally contradictory sentences might meet the same criterion. To the extent to which this is compatible with the idea of a field-restricted language of the human sciences, and necessary to the discursive validity of such a language, it is not a defect. In languages of that sort, legitimate and meaningful sentences are to be expected that, when reduced to (and thereby transformed by) a strictly logical form, appear contradictory. Such sentences are unavoidable whenever the language is realized in discourse. This may have to do with the requirement that units of meaning for those languages are internally related, or that meaning is determined holistically, such that more must always be said than can be stated consistently with all that can be or needs to be said. In this sense, consistency and coherence are to some extent at odds.

To explain this further requires a discussion of the nature of the objective field itself insofar as it has to do with what is human about human affairs. For now, it is sufficient to say that there are languages in which the meanings of specific sentences are not necessarily constrained by the formal properties they share with sentences in general because they cannot be taken as separable and therefore comparable units of analysis. It follows that formal adequacy cannot be a criterion for evaluating the legitimacy and intelligibility of statements in such languages. One way in which the discourse of such a language operates is by allowing each apparently conflicting sentence the benefit of the doubt, necessary for discursive validity, but at the cost of finally settling whatever is at issue. I later attempt to defend this idea and refer to "giving the benefit of the doubt" as an "attitude of waiting," which is an essential feature of the discursively assertive character of what is said in regard to *and* in the course of human affairs.

In passing, one would expect such cases to generate what might be called competing discursive paradigms, what are often called frames of reference, where the terms of the competition do not provide a basis for deciding in favor of one over the other. The circumstances under which the benefit of the doubt is given or is likely to be given certainly needs discussion, but my point here is a familiar one—that logic cannot provide universal criteria of intelligibility for the sentences of a language suitable for a human science. This is the nature of the case and not a disability of the human sciences waiting for a cure. The validity of their claims depends on a language that encompasses an objective field of unrepeatable motions for which no description or analysis can be more than only apparently complete. Its concepts, the objects of its signifiers, cannot be divorced from the volatile life and lives whose existence they presume to realize. This means that two contradictory sentences in the human sciences can be intelligible and even valid at the same time. Their evident contradiction need not be a reason to reject one or to look forward to an eventual solution that overcomes or resolves the contradiction. This is discussed later in regard to agency-dependent objectivity.

Looked at from the side of content, the plausibility of a proposition is sufficient to its truth. That this involves a weak notion of truth derives from the fact that not all sorts of language are appropriate to what is human about human affairs. An interesting corollary is that it is possible to disagree with a proposition without meaning to say that it is false. The reason is that, given this concept of truth, the weakness of which is the strength of the universe of propositions to which it applies, what is usually at stake in a dispute about a particular proposition is the language that makes it possible, and not the particular statement taken alone or in its immediately local discursive context. Another corollary is that a true statement need not be accompanied by the more general self-sustaining feeling of certainty associated with a positive result of testing a discrete claim by its correspondence with an unforgiving reality, by its consistency with other such true claims taken one by one, or by a demonstration that its subsidiary claims (or a sufficient number of them in the proper order) have proven factually true.

According to this, what is known as true about human affairs is what is intelligible under continuing challenges—meaning the intelligibility of the proposition at issue according to its legitimacy within a language that inscribes the universe to which the proposition applies and in which its content is informative (has value in the sense of making a difference). Given this holistic criterion, and given that an assertion of the knowledge that it tests is either prior to a declaration of the truth of the assertion or is logically independent of justifying the declaration yet inseparable from it, it is possible to agree with the following hypothesis. If the argument can be extended throughout the human sciences, "truth" in those disciplines is a secondary property added post hoc to a knowledge-asserting proposition after it is formed and takes its place in a socializing language. The proposition is independently available to parties to that "linguistic community" as an instance of knowledge available to them in their limited capacities as momentary members of just that community, as subjects to its universe of possible reference, despite the fact that any particular referent is likely to be fleeting, ephemeral, or self-deconstructing. It confirms the community by confirming each member's sense of dwelling in the referential field by which the community retains its being as the immanent agency of a "social stock of knowledge." It is in that sense that a proposition is true insofar as it is evidently embedded in such a community-constituting language. A weaker and perhaps less controversial idea would be that an assertion about the state of a certain universe based on a particular claim about an object that is *of* that universe is knowledge to the extent to which it is not confronted with another proposition that immediately undoes the evident holistic entailments of the first one. When this happens, the universe of reference from which the first proposition drew its validity is transformed. The failure of its validity in the face of a competing proposition is derived from the fact that the latter instates a diachronically new universe. *The two propositions in effect occupy different worlds and each appears, at most, as metaphorical to the world of the other.*

From this point of view, knowledge of human affairs is a matter of participating in a socially valid universe of reference, not something that is decided exclusively by logic and correspondence with an independent reality. For example, to "test" whether someone knows what it is to be a citizen of a "liberal constitutional democracy," as Rawls describes it, one must hear her speak dialogically, in an attitude of waiting consistent with the ambiguities inherent in all such discourse. It would be irrelevant and untoward to ask questions about specific beliefs that demand answers independent of their social and discursive validity. For the disciplines of the human sciences, truth is an internal feature of the ongoing accomplishment of knowledge and not a socially independent standard of the rightness of a belief. Again, this means that every signifying moment, which, in a different register, is to say every idea that appears to be signified by a word, gesture, or token, carries the weight of the totalizing field of ideas in which it too is an idea. In this respect, the social life of ideas uncannily resembles the social life of human beings: the truth of an idea, like the subjective aspect of the Rousseauian "first convention," lies both in the value it yields (the difference it makes) and in the value it receives—insofar as it is constituted in the course of an activity in which it is implicated. In that case, one might say that instances of knowledge of what is human about human affairs have more in common with what we think of as metaphors and symbols than with the putative units of meaning that can be defined, summarized, translated, and studied statistically, according to what is then taken to be "their" usage. This account allows us to understand the sense of discovery and enlightenment that accompanies the dialogical realization of this sort of truth, just as the presence of another is immediately apprehended as a likelihood of being surprised. It is an experience of something specific that has immediate ramifications throughout all experience, as if one had suddenly encountered the universal in the particular.

In this conception of truth, a community reveals itself as a course of activity the moment a proposition is asserted that immediately engages more than its statement literally includes, which is also a moment that implicates *responsiveness*. Assertions, like expressions of need, perform a timeless reason for anyone to respond. The momentary completion of a statement substantiates a universe of reference and, with it, the social conditions of the possibility of that universe. We can describe the consciousness associated with this as a sudden and overwhelming realization of the dependence of each gesture or utterance on the greater world from which it receives its quality of *meaningfulness* and to which it contributes value in the form of a difference beyond its apparently immediate scope. As that universe is brought to notice by an ostensible particularity, it is "the basic fact" about meaning. This is how each of us discovers in everything we say as well as what we do the truth of the social contract, the equality constituted by the dependence of each on all. That experience is certain of itself, self-sufficient, at the very moment the universe appears within the particular as a subsumption that gives presence and form to particularity. Parenthetically, the idea of such an experience illustrates the distinction between apodictic certainty, new each time the rediscovery of the basic fact about meaning occurs, and the merely renewable, deliberative sense of certainty, on reflection, associated with a factual demonstration, proof, or logically sound argument from realistic premises. There is still the question of how and by whom or by what such a truth is held, which is to say the relationship between subjectivity, objectivity, and agency, and there is no way of addressing this without going beyond what has been discussed so far.

One problem with this criterion of truth, and therefore with the strategies it authorizes, is that the conditions of applying it are uncertain absent an adequate account of the sociality in which a totalizing language would have to be situated; and it needs to be applied in some sense if the claim that the human sciences are knowledge-constituting disciplines is to be satisfied. This is what makes the conception so far merely programmatic, not the fact that such a language cannot, by the very nature of its obligation to include without limit, live up to the promise of representational adequacy. Speaking not only reflects but performs the inability of language, understood formally, to overcome the anxiety of inevitably failed representation. It is no more detrimental to the sense of truth than the practical difficulty of limiting the number of presupposed propositions that have to be confirmed is to a formal theory of truth extended to natural languages, where rules are guides as much as instructions, intentions are ambiguous, and meaning is indefinite. A formal theory might say, for such languages, that the truth of a proposition depends on the truth of the unambiguous propositions it presupposes. That test, such a truth, is rarely available to the natural languages and in discourse, and the very notion of truth draws its significance as well as its inherent ambiguity and its social aspect from the interaction of speaking and codification, with the former outweighing the latter.

Despite attempts to challenge the distinction between the natural and human sciences, or at least to make it appear less extreme, the second strategy remains programmatic in both the philosophy of natural science and social science (see Fay and Moon 1994, chap. 2). This has taken form in the latter as a debate over the relative priority to be given quantitative and qualitative methodologies. In part, the debate speaks to what appears to be a radical distinction between two types of knowing and the difficulty of reconciling them according to a naturalist philosophy of knowledge. One involves "understanding," which, for Schutz (1967), following Weber, requires respect for the uniqueness of social phenomena and a sympathetic grasp of reasons in contrast with causes. The other involves causal explanation, which many philosophers now argue includes reasons as part of the "causal picture" in an account of action. As such, reasons are themselves often thought of quantitatively (as in strong or weak), especially when people are understood as essentially rational in the utilitarian sense and only incidentally reasonable in the Rawlsian sense of deliberating in a way consistent with the norm of reciprocity.[1] Both sides typically evade the question that Theodor Adorno (1976, 68–86) considered fundamental, and the choice of methodologies may depend on how it is answered: What conception of the object is at stake? Insofar as the social is now theorized primarily within the humanities, the tendency of sociology, political science, economics, and psychology to ignore the connection between critical literary studies and social theory may be one thing Edward Said had in mind when he characterized sociology, with other "ideological and policy sciences," as a "scandal" (1979, 15).[2] As a result, theories for which the notion of sociality is of central concern are often left outside of what the social sciences take to be the limits of their disciplines—which, ironically, continue to show relatively little interest in the problem despite the fact that some such notion is almost always taken for granted. Among those who refuse or find it otherwise impossible to ignore the internal aspect of the relationship between "human" and "social," there is an overriding and I believe ultimately self-defeating meta-theoretical debate about the status of comprehensive claims of that sort. On one side are the historicists who argue that totalizing claims and the experiences they are said to *re-present* are fundamentally ideological. This does not necessarily disqualify them from theoretical consideration. Indeed, to assume that it does risks the paradox of disqualifying "disqualifying." The historicist's point is, rather, that all such claims must ultimately be liable to criticism; and this is so despite the fact that we may need at least some of them to organize our conceptions of ourselves and of the world, as well as those of our undertakings that require an exceptional degree of confidence based, in part, on the plausibility of just such propositions.[3] In that case, nothing invidious is intended in the historicist's use of the term "ideological." Totalizing propositions may be ideological in that a willingness to rely on them can be understood as reflecting two facts: that all representations are contingent and mediated, and that representation at increasing levels of abstraction is thought to be indispensable for theorizing human affairs. It is in regard to its emphasis on contingency that I refer to this position as historicist, in contrast with the anti-historicist idea that certain totalizing propositions are beyond legitimate criticism but are not ideological (see the next section).[4]

A familiar expression of historicism says that the term "social" refers to a concept distilled from a particular type of collective experience (e.g., capitalism, industrialism, modernization, technological innovation, globalization) and that, when used theoretically, it cannot but reflect that experience. Consider the following two examples of the logic of this position: (1) "social" refers to people acting to satisfy their desires through their relations and interactions with others; (2) "social" refers to individualized "role performances," where "self" and "role" are always distinguished, and where the former is not a theoretical term but one designed to preserve a space for statements about such putatively asocial performances as withdrawal, suicide, solitude, and, to some extent, innovation, within what is nevertheless posited as a virtually seamless and morally dense social life (see Emmet 1975). For the second example, both self and role depend on an inclusive notion of structure as system and, therefore, on a distinction between functions and dysfunctions. The first example is often identified as social psychological. It relies on an idea of exchange among rational actors in which there is little choice but for every actor to come to terms with at least one other actor, and it is possible for each to do so, regardless of value differences or divergent "comprehensive doctrines." The second example classically deploys concepts that have to do with (1) the rational organization of action, which is to say joint problem solving thought of as a task-oriented objectively accountable expression of a division of labor; (2) nonproblematic values that, by virtue of the intentions they disqualify, direct or limit the selection of means and ends; and (3) operations geared to efficiency as the most general principle of rational organization and, therefore, the only principle (or value) that can be shared as such by all authentic members. Efficiency is conceived of as a unique value in that it provides the most general criterion of rational participation. Therefore, its conditions are thought of as conditions of rational action for all members of a successfully adaptive society. But, while all members are held to accept it as members, it may or may not apply to any collection of members considered as individuals independent of their social connections.

For the moment, I will ignore the historicist version of exchange (the first example). In any case, the organizational model is more important in regard to how models relate to our general conceptions of the sociality of human affairs and to the possibility that reason and agency characterize supra-personal human entities such as ensembles, groups, firms, or societies. It has been used to account for a wide range of instances of collective action, including large-scale organizations, cooperative ventures, religious movements, political and quasi-political organizations (e.g., social movements), and occasionally smaller groupings and sustained encounters, such as families, localized or distributed networks, and teams, thought to allow more immediate access of parties to one another than is possible on a larger scale where impersonality is positively valued. This model has the advantage of being based on a widely accepted concept of rational action and at least some notion of how ideal types are related to the human affairs they are purported to typify. At least one of its classical versions analyzes the degree to which actual ensembles approximate rational organizational form, and what processes are put into play by the gap between the approximation and the ideal, assuming that approximating such a type is a fundamental tendency of ensembles and that there is a rational continuum of approximation.[5] This model of "organization" identifies agency with the anticipated and therefore self-less activities of utterly nonplayful and non-ironical functionaries, where, "anticipation" means objectively expected by the nature of a task situation that reflects the imperatives of administration. The latter is the objective form of agency that corresponds to an image of the organization as a whole, once values that place limits on purposes and goals are in place. The anticipated activities of functionaries constitute agency conceived of under the aspect of "participation." They are, in that respect, formal extensions of administration. It is nevertheless recognized that they are subject to unanticipated exigencies in the task situation, including the presence of others beyond their complementary actions as functionaries. Where others are involved, the actions have been thought of, since the end of the 1950s, as results of "informal organization" or, in the older organization literature, "spontaneous contribution."

At the same time, the theoretical characterization of organization as a ratification of official imperatives requires systematic indifference to another, sub-theoretical notion of agency on which is predicated the model's more general conception of rational organization as a socially exemplary form of life. It has to do with whatever informally, and therefore extra-organizationally, makes workable the putatively nonproblematic system values that legitimize the coordination and administration of effort by criteria associated with the overarching values of efficiency and limitations on risk. The sub-theoretical notion does not support a theory that specializes in typifying officially designated quasi-legal or legal entities since they are designed to suppress sociality wherever possible, or treating it as a cost. Rather, it corresponds to the more general perspective of people among people, and, to that extent, to what might be called "found sociality."

Derrida might have referred to this as an example of "the play of structure," and Marx as the ongoing activity that constitutes the concreteness, the materiality, of concrete labor relative to and in contradiction with its exploitation as abstract labor (Derrida 1976, 289). These analogies are no doubt suggestive, but they may be somewhat misdirected, since it appears, especially in the most rigorous statements of the rational organizational model, that informality is taken to be an external fact as far as rationality is concerned, and therefore something beyond the intended purview of the theory.[6] The model, plus Weber's "law" of progressive rationalization, is often taken, with many qualifications, to be a general theory of social life. But it is social life thought of as a common orientation on the part of members, those for whom the boundaries of membership are not an issue, to something outside of that life—for example, the organizational environment. The orientation is presumably expressed in practices that are essentially rule-governed, in the sense of "rule" associated with a concept of coherent and adaptive sociality as a rationally ordered state of affairs. But the common object of orientation, the task or problem to be solved, falls outside of the social so conceived.

It appears, then, that the organizational model does not represent the nonformal aspects of what people do together as an internal feature of its object—which is social life conceived of as tending toward rational organization and away from what rationality is said to supersede—charisma, tradition, feeling. Rationality in this evolutionary sense refers to two tendencies inconsistent with what I have referred to as the sub-theoretical notion that the model was presumably designed to illuminate and therefore to re-present as the ultimate object of theory. The first involves an extra-organizational transformation of categorically specific practices into idealized functions (a decision enforced prior to the constitution of legitimacy). These are then impersonally administered and formally accounted for by reference to inclusive and settled organizationally instrumental values (efficiency and effectiveness) that legitimize specific goals, the exercise of authority, the selection of means, and the institutionalization of impersonal rules and task-oriented practices. The second tendency involves the progressive formalization of norms that effectively assimilate whatever appears at any given time to be momentarily informal, spontaneous, improvised, or irreducibly social.

The model can be applied to human affairs only if what people do together is taken into account; however, what has been referred to so far as sociality is excluded by its terms. At best, it appears as a deviation from rather than an internal feature of the rationalizing tendency, as momentary and correctible imperfections in realizing the conditions of rational action (see March and Simon 1958). At worst, it is a noisy factor that threatens rational organization. To that extent, the universe it posits—of subjects, objects, and conditions—does not allow for what is required of the universe of human affairs. Instead, it resembles a world, like that of Lewis Carroll's "Queen of Hearts" or Franz Kafka's "Castle," in which individuals are subject to a stipulated value prior to the subordinate value of efficiency, one that they cannot have chosen and therefore cannot know as products of the application of reason. They must not attempt even to ratify it but only to account for themselves in its terms (or face the Oedipal consequence of becoming unintelligible and therefore possibly monstrous relative to organizational imperatives). As functionaries, they must remain indifferent to the facts and to their own possible fate. The subjects envisioned by such a model are not instances of subjectivity in the sense we mean when we speak, as we always must when discussing such matters, of people among people.

It may be better, then, to say that the model is not so much a description and an explanation as it is the metaphorical expression of a *project*. As such, it expresses a will foreign to the social it is presumably intended to comprehend, a substitution by metaphor. By this I mean that it accounts only for what it institutes or what is instituted in its name and then imposes that on an altogether different referential universe. Beyond that, and aside from the coercion envisioned by such a project, it lacks the naturalistic explanatory power it claims for itself. The reason is that the model, for all its elegance and the convenience of the simplification on which it relies, represents a different universe from the one that is familiar from the perspective of people among people. On the one hand, since it is inconceivable that a model of anything involving people among people can exclude theorizing their sociality and still be consistent with its being justified as an account of even an ideal type of sociality, it cannot be considered a model in the usual scientific sense of the term.[7] On the other hand, as indicated, it can be taken to be a project awaiting implementation, as always, against its possible negation and in that regard against what is occasionally referred to as "resistance." In that respect, it is normative rather than explanatory, but normative in a way that disguises its projective aspect. If one accepts the claim that it is a model capable of being generalized beyond its paradigmatic case, the business firm, what had been thought to be sociality now appears, paradoxically, as the negation of what is supposed to represent it. The social represented by the model is the antithesis of the initial conception. Either the initial conception is an idealization without concrete instances, or the concrete instances from which the model generalizes are not instances of sociality. *The model posits a basic tendency toward a rationality that gradually frees the rational entity of the definitive exception to "rationality," which is, ironically, the alien and disruptive social.*

Specifically, the model treats what it picks out as instances of "organization," as approximate realizations of ideals, classically, "bureaucracy," and more recently, "apparatuses" designed to expand and implement the independent powers of management, understood as authority, and the special entitlements of ownership. This translates the collective activity, without which the approximations of such ideals are unintelligible, into ungrounded abstractions (divisions of function, institutional practices, or performances) rationalized by reference to organizational goals that, by definition, are beyond dispute and therefore beyond both reasonable objection and commitment. As a result of what is lost in translating something sub-theoretical into something purely theoretical, the lack of comprehensiveness to which the model aspires can be overcome only by adding something to it as a supplementary construct. The most prominent ad hoc supplement in the standard literature on social organization has been a distinction between formal and informal aspects of organizational life in which the informal comes to represent the dimension of sociality that had been excluded by the formal model that was intended to *re-present* it.

The underlying concept of the social in models of exchange and in models of organization appears to be limited in the ways the historicist predicts. This does not necessarily make it irrelevant to what we can understand about human affairs that transcends specific circumstances. The reason is that, in following the historicist's lead, we find ourselves in a position to learn about the limits of the theories by reflecting on those instances and qualities of human affairs that seem by their very nature to fall outside the range of the theories, and perhaps outside the range of all theories conceived of according to the simulationist logic of modeling. Clearly, to the extent to which we are sincere in theorizing, which is to say committed to the life of the sub-theoretical object, we cannot simply choose when to confront a given concept or theory, and we cannot learn about the latter's limits on our own. The attempt to apply a theory, to enter it into a universe about which it might be true, engages the question of what the theory systematically omits; this unavoidably public gesture provides the opportunity and the impulse to reflect on limits that cannot be anticipated in the actual course of theorizing.

Learning those limits is bound to be difficult, since to theorize sincerely is to allow oneself to be submerged in a course of activity that has its own inexorable momentum and therefore cannot but extend itself. This totalizing but not centralizing tendency exists regardless of what might be said about its ostensible product, a given theory; and, in regard to what it is in itself, it is opposed to the very possibility of a product or any other sign indicating the termination of theorizing.[8] It is with respect to the relationship between the activity of theorizing and the putative product of that activity—namely, a given theory as an instance of "theory"—that certain concepts can be said to be incorrigible. If we mean by "a theory" the merely *momentary, ostensible*, product of a certain course of activity, and it is not clear what else it could mean if the idea of a theory is to be compatible with the idea of a human form of life, then it is clear that theoretical concepts are misunderstood when they are taken apart from that activity—though that does not defeat the possibility of their being otherwise useful.[9]

That is, if concepts in the human sciences are taken as products of theorizing, they can be understood *as theoretical* only when seen as intrinsically reflexive to the struggle, characteristic of any course of activity, that they momentarily concentrate, and thereby make obscure, in a word or in an ostensibly (that is, post-theorizing) clear and distinct idea. This is so independently of other criteria. To try and understand them apart from those irreducibly tense and self-transforming conditions of their possibility is to constitute a reality quite different from the reality that corresponds to the moment of engagement (or *commitment*) that gives them their essential precariousness, or makes them "essentially contested" within and only within the course of theorizing.[10] This cannot be the sort of reality that is correspondent with the human sciences insofar as they are responsive and ultimately reflexive to their common object, which is, by hypothesis, what is human about human affairs. One can no more theorize without losing oneself in the life of the object/concept than one can perform, in contrast with merely play, a piece of music without getting lost in the totalizing life of its figures, phrases, passages, transitions, and inflections. No moment is free of that life. "Being lost in the object," in contrast with having insight or forming a concept in Black's sense of refining a "paradigm case" is, I believe, the characteristic feature of those courses of activity that can be identified with theorizing, often designated as "the order of discovery" (Black 1990a, 4–5, 101). *It is why writing that sacrifices its own impulse toward the order of discovery to the impulse to justify cannot teach the possibility of what it presents.*

It follows from this idea of commitment that post-theoretical reflection on what a theory has left out occurs only on condition of recognizing that suspending theoretical concepts, and, therefore, suspending the sense of what each concept excludes, is not simply a matter of choice: the theoretician, the ostensible theorizing subject, becomes post-theoretically oriented regardless of his or her particular will—if theorizing is to be maintained. The recognition that one is not free to do with concepts what one wishes also cannot be a result of an argument in the formal sense. It could only be that, in a way that is irrelevant to the course of theorizing, where the concepts make themselves felt in the first place as momentary points of concentration motivated, as it were, by a sub-theoretical notion that, at the same time, appears to defy that momentarily finalizing concentration. Rather, that recognition, too, must be considered momentary, which is to say actively and intensely problematic within a course of activity over which the ostensibly particular theoretician holds little sway. The best that can be said now is that, if it occurs, it is on the part of the momentarily self-abstracting theoretician. Sooner or later, we will have to consider how that abstraction takes place and how it can be known to be taking or to have taken place. For now, the idea of a commitment, which is the aspect of subjectivity within a course of theorizing, implies that the theorizing subject is not in a position to decide freely what aspect of the ostensible object should be systematically omitted and, therefore, when the limits of theory have been reached. Yet the very course of the activity of theorizing *immanently* creates a sense of the *imminence* of just such limits.

In one respect, then, commitment amounts to knowing that one is not free to suspend certain concepts, that one can do so only arbitrarily. That is, the question of when to suspend does not arise in the course of theorizing, though concepts may become suspended as that course transpires. It is in that regard that we can think of the concepts as internal to theorizing rather than as names of topics or objects brought to it from outside or fixed by a theory. It may be sufficient to say, then, that commitment involves acting, being drawn along, in regard to such concepts as if they have lives of their own, as if subjectivity belonged only to them.[11] This guarantees that the theorizing subject will be confronted with the limits of a given theory in the course of discovering that something, for the moment indefinite, has been left out in the post-theorizing formation of concepts as clear and distinct ideas. The sense of discovery depends on the fact that it is the nature of concepts that they cannot, in themselves, be even approximately complete, consistent, and reliable representations of their sub-theoretically compelling objects and that confidence in their objectivity (the sense of their connectedness to a universe of human affairs) is necessarily lessened in the course of their being refined purely in relation to one another and presented as elements of a theory, what I call the theory-product. That is—and this is something of a paradox—they can only represent their objects as reasonably or approximately complete to the extent to which they constitute them as other than the sub-theoretical objectualities in regard to which theorizing presumably has taken and continues to take place.[12]

It follows that the discovery of what is missing, which is a moment of critical reflection, depends on the fact that concepts eventually show themselves to be metaphorical in that what they purport to grasp can be grasped only sub-theoretically and through a course of activity and not in a particularizing way. This, however, takes the theorizing subject only part way to recognizing that what has been omitted is in fact familiar, sub-theoretically, and that it is the theory, the objectivity it constructs, that ends by being unfamiliar. What has been left out appears instead to be of the very domain of objectivity, the region of being that authorizes intelligible reference, which the theorizing subject might, in the first instance, have claimed to be able to know. This domain now appears to correspond to the greater course of activity of which theorizing is merely a moment, in radical contrast with the theory that purports to represent it.

Within a course of theorizing, there seem to be two necessary conditions of the sudden and overwhelming sense that a concept or theory found or otherwise present within the course of theorizing is absolutely limited. As such, they are also necessary conditions of the post-theoretical reflection that affirms that something of the object has been omitted in a theory-product that, for the sake of that very object, cannot be omitted without omitting, or eliding, the activity of theorizing itself, and with it the life of the sub-theoretical notion. First, the possibility may be raised by an encounter with what is beyond the scope of theory but is unmistakably of the order of its object, which thereby appears unknowable from the point of view of the theory-product. Second, there is a prior, meta-theoretical or extra-theoretical norm at the center of the version of historicism under discussion. It requires resisting too easy an assimilation of what is unknown to what is stipulated as known, as if it is not in any sense unknowable. This logically prior limit on theorizing is already a condition of the self-consciousness of the theorizing subject that qualifies commitment and in so doing undermines it. It involves moving from the activity of theorizing to a post-theoretical reflection on its momentary product (a concept, proposition, or theory), effectively suspending the activity of theorizing. The fact that the norm is formally external and logically prior weakens the sort of theoretical activity recognized as such by the historicist since it entails that the burden of proof on theory favors the *activity of theorizing*, and the historicist is primarily interested in the post-theorizing conditions under which *a theory* can be said to be valid and more or less likely to be true.

Even without this norm, however, critical self-reflection is unavoidable and immediate; so the historicist version adds little to the idea of a relationship between theorizing and theory and, in any case, does not diminish the temptation, immanent to theorizing itself, to move from activity to an ostensible product that might be taken *in retrospect* to have been its project. What it adds has to do with that relationship from the point of view of its being observed. The norm seems to operate as a variable that is likely to be but is not necessarily skewed prematurely in the direction of trading commitment, activity, for its ostensible product. In that case, theorizing is no longer sustainable as the activity of following the life of the concept of the sub-theoretical object. In other words, the historicist's norm, such as it is, insists on the distinction between the concept and its object, something theorizing cannot tolerate; but it may turn out that theorizing, by its own nature, cannot avoid that same distinction. The life of the concept, which is itself sub-theoretical and part of the object of theorizing, consists not only of a promise to be connected to other concepts but of its relations with what it is intended to realize insofar as the object resists conceptualization, by virtue of what it must be taken to be if it is to be an instance of life, or an instance of what I call "human affairs."

7

Theorizing

Theorizing is an activity that undermines received concepts, first by identifying the universe to which they refer and second by showing that their meaning depends on something necessarily omitted—on a different referential universe for which what is omitted has its possible concept. It begins with an idea among ideas each of which must be understood as *for* the other ideas, as if part of a system. What is left out, then, is not merely something specific but the sense of an alternative universe to the "known universe." Given that the two universes qualify each other *with respect to what is left out in one*, theorizing is caught up in unresolvable ambiguities. This means that the work of theorizing cannot be directed toward resolving ambiguity; that is what *theories* are said to do. Instead, the activity of theorizing involves sustaining ambiguity, even though it may, despite itself, occasionally support a temptation to resolve the unresolvable, thereby envisioning its own end. Consequently, it is fundamentally ambivalent: *every move toward appreciating the universal significance of an idea is also a move toward appreciating a universe that is thereby excluded.* The moment at which a given referential universe appears as a determinate and encompassing reality is also the moment at which what was omitted appears either unreal or to exist elsewhere.

Ambiguity is always present in the course of theorizing. It constitutes a continuing basis of critical reflection in which theorizing has no choice but to confront its own tendency to become other than what it is. Theorizing is the work involved in discovering a lost world, where its having been lost is both newsworthy and arbitrary. It is newsworthy to the extent to which the apparent totality of the known world *suddenly* appears dependent on *and* vulnerable to what is lost: what is discovered about the known world in the course of theorizing is that it entails the existence of a competing universe based on the fact that what had been omitted must not have been. The omission is arbitrary in that *what is ostensibly known depends on indifference to the fact of the omission.* The following expands on the distinction between theory and theorizing, which is fundamental to understanding how, in the study of human affairs, theory and its object are internally related so that each finds itself—is found— in the other. Otherwise, theory would be conceived of as external to and not an instance of human affairs, and what it acknowledges as human would lack any capacity to theorize itself.

The tragic aspect of theorizing is a consequence of two opposing conditions. First, it is constituted as an ongoing commitment to what Heidegger referred to as "the life of the concept" and, by virtue of that, to the life of its object. Second, the ambivalence that motivates the activity is internal to it: the objectivity of the referent can be imagined as active only relative to its concept and, therefore, relative to the activity of formulating and refining the concept in opposition to its referent.[1] On the one hand, the active unspecifiable object evades positive knowledge; consequently, it anticipates the failure of the concept in the very course of its being formed and refined. The relation of the evasive object and the increasingly determinate concept is part of what is meant by saying that the concept has a life. "Theorizing," in contrast with "a theory," can then be understood as an activity committed to the opposition of idea and sub-theoretical object. But, the fact that the object cannot be specified without being lost undermines the absorption of the activity of theorizing in and its subjection to the life of the concept. On the other hand, theorizing involves more than a positive, forward-looking commitment: the antagonism between its positive aspect and the ambivalence that motivates it implies that more is involved than sacrificing subjectivity to the logical and empirical requirements of the concept. This includes attempting to expel the increasingly ominous shadow of the sub-theoretical object as the concept approaches the limit of its progressive refinement—becoming nothing but an empty signifier within a field of more or less empty signifiers, one of a system of signifiers that have "value" but no meaning. This transfers the risk of a loss of life from the *concept* to the *activity of theorizing.* What is positive about commitment diminishes with the attempt to sustain it: a theoretical continuation of theorizing implicates turning against its own possibility, which is the conceptually unknowable, unspecifiable object.

Such a contradiction is immanent to all courses of activity and, therefore, to all instances of human affairs. Here, it asserts itself as the immanence of a post-theoretical moment of theorizing in which the latter is little more than the construction and evaluation of a theory-product. It is in that respect that the activity undoes itself in its course. The sub-theoretical object to which theorizing had owed its existence and welcomed its obligation now takes an ominous form as it expresses the same ambivalence on its own side: the ambivalence of the theorizing subject is coordinate with the ambivalence of the object—constituted on the one hand as a perfectly signified idea and on the other as a sub-theoretical notion of a life resisting signification.

The play of ambivalence demands an attitude of detachment that violates the first condition of theorizing. It is realized by the segregation of the concept from its unspecified object. This is often called "concept formation" but consists, from what has been said, in the deformation of the object. The latter is thereby reconstituted in a form that *indicates* but in no way *resembles* life. The concept, progressively refined to the point of imaginable purity, is itself reconstituted as thing-like and inertial and is now something that has also lost its life in that struggle: what it stands for is an object that cannot account for its *re-presentation* as a concept. Under the circumstances, the concept, now a purified signifier, can only be indifferent to what it still must be said to re-present; and the object it presumes to re-present now lacks the quality of life that makes the logical conditions of theorizing—namely, commitment and activity—intelligible. The activity of theorizing requires motivation, and this can arise only from the object—not from what it *is* but for what it *does* by way of disturbing a course of activity already under way—in other words, by being in its very nature sub-theoretically irrepressible and, in that respect, engaging. What it is for an object to be "in its nature irrepressible" is discussed later; for now, it can only be imagined as the object of a theorizing subjectivity if it is active on its own behalf. Otherwise, there is no intelligible idea of *theorizing* in contrast with the idea of a *theory* constructed on the order of a formally justified belief.

Such a resolution of ambivalence cannot be sustained: it sacrifices two mutually indispensable lives, that of the object becoming signified and that of the concept becoming a signifier, and thereby reduces the life of theorizing to accounting for concepts by concepts. To that extent, the course of theorizing comes to be abhorrent to itself and is finally suppressed by or erased from the memory of the possibility of producing an ostensible product in the course of theorizing. That is, it constitutes that very exclusion. Therefore, like commodities understood as objective only within a universe of exchange, it cannot account for itself (be accounted for) as a product and, therefore, cannot teach what is involved in arriving at what it has become. Parenthetically, it is important to remember that the minimal condition of the validity of a theory in the human sciences is that it must find its object in itself and itself in its object. A failure to do this is always a sufficient reason for criticism and a reinvigoration of theorizing.

This can be considered from another point of view. The iteration of a full-blown theory is incompatible with the possibility of a theorizing subjectivity. Moreover, the necessary disinterest in an explicit account of the activity of theorizing within its course is undermined by the undoing of both the life of the object to which the concept is obliged and the life of the concept to which theorizing is obliged. Theorizing can only be interested in and make room for an account of itself if it is the sort of thing that needs a justification beyond the requirements imposed on it by its object. But it is inextricably tied to the object. When it gives way to a concrete theory-product, theorizing is placed under a different obligation that can only be met by dissolving itself as an activity of discovery. This requires acts of accounting or justifying that a *course* of activity cannot tolerate. It follows that the only life to which theorizing can respond under the circumstances is the prospect of activity without exemplary instances, a prospect that resides in whatever is left of the life of theorizing after the lives of the concept and object are undone; and, according to the analysis so far, that can be nothing more than a *resistance to theory* (an attempt to preserve what is necessary in principle but cannot be plausibly exemplified) merely illustrated by something taken momentarily and only in passing to be concrete.

It is fair to say, then, that theorizing, under the retrospectively determinate auspices of its ostensible product, a theory, ultimately intends nothing more than itself, which is nothing more than pure critique, the skeptic's impossible version of doubt, or what de Man (1986) listed as one type of "resistance to theory," resistance in the interest of life itself. Intending nothing more than itself, its activity appears to be endless and even idle motion, and not at all progressive in the sense of being transformed in the course of realizing its obligation to the activity that is both its condition and its object. In this respect, theorizing burdened with a theory projects a point of view outside of itself to which it appears as a problem to be overcome in favor of a product that appears retrospectively to have been its goal. It is appropriate to refer to this as motion rather than action or movement insofar as the element of intentionality is distorted if not suppressed by the death of the object.

This subjectivity, bound to its product, posits only itself, thereby consolidating the bad faith that is the negative aspect of theorizing and then revaluing it as the good faith of "hard science." Yet it nevertheless retains what the theory-product cannot tolerate, inchoate traces of a process that otherwise defies memory. Despite itself, the publication of a theory involves a course of activity. It thereby inadvertently reaffirms the priority of life. Whether or not this reinstates self-critical reflection beyond mere negativity depends on another condition, to be discussed in the next section. Before that can become an issue, it is necessary to acknowledge that the theorizing subjectivity at the cusp of a fully formed theory is immersed in a potentially fatal predicament. It must defer its commitment to the life of the concept—its own history. It momentarily accepts something inert that merely stands for life. It lacks all value but what is externally imposed: it draws meaning and force from its formal relations with other equally degraded concepts. In this respect, the language of human affairs, increasingly restricted by the problem it has to solve as theorizing begins to turn away from itself, finally surpasses, in one theory or another, what it is supposed to be about; and it does so as a repression of whatever could possibly restore the intelligibility of a course of activity in which critical self-reflection is an aspect of subjectivity and, through that, the certainty that the most important facts about any theory are its limitations.

So far, I have argued that the course of theorizing is predicated on the opposition of concept and object, an opposition that is internal to each and that constitutes the life of the concept to which theorizing is committed *insofar as theorizing is a course of activity* rather than a function of an intention to form a theory. Subjection to that life is the definitive commitment and attitude of the theorizing subjectivity. This involves reckoning with the concept's analogous involvement in the life of the object it purports to re-present.[2] Insofar as this complex tendency is ambivalent, as it must be, it implicates an aspect that threatens and ultimately undoes both the life that is the course of theorizing and the life of the concept that theorizing engages, contrary to itself, under the post-theorizing aspect of the ostensible product, in this case, *a* theory.

The very notion of the life of a concept entails an actively resistant but mysterious object from which it cannot be separated but which nevertheless threatens to undo it and, in this regard, threatens to undo the connection between the course of theorizing and the theory that is its ostensible product. *Thus, the first condition of the sense of an absolute limit of theory in the midst of theorizing is the possible succession of theorizing by a theory or theories, and of the theorizing subjectivity by a subjectivity that is no longer motivated by its material.* This is also a condition of a possible return to theorizing, a reengagement with the object—that now can only return in the somewhat different guise of an object detached from the conditions of its being an instance of objectivity. As such, it returns bearing the history of its *objectivity in the course of being theorized*, the self-deconstructing history of its reification as the inert referent of a totalistic theory, and the history of that very opposition. It is the latter that, in this momentary renewal, theorizing now undertakes as its remaining possibility, given that it moves beyond the temptation to maintain itself solely through a resistance that requires fixed objects, or the progressive and futile temptation to return to a now-idealized condition prior to those histories.

————————

B eing absorbed in the life of the concept is not identical with that life, since the fate of theorizing is not invariably tied to that of the concept, though their fates are similar. We have seen that the only way in which theorizing sustains itself is by means of the refinement of its object—a living concept that, in living, defies above all just such refinement (as does its own sub-theoretical referent). It does this in order to eliminate a threat to the *possibility* of a theory-product. The threat is, paradoxically, envisioned in a difference internal to theorizing, between conceptual and sub-theoretical object. It is made substantive by the shadow of what that very activity constitutes as unknowable, a quality only a theory can eliminate. However, this solution negates the source of commitment to the contradictory relation of concept and object that gives theorizing its own life as a course of activity, rather than constitutes it as a means to an end.

To refine the concept, to purify it, means to insulate it progressively against the threat of the unknown—which is what is left out of the theory-product in the latter's displacement of theorizing. Doing so increases the apparent self-sufficiency of the theory relative to whatever about the object might have threatened it. However, in this attempt to neutralize its object, thereby neutralizing the course of activity of which it is merely an ostensible product, progress toward a theory also institutes a second condition of self-reflection: *the encounter, the moment at which the unknowable makes itself felt, appears as a confrontation first with the sub-theoretical object as "other" and then with the "self"* that is the theorizing subjectivity in contrast with the very different subjectivity of the theoretician whose aim is to present and justify a theory. Later, I discuss what sort of character must be attributed to the object for it to be possible to imagine such a confrontation. For now, it seems that the attempt to fulfill the imperative to construct a theory, yet to be explained other than by the weak hypothesis of an externally constituted norm, creates a condition that not only threatens the applicability of the particular theory to its sub-theoretical object but raises questions about the very enterprise of treating any *ostensible* product as if it refers to something beyond itself and other such products—and, correlatively, about characterizing the dialectic in which it appears retrospectively *to* have been nothing more than a preliminary stage of concept formation and theory construction (which then appears to be a result of the application of pure reason.

However, given the conditions of theorizing, its necessarily ambivalent commitment, self-critical reflection is possible but for the compelling temptation to withhold any interest in what is humanly objective in and about human affairs. Given the paradoxical implication of the possibility of a theory *within the course of theorizing*, self-critical reflection is possible, but, oddly enough, only to the extent to which it is imposed or "taught" by whatever appears, from the point of view of the imagined end, the theory/product, unknowable. We say "oddly" because *we can conceive of being taught by the object only by way of what a fully realized theory makes inconceivable about that very object*. Another way of saying this is that we can learn about the sub-theoretical object of a theory only by attending to what its theoretical object is not. This is not to say that we are instead directed to or need to attend to some other objects. Rather, we can learn, in the prospect or aftermath of a theory, only from what could not, in principle, be the theoretically completed object, what is putatively re-presented as a pure concept. This momentary negativity constitutes, as we have seen, a course of activity analogous to theorizing. This is the suppressed and displaced sub-theoretical objectivity that, by its demands within the activity of theorizing, defies conceptual specification. In this respect, such an objectivity constitutes a moment of resistance because its objectivity is available to the theorizing subjectivity precisely as the contradiction of what seems theoretically stable and what such ostensible stability reveals about its own impossibility.

Self-critical reflection is not yet conceivable as life, as a feature of activity in its course, since, for the moment, it belongs to a life excluded by the theory-product or threatened by its prospect. The excluded life loses its familiarity by virtue of its systematic expulsion or threat of expulsion from the theory. It nevertheless remains inchoately present as a shadow of life accompanying the nonliving reality constituted as conceptually complete and as a candidate for an alternative familiarity to a nontheorizing subjectivity that knows only categories. This is why the excluded life—and with it self-critical reflection, momentum, spontaneity, morality in the sense of realizing a subjectivity that can only be shared, and so forth—can only be known if it teaches on its own behalf or otherwise imposes itself on a theory-dependent ostensible knower who is now indifferent to it as a matter of principle. This means that the sub-theoretical object can only be known as such if the life of knowing, the activity of self-critical reflection, becomes an object, as it were, to itself. To the extent that it does, it returns to the *life* of the concept and what had been left out by its purification. Self-critical reflection becomes an object to itself insofar as it is an activity in which what is left out makes itself apprehendable against what appears to be known. That is, self-critical reflection's own *concept* is recovered for the activity of theorizing, though it remains burdened by the fact that the notion of life remains sub-theoretical and opposed not only to the theoretical object but even to the apparent realization of life against theory. *The obligation undertaken by theorizing now centers on the life of that concept, and therefore on life as such.* Initially, theorizing rediscovers that there is more to itself than its ostensible product; and it begins to take form as a praxis, a movement toward a self-explication it will never reach but that is beyond its now subsidiary commitment to the life of a concept of the sub-theoretical life of a sub-theoretical object. In this way, coming to reengage what was left out of the theory allows the activity of theorizing to know itself through its newfound respect for the sub-theoretical life of the object. But that is at the expense of what had seemed to give theorizing its public reason and some of its own impulse—namely, the possibility of a product, *a* theory.

Given the relation of theory to theorizing, it might seem that a certain doubling takes place within the latter. One activity follows the life of the concept; another is predicated on both that life (against theory) and a refined concept of "life" (against theorizing). The two are internally related despite the fact that it is impossible to think about them without concluding that they are distinct, in that the first is destined to be lost in the product- or outcome-orientation of the second. In that case, one might expect an accumulation of courses of theorizing about courses of theorizing, and so forth, until the original sub-theoretical object has lost all significance. This is, of course, one common criticism of deconstruction, but it is premature and, as such, misplaced. The problem can be addressed by considering some of the phenomenological conditions and metaphysical presuppositions of the ideas of a course of activity, internal relations, the life of a concept and the life of an object, objectivity, and the like. I offer, in anticipation, some additional comments on how and in what sense theorizing can be a course of activity, how a course of activity can be self-reflective, and how being self-reflective can be an object of self-critical reflection. In what follows, it is convenient to refer to the latter as "reflection," though in some contexts it will be necessary to distinguish between them.

I have argued that reflection becomes an object to itself when the theorizing subject takes its own commitment to the life of the concept as an occasion for further theorizing—that is, when the course of theorizing is momentarily undone by the post-theoretical hypostatization of an ostensible product, a fixed concept or a theory, leaving theorizing in the generative but potentially dangerous mode of self-conscious resistance to theory, or what is occasionally meant by "critique." It is tempting to say that the hypostatization takes form in "the order of justification" distinguished from "the order of discovery," and to conclude that there are essentially two alternating mutually external subjectivities involved in theoretical work. While this evades the problem that theorizing poses to theory, it corresponds to an intuition about the return of the former in the course of the latter's crisis of the loss of its sub-theoretical object. The suppression of the history of the concept (its life) in the order of justification is appropriate to a theory whose *object* can have no history because it has no life. It is in this regard that the sub-theoretical objectivity that is lost to theory reappears as the unknowable. As such, it becomes dramatically problematic and newly motivating but only as a feature of the internal relation of theorizing and theory—for which the denial of one in favor of the other consists in the suppression of theorizing. It is in this regard that the sort of work represented by the expression "the order of justification" finds itself in an unfortunate predicament. On the one hand, it can represent only what can be *re-presented* without resistance, so that omitting its own history is a matter of principle. On the other hand, it finds itself enmeshed in another predicament in the post-theoretical process of eliminating the very possibility of theorizing by focusing on its ostensible product. The hypostatization makes it impossible to teach the possibility of the theory, how it could have come about. That is, it becomes impossible to make the theory intelligible in a self-critically reflective way, according to the labor, the struggles, involved in its production.

It follows that the order of justification is faced with a dilemma. On the one hand, the object of justification is a hypostasized product, in this case a theory without a history and, therefore, indifferent to its conditions of possibility. Since justification is a function of such a theory, its way of presenting itself, the justified theory is likely to appear ideological. As such, it becomes an untoward object of ambivalence on the order of an opinion, regardless of the specific reasons given in its defense—it implies no commitment beyond itself. On the other hand, it can attempt, paradoxically, to repair its loss of referential validity by reengaging what it, as justified, cannot possibly know. The best that can be said is that this capitulates to the very activity of theorizing whose expulsion was a necessary condition of the justified theory. Since the theory claims to know, it cannot acknowledge that unknown. It follows that the order of justification either undoes itself in favor of being nothing more than the exercise of a formal ordering principle, in which case it appears as utterly self-reflexive or dogmatic, or the justified theory assumes a *stance* toward what it cannot claim to *know* thereby throwing into question its own refined concept. This amounts to assuming a stance against itself—not merely against the particular theory but against the possibility of a theory, including the possibility of solving whatever problems theory claims for itself within the universe of refined concepts. Both are temptations within the order of justification, and neither can be realized without contradiction.

When felt as temptations, however, it momentarily appears as if there is an authentic situation of choice, which implies that the theory has not yet turned against itself. Within those limitations, each side of the dilemma may seem to offer at least the prospect of social validation, though that was certainly not what justification was intended to bring to mind. This suggests that one side might be more plausible than the other and that this can be accounted for by reference to one norm that might legitimize an ideology and another that might legitimize the irony of both relying on and denying history. If we look beyond temptation, we see that each option is internally contradictory, so that there is no meaningful possibility of social validation: the issue is not how to resolve an ambiguity but how to restore what has been eliminated to the very formation that existed only on condition of that elimination. In other words, *it is difficult to imagine a socially valid ideology, which is not the same as an ideology that is taken for granted; and it is no less difficult to imagine how accepting the theoretically necessary unknown by ignoring it can be valid in any sense.* But we are now in a position to test the adequacy of the term "norm" for what it is supposed to explain and for what it still might enlighten, when we identify it with an activity rather than something inert, say, in the sense of a rule or a statistically prevalent, "normal" practice.

In this context, the idea of a validating norm can be understood as a movement immanent to the activity of justification in contrast with something brought to it. It is a tendency toward justification in favor of acknowledging the inability of a justified theory to know what it excludes, and the fact that this very unknowable must be apprehended if there is to be an objectively justifiable theory. This constitutes an admission that no order of knowledge can be sustained when what must be known is excluded as a matter of principle, which implies that a theory cannot be an order of knowledge. The principle of exclusion is, then, fateful since it precludes theory from recovering a sense of its history within a course of theorizing. Without this, it cannot teach its own possibility: the only way it can teach is by *not* being what it *is*. But this pathos is a condition of thinking about theory and in that respect a condition of theorizing. This is because the only way to overcome exclusion is to engage it *as a course of activity in itself* and, therefore, as an instance of life. In this way, the justification of a theory, when under duress, as in Marx's critique of political economy, displays its essential reflexivity to theorizing.

A theory may mark the exclusion on which it relies, but it cannot incorporate this condition of its possibility into itself. An admission that it denies the reality it purports to re-present remains external to the theory. This externalized opposition between a theory and its antithetic condition constitutes a new value since it no longer constitutes a basis for a standardized comparison within a universe of comparable theories. The difference now transpires within the life of a theorizing subjectivity committed to the sub-theoretical object *and* to the attempt to eliminate it in favor of a purified positive category within an ostensible order of knowledge. It has come to be imbedded in a course of activity that is an ongoing life. In the case of the theory, the sudden recovery of commitment is necessarily limited to what the incompleteness of its hypostatization now allows—as if there had been no refinement and purification of concepts and no completed justification. *It is, then, as if the only activity that counts is insisting on doing what cannot be done.* This fragile moment of recovered memory returns what is logically post-theoretical—namely, the theory—to a course of theorizing. It thereby allows for a supersession of the very order of justification that had ratified the hypostatized product, the *theory*. But it constitutes a more expansive supersession of the original ambivalent relationship between theorizing and theory. The relationship now intends its history in the course of rediscovering itself, hereby restoring a sense of the life of the object. The latter now includes, however, a trace of what makes it mysterious, what is occasionally referred to as the "presence of what is absent" and what I call its "sub-theoretical" objectivity. As a result, the course of theorizing is no longer innocent or passive in its commitment to the life of the concept. It now extends beyond commitment to the resistance that was all that seemed to remain at the completion of the theoretical refinement of the concept. It is still burdened by the temptation to effectuate a durable product, which accounts for the continuing ambivalence of its self-reflection. It includes not only the life of the concept, and therefore the life of the object, but a commitment to the relationship between these and the sub-theoretical objectivity on which theorizing depends. *Therefore, it necessarily includes a commitment to its own life, which implies a self-reflective commitment to life itself as a course of activity.*

The following proposition is premature, given what is still necessary in order to grasp its force as an idea. However, it is appropriate to state it at this point. In this movement of commitment, theorizing discovers (can assert in due course) its object, which is the life to which it was originally committed through its commitment to the life of the concept. *Insofar as it finds itself on the side of the object, it discovers the object within itself and thereby discovers itself as activity.* At this point, we can see why it is meaningful to speak of theorizing as a course of activity—meaningful because theorizing comprehends itself only *within* a course of activity. It is because of this that it is possible to raise the question "What is human about human affairs?" and expect to arrive at both an answer and some plausible conclusions about what it is to know such affairs in contrast with knowing what is nonhuman about the world.

––––––

Talk of a norm of justification turns out to have been expedient. It is now clear that theory itself is an emergent of a course of activity and that it excludes activity from what it presents as its object. This suspends the order of justification, and with it the ostensible wholeness of the hypostatized product and therefore the raison d'être of the order of justification. The unknowable, which makes itself felt as a sense of an ineffably sub-theoretical object, remains unknowable since that status is inherited from the relationship between theorizing and its post-theoretical, hypostatizing moment. Thus, in returning to the life of the concept, theorizing returns to the relationship between the concept and its object, but with the qualifications previously noted, including the relationship between those lives and the life that theorizing has discovered, in the prospect of loss, as its own. It remains to be seen how the theoretically unknowable asserts itself such that we can speak of a return to a theorizing that has at least begun to apprehend itself in its object.

First, the theorizing subject cannot be said to "know" the unknowable, what cannot be known by a theory, as it presumably "knows" agency-independent objects. The best we can say is that it apprehends the object in its special objectivity, as the life of a concept that now includes theorizing as an instance of life. This means that theorizing remains burdened with the shadow of an unknowable opposed to any refinement of a concept that denies that something is missing. That sense of a sub-theoretical necessity becomes the focus of the commitment of the theorizing subject—a commitment momentarily caught up in resistance as the appearance of the mode of "being unknowable." Parenthetically, the reflexivity of theorizing is by no means complete since, as an instance of life, theorizing remains partly on the side of the unknowable. It is in this regard that we can say that theorizing is self-motivating, or generative, *as if it is constantly trying to find itself.* Because the sub-theoretical unknowable appears as resistance, theorizing becomes committed to confrontation, which becomes, in effect, a confrontation of theorizing with itself—but with a subjectivity that has momentarily surpassed the inauthentic commitment to the ostensible product (a theory). I have noted that such a confrontation is initially predicated on what is presumably dispelled, which is the mysterious quality of what had been excluded. It relies, then, on what is consolidated as a theory in the course of attempting to dispel that quality: the unknowable has not yet appeared as resistance and, therefore, cannot have yielded a return to theorizing in its initial form. Yet in having come to terms with the fact that the product of *theorizing* is merely ostensible, as the value-realizing product is, for Marx, only ostensibly the qualitatively distinct thing, theorizing surpasses the inauthentic subjectivity that takes a theory to be nothing more than a product the "becoming" of which is irrelevant to its justification and therefore its truth. Therefore, it surpasses the original theorizing subjectivity that was unable to avoid the hypostatization.

———

This account of the confrontation of theorizing with itself appears to invoke a transcendental subject external to activity. While this is not my intention, it is admittedly difficult to avoid such a conclusion since the confrontation seems to involve a higher subjectivity that takes the theorizing subjectivity as its object rather than theorizing as such. How that critical position can be internal to theorizing, rather than independent and external, has yet to be shown, but we can at least account for its possibility. Given that theorizing intends itself, we can ask what is involved in such a reflexivity. Above all, it must display the aspect of commitment. Given its history, this can be thought of as a recommitment to the life of the concept as an instance of a more general notion of life. In that sense, it is a commitment that has become radical. This still seems to entail a separation of subjectivity from activity. If so, we would be led to conclude, by the same route we have followed so far, that the rejection of theorizing by itself is not, as I have argued, intrinsically incomplete but still capable of becoming complete. In that case, we would have to conclude that theorizing inevitably comes to reject itself, which is different from saying that it is nullified by the formation of a theory. In that case, it can never realize the life it needs to realize if it is to go beyond the hypostatized concept-object, which, as we have seen, it cannot avoid. If it is lost to theory and cannot find a way to return to itself, then the very notion of theorizing is unintelligible, and with it the analysis of the relationship between the activity and the product, thereby undermining the very possibility of a theory. The only way out would seem to involve a metaphysics of the theorizing subject in which the development of a theory is something altogether different from the sort of activity associated with what is human about human affairs. Theory would then be conceivable only as a transcendental accomplishment. As such, it cannot intend its own possibility and therefore cannot take as its object anything like itself, including mentality, action, intention, and the like. Lacking an object but the nonhuman thing that it asserts, theory stands alone. We would have no choice but to conclude that if theorizing is impossible because it is unintelligible from the point of view of theory, theory is unintelligible because it is impossible from the point of view of its own possibility.

This result is unacceptable. Therefore, we should reject the proposition from which it follows: that the rejection of theorizing by itself can be complete. There must be a more compelling version of "theorizing intending itself." The problem is posed by the following paradox. Theorizing cannot tolerate itself because it returns from a moment, a theory, in which life itself cannot be tolerated. But it cannot be conceived of as other than a course of activity. It never loses the aspect of life, though it may appear to have lost its object, and, indeed, it cannot help but reaffirm life even in its most extreme circumstance—namely, where life is re-presented as something lifeless by a theoretical refinement of its concept. A theory cannot intend the content of the unknowable that nevertheless haunts it as its occasion; and that sub-theoretical factuality is what yields the aspect of human activity I call "theorizing." In effect, theorizing is left with what theory rejects but cannot do without. Since that factuality appears as nothing more than resistance to theory, theorizing is left with the fact of resistance as such, which is, from the standpoint of the theory, irrational. However, it is not that theorizing has lost its object so much as discovered what is objective about it, which is that it too is active, though "it" momentarily appears as nothing more than the negativity of pure activity.

It follows that what was thought to be transcendental is only apparently so. The confrontation of theorizing with itself is immanent and not something brought by a separate subjectivity to the course of being committed to life. The activity of the sub-theoretical object, its force, remains both the occasion for and the material base of theorizing. In apprehending that object as "resistance to what is contrary to theorizing," theorizing reanimates the intimacy of its connection to its object within that resistance and thereby rediscovers what is historical about itself. That is, the course of activity always reveals itself as a course, in contrast with the sort of finality that is typically referred to as an action. It is in this way that the idea of a course of theorizing includes the sense of a struggle or an opposition between that activity (and its commitment) and what impels it, on its own behalf, to undermine activity as such in favor of a merely ostensible product. It is important to remember that the confrontation is superficially one of refined concepts with the fact of an omission, and *only in that regard* a confrontation of post-theoretical subjectivity with subjectivity in the throes of theorizing. One result is that theorizing takes the momentary form of a virtual passivity that is subordinate in general—*that it operates in an attitude of waiting*—which means that it is continually open to surprise. "Attitude" refers here to a submission to or a being subsumed by a course of activity. In that respect, it effectively acknowledges the unknowable as beyond what theory takes as objective. In what does this acknowledgment consist? How is this passivity realized? How should we characterize it? What are its implications for the idea of theorizing as a course of activity? These questions can be further developed in regard to the "norm" introduced previously, and then qualified, as a first approximation of the return of the unknown.

By "norm," in this new context, I mean to indicate a necessary quality of a course of activity and therefore of any commitment—namely, that it is exigent. Exigency is normative where it is difficult to distinguish between subjectivity and objectivity. Its normativity lies in the difficulty the former has in ignoring or resisting the latter, as if the object makes its own demands, or "beckons" the subject. If we, as we must, do away with the normal sense of "as if" and its ironical suggestion of a transcendental knower of the relation of subject to object, we are led to the notion of "internal relations" as part of what is essential to understanding what is human about human affairs. An approximation of what this means is that *a subject cannot "know" an object without seeing in it the source of a norm and therefore as having an aspect of subjectivity in its own right*: to even speak of a "structure of relevance" is to speak of objects making demands, which, in turn, implies that a subject "approaches" its object in an attitude of waiting. To try to avoid this is to substitute biology for intentionality, nonhuman for human affairs.

The norm is that exigent quality in which theorizing reinstates itself by its unavoidable repudiation of the order of justification implicit in the confrontation of theorizing with a theory. It is internal to the reflexivity of theorizing; and the obligation of responsiveness, predicated on waiting, is the categorical imperative of that course of activity. The return of theorizing as an instance of a norm of return constitutes a turn toward the life of a new concept and its ambivalent connection with *its* object. But it is not clear how we can say that it is a "turn toward" since there is nothing known toward which a turning is possible. It is better to say that theorizing *re-turns* to the absence of life in the old refined concept such that the latter is now available to life itself. That renewed sense of the availability of life nevertheless amounts to acknowledging it without any reference to content or substance. The use of the word "norm" seems now to serve a rhetorical function. It dramatizes an essential aspect of theorizing, that it is always renewing its encounter with the theoretically unknowable without the necessity of adding anything significant to that aspect.

We have seen that the activity of theorizing is no less an instance of life than the life of the concept predicated, as it must be, on the life of its object—which, in turn, is predicated on the threat to its sub-theoretical objectivity posed by refined conceptualization. What the theorizing subject now recognizes above all is its own possibility, the possibility of a theorizing subjectivity that, to echo Nagel's account of altruism, anyone can occupy and all do—which is nothing more than the commitment implicit in any authentic course of activity. Such a commitment is passive relative to the internality of the concept-object relationship to which the theorizing subject is committed. That is, the commitment is *actively* passive, in the sense that it is exigent in a permissive mode. In other words, the norm that qualifies the activity of theorizing, that specifies its exigent character, qualifies the course of activity as such; and it momentarily appears as an instance of the activity of re-turning. The moment of the encounter with the unknowable, with the sub-theoretical "present absence" within the ostensible product (a theory), constitutes a commitment that is passive in the specific sense of a subjectivity that is dependent on the concept and its troubled relationship with its troubled and troubling object. In this sense, *the theorizing subjectivity, the concept, and its object are lives dependent on lives.* Passivity in relation to *life* is conceivable only if there is a life to which commitment is possible. In this case, it is the life of the concept as that life returns through the disruption (engendered by the encounter) of what appeared to be the concept's death (as it is refined in the form of a theory and made subject to the inauthentic activity of completing the order of justification conventionally identified as an essential condition of knowledge).

The norm of "re-turn" is not a "norm" in the usual sense of a historically accomplished rule subject to self-reflection oriented by reasons (e.g., according to what sociologists refer to as possible definitions of the situation), except from the point of view of a theory taken apart from its being a product of theorizing (Emmet 1975, 6–16). From the point of view of theorizing, and its opposition to theory, it constitutes the exigent character of the course of activity and pertains to the commitment implicit in that conception. This is not to say that the exigency has to do with the urgency of a particular action engendered by or derived from external conditions (e.g., reasons).[3] Rather, the commitment that qualifies theorizing is urgent in the sense of having its own inexorable momentum. The latter must be thought of as subsuming the theorizing subject and not as an effect of a prior or intervening intention. To the extent to which this clarifies what is implicit in the notion of theorizing, it can be thought of as part of what is intended by the term. As such, *theorizing can be said to display itself as an attitude of waiting within the subsuming momentum of the commitment that constitutes the intimacy of its relation to the concept.* The sense of intimacy I have in mind is a connection between one instance of subjectivity, or life, and another, in this case, between the life constituted as a course of theorizing and the life of the concept.

Commitment facilitates self-criticism in the sense of including it and not in the sense of being a contingent contribution to it. It does this by the priority it necessarily confers on the object over the concept. That priority belongs to the definition of "commitment"; it is a necessary feature of it. The norm, the exigency we now recognize as a feature of the course of activity, is constitutive of the relationship between theorizing and the life of the concept. At the same time, that relationship seems unsustainable insofar as it includes what theorizing anticipates but cannot tolerate—namely, the sense of an obligation to bring about a distinctive product (a theory). The inability to tolerate what it cannot refuse makes theorizing *essentially* reflexive. I conclude that it is implicit in the twin notions of exigency and momentum that the commitment to the object, the dependence of theorizing on the troubled life of the sub-theoretical object's concept, is at the same time a commitment *of* and *to* theorizing. Theorizing is constituted in one respect by the impossibility of reconciling two tendencies that must be reconciled—namely, its own continuation as a course of activity and its self-denying tendency to bring itself to a post-theoretical end through the refinement of the concept against the life of its object. One might say, in regard to its aspect of exigency, that theorizing is passive in regard to the former (which negates itself) and aggressive in regard to the latter (commitment to its own negation). In regard to the relationship between the two tendencies or aspects, it is actively passive.

It is well known that such refined concepts of human affairs as organization, institution, network, function, exchange, role, norm, value, interaction, and system of action are intended to represent the possibility of a complete theory of social life. Their use is by no means intended as merely heuristic or descriptive. To that extent, they articulate a hope that disguises a desperate but futile attempt to preserve the notion of human life *as such* by specifying units of analysis or a settled frame of reference that by their nature does away with life. The hope is that the universe identified by such radically refined concepts will come to replace the theory-defying movement of the objectivity that the concepts were supposed to indicate or signify, which I have identified with the life of the concept. Insofar as that hope prevails regardless of its apparent futility, it envisions a domain of objects knowable only by an appeal to the theory-product and not from within the course of theorizing itself; and it envisions knowledge apart from and in opposition to the course of activity that makes knowledge possible, a theory in contrast with its condition of possibility. Those objects are conceived of as independent of all forms of agency. They are positively empirical in the sense that they are dead things picked out by the theory: "dead" in that they place no significant demands on the theory that might threaten its integrity. Theirs is a fantastic particularized existence knowable only by reference to its theoretical ideal and an untheorizable *tendency* toward that ideal. But the abandoned sub-theoretical region of being, the agency-dependent object domain that authorizes a commitment to the life of the concept, now makes its own demand. It demands that the theory submit itself to the very questions that give rise to theorizing (and therefore to theorizing as the condition of imagining and intending an ostensible product); and because these questions arise in regard to the abandoned region of being, they can have, for the theory, no concrete answers. They remain the ongoing occasions for theorizing.

What is remarkable is that, in regard to that region and without any irony whatsoever, the refined concepts operate in effect as *metaphors*. They describe one object, the dead one now identical to its purified concept, and then submit it to the universe of an altogether different objectivity, one virtually identified with resistance to that death, including the loss of memory and self-reflection that it entails. For example, action is typically conceived of as the execution of an intention, and therefore as a particular event that either occurs or does not occur. When it is normally used in a theoretical argument, at least one qualification is considered necessary if the properties attributed to the act are to characterize it as a whole, as they must if it is a particular event. Weber famously referred to social action as oriented and, then, as "oriented in its course." The latter introduces the quality of indefinite temporality that betrays the idea of an event (1947, 88). The point is that the refined concept necessarily refers to a universe of self-sufficient particulars (mental states, other sorts of action, other actors and events, and the like). But its use in propositions intended to be linked to other propositions (theory) requires precisely the quality that undermines the priority of a specific mental state and therefore of the idea that what is being done is the particular execution of a particular intention by a particular individuated agent. Despite itself, the concept loses its meaningfulness, its applicability to human affairs, without allowing for a sense of something beyond what the concept attempts to circumscribe that abides within an altogether different universe in which temporality is indefinite and particularity is problematic.

The concept of "social action" purports to fix its objective referent. But its use is unavoidably metaphorical in that it invokes an alternative universe in order to preserve a different sense of action from what is stated in Weber's definition, a sense that is presupposed in the programmatic claim that "social action" refers to human affairs. That is, the *concept* is necessarily betrayed in subsequent propositions—for example, where "corporate groups" are said to derive their coherence from overlapping or compatible purposes (Weber 1947, 151). The concept aims to represent its object without anything left over; but insofar as it purports to be about human affairs, it presupposes the sub-theoretical objectivity on which theorizing, and therefore both the concept and its meaning, depend. Both the concept of "action" and reference to its "course" are metaphors, though the first is a privileged member of a theory and the latter appears as nothing more than a minor qualification without privilege. Since each metaphor is effective only if it implicates a universe that provides for and sustains its meaningfulness, the expression of the theory in a succession of propositions appears as a series of totalizing alternations in which the assertion of one sort of thing is followed by the assertion of something altogether different. *"Social action" and "[action] oriented in its course" are, in relation to one another, figurative expressions.* This suggests the following hypothesis: insofar as it is intended to apply to an instance of human affairs, an attempt to formulate a theory will be accompanied by otherwise unaccountable glosses and other textualizing and rhetorical devices necessary for sustaining the sense of privilege attached by the theory to one universe despite its necessary reliance on another to which privilege is denied. I mention in passing two other examples: (1) alternating uses of "interaction" and "community," where "interaction" invokes a logic of exchange and "community" the very different principles of mutuality, reciprocity, and inter-dependence; and (2) "agreement" and "sharing," where the former relies on the idea of a meeting of minds and the latter on the idea of being in common about something.

This is why, despite itself, theory takes on a literary cast the more it is obliged to reckon with the very reality it had abandoned in order to complete the perfection of its concepts. This contradicts the idea that the goodness of a particular theory— its capacity to be understood and its prospects for success in regard to one or another scientific aspiration—depends on purging it of metaphor and purging it of the very possibility that its propositions might be understood as metaphorical.

———

To summarize, theoretically refined concepts are intrinsically metaphorical to the extent to which they are intended to represent something that can only be objective within the *course of theorizing*. The desire for a universe in which life prevails cannot be satisfied when the theory projects a universe that excludes the possibility of theorizing because it excludes the life of its concept. It seems evident that the idea of human life cannot be realized by opposing what it might mean *within* a course of theorizing. In other words, it cannot be realized as a reality independent of agency. The sociality that theory finds within its refined concepts and their propositions is not the sort of object that allows for a justification by reference to what is human about human affairs. That extension of reference has been omitted as a matter of principle. All that remains is what the metaphor allows the theory to omit, without its having to question itself in a last and therefore an atheoretical moment of self-critical reflection.

For the historicist, concepts that totalize their objects are ideological inasmuch as the desire they embody and their conditions of possibility depend on omitting what might undermine hope but is nevertheless presupposed by the desire. At the same time, since the purified notion of the social is what allows theory to be justified, a justified theory supports a commitment to the omission that amounts to a resistance to self-critical reflection. The resistance is undermined when reflection appears to itself as an effect of encountering the strange or unknown, or, what amounts to the same thing, as a sudden and overwhelming opportunity to rediscover theorizing and, therefore, its own possibility.

What the historicist considers ideological does not necessarily lack a *capacity* for self-critical reflection, though ideological subjectivity is reflective only after the exclusion. Post hoc reflection takes a contemplative form, since it is retrospective as a matter of principle. In this respect, there is an analogy to the connoisseur's appreciation of a virtually perfect object whose perfection, or its approximation thereof, appears as her own discovery. This self-elevating subjectivity wishes to be consumed by the object that, on its own part and for its own reasons, it has constituted as fixed and eternal. It is therefore governed by a desire for finality that is incompatible with what it desires—namely, the possibility of the object. Ultimately, this subjectivity finds itself in its own insistence on its superiority, as inspired, rigorous, expert, anything that attests to the highest degree of appreciation appropriate to perfection. Its tragedy derives from the only thing that it can actually discover: it can only fully acknowledge itself as a "self" surrounded by other discovering selves striving to out-appreciate each other—that is, it cannot do without rivals, real or imagined. However, the ideological condition of this subjectivity is inconsistent with its having arrived at the theory by which it justifies itself. In order for it to have moved from theory to the appreciation of perfection, it must have displaced a sub-theoretical objectivity that resists all representation in favor of a final signification. Its constitutive desire cannot be relieved, since it wishes to grasp not only the perfection of its object but the impossible perfection of that object's perfection, the latter as the possibility of hegemony across the field of human studies. At best, the futility of this desire can be suppressed, which is the bad faith of ideology. At worst, it takes both itself and its object as sublime, beyond any grasp of language and, therefore, self-critical reflection.

Because suppression is unstable, ideological subjectivity is forced to confront itself by virtue of the unrelieved difference internal to its object. This brings it closer than it can endure to the engaged reflection internal to theorizing, and thus to the very principle of life that must be rejected for connoisseurship to be faithful to itself. The historicist position is complete when it shows, despite the contingency of totalizing propositions, such as "human beings are essentially social," that it is still possible, and probably necessary, to accept that position while acting momentarily as if the propositions are not contingent. The reason is that contingency is bound to return regardless of the will of the theoretician, ultimately as a challenge to theory. This is so insofar as the idea of "contingency" brings us back to the social and its mode of being as a course of activity that defies all representation.

8

Historicism and Its Alternative

gainst historicism is the claim that certain ideas about human affairs
are necessarily beyond criticism, either because they are obviously true
or because knowledge of human affairs is possible only if they are not
put into question.[1] It is often the case that inconsistent ideas are maintained
in a text, by a theoretician, or within a discipline. For example, the idea that
the skin is a natural boundary, dividing subjects and thereby particularizing
expressions of agency, is often taken for granted in the human sciences. It is not
obviously consistent with another proposition also taken for granted—namely,
that humans are essentially social in the sense that actions are only recognizably complete across bodies and according to an intentionality that is an ongoing accomplishment for which no *one* can be decisively responsible. Both ideas
are virtually axiomatic: a theory that purports to cover the subject matter of
a discipline or subdiscipline (e.g., exchange theory, system theory, or network
theory in sociology) would fail unless the apparent contradiction between the
two ideas is explained, neutralized, or resolved. Avoiding the issue would raise
the very threat of skepticism that is otherwise forestalled by acting as if neither
idea is problematic or needs to be expressed for the sake of such a theory. The
threat is reduced when they are allowed to remain latent—if, in other words,
they are *systematically* excluded from the formal statements of a theory, remaining at its margins along with other ideas "taken for granted"—such as
tendencies of entities to endure and people to resist dissonance, the rational
tendentiousness of action, and the idea, currently being incorporated into the
neuroscience of reading, that "culture" draws its apparent continuity from the
ways in which cultural facts come to be structured in the brain (Dehaene 2009).
Another way of saying this is that those ideas remain beyond question to the

extent to which they remain outside of theory, with the likely consequence that the refinement of concepts becomes even more urgent, increasingly defensive, and increasingly likely to undermine claims of representational adequacy.

A further consequence of ignoring the contradiction between the skin as a natural boundary and the social as incompatible with such a boundary has been a separation of the social sciences from the critical discourses, professional and lay, from which most of their topics, issues, and pre-concepts derive. It is a small step to declare that those discourses are about matters of "value" rather than possible "truths," and, though they may enrich our lives and give direction and significance to what we do, they do not provide knowledge (for a critique of the distinction, see Putnam 2002). This thesis is usually accompanied by a historical narrative in which social science develops as the progressive application of the methods of natural science to human affairs, disregarding those humanistic fields that rely on the essential sociality of humans and the irreducibility of the social (Gordon 1991). The attempt to graft the methodology of one sort of science onto another allows a mass of received topics unaccountable in disciplinary terms to appear to be what it cannot be—namely, a basis for a progressive accumulation of knowledge about human affairs. The overall effect is familiar—that the disciplinary aspect of social science, its claim to specialize within an ostensibly rational division of knowledge, is increasingly subordinate to its departmental divisions and status, its content subsumed by the form and rhetoric of its own socially alienated discourse. In this respect, one might say that theorizing is replaced by theory (refined concepts) and, therefore, by a tendency to subordinate the idea of human affairs to the activity of comparing and synthesizing theories of what such affairs cannot be.

A second, related, consequence may be philosophically more significant. It involves a narrowing of the criteria for deciding what topics, among those received, are worthy of the attention of the social scientist when social science is abstracted from the human sciences and thereby thought of apart from their common sub-theoretical object. It then becomes possible to speak loosely of a humanist discipline—say, sociology, economics, or politics—without having to refer to the "basic fact" that all topics are implicated in what is human about human affairs. This provides a convenient way out of one difficulty posed by the contradiction between the skin as a natural boundary and activity that transpires across bodies—that is, how to rationalize what is social in social research. From this point of view, the significant research questions are received from beyond the discipline of sociology, indeed from beyond all disciplines (see Lazarsfeld, Sewell, and Wilensky 1967). This is because they are essentially practical, and the reality that they are about is understood to be independent of the conceptual commitments of disciplines. To that extent, each discipline is defined by its specialization in one or another domain, though each intends a greater scope of *application* for what it claims to *know*. For the sort of social science under discussion, the domain of immediate reference is the orderliness of *organizationally* practical affairs, though its concepts and generalizations are intended to apply even more generally—namely, to what people do together in regard to the continuity of their association. Its task is, then, to provide tentative answers to non-tentative practical questions by employing well-tested methods of analysis largely on the model of natural science. Its concepts are correspondingly formed in regard to the independent reality of organizationally practical affairs, specifically from the results of testing propositions about them. Social science becomes, in effect, a placeholder for a science that has little or no interest in the idea of the social that underlies and qualifies the idea of organizationally practical affairs, in what is involved in imagining what is human about human affairs, or in demonstrating how topics of research are implicated in those affairs. The contradiction between the skin as a boundary and activity across bodies is irrelevant as long as both ideas remain latent and inquiry remains strictly topical. If both conditions are met, then research and theory are likely to find themselves on the side of skin-bound subjectivity, therefore confined within a paradigm in which the main issues have to do with identifying units of analysis, selecting a methodology adapted primarily to the referential context in which the usefulness of findings (and their concepts) is tested, and deciding what evidence is probabilistically significant to the choice among available theories.

By way of illustration, studies of interpersonal relations traditionally operate on the premise that the skin is a natural boundary to agency, while studies of deviance from and participation in social structures have generally taken for granted that human beings are essentially social, which means that descriptions of agency are adequate only if the factors they identify are themselves essentially social, therefore extra-personal. The emphasis in each is different, the one focusing on intentions, influences, and effects of the exercise of particular intentions, the other focusing on types, mediation, and structural causes. The first tends to "center on the *person* as the basic unit to be investigated."[2] The second takes the person largely as a symptom or index of situations that are more or less structured and more or less overlapping: thus the emphasis on the resolution of personhood as membership, where the latter is internally related to superordinate conditions of action and where both member and situation are social facts. The "person" of the second is, in effect, a summary of such situations over the course of membership. This does not mean that there is no distance between, say, self and role, in regard to what is being done, or that there are no intentions that belong to the person independent of the action implications of the role. Rather, the idea of a personal self apart from others is not the incorrigible foundation of research and theory that the idea of membership is, with the latter's implication of the essential sociality of every instance or expression of agency. To the extent to which this leaves open questions about freedom and the possibility of the imposition of particular wills on others (either positively, say as guidance, or negatively, as in exploitation), this frame of reference focuses on the social conditions of rational action, where such action, the very idea of it, always anticipates a transcendent judgmental subjectivity.[3]

In a different register, one might argue that the use of "person" in each context is different, so it is not that the two perspectives disagree but that they represent different aspects of the same reality—one having to do with participating in an ensemble and another with deliberating or forming an intention prior to a particular act.[4] However, it does not follow from the difference that the two are complementary. The first takes activity as originating in someone, as realizing individualized intentions, and as taking account of others in the same way that inanimate objects are taken into account. The second might look at the same activity (e.g., kicking a football in a game) and describe it as behavior with a reason, where the reason expresses the nature of the sort of practice that has institutional characteristics (is rule-governed according to a system value) and a position relative to other such practices.[5]

The reason cited may be, in Nagel's sense, "someone's" reason. The person kicking may represent a weak version of agency, as far as concerns *the ball being kicked within the game.* That agency is vested in the practice itself and the commitments it authorizes, in the implication that its rules and operating principles are expressed or enacted collectively rather than decided on again and again. If the person is considered under the aspect of agency, it is as an agent of quite a different act—namely, one entering the game in the sense of undertaking to express or be part of its coherence. The specific intention in that case is a desire to be part of realizing the social reality of a game of football. Whatever is added on the part of the individual person to the agentic aspect of the game is of minimal explanatory significance to understanding what is actually done in that context, though there is no doubt that the individual intends to do something appropriate to the game: to kick a field goal is not to kick in any other sense. It is not just that the player knows the rules and then acts with the appropriate reasons, as if the reasons are still external to the practice (inside the individual's mind). As a member, she is implicated in the execution and elaboration of what the rules permit and require according to legitimate team purposes—it is tempting to say "part of," but that would suggest precisely the duality of person and membership that needs to be avoided. What is done remains intelligible as action only within the agency constituted by the game, not merely the situation—which is, again, an agency that does not translate as a particular individual (or individuals) or mentality (or mentalities) but is one over which no particular individual or mentality holds sway.

However, it seems impossible to decide whether agency requires a frame of reference that gives priority to individuality (agency essentially within the skin) or one that gives priority to a structure or course of activity for which the skin cannot be a natural boundary. It is not enough to say that it depends on what one is trying to explain, since both individuals and structures or courses of activity seem to be involved in any case. Nor is it sufficient to reflect on tragic or complementary relationships between personality and social structure since each assumes that both of the original propositions are necessarily true; and if they are, there can be no relationship between them that could support the interactions of individual and society supposed by the concepts of tragedy and complementarity. Moreover, it is not sufficient to consider them as two distinct levels of explanation since each not only appeals to the other but relies on it in ways that violate the concept of a level. "Membership" requires persons (intentional beings) to initiate, execute, possibly extend or elaborate, and evaluate legitimate performances, and "individuality" requires that there be sustaining conditions of rational action (including of speech and thought), therefore a structure of reasons external to the individual. Neither "member" nor "person" can be defined independently of those requirements, at least not in the current languages of the social sciences and the extra-disciplinary discourses with which they are correspondent. Each possible solution relies on the two sub-theoretical notions remaining sub-theoretical and on a principle that allows theory to avoid appealing explicitly to either by simply picking and choosing according to common sense, as when one says that the structuring of reasons external to the individual is somehow "internalized" such that a subsequent action by that individual can be seen to execute as well as express the particular intention that belongs, at that moment, exclusively to her.

R egardless of which position is adopted (historicism or anti-historicism), it is necessary to consider the proposition "human beings are essentially social" as incorrigible, with the implication that sociality is immanent to all that human beings do by way of being human. Whether or not it is subject to the historicist critique, the proposition serves, for each position, as a point of departure for and a regulatory principle of analysis. Moreover, each reserves the right to reject propositions on the grounds that they are ideological in nature, the historicist because no proposition is ultimately beyond criticism and the anti-historicist because it is always necessary to be prepared, when the issue arises, to distinguish between rational, nonrational, and irrational ideas. To apply the proposition "human beings are essentially social" to a description of a particular event, activity, or state of affairs requires a prior judgment that the event, activity, or state of affairs is a particular (has location, form, and boundaries) and that it already falls within the scope of the projected totalization "essentially social." It is not merely that it is a token of a type since that shifts the problem of specificity to the type. Rather, the proposition extends that far because it is only intelligible in extension. Moreover, it is by virtue of the latter that it can be evaluated according to reasonable criteria and rational methods for distinguishing between ideological and nonideological statements.

In contrast with nonideological statements, ideological statements are said to be subject to criticism based at least on the unstated historical specificity of the possible truths of their claims, and on the possibility that the value or form of life they affirm is particular and not general. Nonideological propositions are said to present or be reflexive to conditions of their possible falsification and, in any case, to be framed in such a way that their negative implications can also be contextualized, perhaps by virtue of the way in which they are stated. Whether a proposition is ideological is a problem when its *affirmation* is dogmatic—that is, when it appears to negate another value or form of life and, in so doing, to deny what the negation makes clear, that it depends on what it negates.[6] The difficulty is to distinguish totalistic propositions that are ideological from those that are not—in a way that provides sufficient reason and confidence to continue reasoning. This is acknowledged by both the historicist and the anti-historicist. It is important because the latter wants to argue that the totalistic proposition "human beings are essentially social" is beyond legitimate criticism and is nonideological as well as at least effectively true. A weak version, the last clause of which the historicist is likely to reject, is that the burden of proof is on the denial, analogous to the burden of demonstrating guilt beyond a reasonable doubt.[7] Since its being beyond criticism depends on its being nonideological, the reasonableness of the second thesis, that the proposition should be taken as beyond criticism, depends on the possibility of distinguishing reliably between the two types of proposition in the appropriate case. Unfortunately, there appear to be no decisive methods or criteria available, and none seem on the horizon that are sufficiently noncontroversial to put the issue to rest for any given case and therefore for cases of its type. Does it follow that there is no reasonable basis for distinguishing ideological propositions that are totalistic from other equally totalistic propositions that nevertheless can be evaluated for the possibility that they are beyond reasonable doubt and, if so, for the legitimacy of acting as if they are true? From the point of view of the observer of the debate, it may be more accurate to formulate the question in the following way: in understanding an ostensibly disciplinary human science, is it illegitimate or otherwise unreasonable for its practitioner to act as if any received totalizing proposition whatsoever is more than merely momentarily incorrigible? Is this important, in any case, to the science?

It is possible to maintain the anti-historicist position even without criteria or methods for making the distinction—though it would be difficult in that case to teach it as reasonable. Consider those who assertively, without qualification, endorse the materialist/scientific worldview (in contrast with, say, idealist, substance dualist, skeptical, or religious views), and do so as a matter of principle rather than merely as a working hypothesis, a frame of reference, a point of view, or a matter of course. Searle describes the "'scientific' conception of the world as made up of material things" (1984, 15; 1994, 85, chap. 2; Searle, Dennett, and Chalmers 1997), where this cannot be taken to exclude intentionality and subjective facts.[8] That is, science is ultimately about agency-independent objects, but it fails if it excludes, as phenomena to be explained in those very terms, consciousness—which appears, but only at first, to be an exception that challenges the scientific view. Searle and his colleagues conclude that "the mystery of consciousness will gradually be removed when we solve the biological problem of consciousness," which seems to assume that the way in which we now specify and describe consciousness certifies precisely the sort of phenomenon that biology might explain (Searle, Dennett, and Chalmers 1997, 201; but see Searle 1994, chap. 8, for a sense of the subtlety and complexity of Searle's position despite what may be fatal to it—namely, his determination to start and to some extent end with what consciousness appears to be according to prevailing categories and concepts).

Whatever justification is offered for this move, no matter how compelling it might be, no matter how sophisticated it has become in the course of philosophical inquiry and discussion, and whatever the benefits of it beyond philosophy, it is important to consider some negative consequences of premature solutions to two problems: What is epistemically at stake and what are the possible limitations of current accounts of consciousness based on the ontological presuppositions of its critique of dualism? Specifically, what possible consequences ought we to consider in evaluating attempts to establish a clear division between scientific knowledge and nonscientific opinion, belief, or point of view, not only in regard to consciousness but in regard to the objects of consciousness and the conditions of the sort of relationships presupposed by that division? One important consequence has to do with the mode of thinking that the most prevalent nonreductive accounts authorize in regard to adjudicating between pure and apparently skeptical views of natural science as *the* knowledge-constituting field.[9] In passing, the debate often misrepresents the aims of subdisciplines such as "science studies" at the same time that it leaves room for a critical inquiry into the structure and intellectual conditions of the purist idea, the ideal seen to be under attack (Kitcher 2001). The debate itself, when conducted according to these terms, has been promoted largely in regard to dangers to rationality posed by religion (notably by Dawkins 2006 and Grünbaum 2001), perhaps more often in regard to dangers posed by specific characterizations of literatures identified as "postmodernist" (for examples, see Harvey 1990 and Sokal and Bricmont 1998), and certainly in regard to the ways in which science was distorted and its possible contribution to policy significantly undermined during the presidency of George W. Bush, something discussed in numerous journals, magazines, and newspapers.

My discussion is too brief for the treatment the topic deserves, and I oversimplify what are far more complex issues, though I believe that the simplification is in keeping with the way in which the debate has been framed at the intersection of philosophy and public discourse. I do not believe that it will seem oversimplified, however, to those familiar with the social sciences and psychology, where debate continues between those who adhere to the model derived from the natural sciences and those who have questioned the propriety of excluding other ideas about knowledge and ways of knowing, given the nature of the subject matter and the urgency of questions about the moral, practical, and political consequences of treating human affairs according to methods appropriate to agency-independent reality.[10] In regard to the question of what ought to be included under a legitimate conception of science, Kitcher (2001) discusses the encounter between realism and its apparent other, though with purposes and conclusions quite different from those of the present inquiry. His attempt to accommodate criticisms of realism from within a realist philosophy draws on a more capacious view of science than the absolutist realist would accept and relies on observations about the actual practices involved in scientific work and conditions of those practices that inevitably compromise any ideal—where scientific "practice" includes such activities as the selection of projects according to their significance; the choice of methods; the actual conduct of research; and the attempt to maintain the material conditions, including financing and public support, of undertaking projects. I am concerned here with possible consequences of defending the purist idea of science by adopting a principle of exclusion based on a problematic distinction between scientific inquiry and something else that might otherwise be confused with science. The distinction also allows for an identification of knowledge with the sciences of agency-independent reality, presumably in contrast with "values" and "opinions."

One remarkable consequence of absolutist materialism arises directly from the exclusion. It inscribes a political divide in the name of a philosophy of knowledge that aims to distinguish itself from politics no less than religion. The distinction is said to be necessary in order to preserve the detachment appropriate to the type of rationality imputed to science, what might be thought of as the "original position" of the observer, and the way of being reasonable that presumably derives from science itself—where "science" refers fundamentally to physics and chemistry, and "politics" is understood according to received wisdom about how opinions are formed within and across what Rawls calls "comprehensive doctrines."[11] The divide is, familiarly, between the proponents of an unqualified scientific/materialist worldview, in which "materialism" stands for agency-independence, for whom permissible answers to philosophical questions about reality fall within the scope of an artificial (specialized) language and a specific type of analysis, and those identified as the principal antagonists of that worldview and therefore to knowledge itself and to the very notion of a knowable reality. When they claim to constitute or provide knowledge, the latter are regarded, at worst, as falling on the side of ignorance, superstition, religious speculation, idealism, folklore, naïveté, nihilism, ideology, or self-exempting skepticism. At most, they are taken to be part of culture, understood as meanings and values subject to an altogether different function of mind than is appropriate to the attainment of reliable knowledge, and not part of understanding how the world works on its own account.

I believe that this way of framing the debate misreads most of the literature listed under "science studies," and the caricatures of the field of study are best understood as attempts to delineate an absolute "other" posited by the absolutist position itself in the interest of protecting a view of science that, despite itself, cannot be generalized beyond agency-independent objectivity. It is as if the proponents of the exclusionary rule are driven to that excess by an overwhelming fear that reason itself is currently in peril in ways unprecedented in recent history. This often takes as its primary objects critical literatures that challenge assertions about unity, homogeneity, boundedness, originality, and so forth, in the study of human affairs. In effect, what is at stake is the very idea of theory under its aspect of critical reason as that has been understood since the 1950s. For opponents of these literatures, such as Alan Sokal, it is essential above all else to preserve with the greatest of vigilance the purest ideals of epistemic interest and truth against whatever, in light of the fear itself, appears to threaten that purity. Unfortunately, like all principles of exclusion that necessarily idealize what they mean to preserve and demonize what makes that idealization possible, this one also ends by excluding too much. To that extent, it reveals itself as a version of the very thing it most fears, excessive vigilance in regard to creative endeavors of all sorts.

This cannot be translated into a pedagogical policy without undermining the humanistic aspect of pedagogy itself; and, to that extent, the materialist/ scientific worldview cannot be taught in the same way that it is possible to teach that reasons may or may not be causally related to actions, or that there is or is not a temporally extended and deep agentic self (or what psychologists used to refer to as a self-reflective "personality"), or that society is or is not an aggregate, or that action may or may not be an "event." In effect, it expresses a rule that imposes a prior limitation on philosophy at the very point at which the discipline begins describing its own history as an accumulated set of conditions of the possibility of reasoning about the world: philosophy exempt from philosophy. It not only appears that philosophy is virtually impossible for those putatively nonphilosophical others who fall on the side of antagonism to science, but that the latter's answers to even reasonable questions can only be lacking in the precision, rationality, and realism that lie on the side of scientific materialism. In other words, there are questions on the side of negativity to which there may be understandable reactions but for which rational and reasonable answers are impossible; on the positive side there are ways of identifying what sorts of question might be answerable in principle if not in fact, though there seems no non-tautological way to determine how such questions can be distinguished from and given preference over other questions.

On this analogy, the least that can be said in favor of the anti-historicist thesis, that the proposition "human beings are essentially social" is true beyond criticism, is that it declares a definitive boundary between totalistic statements that are intelligible and those that are not. While the thesis points to the possibility of a nonreductive sociology, it is not clear how any such essentiality can be expressed non-paradoxically within the decisive metaphors of materialist sociology (e.g., structure, institution, organization, system, and rational exchange). It seems, then, that it is best understood as a language-constituting rule that a certain class of statements is excluded, as not sociological, from the mutually dependent propositions of the science. A stronger interpretation of the rule is that it defines what constitutes an authentic sociological proposition, given the nature of the reality to which the language organized by the rule corresponds—thereby envisioning an incorrigible distinction, often based reductively on a notion of levels of explanation, between sociological propositions and others, possibly psychological. However, this stronger interpretation cannot be realized without generating problems that demand more than it can provide. Therefore, I discount it in what follows. The most that can be said for the second thesis is that it constitutes a moral and a practical foundation for a science enjoined to rely on the certainty of the original totalistic proposition out of respect for its subject matter, human affairs. In either case, a pragmatic criterion is applied for evaluating the thesis: at the least, it speaks to the need to maintain coherence and, at most, it speaks to the duty owed the object of study, which is identified precisely as what deserves the exercise of just such a duty.

While the difference between historicism and anti-historicism is fairly clear, it may be, as a jurist might say, a distinction without a difference. It can be argued that the consequences of assuming the one position simply by denying the other are not obvious and may, indeed, be insignificant to the development of the scientific aspect of the social sciences. This argument seems strongest in regard to the actual conduct of research and its accumulation of findings that, unlike totalistic or totalizing propositions that purport to cover what mere facts do not, appear to be governed by rules of observation and inference that cannot accommodate such speculations. The latter are, therefore, considered irrelevant to the scientific character of those fields. However, it is a mistake to identify the disciplinary status of a social science with the notion of a progressively systematic accumulation of findings from empirical research if only because this begs questions that bear on the relationship between the subject matters of particular projects and the content domain of each field as a whole. This is crucial in those sciences that attempt to clarify what is human about human affairs, since they cannot avoid such questions. For example, what is the rational basis, within the study of human affairs, of choosing one project over another? By means of what principle(s) is it possible to decide what is and what is not to be considered information relative to a given project and to its relations with other projects? Is there a noncontroversial way of deciding the disciplinary validity of claims? What sorts of observation and what principles of comparison are necessary to decide whether something contributes to knowledge? What must "knowledge" mean, and what can we be said to "know" when we have it, if such evaluations can be taken to apply across the disciplinary universe of instances of research? Conversely, what must "knowledge" mean and what can we be said to "know" if disciplinary considerations are of no account? How can we know that there is progress in a field when its discipline is divided about the proper measure of progress and when that division has to do with the fundamental question of what object the field is designed or destined to study?[12]

If the latter difficulty is insurmountable as things stand, then this may not be the time to identify disciplinary coherence in any of the human sciences with an accumulation of "findings." Indeed, there may be no such time. In that case, it appears that one cannot simply dismiss totalistic or totalizing propositions as irrelevant to disciplinary coherence. Indeed, they may be, at least for the moment, indispensable. However, if they are indispensable, it is not clear whether that is because of practical exigencies or because of the nature of the object or our capacity to grasp it, not to mention what sort of intentionality does the grasping and, therefore, in what way and in regard to what history the object is grasped. This makes it difficult to say how we should conceive of disciplinary coherence, but it is just as difficult to avoid raising that question if the proposition that human beings are essentially social is either true or should be taken as true for all practical purposes.

Few would defend the claim that there is so radical a division between the level of totalistic or totalizing conception and the level of hypothesis, research, and finding that the first is either hopelessly irrelevant to the second or, at best, merely conjecture based solely on an accumulation of empirical findings but not justifiable by it. If either option is true, the *disciplinary* quality of projects, which should be an important factor in evaluating their contributions to knowledge, is inexplicable. It is tempting to conclude that the totalistic or totalizing propositions said to account for coherence as such are arbitrary (for example, received as a matter of tradition or authority) or uninterpretable. Since we cannot do without some notion of disciplinary coherence and since that seems to depend on just such propositions, at least in the disciplinary claims of the social sciences, it is likely that both the historicist and the anti-historicist would have to moderate their view in regard to the other. In that case, it is necessary to ask how this can be done and, if so, with what consequences.

There is an unfortunate aspect of moderation on each side. The moderate historicist can say that her research must always take account of the social dimension of what she studies, and do so in detail and without exception; it follows that she must also take account, in the very course of doing research, of the sociality of studying, which is also an instance of human affairs. This refusal to abstract the moments of observation and analysis, to take them out of their own histories, is an invitation to research without limits. In this respect, such a refusal is admirable, but it risks a regression for which there is no apparent relief, the only reward being a relativism that cannot be theorized and that equates and thereby neutralizes the truth value of all propositions. There is also a practical consequence of moderating the historicist thesis—namely, the risk of paralysis. The degree of self-reflection that it requires increases the likelihood of impatience and therefore the danger of capitulating to the anti-historicist thesis in frustration and by default. Whether or not these problems can be overcome, they are bound to recur as long as the social remains inchoate, is purely theoretical in the sense of withdrawn from ordinary discourse, or is treated exclusively as a matter of linguistic usage.[13]

Moderate proponents of the anti-historicist thesis are less preoccupied with the problems involved in begging the question of how the knower can be in or imagine herself in a sufficiently unmediated position to have the sort of positive knowledge that warrants absolute confidence—in the sense of confidence that looks forward and, at the same time, disavows hindsight. They must nevertheless admit that we cannot have the certainty we need even though, as they see it, we must be certain about something about the world. This need for certainty risks becoming dogmatic—for example, when the certainty is said to be vested in a community of likeminded thinkers, perhaps as a way out of what may appear otherwise to be a tragic contradiction of theory and practice. One possible consequence of even so circumscribed a dogmatism is a loss of confidence in the knowledge-constituting value of empirical research to the extent to which recourse is taken to what was originally rejected—namely, reliance on totalistic propositions and the uncritical comprehensive doctrines they inevitably invoke. This ironically reinstates the immoderate version of the anti-historicist thesis against a moderation that can defend itself only by denying its own history.

The point of view supported by this regressive immoderation only appears identical with anti-historicism, but it has been profoundly transformed by having no option but dogmatism. Moderation now appears, in retrospect, as intolerable, as a heresy. It is, however, easily overcome by assertiveness and community building, both of which beg the question of the relationship between studying society and being of society that led the historicist to moderate her position in the first place. Consequently, it is likely to leave the philosophical discussion of hypothesis and research in the hands of the least moderate proponents of historicism, in effect yielding to its original immoderate position where it most counts, as far as the positive idea of scientific knowledge is concerned, while rejecting it in principle. The moderate version of the second, anti-historicist, thesis becomes, in turn, an orthodox ontology at the expense of what the problematic of ontology cannot do without—namely, a theory of *how* what is can be known as *what* it is.

Given this distressing play of moderations, it may not be going too far to conclude that what is at stake in the difference between the two theses is how social science should be construed—as far as it is relevant to the human sciences taken as a whole and therefore to social science as an instance. For historicism, it appears to be a discipline that theorizes human affairs as immanently social, but in such a way as to make apparent the self-critical aspect of theory regardless of the risks in doing so. Whether this can be done and if so how it can be done, remain to be seen. For the anti-historicist, "social science" appears fundamentally to refer to a language designed to exclude certain statements rather than to a self-disciplining activity organized around the construction, gathering, or accumulation of knowledge appropriate to its sub-theoretical object. As such, it corresponds to the region of being or domain of possible reference I have been calling "human affairs." The nature of that correspondence is that the rules of the language establish what cannot be intelligibly said, or what cannot be proposed from the point of view of the referential function of that language. One of the rules of social science, understood as this sort of language, is that each proposition about human affairs must be consistent, or at least not inconsistent, with all other such propositions and with relatively few axioms about humans as social beings. This means that social science *defines* a field of reference rather than *finds* it. It is in that regard that such a discipline, constituted from the anti-historicist point of view, can be described as political.

What is significant about the *difference* between the two theses is, then, that it marks a more or less critical attitude toward theory, not that it pits two radically different philosophies of knowledge against one another or that it points to different consequences of having no choice but to act as if it is true that human beings are essentially social. Even so, the idea of criticism depends on what is meant by "social," just as it depends on whether some totalizing propositions are exempt from criticism or none are and on whether we can get back to the idea of theorizing. If some are exempt, and if the proposition that "human beings are essentially social" is an instance, there will always be a problem of how a theory can legitimately distinguish itself from what it studies when that implies that its object is essentially incapable of self-reflection and therefore unable to theorize (see Clastres 1977). If none are exempt, the problem is no less pressing, but it is now an internal one that must be addressed, as it were, from within. The two theses suggest that there are different ways to address the question "In what sense of 'social' are human beings essentially social?" But neither has much to offer beyond that, except in one respect. They disagree about whether sociality is a contingent or necessary and immanent feature of human affairs, and we have seen that the proponents of the first thesis have little choice but to act as if favoring the second, at least up to a point, and those who opt for the second seem to have little choice but to abandon claims to any sort of concrete knowledge.

9

Social Facts, Situations, and Moral Stakes

To say that human beings are essentially social is to say that they and their affairs cannot be understood on the model of a science of agency-independent reality. Otherwise, the human sciences appear as parodies of something they cannot be, because they lack an authentic object, or the object they claim to study can be justifiably known only by its reconstitution as an object of natural science, or they are "immature sciences." To the extent to which the truth of a proposition depends on the truth of other propositions, theory is crucial to the constitution of knowledge. It is necessary, then, to ask what is meant by "a theory of human affairs" when its object necessarily resists signification, and what "truth" can mean when applied to statements about such an object. Addressing these questions requires deciding on appropriate intellectual resources. I have argued that two lines of theorizing are most promising: Rousseau's version of the social contract and some combination of the Marxian critique of political economy and the post-structural critique of the theory of the sign. Both acknowledge the irreducibility of the social and the obligation of theory to find itself in its object and its object in itself.

One cost of ignoring or minimizing these two positions derives from the lack of other well-founded, nonreductive options for coming to terms with what is human about any and every instance of human affairs. This accounts, in part, for the implausibility of formal models that rely on reductive simplifications, such as those based on social facilitation, exchange, or concepts derived from face-to-face interaction. The difficulty of theorizing sociality cannot be explained as a matter of its relative complexity, since none of the standard simplifications are arrived at through analysis of the phenomenon as such. They most often depend on characterizations of individual actors projected onto situations in which other such actors are present—in a sense of "being present" that itself requires analysis. As a result, the models express something that is inconsistent with what is required if the fact that *more than one person is involved* is to be taken into account—as the type of "more" that is not simply a particular one plus a number of particular others (see Adorno 1976; Müller-Doohm 2005, 442).

Another sense of the social is involved when "society" is distinguished from statistical categories such as populations or from arbitrarily delimited entities such as civilizations or nations (Brown 2009). The latter allow the history of societies, "peoples," to be written as the realization of socially progressive movements beyond both mere aggregation and apparatuses of power—though this does not in itself implicate the idea of sociality. The point is that it is necessary to conceive of people among people as comprising something beyond a gathering, a deliberate congregation, and what can be said about individuals taken one by one. Even where the idea of a society might seem relatively clear, it is important to avoid expressing it in the familiar terms of a utilitarian conception of agency or in regard to ethnological historicizing accounts of "tradition," which most often end with a hypostasis of the "past" and an apotheosis of the observer. The first is the most common error because it draws on an established philosophy of action. The social is then represented as an instance of tendentiously rational "organization" that is justified at the level of goal- or value-oriented individuals taking account of others. Weber drew an obvious inference from this when, in his discussion of rationally instituted "imperative coordination," he referred to the "supreme head" and the "administrative staff" of a "corporate group" as comprising the representative voice of the whole, as if it were a body politic, without any evident process of *representing* as such beyond imperative coordination and without any evident structure of representation beyond a hierarchy whose highest point is, by definition, unaccountable or an unassailable limit on rationality. As a result, total administration is, in the end, subordinate to the "supreme head." Parenthetically, this, and not the "iron cage" is the negative image that most clearly emerges from Weber's account of rational organization (Weber 1947, 145–157, 330–333).[1]

When models are about received topics, they are limited by the discourses in which they are generalized in ways that defy disciplinary realization. This contradicts the claim that they constitute foundational paradigms for the accumulation, organization, and progress of knowledge of human affairs. To the extent to which their proponents acknowledge the need for disciplinary justification, it is likely to be assimilated to a concept of "the discipline" as "what its practitioners do." This is contrary to the critical sense of theory for which the activity of theorizing is an instance of its object. Therefore, it creates *in itself* an unacceptable exception to its claim to be a paradigm. Initially, the problem might seem to involve the status of the proposition "human beings are essentially social." In Chapter 8, I discuss two options, one in which the legitimacy of such a proposition requires strict surveillance and another in which certain general propositions, including that human beings are essentially social, are taken to be true beyond reasonable doubt. The first characterizes them as having heuristic value while the second considers them fundamental in the way in which metaphysics is said to be implicit in any conception of a reality. However, both permit treating the proposition that humans are essentially social as true whether or not it meets any standard of truth but that of intuition (e.g., "I know what I saw and heard!"). The anti-historicist considers it true as a matter of principle, while the historicist treats it as true insofar as one takes sociality as a starting point, subject to criticism only after the construction of a theory that locates its topic within a referential universe, often referred to as a frame of reference, and according to the interest that it informs.

The problem is that it is difficult to say when a theory is sufficiently complete to justify such a fundamental criticism, in other words to identify the point at which criticism finds itself as part of the activity of completing the theory and, therefore, operating as an immanent critique. This again raises a question about the relationship between theorizing and theory and about the legitimacy of the distinction between discovery and justification. The activity of theorizing involves engaging the tense lives of concepts. To the extent to which the product/theory denies that tension in the course of the refinement of each concept (and all taken together), it is thereby caught up in a logic of justification that, by its nature, suppresses its own conditions of possibility. At best, the result is a theoretical truth that cannot know its own history and therefore cannot teach; which is a truth that abides only among similar truths that, together, constitute a suppression of their joint history and therefore of what that history (e.g., of resolving ambiguities) might make possible for criticism and pedagogy. Yet the idea of a reasonably complete and consistent theory of the social seems necessary to address the questions one might have about the truth or falsity of the claim that "human beings are essentially social"—leaving open whether "true" and "false" can mean the same thing for the disciplines of the human sciences as they mean for the natural sciences.

The distinction between theorizing and theory, like that between what Marx called "concrete labor" and formally defined "abstract labor" (monetarized as a factor and a commodity) falls under a more general distinction between a course of activity and its negation *as a course*. The latter refers to the negation of *activity* and not of *something* that is active (e.g., a conversation, an exchange, or a series of task-driven acts). If the *distinction* between theorizing and theory is theoretical and not merely categorical (as between doing and succeeding or failing), then the proposition that humans are social must appeal to it, or at least to the greater distinction of which it is an instance. At any rate, there appears to be an impasse in the distinction that has to do with not only the "formal" quality of any theory but conditions of possible formality. The latter already belong to the universe of refined concepts and therefore to the logic of justification; they are not conditions of objectification, predication, and simplification in the face of ambiguity and ambivalence. As a result, the objectivity of what is justifiable is already settled, as if *reason* had finally overcome what the logic of justification can only see as the "genetic fallacy" of attributing the history of their being realized to the theoretically certified objects themselves.

This impasse suggests what human affairs must be if they are essentially social and if theorizing is an instance of what is human about them. The incompatibility of theorizing and theory, despite their necessary connection, lies in the fact that the former shares the qualities of momentum and reflexivity with all instances of sociality and, therefore, with every committed course of activity. Activity necessarily resists the particularity of definitive content precisely because it *is* and does not simply *have* a course. Sociality and theorizing are courses of activity, which implies that theorizing the social involves acknowledging the latter's aspect of theorizing and theorizing's aspect of sociality, regardless of the sort of content that theory presents in its own transmissible form and of its comparability with others of its kind. For now, it seems that it is not the status but the meaning of the original proposition that is at stake: in particular the meaning of "sociality" and the idea that it is essential to what it is to be human.

What is at stake philosophically is not just the meaning of "essential sociality" but also the moral principles associated with progressive imperatives—"society" (equality), community (mutuality), democracy (voice), law (justice), and human beings as ends rather than means—in contrast with what then appear as antiprogressive and effectively authoritarian values—civilization (spirit versus those without spirit), loyalty (pride and exclusiveness), order (power and indifference), utility (particular will against the general will), individualism (society as nothing more than a population), and a corresponding presumption against claims of need relative to quantifiable claims of merit. The mere suggestion that theory and justification depend on and are constituted in the course of theorizing reinforces the value of the progressive position. It implies that theory without self-criticism is paradoxical and that self-criticism begins as a confrontation with what resists the refinement of concepts. This is how theory learns from what it cannot know. This is to say that it is intrinsically superseded by theorizing, which is the activity that makes it conceivable. While I believe that there are such moral/political stakes in this discussion, more is necessary to demonstrate that the human sciences share an object about which knowledge is possible—though not the sort of knowledge identified with the natural sciences or based on particularistic concepts of action, agency, intention, person, and event. In the remainder of this chapter, I explore some further implications of the historicist and anti-historicist positions, and some of what is morally at stake in the discussion of sociality—specifically, in the idea of a "situation." This begins a consideration of the connection between the idea that humans are essentially social and the apparently more general idea that humans are situated beings.

———————

Despite the difficulties that moderate versions of historicism and anti-historicism have in maintaining a moderation they cannot help but turn to in the context of their mutual understanding, and in maintaining their sense of "theory," and despite the problems involved in rationalizing both in ways that clearly show their differences, there appears to be a compelling reason for continuing to insist on the terms of the debate and, therefore, on the possibility of choosing between the two sides. The consequences of deciding one way or the other may be significantly different in regard to important nontheoretical values. The choice appears morally significant when we focus on the differences: either the decision affirms an orientation to human affairs according to progressive principles or it consigns them to antiprogressive principles. The alternative is to say that each has heuristic value for approaching problems that have nothing explicitly to do with theory. Neither option provides a satisfactory reason to continue the debate and choose one side or the other—if we are concerned with the relationship between theory and theorizing and, therefore, with the question of knowledge as it pertains to the human sciences. An orientation satisfied merely by assertion lacks guidelines for dialogue, where the latter means a juxtaposition within a committed course of activity in which none of what is juxtaposed is neglected. Since dialogue, what Hampshire (2000) refers to as "negative thinking," is a necessary feature of theorizing, maintaining it should be one aim of each side of the debate if each wishes to justify its theory as a result of considering alternatives. Moreover, the idea of heuristic value is intelligible here only if the heuristics, guidelines and hints in contrast with rules and algorithms, fill gaps in decision making or provide reliable glosses of a rule-governed procedure.

So far, then, it is difficult to imagine any consequence of choosing one thesis over the other on the basis of anticipated nontheoretical consequences that do not undermine the theoretical enterprise. No matter how compelling nontheoretical reasons might be for accepting the terms of debate and choosing between its sides, the result will be detrimental to any attempt to clarify what is involved in establishing the conditions and character of knowledge of what is human about human affairs. In passing, though one cannot discount the positive effects of serendipity, they tend to reinforce theory at the expense of theorizing, with all that entails.

There is a different question that makes it difficult to evaluate the proposition that humans are essentially social. It has to do with the distinction between "social" as a criterial attribute of what it is to be human, which is the anti-historicist thesis, and "social" as a condition of what human beings do by way of being human, reflecting historicism. We have seen that there is a sense of each thesis in which their distinction is irrelevant, but it is significant when we try to conceive of the subject matter of the human sciences. Historicism presumes in favor of redirecting what are usually thought of as predicates of the decision aspect of action, such as rationality, intensity, and complexity, to something about agency that is social. *What is important is the suggestion that agency and its attributes are immanently social however persons are described.*

It should be remembered that adopting the historicist presumption limits the prospect of conceptualizing and then accounting for possible exceptions to the proposition that humans are essentially social. Yet the requirement of self-criticism that historicism places on theory suggests that exceptions are possible, that there are nonsocial activities that are also distinctively human. But acknowledging exceptions contradicts the force of historicism insofar as its thesis requires, for all practical purposes, a commitment to the claim that humans are essentially social. Its self-critical aspect does not have to do with imagining something nonsocial about humans, but with recognizing that it might be possible to imagine it, so that the question of the validity of the proposition remains open. This is so even though the defense of the thesis precludes theoretical adjustments to account for what appears to be nonsocial. It says that what appears to be an exception is probably not since if it is, no general theory is possible and there is nothing essentially human about human affairs. In that case, historicism appears incoherent since all the theories it projects are disqualified by a possibility that its reservations about the truth of the claim that humans are essentially social seem to commit it to recognize.

Admitting the possibility of an exception would be fatal to historicism, and not merely to specific theories under its warrant, since continuing to act on the basis of the premise in light of its own disposition to self-criticism effectively places it on the side of the anti-historicist thesis. This terminates the debate and the condition of the intelligibility of historicism—namely, that it justify itself *in contrast with* anti-historicism, and this is possible only if the debate is sustained. It seems better, then, to focus less on the meaning of the proposition than on its logical status if we are to appreciate the significance of the difference between the positions. I have claimed that this has to do with whether "social" applies to humans taken one by one or to human affairs as such. If it applies to the former, then even the anticipation of an exception is fatal in that one cannot be confident about whether something identified as human is or is not social. If it applies to the latter, then the existence of exceptions is largely irrelevant—though one upshot is that human affairs might include or even be entirely composed of activities of nonhumans. To think about humans and their affairs as social is to extend that thought to everything connected to human life. The alternative, to act as if exceptions exist, is not available to the proponents of either thesis to the extent to which each is intended to theorize human affairs in terms of what is human about them. It is available only if we assume that human activities can be reliably distinguished by whether they are social. I reject the assumption because, in addition to reasons given previously, tied to the ideas of "human" and "social," it seems impossible to show that applications of the distinction are not arbitrary and, therefore, that it is valid for all practical purposes.

———

There is a logical problem in rejecting the possibility of nonsocial instances of human affairs. For the historicist, rejection is necessary to the progress of research. For the anti-historicist, it is part of what it is to recognize the truth of the a priori proposition that all human beings are social: sociality is not a contingent property of humans or what they do. This means that predicates, like "rational," apply directly only to social facts and do not apply directly to persons and acts, given that such predicates have to do with people living together and not with individuals taking account of specific others and their conduct. Asserting that human beings are essentially social adds nothing to the definition of "human." There is nothing else they could be since there is nothing else they can do but act in concert; and nothing else can act and be in this sense. Both positions agree on this, though their agreement takes them in different directions, the historicist toward a progressive view of society and the anti-historicist toward the more obvious instances of sociality, such as authority, tradition, culture, and vigilance against mistaking something nonhuman for human. The historicist moves to include while the anti-historicist is unable to do so.

If we want to preserve something of individuality in order to distinguish differences in degrees of rationality, we would have to disentangle specific intentions and attribute each to someone as a portion or momentarily particular realization of the intentionality that operates across bodies and, therefore, persons. The idea that humans are essentially social does not preclude imagining an entity that operates according to utilitarian principles or beliefs and desires. It is simply that this would not be about human affairs or what is human about human activity unless it takes account of the ongoing social aspect of beliefs, desires, and utilitarian principles. Otherwise, it is about something already reduced to something else. Simulating such an entity, itself a reductive representation that is then re-presented in a further reduction, may be the aim of a theory; but it requires prematurely taking leave of the activity of theorizing, which is a problem faced by both the historicists and the anti-historicists. There is a further irony: that creating an image (of agency) of what is already an image involves stipulating that what the latter is an image of is, in fact, human and assuming that this actuality can be represented by something radically different from it. The simulation, which *re-presents* a representation is conveniently understood as providing criteria by which the "real" entity's behavior should be evaluated and treated.

The problem posed by simulations of this sort is logical and not simply pragmatic or methodological. An entity taken as a human being may be subjected to conditions that determine a certain motion, or be prepared to move and make gestures and utterances that are in no sense social—that is, indifferent to the possibility of its being restored to the company of consociate humans, as if in a state of nature.[2] Such a restoration would be one test of the representative quality of the simulation; but it relies on certain presuppositions, the most important of which is that the other humans must also have been prepared to accept the validity of the simulation and therefore not to be curious about how the restored being might behave, in the sense of what it might do next.

Otherwise, they would not be able to connect the simulation to what they take as real and no restoration would have occurred. The conclusion seems inescapable that a simulation is intelligible when it is conceived of by competent parties as belonging to a universe comprising nothing but simulations of simulations (plus a different sort of entity that initiates simulation—e.g., a god or a scientist). If so, it is clear that simulationist models of decision and choice can only satisfy Strawson's claim that humans are essentially social and social through and through if the universe they refer to excludes humans from whatever it allows as sociality or if what is social about human affairs is unimportant.[3]

We have seen that historicism is committed to the idea that the original proposition is incorrigible as a practical matter and out of due respect to its subject matter. It follows that the historicist is also committed to acting as if it is true—with the weak extra-theoretical provision that the possibility of criticism must be invoked somehow and at some point beyond the historicist's theoretical activity.[4] The nature of the commitment, its immanence to theorizing, implies that the possibility of criticism arises only *after* the commitment is through, and that it, the possibility, cannot be acknowledged in or incorporated into the course of fulfilling the commitment. It is important to remember that the commitment does not envision its own end and thus can posit nothing about its own course that can be evaluated as a fulfillment of an originating intention.

Historicism and its antithesis may support the same sort of theory, though they differ in their understanding of the relationship between theory and theorizing. Yet the point at which criticism of a given theory is appropriate is difficult to determine. Historicism requires such a determination and therefore such a "point," but it remains an empty prospect: whatever comes to stand for "criticism" represents a mere possibility, which, if realized as an event, would be inconsistent with the basic proposition that humans are essentially social. This is why what stands for "criticism" generally has had such little impact on the debate: it always seems premature and questionable in principle. I conclude with what appears to be a paradox and therefore requires reconsidering the meaning of the terms "social" and "essentially." The historicist's thesis cannot be stated without the possibility of an exception to the social *and* it cannot, any more than its antithesis, abide such an exception. This suggests that historicism must be rejected, but not in favor of anti-historicism. This conclusion is, however, not satisfactory. There remains a sense that something of extra-theoretical, perhaps moral, urgency hangs in the balance—whether or not the terms of the debate are clear, whether or not one or the other side flounders on the question of the possibility of exceptions, and whether or not the distinctions discussed so far are significant ones. For example, Rawlsian approaches to justice often appeal to the idea that sociality (in the sense of an *active* orientation to all) is something achieved and not immanent, and that it is achieved by a universalizing act of identification (the original position as Rawls's weak early gesture toward

Rousseau)—with the compelling but controversial suggestion that distributive justice is necessary to the form and durability of anything that can properly be called a society.

This is more than simply compatible with the historicist position. It presupposes that "society" signifies an activity in which participants are bound to return to the question of conditions, which is to say that it is at least minimally rational and that the meaning of "rationality" depends on those conditions. To the extent to which there is a momentary obligation to attend to principles of distribution on which all reasonable parties should be expected to agree, we can say that those parties are expressing an interest in a type of equality— namely, equal vulnerability—that is possible only in society, where the latter is conceived of as a self-regulating law-governed entity made up of more than one moral type (see Rawls 1999a). But the idea of the original position, and the reasonableness that it enables, has something in common with the idea that activity transpires across bodies and their persons—since reason operates precisely in that way, which is to say that *it is irrelevant to our understanding of reason whether or not agency is invested in individuals.*

There is more to this than a gesture toward Rousseau, though Rawls apparently does not consider the conditions of conceiving of society per se to be problematic and seems to believe that a state-structural description is sufficient (Rawls 1996; 1999a, 31). For Rawls, the importance of justice goes beyond the legitimacy of administrative policies; and if the attainment of the "original position" (in which the particularity of particular wills is momentarily suspended in the interest of reasoning together, though Rawls writes as if reasoning is, ideally, done alone) is conceivable it can only be because, and here one must depart from Rawls, it need not and probably cannot be understood as undertaken voluntarily. In what, then, does its necessity lie? *Rousseau's answer is that it lies in the very fact that participation in a system of law (authority) in contrast with subjugation (power) is possible only if members cannot avoid reflecting on their dependence on all others for their rights, protection, and their very being as social creatures and all else that is entailed by that "basic fact."* Admittedly, it seems unlikely that enough members will reflect on this at the same time to reconstitute, to bring to notice, the active aspect of the general will. But to the extent to which laws operate effectively, though differently, in what we refer to as "society" and "everyday life," one can reasonably expect such reflection to occur regularly (though imperfectly) for everyone in the course of their everyday lives whether or not it is enunciated or otherwise immediately notable from a position external to that course.

This appears to be so for individual members experiencing (and being able to recall) moments of choice and benefit and displaying the sort of modest gratitude and acknowledgment that can be addressed only to indefinite others (or "someones"). It is because its referent is the body politic that gratitude is easily generalized beyond the gifts, affections, and mercies of particular others. It feels true to its object and is, in that regard, both reasonable and rational;

yet gratitude knows no bounds, no definite limits. Durkheim's discussion of the moral basis of law can be read as interpreting the recurrence of such moments as basic to a distinctively modern type of "solidarity," what he refers to as "organic solidarity"—and here one must again appeal to Rousseau since Durkheim did not systematically address the issues posed by the "basic fact" (see Durkheim 1964, preface). It depends on the impossibility of any reasoning individual, no matter how uncontrolled her particular will and no matter how anomic her situation, imagining her life apart from others in general and therefore outside of society. It is not just the concept of democracy that is at stake in the debate, but the notion of equality, of the dependence of each on all, which is foundational to any concept of justice that is not divorced from social considerations and that is therefore consistent with the imperative that humans should be treated as ends and not means.

Whatever difficulties historicism has with the consistency of its thesis, it at least pays lip service to the ideas that theory must be true to itself as an instance of its own object and that it can be true in this way only by being self-critical. Otherwise, it is inconsistent with the idea that humans are essentially social. For a theory acceptable to the historicist to be true, sociality needs to be understood as self-critical in its very course, and not as something done, say on impulse or by virtue of a decision, by individuals taken one by one. We have seen that neither thesis clearly provides for that possibility. Historicism at least insists on it but at the cost of undermining itself. But we might still wonder why it is necessary to decide whether being "social" is contingent or necessary since the moderate positions come close to agreeing that whether or not "sociality" is essential, we should proceed as if it is. Again, there are significant moral stakes that need to be revisited.

One has to do with the consistency of any portrayal of human affairs with the self-reflexivity of universal respect, including the imperative to characterize and treat human beings as ends. In this regard, the historicist's thesis may be superior, if only because of its compatibility with the idea of the moral equality of humans based on the immanence of sociality to human affairs. Hampshire's (2000) theory of justice draws its strength from the concession that this equality is far from transparent because people live and grow up under diverse conditions and are susceptible in any case to the particularizing effects of every exercise of will. Because will takes form and has its orientation, always momentarily, under fluid circumstances that are neither certain nor the same, expressions of equality are bound to vary, which is how deference, or reciprocity, unavoidable in any case, becomes morally significant. Hampshire's theory implies that it is evident in all courses of activity, even if only as a need to hear other voices in order to have one's own. Hearing what is said requires listening, which is an activity predicated on a prior activity. Otherwise, it is voluntary and recognition of the other as "someone" is merely contingent, suggesting the possibility of a hearing that has no need to listen. Such an activity is unthinkable—except as the disposition of a machine or the behavior of a creature in a state of nature altogether separate from society. The prior condition must be immanent to every course of human activity. Studies of conversational speech invariably describe discourse such that deference is an intrinsic feature displayed, for example, in gestures, postural adjustments, and the poetics or musicality of speaking (including momentum, emphasis, hesitation, rhythm, and the like)—namely, as what I call an "attitude of waiting" that acknowledges in itself the presence of an indivisible "someone" in every course of activity and in its every moment.

While moral considerations may be important in choosing one position over the other, neither historicism nor anti-historicism helps us understand in what way humans are social or decide whether sociality is immanent and constitutive, or merely contingent, whether constitutive or not, since both are committed to acting as if the basic fact is true regardless of how we answer such questions. Choosing one position over the other may be irrelevant to what is most important: to avoid sacrificing an indispensable idea to a suspicion that we have no good reasons to trust—namely, that there might be nonsocial exceptions inconsistent with the proposition that human affairs are *essentially* social. Even though the commitment to theories compatible with the basic fact is moral, the injunction is, in its application to science, universal. It is intended, at the least, to protect the theoretical enterprise, of which the social is both the beginning and the ultimate referent, from contamination by extra-theoretical considerations, in this case by separating what pertains to "morality" from the "morally indifferent" development and evaluation of alternative theories according to their compatibility with the basic fact. However, it does this only for theories warranted by either the humanist or anti-humanist point of view as described; one cannot presume that the injunction has no substantive effects on theories that fall outside of both. That is, it attributes moral virtue to the adoption of an exclusionary rule that effectively determines what counts as theory: what it excludes, then, it excludes by definition, and defining terms and establishing their value within a field of reference are normally taken to be theoretical issues. It will turn out that virtually any serious attempt to clarify what it is to be social is likely to run up against the exclusionary rule, especially where the social is thought of as other than a predicate, a state of affairs, interpersonal interaction, communicative action, or a type of agency analogous to a system of action, rational or not.

Since every refined theory is a recommendation, whatever else it is or does, more must be involved if our choice between humanism and anti-humanism is to be reasonable as well as rational. Perhaps we should not neglect the possible nontheoretical consequences of our intellectual choices and the theoretical consequences of our moral choices. Kitcher (2001) is one among a number of philosophers, writing from the point of view of governing a relatively democratic society, who have reluctantly conceded that it is occasionally necessary to consider possible negative consequences of scientific work as reasons to restrict or otherwise regulate it. At any rate, our sense of the original proposition,

including its theoretical relevance, must depend to some extent on various
loose criteria, including how any given theory stands with certain basic principles designed to make what we do in general, including how we interpret human affairs, morally tendentious without being moralistic. Yet worrying about
nontheoretical consequences in this way suggests that there might be a theory
of human affairs adequate to its subject matter even though it recommends
policies that violate what is morally implicit in acknowledging our essential sociality and its immanence to human affairs. The key question here is whether
it is possible for a theory incompatible with the basic fact to be intelligible, or
whether whatever it might be intelligible about cannot be an instance of human
affairs.

The thesis that the idea of the essential sociality of human beings is necessarily beyond criticism risks reinforcing teleological notions of "development," self-serving justifications of war as "bringing civilization to those who
lack it," an emphasis on discipline as a purging of the asocial tendencies of the
immature in favor of the social tendencies of the mature, and a confusion of social life *as things stand* with a stage in the progressive approximation of an ideal
sociality that can be taught and for which concrete exemplars exist. From this
point of view, "essentiality" means "of the nature of the abstract kind or type,"
whereas, for the historicist, it means "what must be said as things stand"—
subject to the possibility of a critique of where things stand. The anti-historicist
thesis is not obviously compatible with the ideas that human beings are moral
equals and that the categorical imperative should prevail both in our understanding of "others" and in what we choose to do or not to do. In the alternative, it may be compatible with the categorical imperative if it can claim that
ends are not of equal moral value. In that case, people may be ends, but that
does not imply that they are morally equal.

The problem is that there is no position from which such a judgment can
reasonably be made. Either the judgment is arbitrary and therefore indefensible
or the judge is left in the unenviable position of having to decide, presumably
on moral grounds, whether it is better to risk the possibility that assigning a
value status is not deserved by the assignee or to risk refusing to distinguish
people on the basis of moral worth when some are actually inferior to others.
There can be no nonmorally rational basis for such a decision. Therefore, the
question of preferable risk assumes that anyone is entitled to decide and therefore that all are, at least in that respect, morally equal. It follows that there can
be no moral justification for attempting to decide in which case one's obligation is to accept the risk of overvaluation regardless of possible disappointment
since this is uniquely consistent with seeing the other as an end or value rather
than a means or thing.

Rejecting the anti-historicist thesis on humanist grounds does not, however, entail accepting historicism. But it does make the latter more attractive.

What reinforces its attractiveness is the exception entailed by absolutism, the exemption of the judge from the condition of the judged. The historicist is able to maintain a critical attitude by avoiding this contradiction as a matter of principle; and it is in this regard that historicism finds its best defense. The interpretive practices of the human sciences unfortunately often assume that whatever is done that has to do with "people living among people" is contingent and circumstantial. Interpretations ultimately display how things stand relative to a specific problem or issue under consideration. In that sense, they can be held to the vague but meaningful standard that they should be the best we can do. Unfortunately, in regard to the idea of sociality, which is a necessary ingredient in deciding that we are doing our "best," we are left with practices, moral considerations, and a language that presuppose a sub-theoretical notion that remains to be clarified. What is important for present purposes is that the internal relation of "human" and "social" is taken to correspond to an internal relation of their concepts, *and at least one term of that relation is unclear.* As a result, and given the division among the human sciences based on the way they view sociality, the proposition that humans are essentially social has not been as useful in rationalizing their joint interest in human affairs as one might have expected. Despite differences in topics, methods, and, to some extent, language, I have argued that they express that interest by indicating what it takes for granted, which is that the human is a "being in a situation" and that being in a situation is to be caught up in a course of activity irreducible to individuals taken one by one. It has occasionally been suggested, in contrast with the standard views of human affairs that Goffman refers to as "individualistic modes of thought," that it "might be better to start from outside the individual and work inward than to start from inside the individual and work out" (1959, 81n). The caveat "might be better" suggests that the injunction is intended to apply only when individuals are intricately caught up in situations that are clearly social. It seems, then, to do no more than restate one's obligation to the facts. In that case, the injunction does not adequately reflect the theoretical significance of the idea that human beings are essentially social. Rather, it trivializes it: even if one agrees that it is "better to start from the outside," one might eventually need to refer to properties of and processes identified with individual intentionality to understand how individuals are caught up in their social situations.

However, I do not believe that Goffman's work on "total institutions," the "culture of the situation," the inevitable predicaments imposed on groups by the intrinsic politicality of a dispositional language, and the range of human affairs to which he so perspicaciously directed his critically ethnological imagination can be read as if he intended to adopt the expedient view of methodological individualism. That would beg the ontological question crucial to our being able to think not only of the objective domain of the social sciences but of the human sciences as an overarching field of study. Rather, I see his work as attempting to clarify and illustrate virtually axiomatic propositions. First, characterizing humans as social entails a situation that transcends individuality and cannot be reduced to what otherwise can be said about the situated individuals. Second, this is not merely the exception to the principle of agency that methodological individualism requires. For Goffman, the idea of a transcendent situation is a logical condition of considering what is human about human affairs. It is true that he makes room for a self that embodies resistance. But this is always characterized, without any recourse to psychology, as internal to the processes of objectification, typification, and control (1961b, 1963). He conceives of resistance as eventful within the course of communication and as inevitable rather than an expression of a resistant disposition. It follows that his notion of the resistant self can be understood only from the point of view of a situation and what the latter constitutes as a field of resistance.

There is considerable research in psychology, social psychology, history, and sociology that presupposes the transcendental aspect of situations. But it is not often acknowledged that this has to do with the essential sociality of humans or that it implies that the social is an irreducible fact. This diminishes the significance of concrete analyses to the overall projects to which they ultimately must appeal (e.g., the analysis of "action" such that it bears on our understanding of the conduct of ordinary affairs no less than on scientific practice). Rather, this transcendental aspect appears rhetorically, as a matter of emphasis, where the description of an ostensibly particular and definite situation is paired with a conception of the individual person ("in" that situation) as a creature that "cognitively maps" environments and responds or reacts fundamentally according to a principle of least effort—as far as that is possible under conditions of what Herbert Simon (1990) famously, and ambiguously, called "bounded rationality." In that case, it appears that the individual is variously disposed but only in ways that can be typified, and that he or she thinks and acts such that those typical dispositions are realized in types of action that are logically compatible with what is mapped objectively about the situation.[5]

The failure to address what is implicit in the idea of a transcendental situation is evident in how the various disciplines address the question of what is distinctively human about human affairs. Descriptions of action under specific circumstances, no matter how rich, typically fail to provide for the immanence of sociality. This leaves theory with a host of problems caused by the default position that says that social facts are external to what people do, and that therefore actions (and intentionality itself) are ultimately to be understood in psychological terms. Thus, we cannot be certain that a particular behavior is exemplarily social and therefore not a proper object of psychological explanation. It is nevertheless necessary to say that whatever is involved in something being social must, at the same time, be reflexive to sociality. So when we refer to social behavior or social action, we are invoking a more general notion, though it is one about which we remain confused.

It is one thing to entertain the idea, common to symbolic interactionists and functionalists, that when someone communicates with someone else, she simultaneously hears what she is saying as if it is the other who is initiating the act of communication and who is, in a sense, the author of their discourse. It is another thing to recognize that this is theoretically intelligible only if the idea of communication is consistent with the basic idea of the social, and it is the common failure to consider the meaning of the social that is the crux of the problem. Otherwise, we are likely to seek individualistic accounts of what Parsons seems to have thought of, somewhat mysteriously and with an apparent gesture toward Alfred North Whitehead, as the "interpenetration" of communicative actions—as when communication is described as mutual interpretation conceived of as a series of discrete exchanges oriented to the possibility of a meeting of minds. It takes only a moment to see that such solutions are inadequate to the problem posed by the need to acknowledge the essential sociality of communication and the essentially social character of communicative agency.

The best we can do when we fail to acknowledge the radical nature of the problem posed by the sub-theoretical notion of sociality is to add a modifying clause to the proposition that, "in speaking, or gesturing toward another, one speaks for oneself." However, this is "best" only when carried out to the next degree. The proposition then becomes more elaborate: "in speaking or gesturing toward another, one speaks for oneself *as for that other* and, therefore, *as if that other is in fact the speaking self.*" In saying that one speaks for oneself, it is presumably for a self that is not, at the moment of the speaking, distinguishable from the other: therefore, "someone is speaking" is a more accurate description of the activity than "John is speaking." It follows that when an ostensible communicative gesture appears, as if issued from a distinct body, its meaning is at that very moment estranged from the one who emitted the words or made the physical movements, the intentionality of that body. That estrangement is not problematic as far as the continuity of communicating is concerned. Even when we agree that human beings are essentially social but describe what they do conventionally—that is, based on individualistic premises (as in "one speaks for oneself")—we are led to a conclusion that seems to contradict those premises: the "knowing" of what a social being is doing (which is itself social) involves an extrusion of the meaning of what is being done from within a self-socializing course of activity.[6] In that case, "knowing" can be understood only from the point of view of participating in (being "of") an ongoing activity (that we might want to call "knowing"), and it cannot mean the individuated mental state of "having beliefs" that are standardly said to constitute knowledge.

When we move from the artificial case of two persons speaking in turn, monologically, to speaking occurring among people, we find that boundaries are uncertain, time is of the essence, and contexts are fluid. I consider this a minimal description of the "typical speech situation," in contrast with Searle's description of speech as "involving a speaker, a hearer, and an utterance by the speaker" (1971, 39). If I am correct, it is even clearer that the notion of the social cannot be predicated either on the idea of interpersonal interaction or the idea of rule-governed practices, including models consistent with Davidson's concept of "triangulation" (2001a) and those that expand on Rawls's early definition of "practice" as a "structure" ordered by a "system of rules" (1999b, 20n).[7] Another way of saying this is that speaking, like everything typically referred to as "action," is reflexive to sociality, and, as discussed previously, this cannot be summarized as taking account of others and their conduct. Whatever persons do as human beings presents itself immediately as intrinsically social beyond whatever their interactions or cooperation with concrete and familiar others might reveal. If so, then the intentionality of actions considered under their distinctively social aspect, including speaking, refers to two related propositions: first, *that what is being done beyond mere bodily movement is social before its content is clarified and before its intentionality is attributed or ascribed to anyone or anything in particular*; second, *the sense in which actors are said to be acting, including speaking, entails that they do what they are doing in "an attitude of waiting."* That is, the intentionality of the deed has to do with the transcendental aspect of its momentary situation such that it assumes its form and has its content as a feature of the situation before it can be said to express something about its agency or its origin as, perhaps, a distinct utterance.

The moment we consider what is being done according to the idea of the transcendental aspect of its situation, we are effectively acknowledging that human beings are social in a way that disqualifies even the most compelling and detailed individualized depictions of what they do. Nevertheless, we may still be tempted to rely on such depictions in, for example, how we assign responsibility, how we evaluate others, and how we interpret research. This is a problem only if we fail to recognize the issues these depictions raise and to acknowledge that those can be put into perspective, and perhaps resolved, only to the extent to which we consider what "situation," "social," and "individual" must mean if statements about what is occurring among humans (speaking, doing, etc.) are to be compatible with what is human about human affairs. So far, we have been exploring some of the ramifications of the idea that the social is "the basic fact," and that it is not possible to imagine being human outside of society, though the idea of it remains unclear; and we have considered some of the difficulties that are bound to arise when the significance of sociality is ignored, and have, accordingly, considered some of what is entailed by even a minimal sense of it.

The lack of clarity exists even among those who agree that social facts are different in important respects from other facts. However, this distinction, which also lacks clarity since the first term is vague, makes it possible to imagine that humans, and what they do, are sometimes *of* and sometimes merely *in* society. This is, as we have seen, unacceptable. Yet it is implicit in the distinction between social and nonsocial facts when both are considered as logically identical in accounting for human activity (e.g., both social and nonsocial facts are "coercive" in Durkheim's sense). We must assume the social nature of humans even when situations appear to de-socialize them. But we cannot simply dispense with the distinction between social and nonsocial facts even though it appears inconsistent with the claim that humans are essentially and irreducibly social. The latter must come to terms with the fact that it seems difficult to avoid relying on the distinction. Yet challenging it involves a critique of both terms that is more likely to undermine the significance of the idea of a "social fact" than the idea of a "fact." The problem may lie in what we mean by "fact" when "social" is its predicate; or it may lie in how we understand the distinction, which may depend less on what we mean by "social" than on what can be said to be a "fact" from within the perspective of sociality. I later consider the possibility that objects that appear to confront individual subjects are not the same as objects whose subjects are essentially social, therefore that the situations in which those subjects exist are not themselves objective in the ways they are often said to be. For now, we can focus on the idea of the social in order to consider the assumption that there are distinctively nonsocial facts relevant to persons as agents to be problematic rather than obviously true. This requires some discussion of the disciplines that explicitly take the social as their subject matter, or object, especially sociology.

II
Social Action

Insofar as the social sciences purport to provide useful knowledge, as opposed to emotionally satisfying intelligibility or practically sterile understanding, these disciplines must uncover the causal mechanisms of human behavior. . . . [But] if every species is an individual spatiotemporally restricted scattered object, then the term *Homo sapiens* can no more find its way into nomological generalizations than the term "Mona Lisa." For laws have a kind of generality lacked by statements about particular objects; they cannot *refer* to particular objects, places or times if they are to retain their explanatory power. And so there can be no laws about *Homo sapiens* or any laws about properties distinctive of *Homo sapiens*. But this means we can expect no laws about actions, beliefs, desires, or any of their cognates; preference, expectation, fear, anxiety, hope, want, dislike, or any other intentional term. For all such terms are conceptually tied to the notion of *Homo sapiens*. . . . Here at last we have an explanation of why the social sciences have failed to find improvable generalizations. . . . Their error has been to believe that the natural kinds which describe human behavior, and its causes, are *intentional*. . . . If the intentional vocabulary in which we have hitherto described human behavior and its determinants is the wrong one, for any attempt to uncover improvable generalizations in the social sciences, what is the correct one?

—ALEXANDER ROSENBERG, "Human Science and Biological Science"

Feuerbach resolves the religious essence into the human essence. But the human essence is no abstraction inherent in each single individual. In its reality it is the ensemble of the social relations.

Feuerbach, who does not enter upon a criticism of this real essence, is consequently compelled:

(1) To abstract from the historical process and to fix the religious sentiment as something by itself and to presuppose an abstract—*isolated*—human individual.

(2) The human essence, therefore, can with him be comprehended only as "genus," as an internal, dumb generality which merely *naturally* unites the many individuals. . . .

Feuerbach, consequently, does not see that the "religious sentiment" is itself a social product, and that the abstract individual whom he analyses belongs in reality to a particular form of society. . . .

The highest point attained by contemplative materialism, that is, materialism which does not comprehend sensuousness as practical activity, is the contemplation of single individuals in civil society. . . .

The standpoint of the old materialism is "civil" society; the standpoint of the new is *human* society, or socialized humanity.

—KARL MARX, "Theses on Feuerbach"

A cabinetmaker's apprentice, someone who is learning to build cabinets and the like, will serve as an example. His learning is not mere practice, to gain facility in the use of tools. Nor does he merely gather knowledge about the customary forms of the things he is to build. If he is to become a true cabinetmaker, he makes himself answer and respond above all to the different kinds of wood and to the shapes slumbering within the wood—to wood as it enters into man's dwelling with all the hidden riches of its nature. In fact, this relatedness to wood is what maintains the whole craft. Without that relatedness, the craft will never be anything but empty busywork, any occupation with it will be determined exclusively by business concerns. Every handicraft, all human dealings are constantly in that danger. The writing of poetry is no more exempt from it than is thinking.

—MARTIN HEIDEGGER, *What Is Called Thinking?*

O body swayed to music, O brightening glance,
How can we know the dancer from the dance?

—WILLIAM BUTLER YEATS, "Among School Children"

Never before have the conceptual boundaries of humanity been less secure.

—JAMES J. SHEEHAN, "Coda"

10

Can "the Social" Be a Proper Object of Theory?

It is often taken as axiomatic that human beings are essentially social, where "social" refers to more than the fact that people, like many nonhuman creatures, are never wholly apart from others of their kind. Despite this, the proposition has, with few exceptions, served as a resource for but not been directly submitted to theoretical inquiry.[1] There may be good reasons for this, whether it stems from a philosophical principle, simple indifference, or momentary neglect. At best, it appears difficult to identify the social, as we must, apart from aggregation, institutional patterns, congregation, familiarity, interpersonal relations, overlapping intentions, rules of social reference, individuals taking account of the conduct of others, systems of social facts, and exchange. Consequently, it may be enough to grant that humans are social and to continue from that point; as indicated previously, this seems to have been Strawson's (1992) strategy. I try to show that the reasons for ignoring the theoretical issue justify the converse. One reason is that referring to and describing sociality typically rely on two distinctions so fundamental that questioning their validity would make it virtually impossible to rely on the idea as a resource. The first is between active subjectivity ("ego") and its other ("alter"). The second distinguishes human beings (agents) from things (agency-independent objects). Taken together, they differentiate what is social from what might mistakenly appear to be social and from the indicative meaning inferred from ordinary linguistic practice. A successful challenge to the validity of both distinctions leads in different directions from what can be imagined within their limits.[2]

The first distinction is between particular subjects understood as agents and the concrete others with whom they are associated as a matter of practice, and whom they presumably take into account. It is realized in depictions of one person doing something in the presence of another as an external relation between a projective subjectivity and a reactive body. An "external relation" is one in which the terms remain as they were prior to their connection and are invariant throughout its course (see Wollheim 1960, 92–128). The distinction presupposes, on the one hand, that the actor and her other "share meanings" so that the actor's intention can be known by both her other and an observer from what she says or does (Weber 1947, 88–115); that is, an act must be understandable to the relevant others if it is to succeed in that part of its intention that anticipates consequences. Therefore, it is described as undertaken in anticipation of reactions of another that test whether it represents the actor's intention. This means that an act is public *before* it is completed by the other's reaction. On the other hand, it is clear that no act in which others have to be taken into account can be sufficiently intelligible as to its initiating intention. Therefore, the test can never be complete. In other words, the idea of "shared meaning" is utopian as long as "taking others into account" defines "social action." Since the conditions of an action being intelligible as an expression of someone's intention that can be shared (and therefore realized by what another does) will vary from moment to moment, we can say that to act is to undertake a certain *labor* that constitutes the meaning of the act within the course of activity necessary to its completion. The outcome cannot be anticipated sufficiently to bring the problem of meaning posed by the act to a solution in a meeting of minds (real or stipulated by an observer).

Part of what is presumably intended by every act, whether goal-oriented, expressive, or imitative, is that someone else will react. In this respect, it appears to support a theory of action that relies on an equalizing notion of "intersubjectivity," thought of as an interaction of agents. However, the reaction of a designated other is not conceived of as an instance of agency in the same sense of "agency" ascribed to the designated actor. To refer to something as an act is to assume it expresses the intention of a particular agent for which everything else is either a condition or an effect. To refer to something as a reaction, actual or anticipated, is to take it as dependent and conjectural, though not as inert or merely passive. A reaction is conjectural insofar as it is taken as an occasion for the continuation of the agency of the original actor beyond the particularity of the undertaking, presumably until there is no longer a question of "meaning": of course, this cannot be interpreted as a settling of the question, and, in any case, it is not yet clear how agency can continue (as more than a mere capacity) beyond the act, and in what way it remains vested in the designated actor.

———

The perspective assumed by this account of the relations of actor, intention, action, agency, meaning, and other is the prospect of realizing an originating intention in an act that persists beyond the moment of the undertaking, in other words the prospect of realizing agency. To the extent to which "agency" is ascribed to the other, however, it refers to a sequence of reactive gestures the completion of which is mediated throughout by the actor according to her recognition of an intention in the other's gesture consistent with her own original intention. This other is stipulated to be tendentiously rational, but this can only be the derived rationality of one whose tendency is to represent an originary subjectivity that is incomplete from the start and therefore impossible to duplicate. The other represented as an instance of agency is such only in the legal sense of an intermediary that either executes or attempts to realize an intention not its own and does so under the uncertainty of an incomplete origin of which the incompleteness of the signifier is merely a symptom. As such, the other appears inflexible in its purpose and hyperrational in its attempt to complete (and duplicate) an intention it has already conceded to be rational despite the fact that it must have been incomplete and, as such, impossible to duplicate. In contrast, an active subject, the designated actor, anticipates the reaction of her others and, consequently, conforms to a more general, flexible, and self-respecting model of rational action. What makes this plausible is that both subjects and their others are recognizably human despite the sense of a "subject" as something active on its own behalf and "the other to such a subject" as, correspondingly, a mere reflection of agency. This means that the presence of another cannot be analogous to the presence of a mere thing, and that this registers itself in such a way that the relation of the designated agent to its putatively representative other frames and thereby limits the scope and generalizing operations of the former's definitive consciousness.[3]

But the recognition of the other as definitely not a thing is insufficiently egalitarian for an idea of sociality consistent with the idea that humans are essentially social. *To grant a degree of independence to what is conceived of as a reactive other within a relation of mutual dependence (and therefore even a modicum of agency) seems inconsistent with the theory of social action as a taking of others into account.* The theory requires nothing more than a one-sided connection of an actor to a re-actor, while the sort of relation that satisfies the requirements of sociality seems to be a "relation with" in contrast with a "relationship to." It is for that reason occasionally referred to as inter-subjective or interpersonal, though we will see that these expressions are disturbingly ambiguous and intended to defer more significant philosophical questions about the nature of sociality.[4] The ambiguity appears to be reduced by replacing inter-subjectivity with inter-dependence, and, consequently, internal with external relations. This has the virtue of emphasizing motivation and behavior over the attribution of a social essence to each separable individual. But it fails to account for the transformation of desire into participation, misunderstanding the senses of inter-dependence and essential sociality that belong to the perspective of a durable society and the freedom of humans who cannot conceive of being nonsocial. In other words, the ambiguity remains, and glossing over it effectively avoids attempting to theorize the idea of the social in order to rely on it for other purposes.

For example, inter-dependence, like exchange, suggests that intentional reciprocity is a feature if not a defining attribute of whatever is referred to as social; it is then possible to infer that the "common" constituted by people together supports mutual recognition and responsiveness to the needs of even unfamiliar others. In that case, there is a sense that subjectivity is *prior to the connection* of one person with others, and a concomitant sense of the social as contingent rather than immanent. Otherwise, when intentionality is thought of as a property of agency per se, and not merely of individuals taken one by one, it is crucial to think through what might be meant by saying that something is social. There is no longer a reason to think of it in terms of relations among individuals constituted by, say, the convergence or overlapping of intentions. But there is good reason to think of every ostensible instance of action as imbued with intentionality no matter how and in what medium agency is vested. This is one sense in which human relations can be described as "with" rather than "to." In other words, *under the aspect of subjectivity, "agency" indicates nothing more than activity as such.*

We might try to redefine "inter-dependence" according to these ideas, perhaps as an intentionality that cannot be attributed to any individual or individuals, or realized individually. We can then say that inter-dependence has to do with relations *within* agency. However, the idea of dependence is part of the concept, which therefore remains problematic: it is not clear what depends on what, so we are left with the idea that "relation" designates movement as such. This allows for the possibility of identifying sociality with a *course* of activity that cannot be represented adequately as "*inter*-dependence" even though it was originally predicated on that idea. The idea of the social expressed as inter-dependence, and now understood as a principle of agency that authorizes different subjectivities, is not compatible with a theory of action that begins by referring to distinct mentally disposed subjects or distinct mental dispositions. For the notion of intentionality as a property of activity regardless of content, the most that can be said about ostensibly distinct acts is that the sense of their being distinct invokes a subjectivity that cannot be reduced to individuals or particular intentions. However, it remains to distinguish subjectivities from other facts, and it is necessary to do so if we are to conceive of inter-dependence apart from individualized relations of dependence and if we are to distinguish persons from things. Do we need psychological facts or mental states to account for differences among the courses of activity typically taken to constitute specific instances of "someone doing something?"

The first version of the intentionality of reciprocal effect easily slips into a pragmatics in which each separate individual pursues her interest by relying on some others as a condition of possible success. When that occurs repeatedly, we are tempted to speak of a relationship between or among individuals who retain their integrity and their identities throughout. We do not have to consider it as having a life of its own since it is merely what individuals continue to do in the presence of others based on expectations related to the past, and otherwise weighted, ratio of success to failure. In that case, the prefix "inter" is misleading: "inter-dependence" is supposed to interpret the sub-theoretical notion of sociality insofar as the latter suggests a connection that cannot be undone without undoing the elements that are connected. It follows that the idea of the social conceived of according to the first version of inter-dependence can be reduced to the simpler idea of dependence, where that means "only able to pursue one's goals with the cooperation or passivity of some others" and does not mean "being constituted as a subject by that relationship." Without the idea of a connection that constitutes its elements, this seems too narrow to capture what we need to mean by inter-dependence if it is to refer to the social, and what we need to mean by the intentionality of reciprocal effect if "inter-dependence" is to mean more than "individuals being affected by one another." The second version of inter-dependence, in which subjectivity is a property of agency, seems closer to the point, at least to the extent to which agency is not identified with particular individuals or particular acts. In other words, if equating the social with inter-dependence takes subjectivity as a property of agency and agency as a logical condition of something being humanly active, the sense in which subjectivity is a logical condition of activity does not require that it be the subjectivity of anyone in particular or that it conform to a person's intention or a convergence of such intentions. It follows that sociality need not be accounted for by reference to individual persons and their relations with other such individuals.

We still might be reluctant to give up on the idea that whatever is a property of agency is a property of some individual, or individuals taken one by one. One reason has to do with the difficulty imposed by language on any attempt to connect agency to sociality without individualizing it. Another is that it is virtually impossible to find terms that adequately capture the sub-theoretical sense of sociality, terms that are not freighted with reductionist implications. However, some theoretical formulations are clearly intended to avoid reduction. For example, Sartre's reference to "practical ensembles" (1976) and Marx's reference to "manifold relations" (1979, 187) avoid characterizing inter-dependence as the dependence of each person on specific others: both are distinct from a mere assembly and have properties of their own that cannot be reduced to properties, dispositions, or accomplishments of their incorporated individuals.

There are, of course, other expressions that seem to overlap enough to suggest something of a discursive paradigm—if we read "inter" against the grain of its suggestion of exchange and the problem the latter poses to the sub-theoretical notion of the social as immanent and irreducible. Discourse about sociality nevertheless easily breaks down when attempts are made to cure the problem by "closer" and more intricate descriptions of what individuals think and do and by extending the notion of context to "structural constraints" that beg the question of how to avoid a theoretically fatal reduction. As things stand, while "inter-dependence" seems to be the least troubling expression, it is not clear how it can avoid becoming increasingly misleading as its use becomes more formal and rule-governed. For sociologists, what is important about this for the idea that human beings are essentially social is the convenient suggestion that individualized subjects take others into account in what they do and how they do it. What this glosses over is that, conceived of as "subjects," they cannot but take others into account, which means that there is no variation in the sheer taking of others into account though there may be variation in how it is done and how it transpires. The point is *that taking others into account is what subjects do as a matter of the subjectivity of which they are moments, not something they might or might not do as independent individuals.*

The second radically qualifying distinction is between subjects and nonhuman objects or things, between what is animate and what is inert. That it is radical is expressed in transcendental characterizations of the mode of being a subject as independent of all particular objects and the mode of being of things as perfectly indifferent to their subjects. Relations of the former to the latter then appear as non-constitutive—as in accounts of action in which reasons based on beliefs about objective facts are said to cause or contribute causally to an undertaking, *but not to transform the actor as such.* When the term "object" is used, as in the expression "object of orientation," certain descriptions suggest that a subject-object relation might be constitutive—for example, when mention is made of a subjectively organized structure of relevance in which actually or virtually referenced objects are said to be "represented" within a "structure of conditions of rational action." But this is not what is provided by a strict interpretation of the distinction. A relation of subject and object appears to be constitutive, as a subjectively decisive and self-generalizing instance of object relations, when it is described as tacitly attributing to the subject a state of need that determines the instance as a structure of relevance and, in that light, considers the subject to be significantly constituted, if only momentarily, by that structure, beyond any specific lack.[5]

The problem is that the only principle of activity provided by such a description is "need" understood as a lack to be overcome by some sort of fulfilling experience. The relations among objects that are initially brought into play by this remain external to the subject, as causes or conditions. The *subjectivity* of the subject is, then, not constituted by relations among objects or relations between objects and the subject, though it is, in a different sense, influenced by both. Parenthetically, one can imagine a series of descriptions in which the subject is seen as a variably needful self and the related objects in her situation are all that count as possible sources of satisfaction, in contrast with, say, a self beyond all particular needs that happens momentarily to lack something for which objects, present or anticipated, may or may not be possible sources of satisfaction. But imagining such a series takes one beyond the limits introduced by this notion of need, *given a radical distinction between subjects and things*. In other words, according to the distinction between persons and things, objects and their connections with one another are described as *affecting* but not *effecting* subjects. They do not constitute subjectivity; rather the reverse. Subjectivity selectively imposes itself on objects such that the latter become "related" and "relevant" to what, in light of that imposition, must be thought of as a range of subject options (e.g., for action)—as when a subject is said to objectify or appropriate something but not *to be* an objectifying or appropriative subject. If we say that subjects are constituted by the relations their needs impose on objects, then the idea of subjectivity is trivial in that it is exhausted by immediate tendencies most likely expressed as bodily movements, not to mention that subjectivity and need are now impossibly distinct. Given this and given that those bodily movements are, in some sense, caused (at the conceptual level of intentionality), the idea that objects and their relations can constitute subjectivity is at best insignificant and at worst question-begging.[6]

In terms of these radical distinctions, then, we are able to speak in a useful though fatefully qualified way about the social implications of relations among people and relations between people and things; and certain interesting hypotheses can undoubtedly be formulated about how the two types of relation interact and about the likely effects of their interaction. For example, one might hypothesize that the closer and less mediated the relationship between persons, the less likely they are to be in conflict with each other and the more likely they are to share both the risks and the benefits inherent in their individual and collective affairs. Similarly, one might expect that the scarcer a resource the more precarious relations are likely to be among those for whom it is a resource, controlling for degrees of closeness of the parties and external mediations. Both hypotheses take the idea of the social for granted by presupposing it in a fundamental conception of emergent types of concrete relationship that obtain among distinct individuals and between such individuals and distinct things under definite types of circumstance. The fact that such individuals are said to be socialized over time in no way changes the reductive character of the hypotheses, since this merely accounts for some of their traits and dispositions—"socialization" typically referring to how persons acquire qualities that fit them for membership and eliminate those that do not. The point is that given the two distinctions, how to conceive of the social does not arise as a theoretical problem—beyond the apparently simple observation that people always find themselves among others and act and feel in regard to nonhuman things.

It will eventually appear that the two distinctions are not quite as compatible as they had seemed to be, since the idea of a subject's relation *with* some other(s) may be inconsistent with the idea that the distinction between subjects and objects is rarely if ever ambiguous and, in any case, cannot be treated as ambiguous if one is to proceed in understanding how persons are in their surroundings. For now, we are concerned primarily with the first, though it will

eventually appear that its bearing on theory has to do with problems introduced by the possibility that subjects and objects are never sufficiently distinct
to warrant treating them even provisionally as if they are radically distinct.

I have claimed that relying on the two apparently necessary distinctions explains in part why so little attention has been paid to the possibility of coming to terms with what is required by the ideas that human beings are essentially
social and that the social is irreducible.[7] They make it unnecessary, since it is
enough to know that relations among persons and between persons and things
are different and that the difference does not pose a contradiction; thus, one
conveniently says that relations *among* persons are usually *about* objects and
relations among objects are *socially constructed*. Other reasons for this lack of
attention have to do with less basic but equally plausible presuppositions. For
one, social psychological models typically analyze "sociality" as "interpersonal
behavior" or "interpersonal interaction." As such, they are predicated on the
conception of a person individuated by natural boundaries and particularized
in space and time. It is in this sense that personal identity appears both necessary in accounting for social life and logically unproblematic. That is, reference
to identity is a theoretical resource in that it conceives of persons as complete
self-presenting particulars, and the acknowledgment of a plurality of singular
skin-bound identities, as in Gutmann's (2003) account of identity politics, constitutes a nonpolitical standard of theoretical validity.[8]

Given this, there is no pressing need for further inquiry into possible meanings of "sociality." This indifference may be reinforced by taking the term
"social" to be theoretically primitive, in the sense that it is where one simply
begins—though that would not bode well for a sociological imaginary that constantly reaffirms the necessity of such quasi-concepts as equilibrium, socialization, moral density, structures of authority and communication, and structural
tension or strain, and is thereby committed to a language that refers to entities,
processes, or dialectics that cannot easily be made intelligible when reduced
to specifiable persons, actions, and interactions. If it is not a primitive construct, it still may be difficult to say what sort of word "social" is. For example,
does it refer to a concept in the formal sense of the term, or does it belong "to
a sophisticated self-referential level of language," in which case it may not be
possible to define it in a straightforward way (Black 1990b, 13–29)? Even so
clearly referential an expression as "interpersonal behavior" may be vulnerable
to the conceptual limits of any theory of human affairs written in a natural language and subject to the difficulties involved in trying to settle the sort of issues
brought to notice most poignantly by literary theorists in regard to representation, interpretation, textualization, translation, voice, ambiguity, metaphor,
and dialogue. Even if such difficulties are overcome, "interpersonal behavior"
seems inadequate to the idea of the social. Without an idea of a "person" that
specifies boundaries, form, and mode of autonomous existence, it is not clear

what is meant by "behavior." If that is included, and "interpersonal behavior" means "interactions *between or among* particular skin-bounded persons," it does not describe what must be meant by "social" and its cognates for there to be disciplines like sociology and the humanities that rely on its sub-theoretical meaning and for it to be possible to speak of human beings as essentially social.

There is yet another reason why one might be indifferent to the problem of how to characterize the social and therefore be surprised when someone else is not indifferent. It is often said that sociality is so pervasive a feature of human life, and so obvious in its meaning, that it is trivial and therefore distracting to say that it is an essential feature of being human. In other words, there is nothing for philosophy to add to theories for which the term is a resource rather than a topic (e.g., crime rates, suicide rates, leadership, rational choice, cooperation, conflict, institutionalization, organizational change, political mobilization). The argument might look something like the following. First, sociality involves nothing more than persons being together in ways that, over time, become familiar and morally compelling. Second, this is a species-specific fact that is relatively invariant within the kind. Third, characteristics of that sort that distinguish humanity from other forms of life are not basic to theorizing the inner workings of *human* affairs.[9] A few comments are in order since the claim is plausible on its face and it has been used to criticize philosophers, literary scholars, and sociologists who have attempted to develop a radical idea of sociality connected to what is distinctively human about human affairs.[10]

There is no reason, on the face of it, to challenge the thesis of the pervasiveness of the social, although it assumes what it is supposed to explain, that the meaning of "social" is unproblematic. One might well dispute the related claim that its meaning is unambiguous and obvious to every reasonable person. However, that something is pervasive is by no means a trivial fact, even if the meaning of whatever pervades is obvious and unproblematic. For one thing, neither the charge of triviality nor the claim of pervasiveness is trivial. Therefore, it must be admitted that they invite critical inquiry. Taken together, these propositions, one normative and the other empirical, are self-defeating, since if they are nontrivial it cannot be presumed that questioning the meaning of their object is trivial.[11] That is, they end up by justifying what they deny, that it is by no means trivial to attempt to identify and theorize the social. More to the point, indifference nontrivially trivializes the very social reality that it aims to protect from the intrusion of trivialization by theory. The mere statement that a question or idea is trivial because its object is not problematic assumes what cannot be true but is certainly nontrivial—namely, that the object is not problematic. It cannot be true because the claim that the object is not problematic is a claim about what theory should not tolerate, and that is largely a matter of normative judgment. All that is true in this is that a particular theory or theoretical point of view cannot tolerate the possibility that the meanings of the words that refer to its object are problematic, and this is, at best, a practical truth established by decision. Furthermore, for such an intolerantly positive frame of reference to deny that the object could be problematic amounts, paradoxically, to trivializing the object and trivializing its own reliance on the object and the theoretical presuppositions associated with it as a foundational resource.

Certainly, what may appear to be perfectly obvious in the human sciences and accepted as such by reasonable people should not thereby be exempt from critical inquiry, especially when there might be significant consequences of relying on its being obvious and when there is any reason to doubt that it is obvious. In this regard, many of the apparently deep problems of the social sciences and humanities may appear less than fateful under different conditions of their conception. Among these are problems that have to do with the following antinomies: individual and society, identity and performance, formal and informal aspects of "social order," "local" and "cosmopolitan" principles of organization, history or process and structure, long-term and short-term, nature and culture, economy and society, self-reflection and collectivity, and thought and action. Certainly, one of the conditions that make these antinomies unresolvable is the idea of the social on which their terms are predicated. That they might be transformed by reconsidering that idea, by taking it seriously, is enough reason to ignore the possibility of triviality based on the presupposition that the meaning of "social" is unproblematic and needs no further definition than what is indicated by the ways in which it is typically used.

––––––––

There is a further problem with the claim that the pervasiveness of the social and the obviousness of the idea of it makes it trivial to focus on it and therefore unnecessarily disruptive to do so. The very *assertion* of such a claim is itself not free of theoretical entanglements. Remember that its propositional content consists of the following: *that the social is pervasive, its meaning is obvious, and it would be trivial to raise doubts about that meaning.* The first entanglement has to do with the assumption that the manifest propositional content reflects what is latent to the experience of social life: it is that latency that is presumably made manifest *and* represented by the assertion. It is as if the latter picks out a proposition that is already preconsciously available to the mind and subconsciously effective in what people ordinarily do.

The assertion is justified by the assumption that it corresponds to an experience that is not self-explicating but that can be sufficiently represented by something altogether different from itself: it corresponds to that experience in the form of an explication of what is already virtually, but not actually, explicit. This is sufficiently problematic to require further discussion. It says, in regard to typical behavior, that people are preconsciously mindful of both the pervasiveness of the social *and* the obviousness of its meaning in ways that prepare them to recognize the folly of attempting to theorize it; and it says that since the assertion registers the fact that they are so mindful it is therefore true to their experience—which in turn justifies the charge of triviality. So *asserting* that it would be trivial and uninformative to try to theorize sociality may or may not be true, but it is in itself not trivial. *In that case, the proposition, that it would be trivial to theorize the social because it does not pose a problem for experience or theory, is true only if asserting it is nontrivial.*

To ascribe a representational function to the assertion presupposes that making the notion of the social explicit on the grounds that the experience of it is otherwise latent is not a theoretical comment about sociality and therefore not an example of trivializing—or that if it is such a comment it is not theoretical in a way that could disturb the obviousness of what it purports to be about. But this cannot be true. The idea that the experience of the social and a sense of the obviousness of its meaning are latent to the course of experience, and the further idea that those latent contents can be made directly explicit by the assertion of a proposition, are ideas about the social; and they are about it in a way that is by no means theoretically insignificant.[12] If the assertion of the original proposition is theoretically significant, and it seems to be, then there is at least one sense in which making sociality a topic is not trivial: when there is a desire to say publicly that it is trivial to try to theorize the social, given that the assertion presupposes that the latter has both a latent and manifest aspect. One might still say that it is trivial to focus on the meaning of "social," but one cannot say, as the justification requires, that it is trivial to focus on where that meaning is lodged—in this case, dynamically, as it were, in the preconsciousness of experience. Moreover, it is evident that the meaning and where it is lodged cannot be separated. The lodging of a meaning (e.g., preconscious or conscious) is part of the problem posed in this case by the question of meaning; and until the latter question is posed, the idea of a location of meaning, which allows one to say that the assertion has a representative function, is not intelligible. It seems, then, that the question of meaning is not trivial, and this means that the original proposition is false—at least that part of it that says that the meaning of "social" is obvious and, on that basis, it is trivializing and unnecessarily disruptive to theorize it. It should also be noted that if the meaning is not obvious, it is no longer clear what is supposed to pervade when it is said that sociality is pervasive.

What remains is a potentially significant theoretical statement about the latency of the idea and reality of the social. But to evaluate it, we need to address a number of questions. For example, what is the sense of the social such that it can have, for the psyche of its ostensible individuals, the aspects of latency and manifestation? What is that sense such that the latent aspect can be represented by a manifest propositional content of a different logical order? How is it possible for such a representation to be recognized as valid by those for whom its object had been latent? What happens to the latency of the idea of the social, and sociality itself, when it becomes manifest; and what happens to the manifestation when it takes leave of the latency?

One cannot underestimate the difficulty such questions have posed and continue to pose to sociological thought and the possible unity of the human sciences. To theorize activity as if its latent content can be made explicit without significantly changing or distorting its character is a dubious strategy at best. Beyond that, it is hard to see how an external observer can gain access to that latency prior to deciding what might manifest it, and access is necessary if the charge of triviality is to be maintained. Assuming the possibility of access is certainly not trivial since it implies at least two nonobvious propositions that are theoretically significant: (1) that the experience of the social is not only latent but readily accessible to someone already free of the latency and therefore able to make it manifest and (2) that those first parties for whom it is accessed and then made manifest will see that the social is theoretically unproblematic without need of further reflection. It is important to keep in mind that the appeal to latency is indispensable to showing that it is unreasonable to attempt to theorize the idea of the social; yet the appeal is itself theoretical and therefore difficult to reconcile with the assumptions of the first proposition and all that needs to be added to the second if it is to be plausible.

We need to go further, since the claim is empirical and can be presumed to bear the same burdens of judgment that would apply to any such hypothesis. It says, in effect, that the conclusion that the social is pervasive, the meaning of the term obvious, and its idea unproblematic, derives from either an induction from or a description of what is otherwise evident in particular cases. The first eliminates the possibility of obviousness, since such an induction has not and probably cannot be done. The second begs the questions under consideration. Despite this, and disregarding what has already been discussed, one might still claim that the meaning of "social" is obvious but that its truth is guaranteed by other, nonempirical considerations or by nonempirical means. This would allow the validity of the original compound claim to be based on considerations other than what would normally be required. In that case, it cannot be said to be empirical as it stands and therefore to be true in that sense. Finally, the idea of the social may still be considered obvious without appealing to conditions of proof or demonstration. But if this is so, it is also not a trivial fact about the idea of the social, since the obviousness of its meaning regardless of evidence is now alleged, for whatever reason, to be an important feature of it. Again, the attempt to demonstrate the truth of the claim of triviality leads, paradoxically, to its denial.

The crucial point is that *the following proposition is in fact a nontrivial instance of doing what it says should not be done—namely, theorizing the social: that sociality is an immediate and self-presenting feature of experience, that this can be fully and directly represented in the form of a sentential proposition, and that the representation brings to notice what the socialized mind is already prepared to recognize as the truth of its experience such that any attempt to theorize the social (presumably other than by saying this) ends in triviality.* It should be added that this does not mean that such a proposition should be dismissed out of hand. It means only that it has nothing to say that could lead to a reasonable denial of the legitimacy of theoretical work.

This leads me to suspect that the claim might be better understood as a symptom of something that needs further discussion, perhaps even a symptom of the social as such. In that regard, one can imagine a question that might engage just such a symptom: What is it about the social that leads us to wonder how it is that in discussing it we are led to wonder why it is being discussed at all? In this regard, Garfinkel's early work can be understood as a description of a course of activity such that (1) the parties to it do not feel impelled to ask, and might well object to being asked, "Why aren't we doing other than what we are doing?" and yet (2) those parties behave as if they require permission to ask that very objectionable question (1967, 7–9).

11

Further Problems in Theorizing the Social

There is a plausible nonradical alternative to the conclusion that the original theory-rejecting claim about the social is, or might be, symptomatic of the phenomenon itself, that sociality is by its nature resistant to being theorized. It is nonradical in that it does not address the relationship between theory and theorizing, and it is necessary to do that if, as I have tried to show, the conception of sociality as a course of activity implies that there is an opposition between ostensible products such as theories, justified beliefs, and gestures, and the activity from which they appear to issue as products. The relationship between theory and theorizing provides a standpoint for inquiring into the human aspect of anything that might be seen as an instance of human affairs. I return to that relationship after briefly considering the nonradical alternative in connection with what might be thought of as the pragmatics of intellectual work, a pragmatics that does not yet find itself internal to a course of activity.

The alternative begins with the familiar idea that the social manifests itself in what people do as a vaguely coherent set of background assumptions that are "taken for granted." Their coherence constitutes a latency that operates generatively as a condition of motivation and self-regulation in regard to conduct that would otherwise be seen as purely instrumental or utilitarian. Imagine an ethnographer of a certain persuasion who observes the following behavior of members of a given community on a number of occasions: an individual stands aside and allows an older person who arrived later to pass through an entrance to a public facility. Our observer also knows that members typically follow a rule governing coming and going that regulates taking turns by sanctioning an order of turns in which the first to come is the first to be served. Exceptions may be deviant to the rule but are not for that reason untoward. Like most rules that bear on the relationship between expectations and obligations, those about turn taking operate only on the possibility of legitimate exceptions. Therefore, we might expect such rules to promote decision making or to justify some subsidiary behavior that can be thought of as deliberative to the point of acting in light of but not necessarily in strict accordance with the rule. Without further information other than the knowledge that such a rule is bound to support or tolerate exceptions, the observer might conclude that the member has performed an act of deference that suggests the existence of a social fact.

This conclusion could be corroborated by reference to other social facts that seem compatible with such deference (e.g., the existence of speech patterns correlated with the relative ages of the interacting parties), or that appear to support deference in general (e.g., other morally distributive practices), or are supported by it (e.g., practices related to the relative segregation of the elderly, or attitudes toward different body types based on an emphasis on stipulated no less than natural marks of aging). Perhaps the member has taken for granted a coherent normative structure that, as one of its many possible effects, contributes to a range of obligations on any member to subordinate herself to a certain type of other and to do so in a way that precisely displays the principle of subordination as such and displays it as modified by the category of age as one of relatively few properties sufficient, under certain circumstances, to activate that obligation.

The idea of "taking for granted" suggests that a doing is a particular event or instance of a type in regard to conditions that are not themselves objects of attention. The way in which the social is taken for granted allows what is being done to appear as a content originating in the intention of an agent and taking form in a way that allows whatever happens to refer back to that very intention. That is, the idea that the social is something sufficiently fixed to be taken for granted in what people do tends to support the ideas of a determinate intention, a fixed object, and meaning and an intention that are also fixed. What is lost is the notion of a course of activity, what happens after the moment of the undertaking and therefore the constant changes of conditions of activity as it transpires, as it must, among people (Sacks 1974). Without going into detail, to avoid the fact that the idea of sociality is lost the moment it is said to be taken for granted, one would have to imagine a course of activity that is somehow dynamically sustained, which is to say that it and its participants are subject to internal tensions that are beyond the possibility of immediate relief.

To the extent to which the alternative is designed to reconcile a commonsense understanding of "social" as referring to entities (e.g., groups) with the theoretical proposition that sociality is conceivable only as in flux, it is bound to admit that elisions, paradoxes, and potentially fatal tautologies are unavoidable in taking the social as an object of theory even when one takes seriously the claim that the social is pervasive and that its meaning is obvious. But endorsing that claim requires concluding that these unavoidable features are not significant enough to justify raising fundamental questions about the nature of sociality: elisions, paradoxes, and tautologies may accompany sociality but they do not qualify its concept. That is, it is not rational to focus on the idea that sociality is an ongoing project since whatever the project turns out to be, *as project*, can be understood in large part as persons together coming to terms with what appear from their points of view to be unforeseen conditions or a momentary looseness in their relations—and that this "coming to terms" can be adequately understood in general as acting according to established concepts of mutually regulative practices such as exchange, negotiation, or normalizing reciprocity through demonstrations of trustworthiness. The scientific normalcy of those concepts places apparent departures from the normalcy of the world they represent beyond the phenomena under investigation, and within the realm of accident or luck.

Unless the idea of the social is submitted to a critique aimed at establishing what is distinctive about it, normalization, the act of marginalizing, seems to draw its force and sense of its legitimacy from the sheer insistence with which it declares in favor of research over theory. Particularly in the case of the social, aggressive normalization is sufficient to justify its exemption from theoretical concern—thereby affirming its status as something to be taken for granted and confirming the independence of whatever theory is at issue from how it came about (or its conditions of possibility). However, deciding to place sociality beyond dispute on pragmatic grounds need not be thought of as merely a matter of convenience. There are substantive effects that need to be taken into account. For one thing, it reinforces a positive idea of theory tied to a positive kind of research, so rejecting theorizing the social is not tantamount to rejecting theory. We have already seen that denying the legitimacy of theorizing the social amounts to a theoretical claim about it and that this is contrary to insisting that pragmatics can actually take precedence over theoretical work. Of course, the pragmatist can claim that the priority of research does not imply the absence of theory; rather, there are certain special and possibly rare cases in which theorizing the social may be necessary. For most of such cases, doubt about a given conception of the social may naturally arise—for example, in studies of momentous social change such as rebellion or revolution, or when relations among system-functional institutions are in strain, requiring a theorization of the noninstitutional forms of action once described as "collective behavior."

The second argument for excluding or limiting theorizing begs the question of how to decide whether a given instance of research requires an application of the exclusionary rule. It says that while a critical examination of the idea of the social is normally not a formal element in the analysis of a particular study, it may be relevant to establishing the authority of the total field insofar as that is understood as a progressive accumulation of a type of knowledge. The requirement is that the study in question rely on the social only as an implicit frame of reference. For the discipline taken as a whole, however, the idea might well be part of its rationalization as a field. In other words, the second may be part of what practitioners are taught about the general orientation of their discipline, and may even be able to stand on its own as a referent of a comprehensive literature, but it is not directly implicated in what is done locally and specifically in the name of the discipline. This is not to say that theorizing the social is of merely historical significance. Rather, the force of the idea is acknowledged tacitly in each study—perhaps by what is necessarily omitted and by the fact that publication itself attempts, in one way or another, to establish a link between a text and the progress of disciplinary knowledge. This middle ground suggests that the problem posed by theorizing the social might be raised at the level of the discipline—if the issue of disciplinary coherence has already been raised—but not at the level of individual studies. In this respect, the nonradical alternative ends by agreeing that theorizing the social is reasonable at the level of the discipline and unreasonable at the level of its practice.

To say that such a theory-rejecting claim should be beyond challenge because of the importance of linking particular studies to an available stock of knowledge and because doing so requires focusing on specific problems and specific bodies of information is tantamount to saying that the argument that theorizing the social is disruptive is true for all practical purposes. But this argument does not imply that truths may not be found about the social, and, in fact, it must nevertheless be admitted that the claims of triviality and disruptiveness are contingent and therefore always subject to review. This, in turn, suggests that they cannot be taken to disqualify the very attempt to theorize the social that they intend to disqualify, since that is the only way that they can remain subject to review.

Parenthetically, there is at least one reason why the non-ironical "truth" may be preferable to the ironical "incorrigible," even though it may turn out that we are dealing with only a *sense* that something is true (e.g., the hypothesis about disruption or the very different kind of hypothesis about the essentiality of the social) whether it is or is not true according to formal criteria. To *assert* that theorizing the social is inessential though the social may be essential is to adopt the form of incorrigibility since the assertion appears to exclude what it must not—namely, the necessity of keeping what is asserted open to review. That is, the assertion appears dogmatic insofar as it not only rejects theorizing (or identifies a point in the research process at which it can be rejected) but rejects the very *question* of whether one should bother theorizing. This impression cannot be relieved by the qualification that indifference to theorizing is appropriate only to some instances of research, since that begs the questions of how the line can be drawn, when such a decision should be made, and what an instance of research would look like if it were even momentarily free of theoretical entanglements—in other words, what would be meant by "research" and "the research process."

We can nevertheless consider some aspects of this argument that have to do with what it does or does not imply about the proposal to theorize the social on the grounds that it is necessary to do so if research and knowledge are to have recognizable disciplinary significance—to bear on a definite domain of objectivity, in this case, as it turns out, agency-dependent reality. First, there may be a good reason to refuse to examine the proposition that it is trivial to theorize the social because it is related to other truths about what is or is not significant enough to justify theoretical inquiry at the momentary expense of research (see Kitcher 2001). But the claim that theorizing the social would be trivial and disruptive does not imply that human affairs are not immanently social or that accepting the idea that sociality is immanent raises no important questions. In fact, it is usually taken to mean that the possibility of immanence, or essentiality, is not likely to raise questions urgent enough to require immediate *theoretical* attention. The implicit substitution of "indifference" for "rejection" sustains the priorities of the more modest idea that theorizing should not be supported if it threatens to paralyze the research imagination—as it does if that imagination is taken to exclude theorizing.

So if we ignore the rhetorical aspect of the assertion, we can say that dedicated indifference to theorizing is defensible from the point of view of the pragmatic and aesthetic features of research, its focus or problem-orientation and its movement toward increasing the clarity and distinctiveness of what it constitutes as its object of study. However, this still does not justify a general proscription against theorizing the immanence of the social to human affairs. Even if we accept the practical and aesthetic justifications of indifference, it does not follow that the researcher should reject the theoretical interventions of those who disagree, especially since both the object of research and the latter's status as knowledge-constituting, including the implications for which it is responsible, depend on the status of the concepts on which it inevitably relies. Those who initially defend indifference must finally admit that it should not extend beyond their most immediate practical concerns, that it cannot represent a philosophical principle, and that nothing about it justifies a general priority in favor of research over theory. At best, they can defend it only against an equally mistaken claim that theory is prior to research or that nothing conceptual should be taken for granted at the point at which research is undertaken. But it should be clear that when we consider the relation of theory to research, we can no longer rely on the standard meanings of the terms, each of which conventionally presupposes a radical difference evident both in the curriculum of the disciplines and in professional journals and monographs.

Insisting on protecting the research process against the distractions of theorizing poses a theoretical and critical problem of yet another order, one that also cannot easily be deferred: What is it to say that our knowledge of human affairs "accumulates" if "accumulation" refers to a "social stock of knowledge"? What does "social" mean in this phrase, and how is knowledge organized and made sustainable as a "stock"? These are not merely questions in the sociology of knowledge; nor do they invoke the ideas of "paradigm" and "normal science." They are, rather, questions about the object-related concepts on which every instance of research relies, and they have to do with how research "finds" itself, its own form of life, in its object and its object in itself (therefore, itself as a form of life). None of these questions can be separated from the research process itself, unless that is defined solely by the technical aspects of statistical analysis, and if "findings" means nothing more than one set of insufficiently interpreted statistics after another, and "research process" refers to a discrete event. All this suggests an internal relationship, as yet only hinted at, between theorizing and criticism. From this point of view, criticism is necessary and permissible, but it has no determinate beginning and its end never comes. Our sense of the significance of this depends on acknowledging that the research process is itself an ongoing course of activity that is not only a human instance of life but subject to all that is implied by the immanence of sociality to every such instance.

T hat it may be possible to justify the *sense* that a statement is true does not mean that it is true as a matter of fact (that it corresponds to an independent reality) or that there are sufficient reasons to endorse it. Moreover, it is possible to have such a sense without denying that it might be legitimately challenged. But we have seen that the content of the claim that theorizing the social is trivial and therefore disruptive needs more than reasons and argument to justify resistance to even the most modest critique; it requires an *assertion* that is preemptive as well as declaratory. If so, it may be that the sense that it is true expresses the insistent character of the claim rather than that insisting expresses, comes after, that sense. The point is that the sense of a statement's being true does not entail that it is or might be actually true—though something about it might make it seem unreasonable to doubt it. If one were to allow that something might obviously be the case without being beyond doubt, still, doubting might be subject to a special burden of proof but it could not be rejected out of hand. The claim that the meaning and significance of "social" are obvious does not, by itself, imply that raising questions about it should be rejected as unnecessarily disturbing, provocative, or irrelevant. However, rejecting those questions may seem necessary if something about the progress of a research project requires momentarily rejecting efforts to theorize the social, though this may be, but is certainly not necessarily, undermined by an evident lack of progress. Above all, rejection is not reasonable if it is based on a denial that there is a legitimate discipline oriented by the idea of the social—unless one is willing to say that research speaks immediately for itself.

Pragmatics may be sufficient for holding that the claim of triviality is virtually true—that is, for protecting the sense of its being true from the consequences of the possibility that it is actually false. This would be so if to allow doubt would effectively bring an end to the discipline as a whole or show its existence as a self-contained field of study to have been illusory. But it may still be possible to justify attributing truth to the claim if the sense of that truth is responsive to some condition or conditions of its being true "in fact." One such condition might be that there is no reason, as things stand, to doubt it in favor of theorizing. We have seen, however, that it fails to meet formal criteria of truth and fails to justify itself against the latency it purports to represent as obvious. This suggests that there may be criteria of truth adequate to justify a sense that a proposition is true (beyond merely incorrigible)[1] other than formal and empirical criteria. The question is whether the *sense* that "a proposition of the sort at issue is true" is legitimate—that is, can be evaluated by a criterion or a convergence of criteria or by a sort of reasoning that otherwise justifies it or fits it into a context otherwise unobjectionable, regardless of the evident fact that the proposition is not and possibly cannot be true according to established, scientific, conceptions of truth. If it is nevertheless believed to be capable of evaluation, there is a further question of what the result would amount to as far as knowledge is concerned. This will be discussed in connection with the relationship between the ideas of objectivity and inter-subjectivity. At this point, I only comment on the aspect of the problem that has to do with the argument at hand, which is how it might be reasonable for someone committed to truth in the scientific sense of the term to accept, with the same degree of certainty appropriate to an empirically true or formally or practically valid claim, certain statements or propositions that are in principle, in their own terms, manifestly and, perhaps, fatefully in doubt.[2]

It is worth noting in passing that there is fairly general agreement that a rule requiring one to reject propositions that do not meet the standard criteria of truth would make it difficult if not impossible to justify many endeavors for which overall justification remains necessary, including in the natural sciences. Some such propositions are often taken to identify reasonable limits to rational justification in specific cases, beyond which one need not go. The problem is well known and has been widely, and even passionately, discussed, especially in regard to the social sciences.[3] Still, it is worth considering how one might legitimately allow for certainty when pursuing a total program apparently designed to undermine certainty in the interest of a somewhat different value—namely, knowledge as an ongoing self-critical affair—especially when it is difficult to distinguish the sense of a proposition as true from whether it is acceptable according to formal standards of truth. The question here is whether the claim that it would be disruptive to theorize something as obvious as the social can be maintained even though it is not justifiable according to the scientific standards it endorses. If it can, then we need to pursue the idea of the social no further than restating that human beings are essentially social—at least in regard to trying to show the relevance of the social sciences to the general project of considering what is human about human affairs. If it cannot, then one cannot legitimately object to engaging the idea of the social as if its constitution and meaning were significant and not obvious. Failing other objections, we can proceed with confidence that those who once objected will now find good reason to support those efforts if not to participate in them.

———

L et us suppose for the moment that a claim that justifies rejecting theorizing the social can be taken as true in some sense if it is legitimate to be indifferent to its own defects, that it is legitimate not to be serious about what it excludes yet to be serious in its defense of the exclusion. The supposition is reasonable if the truth of the rejective claim is subject neither to the usual formal and material criteria nor to other criteria—say, those appropriate to metaphorical truth.[4] The question is, then, what reason can there be for not taking seriously a claim one is bound to accept as "true" in the interest of a *sense* that it is true? One reason might be that some concepts and propositions are thought to be basic in a way that requires doing more than merely giving them the benefit of the doubt. If they are resources on which the course of inquiry in a disciplinary field has come to depend, not to take them for granted as if they are adequate in what they allow and true in what they say is, in effect, to repudiate the progressive or cumulative aspect of the inquiry. If one looks too closely at what is past in order to contribute to a movement toward an acceptable future (e.g., theoretical improvement, increased knowledge), it is quite possible that the latter will suffer, if only because the spontaneity of thought implicit in the idea of progress may be compromised by returning too readily to primitive concepts or propositions. The history of an inquiry can be evaluated for its disciplinary quality only if certain propositions and concepts can be specified in advance. So far, this sounds as if the progress of a science depends on a degree of consensus, justified or not. But this leaves too much room for irony; and the sense of truth attached to the primitive ideas of a total inquiry is never ironic, though such ideas are occasionally presented ironically (as if the assertion is intended to disguise a guilty secret, but not to suppress it altogether).

Progress in the social sciences is usually identified with responses to problems that are for the most part received and neither theoretically generated nor related to a legitimately contested idea of the distinctive object of the field of study. To refer to this as progress requires bracketing the question of the disciplinary significance of the problems themselves. So there is a certain irony attached to research indifferent to the question "What is it intended to illuminate?" The question "What is it about?" can be avoided by an offhand denial of its relevance to what has to be done for the sake of the progress of knowledge. But this is likely to make an attempt to explain a given research project somewhat ironical. For example, classical theories of collective behavior usually begin by referring to an ostensibly social phenomenon, riot, fad, crowd, social movement, demonstration, and the like, the status of which is assigned by interested evaluations of public order before the referent has even been described. They become theories by taking the catalog of instances of "civil unrest" to fall under a distinction between what is noninstitutional in and therefore possibly dysfunctional to society conceived of as a social system, and what is institutional and therefore an articulated part of such a system composed of a logically exhaustive number of such parts. In other words, to use, test, or elaborate such a theory requires as little attention as possible to the basic distinction and to the possibility that there is no rational collection of phenomena that clearly and reasonably exemplify the distinction (Brown and Goldin 1973).

There have been many challenges to classifying one or another phenomenon as extra-institutional and therefore socially irrational. The "social movement" is an example, but the challenge in this case usually depends, ironically, on accepting the idea of an "institutional" phenomenon, therefore the distinction. But the latter has not been challenged, until recently, in the only way it can be, which is to say theoretically. One reason is that the idea of "institution" plays a decisive role in theories of structure, system, and practices, and any elaboration of them requires not only a concept of a system, perhaps as a self-articulating integration of institutions, but a definition of "institution" that delineates its negation, what it is definitely not. In most theories, the negation is taken to be external—a condition that threatens the internal order of the system by operating against one or more of its functional subsystems, and the capacity of the system to sustain itself depends both on a natural tendency to move toward the ideal of rational action and on the absence of internal limits to it as a definite form of life. In its most developed form, the system is conceived of as deathless and relatively immune to changes in form and identity. In other words, the attempt to identify new forms of politics is substantially hindered by a failure to engage theories that sustain the old forms, to engage them at the point at which they are most consistent and coherent, and to engage them by means of an immanent reading aimed at showing where the theory projects, from its own resources and operations, precisely what it is designed to deny. The following brief account is intended to illustrate the importance of challenging the generalization of the idea of a social system to most if not all human affairs and the difficulty of doing so when the theory appears, by virtue of its extraordinary development and refinement, to be vulnerable only at its margins.

First, the noninstitutional comes to include virtually everything attributable to the notion of sociality that, as Mary Douglas (1986) points out, is tied to a weak conception of community. It is, essentially, the denial of all that is presupposed by the idea of "institution," which includes conditions of rational action including systems of rules, normatively reinforced tendencies to approximate ideal types, and clear boundaries that distinguish members from nonmembers. In other words, the "social" envisioned by system theory is precisely what sociality cannot be, role-bound individual decision makers who adhere to conditions of rational action and whose relations with their others are normatively produced and become self-perpetuating or "inertial." The social aspect of system projects, as an altogether different kind of social, an inexhaustible negative category encompassing whatever lies outside of the rationalizing order of institutions. It follows that any theoretical intervention that might relieve the invidiousness of the distinction between what is and what is not institutional has little choice but to challenge the very perspective of social organization, insofar as it exemplifies the idea of a system. The ideal of the social represented by "system" and "system functions" is the negation of the sub-theoretical notion that was supposed to justify the ideal. In effect, the perspective of institution is "the view from nowhere"—which is not, in any meaningful sense, a view; and the corresponding "perspective of the social" becomes a category without substantial reference: it provides nothing that can legitimately be called a perspective—except as the negation of the social sub-theoretically conceived of as what people are and do together. The very idea of a system stands in opposition to the phenomenon it was intended to represent.

Without going into further detail, *given the distinction*, there seems little choice but the system ideal since accepting the logical negation of "institution" as a theoretical concept would be to deny the possibility of the integration of institutions (articulated self-regulation, and therefore action, at the level of the system), hence the possibility of a social system, hence the feasibility of developing an empirically interpretable theory of society represented as such a system. Yet, ironically, the theoretical solution makes such an interpretation impossible. To the extent to which this is correct, it is clearly in the interest of the progress of such a theory that questions not be raised about the distinction between the articulated order of institutions and its negation, and about the phenomena used to exemplify the latter. It is only in confrontation with the theory and, especially, with what it presupposes, that reengaging the idea of the social becomes possible. For the idea of progress in the social sciences, conceived of as the increasing clarification of their ideal theoretical objects, certain basic concepts, and "social" is one, may need to be taken as incorrigible. This is especially so if those disciplines are to remain relevant to what is human about human affairs.

The irony of a representation that denies precisely what it purports to represent exposes the weakness of the claim that it is trivial and distracting to theorize the social, and this is what is at issue. It reduces the claim to a pragmatic methodological proposal—namely, that because a great deal of useful research and analysis is predicated on the idea that "sociality" is a primitive concept, inquiry in the human sciences should begin by taking that for granted. The scientific program it warrants, whatever other value it has, does not pertain to the concept of the social so much as it confirms the concept of a particular concept—the social as an ideal of the orderliness of human affairs without any corresponding idea of the principle of *ordering*, which is, we now see in regard to that ideal, conceived of as the negation of *order*.

It is not unreasonable, however, at a given moment, to take the concept of the social as a primitive notion for the sake of freeing a certain line of research or analysis from the burden of theorizing it; and there are undoubtedly conditions under which that will seem necessary. But, from a disciplinary point of view, this only means that there may be occasional exceptions to the principle that requires theorizing in all possible respects. The fact that the idea of the social has been ignored, elided, or suppressed, more or less at various times, says something about the ideological aspect of the history of the human sciences. The willingness to exclude the basic fact from inquiry expresses an attitude and affirms an intellectual strategy that idealizes practice by denying that most research problems are received and idealizes a kind of knowledge that undermines and finally contradicts its stipulated object. Indifference to the sub-theoretical notion of the social is in that respect anti-sociological and, more importantly, inconsistent with the notion of human affairs. In that respect, it may indicate a desire to police the boundaries of a certain discourse for which a received or established idea of the social can be a resource—though not a topic. But however driven, the constitution and reinforcement of boundaries is certainly a consequence of indifference. The tautology of allowing the claim that theorizing the social is trivial and disruptive to stand as its own evidence allows a nontrivial move to be made against raising the issues of the meaning and theoretical significance of "sociality" and, of course, against considering whether what is sub-theoretical about the social can be validly represented by explicit propositions, however derived.[5] Thus, the original insistence against theorizing can be seen as having a polemical and even political aspect inasmuch as it draws a boundary and justifies the exclusion on the populist grounds that what lies within is familiar and is, as such, obvious beyond reasonable dispute. There is, of course, another related issue, which is that theorizing the social threatens to undermine the vestiges of individualism and the corresponding idealization of the social against itself. That is, it seems incompatible with certain ideas about justice and morality that are admittedly difficult to resist. The desire to preserve disciplinary normalcy and the desire to preserve the rationality and rightness of certain values provide a formidable justification of indifference to theorizing the social, the weaknesses of each being compensated for by the strengths of the other.

Policing borders reinforces normal ways of doing inquiry and protects the moral imperative that humans must be thought of in their individuality and, in that respect only, as essentially or tendentiously rational. This preserves standard ideas of action, intention, and moral personality in the following ways. First, for something to be an action, it cannot be merely reflex or motion. This is often taken to mean that it must have reasons, and it must be reasonable to ask an actor to justify what she did and to assign responsibility for its consequences. Action appears, then, as a particular event rather than a course of activity. Second, it is part of the idea of "a person" that persons are the ultimate referents of moral discourse and theory. This means that a concept of justice, and therefore a theory of justice, is necessary if the moral status of persons is to be clarified in a way that preserves the social validity and significance of the concept. This risks sacrificing any idea of the social as the basic fact to pre-social particularistic notions of person and personal identity. Third, a theory of justice (as fairness) is valid for and presupposes a universe of rational beings taken as ends rather than means. The emphasis on individuality is adequate to the idea of justice under a law that admits only individuals (with their "comprehensive doctrines" as well as personalities), but it is evidently incompatible with the idea that agency refers to something like the subjectivity of inter-subjectivity, or to a sociality that is irreducible and irrepressible.

Still, these principles are consistent with the idea that such a theory must be compatible with an expansive culture of respect and mutuality beyond the idea of exchange or expedience, in which limits are necessarily placed on inequality and the powers of particular wills. They are not incompatible with challenging situational constraints that normally seem beyond question. Finally, if *theorizing* justice is implicit in considering persons as ends and as rational, to the extent to which being an end and being rational are part of what it is to be essentially social, then a reasonable *theory* would have to allow that reflection corresponds in some measure to what otherwise appears to exclude it—namely, experience (see Peacocke 2000, 336; Morrison 1994, 553; Quine and Ullian 1970, 20–34). What makes this possible includes eliminating what theory seems unable to address fruitfully when constrained by the well-established but pre-theoretical figurations of the pre-social individual. Indifference to theorizing the social may express a desire to maintain an individualistic paradigm for all the reasons mentioned previously. But it does not follow that this entails abandoning the appeal to an immanent sociality beyond relations *among* specifiable persons—especially since one upshot of latent individualism is that the idea of such particulars is preserved in a way that makes it unproblematic to be concerned with these problems of reference and unacceptably trivial to theorize the idea of the social, and therefore to attempt to clarify what is taken to be human about human affairs as things stand. In this regard, indifference or hostility to attempts to consider the idea of the social in connection with the question of what is human has a political aspect that is bound to raise the question of the social dimension of politics itself, latent no less than manifest.

12

Social Action as Action

Regardless of the problems involved in assigning meaning to the term "social" and regardless of the criticisms of the argument that dwelling on those problems disrupts the accumulation of knowledge, the idea that humans are essentially social is insinuated in most of what is written in the human sciences—though differences exist about whether this needs further ontological enrichment or should be simplified for purposes of fitting it to current debates.[1] Consider again Strawson's comment:

> It has often been quite normal, quite conventional, in the philosophical tradition to work through epistemological and ontological questions in abstraction from the great fact of the concept-user's role as a social being. All the same it is strange. For it is not as if each one of us builds up his cognitive picture of the world, acquires his concepts, develops his techniques and habits of action in isolation; and then, as it were, at a certain point, enters into relation with other human beings and confronts a new set of questions and problems. On the contrary, all this cognitive, conceptual, and behavioural development takes place in a social context; and, in particular, the acquisition of language, without which thinking is inconceivable, depends on interpersonal contact and communication. I have often used such expressions as "*our* conceptual system," "the general structure of *our* thought," etc., in speaking of the basic or fundamental features of that system and that structure. (1992, 80–81; emphasis in original)

It is not clear from this whether Strawson wants to say that the social is a necessary feature or a condition of what people do and think. Yet his characterization of the "normal" or "conventional" tendency to abstract from it as "strange" suggests a belief that the choice has significant consequences. The same ambiguity and concern for consequences appear in the following quotation, though it is more assertive and reflects a philosophy that begins with a different set of problems from those that motivate much of Anglo-American philosophy:

> But this relation of exteriority is itself inconceivable except as a reification of an objective relation of interiority. History determines the content of human relations in its totality, and all these relations, even the briefest and most private, refer to the whole. But History itself does not cause there to be human relations in general. The relations which have established themselves between those *initially separate objects*, men, were not products of problems of the organisation and division of labour. On the contrary, the very possibility of a group or society being constituted—around a set of technical problems and a given collection of instruments—depends on the permanent actuality of the human relation (whatever its content) at every moment in History, even between two separate individuals belonging to societies with different systems and entirely ignorant of one another. (Sartre 1976, 96; emphasis in original).

The passage also suggests that nothing of what humans do and think can be identified and described apart from its being essentially, immanently, social; yet it seems to allow that the social is a condition distinct from the "technical" organization of effort—unless one reads Sartre's reference to "the permanent actuality of the human relation" as constituting the very structure of "intentionality."[2]

Emmet expresses this same ambivalence toward the theoretical status of the "social" by raising the issue and then neutralizing it: "A common starting-point for both sociology and ethics [is] the fact that people need to live in social relationships with each other, not only for survival but if they are to carry out any of the characteristically human enterprises" (1975, 33; see also 178). Emmet is trying to sustain the idea that living collectively cannot be separated from the "characteristically human enterprises"; and, to the extent to which "any" means "every," she seems to say that being social is characteristically (necessarily?) human about what people do—despite the uneasy grammar that allows activities to occur "*in* human relationships," as if the latter were containers, and as if humans might operate in ways that are not necessarily social (though they may always turn out to be) and be only externally related to their sociality. The phrase beginning with "but if they are to carry out" raises and then begs the question of whether being social is merely a matter of function or instrumentality (in which case there might be adequate substitutes depending on what enterprises one has in mind) or defines the distinctive quality of human enterprises such

that they are characteristically social and not characteristically anything else
and such that they comprise what humans do by way of being human.

Emmet's approach, which I treat as exemplary, is compatible with and relies
on a general theory of action that she does not make explicit and that is, on
three counts, inhospitable to the idea that sociality is an immanent feature of
what people do. First, it separates activity and agency by way of a distinction
between doing and being. This allows "being social," which presumably has
to do with agency, to appear as a contingent and continuously variable property of what people decide to do and then do. But it leaves us with an unenviable obligation to imagine what subjectivity might look like without the aspect
of activity—as inert, diffuse, or somehow indifferent, or even, as Emmet says,
a "romantic notion of the bare subjective 'I'" (178), and to imagine what human activity might look like without intentionality in all its aspects. She addresses this problem when she considers how far the notion of "role" should be
extended in accounting for the relationship between "persons and personae,"
though she characterizes it as, primarily, a methodological issue. In this regard, she asks the unfortunately appropriate practical question: "But in actual
fact can we identify the pure subject in action apart from the social and institutional support represented by the notion of the human person?" (178).[3] The
question is unfortunate not only because she seems to exempt a certain type
or register of theory, with which she understandably has little sympathy, but
because it risks losing the sense of subjectivity necessary to consider subjects
as *subjects* and because its concept of representation is dangerously ambiguous.

It is, then, in "actual fact" that the "pure subject" cannot be identified;
whereas, in apparent contrast with Sartre's proposal, the most general things
that can reasonably be said about subjectivity depend on the concrete historical contexts in which alone it is realized as a personal subject (or as subjects,
plural). I say "apparent contrast" because Sartre is not in fact defending an idea
of pure subjectivity. He is claiming that it is not possible, as things stand, to
think the concept of "subject" without leaving room for at least an intimation of
something sub-theoretical about it that is independent of whatever is invoked
as context. He is not guilty of assuming that theory should study only what is
pure on the grounds of principle or even because any concrete identification of
subjectivity that fails to include its essential disunity fundamentally distorts
the proper sense of the object. If "actual fact" is given the exclusive privilege of
grounding theory (not merely clarifying usage), then it is difficult to avoid the
conclusion that talk of a plurality of subjects assumes what the rational basis of
such talk seems to exclude—namely, subjectivity.

What is most unfortunate about the practicality of the question Emmet
is obliged to ask is that more needs to be said about how, in what sense, "the
notion of the human person" represents "the social and institutional support"
(structure?) and how that representation can avoid implicating "the pure subject." She seems to want to say what she apparently cannot, to say what is meant
by using the expression "human person" to refer to a social being; and it is not

at all clear how to distinguish a concrete subject in action from what seems to "support" it without instituting the sort of metaphysics Emmet rejects—since what appears to "support" may constitute the "subject" (to the extent to which the latter refers to or is equivalent to "'the human person' and her 'characteristic enterprises'"). The problem is exacerbated when the referents of her question appear to be state-like conceptions of "person" and "social and institutional support" without regard to the relationship between activity and states presupposed by the "reasons" she brings into play in clarifying the ideas of "person" and "social," thereby glossing over the possibility that the two conceptions are not at all complementary and may be incompatible.

The second point that is inhospitable to the implication that is essential to Emmet's view of human affairs as immanently social is that the underlying theory of action addresses, as a possible basis of sociality, "conduct which is partly at least rule directed" and therefore subject to mentally instituted reasons conforming to rules (1975, 11). This says that being rule-directed, and, possibly, therefore being social, is contingent (thereby preserving the distinctions between actor and action and between action that is and action that is not social). But it also seems to say—in conjunction with features of her account discussed previously and to the extent to which "being rule-governed" is either equivalent to "being social" or a fact that merely happens to be about all instances of social action—that it is a necessary feature of whatever can legitimately be called human conduct (obliterating those distinctions).

Third, "being rule directed" summarizes the idea that the sociality of action "depends on there being common expectations as to how people are likely to act, and on these expectations not being too often disappointed" (7). This allows that people decide what to do in regard to what they expect to happen as a result of being with others, and that their expectations operate as prior mental states corresponding to or representing their experience. Note that it says nothing about how the possibility of being disappointed fits into the structure of the sociality of action, and that structure, such as it is, must be held to include it. In other words, it leaves open how mutuality and reciprocity are constituted and how they work to produce and sustain an act; yet they are presumed to be prior to the formation of expectations that are said either to be based on them or to express them. The idea seems to be that actors' generalizations of their expectations are individually personal facts that somehow fit rules that are quintessentially social facts, and that the mental ordering of their experiences accordingly corresponds to the intimacy of the relationship between generalization (which is compromised by an uncountable possibility of exceptions) and rule (the concept of which seems incompatible with the possibility of compromise). To the extent to which this is a fair interpretation, it begs the key question of what it is for an action to be social in such a way that actors generalize their expectations and, in so doing, take them as rules that project those expectations as independent social facts that transcend application to particularly specifiable others—that is, extend to others in general.[4]

Possible answers to the question of how to identify subjectivity apart from particular subjects are typically limited by two problematic and possibly self-defeating assumptions about the relationship between mind and action, beyond the fact that generalizations of the sort mentioned are effectively compromised by the possibility of their being violated. The first says that what counts in explaining an instance of action by reference to its intentionality is, primarily, what is present as an intention in the mind of a putative actor, especially beliefs and desires, which are largely inferred after the fact. It is in this regard that the second assumption is fatal. It says that whatever intentionality is involved in an instance of action must be of a sort that can explain that very instance as representing, expressing, or otherwise realizing a prior intention to do just what was done (or would have been but for a failure of conditions or, perhaps, a weakness of will). It requires that what has been done realizes a prior intention to do just that—where what has been done is independently understood according to its ostensible, or public, content and considered as such to have been the aim of the (nonpublic) intention. It amounts to saying that actors generally intend to do what others either hold them to have done (this or that type of meaningful action) or can reasonably be said to hold them to have done. Thus, it is not surprising that Emmet concludes that the idea of the social is "at least partly a matter of terminology" (168). It is, however, surprising that she leaves us with the very question she seemed about to answer when she initially noted that virtually all that human beings do as "characteristically" human is social. If what is human about human affairs is that they are social and the appeal to rules is not adequate to that characterization, we are still far from reducing the vagueness of the term and, therefore, not much closer to showing that the proposal is valid than we were when it was merely stated. It seems, then, that the underlying theory of action provides no solace for one claiming, as I believe Emmet, Strawson, and Sartre are, that sociality is either a necessary feature of human affairs or immanent to them, and, if it is neither, then both it and what it presumably qualifies are theoretically unmanageable.

———

The history of modern philosophy has taught us to be wary of essentialist concepts and, in any case, of trying to decide what is or is not essentially human. Yet the question is on the agenda the moment one attempts to account for the subjectivity of an instance of behavior according to the idea of a context (including "support") and, especially, the moment it is admitted that a context necessarily involves other humans being "characteristically human" in their "enterprises." If this begins with individuals and their mental states and treats social facts as "*shared* representations," it still raises the possibility that such facts exist objectively, apart from specific individuals, and that they operate independently of the sort of experience normally taken to register facts or relations among facts and to project expectations as reasons. Certainly one would be hard-pressed to disagree with the proposition that persons cannot be understood in their personhood apart from their social settings and from society as a vast community of strangers. But this depends on an idea of context that goes beyond its reference to relatively invariant, more or less interrelated, properties of a situation, and therefore on an idea of personhood (or agency) quite different from the idea of a person (or agent) as a particular in a relatively fixed, reliable, and recordable context. This may be enough to justify asking how and what we think when we take for granted that there is something distinctively human about human affairs that has something to do with what we take sub-theoretically to be social—which includes more and perhaps other than what is merely indicated by references to mediation, representation, control, regulation, influence, rules, norms, affections, groups, background factors, contexts, and the like. This is all the more significant when we allow for the possibility that "social" refers not so much to the quality of the act as to the nature of agency itself and that it does so necessarily and not as a matter of contingency or pragmatics. Taking "social" to be a quality of "agency" rather than "the act" is consistent with one important implication of Emmet's account, that all that humans do that is "characteristically human" is, in some respect, social. It is a short step from there to say that what is social about human affairs is what is human about them and not merely a property of something humans might choose to do. In other words, the gains from studying humans according to what they do as ostensibly individual persons are not sufficient to offset a failure to inquire into what makes what they do recognizably human in the first place, as instances of human affairs and therefore as constitutively social.

———

There seems little reason to doubt that accounts of mind, reason, value, individuality, action, language, agency, instrumentality, intentionality, utility, identity, justice, rationality, consciousness, reflection, institutions, and morality depend, in important respects, on the pre-theoretical notion that human beings are essentially social and the sub-theoretical intuition that sociality is irrepressible and irreducible. This is so regardless of what the word is taken to mean and how it is ordinarily used; and it can be left out of inquiry only by ignoring crucial features of whatever topic is being studied. There is little reason to doubt the dependency of those topics on intuitions about sociality because there seem to be few if any examples of inquiry that do not rely on unanalyzed sociological constructs—such as sharing, communicating, speaking, participating, agreeing, taking into account, understanding, and conversing. To the extent to which an inquiry relies on the informal language of sociality, with its individualistic presuppositions, formal analysis leaves crucial aspects of its material helpless to associations bound to undermine the completeness and clarity toward which it is aimed.

Nevertheless, one inference is in certain respects counterintuitive, though it is nevertheless reinforced by certain currents in the philosophies of mind and action. It seems to contradict intuitions based on the premise of most discussions of agency that the skin is a natural boundary, thereby challenging empiricism and individualism at their most fundamental level of expression and most immediate level of application. The conclusion is that mind, considered as coterminous with what is distinctively human and as encompassing most of what is identified with agency, is constitutionally social—at least in the sense that it transpires across and not within bodies and therefore is identifiable as a course of activity and not as self-individuating states of being. Much of this book is occupied with the logical conditions of the intuition that supports this conclusion as part of coming to terms with the sense in which human beings can be said to be essentially social and in regard to what that entails for knowledge of human affairs. To the extent to which this conclusion about mind derives from the more inclusive proposition about sociality, it reveals what is philosophically at stake in theorizing the latter.

Part of this has to do with the widespread but by no means unanimous agreement in the human sciences that the sociality of human affairs differs radically from the collective life of nonhumans—regardless of morally compelling analogies by some sociobiologists and theorists of artificial intelligence, naturalists, fabulists, and many writers of children's stories. The point is not that humans are not animals but that what they are as humans cannot be expressed in the language we use to discuss nonhumans (which may or may not include animals).[5] The fate of behaviorism in psychology testifies to the intractability of the distinction, not as a matter of "folk psychology" but as a matter of what is understood as the very phenomenon to which a science of human affairs must respond if it is to be a science. Accordingly, it is not just that human beings are abstractly social but that sociality is essentially human as things stand (no matter to what else it might be extended) and can be neither reduced to the simple and apparently more general fact of collectivization (or even to the operation of rules) nor separated from the human aspect of human affairs without undoing the meaningfulness of both "social" and "human."[6]

This idea is represented by an ancient distinction, significantly emphasized in modern times by Rousseau, between "society" as the "realm" (or course of activity) in which human beings are identifiable to one another, and to themselves, in their humanness and to that extent are mutually substitutable as absolute values, and a mere collection of individuals, mobilized accidentally or by means of coercion (e.g., as means rather than ends), in the form of a "multitude." This implies that such beings cannot be considered in their humanity as members of a category or collection, including as instances of a type, or as exemplars of a species-kind in the biological evolutionary sense of the word. They must be thought of instead as manifesting a preconception of life that we are unable to do without as things stand, and that we must, therefore, bring to some degree of clarity in order to make of that preconception a conception of a "natural kind"—to bring a certain nature, objective and moral, to critical light.[7]

The notion that behavior is essentially social is often interpreted by a severely reduced concept of social action that, like any such reduction or simplification, and regardless of whatever advantages it might offer to analysis, threatens the discursive connection to what gives it its sub-theoretical force as an idea. The concept is typically identified with Weber's attempt to delineate the limits and conditions of sociology relative to the other human sciences:

> Sociology (in the sense in which this highly ambiguous word is used here) is a science which attempts the interpretive understanding of social action in order thereby to arrive at a causal explanation of its course and effects. . . . Action is social in so far as, by virtue of the subjective meaning attached to it by the acting individual (or individuals), it takes account of the behaviour of others and is thereby oriented in its course. (1947, 88)

Its immediate relevance to contemporary theory derives in part from the fact that it is consistent with a philosophically well-established intentionalist theory of action that gives focus to discourses that validate a dramatic move from a dependence on motivational psychology (hence the constant reference in the earlier literature to the relationship between the individual and society) to a rational choice, decisionist, or, more broadly, transactional paradigm in which "individual" refers to an actor, or instance of agency, that need not be a person in the psychological sense that includes "personality" and takes the skin to be the natural boundary of mind and agency. This move is supported largely by the effects of four disciplinary projects that coincided in the last third of the twentieth century and remain active today.

The first such project attempts to make institutional politics intelligible beyond immediate settings (often by extending theories of organization that emphasize adaptation), and to make noninstitutional politics (e.g., social movements) intelligible as variations of institutional or "civil" processes, with the special moral and political dispositions that authorize, or deputize, such processes.[8] This momentarily overcomes the appearance of arbitrariness in the classical distinction between collective *action*, defined in an underdetermined way that allows a great deal that is not theoretically situated to be taken theoretically for granted, and collective *behavior*, defined in an overdetermined way that threatens the applicability of the very category of politics, thereby giving impetus to the desire for a theory of democracy compatible with late modernist reflections on two possibilities that are always, in one way or another, anticipated: (1) differences within society that cannot be assimilated to a single value or resolved along a single scale or by combining scales, and that therefore cannot be resolved in the sense required by classical theories of social order and social conflict, and (2) the intrinsically decentering aspects of membership and identity and the corresponding diffuseness of their ideas.[9] At the same time, it creates problems for theories of representation that cannot be addressed without rethinking the very meaning and theoretical location of "representation," no less than "politics." Moreover, and in this regard, it leaves the concept of "institutional action," with "function" as a standard, particularly vulnerable to questions having to do with the historiography, political determination, and axiology by which it, and whatever it authorizes, comes to appear as transhistorical, or system-logical and, in that respect, rational; and it leaves it open to the charge that it appropriates the concept of instrumental action to a strictly moral/political project.

The second project can be identified in regard to the prominence of decision theories of the firm. These tend to emphasize computational procedures, within a game theoretical model of situations, and the structures that inhere in and support them. These theories converge on a self-elaborating logic of agency that does not require, except perhaps at its margins, a psychology of individuals. If we ignore the considerable problems this creates for moral and other value considerations, it risks trivializing the notion of agency—not by failing to take account of the human element but by instituting a reduced concept of decision incompatible with other notions of agency more clearly identified with human affairs under the aspect of their being distinctively human (see Kahneman 2011).

The third project advances structural/system theoretical conceptions of "situation" and "context" in regard to which action—understood as a choice among means relative to attainable ends or to noninstrumental values based on specifiable beliefs and desires, with their weights and priorities—consists largely of attempts to work out the practical implications of objective, reproducible circumstances. The significance of this is apparent in *the fourth project*, which attempts to demonstrate the feasibility of generalizing a radically commercial notion of exchange, according to cost-benefit analysis suited to a generalized idea of a "price-making money market," to all aspects of human affairs subject to those conceptions of system and context. This eliminates from the category of rationality all that is inconsistent with the logic of such exchange; or, better, it constitutes the category of "collective behavior" from activities, dispositions, or conditions that seem to negate exchange—for example, love of the object, token, or medium of exchange, concern for others including one's partners in exchange, nonutilitarian forms of self-interest, and whatever is associated with noninstrumental, nonexpedient sociality.

The latter two projects have been deployed at the service of neoliberal educational policies ostensibly aimed at increasing the sophistication of the consumer population in the interest of easing inequalities among individuals in their capacity as risk-taking participants in universal exchange.[10] As is well known, this emphasis on formal, or relative (post-social), equality justifies placing the burden and associated risks of overcoming substantive inequalities on individuals or families, and avoids challenging the structural conditions under which it is deemed desirable to identify equality with the opportunity to gain over and against others. In this regard, one can say that such policies have a reactionary aspect no matter how humane their intentions. The politics of this are fairly clear from the point of view of class and class hegemony, which makes the philosophical and theoretical limitations of generalizing decision theories less obvious but no less informative.

For one thing, such policies are tied to an evolutionary, and consequently narrow and increasingly less inclusive view of social progress, which, unless one introduces justice as an ad hoc principle, requires tolerating inequalities in conditions of life that are inconsistent with the more general notion of a just society often used to account for those very neoliberal reforms (see Murphy and Nagel 2002). From the point of view of economic philosophy, and consistent with late eighteenth and early nineteenth century notions of the "sweetness" of commerce, they reduce the referents of "action" to those clearly definable forms most adequately suited to the "price-making money market," thereby excluding the form of life implicit in what is human about human affairs. One thinks in this regard of Marx's (1990a) account of the ideal of universal exchange and the policies associated with that ideal in rationalizing commerce—in which every distinguishable thing comes to represent a currency that distinguishes among things exclusively by ratio thereby constituting them as self-disqualifying instances of the incessant movement of money itself. Marx demonstrates that this contradicts another condition of rationalization—namely, the capacity to distinguish rigorously among points of production, among system functions, between producers and consumers, between goods and their ostensible tokens, and, especially important for the very notion of commerce, between buyers (buying) and sellers (selling). That is, for Marx's understanding of how capitalist production rationalizes itself in its own terms, the move toward universal exchange is the project on which the rationalization of commerce depends, though exchange remains beholden to what it is intended to suppress—namely, its negation in the progress of production, consumption, enjoyment, sociality, and so on. Yet, as he shows, the attempt to clarify the concept of exchange is forced to replace it by a concept of circulation. This, in turn, is conceivable only as a circulation of money that makes irrational what most needs to be rational—the relationship of money to an independent measure of value (the proportion of the pool of labor power productively employed, or value as productive capacity). This has the further effect of undermining the distinctions between purchase and sale and value and price on which the idea and the common sense of the self-generalizing market depend. It is in this respect that the very idea of universal exchange is equivalent, as a matter of its own logic, to the "circulation of fictitious capital."

In regard to strictly disciplinary concerns, and independent of the moral and political dispositions that they affirm and on which they may well be predicated, these four projects respond, first, to the failure of the psychological model of agency to account for what people do together and what being together does to them, and, second, to the unwieldy accumulation of increasingly elaborate quasi-concepts (e.g., norm, role, and rule), by which I mean concepts insufficiently coherent with other concepts and propositions in a theoretically interpretable way. Both are obstacles to reflecting on the implications of the idea of sociality as what is human about human affairs. The fact that such quasi-concepts arise, proliferate, and become increasingly elaborate has the effect of sustaining individualism as the default model for the failure to clarify the idea of the social. However, this merely shifts emphasis from the internal life, or intentionality, of the actor to what lies outside of the actor, as objective situation, ultimately reducing the model and what it purports to represent—namely, agency—to marginal notations; it thereby leaves the center, as it were, theoretically unoccupied. In that case, the durability of individualism poses problems that remain to be addressed, at least by a sociology that appears committed to it despite a history of disclaiming it; and "agency" remains fatefully bound to a metaphysics of particulars.

Weber's concept of social action is typically taken to characterize what it is to be social—with room, later, for nonrational, pathological, parasitical, or marginal cases. It says that a great deal if not most of what individuals do can be understood only if some reference is made to their "taking account" of the straightforward and more or less immediate presence of "others."[11] The general formula might be stated as follows: an act, defined by its reason, is a function of an actor in a situation that includes others as irresistible action-salient facts. The reference to that connection between actor and other subsumes and in that sense qualifies whatever additional facts might further our understanding of the act, but it does not exclude the relevance of such facts. The "others" who, apparently individual by individual or as a plurality, figure in the idea of "a presence or presences taken into account by an individual actor," are, in that capacity, exceptions to the dictum that humans cannot be "understood" according to whatever allows them formally to be characterized as members of a collection, though, as others *to* an actor or actors, they are identified with a special class of situated objects. These comprise a topographically coherent space, a context or "structure of relevance" (Schutz 1970, 39) composed of relatively invariant relations in which action has its orientation and intention, and has the unintended effect of determining variations in those relations, thereby inadvertently reconstituting the context of further instances of oriented action.

Despite its initial plausibility, the relationship between actor/action and context (ostensible objects of action-relevant belief) poses difficulties for the concept of "taking account of others." These arise in regard to the dissociation of the situated others taken into account from the conception of humanity that unites them with those who take them into account; and it is this conception that imposed, in the first place, the theoretical need to introduce the concept of taking others into account. The difficulty arises because the concept does not provide for the distinction of kind it assumes between actor and others. Yet fitting the idea of others to the idea of contexts that are externally related to action, to situations that indifferently include things and people, relies on just such a distinction. To the extent to which the others to be taken into account are human beings, taking them into account must involve a certain alertness, sensitivity, and openness on the part of the actor, as well as skill at recording features, recalling, drawing inferences, and calculating; and it must involve a degree of alertness, sensitivity, and openness that cannot be assimilated to the notion of an external relation of actor to situation in which things and others are treated as presenting to the actor the same sort of accountable fact.

The others' membership in the collection of situated and accountable objects is defined by their otherness to actors, their being for the moment non-agents. Actors, who are in principle human, are of a different order of being as far as the relationship between action and situation is concerned: they are, at the very least, engaged rather than passive. In contrast, Weber's others are in that crucial respect not distinctively human. They are, rather, instances of "something taken into account that does not take anything into account." They are thereby conceived of as opposed to "what takes things into account but is not at that moment taken into account."[12] The way in which they are "other" to actors lies, then, in the fact that their presence, all that it amounts to relative to action, is objectively part of the situation in regard to which actors act, including whatever external characteristics they have that bear on the situation and the calculable residues of whatever experiences they have had of the non-actors in other situations in which they might have been active. It is necessary to sustain this idea of a situation that indifferently adds others to extra-personal situated facts if the theory of the sociality of action is to allow for the kind of objectifying rationality required by "taking account" and if the idea of the actor's way of being social, from which we are allowed to arrive at the idea of a social action, is not to undermine the idea of her individuality. It must be kept in mind, however, that one overriding purpose of most theories of action has been to account for a type of agency that, as far as we know, cannot be duplicated by animals (below a certain threshold of symbolic competence) or simulated by machines.

A special problem arises when "taking account of others" needs to be taken into account. "Taking account of others" cannot be a matter of calculation and it cannot conform to even the most general idea of information processing. For it turns out, according to a strict adherence to the formula given previously, "an act is a function of an actor in a situation that includes others as irresistible action-salient facts," an actor conceived of as a computing machine is no more distinctively human than her situational others.[13] This is because of the stipulation that taking such others into account does not require their being human except in the trivial sense of behaving according to relatively fixed dispositions at the moments the actor forms an intention and then acts on it. These dispositions are present in a way that allows the actor, who is taking account, to assign probabilities to what the others might or might not do, thereby allowing decisions to be reasonably based on those assignments. Given this, the reflexively agentic sense of "actor," without which there would be no interest in a theory of action per se, is trivialized by characterizing actors as a registries of facts and as rationalizing machines that operate primarily on those same facts according to, among other rules, a principle of least effort, qualified by action-independent factors, and according to the actors' own prior dispositions.

Insofar as an actor is conceived of that way, because the standard concept of action requires just that conception, and because, at the precise moment of acting, the actor is taken to be identical with the set of complementary decision functions, her relations with others can be conceived of only as external and, therefore, as relations with particular others—"particular" in the sense of being the exclusive and self-sufficient occupant of a singular point in space-time. Such others, along with the nonhuman things with which they are grouped by the act of taking them into account, are merely givens. They are specific and prior, and are pre-theoretically stipulated as non-thing-like human elements of the situation in which action takes place. The conception of such an actor effectively amounts to little more than those external relations concentrated internally by a disposition of mysterious origin (namely, to register/calculate) and internally regulated by no less mysterious determinative states (or properties of states) such as complete beliefs and complete motives. In other words, in consigning others to the status of situated objects, given the assumption that the skin is a natural boundary to intentionality, this theory of social action leaves us with a similarly reduced conception of the agency implicit in the idea of action. It is so much reduced that agency can no longer be recognized as a referent of the theory and as a property of the "actor." To that extent, the theory is no longer about what it was originally intended to address.

The pedagogy of the theory is similarly affected. The actor is most persuasively represented diagrammatically as a point of origin, qualified by prior states and a current need or desire, relative to a determinate set of parameters within a situation, a space, in which the relations of the originary point and those positions are invariant but the boundaries of the regions that divide the situation a priori, and the "paths" that link those regions, are stable relative to the actor. It is given that the actor is already in motion within that situation, and that her predicaments change (e.g., in regard to time, meaning, and the salience of certain possible choices) as she moves through its various subregions. It is a feature of the temporality of the space, its aspects of invariance and conditions of transformation, that the movement of the originary point, the actor, confirms the relations that constitute its specificity. If the movement is not given, and the constitution of agency thereby becomes an issue, the pedagogical model can be sustained as a re-presentation of action only if something else is added to explain agency, perhaps a concept of a self that contains beliefs and desires and the structure that unites them and that somehow extends, without losing its identity, from before the undertaking to an indefinite future for which, it is presumed, the preservation of that very self is the overriding motive.

Introducing a principle for pedagogical purposes, such as an appeal to the idea of a self, easily takes on conceptual significance and risks incurring theoretical obligations—as if what is offered, by way of illustrating, dramatizing, or even filling in an idea otherwise difficult to clarify, is the idea itself.[14] For example, it might require transforming the theory of action into a theory of conditions that presumably prevail or could prevail apart from any instance of action but that nevertheless address some of what is most often associated with it. In that case, it may be possible to identify sufficient conditions of action, sufficient in the sense of being the last moment of a value-adding process in which there finally are no apparent options. But it becomes difficult to say what they are sufficient for, what might be uncontroversial instances, without seeming to identify the act with its conditions—as when one "derives" intentions from context in such a way that it is possible to characterize the act as an undertaking determined exclusively by its setting—and, so, as "rational." Another possibility involves theorizing enduring dispositions of a self that might inspire or contribute causally to action but, because they are dispositions and are presumably inertial, have no other extra-theoretically recognizable aspect of human agency, much less of sociality.

Both options arise as expressions of obligations incurred when one tries to illustrate an idea of agency that cannot include situational others in the same category of human being as actors and for which the skin is taken to be a natural boundary. Given those restrictions, formulations that are designed to make the idea of social action convenient and intelligible in extra-theoretical ways— that is, pedagogically—inevitably become points of departure for new theories. But the idea that humans are essentially social is intuitively no less valid insofar as it means that what they do by way of being human is immanently and not contingently social. Since this remains sub-theoretical to the idea regardless of how it is presented pedagogically, it is and must be one test of the validity of any theory. For example, a concept of "self" intended to contribute to an account of a particular undertaking would have to be caught up in that immanence, and the latter is essential to a theory of action for which social action involves taking account of others. The undertaking must be explained if taking account of others is to be relevant to action, since to take them into account is already, in some sense, to have already begun the undertaking.

The idea of an essential sociality can accommodate neither conditions of action that are not immanent to the act nor behavior described as external to what are said to be its conditions. It does not support a characterization of the actor as an originary point relative to other, inertial points. It does not provide a perspective from which action implicates a situationally transcendent self. Finally, it does not provide for the sort of individuality that supports the idea of an originary point able to move beyond whatever had already put it into motion and, by virtue of that, able to transform its situation in the interest of bringing itself to an end. If there is to be a self, it must account for the immanence of the social; and this does not seem possible given the logical conditions of such a conception derived from the standard theory of action.

What leads to this particular theoretical impasse is the pedagogical side of reasoning about action as a particular actor's taking account of particular things, such that social action is conceived of as an actor's taking account of others as thing-like. References to conditions of action, others, originary points, movement, invariant relations, and the rest, now appear to be extra-theoretical, designed to make intelligible an unnecessarily weak pre-theoretical notion of what it is to be human and to act accordingly. In this respect, the audience for the standard theory of action as taught is already committed to such notions of origins, individuality, selves, identity, and situations. It is the pre-philosophical audience that philosophy has always taken as its primary addressee beyond even its most technical analyses. Those undoubtedly appealing notions are not formally derived from strict action-theoretical propositions; they are not compelled by empirical fact; and they apparently are not part of the logical development of the concept of action as that occurs in the course of refining the theory, other than as temporary constructs intended to stand in for possible developments internal to theory or drawn from other disciplines.

13

The Self of the Actor

I argue that the theory of social action as conduct that takes account of others is not an adequate interpretation of the idea that humans are essentially social because it categorically distinguishes between the actor who takes others into account and the nonactors taken into account. The theory depicts the actor as solitary insofar as she is taking something (e.g., an "other") into account, so the predicate "social" applies to the action in the course of which "taking account" occurs and not to the actor herself. In this respect, it is occasionally convenient to represent the actor as a predisposed "point" on a space represented topographically as areas, boundaries, and paths that are parameters within which changes in position are possible. The point's movement transforms this space, changing the distances between and relations among the areas, boundaries, and paths, thereby leading to changes of direction or pace. We can imagine such an actor by rough analogy of an automobile driver following a map that must be constantly turned and refolded as she moves from one place or set of circumstances to another. Other drivers are also parametric to what the actor/driver is likely to do next, so they are likely to be taken into account by the actor in the course of acting. If so, what the actor *is doing* qualifies as an instance of social action, although the actor is not thereby a *social being*; and the others taken into account are conditions of action in contrast with actors and social beings. Since taking things into account tends to homogenize them according to a standard, what counts as human about the actor is her predisposition and capacity to take account of things. The actor is, then, conceived of as a pre-social being that occasionally engages in social action. How, then, should her initial state and conditions of orientation be explained? One popular answer invokes the idea of a self that endures beyond the particular situations

in which an actor takes account of things that are present and in regard to relations among persons. But how can a pre-social being have acquired the sort of
self that can explain what is involved in recognizing and then taking account
of others? It cannot; therefore, the actor must be conceived of as social from the
outset, as essentially social. In that case invoking the self is inconsistent with
the model of action that made it appear necessary—which assumes a pre-social
actor who is, therefore, solitary in the course of deliberating. Yet the concept of
a self plays an important role in the extension of the theory of action to situations in which reasons that correspond to immediate conditions are insufficient to explain the undertaking of an act or, as we have seen in the discussion
of Nagel's analysis of altruism, to the fact that people often respond to reasons
that arise in regard to interests that are not momentarily their own. The idea of
a self was supposed to provide for a crucial set of conditions of an action's being
social in Nagel's sense (1970, 99–115) and rational in Searle's (2001, 74). But it
fails if it does nothing more than reify the agentic life of the actor by extending
it from particular concrete situations, in which "agency" is reduced to registering and calculating, to a transcendent situation that embraces the life course of
the individual *qua* individual—that is, as pre-social (independent and autonomous). Among the conceptual problems raised by this point of view, the crucial
problem of accounting for "accounting for *others*" in terms that have to do with
what is human about human affairs remains unsolved and, given the theoretical constraints, appears for the moment unsolvable.

There is another way to introduce the idea of an agentic self in order to deal
with what is missing in the theoretical leap from the activity of taking
things into account to a full-blown action that is both an instance of a type and
an event that can be understood as a structure. It will become apparent that
this effectively frees the problem of agency from the limits placed on it by the
theory of action and reassigns it to a discourse in which the concept of "self"
is subject to different theoretical constraints and intentions. It thereby appears
to supplement the original theory of action without changing it; and, in this
regard, it accounts for what the original theory fails to do—namely, to explain
action both as an undertaking and throughout its course and to provide a basis for evaluating the rationality and reflexivity of particular activities beyond
their immediate situations and reasons strictly derived from those situations
(see Searle 2001).

Hampshire expresses this programmatically:

As soon as one realises that the using of language, both in the practical
calculation that may accompany physical actions and in the making of
statements, is itself a kind of behaviour interwoven with other kinds,
one is free to consider the range of essential human interests afresh and
without prejudice. In particular one is free from the prejudice that the

concept of action itself is by itself sufficient to mark the domain of the essential human virtues. One has before one, for reflection and comment, whether in one's own person, or in the person of another, always a whole person, including the way he thinks and expresses his thoughts and feelings, the things that he notices and neglects, the attitudes that he adopts, the feelings that he restrains and the feelings to which he allows free play, the words that he chooses to use or that he uses unreflectingly, the gestures and physical reactions that he controls or suppresses, the plans that he makes and the sudden impulses that occur to him. (1959, 91)[1]

This alternative is discussed later in this chapter and in other sections of this book. For the moment, it is worth noting that it seems to address what Searle sees as a major problem of theories in which reasons perform the same logical function as causes, where situational constraints may be drawn too narrowly to explain what the simplification is intended to make explainable. He describes the "gap" between reasons and the actions they are supposed to explain[2] and argues that its theoretically disabling effects can be mitigated by positing a structural feature of the individual, presumably learned, that has recourse to reasons apart from what is required by any particular situation and that is continuous across situations and throughout most instances of action. Like Nagel (1970), he chooses the "self," which involves increasing the scope of "rationality in action," and conceptualizes it as narrowly, and therefore as manageably, as possible.

There is a well-known danger in adding such a concept to the theory of action, to which the humanities and social sciences are thought to be particularly vulnerable. To the extent to which it transforms the theory or substitutes another for it, it risks treating a formal representation (e.g., action as an event in a causal nexus of mental states, reasons, and intentions)[3] as referring to a reality against which the adequacy of other such representations, as well as the theories of language on which their intelligibility depends, can and must be judged. That is, "action" will not refer to the same thing in the superseded theory, which does not rely on a refined concept of the self, that it means in the superseding theory organized by just such a concept. In that case, the theories cannot be compared according to a shared object, and the conceptualization of a self fails to address the problem of the gap generated by a theory of action formulated without that concept. To avoid this requires confirming the hypothesis that adding a fertile notion of *a virtually undertaking self* to a theory of *action apart from its being undertaken* leaves the theory intact.[4] This is crucial since it is the latter alone that presents the problem of the gap, and this is what is said to generate the need for a concept of the self and, at the same time, places limits on what it can mean. The hypothesis is supported by a conception of the self as a vehicle for manifesting and then realizing reasons, and by the character attributed to that vehicle insofar as it can impose a sense of its identity on each instance of action, including the formation of an intention, the undertaking, and reflection on consequences. For the imposition to work, the vehicle itself must sustain that identity in a type of entity able to support continuity throughout the "life course." The self is, then, predicated on the existence of an autonomous person for whom the skin is a natural boundary and whose conduct is motivated from within. This allows for the possibility of assigning responsibility and blame while apparently avoiding the problems posed by explicit reference to essential human virtues (see Putnam 2002, 17–18; Taylor 1985b, 15–41, esp. 21). In that case the second theory, which includes the self, complements the first, as a supplement that allows it to complete its account of action. There are now potential, or trans-situational, self-motivating agents who might or might not be faced with the facts of a given situation and who are governed by complex dispositions of long standing and considerable generality; and there are types of action that subsist as templates for what might follow from filling the gaps in the relation between intention-constituting reasons and an undertaking. The situated moment of the actor is identified by such temporarily interrelated states as believing, desiring, and intending, which are insufficient to account for the undertaking but that, taken together and independent of the self, are presumed sufficient to evaluate retrospectively the rationality of the instance of action relative to its immediate situation and, perhaps, the actor's memory. But it now seems that there are two rather different theories with different objects—namely, different conceptions of action.

The problem addressed by this strategy is how to expand the scope of rationality beyond what is required in a particular time-limited situation, and to consider additional reasons that might bring the actor yet closer to the actual undertaking of the act. I argue that introducing the notion of a self—and to tie it, as Searle does, to biological longevity—in order to account for both the final intention and the actual undertaking either fails in its own terms or transforms both the notion and the theory to such a degree that their combination cannot be said to address the same object addressed by the theory of action alone. What is important about this is that the notion of a self is introduced to explain what the theory of action needs if it is to provide an analysis of social action as social. The idea of a self is clearly able to take account of "taking account of others," by virtue of its ability to place those others in a spatially transcendent context, but only if the others taken into account also abide in time and are therefore social beings in contrast with thing-like objects. But more is still necessary for them to be grasped as of the same order of humanity as the actor who takes them into account and for the actor who subsists over time in the form of a self to be understood as identical to the limited actor who subsists within a concrete situation requiring that something be done—the actor as a reflection of that situation somehow imbued with a transcendental principle of agency.

When the strategy is examined in detail, it is no longer clear that adding a self is merely supplemental. Too much is involved to justify the meta-hypothesis that the theory of the self and the theory of action are not significantly transformed by combining them. The strategy ends by assuming what it cannot legitimately assume—namely, that the object of the two added together, which remains stipulated to be "action," will be the same as the object of the one, the theory of action, without the addition of the other, the theory of the self. It seems clear that the properties by which an object is formally delineated limit its *concept* according to the theory in which it is instantiated as such. Action is one such theoretical object, and its availability to more than one theory depends on showing that each theory identifies it by the same features and formal properties and, perhaps, by the same rules for picking out examples in different situations. Hampshire comments in this regard that "it is a philosophical self-deceit to pretend that the proper subjects for evaluation, and for the exercise of the will, are already marked out for us by an ordinary, undisputed concept of action" (1959, 92). But theories that seem to agree about the properties of action and ways of singling out instances of it are not likely to be different enough to be thought of as alternatives or, for that matter, as complements, though the possibility cannot be ignored (see Hebb 1949).

On the one hand, it would be mistaken to assume that a conceptual object formed by a given theory is the same conceptual object formed by a compound of that theory plus another unless the two theories are equivalent. On the other hand, virtually all theories assume that action thought of as an event not only is the consequence of a decision or the acute tension associated with the stimulation of a desire or habit but realizes itself in a definite movement, an actual undertaking that corresponds to the content of an original intention. I eventually criticize both assumptions; but a theory that accepts them must demonstrate that the action *undertaken and in its course* is the same sort of thing as the action *defined by reasons* residing within the person. The latter may be understood as a particular event in some sense (e.g., as the realization of an intention). But the former cannot, since it is likely to be identified with an intention only after the fact, and then, suspiciously and at most, with a remembered or self-ascribed intention: one cannot rely on a concept of the memory of what was done and why and still claim to have a theory of "action," and one cannot take for granted that nothing else happens following the formation of an intention other than continuing to try to realize it.

The introduction of an idea of a self aims, as far as possible, to complete the theory of action at the level of intentionality, which is the site of both the discursive order of its conception and the sub-theoretical sense of its idea. It does this according to the presupposition that the skin is a natural boundary and the requirement that the causal analysis of action must, as a matter of principle, preserve the absolute autonomy, the solitude, of the individual actor. Under the aspect of intentionality, the causes of an action are mental. One cost of adding a self to a theory that has systematically omitted it is that the meaning of "action" changes. To introduce a notion of the self to solidify an account of the undertaking affects the very idea of an action as a realization of a situationally responsive intention, unless the self and its non-situated reasons are distinct from whatever agency is involved in situated reasons and the actions they are supposed to explain. But this vitiates its purpose, since we now have two agents, each of which produces the problem of a gap between the different sorts of reasons and the actions they are said to cause. The risk may appear insignificant if referring to a self is not intended to be theoretical—if the word "self" is to be used heuristically or as a stand-in for a concept yet to be formed or an intuition yet to be substantiated. But even a nontheoretical notion that aims to correct a theory must allow for at least the prospect of its being theorized. For example, Searle lists five "features of the self" that I believe, though he does not seem to agree, raise doubts about the validity of the concept of action as typically defined and about the intuitions the concept is intended to satisfy.[5] This self is conscious, persistent through time, "operates with reasons, under the constraints of rationality" and "under the presupposition of freedom," and "is responsible for at least some of its behavior" (Searle 2001, 95).

While Searle may not intend to undermine the concept of action, his intentions are theoretical despite the fact that his notion of the self is far from what would be required of a concept. He says:

> The subject matter of rationality is not formal argument structures, much less is it marginal utility and indifference curves. The central topic of discussion in a theory of rationality is the activity of human beings (and presumably some other animals, as [Wolfgang] Köhler's apes have convinced us), selves, engaged in the process of reasoning. Just as the central subject matter of the philosophy of language is neither sentences nor propositions, but speech acts, so *the subject matter of the philosophy of rationality is the activity of reasoning, a goal-directed activity of conscious selves.* (2001, 95–96; emphasis in original)

This comes perilously close to endorsing the notion of a course of activity that cannot be understood in the same way action has been understood—namely, as the unequivocal product of individuated intentionality. To go further requires rethinking the meaning of "self"; reconsidering possible options for addressing the problem of the gap; and rethinking the concepts of reason, intention, action, undertaking, and so on, in regard to which the gap appears unbridgeable. *Surely the idea of a self is no clearer or no more easily fit to our other ideas about what people do than the idea that sociality is immanent to all of what they are and do.* As we will see, Searle's choice is not easily reconciled with his statement that action is the execution of an intention according to "the two most important relations in the internal structure of actions," which are "the causal by-means-of relation and the constitutive by-way-of relation" (Searle 2001, 51–52; see also Fay and Moon 1994). It goes almost without saying that his shift from "action" to "activity" is more than a matter of inflection, for ongoing activity is precisely what has been read out of the theory of action.

One option is to think of the word "self" as nothing more than a marker for a complex fact that seems undeniable—namely, that action and everything associated with it take place in a time beyond any specifiable situation and may be subject to some sort of memory. While this does not provide a theoretical solution to the problem of the gap, the mere use of the term is a reminder that any explanation of an act must encompass more than whatever appears as the immediate situation. It also allows for the possibility that values and beliefs may subsist over time, whether or not they are vested as such in individuals. Again, reference to a self necessarily extends the idea of a situation, radically weakens the idea of social action as the action of an individual that takes account of the conduct of others, and inadvertently introduces the idea that the term "action" either does not refer to what humans do or it needs to be rethought as referring to a course of activity. Parenthetically, it is important in this regard to remember that the standard concept of social action implies a difference between a human actor and a quasi-mechanical humanoid other taken into account. If we accent the social dimension rather than the putative pre-social individuality of the self, and if the same humanity is to be ascribed to both the other and the actor, then it is not clear what "taking account of the conduct of another" might mean, though it is clear that both actor and other are no longer individuals in the same way they are when their essential sociality is not taken into account.

It is implicit in the theory of action that, once the execution of an intention begins, which is presumably the moment of the undertaking, doubts about the situation are suspended by the decision to act. However, if we think of the act as a *course* of activity, the situation will be somewhat different from moment to moment and doubt is likely to return; in that case, the intention and the agency of whatever is being done are likely to vary, and this is not accounted for by the theory. If we assume, with Searle, that the self is a structure that operates reliably over the long run, we are also assuming that it does not normally cease to be reliable as the foundation of an identity in the midst of what is being done. Yet to the extent to which the situation changes in the course of activity, the referent of "undertaking" is no longer clear; nor is it clear what the self is doing in regard to those situated intentions that preceded and were fixed prior to the undertaking and those intentions that should be thought of as "ongoing accomplishments" rather than realizations of a fixed intention. In these respects, the existence of a self implies a de-situated aspect of agency, and a profoundly problematic gap between the idea of action as a function of a personalized self and the idea of it as a function of a situation.

The notion of a self nevertheless hints at something that must be taken into account—that social beings are never at rest; they are continually active as parties to courses of activity over which they have far less control than is attributed to them by the standard theory. This requires a conception of agency as reflexive *throughout the course of an action*, something ignored in the current analytical literature. It also requires a logical fit between every instance of action and an intentionality that is already in motion and that displays itself in each moment of the course of the activity. This means that there is no slice of activity, instance of behavior, or cross section that can be extracted and treated as distinct; for whatever activity appears to be a particular event is, by definition, embedded in a changing situation from which it cannot be removed and still intelligibly appear as intended. It also means that the language of agency and the language of individuality are not mutually translatable. This has implications for replacing the self in the theory of action, possibly by an aspect of sociality.

Many proponents of the standard theory endorse two inter-dependent working hypotheses: (1) that the self is the sustaining context of reasons that go beyond the exigencies of specific situations and (2) that the self is an important feature of intentionality, since it corresponds to what is irrepressible in the life of the individual person who acts, and it operates throughout whatever that person does by way of being human. It follows that the closeness of an original intention to a specific undertaking, its causal force, depends on an enduring formation already in motion before the moment of the undertaking. A theory of such a formation would doubtless include the idea that the self contains relatively integrated generalized orientations that determine the limits and to some extent the tendency of the momentarily specific orientation of an undertaking. It would also provide for self-sufficient facts from outside of the concrete situation as part of an explanation of how an action already in motion can change in its course despite no detectable changes in its immediately concrete situation. The course of activity can change if it embodies not only the potential but also a readiness to change—that is, if it is, somehow, the activity of a self as well as a limited reaction of a situated actor to a definite concrete situation. This seems implicit in the claim that the self is a continuing and stable presence throughout the life of the individual, and Searle's more radical implication that little if anything about that life thought of under the aspect of intentionality is intelligible without that presence. The self, or whatever it stands for, must therefore be taken to manifest itself in whatever the person does under whatever conditions she does it and in response to whatever situation immediately presents itself.

This means that both the moment of the undertaking and the activity that it initiates display subjective qualities such as alertness, anticipation, and the like. If all this is implicated by inserting the notion of a self in an account of action, then it is clear that "action" no longer refers to the execution of a specific intention, and that not only the undertaking but the course of activity that ensues must be attended to if there is to be an account of what people do that conforms to whatever intuition adding the self to the theory of action is supposed to satisfy. Among the further issues this raises are the status of the general structure in regard to consciousness, and the nature of the relation of a self that is extended in time (with the stable beliefs, values, and motives it presumably *contains*) to the actor who intends and undertakes according to the composition of a relatively static given situation and, perhaps, by far more unstable and volatile beliefs and desires than those that can be part of the "structure" of a self. Despite the apparent intractability of these and other issues that are bound to arise, reference to a "self" may still be defended on the grounds that it serves heuristic purposes the advantages of which outweigh the problems that arise when it is refined as a concept. It is nevertheless clear that reference to a self at least dramatizes the fact that there is a theoretically significant gap between situated reasons and the moment of the undertaking, even if it is no more than an ad hoc supplement. The latter is by no means innocuous since it brings in more than the theory of action can bear and still remain coherent—at least if it is to be useful beyond its relevance to the simplification of the phenomenon it claims ultimately to address. For one thing, a concept of the self must not be inconsistent with what appears to be an overwhelming and indisputable social psychological fact—namely, that selves are social products or what is not quite the same, emergents. This means that the self is a "product" of socialization agencies and processes that operate throughout the long run of the person's life; and there is no reason to believe that this is either a linear or a cumulative process or that it is deliberate and self-correcting, or that its "continuity" is the sort Searle, for one, requires.

This introduces a degree of complexity that is not anticipated by the theory of action or by most philosophical accounts of rationality in action. Moreover, it opens up the possibility that, whatever "self" refers to in other contexts, it cannot be the self-sustaining structure it seemed to be when it was introduced as a supplement to the theory of action. Rather, it seems that we are left with the idea of a social self. Parenthetically, this is not what Goffman (1963) means by "social identity," which is intended to indicate a typifying moment of a collective process in which the possibility of attributing an identity to someone based on a metonymic figuration of her type becomes, or might become, an issue for others. When there either is such an attribution or one is anticipated, the resulting tension is managed (in the first case) or information is controlled (in the second), and in each case there is a collaboration among all parties to the setting. Goffman is not saying that the attribution of a social identity, or the possibility thereof, is what sociologists used to refer to as "labeling," but that it is a problematic fact about every instance of communication (people among people) and therefore a feature of the "order of human interaction."[6]

Social identity, conceived of in regard to the aspect of action that involves taking account of others who also take account, is apparently sensitive to the irreducibly collective features of its environment, and these cannot be ignored by any attempt to clarify it, say as a structure, and relate it to the idea of an individual self in Searle's sense. We will see that neither identity nor self solve the problem posed when theories of action attempt to take account of an undertaking if *action is conceived of as a course of activity in which individuality is, in some sense, subsumed by sociality and then restored as an instance of it.*

However this may turn out, it remains the case that referring to a self in accounting for action is aimed in part at expanding the scope of "rationality in action," in this way adding explanatory value to the theory of action and enlarging the range of normative considerations to which the idea of rationality might be relevant, both of which are intended by Searle. It is in this capacity that the notion of a self may appear adequate to a theory of action capable of accounting for social action, but only if the latter is sufficient to identify persons as social beings beyond what they do about the presence of others, and we have seen that it is not. Invoking the notion of a self at least points toward possible additional reasons for an actor's choosing whether to do something in particular, apart from those pertaining to the immediate situation. If the course of a life is understood as an ongoing process of socialization, whatever else might be added,[7] these reasons have to do with membership in groups and participation in courses of activity that no individual devises or necessarily intends. It should not be thought obvious that these socialized reasons belong or can be attributed to a particular self, and they do not seem to be the sorts of "reasons" that add up to unified and relatively stable intentions. Even if one claims that they do, the self brought into play in this argument is not the self that Searle and other philosophers have described as relevant to the theory of action.

There is, however, still more to discuss in regard to possible solutions to the problem of the causal gap in standard accounts of action. For the supplement of the self to work, it must complete the theory of action as far as it includes social action conceived of either as a taking account of others or as what transpires within a course of activity. If it cannot, then the individualistic perspective that informs the standard theory of action is liable to the critical charge that it is not consistent with the ideas that humans are essentially social beings and that sociality is irrepressible and irresistible. So far, the discussion has put to the side questions raised earlier about the loss of the human dimension of actor and other in the theory of action. It is now necessary to return to those questions and decide whether any version of the self can restore that dimension— remembering that it can succeed only if it does so for both the actor and those taken as the actor's others.

14

Self and Situation

The theoretical usefulness of the construct of a self depends in part on what it is intended to bring to notice. For the point of view under consideration, that is a complex temporality of action coordinated with the actor conceived of as a particular for which the skin is a natural boundary that individuates certain "events" sufficient to provide a general grounding for motivation and to integrate the various dispositions necessary for the formation and implementation of specific intentions. The integrity of the temporal dimension is confined to and supported by a self-articulating identity the tendencies of which continue throughout the physical life of the person, constituting, mysteriously but by more than mere accretion, a psychical structure. Change is thereby conceived of teleologically, as an effect of a series of total adaptations to external facts without any significant change of identity: there is no internal source of transformation; nor could there be. Such a self-identity is not at all mysterious to the portion of the person's mind that reflects on herself as a spatially and temporally limited totality, what Mead (1962) referred to as the "me" that is knowable in contrast with the ineffable "I" that knows but is not knowable. However, self and mind are, on this view, neither equal nor merely complements. The former is, ultimately, subject to the latter, though the distinction between the two and the subordination of self to mind are as yet confusing parts of the standard picture. Therefore, one is not surprised by who one *had been*, and is able to project, prudently, what one *will be* in making a rational decision in the interest of that continuous, trans-situational self, which may or may not be in the interest of the situationally responsive portion of the self. Concretely situated decisions are brought about by what appears to be either the mind as a portion of the self or something apart from it. Moreover, it is not clear from the standpoint of defining the agentic feature of a projected action whether there is one self or two or whether there is a total subjectivity at work that, in still another guise and under its own local conditions, takes into account the whole self of which it is either a part or moment.

There are, then, endless theoretical problems and a constant need for further supplements whenever the term "self" is deployed. Yet there are two important insights provided by its use. For one, the idea of action in which an individual reconciles desires and beliefs in a particular describable situation is insufficient to account for what that actor appears to be doing—once one acknowledges the problematic aspects of the idea of a situation and the impossibility of extending a severely reductive paradigm to facts only available prior to the reduction (as in adding the idea of a self to overcome the insufficiency of reasons to action in the standard account). The second insight is that the temptation to refer to a self is so fraught with logical difficulties that it appears necessary to think of possible alternatives—to the concept of a self, to the concept of action, or to the individualistic theory of action that cannot resolve on its own terms the problem of the gap. It is important to remember that the supplemental "self" does no more for theory than address the question of how, not whether, individuated intentions are linked to undertakings; in other words, it is designed precisely to leave the reductive simplification in place both for the sake of the standard theory and, paradoxically, for the sake of a universe of human affairs beyond a paradigm that cannot represent such a universe.

One compelling alternative begins negatively, with the counter-supposition that self-identity and individuality are not valid as initial or primary referents for a general account of agency, rationality, and the intelligibility of what has been or is being done by social beings. Positively, it says that an analysis of "sociality" is necessary if the proposition that humans are essentially social is to be taken seriously in trying to understand human affairs, including whatever humans do by way of being human. To the extent to which "action" is intended to stand for just such activities, the theory can be challenged for the adequacy of its paradigmatic simplification. This may afford an opportunity to develop principles from within the ontological field of the human sciences that cover what are supposed to be explained by the standard theory of action and at least some of what that theory fails to take into account beyond what it claims to represent by its simplification of "rationality in action"—including the very possibility of a theory. Before considering this alternative in detail, it is helpful to discuss a related but somewhat different approach that may be more appealing from the point of view of the human sciences thought of as a whole. It does not give priority to the idea of a self but leaves room for it. It says that action is, either generally or fundamentally, a function of its situation. Here, "situation" refers to something far more expansive, uncertain, and self-transformative than is allowed for by the standard theory. The ideas of a skin-bound structure of intentionality and a self may be preserved in one way or another but only as default supplements to or tentative qualifications of a general theory of situations thought of as putting people in motion in the sense of Goffman's (1967, 3) aphorism, which I paraphrase: not persons and their moments (or situations) but moments and their persons.

Despite its limitations, a self of some sort is presupposed in most of what is written about agency, especially in regard to desire, self-interest, sympathy, empathy, identity, choice, weakness of the will, satisfaction, and assignments of blame and responsibility. In each case, there is a veiled reference to virtually coercive features of the situation, either normative or effects of scarcity. When we attempt to extract a theoretical meaning from the use of the term, it brings into play a transcendental conception of an unambiguous super-arching situation within which specific situations or settings—which are always somewhat uncertain, volatile, and ambiguous—impose a sense of urgency on their parties. From the point of view of such settings, "self" is largely a source of that sense, including whatever general interests or values that the setting constitutes as reasons in its own course. It becomes tied to a concrete decision to act only when the situation is in doubt, relative to coming to a decision, and when doubt requires displays of commitment. As such, this is a far weaker version than the idea of a self as narrowing or perhaps closing the gap between reasons and undertaking. To say that specific situations are uncertain, ambiguous, and volatile is to admit, contrary to what is required by the supplemented theory of action, that the self and its relevance to what is done or is being done are contingent. In that case, the general idea of a superordinate self seems contradictory to the setting-specific version of agency, since it supposes a temporally ordered but simultaneously accessible set of momentary situations in which conditions of rational action are more or less generalized for each actor who can then be judged both by how appropriate her specific act-type is to *its* situation-type *and*, oddly, how appropriate it is *across* situations and therefore beyond the immediate urgency that brings the contingent self into play in the making of a decision.

―――――――

M aintaining the idea of a superordinate self in a theory of situations requires thinking of it as a kind of storehouse of past and possible future reasons that retain the momentous quality of intentionality independent of particular orientations and concerns. In this storehouse, the differences that had once marked the subjectivity of those experiences, including their accessibility to recall, are irrelevant. They not only are transformed into a general form that the self knows independently of specific memories; their formerly situated content also is lost to whatever they have in common with all the experiences that add up to the self at any time it is manifestly in play. In effect, the object of the self is not the array or sum of the objects of prior acts or imagined acts; nor is it the result of what had been learned from encounters with reality. The psychic economy of the self, for a theory that emphasizes situations and experience, involves a fully and coherently generalized subjectivity that can be extracted from the experiences of the past and of the different objects to which the person was subject; and that seems very much like the pure and autonomous self that Emmet (1975) found theoretically unsustainable.

As conceptualized, there is no additional content to the self but an abstract presence, which is a resultant but not a compendium of past experiences. Therefore, the most we can conclude about its relevance to action is that it appears, within the process of coming to a decision, as an index of the need to survive or, in the language of a situational theory, to "fit in." It contributes to rationality only at the ultimate, or ideal, limit of an intention, and it does not otherwise bear on what in particular needs to be done. But because my survival at time a is intelligible only as my survival at times a and b . . . n—that is, as survival per se—the superordinate self has an immediate but still only a highly abstract relationship to the possible prudence of a given intention, though not, for reasons discussed previously, to altruism: it may account for a certain nervousness or anxiety, an anticipation of guilt or regret, or even a vague sense of a positive outcome relative to the possibility of other, non-immediate reasons logically at odds with situated reasons. In this respect, it does not provide a general solution to the problem of the gap between current situated reasons and the moment of the undertaking as discussed earlier; and it is difficult to see how it does so even in the case in which, by hypothesis, it appears to matter—namely, prudential action. Note that my interpretation of Nagel's theory of altruism points to the social dimension of the relationship between "someone's" reason as a reason for another "someone" to act—not because universally recognizable reasons are in play but because "someones" are social beings through and through and this is revealed when an appeal (e.g., the expression of a need) is directly made to the basic fact of sociality (inter-dependence).

Given these complex conditions of self-oriented action, prudential reasons that arise in anticipating a future are, as Nagel says, current reasons (of the person at the moment of decision) that reflect on a projected past in order to provide some governance to the choice of a future. Their currency, which derives from the self, applies to the extent to which what is indicated is a vast present, in light of which the immediate situation is only a small element. The subjective apprehension of its vastness includes that life and those projections, all of which the self is obliged to attribute to the person of which it is the self, as conditions of rational action in each state of mind in which personhood appears as an object of consciousness as well as according to the immediately restrictive conditions of each situation on that state. It is assumed that the total order of reasons and beliefs are self-organizing, however that is determined and along with other personal facts, such that the person, as a conscious being, always finds herself with a self and, even more importantly, is confirmed as an agent by that self—and therefore finds herself possessed of a rational obligation to sustain that self largely by means of a comparison of costs and benefits apparently derived from reflection on the self's unlimited continuity until death.

The dependence of the idea of a superordinate self on the idea of a superordinate situation poses another problem: without clarifying the idea of a situation beyond the notion of a given set of specifiable circumstances, it seems impossible to theorize the self beyond what has just been summarized, and no such concept is available that can do what is required by the standard ideas of action and agency—namely, that a concept of a situation that allows for a taking account of others that distinguishes those others from nonhuman things identifies them as the same sort of being that takes them into account, and that is compatible with the idea that human beings are essentially social. The problem is a special one because it also calls into question the relationship of possession insinuated between self (possessed but morally active) and person (possessing but morally inert) as those are characterized and distinguished by theory and in the informal discourses that support it. The problem may be less evident in refined accounts. For example, according to Davidson, "a person is a physical object which in detail and as a whole functions according to physical laws" (2004b, 87). But, he continues, there is a way of that object's functioning, or a way we interpret it as functioning, that distinguishes it from other such objects and places it beyond its physicality. For one thing, it thinks in ways that we cannot identify with artificial thinkers, and it learns and "has learned from causal interactions with the world" (89). Since "beliefs and desires exist only in the context of a very rich conceptual system," anything that is or acts like a person must be held to operate on the basis of such a system (according to the norms by which we interpret behavior as relating a person to the world) and not, say, merely according to a program of rules, or sequentially according to what simply comes up (90). Davidson concludes that the "vocabulary we reserve for the intentional" applies uniquely to persons (or anything that we see as personlike) to the extent to which the "classificatory concepts" of the "mental and the physical" are different, though they "share ontologies."[1] A person is, beyond its physicality, a being we interpret as essentially rational; and by interpreting the object in this way we are effectively endorsing the proposition, and the practices it implicates, that "interpretation involves the use of normative concepts like consistency, reasonableness, and plausibility, and these concepts have no role in the understanding of a syntactically specified program" (99).

However, to say that we identify persons as rational because we are rational (and presumably can acknowledge that in ourselves only by acknowledging it in general), and to say that what makes something a person for us is that we interpret its activity consistent with our own self-understanding, and therefore in a way that involves appealing to norms, solves only a part of the problem posed by the need to preserve the directedness and continuity of intentionality in the theory of action. The divisions made between a nameable actor in a concrete situation acting according to present beliefs and desires and the anonymous theorized actor who takes things into account that are in no sense part of the immediate situation, and between a sense of personal integrity, necessary for continuity to be meaningful, and the fact of it, necessary for the continuity of the self to be true, requires more than a concept adequate to distinguishing between the conduct of things that resemble persons and the conduct of persons who cannot be things. The issue for us is not how "person" is defined such that it is possible to distinguish it from something artificial, like a thinking machine. *The discussion of the theory of action so far has been directed at evaluating its capacity to explain social action, and this is important insofar as that theory purports to re-present the idea that human beings are essentially social—with the necessary addition that this involves certain properties of situations.* The problem is to show how action can be rational relative to the "total life" of the actor when no definite description of a situation can be sufficient to account for that rationality or adequate to identify in a useful way rationality within the limits of uncertainty and nonrational factors. The theory of action under discussion, to the extent to which it has general application, seems to require reference to the idea of a "total life," implicating as well something like a total situation; and without both it is not clear how to come to terms with what is theoretically involved in taking account of others, hence with sociality seen from this point of view.

W hen used in conjunction with expressions like "*M* has or has had a certain experience or experiences" or "something has happened to *M*," and in regard to the idea, crucial to the theory of action under consideration, that rationality involves treating the concrete situation as an arbitrarily limiting case of a total life situation (and therefore no longer sufficient to the act in the sense required by the standard theory), the person is conceived of as an integrated instance of agency that operates largely through the medium of memory and, by virtue of that, across situations, and in regard to others whose theoretical status as selves and whose capacities as agents are in principle either unclear, denied, deniable, or otherwise in doubt.[2] As a result, interactions among persons "having selves" (being such instances of agency) can be represented only from the point of view of a single agent. The others and their behavior appear as properties of that agent's situation. Note that in this case, the intentionality of the originary agent, which is at least attached to or constitutive of some indeterminacy, is not a property attributable to the others who are stipulated to be predictably disposed: they have intentions without intentionality, dispositions, and are therefore able to be taken into account.

However, instead of extending the theory of action from its limited application in immediately concrete situations to contexts of agency conceived across situations, this idea of a person with a self leaves the theory intact as long as it applies exclusively to whatever falls within local settings described as concrete particulars, with, as Nagel (1970) points out, relatively little provision made for prudential reasoning. It is as if there are now two theories of action. One excludes the self in order to deal with the results of decisions based on reasons derived from what the actor believes about immediately present circumstances and estimates of what is likely to happen over the appropriate "short run," subject to certain parameters such as incentive values, language, and the like. In contrast, by including the self, one can deal with decisions that might bear on the continuity of the life of the actor across situations and, therefore, are subject to different sorts of reason and different parameters. It is not enough to say, by way of denying that the two theories are radically different, that one merely adds a construct to the other, though doing so suggests three hypotheses apart from the possibility of a theory of the self: it might expand the domain of legitimate reasons for making a decision to act, it might imply that all reasons are "timeless" in Nagel's sense, or it might suggest that those who use the construct may have no intention to theorize it. In regard to the last hypothesis, there seems little doubt from his examples that Searle, for one, intends to conceptualize the idea of the self and situate it within a theory (or something like a theory) of the total course of a life, though, to my knowledge, he has not undertaken such a project. The other two hypotheses presuppose a theory that goes beyond situated action, thereby pitting them against the idea that "self" is meaningful without any further need for a theory of its referent, apparently for two reasons: the idea of a concrete situation is sufficient to support a rational relationship between belief and desire and the idea that relationship is sufficient to justify the use of the word. It is the self that is rational when an intention or an act is rational and irrational when neither is rational; and no more need be said, though it is clear that this is itself a kind of theory.

If there are now two theories, it is not obvious how they can be combined without a third that accounts for the included propositions, not to mention for why they were selected for inclusion. Certainly they cannot be combined if they are both equally theoretical (with refined concepts and propositions constrained by overarching principles), and it seems to me that they are in principle, though not as typically articulated. As a result, the word "action" is systematically misleading in its suggestion that both theories—of action based on a self that subsists beyond every situation and action bounded by a situation—have the same referent and address the same object, and, as we see, this cannot be true. In regard to the theory that relies on the sufficiency of the immediate situation of the actor, "action" refers to something that can be identified as a concrete particular (e.g., an event), with a distinct content, boundaries, and a clear beginning and end. It is in this sense that "action" can be defined as "behavior with reasons" proximal to the undertaking (Shwayder 1965) or even that "human actions can be taken to constitute a class of events, in which a subject (the agent) brings about some change or changes" (McCann 1995, 6) that, presumably, reflect on that subject in ways that matter among assembled parties but that may have nothing in fact to do with her. In regard to the possibility that "self" marks the totality of a life, gives it an aura of subjectivity, and the corresponding implication of a transcendental situation, the word "action" lacks sufficient clarity and definition to designate a concrete particular or an event. In other words, the concept of action appropriate to the standard theory is not appropriate for a theory that depends on a notion of a self when the latter is required by that theory. In effect, each theory discredits the other.

Philosophy has not yet provided the degree of clarity about action when the self is offered as an organizing principle of a theory that relies on the idea of an immediate situation. Consequently, we are left without guidance about how to formulate the relationship between what people do in their capacity as selves and what is human about what they do in that capacity, and about how to conceive of taking others into account in a way that respects what is indicated about life by referring to the self. As a result, the concept of agency is bound to seem trivial in the theory of action, at least to anyone interested in generalizing the latter, insofar as it merely refers to the execution of a decision, refined and conceived of in hindsight as an event; and it is problematic in regard to activities undertaken in regard to or as part of the course of a life (presumably known as a "totality" from the point of view of its death). The distinction is marked and then glossed by McCann:

> At the foundation of human action lies the enigma of agency: the phenomenon whereby, as it seems to us at least, our actions are finally to be accounted for solely in terms of our performing them. Agency is an enigma first because it is hard to say what it is. Exercises of agency are at best difficult to describe, and the concept resists any effort at reductive analysis. . . . On the other hand, to relinquish the idea of agency is to jeopardize the entire concept of human action, and with it our sense that we are responsible in a distinctive way for the changes we produce in the world. (1998, 170)[3]

———

To the extent to which this critique is valid, the concepts typically employed in theories of action cannot be used as a foundation on which to build a theory that extends the ideas of intention, actor, and action throughout the sequence of life situations presumably indicated by reference to a self. This does not deny that each theory might be suggestive about the other—only that, as things stand, they cannot be synthesized as a comprehensive theory. Nor do they stand in relation to one another as comparable theoretical options, each of which might eventually cover what the other covers. Either the standard idea of action as concretely situated and temporally limited merely deploys the notion of action heuristically over the course of a life or the idea of a self that requires flexibility in restricting the concept of a situation is merely heuristic to applications of the standard theory and in that capacity is bound to be misleading. It seems, again, that we have not two theories about the same thing but only one theory coupled with a notion brought in nontheoretically in order to complete the other theory but that can only complete what the theoretician might wish to say about its possible extra-theoretical scope of application or interpretation. The irony is that we cannot tell which of the two we have been considering is the theory we need and which is merely a notion that, regardless of whether it looks theoretical, only allows such a need to be satisfied extra-theoretically. If the only alternative to the standard theory is a theory of the self or if reference to the self is taken as a complement to that theory, attempts to extend it beyond the limits of its paradigm inevitably implicate an idea that is incompatible with it.

Similarly, attempts to tie the pre-theoretical idea of a relationship between agency and self to a standard conception of action fatally compromise the latter. Later, I discuss how it is that the movement from the idea of temporally restricted action to the idea of activity as such becomes more important than any reference to individuality. For now, *we again see the beginning of a breakdown of the concept of action, leaving in its place the shadow of a different idea—namely, a "course of activity"—that requires a different way of theorizing and a different attitude toward theory.* We have already seen that there are good reasons to believe that the theory of action by itself cannot solve the problems that are bound to arise when social action is said to be action in which others as well as things are taken into account; and we have seen that the idea of a self leaves gaps where there should be none that are significant to explanation. For the moment, we need to pay a bit more attention to the relationship between theory and heuristics in the context of the present discussion.

If reference to a self serves a merely heuristic function for the theory of action, an informal way of extending the theory's scope or applying empirically, it does not disturb the theory though it may come to disturb the theoretician. In contrast, the theoretical implications of the idea of a self might be looked at under the aspect of its being tendentiously theoretical—in contrast with being theoretically tendentious. By this I mean that it might present itself positively, as in need of a certain sort of theorization, but not as inclined toward one available model among others. To that extent it is understandable why attempts to explicate the idea of a self for the sake of understanding the action of someone as a realization of desires and beliefs often appear so desperate. Such attempts are aimed at sustaining a notion for which concept formation and explication seem to pose overwhelming problems and, at the same time, to invoke, by means of association and often by the use of terms notorious for the unpredictability of the effects of their use, the possibility of establishing reasonable conditions of theoretical discussion.

From a slightly different point of view, the value of referring to a self appears in both cases to be heuristic and not theoretical. In the one case, it keeps open the possibility that more may need to be said about a given instance of action than what can be said within the standard theory. In the other, it introduces what might be seen as a methodological principle of commonsensically insisting that any imputation of a fully coherent identity be tested against the possibilities of division and multiplicity, that every figure of speech or organizing principle be examined for the difference on which it relies that makes for the appearance of a unity that it cannot sustain. This is appropriate to the otherwise limitless temporality of the life of the actor (for whom a self is conceivable) who must decide what to do in a given situation according to whatever is introduced as relevant based on (1) the fact that it is merely one among many situations she has faced and can anticipate facing and (2) the principle that if decisions about a given situation are to be evaluated according to a rationality that has to do with the self and the limitless plurality of situations it indicates, then they are thereby subject to whatever values, decision rules, and so on derive from or are taken to represent such a plurality. But if there is no satisfactory theory of the self that is adequate to the task posed by the limitations of the theory of action, and if the theory of action cannot be sustained on its own, then we are once again forced to consider the possibility that something has been lost between the commitment to determine what is human about human affairs and the employment of the framework of the theory of action to meet the conceptual demands of that commitment, at least the demand for an account of the sociality of social action.

It is still necessary to consider what difference a heuristic notion might make to the theory of action once the latter is extended beyond the restrictions of its paradigm. It is in this light that the question cannot be begged as to whether the concept of the actor needs to be rethought in terms of what is introduced by even casual references to the self. This is because the actor can no longer be conceived of in the way required by the theory—that is, as a decision maker effectively constituted by a situation understood as a locally restricted set of conditions of action, including whatever immediately precedes it in the theoretically articulated forms of mental states such as beliefs and dispositions and, perhaps, the possible addition of "timeless reasons." With the reference to the self, and through that to problematic conceptual extensions of the ideas of situation, belief, reason, and all else that have to do with intentionality, the actor appears to be part of a greater situation in which her immediately concrete situation is inert and consists of nothing more than specifically accountable facts. But this is likely to require a different notion of situation from what had been clearly defined by the theory, and a different idea about how to conceive of a plurality of situations and, therefore, of relations among them such that it is possible to imagine an actor entering one situation from or in light of another (Goffman 1961a). All this threatens the notion of a continuous, relatively fixed identity that Searle considers necessary to resolving the problem of the gap between intentionality and behavior, and Nagel requires in his account of the force of prudential and altruistic reasons.

In expanding the temporal horizon of the actor and, therefore, the context in which she can be said to act, "self" operates as a construct, a discursively mobile sign that stands for a set of problems, and not as a concept, which is a severely restricted signifier that resolves a theoretical problem.[4] Even so, the history, complexity, and moral status of the idea impose an extraordinary obligation to rethink the basic concepts of action theory, precisely the burden it was intended to defer: "extraordinary" because the construct, as received, takes us beyond the resources of the standard theory and possibly any theory that relies on a paradigmatic simplification of what people do and on a reductive theory of agency. The best it can do is to extend the idea of an action in such a way that it no longer has clear boundaries, an identifiable form, and the sort of context implied by the original theory. The intention in using the construct may be to continue working within the logic of the theory until its limitations are accounted for. However, it is more likely that the limitations will become evident in ways that make it impossible to defer *theorizing*. Either reference to the self is eliminated or somehow modified, in which case the questions that invited that reference are begged, or the theory is radically revised whether or not the revision can include the self as a concept.

In passing, it is, of course, possible that the use of the construct is intended to be casual in the limited sense of standing in for something yet to be discovered that might mediate action. The need here is to avoid insinuating something that cannot be represented without rethinking the ontological presuppositions of "action"—especially in regard to what is human about it. For example, theoreticians who begin on the other end, by problematizing the idea of a situation, may be led to refer to "interactions" between actor and situation—as when social psychologists speak of "negotiating" a situation. This momentarily appears to preserve the standard theory by enlarging its idea of a context, but it presents its own difficulties not so different from those we have reviewed in regard to the self. The most important of these has to do with the peculiar polarizing effects of the ambiguity of the metaphor. Does "to negotiate" mean to maneuver, to forge through, to get around, or to surmount? In those cases, the situation is conceived of as relatively inert, requiring little more of the actor than that she observe and compute. Or does it mean to bargain, arbitrate, settle, arrange, or come to terms, in which case the situation appears to be active in its own right. Nevertheless, it avoids problems of at least equal magnitude that follow from the standard assumption of a relatively fixed situation in regard to which the actor performs a purely cognitive function prior and possibly sufficient to the undertaking. For that assumption, the actor is imagined as forming a mental image of what is *within* the situation as well as its *form as a totality*. Only then does she take account of both; and, while "taking account" may but need not be assumed to continue throughout the course of what is being done, it is not conceived of as identical with, incorporated within, or overlapping the actual doing, since that is conceived of as a purely executive function relative to a prior intention.

Deferring theory by deferring criticism, as in the use of "self" as a gloss, is often intended to leave a particular theory in place on the grounds that criticism, the demand for a return to theorizing, is premature. We have seen that there may be pragmatic reasons for doing so and that it is not unreasonable to want to see an idea through to its logical consequences and to the possibility of evaluating it according to what lies behind the simplified paradigmatic case. For that, it is best to allow a theory to remain free, subject to its own devices. The burdens of radical criticism are, after all, burdens the theory will eventually have to bear if it is to be of general interest in the human sciences, but for the sake of the theoretical work, they should be deferred. However, theory cannot earn the right to be free merely by justifying that right by its own criticisms of putative alternatives, since the latter can also be presumed to deserve immunity on the same grounds: the reasons that justify deferring theorizing (criticism) in the one case can also justify it in the other.

Whether or not the standard theory of action works on its own account, it provides no logical basis for criticizing either its own critics or alternative theories—other than by focusing exclusively on obvious problems as if critical decisions about what are *obviously* problematic are also beyond question. The counter-critique is, in any case, appropriate only on the basis of an unjustified distinction between theorizing and theory that leaves only the idea of the latter intact. As such, it is not consistent with the requirements that the critic consider the intellectual conditions under which the alternative is possible and that she account for the possibility of her own criticism as an instance of theory. Both involve theorizing, and this cannot be ignored if criticism is to succeed in both its aims: addressing the apparent defects of alternative theories without denying the conditions of possibility of those theories, and making itself accountable as a theoretical position whose conditions of possibility also count. At the least, one should be able to evaluate the countercriticism in part by how a reader might come to share rather than simply receive the critic's conclusions about what aspects of the object of her criticism should be considered in evaluating those conclusions.

In passing, there is a related problem in defending the standard theory by criticizing alternatives according to the same logic one rejects on the part of those criticizing the standard theory. Relying on the simplifications of "action" as essentially instrumental and "sociality" as taking account of others makes it difficult to imagine how to compare action theory with possible alternatives, either because the latter are concerned with something beyond such simplification or, if they also simplify, the model they adopt is almost certain to be logically different from that of the standard theory. It seems that the exclusion of readers' questions, insofar as they attempt to reopen the theoretical issue, is part of the strategy of retaining the self-less theory of action despite the insinuation of a notion behind the construct that can operate only sub-theoretically and therefore problematically. It calls for a theoretical transformation from the very outset. Note that what is at stake is how to identify the object, action, agency, and situation. If there is a question about the initial simplification, this can be begged legitimately only if there is reason to believe that it will finally prove adequate to the phenomenon, joining what must remain sub-theoretical with what is explicitly theoretical.

I suggest that the construct is valuable if it is intended to stimulate thinking, but not at the cost of isolating the theoretician and protecting her from questions her readers can avoid only as passive-dependent recipients of whatever follows from the initial simplification. If what is at issue is the capacity of the theoretician to think through her ideas, it seems to me that it is unduly limited by refusing to do what is necessary to end up with a comprehensible theory, which is to ensure that the simplification, including what it progressively omits, is accountable throughout the course of theoretical work. Without continual reference to the struggle to sustain the simplification, the result is a theory that can be justified but not taught as a possible idea, which is to say as a momentary outcome of theorizing. In that case, readers are no less passive recipients—consumers—of the completed theory than they would have been had they been invited to follow the work from the outset in exchange for deferring criticism. In other words, what facilitates the development of a theory that stands apart from how it came about also constitutes a reader who cannot theorize, just as the idea of social action as taking account of others' behavior requires that those others be passive-reactive, that they not be beings who "take account."

The theoretician who constructs the notion of a self as a supplement to the theory of action works on her own, with her readers idealized as passive throughout the course of reading. In contrast, for readers allowed to be interested not only in *a* theory but in the activity of *theorizing*, work begins immediately and continues throughout the course of resolving ambiguities and deferring criticism while remaining aware of its possibility. The *theoretical text*, the ostensible product of theorizing, is itself an object for an audience. From that point of view, it becomes a virtually open source site, but too late for that audience to theorize: it can be shared as a thing, but not appreciated for how it was possible and therefore for how it might have been different. By contrast, *theorizing* is in the interest of readers continually concerned with the subtheoretical objectivity that warranted their attention and desire to theorize in the first place and not with the theoretical object already simplified and made abstract as one such object among, and comparable with, many.

No matter how the "self" is interpreted—as a construct to be deployed or a pre-concept designed to create a disturbance in a given theory, or as subtheoretical in the sense of being tied to what seems momentarily to be an incorrigible intuition—it seems that theory is bound to get involved in reconsidering the nature of action as such and its possible fit to the idea of the "whole continuous person" of the actor and how, in turn, that personhood fits the concept of the actor as originally theorized according to the equally imperiled concept of the situation. As useful as the notion of a self might be to the theoretician operating on the basis of a rational simplification of the object, in either reopening questions or expanding the scope of well-formed concepts, it remains to be seen how it can add to the explanation of the undertaking of an action if what counts is the elimination of the gap between reasons (causes) and act (effect) that arises when individual persons are the putative locations of agency and origins of what will count as instances of action.

————

One might still argue that there is a possible gain in explanatory power that does not challenge the integrity of the theory of action. For example, what is brought in by referring to the self might be thought to add value to the theory (e.g., by narrowing the range of expected actions because of indications, incorporated in the notion of the term "self," that there are reasons regulating action beyond those set in motion by the immediately concrete situation). That is, the gain in explanatory power presumably comes at the point at which the theory of action has exhausted what might be expected from the context it identifies as the actor's objective situation that gives focus to beliefs and limits the experience and expression of desires. This requires distinguishing the moment of the undertaking from the moment of the decision to act based largely on situationally induced reasons qualified by other mental states.[5] This can be interpreted as saying that the moment of the undertaking is no less a matter of deliberation, or something approximating it, than that of fitting reasons to preferences and beliefs about prevailing facts, since adding a self suggests that no matter how certain the decision prior to the undertaking (based largely on situational considerations), there still remains in the mind of the actor a plurality of options for acting—a mind, it should be noted, that is now coordinate with the self and not, as before, a mere reflection of or operation on the concrete situation.

It follows either that the action undertaken is not determined at the level of intentionality made manifest by the standard theory of action, and by extension the standard theory of social action, or that "intentionality" does not now mean quite what it had seemed to mean. If the term refers to more and other than what appears uniquely determined by the immediately concrete situation, then it cannot refer as well to the processes and factors identified by the standard theory as essential conditions of action. In this respect also, adding a self does not sustain the integrity of the theory; instead, it invalidates it. If so, it may be that what needs to be explained is neither the point at which a decision is made nor the point at which the act is undertaken, but how what is done is part of the activity of determining what is to be done (and vice versa), so that what appear as the making of a decision and the undertaking are no longer separated by a gap but must be considered part of the same concept and, indeed, the same event.[6] The question is can this be possible on the assumptions of unitary and distinct actors—that is, individual persons—and actions as particulars with beginnings, ends, and definitive reasons? It evidently cannot. *If not, then it may be necessary to rethink the very notion of agency according to the idea that began this discussion, which is that humans are essentially social.* As things stand, this is not explicated by the standard theory of action, or clarified by adding the idea of a self, or by using it to refer to a concept in a different but possibly complementary theory of what human beings do by way of being human, or, one must add, by thinking of reasons as "timeless" for the putative individuated actor without considering the sociality that must be part of any account of timelessness. Parenthetically, timeless reasons, in Nagel's sense of being recognizable by all members of the community as reasons for acting, are only atemporal, ungoverned by the concrete moment, for a hypothetical individual actor. Even then, for the moment of the undertaking, they are anything but timeless; and the metaphor of timelessness is bound to be misleading both in regard to the individual and to the context in which timeless reasons must somehow reside.

Nagel's theory of altruistic action returns us to the individual, but his characterization of the timelessness of certain reasons (e.g., a plea from "someone" for help) suggests a different hypothesis, one that requires deferring any discussion of individuality, and anything that presupposes it, until after a reasonable clarification of Strawson's observation that thought and action begin in the midst of sociality and bear in their very being its immanence. What, after all, gives such reasons their immediacy, and to what is that immediacy given? *I have argued, first, that we can understand the immediacy of any reason—either how it comes to be commonly recognized or its evident contribution to the undertaking and the sense of spontaneity that accompanies it—only from the point of view of the sociality of human activity and, second, that it can be understood as an immediacy only in regard to a course of activity that is intrinsically and irreducibility social.*

Rethinking the meaning of "agency" is an essential part of such a project. It is likely to change how one might theorize the relationship between specific circumstances, which can no longer be conceived of as prior to subjectivity and therefore to the decision to act and the undertaking, and the more general circumstances and causal complexity brought to notice by referring to a self. The latter can no longer be taken simply to qualify the immediate situation and its implication of a reflected individual subjectivity. The relationship is now reversed: the abstract and complex general circumstances have logical priority over the immediate concrete situation—unless one is willing to say that what is brought in by way of the self is less important than the self-less considerations of an altruistic actor in a definite situation of which his or her subjectivity is nevertheless largely a reflection. To rethink agency requires different initial representations of what is being done, its conditions, and the actor and her others, from those of the standard theory of action. It would have to begin by reinstating the theoretically independent *sub-theoretical* sense of action, which provides the reason for theorizing in the first place, in place of a theoretically dependent *pre-theoretical* intuition. The latter is designed to eliminate any sense of the phenomenon that cannot support consensus at the theoretically most basic level of reference—and that, we have seen, allows no room for a self. Since the sub-theoretical sense of action, perhaps as both individual and social such that each is internally related to the other, resides in non-formal discourses that resist rigid designation, it might appear that a question is being begged by refusing to be specific or to provide reasonable alternatives to the standard definitions, or that going on about something inchoate, to which the concept is alleged to have no choice but to appeal, is discursive in ways that cannot provide a basis for theorizing.

A subject matter that defies simplification and division into units cannot serve as an object of a theory that depends on precisely that sort of analysis.[7] But what constitutes a proper version of theory is part of what is at stake when we ask what is human about human affairs. McCann's summary of the standard conception of action illustrates the problem: "In general, human actions constitute a class of events, in which a subject (the agent) brings about some change or changes" (1995, 6–7).[8] And it does so in a situation conceived of as immediately concrete and limited (though McCann does not discuss this directly). This holds that actions can, in general, be unambiguously specified, that they change with changes in their intention, that intentions are subjective facts that belong to and are normally accessible to the individual actors, and that action, so understood, occurs in a situation that allows the actor to evaluate the changes she has brought about and therefore to see whether her intention has been realized. A great deal is predicated on this rigorously simplified, individualistic model, including much of what is said about the ideas of deliberation, rationality, choice, and self-reflection; and all this is placed in jeopardy the moment a theoretically competent notion of a self is introduced.

To think of the "self" not as a supplement but as providing an opportunity to reconsider the theory of action for what it systematically omits seems to invoke principles that philosophers committed to ontological individualism have largely rejected, though not for that reason alone. Among those are the independence of the mind, which is occasionally brought into play by some notions of "reason" and "the self"—that is, by recourse to the idea of a transcendental agency able to eliminate the threat to a naturalist explanation of action posed by the progressive accumulation of gaps between the readiness to act and the undertaking and by the possibility that actions are in some sense uncaused.[9] If, however, we appear to have little choice but to make use of the idea of a homogeneous and continuous self, with its own reasons, and if doing so risks philosophically undesirable consequences, then it is not unreasonable to shift our frame of reference in order to consider the possibility that the word "self" operates as a figure of speech. This may still appear to beg the question but only momentarily, appropriately so because of the limitations of the discussion thus far. It avoids the possibility that some of the undesirable consequences might, on further reflection, come to be transformed into defensible and even necessary ideas, or, at least, formulated in ways congenial to the sort of self-critically dialectical disposition I defend in this book (see, for example, Foster 1991 and Cottingham 1998). For now, a shift to the poetics of the philosophy of action seems warranted. It suggests that the use of the word "self" is *intended* as a rhetorical device, or should be treated that way in order to avoid the perils of treating it as referring to a concept and to be able to rethink the concept of a situation taken as fundamental to the idea of agency. As such, it usually invokes de-situated and therefore external factors presumably accumulated (and stored) "*in* memory" over the *longue durée* of experience or that otherwise correspond to a mode of existence (as an "identity") and a temporality beyond that of the actor's immediate situation. These add, figuratively, to the mass of reasons that must be attributed to her if she is to be seen as attempting to respond to her situation as rationally as possible. That is, they provide a total and homogeneous image of a self.[10] These are thought of loosely as elements, which "add" to what Searle refers to as a "causal picture" that, given suitable information, are incorporated in beliefs relevant to the actor's acting rationally but that are not standardly taken into account, hence the gaps. Favoring the naturalist idea that "self" refers, in one way or another, to something substantial still requires a fairly expansive view of what the self brings to the action situation, difficult to manage under naturalistic assumptions; so that one might still take it as provisional to the formation of another identity-related concept that might better capture that expansiveness. In either case, however, any attempt, in everyday practice, to rely on this way of enlarging the scope of the actor's intentionality without acknowledging the effect of doing so on the very idea of rationality in action is likely to run into problems.

This is illustrated by Searle's (2001) report of an encounter with a student over the issue of her smoking cigarettes, a contingency that poses a risk, depending on all sorts of condition. Searle judges her decision to smoke as irrational because of her failure to take into account the greater interest of the self. As I read him, the point is that the continuity of one's life is a valid present reason and should be expected to influence every decision that might bear on longevity or quality of life. He considers her attempts to justify rejecting his point as compounding the irrationality. My argument with Searle is not about his evaluation of smoking, but about his assuming more than he reasonably can; and he seems to underestimate the student's capacity to think through a range of contingencies and probabilities available to her and not to him, in coming to a decision. His judgment of her irrationality depends on his selection and isolation of one contingency from the tremendous scope presumably brought into play by his theoretical concept of the self—as if her future is determined by her decision to smoke rather than that smoking presents one contingency among others, in a complex web of probabilities, that might justify a different decision from the one Searle preferred. Searle is surely correct in saying that it is irrational to disregard what might happen in the future when a present might bear on that future. But it is wrong to assume that only the contingency he identifies should count, since his judgment comes from outside of the student's self and, therefore, the full range of reasons that she may be competent to consider by virtue of experience or reasonable expectation. Searle has confused giving advice, which can be based only on a limited sense of what is likely to happen and should always be open to disagreement based on the subject's superior knowledge of herself and the proper scope of her concerns, with judging another's action as irrational. From this point of view, her resistance to Searle's injunction was rational, either on the grounds that he did not have enough information to judge her or that she was right to feel insulted by his insistence that only one contingency, with its probabilities, be considered as a sufficient reason for her decision. Searle's desire that she stop smoking is not unreasonable; but his judgment is since it was based on the simplifying logic of advice but failed to respect the limitations of that logic in his immodest insistence on judging her.

Searle based his judgment on only one contingency, as one might do if one were committed to the simplification of the standard theory despite introducing a construct inconsistent with it. While emphasizing one contingency is sufficient to warrant giving someone advice, it is not relevant to deciding whether Searle's student was or was not rational in her decision to smoke.

A theory of action supplemented by the self remains inadequate to its object if it simplifies the greater self-totalizing situation as a way of remaining at the same level of abstraction as before. That either favors the immediately concrete situation, which makes it difficult if not impossible to gauge the contribution of the self, or overemphasizes the expansive future relative to the restrictive present, which weakens the idea of rationality based on individually held reasons as causes. An actor who responds primarily to the underdetermined and expansive situation of the self is no longer merely a respondent, reflecting on specific facts according to specific desires and justifiable beliefs, since the facts associated with possible futures of that actor are not likely to be specific or determinate enough to warrant responding in the way one can respond to a situation in which there are relatively few imaginable outcomes with assignable probabilities. All this contributes to the impression of the "self" as a rhetorical figure, forcing us to acknowledge a problem that goes beyond correcting or designing a theory—namely, the possibility of having to rethink the idea of theory itself.

What is sub-theoretically projected by the use of "self" does not seem to fit either a model in which both actor and actions are concretely situated or one in which the reason of a self is unambiguously causal to the undertaking. It seems that the intuition that warrants an appeal to the self is at odds with the intuition that warrants a theory of action that excludes the self. Whether or not it is used as a figure of speech, reference to the self jeopardizes the theory of action. However, understanding it that way brings us closer to the possibility that Strawson's claim about the priority of the social identifies far more crucial problems in advancing our understanding of thought and action than those identified with the priority of the individual (e.g., the gap between intention and undertaking). One positive consequence of acknowledging the rhetorical function of the "self" is that it begins to suggest a more comprehensive, and I believe less burdened, alternative for theorizing agency commensurate with the idea that humans and what they do are essentially social in ways that cannot be imagined from the point of view of individuality and the corresponding particularity of an action.

If activity is individual only inasmuch as it is constitutively social, then, as we will see, it cannot be realized theoretically by the use of a referential language that points to spatially and temporally specific particulars in the ways discussed so far, or that identifies what can be said about agency with what can be said about individuality. Moreover, if "sociality" no longer means actors taking account of others such that doing so can be described as an event and such that those others can be taken to be elements of a given state of affairs, then we have to consider the possibility that the word "social," like the word "self," must now stand for something that cannot be described in a language that knows only identities, events, and structures, including those self-expanding quasi-structures that are now referred to as "networks." Correspondingly, it might be necessary to think of situations as radically different from the standard notion of a state of affairs subject to evaluation prior to the undertaking. In that case, the significance of the gap shifts from the need to account for a missing cause on the order of reasons to the problem of rethinking the meaning and theoretical status of "action" and "agency."

15

Self and Agency

L et us suppose that the concept of the situation in which an action takes place is radically different from what is required by the standard theory. How might it be characterized and what theoretical issues does it bring to notice? One possibility is derived from an early idea in social psychology: what a person does in her capacity as an agent—as a bearer of intentionality—expresses a subjective state at least partially constituted under circumstances that call for meaningful as well as effective behavior and therefore behavior with reasons that could be reasons for any party *and* appreciated as such by any competent observer. Since these are reasons "someone" might have, there is a social aspect to the subjective state and, in some sense, a subjective aspect to the situation. In other words, there is far more to a situation than the ordered collection of circumstances presumably found by its parties *and* knowable as such to an observer. Moreover, from this point of view, a condition of meaningful action is the ability to distinguish between persons with their subjective states and mere things (see Heider 1958). Later, we will see that this is not as clear or robust as it might seem, though for the moment it points to an apparent difference between intending a particular effect and behaving meaningfully and therefore acting inter-subjectively in a way that constantly invokes, is reflexive to, the social aspect of whatever humans do.

Inter-subjectivity implies, in this regard, that neither subjective states nor objective circumstances are static or inert. Consequently, neither can be conceptualized as stable or formally complete. Subjectivity is always a multiplicity, so that its instances change in the very course of activity. It is not that subjects redefine their situations as needed so much as the very fact of being an instance of subjectivity entails a constant process of subjectification and therefore a constant transformation of conditions (see Lewin 1936; Schutz 1967). But these are still thought of as conditions of *action* rather than conditions implicated in *activity* itself. When our point of view shifts to the latter, the difference between subjectivity and objectivity becomes problematic in ways that it is not under the auspices of the standard theory of action. Since the critique of the latter entails just such a shift, the problem cannot be dismissed and must be worked through regardless of where it leads. What follows is written with this hypothesis in mind. One aspect of the problem has to do with the difficulty of reconciling the self, as designed to supplement the standard theory, with the agency initially posited by that theory. We might, then, say that each person's past experience, coherently ordered or not—in memory and as accumulated tendencies—mediates and is mediated by a present situation that has its own temporality. But the question remains as to what is meant here by mediation, and this is a theoretical problem and not merely a problem of synthesizing two theories, one of the self and another of situated agency. What is at stake in this chapter is the relative priority of sociality and individuality in our knowledge of what is human about human affairs, given that the languages of individuality and agency are distinct in the sense that neither can be reduced to or explained by the other.

Without the presuppositions of individuality and a self that embodies both the past and general orientations and aspirations of the person, this might be stated as follows: agency operates as a feature of its situation regardless of whatever else might account for changes in that situation. Another way of putting this is that agency, situation, and action are what Garfinkel (1967) calls "ongoing accomplishments." But we are not yet at the point at which this can be clarified; rather, we are still caught up in an individualistic ontology qualified and modified though it has become. I will, then, continue to speak of two referents of "situation." One comprises present circumstances and the other represents a history of being in situations. I refer to the former as the immediate situation and the latter as the greater situation. For the moment, the problem has to do with their relationship in regard to the difficulties they pose to a viable conception of the self as key to understanding the form and activity of agency. The greater situation taken over the course of the life of the actor must be seen as essentially social in a way that is not adequately represented by saying that social action involves actors taking account of others; and, as we have seen, the immediate situation of action is not adequately represented by the encounter of an individual agent with specifiably objective circumstances. To that extent, there needs to be a reexamination of the theoretical status of reasons and the meaning of "rationality," as thinkers as diverse as Schutz, Habermas, Rawls, Garfinkel, Davidson, Simon, Kahneman, Douglas, and de Man have in one way or another recommended, as well as the status of terms used to substantiate the idea of intentionality (e.g., belief and desire). Short of that, the problem of how to account for what persons do among people seems unsolvable. Reference to a "self" implicates more facts and possible consequences that the actor has to consider in deciding what to do; however, it still leaves the gap between the readiness to act and the undertaking where it was in the first place. This is so if the self is intended merely to add to the causal picture of action, with its identification of agency with individuality, and to the capacity to evaluate the rationality of particular acts. If it is not so interpreted, it might still be considered a matter of pragmatics, "self" operating as a rhetorical device designed to encourage theory, despite itself, to include more than what immediate circumstances allow. The anticipated enrichment of explanation does not solve the problem of the explanatory gap between reasons and undertaking that warranted referring to a self in the first place; nor does it offer a way of reconciling the greater situation of the self with the strictly limited situation posited by the standard theory.

The idea of a self might be considered pre-theoretical, which is to say dependent on a given theory or theories for its justification as a primitive notion. This would allow for an accumulation of associations with reasonably established concepts from other fields until it becomes possible to see more clearly how the gap between intention based on reasons and an undertaking might at least be reduced, or how it might eventually cease to be a problem. Initially, this might involve using the word as a kind of metaphor to evoke a sense of something subsisting within the gap as a carrier of some sort, perhaps by marking a place for a function yet to be identified that effectively oversees the gap and acts on it, or for what Bruno Latour (2005) calls "mediators" that, operating serially, either add value to the causal picture of action or constitute a different picture of intentionality. This last suggestion seems less problematic than the first two. Therefore, it may be the most appropriate candidate for filling the place of what is otherwise missing in the theory of action insofar as that theory is open to being adjusted to the limitations imposed by the initial simplification of the idea of an action (and in the case at hand, social action) on which it depended for its development as a formal theory.

Whatever its relevance to solving the problem of the gap, the metaphor is self-expanding by virtue of its capacity to attract predictable associations; and the diffuseness of its associational field provides fertile ground for an imagination that cannot be constrained even by the rigors of theories whose concepts are fundamentally associated with a preconceptual notion of the self. Given this, the purpose of using the word is bound to seem rhetorical or pedagogical rather than theoretical, and perhaps that is the best one can hope for in a figure of speech designed to reduce the gap between what is required by the standard account of action and the recalcitrant reality that corresponds to it. One consequence is the possibility of a reconnection of the theory to the informal discourses in which both "self" and "action" operate as metaphors—discourses crucial to the sense of the theory's validity as a whole. In this capacity, use of "the self" does not require adding one theory to another any more than it can be treated as a well-formed concept.

The theory of action, extended to social action without the addition of a self, constitutes a logic connecting beliefs, desires, and intentions with actions and the possibility of their being evaluated under circumstances that are immediately objective to the actor. This assumes that all of these but the situation belong to individually distinct agents who intend to cause a difference by what they do and who, in some manner, take account of others in the course of executing their intention. To complete the causal picture, or close the gap between the causes and their effect, it would be necessary to do what Searle says the pure theory of "action as situated" cannot do—namely, state what are required for reasons to be virtually sufficient to an undertaking. The introduction of the self is intended to do that but only indirectly. In effect, it names a project and not a theoretical accomplishment. This is why it is allowed to function as a pre-conceptual construct that attracts associated notions hopefully able to enrich it to the point of discovering an appropriate referent. It also appears to allow for moral considerations in evaluating what someone has done that are glossed over in the standard theory—though a proper evaluation would still depend on the adequacy of the account of the undertaking.

Deploying such an expansive construct leaves open another possibility, of identifying the intentionality of what is being done with what it is to be human and therefore with the prospect of the theory, *taken as a whole*, returning to the sub-theoretical intuition on which is predicated the possibility of its being applied. Rather than take recourse to biology, say to sufficient conditions of bodily movement as a function of the organism, the construct of a self makes room, discursively, for the possibility of adding to the causal picture at the level of intentionality at which the theory's problems are set and its elements are conceived. However, this is to admit that the functions of the construct are pedagogical and rhetorical. When "the self" is mistaken for a concept, its use may lead to ungoverned speculation.

The *rhetorical* function may lie, specifically, in indicating a vague but compelling sense that something continuously self-presenting resides in the theoretical gap between reasons and action, or subsumes the gap, and that this accounts for what otherwise appears to be a leap beyond the intentionalist synthesis of beliefs, desires, and the like to the contingent undertaking of an act. It dramatizes what is presupposed by theories that otherwise seem satisfied with the gap between reasons and undertaking and are committed to the ontological independence of reasons and the act itself. The related *pedagogical* function may have to do with the fact that "self," when used in ways that evoke associations to Searle's "irreducible notion of the self" (2001, 88), brings to mind an open-ended list of properties, including capacities and tendencies, identified with an earlier philosophy of mind. In this, we are reminded of why it was important in the first place to theorize action and, through that, social action.[1] In that regard, inserting the construct into an account that depends on a far more limited theory of action renews long-standing concerns about the entailments of the idea of a continuous and independently active principle of agency, an idea that had been largely put to the side as part of rejecting Cartesian dualism and, in particular, with the idea of "the thinking self as essentially incorporeal."[2] As Searle points out, "The self is one of the most scandalous notions in philosophy" (2001, 76). Yet "agency requires an entity that can consciously try to do something" (83).[3]

But this consequence of the use of "self" may be inadvertent since the theory of action, which seems to require such an expansive construct, is designed in the first instance to avoid it. At any rate, the theory is jeopardized: it cannot be completed by the simple addition of a notion of a self; nor can it be renewed by using the term as an aid to identifying factors that add causal value to what is already assumed to be a plausible and adequate view of how actions occur. However, it can be made to highlight precisely what it was intended to eliminate, the social, thereby ushering in a radically different conception of its ostensible object, action.

———————

It would be difficult if not impossible to reinstate the sub-theoretical notion that leads to theorizing "action" without challenging the validity of the basic concepts of the standard theory—if I am correct in concluding that the latter has lost its purpose in what it requires for completion. At least such a challenge involves considering the possibility that the object is more and other than *action* conceived of as the realization of an individualized state of intentionality in the form of an event.[4] This allows for several possibilities. First, actions may not be things that can be sufficiently caused—or conditions can be imagined under which it would be necessary to say that they are not such things. Second, they may not be things that can be temporally extended such that the conditions of identifying them can be satisfied in regard to the idea of a situationally transcendent individualized unity of agency (see McCann 1998, 4). Third, individually held reasons may not be as significant in explaining what people do as they are said to be in the standard theory. Finally, the ostensible temporal continuity of the actor unified across a series of situations may lead to the dissolution of the very idea of the actor as a unified instance of agency.

I have argued that, given the idea of a transcendent actor across situations, the horizon of rational agency and the relationship between form and content no longer correspond to the conditions of rationality that obtain in the paradigmatic instances of the standard theory of action. The typical object of that theory is concretely situated action. To consider the possible rationality of an instance, it is necessary not only that the beliefs and desires to which it presumably responds are relevant according to some principle of decision but that, logically, they are capable of being composed mentally, as a state of motivation disposing an actor to act or that only realizes itself reflexively in action. Moreover, the mental composition must by conceived of as contributing causally to the act in question, which means that it contributes to the intention to undertake the act in a way that realizes the principle of relevance; and it must be such that the relation between that intention (what is composed) and the completed act (what the intention is composed for) can be retained fully in the actor's memory and, as such, constitutes a unified object of reflection. This is possible only if there are clear and stable boundaries between the situation, which is presumably external to the actor and the situation's own externalities, and only if the form of the mental state fits its content (e.g., facts about things and/or features of beings, and preferences that are reliable, value related, and coherent among themselves).

I argue, beyond what has already been said in this regard, that such transcendence is conceivable without the embarrassment of an incorporeal yet substantial self only if agency is conceived of as essentially social. If reference to an individual actor is intended to conserve the volitional principle of agency, it cannot be the same principle identified by the standard theory since the latter does not provide a sound basis for a theory of social action. That is, if the actor is transcendent in the sense of operating across situations, and the difference between taking account of others and taking account of nonhuman things is not trivial, and if this transcendence is intelligible on the interpretation that such an actor is essentially social, then whatever the term "action" stands for, it cannot be both an effect of a transcendent agency and the product of the mundane agency vested in a concretely situated individual actor. Whatever is explained by the sort of agency that corresponds to an external relation of concrete situation to individual actor, it is not action in the sense of something people do by way of being human, though it may be action in the limited sense of being the execution of something like a decision, regardless of whether one agrees with my conclusion that this will not explain what is actually done. *In explaining what people do as part of what is actively human about them, there is no better reason to rely on an individualistic ontology and a corresponding theory of the interactions of specific and directly expressible referents such as persons, situations, reasons, and actions, then to rely on the proposition that it is both necessary and possible to begin theorizing what people do on altogether different grounds derived from their essential sociality and, correspondingly, with rather different procedures.*

One can find warrants for such an enterprise in those fields that attempt to make human activity understandable in its human aspect, and in a considerable body of literature that criticizes the common sense of straightforward reference and predication on which the standard theory of action relies. There are also philosophies not identified with the Anglo-American tradition, though not necessarily incompatible with it, that have attempted to address irreducibly human aspects of human affairs. Presumably, these are aspects that cannot be otherwise categorized or broken down into simpler elements and still remain intelligible as the sorts of things that lead both to a desire for just such an analysis and to accounts that rely on an idea of *activity* as fundamentally resistant to objectification, reduction, and specification—thereby breaking with the ontology presupposed by standard models and the procedures they require.

There is still another source of authority for undertaking to theorize what people do by way of being distinctively human—namely, that philosophy has not had the desired success in showing how agency can be specified when the contexts of performances, activities, expressions, and so on are simplified in the form of immediate concrete situations composed of relatively unambiguous entities, about which ambivalence is either unlikely to be or is not theoretically significant. In this regard, McCann's comment seems fairly representative:

> Action theory is also important to our understanding the relation between mind and body, action and perception being the two major arenas in which, as thinking beings, we interact with the world. Action is especially important here because it involves the mysterious phenomenon of agency, the operations of which resist representation in terms of familiar causal processes, and may require irreducibly teleological conceptions in order to be understood. (1998, 1)

McCann is suggesting that the literature on agency has left us with mysteries that try us at the very limits of our disciplines, and that these have to do with the ontology of action, which I have claimed has to do with the ontology of the social. His discussion brings the theory of action and its assumptions about volition to a point at which it becomes imperative to ask whether it can be sustained in its standard version. That is, he fails to solve the mysteries, not because of any obvious lack on his part but because he approaches the limits of the standard theory in such a way that its ontological problems can no longer be glossed over and, in any case, cannot be resolved in terms of what is presumably given to common sense. The solution he offers, which is to admit "intrinsically practical reasoning into the theory of action" (233), requires giving up significant expectations of what a theory needs to do if it is to live up to its original sub-theoretically induced purpose.

The predicament involves an inability to clarify the conditions under which a standard theory of action can be sustained in connection with other theoretical domains and in regard to nontrivial applications. This is so to the extent to which clarification accepts the ontology that excludes what it most needs: an idea of agency sufficiently robust, and therefore ontologically exceptional, to shed light on problems associated with the sorts of ideas (e.g., of will, weakness of the will, intention, reflexivity, and freedom) with which the theory was supposed to deal from the start. This suggests, again, that it is worthwhile reconsidering the very concept of action, despite the understandable desire to risk error on the side of caution by giving the standard theory the benefit of the doubt. It is reasonable to do so because the attempts to salvage the concept of strictly situated action have placed it into question, and one can no longer be confident that it is legitimate to avoid rethinking the reasons for absolutely rejecting older metaphysical views.[5]

The fact that this might risk the embarrassment of an incorporeal or depersonalized self—that is, selves not vested in the bodies of skin-bound individual persons—cannot justify ignoring what seems unavoidable if there is to be any general understanding of how what people do can be consistent with what is human about human affairs. In other words, given that one cannot help but speculate with Searle about the possibility of a "non-Humean self," "action" cannot refer to what it refers to in the original theory, and what "self" refers to may not be what it might have been thought to be. On the one hand, it cannot be a self-reflective effect of causes or a direct outcome of reasons located fundamentally within the individual over the course of a life; and it cannot be a totality with a distinct form and a beginning and an end, where bodily movements are taken either as definitive or indicative of the action at issue. On the other hand, given the available concepts, and the need for a reformation of the theory of action, it is not unreasonable to proceed as if action might still turn out to be a matter of individual reasoning and reflexivity, or that the latter might turn out to be aspects or features of individual action. As we have seen, however, these options beg legitimate questions about the viability of the ontology on which they depend, and this seems to be where the most important problems lie. One way out involves arguing that a construct such as the self can operate theoretically in regard to the theory of action as a whole even though it cannot be formally part of it. In that case, the ontology of action is no longer a key issue. But the same cannot be said for the ontology of the self.

The argument is that the notion of a self may perform a formal theoretical function, but, at most, only *for the theory of action taken as a whole.* In this regard, it addresses the insufficiency of the theory to explain the undertaking. That is, what the theory actually addresses is deciding rather than acting. To the extent to which deciding is trivialized by its separation from the undertaking (and from a commitment to what is undertaken), something needs to be added in order to complete the object—not the reduced and refined object of the theory but the object to which it is intended to return. The theory does not and cannot account for the gap between reasons and action since its object is essentially the former and the object to which it is applied is precisely the one that displays the gap. Since it is not possible to add the notion of a self to such a theory without undoing the theory itself, its only legitimate function, given the desire to preserve the basic components of the theory, is to connect the representation of situations by reasons based on beliefs to the undertaking, which seems, then, to constitute an object of a different order. While one might argue that "self" names another reason—namely, the integrity of the agent over time—this is not the same sort of reason that represents a situation, and that sort is a necessary part of the theory of action as things stand.

The usefulness of an idea of a self requires the idea of an undertaking. But it does not follow that an evaluation of a situation accounts for a decision to act. The proposition that "we are what we do" satisfies part of what the idea of a self is supposed to add to our understanding of what we do. But it leaves open the question of what is meant by a "self," allowing for speculations that are risky enough to put into question the very enterprise the construct was supposed to preserve. Referring to a self may shift theoretical interest from reasons to act to the undertaking and, in doing so, from the pre-theoretical notion of a "structure of action" to the sub-theoretical notion of a "course of activity" in which commitment is not problematic. While this does not require speculation about the self, it does allow for a different, nonindividualistic conception of agency from the individualistic conception associated with the theory of action.[6] Davidson hints at this when he says that propositional thought requires communication (2001d, 130, 209–210, 213). But he preserves individualism by identifying what he calls (but does not analyze) "community" with norms (215, 217) and by illustrating the social dimension of thought, and I assume action, by saying that "it takes two points of view to give a location to the cause of a thought, and thus to define its content." Parenthetically, since each of the two points of view is a thought, and so is their coupling, more points of view are needed ad infinitum, and this threatens to undo the idea of a definitive content just as it places into jeopardy the very notion of a point of view.

In other words, it would seem necessary to develop a very different, non-normative notion of society (or community) in order to sustain Davidson's otherwise prescient conclusion that there is a social dimension to what we think and do that is generally prior to any other dimension, possibly excepting what cannot easily be assimilated to a theory of mind—that is, pure and immediate sensation. Then, to the extent to which one wishes to connect what is presumably covered by the theory of mind with what is presumably covered by the theory of action, thinking with doing, and to do so according to the notion of intentionality, it is necessary to rethink both the origin of doing (agency) and the sort of deliberative processes that presumably take place during the course of activity that constitutes doing. A robust concept of sociality consistent with what appears to be the intent of Davidson's claim would effectively challenge the ontology that locates thought and action within individuals subject to interpretive norms and shared meanings.[7]

It is important to remember that even without such a reconceptualization theorists of action are still committed to an informal meta-theoretical constraint that is admitted in principle but elided in virtually all their theories. On the one hand, that constraint requires at least some reference to an irreducibly social aspect of what, as Emmet (1975) says, people characteristically do. As we have seen, introducing the construct of the self is one way of avoiding the issue. It effectively sustains the belief that understanding human conduct requires an individualistic model of agency that runs counter to that constraint. On the other hand, it attributes continuity to the actor beyond his or her situation. In this respect, it suggests that it is necessary to conceptualize agency in such a way that the individuality that lies at the center of the theories is fundamentally compromised. Since the history of each individual is intelligible only as a history of the social being of that individual, and his or her memory is at least mediated and at most constituted as a social fact, any reconceptualization consistent with the meta-theoretical constraint is bound to make trouble for the most fundamental ideas associated with prevailing theories of mind and action, at least as far as the two are considered, as Davidson does, to be necessarily connected. This is likely to lead one back to the decision-theoretical frame of reference that produces the theoretical gap as a permanent feature of the individualistic theory of action. But it need not do so. It can also lead one to doubt the adequacy of the more inclusive frame of reference or ontology, therefore to doubt the reasonableness of taking individuals to be the locus of efficacy, determination, and effect. In that case, one must acknowledge the possibility of an idea of social agency that relies on the irreducibility of the social and that is more than individuals taking account of one another, responding to norms, or connecting, or even trying to connect, personally individualized mental contents to behavior.

Since both the social and the self are conceived of as irreducible, the reason to choose the latter over the former may be a desire to avoid the risk of reification. But it is the nature of any risk that it might be avoided, and there are certainly similar and possibly more dangerous risks associated with speculating about an irreducible and continuous self. Later, I try to show what a radically nonindividualistic account of what people do might look like, and I argue that accounting for what people do according to the idea that what is human about human affairs has to do with their essential sociality requires pursuing this option as radically as possible.

I have argued that recourse to the idea of a self is one possible result of reflecting on the limitations of a theory aimed at explaining individual action in situations in which the actor can be represented as a relatively autonomous moving point on a space of invariant relations the transformations of which depend on the movement of that point. In that case, the standard account fails to provide sufficient conditions of the transition from the disposition to act to acting according to that disposition. A corollary is that this solution to the problem of the gap, between the various factors that are said to operate as proximal causes of action and the actions they are supposed to cause, is especially appealing when the account of action is predicated on the designation of a closed set of situated objects, including other persons, consideration of which provides the actor with the sorts of mental state or disposition (e.g., beliefs, desires, intentions, and reasons) that are insufficient to explain the moment of the actual undertaking. The solution seeks to address those limitations by redeeming the "non-Humean" self, but to do so within the model and not against it. This is why, if social action involves taking others into account, the distribution of selves that the theory requires leads to the paradoxes described previously. The self that can be attributed to the actor as theorized is either negligible, insofar as it allows the situated others to be selves in an extremely limited sense, or it is the only self that operates as such in the situation in which action transpires. But referring to a self in order to connect the disposition to act to the undertaking leads to other gaps and in any case ultimately threatens the theory it was intended to supplement and thereby preserve.

I have also suggested that the model and its ontological assumptions are at fault, not just that the theory is incomplete. This is all the more likely when what is at stake is not merely how to account for the coupling of reasons and bodily movements but to account for the social aspect of whatever human beings do by way of being human. The problem is perhaps more obvious in regard to the idea of an actor's taking account of others according to an individualistic theory of action, which is one version of the idea that human beings are essentially social. Earlier, I tried to show that, for an actor to take account of others as a subset of a set of objective elements delimiting a given situation (that constitutes, theoretically, the universe in which the action transpires as a theoretically accountable event), either there is only the actor's self or there are no selves. If the former, there are still, effectively, no selves—since the idea of a universe composed of a single self and no others is incoherent; if the latter, there is no theory of action that is also a theory of social action, and we are left with our original problem: In what sense can human beings be said to be essentially social? Insofar as the self is reserved for the one identified as the actor in advance of any such reservation, and denied the others insofar as they constitute part of that actor's situation, it allows for nothing about the actor that has to do with taking other *human beings* (or their conduct) into account or, for that matter, with any other version of human sociality. As we have seen, the actor whose life beyond an immediate concrete situation is presumably confirmed by the attribution of a self turns out to be no less a nonhuman thing than its situated others, or at least is severely reduced. The way the attribution is said to allow for the actor's taking others into account begs the question of what this can mean beyond the sort of registering and calculating that needs no reference to a self. Under these circumstances, referring to a self has no other logical justification than that it names whatever reduces or fills the gap between reasons and undertakings, though, as we have seen, it creates new ones. This is so given the mysteries introduced by a theory that defines social action as action that takes account of others, and given that the value of adding the construct of a self depends on being able to add properties to it that go beyond the standard ontology of action, to go beyond it as mere construct. In that case, it begins to look less like a supplement to a viable theory of action than the beginning of a new theory destined to challenge and then displace the theory of action. To that extent, it disqualifies at least some of the philosophical considerations that the theory was intended to satisfy in the first place, possibly even the most basic ones. What moderates this radicalism are, presumably, constraints on the concept designed to protect it from metaphysical doctrines thought impossible to defend, constraints that, as things stand, appear to defeat the attempt to substantiate the self.

What constrains the list of properties, capacities, and modes of existence incorporated in the sense of a self (e.g., memory, freedom, the capacity to deliberate, evaluate and learn, and relative autonomy), allowing it to be converted from a mere construct to a concept among concepts, is the desire to maintain a necessary distinction between the actor as an active living entity and what the actor does in undertaking an act (e.g., between something like a decision and something like the execution of a decision). But maintaining it means that the action that had been the essential referent of the theory, what the theorized disposition is presumably about, is in danger of displacement by an older and unmanageably richer conception of an active self—that somehow emits activity rather than instigates or initiates it. Such an entity presumably subsists beyond the immediate scene of any particular, self-presenting action. What is gained in substantiating a life (and agency) beyond the actions called for in immediate concrete situations is lost in the failure to connect that life to the undertaking in a way that allows responsibility for what is undertaken to be reliably assigned, including responsibility for justifying what has been done. The notion of a self is either too meager to meet the needs of theory or too robust to be limited by any specific situation and, indeed, by anything that can be called a situation according to the standard theory.

The point is not that there is something wrong with the intuition that authorizes the notion but that there are other and, given the preceding discussion, better ways that intuition can be satisfied. The notion of a self is not the only possible solution to the problems of understanding human activity according to a principle of agency and in such a way that activity is seen as an upshot or outcome of conditions beyond those restricted to individuals in immediate concrete situations. It is necessary to consider an alternative to the extent to which we are interested in understanding what people do according to what is essentially social about human affairs. But the alternative cannot be merely another construct, or a concept compatible with the standard ontology of action. I try to show that in considering the problem of what people do that expresses what is human about human affairs, it is necessary to reverse the normal order of inquiry and analysis. Rather than start with individuals who are then shown to be social, we need, as Strawson and Goffman remind us, to begin with the idea of the social as such, first asking what it tells us about the nature of human activity and only then what it tells us about the conditions of individuation. Since this does not require an investigation of the sort of mentality associated with individuation, that mentality, such as it might be, is not directly relevant to this inquiry. Nevertheless, it will become apparent that even an investigation of that mentality will produce different results from beginning with the individual as only formally or contingently social.

————

To summarize and conclude, the idea that human beings are essentially social seemed to be adequately represented by saying that actors take others into account. Since this depends on the standard theory of action, it works only if the latter can be defended. Problems with it, in particular the insufficiency of reasons as causes of the undertaking, have been addressed by a number of philosophers, including Hampshire, Hornsby, Nagel, and Searle. For Nagel and Searle, the term "self" indicates a structured and durable volitional capacity capable of adding to situationally specific reasons, thereby bringing the intention closer to the undertaking. However, this solution was either insufficiently developed or it created more problems than it solved. Moreover, it appeared that it either could not contribute to a general theory applicable to social action or could do so only under the auspices of a different ontology from that affirmed by the standard theory. Ironically, both cases undermine the very idea of a self, though not the intuition for which it stands—namely, that human activity involves more and other than what is conceivable under the standard theory, including what falls under the category of activity, the status of reasons, and the idea of agency.

Parenthetically, the persistence of this use of the self despite its problems reinforces the hypothesis that the intuition is *sub-theoretical* to the standard theory of action and, as such, is an obstacle to its realization as a general theory. If so, the validity of the theory is open to challenge for the different, individualistic ontology that it affirms on its own account as essentially *pre-theoretical*. To that extent, it is necessary to consider what is human about human affairs and to take seriously the entailments of the idea that human beings are essentially social—and, it must be added, to look elsewhere for a useful notion of the social than the idea of action in which others, like situated nonhuman objects, are taken into account. Instead of trying to account for the relationship between the mental states and the actions or undertakings of persons, where those actions or undertakings are taken as events that realize such states in specific situations, we may be led to conclude that there is no generally explainable relationship because there is no directly theoretical relationship, that what we are prone to call an instance of action does not point in the way indicated to personally held mental states, at least to those mental states that are supposed to determine what is actually done. Nor, for the same reasons, does it seem likely that a theory of action plus a self will provide an adequate account of social action. We have arrived at this point because taking others into account was supposed to be a sufficient description of being social; and this floundered on the insufficiency of connecting mental states to action and on the failure of the construct of a personal self to fill that gap and, beyond that, to provide for the characteristic features of the others such that they can be taken into account as other human beings.

What turns out to be significant in referring to a self is not that it does or does not contribute to the standard theory but that it invokes a sub-theoretical principle inconsistent with the idea that an instance of action can be specific enough, and sufficiently constrained, to be reasonably attributed to a particular person responding to a particular situation. That is, the solution provided by the self to the problem of the gap, when carried far enough, separates agency as a general capacity from individual intentionality and, therefore, from the idea that an action is something done by individuals considered as entities whose undertakings depend on their registering facts and calculating possible options prior to acting.[8] The following discussion adds to the last few chapters by focusing on Searle's attempt to reconcile a "non-Humean" self with a Humean idea of action, and on some of what is involved in theorizing such a self. In later sections, I consider the relationship between sociality and the notion of a course of activity, and what this involves for the idea of human affairs.

Searle's work on "rationality in action" attempts to bridge the gap between mental states and action by reference to a "self" conceived of at the level of intentionality. This presumably extends the contents to which the mind applies itself, when forming an intention to act, to conditions that are not immediately present in the concrete situation, in light of which he reconsiders what other reasons are relevant to the rationality of an act. He begins his "summary of the argument for the existence of an irreducible, non-Humean self" by stating that its existence is necessary if we are to speak coherently of responsibility, blame, approval, and so forth (2001, 90–91). He might have added that the determination to give moral energies their focus by settling issues involved in coherent assignments of responsibility, blame, and so on has its own complex context that is at once discursive, ideological, political, and conventional. It includes what we typically but do not necessarily mean when we speak of responsibility, blame, approval, and the like. In that case, it seems unreasonable to make the test of the adequacy of the conception of the self its compatibility with the meanings and uses of terms that *already* incorporate a vague notion of the self that is the very one in question. Moreover, it should be fairly clear that raising questions about this notion of a self is bound to challenge the foundations of a moral discourse that cannot do without such a conception. Until a critique is undertaken, we cannot take it for granted that a failure of the construct to become a concept would be fatal to the idea that there is an ultimate referent of moral discourse that at least includes individuals. We cannot take it for granted because we have deferred the problem of individuation in anticipation of a clarification of the idea of sociality sufficient to allow us to rethink what might be said about the relationship between moral discourse and individuality no less than what might be said about each. Until the notion of the social is clarified, at least in its general features, we cannot presume to know what conclusions would follow from such a critique. It seems better to try and discover what sense can be made of that notion before assuming the very type of moral discourse that presupposes sociality in a way that, as we have seen, is difficult if not impossible to defend.

Independently of these important but momentarily marginal considerations, Searle clarifies his idea as follows:

> The requirement that I state the reasons I acted on requires a reference to a self. The truth conditions of sentences of the form "X performed act A for reason R" require not just the existence of events, psychological states, and causal relations between them, they require a self (which is something more than an agent) that makes a reason effective by acting on it. (2001, 87)[9]

In other words, the insufficiency of what are ordinarily said to be causes at the level of intentionality requires not more of the same, but the construct of a self that invokes, uncharacteristically and somewhat cavalierly, a principle of vitality. This is given properties designed to complete the causal picture provided by the theory of action, without otherwise disturbing the self-less analysis, "X performed act A for reason R," except to suggest the following translation: "X is the actor who performed act A for reason R." What of X is left over is not formally relevant to the theory of action unless the theory is modified to allow X to be a repository of reasons that arise from something de-situated about X, in which case X is continuous across situations and, presumably, situated at a more general level, requiring, on the one hand, a redefinition of "situation," and, on the other, a notion of the actor, in her greater identity, as *essentially* unsituated.

This self, or the entity that is, as Searle says, "also" a self, must be "capable of conscious reasoning about its actions. It must be an entity capable of perception, memory, belief, desire, thought, inference, and cognition generally" (2001, 92). That is, "in order to account for rational agency, we must postulate a self that combines the capacities of rationality and agency" (95). Its features are that it is conscious, "persists through time," "operates with reasons, under the constraints of rationality," presupposes freedom, and is "responsible for at least some of its behavior" (95)—presumably that portion that is, for the sake of judgment, easily enough distinguished from the portion for which the individual is not responsible. What Searle seems to have in mind is not just the need to make human sense of acts already done but to bolster the theory of how they get done in the first place by imagining a centripetal tendency that brings the various conditions of action together as a coherent whole that can be identified with whatever person (or persons), X, is assigned the status of actor in the formula "X performed act A for reason R." The aim is not merely to account for how acts are justified but to explain how they occur or might occur. It is important to recognize, however, that the explanation presupposes the incorrigibility of the practices presumably integrated by the concept of a self as a self-ideal, and in that sense Searle is offering a moral theory.

On the one hand, it might be said that this integration of conditions is strictly formal, amounting to no more than naming our ignorance. This would not be the case if there were previously unidentified conditions; but those listed by Searle are familiar to the standard account of action. On the other hand, knowing that we are ignorant about certain things means that we know something about them; and it is in that regard that Searle's solution may be suggestive. For one thing, it seems to suggest that there is no problem for the theory of action to solve, that the insufficiency of reasons to the undertaking is no longer an issue—not because the idea of a self completes or reinforces the theory but because it insulates the theory against its own apparent defect. It thus protects the attribution of causal efficacy to privately held reasons. But, given an adequate development of a theory of the sort of "self" Searle has in mind, there is no reason to expect that the now-marginalized theory of action will have the theoretical properties and advantages it had when its limitations gave rise to a need to posit such a far-ranging and deliberately vague construct.

If adding the notion of a self must change our ideas about reason and action, not to mention our ideas of rationality and causality at the level of intentionality, Searle's main achievement may well have been to discredit any claim to generality for the theory of action. If the theory was originally designed to avoid the metaphysical problems associated with the concept of a non-Humean self, it loses whatever advantage it had when just such a self is now said to be essential in accounting for its object. At best it is marginal and at worst no longer relevant. If Searle is correct in his description of what such a self would have to look like and be able to do, then the problem that gave rise to it, the reason he formulated it, no longer obtains. The problem was a feature of the very theory that he is trying to preserve with the addition of the non-Humean self. We have to conclude that he leaves us with an idea for which there is no apparent theoretical reason. There is no reason because there is no gap; and there is no gap because, in having named the filler of what was once a gap, "self" takes over the task of explanation. If it leaves the original model intact, then the gap remains unless the self somehow constantly asserts itself against it, in which case what is important is not the self as he describes it but its tendency (or some as yet unmentioned tendency of the actor) to assert itself. If this is a constant tendency, then it must be immanent to the reasons adduced for a decision to act. It is not yet clear how this could be the case or what reason would be like if it were the case, unless "reason" simply means a tendency to act according to a content, and for that the concept of a self is unnecessary.

There are views of action that hint at this possibility, but they are not Searle's. If the notion of a self makes the original model obsolete, as seems to be the case, then the conditions of the gap no longer exist (since they had to do with the connection between discrete reasons that are not tendencies and discrete actions), but there is also no theory of action for the idea of a self to complete. What began as an attempt to repair an otherwise workable theory ends by either requiring something (e.g., self-assertiveness) that it does not theorize, or it presents itself as an altogether different theory of something that used to be called "action" but now may need to be reimagined in different terms.[10]

16

Social Action Reconsidered

We have been considering an application of the theory of action that identifies the sociality of action with actors taking account of others. While this need not be thought of as exhausting the meaning of "social," there is considerable agreement that it provides a basis for a reasonable account of conduct in the presence of others. However, this application depends on taking action and human association as ontologically distinct. If the distinction is rejected, as I have suggested, one has little choice but to begin with the idea of the social and derive individuality from it, in contrast with what now seems to be impossible—namely, beginning with individuality and attempting to derive sociality from assumptions about how individuals relate to each other and how those relations can lead to the formation of social entities. The version identified with Weber has to do with "type concepts" and a utilitarian distinction between rational and nonrational reasons for action. The paradigmatic form of action is rational/instrumental; everything else falls under the negative categories of nonrationality and irrationality. Thus, while the Weberian position appears to be methodological, it is nevertheless theoretically significant: "For the purposes of a typological scientific analysis it is convenient to treat all irrational, affectually determined elements of behavior as factors of deviation from a conceptually pure type of rational action" (1947, 92). It apparently includes what Weber refers to as "value" or "substantive" rationality. Its theoretical significance presumably derives from the implications of several assumptions. The major ones are that goals can be specified in advance because they fall within the range of a prior value and are already available as meaningful options in the situation, that actors form expectations by taking account of probabilities they arrive at by appraising their situation, that actors are able to choose accordingly and to evaluate their choices in advance and in retrospect, that they are motivated to act as efficiently as possible according to a principle of least effort, that any lapse in efficiency and judgment will lead them to reflect as rationally as possible on what they either intend to do or did, and that whatever is left of sociality from this conception presumably can be analyzed in relation to it.

The last assumption is implicit in Weber's definition of sociology as "a science which attempts the interpretive understanding of social action in order thereby to arrive at a causal explanation of its course and effects," and in his definition of social action as action that, "by virtue of the subjective meaning attached to it by the acting individual (or individuals) . . . , takes account of the behaviour of others and is thereby oriented in its course" (1947, 88). It is clear, from the qualification imposed by the former definition on the latter, that taking account of the behavior of others involves taking account of those others. Otherwise, being oriented by the behavior of *others* would be no more noteworthy than being oriented by nonhuman things, and there would be no need to speak of social action at all—or, if there were, it would not rely on a sense of sociality that requires "interpretive understanding."

When intended to illuminate an idea of sociality applicable to human affairs, this view precludes a great deal of what otherwise seems important in clarifying the relationship between what people do and what must be thought of as distinctively human about what they do. Weber was interested in delimiting the field of sociology, but, despite his appeal to "ideal type concepts" (concepts among related concepts), his solution relied on a psychological hypothesis about the relationship between orientation and action and a reduction of agency to individualized inclinations. Thus, it does not directly address the problems posed by the basic fact of sociality. As a consequence, the popularity of his theory may, in part, reflect its individualism and the utilitarian basis of his idea of social action as action that "takes account of the conduct of others." However, his approach cannot be reconciled with the ongoing and supra-individual aspects of a course of activity.[1] Conceiving of social action independently of the self-transforming, reflexive movement that comprises a course of its activity is intelligible only if there is nothing distinctively human about human affairs.

To say that social action consists of an actor's taking account of others in deciding what to do begs the question of what is social about it, just as it begs the question of what it means to be oriented. I assume that the idea of orientation implies a self-presenting course of activity that responds to its passing moments and not to an overarching *telos*; I assume also that it does not consist of a path chosen from among other possible futures available to an actor, as if actors are absolutely distinct from what they choose to do and can manipulate their own conduct and its situation for the sake of their own prior ends.[2]

If the situated others are merely things, even somewhat like things, it would be neither necessary nor sensible to refer to behavior oriented to them as social, unless one were prepared to reformulate the idea of the social to include relations with nonhuman objects as well, in which case to claim that action is social is to say something radically different about the objects of action—that they are not merely passive and that, therefore, orientation is not what it seems to be when its objects are things. What is set in motion by others who are active on their own account is, for the actor conceived of in the analysis of action, change—which is not the same as *conditions* of change. One might conclude, then, that action that takes account of others is identifiable as social action primarily by the fact that it is a course of activity; or, as Davidson's account of the social dimension of knowledge seems to suggest, all courses of activity are such by way of others being taken into account (2001e). An action is, then, not to be understood as an instance of a form, a realization of a prior intention or reason, a result of an individual's decision, or something like an event imposed on a world otherwise free of such impositions. However, once the idea of a course of action is on the theoretical agenda, it requires a theory for which sociality is constitutive of action and not merely one of its conditions. Nevertheless, the concepts of individuality and agency are bound to remain problematic to the degree to which it is no longer possible to rely confidently on available methods of analysis or available solutions.[3]

———————

The original formula says that an instance of action is a function of an actor in a situation that includes others as irresistible action-salient facts, where its being such a function depends on meanings attached non-idiosyncratically by the actor to his or her own behavior. The previously discussed paradox makes itself known to the extent to which the formula is applied to actual or imaginable settings, and to the extent to which the actor it posits is taken to be a sufficient substantiation of the relationship between the human and social aspects of action—as the sort of being that takes others into account.

There is a potentially devastating consequence of the way in which the relationship between actor and situation is portrayed: the others are effectively nonhuman, or not human in the sense of the actor's humanity. The nonacting but merely behaving others are posited as entities taken into account in the same way that nonhuman situated entities are taken into account. Taking account of others is, then, not the same as taking account of others as active human beings. For action to be intelligible under the action theoretical limitation of its taking account of the behavior of others, it must appear to treat the others as fixed and their behavior as, correspondingly, a matter of a predictable disposition. It is at the moment of the act that the other is not fully human, and to take account meaningfully of the behavior of others, hence to take account of others, it is necessary that the actor and those others share humanity. It follows that the actor of the theory of action cannot be said to take account of others, and the conception of sociality as a taking account of others fails. Ironically, this makes it difficult if not impossible to connect the human aspect of action to the actor herself, if our *obligation* to interpret meaning (the actor's sense of the meaning of his or her behavior) is to have any meaning.

In other words, actors posited as such by the standard theory of action are no more able to represent the definitively human aspect of social action than the others taken into account who, by hypothesis, complete the social aspect of an action by their passive existence as entities available to be taken into account. Because they take account of others in the same way they take account of things, such actors are effectively alone in their exercise of agency, and in regard to the obligation observers have to interpret the meanings of what they do. This does not mean that there might not be a last person, as it were, who, having been born the moment after the world was destroyed and somehow survived, though without language and the experience of others, forms reasons based solely on the relationship she feels between her needs and the otherwise non-meaningful things around her. It only means that such a person is not a human actor to the extent to which action is social by virtue of the actor taking account of others. The solo actor, incapable of even fantasizing the existence of others like her and therefore unable to form an idea of selves and therefore a self, certainly takes account of things in some sense of the word, but not self-referentially and without the advantage of being able to attribute meaning to her behavior and to the things that it takes into account, presumably moment to moment.[4]

The comparison between the fantastic solo actor and the actor of action theory is not an exaggerated analogy. They are logically identical inasmuch as the actor and the solo actor take account of things and neither takes account of other humans, as now seems to be the case. To take account of something merely given is not to take account of others, and both actors take account primarily of what is given. One might argue that the difference between the two is that the one knows that the others have histories that are histories of intentions, and the other does not. However, while this may explain a sense of obligation on the part of the former, it does not affect the status of the "others as given" in the same sense that nonhuman objects are "given." Indeed, the actor who feels a special obligation to human beings and not to nonhuman things might just as well decide that nonhuman objects also have intentionality and deserve respect. In any case, the sense of obligation may affect how the actor feels about what she is doing, but that does not bear on the logic of the relationship of "taking into account" that characterizes the actor in a situation; and *that relationship is, at the moment identified by theory as causally relevant to action, one of indifference to the distinction between human and nonhuman objects.*

If this taking account of what is merely given exemplifies agency, it is a severely reduced version not so different from the rudimentary agency attributed to the most primitive of animals. On the contrary, the Weberian theory of action is designed not merely to show that what can be called an actor must also be an agent, but that agency is a property of being human such that it cannot but be exercised by persons in regard to the fact that they are always with others. It is the case not only that agency is a property of being human but, as far as the theory is concerned, that being human is a characteristic feature of agency. If being human involves being social, then agency is intrinsically social and therefore requires not only the existence of others but their existence as different from nonhuman things. That difference must be more than merely categorical if it is to be relevant to a theory of action in which social action involves taking account of others. It seems, then, that *one's taking account of others minimally involves something like taking account of others taking account of one—in which case the movement among the activities of taking account becomes the object of theory, and must be taken to supersede any individually intentional content; it follows that the problem theory identifies for interpretation has nothing to do with separable minds or individually situated meanings.*

To summarize, according to this interpretation of the standard formula, (1) only the actor exercises agency; (2) the actor exercises agency in regard to things that cannot be, at that moment, instances of agency; (3) an agent who is not in the presence (or virtual presence) of agents cannot be social; (4) the most general condition of social action is that an actor as agent is in the presence of actors as agents; (5) not being social is not being distinctively human; (6) the capacity to provide for agency in general is a critical test of a theory of action; (7) but, it is incoherent to assert that an actor who takes account of others is or can be social without those taken into account being of the same order of being as the actor; (8) being in the presence of actors as agents means that the actor is not merely taking them into account, since to do so would require fixing them as if they are not human so that accounting in the way prescribed is possible; and (9) against the original intent of the formula, social action cannot be social unless it involves a relationship that is both constitutive and substantive beyond the individuals who are its ostensible elements and is therefore a relationship that is itself neither fixed as such nor reducible to what individuals think and do.

The formula in which social action involves an actor's taking account of others can be seen, like most ideal typical accounts, as a failed metaphor, a rhetorical device issued as a description but without an accountable referential field. That is, it uncritically evokes a sense of mechanism, therefore of simulation, repetition, and duplication, indicating a relationship of one set of facts (actors as calculating devices with relatively motivating dispositions and beliefs manifest at the point at which action becomes possible) with another (dispositions identified as reasonably reliable tendencies of others and more or less registered as such by the actor). Such a type is easily exemplified, can be elaborated on in its own terms, and instates retrospective accounts of actions as events that are immediately plausible as long as one accepts the legitimacy of relying on the metonymic organizing principle. Given these qualities, one can see how it could have been taken as a general enough description to apply to most of what people do, one that adequately substitutes for, and corrects, what some physicalists refer to deprecatingly as a "folk psychological" idea of action as a self-reflective exercise of participatory agency under conditions of divided intentionality, dependence, ambiguity, and uncertainty, and where meanings and consequences are variable in the sense of being what Garfinkel calls "ongoing accomplishments" (1967, vii).[5] It seems clear that too much is lost in such a translation to claim that it clarifies the sub-theoretical notion that creates an urgent need for theory in the first place. As already stated, this is not to deny that the model serves certain purposes. For example, it may be defended as accounting for a limited range of phenomena; and it may have some heuristic value within debates with those who view human affairs as essentially irrational in their foundations, or only secondarily rational. Above all, it seems that the concept of action implied in the standard theory does not easily lend itself to considering what is human about human affairs, even with the addition of discussions about the weakness of the will.[6]

To deal with some of the limitations of the standard theory, facts specifically pertaining to the actor in her capacity as agent are often qualified by epistemic variables such as complexity, ignorance, and shifts in perspective. I eventually identify these with an attitude of waiting that corresponds to the sociality of a course of activity. For now, it is necessary to see them as compromising rationality[7] as that is usually understood. Among the requirements of rationality so compromised are the following: that actors adhere to the principle of least effort; that they form reasonably clear and distinct beliefs relevant to choosing an option; that they be clear enough about preferences that second thoughts do not paralyze their will; and that they be able to reduce what appears to be a complex or multidimensional problem to one as close to a single dimension as possible so that options can be sufficiently specified in regard to their relative availability, desirability, costs, and benefits, compared along those scales with other options and ranked such that they remain options even at the point of the undertaking.

The assumption that deviance from strict morality is motivating, the rigor with which the formula can be elaborated under the auspices of the idea of the moral and practical centrality of problem-solving rationality, and the assumption that there is little if any need to refer to non-propositional mental states, are among the reasons why the introduction of the idea of rational choice to the social sciences seemed to promise a broadly applicable predictive theory able to account for the sociality of action without either mystifying it or exempting it from prevailing views in the philosophy of action and the philosophy of science.[8] When the paradox framed by the need to distinguish between actor and other, and to do so such that "other" refers to what cannot be "actor," became apparent, either directly or indirectly through the pressure of apparently unrelated problems, many of the proponents of the theory shifted from that justification to one in terms of normativity, while others attempted to retain some measure of predictive quality by narrowing the scope of application of the theory.[9] The model that was initially supposed to explain action was thereby transformed into advice for those able to state their interests according to preferred goals that can be ranked and analyzed according to cost, expansively conceived.

This allows that the question of value, which Weber identified with "substantive rationality," does not arise—that is, it can be taken for granted for all practical purposes. In this respect, the normative force of rationality is indifferent to the force of values in regard to which a norm might be relevant to making a choice, or choice being an issue at all. In other words, rational action is conceived of as action indifferent to values (values as parameters of decision making), and, it follows, when the theory is applied, that what people do in ordinary instances of decision has little or nothing seriously to do with values and considerations of value, which are, in other words, given; ordinary action is, then, no less value-free than science. Parenthetically, Parsons, and then Goffman and Garfinkel, attempted to make clear, in different ways but contrary to Weber, that the concept of action is fatally incomplete without the immanence of value, and that there is no point in an instance of action that this element is not immanent—that the notion of a value-free action is incoherent.

Even ignoring the paradox, however, and therefore begging the question of what an actor must be if his or her others are mechanically disposed entities and therefore nonhuman, taking account of others turns out to be more involved than taking account of things and it must be more spontaneous than what is suggested by the expression "taking account." Only through a recognition of the paradox and the limits it imposes on the theory of action is it possible to restore the perspective of the nontrivial sub-conceptual notion of agency implicit in reference to actors. These limits include the inability to establish what is human about human action when absolute distinctions are made between actor and situation and actor and other, and uncertainty about what is active about human action when the behavior it refers to is imagined as reactive and characterized in state-descriptive terms according to a relationship between a mental state and a non-intentional executive function.[10]

The difficulty is clear from the way in which others are typically characterized as human in order to be consistent with the individualized agentic aspect of the actor and an idea of taking something into account that has to do with that very aspect. For this, the quality that marks others as special among situated objects appears to be their unique capacity continually to add motivational value to a given subject's intentions and to modify her expectations predicated on the unpredictability of that value, at least at the point of the undertaking— that is, expectations not arrived at as a rational accumulation of past instances. In other words, if others are presumed, in their human otherness, to be able to motivate an actor in this way, then it is difficult to resist concluding that she is, at the very moment of their presence, aware of her own subjectivity relative to those others as subjects; and they are able to do this in such a way that it is not possible for her to ignore their capacity to motivate in a way that is both self-presenting on their part and irreducibly relational, and not predictable from any point of view that can be assigned to the actor as an individualized instance of agency.

One question raised by this has to do with how others can add motivational value to the actor beyond the concrete needs and interests that are normally thought to dispose her and beyond the incentive value of the various options available. It is of course possible to deny the point, but it seems built into a conception of the other as a human object to be taken into account. One way this has been addressed is by arguing that the other is merely a more complex object than the simple and relatively homogeneous objects that comprise the nonhuman portion of the actor's situation. But this is an ad hoc account that leaves open the question it is intended to address: What is it to take things and others into account in a single moment of decision? In any case, complexity is, in this context, an extremely slippery idea that nevertheless assumes a general theory of the person as actor that lends itself to just this sort of objectification. Moreover, it is difficult to imagine how one can apply it to the actor without losing the sense of agency that allows one to distinguish between actor and others in a substantive and not merely a formal way.

The others, represented as instances of an accountable type of object, are then thought to constitute one part of a context of action. To the extent to which action and context are internally related, so that reasons and desire are what they are only in a situation, action is conceived of fundamentally as a manifestation of an agency denied the others who are taken into account. Or, in terms of the functionalist idea of a system of action, such others are non-material elements of the "conditions of rational action" for actors whose goals can be represented and pursued only in regard to others' intentions and to progressively inclusive institutional contexts.[11] According to this view of the relationship between two kinds of entity of interest in the analysis of action, agent and context, the objectivity of the accountable others lies partly in their capacity to actively motivate subjects. However, this makes it difficult to maintain a clear distinction between agency and alterity. That is, if the other is characterized as adding motivational value to the actor's disposition to act in a particular way, as "alter" to the actor's "ego," this must be attributed to something actor-like about the former, over and above whatever can be said about the complexity of "alter" and about the past experience of the actor with that other. It follows, however, that the existence of others, posited as part of the attempt to explain the sociality of action largely in terms of the actor's taking account of others, makes the difference between context and action sufficiently ambiguous to require rethinking the foundations of the theory—at least in regard to the implicit notion that subjects related to subjects cannot be described as states of affairs, or events, or as activity predicated on particular conditions. One way of rethinking foundations involves a further extension of the logic of the relationship between those actors (putatively originary subjects) who take account of others and those who are taken into account as part of the context of action (in order to preserve the idea of sociality *in* action).

This points to another, related paradox. It is assumed that the other is accounted for by an actor who can be rational only by taking that other into account and that this limitation has something to do with the character of what has to be taken into account—not merely the motion (e.g., behavior such that it can have what Weber calls a "course") but its source. In other words, the limitation is not contingent. It is part of the sense of agency that relates it to others as agents. The theory seems to require that the other be in motion in a way that is inseparable from and of the same order as the motion of an agent, the actor. In other words, there is some sort of identification of the one with the other: each is an instance of agency. This identification of actor and other is not consistent with two theoretical requirements: that the former be originary (a source of motion) and the latter be contextual (either fixed or movable but not an agentic source of motion), and that the two be distinct in regard to the concept of action that inaugurates their status as concepts involving a distinction between activity and passivity.

This means that the identity shared by actor and other leads us beyond indifference to the question of what about being social is distinctively human. That is, if actors are not merely driven by considerations of utility such that taking account of others involves implementing a sense of others as ends and not merely means, and an expectation that the same is true when the positions are reversed, then something irreducibly moral must be recognized in the sociality of action by a theory that had hoped to identify *taking into account* with utility and *being "an other"* with context. The theory allows for but does not rationalize a distinction between the moral being of the actor as a subject and the actor as rational decider, and it is in regard to the latter that others are taken to be different in kind. But this fails to solve the problem. If the logic of action requires referring to the moral quality of the actor, then that logic provides little if any of the explanatory value it promised. Moreover, if that logic is to be more than formal—that is, if it is intended to allow us to approach what is done by people among people from a point of view consistent with an idea of the social as distinctively human—then it must be coherent in itself before one can ask what needs to be added to complete the project of explanation. Therefore, to conceive of action is to place it in a conceptual space that provides for agency, context, and other such notions. These are necessary to the intelligibility of the concept relative to the various sub-theoretical notions a theory of action would have to address if it is to be theoretical in regard to its concepts and not just to the form of their relations.

Finally, it must be remembered that the logic invokes a distinction between what pertains to context and what pertains to action and the actor. This requires an ontology that supports the distinction between what is external and what is internal—if it is to be interpretable as a theory of individuated action;

and while that ontology begins with an absolute distinction between actor and objects, it ends, as we have seen, with the collapse of that distinction. On the one hand, the other appears no less a moral being—that is, engaged—than the actor. On the other hand, the idea of taking account of others seems to require that the others be the same sources of motion that actors must be if they are to take others into account, and it cannot be the case that the motions of each are only externally related and, in that sense, distinct.

Given this line of argument, the way actors take account of others is unaccountable, and attempting to fulfill the conditions of agency by conceiving of the actor as an originary subject does not yield the type of otherness required to sustain the idea of another being taken into account. The source of motion and the moral dimension of action belonged at first to the actor and not to her others, and now it belongs to both; and it seems impossible to avoid the idea that actions involve consequences that are not merely understandable in terms of goals and values but have to do with the very way in which actors and others are related—unless this, too, is thrown into the category of values. Such consequences count only if they are internally related to what it is they count for (e.g., the moral aspect of the person or her acts). This requires that others are ends and not means and that those others are taken into account as actors taking *their* others into account. In that sense, ego's taking account of her others cannot be intelligibly separated from those others' taking ego into account. I try to show later that this cannot be conceived of in terms of interpersonal interaction.

Reference to anything like an originary subject, then, seems at best metaphorical in that surprising way metaphors have of indicating a universe about which, for the moment, it is not possible to say more but more must always be said. The inhabitants of such a universe no longer resemble those who inhabit the universe in which the theory of action allows for none of the ambiguities and paradoxes discussed previously. In that case, we are at the beginning of an attempt to address the question that was the original working title of this book, "What is human about human affairs?" Before that, it is necessary to remind ourselves that any theory of action, of what is being done, must deal with two logically related facts: that the distinction between actor and other cannot be sustained at the level of theory, and, therefore, that the distinction between action and context cannot be sustained—no matter that each distinction may have extra-theoretical value.

It is now clear why we are unable to use the theory of action to explain what is meant by saying that human beings are essentially social. The attempt to clarify the concept of sociality by importing "others" in the explanation of action fails because the explanation of action makes obscure the logical conditions of taking account of others as human beings. Something else must be meant by "social" than "taking others into account" or "taking the behavior of others into account." Whether this can be made clear by beginning with individuated subjects and determining how they might compose a social entity or process or by trying to expand on the pre-theoretical notion in order to bring about the same result does not seem to matter. What counts is describing what is irreducible about the social and being able to refer non-categorically to conditions under which it is possible to conceive of agency and activity as instances of being social.

Perhaps this is why Parsons referred to the relation of an originary subject, or actor, to that subject's situated other as one of "ego" to "alter," and to a "complementarity of expectations," suggesting, even from the point of view of ego, an idea that cannot be expressed as "interaction"—dangerously close, as far as the utilitarian aspect of Parsons's structural-functionalist sociology is concerned, to the mutual fantasizing described by Sigmund Freud in his accounts of the dynamics of the inter-subjective aspect of transference and counter-transference and indicating a conception of the social that cannot be represented by sampling populations (Parsons 1951, esp. 10–11, 40). At the end of his initial discussion of "the unit of action systems," Parsons identifies as among the most significant theoretical problems for social thought that "of the relation between the analysis of the action of a particular concrete actor in a concrete, partly social environment, and that of a total action system including a plurality of actors" (1949, 50–51; 1951, 7–8).

Despite clarifying some implications of the Weberian concept of social action, Parsons's account still depends on the notion of an immediately present other conceived of as a segment of a situation that is, for the originary subject and what she decides to do, given. But while the idea of simply and immediately present others complicates the notion of human action and moderates the strenuous individualism of the utilitarian paradigm, it has proven inadequate to characterizing situations, if only because of the need to refer to norms and other such social facts, including language and courses of activity that transcend and supersede individuality, that appear to operate across situations or to define conditions that cannot be reduced to the anticipated actions or dispositions of specific others.[12]

If conceptualizing the situation is problematic, reference to taking account of others suggests that "situation" can no longer be thought of as referring to externally objective conditions of individual action. Once the other is introduced, the concept itself is changed. Parsons comments in this regard that, unlike action that depends on the interpretation of signs for their cue-functions, "in social interaction alter's possible 'reactions' may cover a considerable range, selection within which is contingent on ego's actions" (1951, 11). This "contingency" must be more than empirically definite in the usual sense, since the characterization of an actor as taking others into account requires a different sense of dependency, and one that does not suppose that the act of one is contingent on the act of another such that there is a natural temporal order to their appearances. For the problem raised is precisely in what this contingency lies, how it manifests itself, and how it is composed. The idea of "simply present others" is also inadequate for describing and understanding action if it is true that what individuals do typically transpires across bodies, and possibly persons, suggesting a need to question the distinction between selves and others—as far as that distinction needs to be rethought as it applies to courses of activity and not merely to actions conceived of as behaviors that execute reasoned intentions.

If we accept the proposition that the social cannot be reduced to what individuals intend, know, or do as individuals, then the problem is to explain behavior from the point of view of its being a course of activity and not merely an instance of a type without recourse to individualistic notions of rationality and processes of deliberation and by rethinking the meaning of key social psychological concepts as communication, social facilitation, mediation, and influence.[13] With these qualifications in mind, the idea of the social seems to refer to something on the order of a structure of action types that cohere as mutually oriented functions at various levels of agency, where agency is not reducible to individual intentions, actions, or beliefs and desires. That is, from the point of view of such a theory, situations cannot clearly be distinguished from what they are purported to situate, and action cannot begin with an individual's intention to act in such and so a way and end with that individual's completion of the intended act. In other words, whatever personal individuals are, as far as social theory is concerned, they are not essentially origins; nor are their intentions essentially the instigators or measures of their activity. This much is, I believe, accepted by quite a few sociologists; and the few philosophers who have tried to clarify the idea of the social have come close to endorsing the independence of agency from persons, though they typically veer away from it at the last moment, largely for epistemological reasons. Thus, Peter Winch poses the following problem for "our understanding of social life":

> It is clear that men do decide how they shall behave on the basis of their view of what is the case in the world around them. For instance, a man who has to catch an early morning train will set his alarm clock in accordance with his belief about the time at which the train is due to leave. If anyone is inclined to object to this example on the grounds of its triviality, let him reflect on the difference that is made to human life by the fact that there are such things as alarm clocks and trains running to schedule, and methods of determining the truth of statements about the times of trains, and so on. ([1958] 1990, 21)

But he goes on to say, crucially, "The concern of philosophy here is with the question: What is involved in 'having knowledge' of facts like these, and what is the general nature of behaviour which is decided on in accordance with such knowledge?" ([1958] 1990, 21).

What is crucial about this is that it is not necessary to assume that the knowledge of social facts is the same as the knowledge an individual "has" in moving his or her body in a certain meaningful way, of undertaking some course of activity. Much of what we, like Winch, refer to as social facts are not on the order of what individuals can "have" as knowledge and still be individuals; and what individuals do, as far as what they do is itself a social fact, need not be predicated on the sort of knowledge that is ordinarily meant by "having knowledge" of, being able to form propositions about, social facts. Thus, Winch's statement might be revised as follows: the concern is with the question of how what gives sense to what an individual does relates to that individual's knowledge (or mental state) at the point of an undertaking and during a course of activity, given that both are social facts such that the individual cannot "have" the sort of knowledge that could explain the very social facts that include and define what she is doing.

This social psychological insight has nevertheless been helpful in shifting emphasis from monadic dispositions of actors, including habits, to contexts of action, and in encouraging a sociological approach to a significant portion of what had formerly been thought of as strictly psychological facts. However, the positive meaning of its key term, "social," remains unclear. Therefore, although it may have heuristic value, it cannot provide a base from which one can derive hypotheses; or attempting to derive hypotheses requires sacrificing significant parts of our sense of the term. It rather offers an opportunity to begin an inquiry for which standard definitions, formulations, and theories are not as useful as might have been expected—except for what they can be shown symptomatically to neglect or elide.

———

The historiography of the idea of society does not help, since nothing is implicit about human relations in either of its two main conceptions, as system and as balance of forces. The identification of system with statics and forces with dynamics was an anachronism by the end of the 1930s, even though they remained difficult to avoid in theoretical practice, largely because addressing social change tended to undermine the theoretical specificity of each paradigm and treating them as complementary required simplifying assumptions that weakened both. Even so, critics now widely acknowledge that the notion of a system implies a dynamic aspect and that reference to forces implies the "practico-inert," which is Sartre's (1976) characterization of statics in terms of the latency of the unresolved problems of the history of every momentary balance of forces—such that they can be "forces." In passing, it may be conjectured that a failure adequately to investigate the logical conditions of sustaining either paradigm or both has made it difficult for American sociology to develop as much theoretically as it has statistically. If so, it may be one reason why many younger sociologists have turned to the work of the post-structuralists and to nontotalizing models of networks that avoid identifying dynamics with the notion of a system and that preserve a growing commitment, not without its own philosophical and theoretical problems, to a purely descriptive ethnography (see Latour 2005).[14]

Each paradigm was originally intended to explain the persistence of certain conditions under which people live together and to account for the durability of regimes, though system has been most fruitfully applied to the former, while the interaction of forces has best served as an account of the history and fate of regimes. The ideas of association, interaction, social action, and sociality have served to explain the affairs of people apart from the systems in which or regimes under which they have lived, but again the terms are not synonymous. Association suggests contiguity, interaction suggests mutual effect, social action is typically identified as having reasons that refer to the presence or possible presence of others, and sociality seems to indicate little more than copresence in which no distinction need be made between crowds or casual gatherings and groups or formally (or officially) instituted ensembles.

The problem has to do with taking account of others, and that is because it was generally assumed in the history of social science that familiarity trumps the perception of difference and that "primary groups" like families are more important than, in the sense of prior to, "secondary associations" like schools. That is, it was assumed that when people take others into account, it is particular others with whom they have particular relations. Those falling outside of those relations may affect them but only by way of reinforcing norms within interactional networks of which each person can know only a part. This is rather different from Rousseau's view of human association, reinforced by my interpretation of Nagel's account of altruism: of most general importance are our relations with indefinite others, those on whom we are equally dependent such that we can have rights and the experience of freedom only in regard to that indefinite "them," which is not Mead's "generalized other" in which the generalization is conceived of as subsequent to and predicated on specific interactions. Immediately confronted with particular wills, people do not construct society but act according to the relative strength of those wills, among other things. This is why those closest to us cannot provide us with a sense of our social being, and why we cannot derive society, and our sense of belonging to it, from our experiences with those immediate "consociates."

It follows that as individuals we attend to indefinite others, which poses the theoretical problem of the social even from an individuated point of view. But it is not clear how this attending relates to what we do and how it helps us to understand the idea of sociality and decide whether understanding it is sufficient to answer the question "What is human about human affairs?" While we know that society must be distinguished from an accumulation of individuals, deciding what we mean when we use the term remains problematic, as does the context brought into play when we attempt to use it to signify. Suppose our context is "What is human about human affairs such that we can ask the questions that motivate philosophy and the human sciences, not just about the true, the good, and the beautiful but about civil order, collective will, empathy, altruism, intuition, and so on?" In that case, we cannot simply mean by "society" only those who are present; nor can we settle for notions of structure that ignore the self-transforming movements of people living among people. Nor can we settle the issue by reference to conditions of rational action, institutions, groups, organizations, and the like. All these presuppose a definition and characterization not yet available but that now at least seems on the horizon.

III
Subjects and Situations

17

Overview

A psychology that is soundly understood cannot attempt to know consciousness by describing it as some sort of analogue to objective reality: it must rather see the fact of consciousness as something irreducible and ultimate, which can only be disclosed as such but which cannot be explained in accordance with the categorial forms of our knowledge of things, and in particular not in accordance with the categories of substantiality and causality.
—ERNST CASSIRER, *The Phenomenology of Knowledge*

Far closer to man than the order of nature stands the order which he finds in that world which is peculiarly his own. Here, too, it is by no means mere arbitrary will that governs. The individual sees himself determined and limited from his first movements by something over which he has no power. It is the power of custom which binds him; it keeps watch over his every step, and it allows scarcely a moment of free play. . . . Custom is the abiding, unaltering atmosphere in which he lives and has his being. . . . It is little wonder, then, that in his thoughts the vision of the physical world cannot free itself from that of the moral world. These two visions belong together and are one in their origin.
—ERNST CASSIRER, *The Logic of the Humanities*

The immanence and irreducibility of the social is virtually axiomatic in the discourse of the human sciences despite the lack of consensus about the meaning of the term and despite the continued prominence of individualism as the default position in the philosophy and practice of social science. In other words, it has proven difficult even to approximate the programmatic obligations imposed by Durkheim's identification of society as an autonomous form of life (1961, 60). Taking the concept as primitive may allow one to select with confidence certain nameable entities (nations, licensed organizations, police, etc.) or "families" of such entities (the "system" of higher education, culture, etc.) for sociological, historical, or political study and provide a basis for generalization. But confidence comes at a cost. Here, it begs three crucial questions: How can such an entity move itself on its own behalf? In what sense is it capable of self-reflection? What kind of knowledge, and knower, corresponds to it? As things stand, intentionality and self-critical reflection are two conditions of recognizing any form of life as human. I have argued that they can be addressed productively by substituting the notion of a course of activity for the concept of an action and by substituting the idea of reflexivity for self-reflection. The positive arguments in favor of these substitutions remain to be developed, and introducing them is the main task of Part III. Parenthetically, it must be remembered that the arguments are intended to expand on an idea of the social that I take to be sub-theoretical to the human sciences taken as a whole, what Foucault refers to as "a sort of de facto axiomatization," and that offer the prospect of coherence to the field of reference that authorizes those disciplines and in regard to which each discipline can legitimately claim to constitute knowledge, with its own objectifying procedures and methods of completing those procedures (2003, 182). In that respect, this investigation should provide support for two critical projects. First, it should open the way toward a critique of the human sciences different in important ways from what has been, for the most part and with the important exception of the intersection of Marxian theory and post-structuralism, available in the contemporary critical literature. Second, it should contribute to a fuller recognition of the incompatibility of many of the most important concepts and models in the social sciences with the intuitively compelling character of the sub-theoretical notion of sociality on which the validity of those concepts and models ultimately depends. I have been arguing that this is so given what appears to be an unavoidable condition of validation—namely, that what is human is intelligible only in the context of the human sciences taken as a whole—on the premise that sociality is, in its irreducibility, irrepressibility, and immanence, the uniquely shared object of those disciplines.

I have discussed some consequences of ignoring the difficulty of clarifying what is meant by "sociality." Several that I now focus on have a special bearing on three important topics: the relationship between the idea of theorizing in contrast with its ostensible product (a theory), the social as a form of life immanent to all instances of human affairs, and the importance of at least deferring and at most challenging the distinction between subjects and objects for the sake of the crucial idea of a course of activity. Again, it should be remembered that I am trying to show that each topic points to ontological presuppositions common to the human sciences as things stand and despite what many of the prevailing models and theories appear to disclaim. It is not that these point to or represent an independent reality beyond what underlies the specialized claims made by the various disciplines with respect to their specialized concerns. To the extent to which these presuppositions represent what the disciplines have in common—and what they must have in common in order to address the question of what is human about human affairs—it is possible to imagine a critique that would be appropriate to reflecting on their limitations when they are taken together as a single knowledge-constituting field. This undoubtedly depends on clarifying, beyond what I have already said, what is assumed about the form of sociality that is, as things stand, distinctively human. I am not directly concerned with the details and methods of such a critique but with the conditions of its possibility.

As we have seen, one consequence of the difficulty of living up to the obligations of the idea of society has been a reluctance to engage the question of definition, possibly on the ground that it is a primitive concept that needs no further elaboration or critique. It follows that addressing it as a topic disrupts the sort of paradigmatic work necessary to the progress of social science. Another has been a tendency to reduce the idea of sociality to analytically manageable units, as in theories of exchange that emphasize a negotiable relationship between culture-based meanings and organizational practices in accounting for a meeting of minds, and theories of rational choice that emphasize conditions of cooperation or composition and agreement where the dimensions along which choices might be made are relatively unambiguous. Such reductions characterize the social as an epiphenomenon of a plurality of particular actions done by particular individuals in the presence, virtual or actual, of others. The actions themselves are embodied in persons conceived of as spatially and temporally specific self-motivated points within a multidimensional field composed of a plurality of such points. What such persons do is analyzed according to concepts imported from psychology that allow this field to be rationalized as distributions of attitudes, expectations, and other intention-driven agency-dependent conditions of action. These are understood either as instrumental (goal-oriented) or as a learned synthesis of instrumental and expressive or value orientations. The result becomes sociologically relevant to the extent to which it substantiates a commonality of experience sufficient for persons, in their individuality, to communicate effectively with one another under the organizationally necessary prospect of a meeting of minds.

A third consequence has to do with a tendency to rely on untheorized criteria, based, for example, on lineage, convenience, familiarity, or a sense of rightness, in choosing points of departure for research and devising simplifications for modeling collectivity, association, cooperation, interaction, conflict, incorporation, and other stipulated instances of sociality. It is typically assumed that these capture something basic about human affairs and that this will become evident in the course of research. Empirical research often begins with a problem at hand, perhaps as a question about structural, causal, or functional relations among factors or variables. These may or may not turn out to be valid approximations of the greater phenomenon that a study was intended to make understandable, but that question is raised, if at all, only after research and analysis are complete. The reduction of its subject matter to a simplified form is designed, among other things, to highlight dimensional variations that can be studied for their specific interactions and to establish the difference between internal and external conditions, on the grounds that arriving at the proper level of complexity will occur when sufficient numbers of dimensions and variables have been identified and their interactions properly analyzed.

These last two points are significant in those histories of sociological thought that emphasize the progressive accumulation of findings and, possibly, the discovery of regularities on the order of laws. However, they have proven to be obstacles to theorizing aimed at testing the possibility of reconciling such a project with the conception of human affairs as essentially social; and such a reconciliation is, presumably, what warrants any such project. Even the most radical empiricist must recognize something like this to the extent to which she claims that her research bears on the history of a discipline and, in particular, on the progressive clarification of an object domain prior to its reductive instantiation in research programs—though it is often said that the received categories represent a body of research that is adequate at least to acknowledging such a domain.

By contrast, it has been argued, notably by Sartre and Ollman, that the idea of the social is made theoretically intelligible as distinctively human only through the application of dialectical reason. For Ollman, the fact that human affairs are always in flux means that every analysis is specific to a definitive level of conceptualization that presumes yet another, more inclusive level. For Sartre,

> the dialectic is both a method *and* a movement of the object. For the dialectician, it is grounded on a fundamental claim both about the structure of the real and about that of our *praxis*. We assert simultaneously that the process of knowledge is dialectical, that the movement of the object (whatever it may be) is *itself* dialectical, and that these two dialectics are one and the same. Taken together, these propositions have a material content; they themselves are a form of organised knowledge, or, to put it differently, they define a rationality of the world. (1976, 20; emphasis in original)

Two things are significant about this in the immediate context. First is Sartre's rejection of the belief that one can analyze human affairs without doing violence to their concept by identifying units that are undivided and therefore static or inertial concrete particulars, and second is that this failure to find movement within every referent and the related perils of simplification can be avoided only if theory finds itself within its object and its object within itself.

The version associated with Ollman offers a conception of internal relations that does not reject analysis into units where the need for it arises because of the insistence of a specific problem having to do with relations and their transformations. But this implies that nothing unitary can be understood without understanding the conditions under which unitariness is asserted or comes into question. Ollman argues that an analysis at the level of units and their relations and an analysis of the very operation of inclusion based on relations between levels preserve the socially relational aspect of human reality. That is, it preserves a limited integrity of the form of life while maintaining its aspect of incessant change.[1] In this way, the relative autonomy of sociality is preserved by reading the whole in each of the parts (see Ollman 1993, 2003); or, when we consider how problematic the idea of totality is, Ollman might be amended to say that the idea of society is preserved by reading each ostensible part as a moment of a course of activity and, therefore, of becoming, as it were, nonidentical with itself. Both Ollman and Sartre reverse the question of how groups or societies come to move themselves, which is to say how they can be agents, by asking how it is that they only occasionally appear to be inert and most often do not appear as identities at all—and why we might come to think and act as if they are fixed entities when they cannot be and still be instances of human life.

However, since theorizing human affairs takes place within the very context it studies, a dialectical approach leads to potentially embarrassing questions about the nature of theory itself, and thereby about what might be called the "production of theory." This heightening of self-consciousness challenges what is normally stipulated as the boundary between the activity of theorizing and the apparently very different activities involved in spontaneous, or informal, discourses. The stipulation determines what of each putative type of activity can be exchanged with the other, or what transformations of each can serve as a reliably operative notion, an effective investment, in the course of the other. It is widely agreed that theory in the human sciences invariably draws on ordinary discourse, at least for what is sub-theoretical about its object; and a given disciplinary theory becomes public and recognizable across disciplines when it is transformed according to features of public discourse no less than according to what transpires in the other disciplines. In these ways, a basis is established for attributing to theory a grounding in common experience and in what appears as knowledge in general. At the same time, it allows theory to operate as a systematically critical reflection on experience that particularizes as it intensifies, and on knowledge that generalizes as it establishes a certain detachment—though not in the sense of what is ordinarily intended by "critical" and "reflection," or, for that matter, "experience." However, this seems to imply a paradox since it means that the stipulation cannot be sustained in the course of theorizing. The very idea of a boundary becomes unworkably vague without reifying theory—as a product distinct from its mode of production, which is also a mode of valuation. This has the unfortunate consequence of nullifying the activity of theorizing on which the very idea of a theory presumably depends (as the objectifying moment of an engagement or course of activity) and which guarantees that it, like all instances of human affairs, including all products, objects submitted to a socially intelligible idea of value, is always, and as a matter of logical necessity, in the course of undergoing change.

Parenthetically, this argument entails a particular way of reading a theory-product against the grain of its self-representation as an ordered set of propositions intended to be inclusive across a referential field. This can be thought of as "reading in the mood of writing." Its necessity and critical force depends on the credibility of what has been said so far about what is human about human affairs. Specifically, it attributes to the theoretical text a logical tendency to be inclusive beyond the boundaries of what it may declare as its referential field,

including what it takes to be its own boundaries. This sort of reading operates on the text as a movement of reclassification and inclusion without logical
limitation. It is, then, seen as laboriously engaged in a self-denying and unsatisfiable intention to textualize, to become a totality, and as fatefully caught
up in a futile and consequently uneasy course of textualization. In that case,
dialectics becomes the very meaning of theory inasmuch as it brings to notice
the complex and irreducible relation of theory to theorizing.[2] It is in that regard
that theory itself must be thought of as reflexive to the idea of the social as a
course of activity. Understood this way, dialectics introduces a certain tension
between theory (the moment of the product) and theorizing (the course of activity of which a theory is such a moment), a tension that is untoward from the
standpoint of the product but that meets the epistemological requirement that a
theory of human affairs be an instance of those same affairs.

Since Rousseau, the word "society" has referred to a form of life that cannot
be described in terms of the modernist organizational dimensions of scale,
complexity, and diversity and still be consistent with the idea of it as human.
This is true to the extent to which those dimensions are associated with distributive categories such as class, race, and gender that are not self-rationalizing, or
apparently goal-oriented and self-rationalizing entities such as nations, ethnici-
ties, and formal organizations on the order of Weber's "corporate groups." As
things stand in the human sciences, the referent of "society" cannot be picked
out unambiguously or substantially designated and observed in the sense in
which we are said to be able to observe or know concrete particulars. Perhaps
it is better to say that "society" refers to something that can only be indicated
and that its putative properties are constructs of the ways in which we indicate
it, though even then it must be admitted that there is an irreducible tension between our indications and our sense of what it is that we are trying to indicate.

In that respect, any name applied to an instance of society, any rigid desig-
nator (e.g., "Queens College") or family sign (e.g., "group," "organization," etc.),
is bound to be misleading—but only if we consider the question of why it seems
to be the case that social life can never be more than merely indicated (see
Goffman 1961a). It may be that behind the *use* of "society" lies an intuition that
our lives together are more dynamic and unpredictable than is suggested by
reductionist theories; by appeals to the legal and cultural coherence of groups,
organizations, and nations; and by the commonplace and often invidious distinction between members and nonmembers. I have suggested that this intuition is part of a sub-theoretical sense of sociality that, as we have seen, can now
be expressed but only negatively and as a matter of pragmatics. There is always
a sense that the desired object of reference has been or is being at least somewhat evaded in any course of activity ostensibly devoted to a topic (see Sacks
1974; Lamont 2009; Goffman 1963; Garfinkel 1967; Blank 1980). Positively, it is

possible to demonstrate that this limitation is inconsistent with asserting that particular descriptions or models of sociality should be taken as generally valid.

In this respect, I have pointed to the need to distinguish between what is sub-theoretical from what is normally thought of as pre-theoretical. The latter is what a given theory posits as non-formal constructs that it projects as its referential base and that it claims ultimately to rely on as its occasion. The former is what every worthwhile theory demands of every other one—namely, that it ultimately return to an intuition about the world to which each can be said to have been a response (where "ultimately" is not simply an opening to "never having to explain"). The sub-theoretical sense of the social makes itself felt as an objectivity that resists theoretical totalization, thereby making all explicit concepts and propositions having to do with human affairs essentially contestable. I argue that it is in the midst of this incessant movement (within the activity of conceiving) that the object of the human sciences makes itself known as a self-transformative movement punctuated by unassimilable moments of particularization—that is, as a dialectic of irreducible sociality and irrepressible self-reductive tendencies endemic to the social itself. In this respect, what is otherwise thought to be an empirical question, to be answered by such procedures as simplification, observation, clarification, reduction, and analysis, is itself problematic. This is because those procedures are not consistent with the object they are said to represent. The object, understood as a course of activity reflexive to itself, resists those procedures—or invariably renders their results unsatisfactory according to what the social is sub-theoretically thought to be before those procedures are put into operation, and not because of a lack of sufficient information or clarity.

This dialectic depends on the idea of a "course of activity" in contrast with "action"; and on a notion of agency that does not presuppose the skin as a natural boundary. For now, we can say that the sense of society that lies behind attempts to define and theorize it is sub-theoretical and not pre-theoretical. It cannot be subjected to the sort of theoretical, experiential, or analytical interventions thought appropriate to constructs or ideas that are pre-theoretical. For one thing, it is not a sense that can be attributed to persons taken apart from society. It is somehow collectivized, so that the word "sense" is somewhat misleading. For another, it is itself a feature of a course of activity, part of the latter's reflexivity. This source of resistance to theory is irrepressible insofar as there is a promise implicit in every theoretical undertaking to go beyond its concepts and propositions and to return to what it necessarily suppresses in the interest of arriving at a determinate product (a theory). One can say, then, that the sub-theoretical sense of the social stands as a test of every standard version of theory in the human sciences, a test that few if any can pass. Since its criteria can never be made sufficiently accessible or clear to establish even a presumption of validity adequate to the disciplinary idealization of cumulative knowledge, the history of theory can be narrated, first, as the history of reasons used to justify various abstractive simplifications (exchange, structure, influence, etc.), the differences among which are bound to appear unresolvable, and, second, as the history of reasons for rejecting those reasons, based on a sub-theoretical sense of the social that necessarily generalizes criticism. The second, the critical narrative, is possible only on condition of that sub-theoretical sense of the social, so there is a criterion for testing the adequacy of a theory. But instead of providing an opportunity for a corrective, this insistently reminds the theoretician of the irreducible tension that exists between theory and theorizing and therefore of the fact that the theoretical enterprise is not only inseparable from its object; it is a feature of that object and not merely something that affects it or our understanding of it.

The sub-theoretical objectivity of society implicates an inter-dependency among people who are, in principle, unknown and unknowable to one another, where "inter-dependent" means "internally related." This is the import of Rousseau's observation that the universality of the social appears in the a priori recognition all human beings have that they depend for their very identity, functioning, and moral status, on countless unknowable others. Such connections doubtless underlie what Émile Durkheim thought of loosely as the "organic solidarity" of contract in contrast with the "mechanical solidarity" of identity. They complicate that distinction because they connect each momentary subject with others in general and, therefore, subjectivity with otherness. Such connections are not adequately described by the word "association," at least as far as it means rule-governed practices among distinct, mutually specifying, and reciprocating individuals. When we speak of the social and intend by that to indicate more than words can say, we mean relations with others in general, though it remains to be seen from what perspective those relations are projected: all we can say at this point is that it cannot be from the perspective of a distinct personality or self.

To speak of relations with *others in general* is to acknowledge that the attributes determining familiarity, sufficient to account for reference to any particular instance of that generality, are socially constituted. Moreover, the determination of those attributes is problematic for two reasons, holding in abeyance the question of perspective. First, the notion of "others in general" implies a limitless and therefore unreliable field of reference. This suggests that referring to *an* other among others in general is socially constituted, not merely influenced or mediated; and, no matter how confident the act of referring might be, the show of that confidence will always display *an attitude of waiting*. In anticipation of what follows, this provides a clue as to how the problem of perspective might be addressed. Second, it implies that there cannot be sharable knowledge of others as separable individuals, that there is no act of reference sufficient to such knowledge. Referring to one or another relies on the ability to cite properties (height, beauty, goodness, friendliness, etc.) but cannot *thereby* realize a sense of any particular other's distinctness and vitality as an instance of life: indeed, from the point of view of referring, there is no familiarity with a specific other that can be communicated as such to a third party, therefore no access to the social by virtue of our knowledge of that or any specific other. There is no exemption from this apparent gap between a subject and its others, "apparent" to the extent to which we are still thinking of subjectivity in terms of individualized agency. This is so even for those normally said to be familiar to a particular subject and immediately or near at hand (as in "face-to-face interaction"). The reason is that every other, simply by virtue of being other to a given subject, partakes of an otherness that compromises even the most concretely distinguishing signifiers.

This presents one application of the familiar problem of the relationship between universality and particularity, and we can see more clearly from this application the justice of Hegel's critique of the adequacy of "perception," given in the contradictions of "sense certainty," to our knowledge of the world (1977). Hegel reminds us that the apprehension of the singularity of an object by citing properties that apply across objects is necessarily caught in an incessant movement from the futile attempt to particularize by grasping the pre-propertied essence of the thing to the equally futile attempt to place what is particular in the generalizing field that allows it to be identified in the first place by the comparisons that field makes possible. The movement is, then, from attempting to specify essence to attempting to specify properties. Each pole relentlessly tears subjectivity from the one and forces it toward the other. It follows that referring is never unequivocal. In that respect, members of society can be thought of individually as "at large," as "someones," and the form assumed by their relations can appear only as a *momentous community of strangers*.

Except for constantly reinforcing the two qualifications, that the idea of society is radically different from the idea of a plurality of people and that human affairs are essentially social, individuals and all instances of individuation must be thought of as moments of such a community's realizing itself—that is, its reflexivity. American theoreticians have generally avoided attempting to clarify the sub-theoretical notion of sociality on which the commitment to theory depends for its rationality (for an exception, see Blum and McHugh 1984). Apart from the difficulty of conceptualizing what cannot be conceptualized in a straightforward way (Black 1990a, 29), there are other forces at work in the theoretical enterprise that help explain why the social sciences have relied on received notions of their subject matter that are neither accountable on disciplinary grounds nor compatible with the Rousseauian intuition on the basis of which one can conceive of a social science in the first place—as a study of what is human about human affairs.

For example, from the 1930s until the 1980s, sociology focused primarily on topics of administrative concern (distribution and regulation) that lend themselves to categorization and quantification. What is generally called "administration" is a sub-corporate response to scarcities of all sorts as they arise from *within* a totalizing project that, by its nature, generates scarcities. A sociology that specializes in the rationalization of that response cannot address the politics that are bound to accompany such a project. Consequently, at least until the 1980s, those politics were depicted as irrational or nonrational "episodes" of "collective behavior" that constituted breaks with the "institutional order of society"—that is, not as politics at all. What Weber referred to as the "corporate" form is designed to avoid distributing the decisive conditions of the Rawlsian "original position" (hence the prospect of shared decision making at the most general level of choice and in regard to the most basic of values). It is intended to keep democracy at bay in the field of business and ensure that the resolution of the problems associated with scarcity do not interfere with the market-driven competitive side of the abstraction we call "business." Insofar as it deals specifically with scarcities, the administrative work of regulation and distribution is understood as technical in the sense of not being subject to value considerations. Those who perform the tasks that are subject to the totalizing project are likely to experience a gap between technical solutions to the essentially utilitarian problem of distribution, such that the cup is both half full and half empty at all times, and values that are immune to general review so that no policy can be justified by an appeal to a pre- or extra-corporate ideal of fairness or social validity. The politics that accompany this attempt to eliminate politics, theoretically as well as practically, are typically left obscure in social scientific projects aimed at studying effects within the limits imposed by the corporate form itself.

Another way of saying this is that the purpose of the corporate form is to eliminate society from the practical world of business and to fill what is left of society with the forms that ratify that world. The elaboration and extension of the corporate form, often labeled "neoliberalism," is currently justified by claims of accelerating scarcity. It is now applied to aspects of life for which it had never before been considered appropriate (education, family, medicine, self-government, etc.), at the least because basic value considerations are thought to be vital to them. This allows us to see that its primary aim is the minimization of society itself in as many respects as possible. Despite the fact that a certain amount of social scientific work has recently moved closer to the humanist's concern with what is human about human affairs, the field remains burdened by concepts and methods that were developed as contributions to solving the very problems of corporate life that, when solved, make it difficult to imagine that there is anything distinctively human at all. If there is not, then the human sciences do not form a field and, indeed, the division between fields that produce knowledge and fields that do not seems destined to make it increasingly difficult even to discuss what humans do that might be improved on in the interest of what is human about them. The result is a theoretically perilous gap between what is thought, sub-theoretically, to be true about human life in general (e.g., that it is essentially social) and what is considered reasonable to say about human tendencies and capacities—that there are problems that are essentially social, that the social aspect of life guarantees that most knowledge is vested, as it were, collectively. In attempting to reconcile what appear to be individual capacities with the general conditions under which they are *collectively* exercised as courses of activity, it must be acknowledged that something crucial is missing in those fields. *If there is a unity of the human sciences, it can be based only on the ideas that humans are essentially social, that human affairs are irreducibly and irrepressibly social, and that sociality, and the "attitude of waiting" that corresponds to it, can be understood, from the perspective of a possible unity, only as a course of activity. It follows that humans are not particulars. This allows for the possibility that what appear from outside of a course of activity to be individuals are moments. Another way of saying this is that intentionality is theorizable, first and foremost, as a social fact rather than an individual one, and individuality as such must therefore be understood as constituted in a course of activity and therefore only momentarily.*

Part I explores several aspects of this problem insofar as it bears on the possibility of knowing human affairs according to what is human about them. That leads to the tentative conclusion that sciences specializing in understanding human affairs have more in common with the humanities, which deal with agency-dependent realities, than with the natural sciences, which deal with reality independent of agency.[3] However, I reject two possible negative interpretations of this claim. The first says that the study of human affairs is not scientific in principle. The second says that, if it is scientific, its ideas and practices stretch the limits of science beyond what is reasonable. Therefore, the human sciences must be thought of either as failed sciences or, developmentally, as pre-scientific or immature and therefore part of the evolution of positive knowledge and the progressive demystification and refinement of the idea of truth.

Human science is said to fail to the extent to which it systematically avoids questions that can be answered reliably in regard to identifiably objective phenomena or conceptual referents that might be observed. From this point of view, it may still be of extra-scientific pragmatic value, and it may contribute to our understanding of certain events. But what it offers cannot be called knowledge because it is not about anything that can be known, strictly speaking. We might come to know something about the causes and effects of what people do and other conditions associated with what they do; however, the very idea of human affairs as distinctively human is at best vague and incurably abstract and at worst an artifact of conventional ways of thinking that are antithetical to the pursuit of reliable knowledge. It follows that any attempt to justify such a discipline by reference to its contribution to knowledge is bound to fail since that is not where its value lies. At its most generous, the first interpretation draws on a notion of the division of intellectual labor that depends on the distinction between fact and value criticized by, among others, Hilary Putnam (2002) according to a logic of specific functions (e.g., knowing and valuing as irreducible features of self-reflective life).[4] The second interpretation assumes that the development of a knowledge-constituting science of human affairs is possible only on the following conditions: (1) that there be greater modesty than has so far prevailed in those disciplines; (2) that a reduction to more basic laws be systematically anticipated so that claims to know about human affairs at the level at which they are found are necessarily ironical as far as their ontological commitments are concerned; and (3) that such inquiry progressively adapt itself, with due respect for the nonquantitative aspect and moral dimension of its subject matter, to models of theory and research derived from the sciences of agency-independent nature. If my conclusion turns out to be correct, that it is legitimate to claim that the human sciences provide knowledge, and if this is so because they share a common object of which they are also instances, then it is reasonable to refer to them as a whole—even though they are currently administered as if they are either logically different or evidently occupied with radically different, though not necessarily antagonistic, concerns.

Parenthetically, when the social sciences are said to be insufficiently mature as sciences, they are all the more unlikely to be placed under the same umbrella as the natural sciences. This is, however, not ordinarily justified by a principle. Rather, because they are typically justified according to a logic of inquiry compatible with and evolving toward the naturalistic model in the philosophy of science, when they are located apart from the natural sciences, their departmental status appears as a temporary convenience until they mature or are otherwise corrected. Allowances are nevertheless made for certain fields, largely on methodological grounds. For example, certain areas of psychology not incorporated into neuroscience may be placed among the natural sciences. In addition, economics, usually represented as most approximating the natural sciences, is typically placed among the immature social sciences (e.g., sociology and political science) or allowed to mingle with other areas with which it is thought to have special affinities tied to the pragmatics of administration and policy, in particular, with law, politics, and business.

To argue that the human sciences are sciences requires evaluating the content and significance of claims about a reality other than agency-independent reality that are true in some sense of the word. These claims depend on whether it is reasonable to say that those disciplines have *a common object that is not available to the naturalist sciences and that this object can be theorized as such only without recourse to individualism and its ontology.* This is not theoretically interesting if it suggests no more than that the social sciences should be located as departments among those humanistic fields that specialize in identifying parameters of mutual orientation such as values and symbolic forms and "structures of meaning and feeling," and extending the range of conceivable behavior beyond the limits of those parameters and structures. This way of describing the humanities as essentially "culturological" may cover some of what is done in the name of humanism. But it disregards their claims to provide knowledge of what is distinctively human about human affairs and reasonable confirmation or criticism of ideas about those affairs on which most people, including scholars, actually rely regardless of their comprehensive doctrines and positions on particular issues. To characterize them in this way either denies their rational connection to truth (and considers them the moral media of a reason that is too harsh when dissociated from the passions) or neutralizes them to the extent to which it becomes impossible to distinguish between claims that are and are not instances of knowledge. If there is something distinctively human about human affairs, and if it is not only reasonable but necessary to distinguish our knowledge of those affairs from convention, opinion, and evaluation, and from our knowledge of nonhuman reality, then questions about objectivity, truth, and reliability of observation in the human sciences significantly bear on philosophy and our understanding of theory and its conditions of possibility.

This is why it is necessary to reconsider what can be meant by "truth" and "validity" in regard to a possible realignment of the human sciences. This requires clarifying the constitution of their common object, what allows the disciplines to be thought of together, in regard to the vexing questions posed by agency-dependent reality. That is, if their objects implicate agency, which is to say at least that their descriptions, no matter how apparently exhaustive, are reflexive to agency, and if that is their ontologically distinctive feature, then it must be admitted that, if it is possible to know such objects, knowing them is different from what we mean when we speak of knowing agency-independent reality and its objects. The significance of what these otherwise disparate fields have in common turns on the intersection of the humanities and the social sciences at the point at which one is bound to raise the related questions of truth and validity in regard to what is human about human affairs. If the claims to provide knowledge are valid, and if this includes some reference to truth or truthfulness, however conceived, it follows that the connection between social science and the humanities does not compromise the scientific status of the social sciences but, indeed, enhances it. This assumes, however, that it is possible to say something about truth and validity adequate to the claim that the study of what is distinctively human provides knowledge that differs in form from what is provided by the knowledge-constituting sciences of agency-independent reality for which what is human about human agency is considered to be irrelevant to their claims.[5]

Crucial to this thesis are the radical implications of the familiar distinction between the two types of reality already alluded to, one depending on and the other independent of agency:

In the ontological sense, "objective" and "subjective" are predicates of entities and types of entities, and they ascribe modes of existence. In the ontological sense, pains are subjective entities because their mode of existence depends on being felt by subjects. But mountains, for

> example, . . . are ontologically objective because their mode of existence
> is independent of any perceiver or any mental state. (Searle 1995, 8)

The distinction is crucial for clarifying the idea of sociality as a course of activity and therefore for completing the thesis of this book. A discussion of it shows how the key ideas discussed in Parts I and II—for example, the differences between theory and theorizing and action and a course of activity—are essential to establishing a valid and useful idea of the social, given the conditions under which defining the term becomes a matter of some urgency. This should have significant though unexpected consequences for a number of philosophical debates within the human sciences pertinent to the question "What is human about human affairs?" Perhaps the most important of these is the conclusion that a theory of human affairs must also be a theory of theory, and, therefore, of theorizing. This and other such results will, I hope, prove helpful in coming to terms with the possibility of a common ontology among the human sciences, thereby providing an opening for a yet more radical critique of the conditions under which just such an inquiry, and its results, might be thought of as a necessary part of the ongoing historicization of society, which is to say a critique of the way things stand in the interest of the way they might.

––––––––––

Chapter 18 reconsiders some ways in which the ontological question and its implications have been generally avoided in the social sciences, perhaps for the sake of sustaining the natural science model, even at the cost of leaving disciplinary claims obscure. It is helpful to recall a number of ideas that have already been discussed and on which the following discussion relies. First, human affairs are most generally conceived of as essentially social, where there is a sub-theoretical sense of the meaning of the term that is at odds with attempts to specify it by reference to categories and types, and by reference to particulars of any sort. Second, to the extent to which sociality is distinctively human, it must be conceived of as a course of activity rather than a structure, a process, or an action, and it is no less resistant to the "categorical forms of our knowledge of things" than consciousness itself. Third, if sociality is conceived of as a course of activity, individuality can be conceived of only as moments and consequently as ostensible. Fourth, a theory of human affairs must make visible in itself all the aspects and details it attributes to its object and it must make equally visible what about its object makes the latter an instance of the activity of theorizing. Fifth, the objective referential field of the human sciences involves agency-dependent reality with all that it entails. Sixth, a universe of agency-dependent objects, a possible world of the sort necessary to make explicit the idea of agency-dependence, is necessarily inter-subjective, which means that it can be analyzed only according to a radical notion of internal relations. Seventh, theoretical work in the human sciences has to do with two distinctions, each of which operates on the order of a motivating contradiction:

(a) between a sub-theoretical virtual reality that ambivalently defies categories and ambivalently resists ostensible and momentary realization largely through "the categorical forms of our knowledge of things," and (b) between theorizing, which is the agentic moment of sub-theoretical objectivity (that appears from the standpoint of its ostensible products as, alternately, the production of theory by virtue of the "power of the negative," or concept formation thought of as a choice from among possible concepts), and theory, which is the ostensibly positive product of an activity to which no overall singular intention can be attributed and that shows itself momentarily as alienated from its own conditions of possibility. I now comment briefly on this last point. The quality of being alienated in this way derives from the necessary reliance on a theory that is indifferent to the activity of theorizing, in other words, one that relies on the logic of justification. One important result of this is that neither the theory nor the theoretician as its ostensible agent can provide a coherent reflection on the origin of the product, yet a reasonable theory must promise just such a reflection if it is to be an embodiment of the general knowledge of which it claims to be an instance, alongside of what it studies. Consequently, it has little to say about the predicaments and ambiguities it takes itself to have resolved—that is, as Hegel reminds us in regard to the first appearance of reason, that it cannot teach or be taught for its possibility.

Eighth and finally, criticism is immanent to every course of activity. It is not to be understood as a type of action—that is, an option for an independent agent that might or might not be undertaken. This means that there are no instances of human affairs that are not immanently critical. This is because human affairs are social and therefore, by definition, *tension-preserving*, and criticism is what is most evident in that fact; and, since a course of activity is driven or made momentous by tensions that are necessary to its being such a course, criticism is a necessary feature of its reflexivity.

18

Causes of Failure in the Social Sciences

When the social sciences are understood as imperfect realizations of the standard model of the natural sciences, their defects are explained in a number of ways. Here I discuss three: complexity, the problem of the observer, and immaturity.[1] My purpose is to expand on the thesis that their weaknesses are not primarily epistemological but ontological; they have to do with sociality as the basic fact. The problem is not that available methods are as yet inadequate to their subject matter, though that may be part of it. Nor is it simply a matter of hubris, though researchers often make too much of too little, or a result of the immodesty of generalizing from hypotheses that have no developed theoretical warrant. Rather, it has to do with the sub-theoretical character of the subject matter and the types of knowledge and knowing it entails, including the appropriate logical and pragmatic conditions of investigation.

Complexity

The most familiar explanation says that the complexity of the subject matter of the social sciences is greater than what intuition, conceptualization, and methodology can bear, which disposes them to pre-scientific complexity-reducing tendencies such as relying on received or official determinations of their topics and problems; emphasizing covariations among surface variables; and speculating about causes, effects, conditions, and mediations based to a large extent on popular representations, common sense, informal reasoning, or hypotheses designed to fit specific sets of findings.[2] Though the notion of complexity is by no means settled in philosophy, it seems difficult to avoid when thinking about the social aspect of life (see Machlup 1994).[3] This suggests that we consider what is at stake in attempts to define it before trying to defend one definition or another. What seems most generally at stake is the significance of certain questions that are invariably raised with respect to what is human about human affairs regardless of whatever concrete answers have been or might be offered.

Before proceeding, it is worth reminding ourselves of the relationship between those questions and the values to which they correspond. These are values that most philosophers believe need to be sustained in whatever is done under the warrant of theory. This is certainly true of those who take the history of philosophy as an inventory of humanity's most serious and abiding problems. Moreover, there is widespread agreement that they can only be effectively addressed holistically—that is, in regard to the internal relations among them. I merely add the qualification that they need to be sustained in any attempt to understand human affairs in line with the principle that what is distinctively human must include theorizing and what is theoretical must show itself to exemplify human life. This qualification is acceptable only when sociality is understood as immanent to human affairs and conceived of as logically necessary for coming to terms with them.

These questions address the very topics that substantiate what I have been referring to as "the way things stand." Keeping them alive is, from that point of view, a necessary condition of the validity of any attempt to theorize instances of human affairs. How, then, does the critique of the social sciences as imperfect, as immature, or simply as weak sciences bear on our capacity to theorize human affairs in a way that does not sacrifice the grounds for thinking holistically about what is human about them? That is, how does it bear on that capacity without dissolving the very connections among intellectual, moral, and political commitments to which every field concerned with human affairs owes the possibility of its justification as a knowledge-constituting discipline? Reference to complexity reinstates these questions by default, regardless of whether Durkheim's assertion that "every individual is an infinity" is taken to bear on social as well as psychological levels of explanation.[4] It implicates a virtually unlimited number of explanatory factors, presumably having to do with the nature of the subject matter. This means that any finite list will be unsatisfactory, or at least too controversial to support confidence in the claim that the human sciences provide "knowledge." Consequently, reference to complexity inevitably returns us to our original questions about social reality, which then reappear as the reproducible content of the field.

In that case, progress in the social sciences is identified with an accelerating complexity of what can be said about their subject matter, which corresponds to a sub-theoretical intuition that the subject matter is intrinsically and irreducibly self-differentiating. This not only invites an untoward degree of uncertainty about referents; it makes the restlessness of theoretical debate, including disputes about what sorts of simplification of social reality can adequately represent it, a primary topic in the historiography of those disciplines. This may be one reason why histories of the social sciences typically focus more on encounters among the proponents of general hypotheses or frames of reference than on the systematic features of their thought and the way in which those features momentarily reduce the force of ambiguities that otherwise resist systematic resolution. In doing so, they contribute to a romantic image of social science, as progressing through encounters among thinkers and, paradoxically, as a purely cognitive process that is exceptional to what is entailed by the very idea of human society.

It is in this regard that reference to complexity reinstates general questions to which classical figures (such as Marx, Weber, Durkheim, Simmel, Lewin, Freud, etc.) are then said to respond, usually in the theory sections of introductory texts, and in almost all twentieth-century histories of the field written in the United States. This conveys an overriding sense of a disciplinarity defined by historically significant thinkers who are thought to establish, in the convergence of their ideas to the exclusion of others, something on the order of a tradition, its subdivisions reflecting differences in, among other things, emphasis (on one or another type of fact—for example, communication or control), the relative priority among otherwise shared concepts (e.g., system and action or structure and process or culture and politics), or programmatic aspects of research according to ideas about how theory and observation can be reconciled (e.g., as a self-rationalizing accumulation of findings in regard to a paradigm or by testing logically critical hypotheses). In many introductory texts, traditions and their variations outweigh what is said about subject matter and, in that respect, what can be said in justification of the various methodologies they describe. That the subject matter, the social, is taken for granted in histories of sociology has always posed one of the more serious difficulties in teaching it and clarifying what is at stake in it for the other human sciences.

Three issues are especially at stake in considering complexity. One is the distinction between nature and culture, often interpreted as a distinction between universal conditions of human affairs and conditions that arise through the operation of sociohistorical forces and that are difficult to represent reliably and that, by their nature, defy causal explanation. A related set of questions has to do with what is theoretically required by the distinction between what is manifestly deliberate about culture and what is latent, accidental, or historical. Finally, there are significant questions about that part of culture that has to do with deliberation and self-reflection and about the boundary between the consequences of rational responses to systemic imperatives and what are determined, as it were, by nonrational and/or political factors. It appears, then, that progress, development, and the persistence of effort in social science have little if anything to do with paradigmatic normalization over time or a rational succession of paradigms, and a great deal to do with the ontological issues that arise when human affairs are taken to be essentially and not contingently social. I conclude from this is that what is at stake in referring to complexity as a justification of the state of social science is the authority of the claim that humans and their affairs are essentially social. If so, it raises the question of whether what is entailed by the idea of sociality can be demonstrated by the sorts of methods appropriate to nonsocial entities. If the idea of complexity includes a sense of progressively disunifying differentiation, as Rescher (1998) seems reluctantly to suggest, then methods that rely on logical reduction, classification, statistical analysis, modeling, and simulation will fail to represent the phenomena as the latter insinuate themselves into discourse subtheoretically, whatever other advantages they might afford. From this, one might suppose that if the social sciences provide knowledge, it is unlikely to be the sort identified with naturalistic scientific procedures and criteria of truth. If they do provide something we feel obliged to call "knowledge," then a prima facie case will have been made for the human sciences as knowledge-constituting disciplines oriented to and by what is human about human affairs.

In addition, complexity may be thought of in somewhat different and more optimistic "value-added" terms—namely, as a manageably finite and stable multiplicity of increasingly specifiable explanatory factors, given that there is a reasonably coherent sense of the object to be explained and some prior knowledge of the types of factors that might contribute to a causal picture. In that case, the problem is epistemological and, ultimately, a matter of technique. This poses several questions, one of which has to do with how that sort of complexity can be known as such, since the object of which it is a property is presumably known independently of its degree of complexity. Moreover, knowing complexity presupposes a basis for comparison that, like the problem of identifying objects as distinct, may require more than is feasible for a relatively immature science. Given this, we might want to say that the history of social science, to the extent to which the complexity of its subject matter only unfolds over time, is not only the history of identifying and then engaging a particular type of entity (e.g., society) but the history of becoming aware of complexity itself as a variable property of that type and managing it as a constant feature of the work of engaging instances of any type. In that case, we are dealing with a history of the development of a subject matter and, therefore, of attempts to deal with what is, conceptually, unmanageably complex at any given time, by trying nevertheless to make it manageable as things stand.

It follows that it is reasonable to expect critics to give more leeway to those disciplines than they are often willing to, since the social sciences are always operating with descriptions that are immeasurably less complex than the subject matter they aim to enlighten and, therefore, the identities of what appear to be instances of that subject matter are always bound to be at issue. This may or may not be true of any other sciences, and an argument has been made that the progress of certain sciences has to do with the development of their capacity to manage complexity—shown by, among other things, an overall increase in predictive power. But it seems true of the social sciences, since evidence for gains in predictive power is insufficient at present even to indicate the possibility of a progressive tendency—possibly for reasons that have to do with what is human about human affairs. From this point of view, a science of the social aspect of life cannot be judged according to standards appropriate to a more developed field, or to one with a less vexing subject matter. An evaluation should be appropriate to the degree of complexity that the discipline is equipped to deal with, given its "stage of development." In that case, however, there appears to be no superior position from which complexity can be seen to vary, allowing one to evaluate the evaluation itself. As a result, a modest and tolerant evaluation of a field should allow provisional claims to stand, given that good reasons can be stated, even though they cannot meet standards of truth that apply when propositions are incorporated into fully developed conceptual schemes with a strong refer-ential base. It seems, then, that a modest and tolerant evaluation begins from the point of view of a developed science based on a well-defined subject matter. However, this risks unduly imposing what is required for understanding one sort of subject matter (as far as its conception is reasonably clear and distinct at a given time) on what is required for understanding another, possibly quite different, subject matter, or, in the alternative, problematically assuming that there is only one history of science and, because it is the history of reason itself, that it is epistemologically independent of subject matter.

Nevertheless, one may still insist that the perception of a complexity mo-mentarily too difficult to manage reflects only technical limitations, so that knowledge can always be improved over time, rather than that it bodes ill for the use of a natural science model in the social sciences, or a general model of reason based, say, on the sort of reason that has proven useful in physics, en-gineering, and biology and that has been well-defended by philosophers. This raises the question of what is entailed by the idea of technical limitations, spe-cifically what sort of reality stands as the measure of *relative* success and how we know it. There is, then, another caveat. In order to complete such a tolerant view, it is necessary to make the case that there is something real, though it may not be clear and distinct enough to be theorized as such, against which it is possible to speak of the weakness of the field in respect of the complexity of its subject matter; and the latter is something unavoidably sub-theoretical in re-gard to which a science's accomplishments, and the validity of their evaluation, must ultimately be measured. Unfortunately, this begs the question, possibly in the interest of normalizing research. It shifts attention from conception and theory to methodology; and it does so by referring to "complexity" despite the arbitrariness of identifying it with the sheer number of factors that are momen-tarily taken into account, relative to some past or projected future. Identifying it that way suggests a continuum running from simplicity to complexity quite different from what we think of when we think of complexity as an *acceleration* of differences that may not lie on a continuum. In other words, that form of identification allows work to proceed without having to account for its suit-ability to its subject matter. Here, method trumps ontology; but in doing so it inevitably turns against its own authority—namely, the reality it purports to clarify and make accountable.

There is a positive side effect of this consistent with the defense of the social sciences on naturalistic grounds. It is implicit in Durkheim's qualifications of his "rules of sociological method," given that the reality one is studying consists largely, but not exclusively, of "collective representations" at the same time one is immersed in them (see Durkheim 1966, 1982), and given the relatively ephemeral facticity of social facts and their bearing on the overall order of such facts (their degree of "normalcy" relative to the historical "stage" and "type of society" under consideration).[5] For Durkheim, these are irreducible features of sociality, and the science of it can never be free of what they entail. The point is that it is possible to classify the social sciences as sciences on the assumption that methods derived from the natural sciences offer the only possibilities of epistemic progress—even though their models are problematic because of the difficulty of modeling human affairs without losing the idea of them as human. Also, key propositions are bound to be ambiguous, and at least some claims can only take a form not amenable to positive verification. Accordingly, accepting the social sciences on these terms does not mean accepting or even tolerating a weak version of science. It means accepting a certain predicament, based on the features of the reality at issue, relative to a given stage, in which the use of reason guarantees neither momentary success nor progress relative to what might appear necessary at a "later stage." What it guarantees are (1) the accumulation of reasonable questions that must be asked at a given time about whatever is said about social life that seems to be true and (2) the proliferation of qualifications that should be made of any claim about sociality and that cannot simply be derived from what is already believed to be true or might "eventually" be taken as true.

Progress in social science appears then as demonstrations, on the one hand, that every question that can be asked about social reality entails further questioning and proving, on the other, that momentary answers are conclusive only as things stand—that is, insofar as they respond logically to questions that cannot be avoided at a particular moment in the history of questioning. What are gathered over the long run are not truths, in the sense of correspondence to a clear and distinct idea of an independent reality, but further related questions and the reasons why none of them can be avoided without undoing their subject matter however that is defined. In effect, it is the *necessity* of the questions that is true; and this reveals itself in the course of discovering what questions are entailed by addressing and answering other questions. This suggests that the sophistication of sociological knowledge lies in our understanding why it is necessary to keep all questions open, even where policy is at stake; and the empirical material social scientists gather constitutes evidence of this necessity. Again, for this interpretation of the implications of Durkheim's "rules," sociology is a science measured more by its incessant generation of questions, given that there appear to be answers, and the knowledge of why they cannot be avoided, than by its accumulation of specifically confirmed true beliefs about the world on a standard set in the indefinite future of ideal knowledge.

————

Despite these caveats, this version of the argument that explains the imperfections of the social sciences by the complexity of their task does not require rejecting their knowledge claims. This is because they may well be at relatively early stages in their development as sciences and their momentary conclusions may represent the only serious options for understanding phenomena that they alone have addressed in a systematic and disciplinary way. This has significant consequences for a philosophy of the human sciences, since it allows for a degree of relativism, and at least caution, in evaluating both the ontological claims and methodologies of those fields, in contrast with a denial of their scientificity or truth based on evaluating them primarily by their conformity or lack thereof to the ideal of reason articulated in the philosophy of science.

One might argue that this is all beside the point, since one task of the historian, critic, or philosopher is to go beyond identifying the historically determined limits of a discipline in order to evaluate the rationality of its claims according to a reasonable conception of truth or, more generally, validity, since the notion of reason, though not necessarily our grasp of it, is said to be timeless and therefore always formulated in its greatest imaginable generality. What is at issue is not whether the practitioners of certain disciplines are reasonable but what sort of reason, what sort of thinking, is necessary to come to terms with a reality whose objectivity is specified, or placed in question, under historical conditions that significantly determine the meanings and procedures of "discovery" and "justification," the latter in terms of what counts as a reason and what is involved in publicity. These may be at odds with the requirements of knowledge based on a specification and description of a subject matter at a later stage or under different conditions of the science and its possible interpretations. To challenge those conditions from the later point of view is to fail to grasp the nature of the reality taken to warrant investigation at the earlier stage—that is, investigation of what can legitimately be taken as objective (i.e., as fitting existing knowledge and as true to experience). But if there is a failure to grasp the objective conditions of knowledge at an earlier stage, the conditions of that failure doubtless apply to understanding the objective conditions and limitations of knowledge at the putatively mature reference stage. It is to fail to reckon with the nature of what can legitimately be taken as real and/or fundamental at any stage, no less than what qualifies as truth in the context of establishing reasons for belief and how those qualifications fit into whatever ideal of reason accounts for the communicability of knowledge and the possibility of consensus or normal practice. It is not simply that earlier human sciences were groping for a reality only disclosed fully at a later stage but that they were dealing with what could only be conceived of as reality—a reality that can be thought in terms of the total body of what stands at any given time for knowledge.

It takes only a moment to recognize that tolerance, relativism, and caution in evaluating disciplines that may be at different stages of development from whatever is taken as a standard involve more than suspending disbelief. This is to acknowledge that the social sciences, and perhaps all sciences, have their deep histories, which are often described as the sudden emergence of knowledge from what it cannot be—namely, opinion, folklore, superstition, or metaphysical speculation. It is also to acknowledge that the appropriate model of knowledge, most generally understood as valid or justified belief (for the most part in relation to other such beliefs), significantly depends on the social, conceptual, and linguistic circumstances in which beliefs are validated and by virtue of which they become teachable and useful—and therefore subject to the mechanisms and processes, both scientific and extra-scientific, rational and extra-rational, institutional and noninstitutional, that presumably account for systematic accumulation. This allows that a reasonable history of any discipline requires acknowledging the comprehensibility, validity, and "truth" of work under different circumstances. Reference to stages is misleading when it grades the circumstances in order to grade the intellectual work. Perhaps it is better to say that such reference is rhetorical; it is part of the pedagogy and politics of a text that is necessarily public. The circumstances include comprehensible conditions under which it is difficult to separate scientific discourse from other discourses and the practices of which they are features, and as difficult to assess the relative adequacy of what might appear only in retrospect to be distinct methodologies.

Rather than disqualifying the social sciences, the argument for the difficulties posed by complexity offers two familiar redemptive conclusions. The first says that any moment in the development of a science of human affairs as an instance of systematic knowledge is likely to be invalid from a later vantage point. That point of view may encourage the mistaken conclusion that there had been little authentic knowledge in earlier times and other places, therefore and perhaps most important, that nothing significant is lost when those claims to know are degraded and replaced (see Cottingham 1998). The second says that validity and truth, like comprehensibility, depend at any moment on the fact that problems are generated within frameworks partially set by work at earlier moments, or in different contexts, which is to say that it depends on the history of the problem-setting aspect of a given field and the assumptions, many of which are bound to be extra-theoretical and extra-disciplinary, on which that history depends.[6]

This familiar version of a historical appreciation of social science is implicit in the idea of the complexity of the latter's subject matter, at least to the extent to which part of the idea is that good science no less than bad has a history and that it is limited by that fact. It is also progressive in that it envisions an evolution of a field toward the standard model—in regard to which ontology is displaced by epistemology. To that extent, scientific knowledge in fields thought to be especially burdened by the complexity of their objects must be seen as changing according to a certain *telos*, a tendency toward greater degrees of articulation and inclusiveness, and therefore as never entirely free of or separable from whatever seems to be its pre-scientific aspect. Similarly, its acceptability as valid knowledge cannot be understood as wholly dependent on the application of reason to reality according to idealized naturalist standards: the latter familiarly include the logical independence of objects of investigation, the separateness of scientific investigation from all other inquiries, the possibility of measurement and computation, and coherence among all propositions whose justification meets these and other such criteria.

It is often tempting to disregard historical considerations in favor of the ideal and, taking the complexity of the subject matter for granted, to try to identify a particular set of practices as constituting a scientifically valid core possibly made obscure by overemphases on its academic aspect. This is what Lazarsfeld and his coauthors attempted to establish in their account of the role of contracted empirical research in the disciplinary development of sociology (1967, ix–xxiii). They suggest that the scientific core of sociology consists, by and large, of whatever propositions are valid according to the criterion of reliable measurement and the appropriate analysis of what has been measured, and according to its predictive quality within the limited area in which the problem initiating research is immediately meaningful. A corollary is that the best that social science theory can do for the imaginable future is to summarize fundamentally descriptive findings, including incidence and regularities, and correlations and possibly to state them in the form of inductively derived generalizations of one or another kind of causal analysis. The reason is that, on this view, the content of sociological knowledge derives from specific research projects, especially those in which the problem is initiated by someone other than the researcher (what Lazarsfeld refers to as the "client"). In this respect it is presumably less likely to be contaminated by self-fulfilling discipline-intensive paradigmatic concerns and less apt to be limited by the pre-scientific or metatheoretical habits (and ideas) that are bound to affect the normal science associated with any disciplinary paradigm. Parenthetically, the normalcy of a science is described by Thomas Kuhn ([1962] 1970) as constantly unsettled by an institutionally mediated tension, which is a constitutive feature of scientific practice, between what is established as normative (beyond merely normal), largely by virtue of the logical coherence of the prevailing paradigm and the weight of consistency within its research history, and whatever rationally threatens that normativity, such as new discoveries, findings, or analyses. The knowledge described by Lazarsfeld and his colleagues is useful before it is either scientifically meaningful or able to be identified as to its discipline. It is, in effect, a matter of practice that projects only the theory it momentarily needs.

However, there is no reason to assume that the practices for which this sort of work can be said to constitute "knowledge" group together as a whole except by, among other things, habit or routine; commercial value; social control; the emergence of informal rules over time and under specifically appropriate circumstances; and the technical, ideological, and practical imperatives of corporate administration established under the auspices of fixed comprehensive values. One might see these as organizational settings in which power is obscure and the interests and values that authorize the research project are therefore either taken to be beside the point of actual research or reasonably noncontroversial. In effect, as enumerable critics have suggested in regard to the increased emphasis in the university on funded research, research projects in the social sciences belong, intellectually as well as practically, to the generalization of administration; thus values, in the sense of what inform the overall problems addressed, are settled in advance, before any values that belong to the researcher can be asserted; and this belonging to administration is a necessary and internal feature of the course of research and not merely accidental, voluntary, or a matter of context.

To the extent to which theory is relevant to any of the social sciences, it can, even on this view, certainly be relevant to their identity as disciplines. The knowledge so authorized takes no more elaborate a theoretical form than is sufficient to cover whatever specific findings are at issue according to a problem set in advance, and those that are already settled, and, presumably, to generate critical hypotheses designed to adjudicate among generalizations having to do with the type of problem at hand. The philosophy that fits this point of view is a version of naturalism modified to meet the practical difficulties involved in attempting to establish the validity of social scientific laws or to justify beliefs associated with specific propositions. It is relatively indifferent to the historical aspect of social science discussed previously, though it acknowledges that different tasks are involved in the theoretical work of devising a research project and interpreting its findings; and, given a requisite degree of clarity of the relevant concepts, it emphasizes conditions under which cases more or less approximate the scientific ideal. As a result, such a philosophy is bound to reject disciplinary claims in favor of those internally coherent and durable bodies of controlled empirical studies nevertheless presumed to have been done under disciplinary auspices.[7]

Such studies, no matter how abstractly represented, cannot in themselves sustain a disciplinary account of the reason for their choice of subject matter. As a result, the reasons why topics are chosen, and therefore, arguably, the parameters of concept formation and hypothesis, are extra-disciplinary, often yielding the illusion that certain topics are simply there to be studied or that their persistence throughout a literature is sufficient to warrant their having been chosen in a specific instance. Indeed, emphasis on received topics and problem solving virtually guarantees that the results of inquiry remain non- and possibly anti-disciplinary in the sense of lacking the intellectual continuity, comprehensiveness, and referential adequacy required of what is thought of as authentic disciplinary knowledge—that is, knowledge oriented to a particular object or type, committed to a methodology that addresses the special qualities of that object or type, organized and made communicable by a distinct body of literature, and given a sense of historical coherence according to a general notion of the movement of the discipline in those regards. Too strong an emphasis on the theoretical sufficiency of empirical research ends by denying the relevance of the disciplines to what is produced in their names. The paradox is that either the selection of a research topic appears arbitrary, or it is determined from outside the discipline and, indeed, outside of all disciplines and disciplinary considerations, in which case the assignment of significance to the research depends fundamentally on ideology or some other comprehensive doctrine, or Lazarsfeld's "administrative context." Or it fails to meet disciplinary standards of justification so that it is likely to be irrelevant to claims about the status and development of the discipline it purports to represent. In either case, the emphasis on research cannot sustain the notion of disciplinarity on which it relies for its own justification as a specialized area of study.

This version of the argument from complexity argues that it is not merely the complexity of the subject matter that accounts for the weakness of certain fields among the social sciences, though that is certainly an issue at least because of the apparently inexhaustible number of dimensions involved in description, classification, and analysis of human affairs. At least as important is the historical complexity of the research situation itself, which includes the mix of client-professional relations, administrative context, public discourses and ideologies, and academic practices intrinsically at odds with those relations and that context, and often with each other (see Lamont 2009). The argument effectively pits the development of knowledge *against* the development and maintenance of disciplines. However, it accepts an essentially localist conception of the practices associated with coming to know that does not seem consistent with its demand that what is known according to these practices must, by virtue of the accumulation of findings, yield something more general and comprehensive. In this regard, it is worth noting that what is understood generally or comprehensively is by no means clear without a rather different notion of theory, one possibly tied to disciplinary considerations. Nor is it obvious how to decide, without reference to those same considerations, whether one finding, or any number of findings, falls within the category of another finding or collection of findings and can therefore be considered an instance of an accumulation.

All but the narrowest interpretations of the idea of disciplinary knowledge agree that it depends on other sources for the validity of its concepts and conclusions, and this aspect of complexity also seems precluded by too great an emphasis on the significance of empirical research to general and comprehensive knowledge in the social sciences. An interpretation of any instance of research that is more than situated problem solving and that can be said to have disciplinary validity can hardly avoid giving priority to received concepts, extra-disciplinary referents, and preconceptual claims or sub-theoretical intuitions over specific findings. Yet it may turn out that this aspect of the complexity of disciplinary work does not contribute to the weakness of the social sciences but to their strength, in particular to their capacity to sustain a sense of a subject matter that has something to do with what is human about human affairs. Parenthetically, it is important to note that this is so only if social science is understood as one of the human sciences, in contrast with a field that studies agency-independent reality, and as inseparable from those disciplines in all respects that have to do with comprehending and theorizing what is human about human affairs.

The upshot of the argument from complexity, whether it refers to the complexity of the subject matter or the complexity of academic practices often said to make obscure the rational core of the science, is that the imperfections may be due either to historical limitations or to a failure to identify scientific knowledge with the independence and therefore practical disposition and flexibility of reason. In either case, the defects appear curable by the judicious application of an independent measurement-based empirical methodology (the methodological option). An alternative strategy within the same frame of reference involves facilitating the development of those disciplines in their own terms and according to the present clarity and distinctness of their ideas, beyond what is possible for research aimed essentially at solving extra-disciplinary problems (the normalizing option). The methodological option requires undistracted commitment, while normalization requires patience and a willingness to entertain the possibility that exclusive reliance on a natural science approach may be too limited in its capacity to identify and address what is human about human affairs. Given the scientific worldview identified with naturalism, the second option requires a greater degree of tolerance of other approaches that are critical of that view from, so to say, within it. The question remains as to what is involved in tolerating such approaches from within a view that is hostile to them in principle.

Both ways of addressing the defects that arise from complexity acknowledge naturalism as the horizon toward which the social sciences must orient themselves (see Gordon 1991). Neither requires considering what is human about human affairs in the actual course of conducting research; *and it is this consideration that opens the possibility that the social sciences have more to do with the humanities than with the natural sciences.* Insofar as this requires re-examining the relationship between "truth" and "knowledge," it opens the further possibilities that the human sciences, taken as a whole, provide knowledge appropriate to the proposition that human affairs are essentially social, and that such knowledge is radically different from what is provided by fields that constitute knowledge of a reality minus intentionality (what I call naturalism).

But this possibility depends, in turn, on whether the object of social science—conceived of as distinctively human—lends itself, as such, to applications of the naturalist philosophy.

Observer and Observed

A related account of the weaknesses of the social sciences begins as an immanent critique of the naturalist perspective and indirectly introduces the problem of the human aspect of human affairs when the latter includes the very process of coming to know. It holds that the imperfections of the social sciences have to do with an apparently necessary condition of scientific inquiry: that the observer and the observed are more than relatively independent.[8] The point is a familiar one: it is difficult, in regard to the social science research process, to imagine how the observer can detach herself from culturally determined preexisting attitudes and categories that tendentiously give order to one's knowledge of others (as momentary objects of research) and to the interpretation of the circumstances in which observation presumably takes place. Even if it might be imagined, and even if it is projected as a matter of degree (allowing for progressive approximations of ideal independence), there seems to be no reliable way to decide for a given project whether it has been contaminated beyond its capacity for self-correction by something about the observer or the conditions under which observation takes place, and for deciding whether a project or any set of projects is more or less on the way to the ideal of the relative independence of the act of observing and the object observed.

In regard to confidence, what counts most is the degree of confidence one can rationally have in the findings of a piece of research done by another; and that depends on the quality of the research as well as other factors that contribute reasons for confidence, including other bodies of research and other knowledge that give weight to one interpretation over others. But the distinction between what warrants the confidence of an audience in findings (e.g., readers, lay or professional) and what warrants accepting them as "findings" because they have satisfied a standard of sufficient independence is often problematic enough to warrant philosophical concern. Confidence in any given case, and I am still speaking of the social sciences (including psychology), depends on conditions that cannot be sufficiently accounted for in the research text to warrant confidence on the part of a reading audience; nor can it be accounted for, I believe in most cases, by the history of any line of research or as a property of any discipline taken on its own. The point is that the rationality of confidence depends on the specific case and not on an overall sense of success, and on the interpretation of its findings (which are themselves interpretations), since what counts as success is at least debatable on grounds the naturalist would prefer not to consider: the interpretation of a piece of research includes more than it can acknowledge in its own terms and it takes place under the very circumstances of social life that seemed to produce the problem of bias in the first place.

In passing, I do not defend skepticism. Rather, I suggest that one important problem in applying naturalist principles in the social sciences lies in the lack of a concept of their object, such as it might be, and this conditions all that is currently said about the possibilities of bias and confidence. As long as subject matter is identified with received topics of research and not clarified in advance of particular projects and according to the requirement that it have something to do with what is human about human affairs, the problem of ascertaining rational degrees of confidence remains a challenge to the knowledge claims of those fields. In any case, merely raising the issue of independence as things stand supports the argument that, just as the claims made in the name of any research project cannot be extracted from its (and their) greater context, the disciplinary claims of any particular social science cannot be separated from the claims of other disciplines.

———————

It is relatively uncontroversial—though the implications may be trouble-some—that even the most rigorous observations and analyses necessarily rely on nonscientific intellectual resources, including inherited and popular discourses. However, this seems to weaken if not defeat the fundamental pre-supposition of confidence, the relative independence of the act of observation from characteristic tendencies of the observer and the corresponding pre-scientific stipulation of the identity of the object apart from its particularity as a point at the intersection of time and space—an idea of purity impossible to make intelligible in the social sciences if they are to deal with social facts, since the facticity of each such fact seems to depend on other more inclusive social facts, such as conventions of temporal and spatial representation.

Needless to say, those conducting research are the same sort of conscious being whose existence authorizes their study. Their training is, by virtue of their own point of view, presumably continuous with a lifelong socialization, some of the most important effects of which are latent to all that they do and capable of becoming manifest and manageable only from within, and qualified by, that same latency. To that extent, the requisite degree of independence for the naturalist is at least unlikely and may be impossible for the social scientist. Does this mean that knowledge is impossible for the social and other human sciences? It does if there is nothing distinctively human about human affairs that reduces, modifies, or nullifies the epistemological relevance of indepen-dence. It does not if "human affairs" refers to a different reality from the reality for which the natural sciences are sufficient guarantors of knowledge and if that difference implies that independence is less relevant to knowing than had been supposed.

Even if it could be established for social science that detached objectivity or neutrality is possible in principle, there is no point at which an observer can know whether her observations are free of dispositions determined by prior attitudes and received categories for which, even if she could bring them to full consciousness, which is unlikely, it would not be rational for her to attach subjective probabilities; or, if we want to say that she is free of such dispositions and knows that about herself, it is not obvious that she can communicate that truth, therefore that she can reasonably be believed—regardless of what might be offered as "corroborating evidence." One might agree that scientific progress depends in part on the constant generation of a plurality of ideas about the significance of particular facts. This seems obvious in one respect, since our conception of thought itself entails just such a plurality. But it is question-begging in another respect, since the problem addressed does not have to do with the difference between one thought and many thoughts but, as I try to show, with both the content and location of thought, in other words with objectivity and agency. Until this argument is made, it might be claimed that the facts I have cited as reasons for suspecting bias are merely conditions that are not only correctable *in principle* in the course of the development of a discipline but bound to be corrected in that course and that this merely qualifies and does not eliminate the confidence one can reasonably have in specific and accumulated findings. A compelling version of this is identified with the work of Simon (1990). It says that we are dealing with the "boundedness" of the rationality of the observer in virtually every case; and while this qualifies what might be cited as reasons for confidence in a belief, it does not defeat the reasonableness of any act or observation under the circumstances and of drawing conclusions from it. It seems simply to indicate that conclusions can only be provisional and, therefore, that it is always necessary in social science to do more work. In that case, what makes the notion of bounded rationality relevant to evaluating a given instance of research is the implicit assumption that what I call bias (and thereby seem to suggest is a latency that cannot but limit self-criticism) needs instead to be thought of as prior inclinations that cannot, in general, be rationalized.

This means, however, that it is unfair to require of the observer of human affairs that her observations and conclusions be subjected to the same standards of objectivity as the natural sciences; though whether it is a matter of fairness or suitability to the subject matter is precisely what is at stake. For one thing, observation in those fields addresses a type of objectivity, agency-dependent, that cannot be described and analyzed independently of its fundamental condition. In that respect, unless one decides that it is wrong to refer to this as "observation," it cannot be considered inferior to the observation of agency-independent objects but must be considered something radically different. It may be more akin to invoking a possible object, and in the process simultaneously constituting its field of objectivity, than to describing a preconceptual thing and holding it up to inspection by "anyone"—which hints at a possible further implication, that object and observer are not even ontologically distinguishable in the ways they are often assumed to be and that objects and observers are not independent of one another (or, minimally, neither observers nor their audiences can rely on a sense of that independence). Perhaps it is better to state the positive claim, which is that they are radically inter-dependent.

In any case, it appears from these two propositions that it may not be differing degrees of objectivity but differing kinds of object that distinguish the two sorts of discipline. Since "lacking independence" is not quantifiable in a way that easily allows for judgments of "more or less," there may well be a qualitative difference that goes to the heart of what constitutes social scientific knowledge and, therefore, knowledge in the human sciences taken together.

If we wish to maintain the criterion of independence, we must still agree that social researchers are never free of the same conditions they study and therefore do not accountably conform to that criterion and that, without some sort of corrective, this compromises the sort of objectivity based on the naturalistic model of knowledge-relevant scientific practice. It is not only that social scientists belong to the very entities and movements they study and are inextricably caught up in relations to self, to others, to collectivities, and to objects according to what those allow but, unsurprisingly, that the organization of their thought, as far as the most immediate possible objectivity is concerned, is significantly local (Hampshire 2000, 11–12, 17) and looks outward under the limitations of that condition. Their sense of reality as well as their models of "rationality in action" cannot be accountably independent of that fact. In that case, it is reasonable to doubt that their propositions and models represent moments in the progressive accumulation of increasingly reliable accounts of independent reality, or that what is produced as knowledge can be evaluated as an approximation of the sort of knowledge that increasingly approximates a final truth.

To argue that imperfections in the social sciences have to do with the difficulty of controlling bias suggests that objectivity is a matter of degree and that bias can be reduced by a judicious critique of interpretive dispositions, including ideologies and culturally determined beliefs, and by methodological advances that allow for greater control and the identification of reliably measurable variables capable of being ordered according to the naturalistic logics of causal, functional, or structural explanation. The image of the self-correcting marketplace of ideas is appropriate to this point of view inasmuch as it suggests that whatever residue of bias is present in a body of research is *recognizably* corrected in the long run by a competition among ideas operating with the force of an evolution of knowledge in the direction of greater and greater approximations of empirical truth—and a greater and greater capacity to recognize it. For this, knowledge is tied to the idea that the truth of a statement is a function of the truth values of its constitutive elementary propositions. This depends on the belief, reasonable but, as we have seen, by no means beyond dispute from the point of view of the human sciences, that objects of research essentially lend themselves to criteria of objectivity provided by the standard model in the philosophy of science. That is, they are, among other things, independent and relatively stable. The epistemological significance of the reliance by social science on the truth functionality of elementary propositions depends on the further belief that observers (and their communities) are able to reflect on their own sources of bias in a sufficiently enlightening way as to preclude the sorts of ambiguity that might undermine confidence in the process if not the results of research. In summary, this account of the imperfections of social science assumes that the relationship between observer and observed is an external one between distinct types (of entity or activity) and that it is possible, under conditions yet to be determined, to treat agency-dependent, meaningful objects with the same analytical techniques used to generate and test propositions about agency-independent objects. Again, this begs the question of whether the lack of independence is a problem to be solved or a constitutive feature of what is human about human affairs and, therefore, what is possible for and significant about theoretical work.

Immaturity

There is a third notable explanation of the lack of strong truths in the social sciences, by which I mean nontrivial propositions that satisfy positive criteria of truth *and* that inspire the sort of confidence needed in order to rely on inferences from them. This holds that those disciplines are overdetermined by their prehistories and are, accordingly, immature, premature, or simply folklore. This means, first, that they remain systematically dependent on common sense, received wisdom or "folk psychology," and, second, that the ways in which at least some key assertions deviate from scientific norms resemble a once popular theory of sociocultural change as an increase in rationality accompanied by irrational reaction on the basis of tradition. It emphasizes degrees of tension between what is taken for granted about human affairs and the attempt to free knowledge claims from the strictures of those affairs by judicious applications of reason guided by experience. From this point of view, the development of social science depends on the ability to identify propositions that are incompatible with what is known more generally about reality and to eliminate them. Apart from what it assumes about the dynamics of scientific development, this explanation assumes that the objects of scientifically appropriate propositions are only contingently agency-dependent and that it is only when left unreformed that agency-dependence places the independent objectivity of objects, and, correspondingly, the reliability of observation, in question. Parenthetically, it is tempting to suppose that purging what is merely received (or depends on it) is necessary for arriving at knowledge, partly because this is thought to loosen the hold that the folklore of agency-dependence places on the rational justification of beliefs about the world. This supposition is crucial to the extent to which science is said to involve the search for what can truly be said or reasonably be considered true about a pre-agentic reality in the face of superstition, idealism, delusions, and dogma that insist on a world determined by mind, spirit, or a designing originator. This critique pits science against primitivism, which conflict is, ironically, itself a kind of superstition.

To summarize, if the measure of success in striving for knowledge in the social sciences is the truth of descriptions and predictions, where truth depends on the sense of a fit to reality, or the prospect of such a fit, then the distinction between them and the natural sciences has to do with defects of the former, which are the result of history, the relative complexity of subject matter, the difficulty of controlling bias, and/or dependence on received wisdom. From a slightly different point of view, the difference and its fatal implication has to do with the failure of the social sciences to separate themselves sufficiently from the humanities. A corollary is that the distinction between the social sciences, understood according to the naturalist project, and the humanities is on the order of the distinction between knowledge and what is loosely called "expression" or, alternatively, "evaluation." From this point of view, Knowledge is the special province of science in contrast with the humanities, whose main concerns are said to be values, sympathies, expressive representations, and morally relevant identities. Between the two presumably lie recalcitrant or eccentric sciences such as psychoanalysis, disciplines like politics that set out to link what is with what ought to be, and synthesizing fields like some versions of cultural studies that might be called interdisciplines.

The synthesizing fields, unlike the humanities taken as opposed to science, reject the idea that their objects represent special functions of the mind (e.g., symbolic and integrative) and typically claim that they constitute or are part of a distinct reality—one that is not, however, independent of mind. In contrast with naturalistic science, they can be understood as attempting to sustain the ambiguity of key referents, such as the general will, society, norm, culture, group, institution, text, interest, art, science, history, and personality, in the interest of sustaining the sort of tension that brings theory and its object increasingly closer. In this respect they emphasize *reasonableness* in fixing belief, which cannot be idealized, over *rationality*, which most often is—where reasonableness involves acknowledging in a committed way the possibility that ambiguity is a social fact that can only be momentarily reduced and is therefore immediately reengaged as a matter of necessity.

Such synthesizing disciplines can also be understood as standing for the possibility of a unity of the human sciences. The reason they work to sustain ambiguity is not merely pragmatic, though practicality is often taken as sufficient justification for the disposition. From this point of view, the reality to which they constantly allude is what I have been referring to as sub-theoretical, with the implication that it is agency-dependent in all theoretically significant respects—where "agency" does not refer to something internally homogeneous or unified, or for that matter psychological. It follows that the distinction between knowledge and expression begs the question of what knowledge consists of when it has to do with agency-dependent reality.

I argue that the naturalistic view of knowledge (as composed of the products of scientific work in regard to agency-independent reality) depends on a qualitative distinction between the humanities and the social sciences and a quantitative one between the latter and the natural sciences. Applied to the social sciences, this view assumes that knowledge is possible only in regard to independent and relatively fixed phenomena, that propositions are true (or not false) only if they conform to or are otherwise compatible with that sort of reality. In that case, natural science, and social science considered as an intended approximation, can be thought of as the study of a reality that is independent of agency—in other words, where agency is not the main issue though it might remain somewhat problematic and though it might be reduced to psychological facts by way of giving it the same objective status.

One purpose of this book is to make a case for a different ordering of the disciplines and for an understanding of knowledge in the human sciences that does not depend on the standard view derived from the sciences of agency-independent reality and that therefore invokes a different methodology from what philosophy typically offers the social sciences. This depends on the plausibility of a radical idea of agency-dependent reality and how that idea illuminates the sub-theoretical sense of a sociality that is the unifying object of the human sciences. It is worth remembering that the latter are taken as a whole when they are said to share a fundamental commitment to what is human about human affairs. In this sense, the social sciences have far more in common with the humanities than with the natural sciences. The strong part of the argument is that rather than compromising their claims to provide knowledge, this enhances those claims. The key lies in understanding how the difference between critical and positive reason cannot be reduced to the difference between what ought to or might be and what is in fact, or between mere opinion and knowledge. It is necessary, then, to discuss certain problems before addressing the theoretical issues surrounding subjectivity, inter-subjectivity, action, situation, and the special objectivity of the referential domain of the human sciences. I begin with an issue in the philosophy of language.

Two famous comments by Bertrand Russell, in his introduction to Wittgenstein's *Tractatus Logico-Philosophicus*, can serve as a point of departure for what follows. The first is that "in practice, language is always more or less vague, so that what we assert is never quite precise" (1974, x). The second is that "the whole function of language is to have meaning, and it only fulfills this function in proportion as it approaches to the ideal language which we postulate" (x). As for the first, when language is considered in its connection to the world of human affairs, this vagueness and lack of precision must be thought of not as something negative about language as used but as an intrinsic feature of language *insofar as it can be used*. In that case, we are not dealing with vagueness and a lack of precision so much as a "function" of language that is quite different from what Russell refers to in his second comment, which, as I read it, has to do with the possibility of a meeting of minds. Parenthetically, Russell was interested in how we can be misled by language, and I am concerned with what he asserted about language such that it might mislead.

I try to make the case that language seems "vague" and "imprecise," given a communicative ideal incompatible with normal speech, because of the nature of its objects of reference, which are agency-dependent, and not because the normal use of language is intended to approximate an ideal of a meeting of minds—which is, then, "ideal" only to the extent to which language is not understood as a social fact. In other words, it is the object and its situation that largely accounts for usage. *The language of which Russell was speaking is not, then, the language he chose to study.* To the extent to which it has the qualities he attributes to it, vagueness and imprecision, it is best thought of as discursive speech, and this cannot be understood as an imperfect version of an ideal language or even as something the motions and operations of which can be illuminated by such a language.

I also defend the weaker proposition that the overall function of language, if it is reasonable to say about something like language that it is an "it" with an overall function, is not to have meaning in the strict sense of providing for a meeting of minds—unless one conceives of sociality as antagonistic to the idea of "the humanness of human affairs for which language might be said to have as its primary function the determination of meaning." To say that the function of language is to have meaning is to imply strongly that the function of meaning must be, in part, to fix usage, hence the emphasis on the ideal. One might then ask what good is attained by fixing language, and more than several goods come to mind. But surely it cannot be the overall function of language to fix itself or to provide a basis for criticizing vagueness and imprecision, unless its function is, finally, to end vagueness and imprecision by producing in their place something quite different from what Russell admits is the normal course of things human when he says that "in practice, language is always more or less vague."

If meaning is to have a function such that language can also have one, then the image of what projects that function is the discrete event—for example, linguistic acts that begin and end and can be understood not for their essentially incomplete participation in the movement of human affairs (e.g., discursivity) but only for how they terminate the activity of speaking in the *discovery* and *institutionalization* of "meaning." To say that "the whole function of language is to have meaning" is, in effect, to say that the whole function of language is to end sociality: it is commonly conceded that to fix speech in the way suggested by Russell is to substitute something formal, accountable according to rules, for what cannot be formal, thereby bringing speaking to an end in the name of something antagonistic to it called "communication." To the extent to which speaking is essentially social such that a theory of language must at least respect that fact, it is fair to say that "meaning" in Russell's sense of the functionality of language is inconsistent with the idea of the social. In considering what is human about human affairs in such a way that knowledge is also possible, it is necessary to think of language and "communication" in somewhat different terms and according to different models, and, with that, to consider the agency-dependent objectivity that gives speaking its own referential quality—language used, as it were, spontaneously in the context of a reflexivity not under the control of the ostensibly individualized speaker.

The reality of which Russell's notion of language is a function does not correspond significantly to what we consider human affairs to be when, for example, we take Russell's own comment about the normalcy of vagueness and imprecision more seriously than he, or some who followed him, once did.[9] If we think of language as something capable of having a function and as having it for the sake of a sociality in which what is vague and imprecise is necessarily so and in which no individual, intention, or act is complete and unambiguously definite as things stand, it is necessary to conclude that its function, speaking rather than a meeting of minds, must be thought of as the *continuation of sociality*. Consider in this regard a rough analogy to certain aspects of money. According to prevailing conceptions, money must circulate. In so doing, it continually constitutes itself as a liquid medium of exchange—thereby continually posing a problem of reference and therefore rationality. It must do this if it is to have the social function of making exchange a moment of a continuous operation of an institutional feature of society rather than the discontinuous and asocial transactions it appears to be when we analyze it into separable but complementary mind-meeting actions, buying and selling. Of course, the circulation of money, and the society that supports continuous exchange, of which that very circulation must be a constitutive feature, is itself a negation of a different sort of entity. It is in important ways opposed to the generative socialized activity of production that makes exchange, therefore money, and now one must add language, conceivable. To put it more succinctly, to consider money, rather than, say, the activity of production, as basic to society is to define "society" as an endless plurality of "meetings of minds" based on the circulation of a means of exchange, or currency (money or meaning)—which is to say to define it as logically opposed to what can be conceived of as humanly social.

Again, the movement of money systematically discounts what it most depends on—namely, what people do together in regard to the agency-dependent objects (products as indices of the disposition of a portion of available human labor and other forms of capital) in regard to which their activities, productive and otherwise, are capable of a rationality consistent with the possibility of the continuation of those very activities. If the analogy holds, to the extent to which language is a function of human affairs, it aims not merely at the manufacture of fixed and therefore repeatable units of meaning but at its own continuation as discursive speech. From a different point of view, it aims at a continuation in which persons are absorbed in a course of activity not of their own devising and in which individuality, such as it might be, is a moment of collective reflexivity before it is anything else. The idea that discourse pursues its own possibility before it can be understood as producing meaning and establishing something like interpersonal communication cannot be accounted for by the substitution of an idealized form of something altogether different from what it is supposed to clarify, for whatever is indicated by the properties of "vagueness" and "imprecision."

19

Objects and Their Subjects

One working hypothesis for what follows is derived from the relationship between agency-dependent reality and the social conceived of as a course of activity. It says that there is an internal relationship between a certain idea of criticism and what is human about human affairs. I have been using the expression "human sciences" to refer to disciplinary fields having to do with agency-dependent reality. In anticipation of what follows, "agency-dependence" refers to the aspect of an object that presupposes subjectivity irreducible to individual mentalities. This is a radical claim if every referent of discourse presupposes such a subjectivity. The point is not that discursively constituted objects are implicated in or caught up in human affairs but might not be; they are already and always instances of those affairs and have their identity and uses uniquely in that connection. As things stand, this reality can be thought of as a region of being that encompasses an internal relation of life and situation.[1] I have discussed the idea of a situation in its relationship to a general notion of human life and its significance to the question of what is human about human affairs. If "situation" refers us to agency-independent reality, there is no serious question about the human quality of such affairs that does not preserve the autonomy of the individual human being, with all that entails (including the absolute distinction between that being and her situation). If it refers to agency-dependent reality, the answer to the question is bound to reorganize our conception of what constitutes knowledge of human affairs, which is where the idea of criticism becomes most important.

We will see that this idea of agency-dependence challenges the standard ontological distinction between subjectivity and objectivity in philosophical accounts of mind and action (see Davidson 2001c for a critical discussion).[2]

Instead, it yields a notion of inter-subjectivity that supersedes subjects in the individual psychological sense and objects insofar as they are agency-dependent. The point is that for agency-dependent reality to be thought of momentarily as a universe (*in order to clarify the concept*)—that is, as if it were all that falls under what can be known by the human sciences—life and situation must be thought of as internally related and, therefore, as *essentially* inter-subjective. However, the expression "inter-subjectivity" suggests a division ("inter") that seems inconsistent with the idea of such a relation. Addressing this problem requires reconsidering the notion of subjectivity according to the more fundamental notion of a course of activity.

As a first approximation, the idea of an internal relation of life and situation suggests that we think of life as essentially differentiated. To be essentially differentiated is to be internally divided in a way that precludes unity. I refer to this sort of division as "oppositional," so that instances of life are conceived of as irrevocably self-differentiating and, in that respect, always motivated. Consequently, an instance of life is not "an instance" in the ordinary sense of the term: it is only momentary in its assumption of both a specific form and a specific content, and, in that sense, apparent in those respects. Therefore, it is only *ostensibly* an instance of a type and only *ostensibly* definite relative to the descriptive requirements of meaning (identifying a type) and reference (picking out an instance). Such an instance can then be characterized as necessarily incomplete, from which it follows that a theory of life is inadequate unless everything it attempts to account for is conceived of as being generative in all respects. One might say that an instance of life is grasped as such in the mode of "sense" (considered as the immanent apprehension of what is being done in the course of its being done) rather than in the mode of either "perception" (according to essence and properties) or "understanding" (according to laws or tendencies). Perhaps it is better to say that perception and understanding, which depend on meaning and reference, are theoretically subordinate to and dependent on a sub-theoretical sense of the object.

This humanly inescapable dynamic mobility can be thought of, as Sartre did, as a "multiplicity"—in contrast with an organic unity that depends on a totalizing impulse aimed at making wholly manifest a totality already in place or something concretely integrated in the manner of a system that depends on an established complementarity of "functions." What this sacrifices is the assuredness and convenience of classifying—for example, designating distinct living entities as instances, and possibly merely tokens, of types. But, no matter what its purpose and no matter how unavoidable it may be in regard to a particular problem, classification effectively denies one aspect of the distinctive objectivity of life, its irrepressibility. It therefore invalidates itself the moment it is rationalized—or clarified according to an explicit principle or by a dimensional analysis capable of justifying a list of types as more or less exhaustive of all possible types defined by the points of intersection of linear dimensions as more or less of various universal properties. What is gained at the cost of losing one's ease with classification is a conception of life in regard to its condition of possibility—namely, its resistance to whatever terminates movement or makes it nonvisible (e.g., specifying and classifying) or its refusal of anything approximating inertia or rigid designation. Acknowledgment of this disposition is necessary if theory is to take itself as an instance of its object, to see its object in itself and itself in its object. But resistance by itself cannot be taken as the starting point of theory. I argue throughout that the opposition of classification and resistance is given by the very idea of the sociality of human affairs understood as an inter-subjective course of activity. This is so for two reasons: (1) there is no other way of understanding what is human about such affairs, and (2) there is no other way of understanding "being in a situation" (discussed in a later section). Thus, as things stand, resistance, no less than the internality of relations, is a logical feature of the concept of life as immanently social.

———

The perspective of multiplicity identifies resistance most generally with the activities of self-differentiation and self-differentiating recomposition. Goffman's (1963) analysis of discursively determined subjectification is a version of that perspective in its description of the interplay of what he calls "virtual" (or attributable) and "actual" (or self-asserted) identities, where identity and the *individuality* of identity have become issues shared by the parties to an encounter, as tends to be the case in many if not most sustained encounters. This play of hopelessly imperative identity claims is, in itself, intrinsically socializing. It constitutes a course of activity without horizon, involving attempts that cannot fully be identified with individual agents or even seen as such in their course to reconcile abstract individuality and abstract sociality according to two demands implicit in discourse itself. These have to do with the discursive tendency Goffman identifies as political in the most expansive sense of the term: the apparently paradoxical tendency of discourse itself, which is constitutionally non-rigid, to make at least some of its designations rigid, just as the apparently paradoxical tendency of theorizing is to deny itself as a course of activity in its ostensible products.

The first imperative is the asymmetrically shared obligation to neutralize the effects of disclosures of "shameful defects," requiring collective efforts at what Goffman calls "tension management." The second is the motivating anticipation of rigid designation, hence over-definition or hyper-objectification. This puts the parties in a shared predicament of having to "control information" that might be seen as personally revealing without knowing in advance what will be relevant or, for that matter, what will constitute "information" in the sense of making a desired difference. Goffman uses the word "information" somewhat ironically, since what needs to be controlled is not the possibility of a discrediting fact's coming to light, but the high degree of probability that any property might become noticeable and therefore possibly discrediting. Because of the ways in which the possibility of becoming noticeable is discursively processed—for example, by ostentatious indifference, perhaps intended to assert a norm of neglect—no party can afford to ignore the possibility that she may be rigidly defined by any property that comes to collective notice.

It follows that, when something is noticed and has become ostensible in the form of a property that can be attributed to someone and possibly anyone, it becomes a predicate awaiting a subject, and any particular assignment initially, but only then, appears to be hypothetical. It arrives at a subject, as it were, or "picks someone out" in the course of the ensemble's projection of itself in the form of a discovery of a proper subject for a totalizing attribution, a commitment to identifying an absolute other. In light of such an attribution the ensemble appears to normalize the self-reflective form of "us" by which a discourse is identified, in retrospect or from outside, as the property of a group self. Of course, not all discourse becomes invested in such a self, and there is no general tendency of parties to a discourse to force that issue. But the issue of "spoiled identity," which is Goffman's topic, places the ensemble (for which it is an issue) at the point of either self-definition or dissolution, and this is where stigmatizing attributions are likely and, as such, are political even in their prospect. Goffman seems to be making two claims here. One is that discursive "encounters" achieve their own identity as a momentary group against something decidedly non-discursive or anti-discursive relative to what they otherwise appear to be, which is to say something unmistakably individuated, hence capable of rigid designation (subject to the deployment of "rigid designators") and is therefore intrinsically tendentious. The second is that every participant is vulnerable to this politics of prospective disassociation simply by virtue of those features of speaking that convey the illusion of determinate meanings and that demand that this illusion nevertheless be experienced as real. As far as speech is conceived of as part of a pragmatics of group identity, each party to speaking is bound to experience something on the order of an Oedipal anticipation of becoming momentarily monstrous and normatively unrecognizable—which is to say becoming absolutely distinct and thereby radically dis-subjectified and disqualified as a possible party to discourse. This is one way in which Goffman sees sociality as momentarily taking on the appearance of a self-reflective entity—specifically against a background possibility of a potentially group-defeating individuality that is converted by designation as such into a resource, an other against which the group takes its own apparent sociality as its *telos* (Goffman 1963).

It follows that at least some part of the work of the collective involves keeping this danger to its parties-in-general at bay by effectively assigning to *someone* the status of anti-discursive other on the basis of a detectable attribute that signifies a possible property of a social identity within a more inclusive, relatively de-situated discourse. This is done largely by individuating that someone as an instance of a type such that it becomes possible for the parties, now freed of their own anticipation of being so individuated, to relax their vigilance toward the prospect of being the next discursive other. This is also why Goffman refers to the process by which a group asserts itself as an identity as "political," just as every explicit assertion of group identity is always in some sense ideological. I take it that this does not mean that sociality is a contrivance of the participating individuals, though Goffman is occasionally interpreted as claiming just that. It takes only a moment to realize that it cannot be unless there is a prior agreement or prior social activity on the basis of which it is possible for the parties actively to contrive together. As I see it, his analysis implies that sociality cannot be explained by the formation of strategies designed to justify the self-assertion of the ensemble in response to the self-assertion of any of its parties (as particular wills) any more than it can be explained by the separate self-consciousnesses of those parties. What appears to be contrivance is, then, one way in which sociality momentarily betrays itself in the form of an identity manifestly guaranteed by the "spoiled identity" of an individuated other, given that self-betrayal is inevitable to, but not definitive of, anything that can be thought of as a course of activity.

———

If we adopt the perspective of multiplicity, we are then committed to the further idea that the self-reflective aspect of sociality cannot be reduced to self-reference; reference to a principle or set of principles; or reference to purpose, goal, or condition. The word most often used to name this aspect is "reflexivity," and it *refers most generally to the way in which something implicates itself as immanent to a course of activity*: what it is immediately shows how it is possible. This involves two related ideas. The first has to do with the incessant totalizing activity (including, beckoning, or reaching out) by which something is immediately recognizable as an instance of life.[3] This activity is often thought to assume its appearance, its momentousness, around the aspects of differentiation, recomposition, and reformation and/or extension of retrospectively ostensible boundaries. The second idea is "work," which is a necessary feature of activity and a legitimate metaphor for its course. We must say that life is active in a certain way before it appears to be individuated if we are to appreciate the distinction between life and things, intentionality and mechanism; and it shows itself as active in that way by returning to itself as an immanent motivation, beyond particular preset tendencies or dispositions, that has to do fundamentally with the idea of a *course of activity* in contrast with an *action*.

In regard to this idea of an activity that always exceeds itself, motivation must not be thought of as an additional element but as an aspect of the necessary relationship between the activity and its capacity to be, to continue being, to produce itself as, activity. One way of thinking about this notion of self-generation is that internal division makes continuation problematic and continuation makes division problematic—the former because division seems at first to lead only to repetition, the latter because continuation seems to lead to identity in the sense of a unified subjectivity. Neither repetition nor identity can support a notion of activity other than as the same sort of caused motion or event identified with agency-independent objectivity. However, the fact that activity always exceeds what can be said, known, and rationalized allows us to identify the noncontingent motivation that we find implicit in the very concept of life independently of individuation. This fact, that life creates a surplus of itself, of activity as such, guarantees that any course of activity will display the effort of its parties beyond any specific intentions and the indexical signs of a "work" that addresses the impossibility of reconciling that surplus with its being and having been produced. Reconciliation is either logically impossible or it is not possible to decide when or if it has occurred or is even being approximated. In either case, it is clear that no part of a course of activity is free of that sort of work. Therefore, we can say that it is an immanent feature or aspect of whatever is being done when doing is conceived of as a course of activity, but not when it is conceived of as action in the sense of a definite, unified, particular event.

"Action" familiarly refers to the virtually automatic executive operation that takes place between intention, formed as a sufficiency of reasons, and result. As such, the actor is most likely to be described as a mechanism preset to select from among a limited set of options, according to a principle of least effort, relatively stable facts in regard to which options are typically weighed according to relative costs and relative benefits, and a more or less unyielding standard or set of standards (e.g., attitudes, preferences, and values). It is typically taken for granted that the actor is generally disposed to act, that the option not to act at all does not count. Whether the actor is a human being or an automaton, its operation so conceived is radically different from work.[4] This description is enough to appreciate the gulf between human activity and the executive operation identified as an event in the theory of action. The former is conceivable only in opposition to mechanism, which is to say that it is conceivable along the very different lines of an internally motivated, nonrepeatable, momentous multiplicity identified with neither a definite prior intention nor a definite result or product. In this respect it is something that can be done only by socially disposed human beings. When work is alluded to in the philosophy of action, it is typically thought of in connection with the category of deliberation prior to that operation, and that deliberation is not ordinarily considered to be a course of activity so much as the application of a method or methods. As such, it is considered to be an economic factor in the strict sense of the term, and defined in a way that begs the unavoidable question posed by every theory of what people do: How can what is called "action" be understood as an instance of what is human about human affairs?[5]

In discussing the immanence of work, I try to develop further the argument that the standard concept of action precludes identifying what have been, are being, might have been, and might be done uniquely as instances of life and that, in this respect, it shifts attention from activity, which is constitutive of life, to what "thought" amounts to under the concept of "action"—that is, when it is considered to be independent of doing and therefore not necessarily related to life. This raises a question that indicates a possible paradox: How is it possible to conceptualize life without thought and thought without life? I have suggested in different ways that the standard concept of action is designed to clarify the language of intentionality, in contrast, say, with expressiveness or reflexivity, on two assumptions: (1) that the skin is a natural boundary to agency and (2) that agency is or, as Davidson claims, should be treated as tendentious to rational action, where the rationality of an act is defined by the actor's realization of the implications of her justified beliefs about feasibility, costs, a certain attitude toward risk, and relatively spontaneous desires limited by more general values and ordered at the moment of decision as a given hierarchy of preferences. It is clear that only if these assumptions are taken as axiomatic can the theory of action constitute a paradigm for the study of human affairs, and, therefore only if those affairs are not essentially social.

In that regard, its specification of certain variable properties of agency (e.g., weakness or strength of will, intensity of effort, complexity of beliefs and/or desires, coherence, memorability, responsiveness to exigent conditions including "social facts" such as rules) is intended to mark what is human about action, beyond describing an ideal of reason abstracted from human affairs and, therefore, from intentionality itself. In examining this paradigm for whether it is adequate to the task of normalizing research and analysis, it must first be noted that each quality can apply to many different sorts of agency (for example, certain animals, certain types of machine, and, in another logical register, certain objects taken as products) and different sorts of activity. Without reference to such qualities, the model of rationality cannot on its own describe what people do. In its pure form, it pertains to human affairs only insofar as they are not distinctively human. This suggests that in order for the attributed properties to be able to pick out something as human, they need to be thought of in combination such that, taken together, they clarify the idea of what might be called an authentic "natural kind" or species, perhaps in this case, human beings as passionate reasoners.[6] The properties being universal, emphasis is on their combination insofar as that bears on the human functions of self-reflective intentionality and deliberation. These are necessarily contained within the skin of the putatively independent entity for which those are functions—namely, the psychological individual.

One problem already discussed is that specifying this entity in terms of its properties alone seems impossible, or it is not possible to tell when an attempt at specification is sufficient, and asserting an underlying essence begs the question that was supposed to be solved by listing (and combining) properties.[7] One might therefore conclude that the action paradigm ends with its object being something altogether insubstantial: an unanchored movement from separable

performances (expressions of intentionality or executions of the results of deliberation) to their connection to something that is independent of the properties but capable of integrating all performances—something that has, in other
words, a necessary function that cannot be specified in terms of sufficient
properties. Whatever the gain in focusing on this movement of assertiveness
(of something like the self) to its dissolution as a distinct identity, it belies the
paradigm that is responsible for it—that requires both the properties and the
essence but cannot take them separately or combine them into the entity it posits as distinctively human.

At best, the concept of action privileges the mental state rather than self-
differentiation. For this, the body is nothing more than the machinery that
integrates and energizes mental states and is somehow directed to execute intentions—or intentions are already actions or parts of actions so that the very
concept of an intention, which is an essential ingredient of the paradigm, loses
its clarity and distinctness. The intellectual tendency that corresponds to this
problem of integrating properties by reference to something that presupposes
just such an integration is to resolve the question of what is human about human life in favor of mental atomism or, more generally, functional particular-
ism. This makes it difficult to avoid either the radical physicalist emphasis on
mind as epiphenomenal or a skeptical resolution of the mind-body problem in
terms of linguistic usage.[8] In those respects the paradigm begs the question of
what "action" means when it is understood according to the lexical field from
which alone it draws its paradigmatic significance, that situates it and allows
it to be used in conjunction with such concepts as intentionality, rationality,
intentionality, and "weakness of the will." This is also to say that it begs the
questions necessarily posed by those disciplines that depend on that field for a
sense of what it is for an object to be agency-dependent and for humans to be
social beings. We have seen that this entails a language of agency independent
of the assumption that the skin is a natural boundary, thereby logically depos-
ing the very individualistic concept of action (as an event) in favor of its opposite, which is the notion of a course of activity.

"Reflexivity" refers, in one aspect, to the immanence of work to anything
thought of as a multiplicity, which is to say life as things stand. This
is because thinking of something as a multiplicity, as self-differentiating, involves acknowledging that its quality of being ongoing, of being incessantly
active (though not diffuse), stems from its constant reckoning with itself, with
its internally contradictory aspect and with its possibility as just such a productive movement. That reckoning is neither something additional to activity
nor something that reflects the dispositional nature of an organism: the biologically determined diffuse restlessness of the latter is not distinctively human
and it does not account for the sort of supra-individual motivation capable of
sustaining and intensifying a course of activity. From this point of view, work is

immanent to the sociality of life and not merely something that might or might not characterize any of its instances. It reinforces the idea of a multiplicity that may appear to be a unity but which is always dividing itself in the endlessly self-transforming prospect of a completeness that it can never achieve. It is in these terms that life can be thought of as irreducibly generative, where generativity has to do with sustaining the negative relationship between activity and its momentary cessation in the situated appearance of unity.

It is evident that such an activity can never be adequately conceived of as a totality (formally complete or approximately so) though it may momentarily appear to be such.[9] To represent it as a unity is not consistent with its reflexivity. Reflexivity implies that the self-transformation of activity is immanent to its course, which is different from the succession of states of affairs ordinarily referred to as change—for example, a reaction to something external to the course of activity, a conscious attempt to realize a given type, an intention merely to disturb whatever seems to be going on, or the result of accident. In each of these cases, what counts is action rather than a course of activity and individual subjects rather than subjectivity as such. It follows that we can describe a life that is internally related to its situation as one in which every momentary ostensible unity displays an unresolvable disunity such that all that can be recognized as distinctively human about it resists specification in terms of that very unity. In other words, reference to reflexivity entails understanding human life as constantly changing the terms of its existence insofar as it can be known in its distinctively human aspect. That life, that sociality, is endlessly self-differentiating and, therefore, always in the course of being composed. This means that it constantly exceeds, or goes beyond, itself. "Going beyond" is, then, implicit in the idea of reflexivity. Otherwise, self-differentiation and recomposition must come to an end in the course of activity, in which case there is no need for the idea of a "course" and no concept of life. This raises obvious problems for the concept of a situation, as in the claim that human beings are beings "in a situation." But these are problems only if the idea of a situation retains the logic in which the location of an action is independent of the action as such, which is not acceptable when what is at stake is what is human about human affairs and when that has to do with agency-dependent objectivity and the idea of a course of activity.

I define "situation" indicatively by its correspondence with this conception of life and according to the condition that life and situation are internally related. The term refers, then, not to a set of independent conditions of action but to what I want to call the "limit subjectivity," which is a feature of all instances of life in its situation by virtue of the fact that, as things stand, subject and object are themselves internally related. This limit subjectivity corresponds to a universe of agency-dependent reality. Another way of saying this is that the term "situation," used in connection with the idea of human life, refers to agency-dependent reality and the sociality that corresponds to that reality. It follows that no instance of apprehending or knowing agency-dependent objects can be complete or whole; therefore, a theory of knowledge that is also a theory of subjectivity cannot provide a general account when it is obliged, in the last instance, to assign knowledge (and the process of knowing) to individuals. Similarly, no instance of such an objectivity can be indicated from a point of view outside of it and remain consistent with the idea that life and situation are internally related. It cannot be indicated as an identity, a particularity, or a composed unity, or according to any set of laws intended to describe it as an enduring totality. If it were to be any of those things, it would be agency-independent and therefore not an instance of human affairs.

According to the logic of its connection to life, the idea of a situation cannot be clarified according to variations in its stability, clarity, and ease of access. Its objectivity is inseparable from the agency it presumably situates and the activity attributed to that agency. In this case, the problem posed by the gap between reasons and undertaking does not arise. The need to conceive of an internal relation of situation and agency supports thinking of the objectivity of a situation as a limit subjectivity.[10] For the moment, however, it is helpful to consider a different idea that may support a positive version of the situation, thereby avoiding the problems, and the advantages, associated with the ideas of internal relations and agency-dependence. For this, the word "situation" might signify something definite and external to individual actors and their actions, thereby accounting for, among other things, "communication," where the latter refers to the prospect of a meeting of minds about something. For this, situation is not merely a collection. It may be composed of entities, norms, representations, and physical conditions that are outside of the minds of individuals taken one by one and that, to the extent to which they are not a mere collection of unrelated facts, can contribute to the rational formation of beliefs and the undertakings of which those beliefs are causally connected. The point is that the standard theory of action requires a distinction between external conditions and agency. This is so even though it is as least as difficult to find a clear definition of "external condition" as it is of "agency," which, we will recall, McCann refers to as a "mysterious phenomenon" (1998, 1).[11] What is significant about this distinction for a theory of action is that it seems to overlap a further distinction between causes and reasons that is difficult to avoid in considering the ontological problem of how action can be individuated when, as Strawson claims, actors must be understood as social beings through and through. However these and related problems are resolved, the notion of a situation (context, conditions, etc.) is conceived of pre-theoretically as a state of affairs that comes to the attention of a particular subject. To that extent, one can say that subjects act according to, among other things, beliefs *about* their situations.[12] Such subjects are presumed to be bearers of particular wills that can be weak or strong, able to focus or not, divided or unitary, and so on but that cannot help but know themselves. This sort of subjectivity has several properties worth mentioning again.

For one thing, it abides across situations (which are there for any actor) and operates in each distinct situation with an ordering function correspondent with the abiding will; for another, it is relatively volatile: it is always found in an attitude of intentionality beyond specific intentions and invariably seeks, in what it does, to make a difference. This is the sort of thing that it is, and it is this restlessness that presumably justifies using the word "will" in trying to give substance to the concept of agency. Given this, the particular will of this positive conception of action in relation to the idea of a situation can be understood as divided into a search mechanism and something, the will itself, for which searching is a necessary operation and often enough efficacious. This idea of how will and situation are defined and then connected, at a point at which both are presumably stabilized, underlies the standard utilitarian model of action, with or without elaborations designed to include what Nozick came to refer to as the "symbolic" aspect of rationality. If I understand him correctly, this involves the agent's adding utilities by virtue of past associations. That is, every situation activates desires, fears, and the like derived from experiences in other situations that add to whatever drives action in the immediate situation (Nozick 1993, 26–35). Thus, every action is both symbolic and instrumental—and it is not clear whether Nozick means "simultaneously"—and every action refers to more than what its immediate situation requires. In passing, it should be remembered that this hypothesis has been discussed in detail by social psychologists and sociologists for over a century, and that part of that discussion has turned on the question of the adequacy of utilitarian assumptions about the nature of both will and situation if one takes account of the essential reflexivity of social action and the essential sociality of human affairs.

On the one hand, a significant problem with the positive model is that it identifies action as external to the "being in a situation" that presumably makes it possible in the first place to conceive of what humans do as humans. Because of this, the model has nothing to say about the activity of arriving at itself, and therefore nothing to say about activity, reflexivity, and, therefore, the theorizing that characterizes the subjectivity the model is purported to re-present. To exempt theorizing in this way is to reduce the conception of the object of the theory (will or intentionality) to one of a nontheorizing entity impossible therefore to identify with what is human about human affairs. *Once situation and will are separated, they can never be reunited satisfactorily, and that problem has beleaguered theories of action influenced by utilitarianism throughout the history of modern thought.*

On the other hand, the very insistence on the validity of the model despite the self-alienating effect of the progressive refinement of its concepts—by which I mean the increasing separation of concept from what is taken subtheoretically as its object domain—does not simply mean, as Nozick (1993) claims, that a major problem with the theory of action is that it has necessarily become too technical for its validity to be appreciated by the average person. Rather, the increasing dissonance between the sub-theoretical notion of what is

human about human affairs and the very act of compounding the initial philosophical error by adding to the formal elegance of an ontologically compromised model raises crucial questions about the validity of the ideas of agency
and subjectivity themselves, insofar as they are defined according to the distinction between situation and will. This, in turn, is bound to draw attention
to the difficulties involved in distinguishing between subject and object that
have never been sufficiently resolved to guarantee the relevance of the theory
of action to the disciplines that it is intended to inform. Indeed, the very idea
of the distinction becomes tenuous and possibly unintelligible in the face of the
refinement of the model as far as it concerns trying to make experiential sense
of human affairs. This does not mean that it should be abandoned—only that,
as things stand, it cannot perform its foundational task without generating the
dissonance that raises questions about its validity.

From within a course of activity, subjectivity is an immediate feature of all
that is situated and not merely a qualification of what is otherwise independently objective. This is implicit in the idea of experience, and it is part of what
is meant by the expression "within" when it is used to capture the idea of experience—in contrast with effects and the process of registering or accounting for
a fact. It is in this regard that it is necessary to ask how it is possible to express
the idea of a situation positively and, at the same time, remain consistent with
what is human about human affairs. It may be theoretically more accurate to
replace the term "within" by the expression "in order to make sense of human
affairs in regard to what is human about them as things stand," which invokes
the possibility of experience, whatever other problems it might pose, given that
experience is itself constitutionally social. The important thing to remember is
that what is essential to human affairs is sociality that is conceivable only as a
course of activity. We can see, then, that referring positively to a situation in order to maintain the distinction between subjectivity and objectivity ends by de-
feating itself. It necessarily invokes a reality of which subjectivity is a necessary
feature of all that is and can be said to be intelligibly objective about it. This
seems to admit what the emphasis on the positive was intended to deny, that situations are agency-dependent in the same sense as agency-dependent objects.

But this is misleading. We usually think about action as if its situation is
composed of objects, agency-dependent or not. This relies, metaphorically, on
the idea of a territory containing distinguishable things where natural boundaries, capable of supporting beliefs about those things are constituted initially
by agency-independent relations among those things. But the relations that
constitute "contents" cannot be taken as invariant, even relatively so, in the way
the metaphor suggests. The compound idea of a container and its contents fails
to represent a relationship between situation and life and, therefore, fails to satisfy the need for concepts of action and situation able to account for the sociality of human activity. We are again forced to admit, even under the auspices of

a positive approach to the relationship between life and situation, that reference to a situation is intelligible on condition that it is consistent with the agency-dependence of its objects and of itself as a form of life. It is to that extent that "situation" can be thought of as the "limit subjectivity" of a course of activity.

We need to ask what the objects have in common as objects that cannot just be particular things in situations, which themselves cannot be a collection of things. What is most obvious about situated objects the moment they come to notice within a course of activity is that their objectivity is inseparable from subjectivity—not merely because they are relevant to a purpose or because of a property they have that attracts the attention of an agent or a plurality of agents. The being of such objects, their objectivity, includes their implication in a course of activity and the subjectivity that defines it as a course, in which they contribute to the very possibility of agency itself. To begin with the distinction between subjectivity and objectivity is to end with a conclusion that contradicts it. States of mind, practices, projects, and activities can be understood as a working out of objectivity every bit as much as a working out of subjectivity, and *nothing establishes a legitimate analytical priority of the one over the other.*

It follows that the involvement of the object in subjectivity and the subject in objectivity is symmetrical. The two are mutually constitutive: subjectivity constitutes its objects and objectivity constitutes its subjects. We are now in a position to answer the question "What do situated objects have in common such that we can learn something about the nature of situations from that commonality?" The answer is implicit in the question: they are, above all, situated. What can we learn from that and from the logical fact that their being situated means that they are with each other only to the extent to which they are with subjects, where "being with" is understood as an internal relation? Being situated is certainly one and perhaps the only thing they share. But this is not a significant fact if it is translated as "they are objects *in* a situation" or "each is relevant to some subject *in* a situation." That simply reproduces the problems already discussed. Its significance is less easily described or illustrated than the common properties listed or structural identities construed in describing the independent objectivity of mere things. Unlike the latter, situated objectivity cannot be dissociated from subjectivity: it not only bears the latter's mark in all significant respects; it carries its very weight.

Let us suppose that we are theoretically committed to the term "subjectivity" despite the qualms we have about it, therefore that our commitment is somewhat ironical; let us suppose that the fundamental reason for this curious and possibly self-defeating obligation is that we are sub-theoretically committed to an intuition that the world of human affairs in some sense reveals subjectivity in everything that can be said about its reality; and let us finally assume that this is not a fallacy created by vague and imprecise language, but a genuine intuition enacted in the very irony with which we use the term and by certain

additional commitments, revealed, for example, in our desire for the artful moment in which life makes itself felt against whatever might simply have been
expected, and in the spontaneity with which we relate altruistically to others—
on the basis of "timeless reasons" that, as Nagel says, could be anyone's. I suggested earlier that Nagel's analysis of altruism concludes by recognizing just
such an intuition, though his purpose was to show that altruism is not contrary
to the standard theory of action; and, while there may be many attitudes toward
art, the emphasis on what it does to our sense of the world when we lend ourselves to it, when we do not resist it, may, as Foucault seemed to say at the end
of *Madness and Civilization* (1965), be further evidence of the point. If all this
is reasonable, it is also not unreasonable, and perhaps it is necessary as things
stand to say that the objectivity of situated objects can only be conceived of as
subjective—not in the sense of those objects being whatever people say they are,
whatever they construe them to be, or whatever in experience constitutes them
as symbols, but in the logical sense of their being instances of subjectivity and
only able to be designated or indicated as such (which is also to say necessarily
agency-dependent and therefore caught up in internal relations).

Situated objects are all the objects there are for humans conceived of as "beings in a situation." The argument so far suggests that they can be thought of
as *subjective objects* and cannot be thought of as things (only possibly or partly
related to subjectivity). In that case, agency-dependence is not identified with
relations of specific things to specific subjects or with the relevance of distinct
objects to distinct purposes. It is important to keep in mind that *the meaning
of "agency-dependence" has changed from the name of a property of a class of
things to a characterization of their special way of being objective.* However, "dependence," which by itself suggests contingency, now seems misleading. The
idea no longer supports the classification of objects as either one sort of thing or
another and therefore does not allow for an interpretation of *activity* as *action*
(behavior with reasons based in part on evaluations of distinct objects and on
correspondingly accountable results) for which it is possible to interpret individually held reasons as causes and for which justifications that, when properly analyzed, are essentially unambiguous. The subjectivity of situated objects
does not, then, support an analytical separation of action and its reasons from,
on the one hand, objects of beliefs or feelings and, on the other, practices, activities, and mental states that rely on the presence of such objects.

This line of criticism implies that the very concept of action as behavior
with reasons is in jeopardy the moment it is made explicit, and with it the familiar corresponding ideas of specifiable actors as initiators of specifiable
actions, of actions as units or events (in contrast with the idea of a course of
activity), of agency as vested in a distinct personal self, of the essential lack of
ambiguity of self-referring expressions, of the possible sufficiency of a justification according to individually held reasons, of total intentions that characterize
action through and through, of the essential irrelevance of ambivalence (often
conceived of in that light as "weakness of the will"), and so forth. The criticism

relies fundamentally on the ideas that human beings are never outside of society, that human affairs are never not social, and that the conception of sociality derived from the analysis of those propositions entails the further concept of a course of activity (which is a minimal specification of the social aspect of human life). It follows from this that one can conceive of what is done by humans only from the point of view of an internal relation of situated objects and experience in which the analytical distinction between subject and object becomes only occasionally useful. Such a relation is in contrast with the sort of relation in which a relatively stable consciousness comes to be filled for the moment with one relatively stable content or another but remains what it was and "is" through changes in content—where "content" refers to individually constituted representations of objects. To the extent to which this argument is plausible, it jeopardizes individualistic theories of choice and rationality that rely on external relations among ostensibly residual totalities such as actions, objects, mental states, actors, and ostensibly accountable others.

———

There are, then, important consequences of recognizing that the objectivity of situated objects cannot be separate from their being situated, and that a situation cannot be disentangled from the subjectivity of which those very objects are, in one aspect, constitutive and, in another aspect, instances. Agency-dependence is not a property. It now must be said to involve the mutual constitution of subjectivity and objectivity, where the former is essentially situated and, *therefore*, its objects are also essentially situated. The fact that this is not the same objectivity that is ascribed to independently identifiable things suggests that what can be said about independent things cannot be sufficient to describing or making knowledgeable assertions about situated objects. However, it remains difficult to clarify the concept of such objects, and I have argued that the difficulty has to do with the fact that their objectivity cannot be separated from their subjective aspect, which is to say from what they have even in common with the sort of subjectivity typically described as if it is apart from them and of a metaphysically different order. Nevertheless, one can say enough about them to clarify their position in an account of human affairs as social and, in that respect, distinctively human.

Situated objects are, on this account, active in contrast with passive or inert (presumably allowing the product of a perception to be confirmed by some other act of perception). *This is the aspect of their objectivity that requires that we consider the internal relation of subject and object to constitute an encounter of subjectivity with subjectivity, which is to say of a course of activity with a course of activity.* Such an encounter implies, first, that the tensions within and between subject and object are immanent and, second, that in certain theoretically crucial respects the two can be exchanged, one for the other.[13] It also implies that there is no theoretically good reason to assume that the skin is a natural boundary as far as intentionality is concerned. To put this more prosaically, the internal relation of subject and object can be most usefully represented as an instance of *work* rather than performance, practice, or action; and there are two ways in which we can consider the sort of work that corresponds to a theoretical recognition of the internality of the relation of subject and object. It involves, first of all, reciprocity in which subject and object (including others to be taken into account) are interchangeable as far as the tension immanent to their immediate encounter is concerned. That is, the same concepts apply to the one as to the other in accounting for the realization of the internality of their relation. Second, it involves motivations that inevitably arise from the intersection of the mutual demands of subject and object indifferent to any metaphysical distinction between them: the momentarily specific object no less than the ostensibly specific subject displays something on the order of intentionality, and this fact about its other is irresistible to each.

To the extent to which tension is a feature of the internal relation of subject and object, it is a feature of each. In that case, there must be something about the momentarily specifiable object that immediately appears as an instance of subjectivity, beyond whatever characteristics it might have as an independent thing such that an utterly individuated subject might be indifferent to it (and therefore might be said to have chosen or rejected it) or such that it might be irrelevant to the determination of the situation. That is, to the extent to which it is necessary to appreciate the internality of the relation of subject and object, it is necessary to see both as bearing the character of subjectivity. This is also to say that each is as much for the other as it is for itself, and neither can refer to a self-sufficient entity. Yet another way of saying this, though its language is bound to be somewhat misleading, is that within the course of their activity, subjects do not *and cannot* fully distinguish the independent identities of their objects from their own identity in the way observers are thought to do, or in a way that is logically appropriate only to an idealization of the external relations of agency-independent objects. Their apprehension of their object, their grasping of it, must be thought of not only as implicit in the course of their activity, but as actively demanding, resisting, motivated, and so forth—just as the sense of their own momentary independence must be thought of as encompassing the same tendencies. What is misleading about this way of stating the idea has to do with the ambiguity of the expression "their apprehension of their object." This seems to say that the object is merely constructed, directly encountered, or represented arbitrarily (or by habit) by a subject who, *within the course of activity*, might have done otherwise. I have tried to show that, when the idea of a course of activity is properly understood, in contrast with the concept of action, this interpretation is false.

The idea of an internal relation of subject and object requires that the subjectivity of the object is both a necessary and immediate feature of its objectivity—that the difference it makes is unavoidable and irresistible: *but not merely to individuals*. This is not conceivable when that relation is characterized as essentially external; and it cannot be characterized in that way without undoing all that allows us to conceive of human affairs as human and sociality as what is human about them. I have tried to show that the forced attribution of externality produces problems for theory insofar as the latter addresses the question of what is human about human affairs. On the one hand, this requires acknowledging the internality of the relation; and to recognize that the notion of sociality implies the internality of relations is to acknowledge that *subjectivity* is *active in ways it could not be unless its objects were also similarly active, which is to say equally of a course of activity*. The very concept of a course of activity dictates this conclusion.[14] On the other hand, the sorts of ostensibly individuated experience that suggest independence, and therefore externality, cannot be denied: the perception of qualities, for example, is certainly part of every instance of experience attributable to skin-bound individuals. But they cannot be meaningfully placed within the theoretically determinate space in which distinct subjects and their objects are at issue when what is human about human affairs is at issue. One can only say that what is directly relevant to a course of activity is at most only indirectly relevant to what can be said about the intentionality of a subject conceived of as essentially independent (or, in effect, pre-social).

The objectivity of situated objects apparently has to do with the *immanent possibility* of their being ordered in one way and then another and therefore in their presenting order at the outset: the idea of an order that arises or is brought about from the absence of order is not intelligible. Nor is it sufficient to speak of degrees of order (or disorder) since it can always be claimed that what, in human affairs, is said to have a low degree of order is really as much order as what is said to have a high degree (therefore what counts has to do with what it is to speak of degrees and what sort of knowing or constructing agency is implicit in such a claim). It must be said, then, that what is objective about situated objects has to do with their participatory implication in a course of activity. This is an altogether different mode of being from, say, having degrees of probable relevance to potential projects, practices, or goal-oriented actions. This version of inter-subjectivity is radically different in its implications about the nature of situations from contextualist models of interaction among separable (and therefore externally related) persons. It confers on the discursive sense of a situation the metaphorical aspect of a field. This is in contrast to a collection or statistical distribution in which each member-thing is quantified by something like attributed value or preference, or is said to be subject to beliefs about it. The conferred metaphor suggests simultaneity. In that respect, it is illuminated by the suggestion, in Rousseau's reference to the indivisibility of the general will, of a spatial rather than temporal relation among socially constituted equals. Given this, the metaphor suggests what theory requires: a lack of total accessibility to any possible instance of individuality—as in Rousseau's notion of the equality of all individuals in the face of the common dependence of each on all (and not particular) others—interpreted as a first, provisional reference to an inter-subjective course of activity.

How does this bear on our understanding of the momentary instances of ostensibly individuated acts of participation if that participation is not to be understood as directly oriented to what can only be collectively determined or as a precipitate of a field? What, in other words, must be conceived of as the universal attribute of such participation? Following an earlier discussion, this is best understood as *waiting*. This is where recent research on conversational activity has been able to take advantage of a profound suspicion of the distinction between subjects and objects in its emphasis on the collective work of sustaining discourse itself.

As situated, objects immediately reveal themselves to be instances of activity within a subjectivity that reveals itself primarily as *an attitude of waiting*. This is what is seen in an "other" insofar as that "other" is seen as distinctively human. Correspondingly, what is made visibly objective by situated objects is the attitude of waiting that they manifest and that they instigate. That is how their objectivity is displayed. One can say that instigating waiting is how they constitute themselves as objects within a course of activity. A more precise way of saying this is that agency-dependent objects appear immediately as agency-dependent and, therefore, as radically implicated in sociality.

From this point of view, waiting cannot be theorized as something skin-bound individuals do as a matter of being human; it is cooperative by its very nature. It is irreducibly social and therefore, one might say, it is the most generally possible and perfect expression of the general will. Yet, despite always being perfectly participatory, waiting may appear momentarily no less individuated than utterances. That this is momentary is shown by the fact that waiting cannot be conceived of as supporting sociality as such if it is individually intended, as a matter of choice or personal disposition, rather than an inevitable feature of sociality (whatever other intentions might be attached to it and for whatever other purpose it might be described). It seems clear that such a concept of waiting is necessary for clarifying the idea of inter-subjectivity implicit in a concept of sociality understood according to the ideas of a course of activity and agency-dependent objectivity. Characterizing it further involves trying to make it correspond to a sub-theoretical intuition; and this requires referring to attributes and examples beyond the concepts theoretically established as logically necessary to a conception of sociality able to satisfy the conditions of answering the question "What is human about human affairs?"

It may be said that to wait is to be available, but not in the voluntaristic sense of making one's self available; this means that waiting is not occasional, passive, or diffuse. Its focus is inward, by which I mean reflexive to itself, to its possible continuation, to availability as such. In this respect, one might say that it is focused not on specific targets but on the situation as a field. Perhaps the better word is "concentrated" since the point is that the attitude of waiting encompasses sociality in its most general aspect though it cannot be said to be particularly focused. What corresponds to waiting is activity and projectivity. Since it is neither passive nor utterly diffuse, it, like any course of activity, has its own momentum. The objects of such an attitude, if we think of attitudes as courses of activity, are also instances of that very same thing—namely, activity that projects itself, as it were, subjectively. It follows that situations, often thought of nontheoretically or pre-theoretically as agency-independent, must be thought of as only *momentarily* specific and, therefore, as only ostensibly so. In that respect, the term refers to an unsustainable totality that only appears to be limited by the particularity of its momentarily specifiable objects. The appearance of something as complete as situations are typically said to be is, then, belied by the fact that no set of ostensibly situation-comprising objects can be taken apart from the prospect of modifications, reidentifications, additions, and subtractions—in a word, change.

Moreover, since the idea of a situation invokes the sort of "waiting subjectivity" that responds only to an actively subjective objectivity, what it seems to refer to may stand out within that relation as momentarily complete and comprehensive; and it is in that moment that reference to a situation seems to express both longing and a sense of futility, lending a tragic aspect to its ostensible completeness. The tragedy, such as it is, lies in the irreducibly relational fact that the situation constitutes, in the midst of the internality that gives it both life and the appearance of conditions of life, the semblance of an unsustainable totality. Its particularity is merely an appearance that, at the very moment that it seems most complete and therefore most reliable, defeats itself in an unavoidable and momentary implication of a possibility against which it most needs to assert itself—namely, its own subjectivity—for the sake, it must be remembered, of the idea of action in contrast with a course of activity.

From this point of view, "situation" refers not only to something that is virtual—that is, possibly but not potentially complete—but to tragedy itself, since what is only *possibly* complete is also incomplete. The movement back and forth—from completeness that defines subjectivity as its negation to subjectivity for which completeness is a negation—ultimately overwhelms what had momentarily come to notice as a possibility of completion. Consequently, "situation" can only refer, in the sense of *continuing* to refer, to a mere vanishing, the corresponding sense of which is a certain restlessness or tension in all respects and in all moments of the relation of subjectivity and objectivity. This sense cannot sustain unambiguous reference or a judgment that one act of reference is more ambiguous than another; therefore, referring to an object cannot be thought of as if it involves naming something that is incorrigibly "there" (though possibly subject to error or confusion) but which vanishes or might vanish only under certain conditions.

We can now see momentariness as a phenomenological feature of both vanishing objectivity and vanishing subjectivity, where vanishing indicates subjectivity as a course of activity and not as individuated states of mind. It follows that situations are necessarily momentary to the extent to which they are constituted in regard to the internality of the relation of subjectivity and objectivity and, through that, to their own connections to life. By this I mean that the word "situation," used to theorize what is human about human affairs, stands for momentariness, that aspect of subjectivity that always indicates something virtually complete that cannot be complete and that therefore constitutes a phenomenology of situations as vanishing—for example, loss of the definiteness of things, of vantage point and perspective, of meaning, relevance, and so on. In this regard, momentariness can be thought of as the life of appearances within the internal relation of subjectivity and objectivity and the basis of the theoretical capacity to acknowledge inter-subjectivity as a fact about subjects and objects taken separately and together. In acknowledging that, *theory begins to recognize its own implication in its object, which is to say in the internality of the relation of life and situation.*[15]

20

The Positive Sense of "Situation"

I have distinguished between the idea of a situation as internally related to life and the more familiar positive idea of situations as independent entities comprising similarly independent entities. It appears, however, that both lead to the same conclusion, that what is typically considered to be external to subjectivity has a subjective aspect that is an irreducible feature of its objectivity. This chapter considers some implications of this conclusion *insofar as it is implicit in the attempt to maintain a positive conception of "situation."*

We often use the term "situation" in a positive way to refer to what had come to an actor's notice prior to her decision to act and is, in that sense, already there. When I sit with someone at a dining table, the food and utensils are in place and effectively fixed in their qualities and amounts, regardless of whether I have an appetite and regardless of whether my purpose is to eat or to keep someone, say John, company. If I do not initially intend to eat, I may nevertheless feel that I should at least nibble, for example, if John is not to feel awkward while eating in front of me. It might be said, then, that I eventually form an intention to eat (rather than ingest) despite the fact that I initially had no such intention and might still have no appetite. It seems necessary to add that I might always have intended to act in whatever ways might make John comfortable. But that changes nothing. He appears in all this as an element in my situation, as the other that I take into account in what I am doing. Yet the intimacy of the moment—its autonomous aspect—imposes no special effort on me, no need to deliberate, in order to fit into the John-laden situation (including, perhaps, nibbling, making small talk, and the like). It makes a difference in how I see John and what I do and do not do in his company. This cannot be a matter of just taking him into account (as part of my being rational in what I choose to do, as in the standard theory of action) but fitting in to a subjectivity in which differences, such as they are, are subordinate to the course of activity. I do not make a decision to nibble. I nibble by way of being *of* a relation that cannot be represented (even by me or John) as two parties externally connected and therefore essentially independent of one another; it would be equally incorrect, and for the same reason, to say that speaking conversationally involves, fundamentally, making one decision after another to speak. A necessary condition of my *being with John* in the intimately situated manner of consociates is, like conversational discourse, the sort of sociality Rousseau referred to as "the basic fact" understood as a course of activity. To be *in* a situation is to be *of* it in a way that constantly reconstitutes subjectivity across parties who are conceived of as independent only in theory.

The food and utensils and even John's mood and what he is doing are, for the positive sense of "situation," like stage props, certain qualities of which will be significant to what I do but which are independent of qualities that might be significant in another situation. The forks, spoons, and knives are nothing more than indications of how eating is done, though attributes of them derived from other courses of activity may interfere with the momentum of dining together, as when the value of the material of which they are made becomes a topic, thereby disrupting the course of activity. Using them realizes the ongoing character of an activity that is not merely ingesting and that has momentum, call it "John and I dining," where, relative to the activity, John and I are exchangeable features of it. So it must be admitted that there is something different about John from the "props," and this difference threatens to undermine the radical distinction between actor (and action) and situation that positive accounts of situations are normally designed to preserve.

John's mood, possibly assessed in advance, has something of this givenness to the situation and so might be considered one of its material elements. But this is not as simple a matter as it might seem, since mood is inseparable from the person as he is situationally found. Neither John nor his bearing can be thought of as elements of the situation in the sense of being objects identified with their properties. For one thing, my attending him includes being subject to his interests, as it were, following them as they play themselves out. This involves what cannot normally be a matter of choice—namely, waiting on him and not merely anticipating that he will express his interests; and this has to do with his being the John I have known and am with and not, say, any persona I might ascribe to him including his incumbency to a role. We are situated and "interested" together; and this is true for *us* and it cannot be represented as distinct for each individual. This unplanned attitude of waiting on my part immediately distinguishes John as an object for me from the other entities that *appear* to be given as independent objects that happen to comprise my situation at a particular time and in a particular place. In other words, he is immediately apprehended as a subject and not a thing. But it is not the case that the *attitude* of waiting creates the special way in which John is objectively real, since the attitude of waiting is what it is, humanly, to be alive in a situation. It is not something I choose to have or that might or might not be my state of mind. It is a feature of me that is also a feature of him insofar as an outside "observer" might want to consider them from the point of view of their sociality.

I am, I find myself, effectively constituted by him in the sense of being continually surprised in the course of everything that indicates his presence and does so as an indication of my own. The general principle is that one cannot be said to be in the presence of an other without being surprised by all displays of intentionality; and this being surprised is a result of the attitude of waiting that characterizes all that is done in a course of activity. Otherwise, the words "presence" and "another" are meaningless to the study of human affairs as distinctively human. That is, from the retrospect of attributing a point of view to John, I become objective to him in a subjective way. Note that it would be improper to say that I allow myself to be led by what he is doing in the same way that it would be improper to say that I allow myself to play the particular notes of a particular passage of a Bach fugue, since in the playing of the piece I *find myself* playing its notes. If the question "What are we doing?" were to be raised in such a way that an account would be expected, and therefore the parties would suddenly be reconstituted as independently waiting for an answer, the break with the course of action would be experienced not only as a break but as sudden. It would suddenly appear necessary, from a theoretical point of view, to do what the distinction between actor and situation did not initially require—namely, *conceptualize* this relationship between John, on whom I incessantly wait, and me for whom waiting is, in effect, what I am (as far as I can be said to be with the other, as my side of mutual recognition in a situation). I say "suddenly" because the original absolute distinction between actor and situation either anticipates the possibility of an unequivocal classification in which John does not fit or it implies, unacceptably, that we are not in a situation together. To make my knowledge of "John in the situation" theoretically intelligible as internal to the course of activity is impossible for me if it involves positing a desire on my part to take account of John's conduct (and therefore to make my own activity accountable). If I were to see him as something to take into account, I would also be attributing to him—from a position outside of the situation we once shared and, in sharing, became absorbed by it—a particular mental state, thereby setting up a relationship between the positive idea of the situation and the positive idea of the actor. I would also have defined myself apart from the situation we had once shared (and in the sharing had been absorbed by it). Both positions are incompatible with the idea that humans are "beings in a situation." The image I would have created is one in which John's "new" status is "one whose conduct is to be taken into account," in which case I act toward him as an object divorced from the subject I now pretend to be.

What is important in this is that my perception of John as an exception to the absolute distinction between actor and situation fits my own sense of being an exception to that same distinction by way of being the subject engaged in the situation and not merely subjected to it, and by way of being in a course of activity but not merely selecting from among behavioral options. Both John and I are radically different from independent entities only accidentally or voluntaristically conjoined or forced together. In that respect, we appear only as *subjects* in the sense of being involved in, being moments of, courses of activity and not as independent actors executing one intention or another. The fact that each side, each momentary activity, intimately involves the other, and it is necessary that it does, means that conceptualizing the relationship between John and me requires, for theory, that I be taken to know, in that relationship and as crucial to it, what we are doing together as inter-subjective beyond what might otherwise be attributed to each of us as individual persons. However, it must be clear that "inter-subjectivity" is not just a theoretical term. It is that, but it also refers, in our example, to an aspect of my own experience of that relationship, even though "initially" I might have felt certain about the difference between me and my situation and, therefore, between me who is not and John who is *of* the situation. In effectively recognizing John in his difference from the other situated objects, I recognize him not only in regard to what about him makes him recognizable to *me* but in regard to the mutually constitutive activities in which what each of us does seems spontaneous and surprising—rather than contrived—and immediately responsive to the other.

Whatever *we* do—that is, whatever is done together, collectively—occurs in an identifiable way on condition that it move through a course of activity without seeming at all out of place or without seeming to belong to one person or another. "Initiating," then, is not the crucial theoretical issue that it is in the standard theory of action. Examples are as apparently definite as placing food on a fork and as spontaneous as conversing, shifting position, looking at one another, and the like. Each must be seen as a continuation of a course of activity that does not simply arise within one of the parties as an expression of her mental state. In all such instances, *we* are rendering the ostensible distinction between us (one being the subject and the other being the object of "taking account") within an inclusive subjectivity; the difference is, theoretically, not between radically different types of subject or types of components of situations. *In the course of doing something with another, it is the case in principle that subjectivity itself must be taken to operate across the biological barrier of the skin.* This is why my use of "inter-subjectivity" should not be interpreted as synonymous with "interpersonal relations," "interaction," or "negotiation." My relationship with John is, for me-as-situated, a matter of inter-subjectivity and not a matter of materiality in the sense associated with agency-independent objectivity. This is what theory requires if sociality is the distinctively human condition, if the term refers to a course of activity rather than a state of affairs, and, above all, if what is theoretical about theory, self-reflective in it, is its commitment to what is human about human affairs.

In contrast, the positive use of "situation" to mean "an arrangement of otherwise independent objects that are normally taken for granted by some otherwise independent subject (but might come to that subject's specific notice from that very background)" confirms a radical distinction that is necessary in attempting to understand sociality according to a theory of action but, paradoxically, cannot be maintained in its terms. This is the familiar one between what is materially objective and what completes and finalizes the interior subjectivity of the independent actor. The theoretical issue that poses what I believe is a fatally intractable problem for this way of understanding the situated aspect of human activity, as both situated and human, is the notion of a subjectivity that, according to the theory that identifies action as the realization of a state of mind, can project itself successfully only across particular bodies and possibly, therefore, across persons taken as particulars. According to this theory, what is *positively* given or already there as situation for me as a rational actor includes John as an independent particular and a nameable referent. As such, an attitude of waiting on my part would be rationally inappropriate or merely epiphenomenal. Here, the distinction between subject and object must be absolute, and that is how the problem arises: being with another such being in a situation institutes an area of nondeterminacy within what is presumably covered by that distinction; and this challenges the latter's theoretical validity.

If we suspend the distinctiveness of John's presence—the fact that he is distinctively human—we eliminate the possibility of inter-subjectivity. The cost of this may be outweighed by the fact that it appears to ease the problem of understanding what it is to be in a situation. But, as we will see, this is an illusion. *This* "situation" refers to the relationship between an actor and relatively inert things solely from the point of view of an unattached observer of ostensibly independent entities. In that case, it refers to a collection of discrete things taken together (as composing a situation) for which the question of whether they are independent is not an issue (for a rational actor whose rationality depends, say, on evaluating their calculable relevance to her choice). The act of making a choice (as being one who chooses) is logically independent of them, though what it amounts to depends on their properties and the values they appear to represent. Here, subjectivity appears to be reducible to person-specific intentions that correspond strictly to linguistically representable, therefore at least potentially third-person, or public, reasons. Parenthetically, this suggests that the significant fact about any situated relation is the outsider who either has had no experience of it or has left behind whatever experience of it she once had, and, in either case, therefore, cannot be said truly to know it as such.

In passing, to the extent to which this "not being an issue of agency-dependence" is somehow displayed in the course of the actor's having acted, some theoreticians would say that agency-dependence remains a latent issue the evasion of which is an irreducible feature of the activity being observed (see Garfinkel 1967). By and large, however, it is assumed that an actor/person takes account of those things the collection of which forms the concrete totality of his or her situation, and does so in the same calculating and evaluating way regardless of their particular properties (that can be taken across situations) or their history in regard to the history of this actor/person. Given the assumption, properties of those situated objects are likely to be represented by the observer as independent variables in the individual's decision making; and that same observer takes them into account as if they are experienced as similarly fixed. The actor/agent then becomes a theoretical point of origin in which the conditions of rational decision are consolidated in an orderly set or series of reasons and representations of conditions. This presumably accounts for the subject's action in choosing and how that action can be accountable to a detached observer and, prospectively or retrospectively, to (and by) the subject herself.

All this depends on being able to isolate something called "action," to distinguish among situated objects according to independently objective principles, and to account for all that is important about the subjective aspect of action in terms of person-specific intentions strictly defined and determined by specifiable elements of the situation mediated by mental facts. The relationship between subjectivity and situation so conceived involves the interaction of variables; an additional person is nothing more than another situated object, though doubtless something more complex than the other such objects that comprise the actor/person's situation. For this to work, however, one must actively dis-attend to what I have been referring to as the course of activity entailed by the concept of action itself, a movement that lies between ostensible conditions and results or effects. Attending to it effectively undermines assumptions that are essential to the positive view—namely, that subjects and objects are ontologically independent, and that subjectivity has to do fundamentally with the rational adaptation of an actor to facts according to prior expectations and gradable value-determined preferences (or susceptibility to just such norms).

Those assumptions are weakened whenever it becomes necessary to account for the coherence of a situation beyond the mere coincidence of things, to allow for at least some distinction between persons and things that involves more than complexity and a similar distinction between things and situated objects, and to acknowledge the shifting identities of such objects in the course of the activity to which they appear relevant or in which they are otherwise implicated. Under those circumstances, subjectivity appears less independent and situated objects appear less discrete than the technical account of the situation originally allowed. Above all, the stipulated presence of someone else is bound to unsettle the idea that we take account of another in the same way that we take account of other objects in our situation, objects that are radically opposed to subjects. Of course, *there cannot be the presence of a distinct other where there is no relief from the foundational dependence of each on all.*

Like the first version of "situation" discussed previously, this also requires a degree of certainty about the constitution of subjectivity and about the distinction between it and situated objects that can be neither justified nor realized. To that extent questions unavoidably arise about the assumptions that the skin is a natural boundary, that objects are independent of one another, and that the concrete particularity of the actor/person is adequate to what is intended by the concept of a subject. In these respects, it also opens up two unexpected possibilities: first, that subjectivity is a constitutive feature of every situated object and, second, that such objects resemble subjects to the extent to which the latter can be said to be "their subjects." It is enough at this point to note that something now seems possible that was not possible until the non-positive idea of a course of activity made itself felt as implicit in the positive idea of a situation.

Each positive conception of the situation entails an external relation of subjectivity and objectivity sufficient to account for those ostensibly objective manifestations of intentionality referred to by most philosophers as acts or actions.[1] To that extent, before it proved impossible to guarantee the distinction between subject and object that they presuppose, both conceptions justify the following hypotheses that I have been arguing are plausible but unacceptable as things stand. *First*, there is no good reason to consider any more expansive a notion of the subjectivity involved in situations than that of a person-specific mental state. The latter is, in principle, objective in the same limited sense that concrete objects are said to be objective—which is to say that they can be identified by universal properties—and represented accordingly. Indeed, there is good reason to reject any more expansive a notion of subjectivity than that of a mental state or condition. A corollary is that the key to understanding the relationship between life and situation is to characterize it as a relationship between independent objects and independent subjects such that subjects can be said to take account of the objects they find in ways that can vary but nevertheless leave the identities of those objects intact. *Second*, there is no valid justification for denying the essentially independent and incorrigible objectivity of the referent of "situation." In that case, a subject is said to be able to take account of a situation as a totality, and to do so in the sense that her relationship to it is external and contingent rather than internal and mutually constitutive: she can never truly be lost in (subjective to) a situation, and therefore there is no need to consider the course of activity as such. It is, then, a fact that situations remain self-identical across subjects, or at least for any given subject taken as self-identical over time, and that subjects must be thought of as remaining self-identical across situations. Situations can modify subjects and subjects can modify their situations, though the former are essentially inert or passive and the latter essentially active and receptive. The key is to understand the different modes of change involved: situations are (possible) conditions of possible actions while the mental states of subjects function as causes having (at least) situated effects (e.g., reasons that operate as causes of action and that invariably exceed the conditions to which they respond). *Third*, relying theoretically on the independence of subjects and the incorrigible objectivity of objects gives a sense of necessity to the proposition that referring to inter-subjectivity is an anachronism of folk psychology. In that case, "inter-subjectivity" is best defined as the behavior of independent persons in regard to conditions that include the presence of objective others and in that sense involve taking others into account.

Taken together, these hypotheses, and the view that supports them, holds that subjectivity refers, at most, to mental states that are positively objective, though possibly only privately accessible, and prior to or correlated with action conceived of without regard to the idea of a course of activity.[2] What is left of the idea of a situation is something independently objective, consisting of independently objective things. The extent to which any one of those turns out to be agency-dependent lies only in the fact that at least one of its properties points to something (involving people) beyond the mere self-identity indicated by its being agency-independent. This in no way compromises the independence of its identity relative to other objects and to specific (or apparently situated) subjects. What remains of the idea of a situated object is a thing that is only momentarily in place and, in that respect, has come into an arbitrarily assigned status among other objects according to criteria such as usefulness, utility, or relevance: the arbitrariness of the assignment has to do with the fact that it corresponds to an attitude and not to something about the object as such. That is, what remain are objects altogether inessential to subjectivity. Their definiteness depends on their possessing universal properties and not on the constitution of their momentary objectivity within courses of activity in which they are themselves constitutive features. From this point of view, such definite objects are conceived of as instances of a plurality of just such definite things that, taken in combination, comprise an objective situation in regard to which certain situationally responsive person-specific mental states operate, somewhat mysteriously, as reasons (e.g., for action).

***

In pursuing this positive strategy for theorizing the relationship between life and situation, and the distinctions on which it depends, we may decide that at least some of the problems that arise, say about inter-subjectivity, have to do with treating units of analysis in an overly particularistic way. One way of redressing this without sacrificing the strategy begins with the idea that what people do in situations derives from or is limited by how they see the situation as a whole, beyond what might be suggested by its components when they are taken by themselves or in series, one by one. While this may limit, and possibly vitiate, application of the utilitarian calculus, it seems to offer a way out of one dilemma of action theory: if actions are particulars, there appears to be a theoretically fatal gap between them and the causes (e.g., reasons) that are said to operate at the level of intentionality at which they are conceived of as particulars. We might, then, think of a situation as a context organizing certain meanings that determine what is expressed, what is otherwise done, how self-reference (e.g., the use of "I" or "we") is interpreted, and so on. This involves acknowledging that what holds the objective components of situations together is not the simple and ordered confluence of things, accidental, structured, or contrived, but a sense of something totalizing that goes beyond what might logically or empirically connect its individual elements, and beyond what can be determined by any person on his or her own. In this respect, agents do not construct their situations but find themselves as situated beings. This proves problematic to the sufficiency of the positive strategy to the extent that it requires a transcendental notion of situation. Even so, it provides for a holistic theory of action that at least mutes the radical distinction between subjects and objects and that brings something like inter-subjectivity into an account of the meaningfulness of anything done as an instance or part of a practice, and, possibly, where most of what is done can be understood as an instance or part of a practice. Its success to any degree will, however, depend on clarifying the concept of a system of rules and on showing that what people do together can be generally understood as participating spontaneously in practices.

Just as we often cannot state a rule for specifying what constitutes membership in a category, though we nevertheless make the determination, we can identify ways in which a given situation invokes, modifies, or restricts types of action or makes certain acts and expressions inappropriate or otherwise unacceptable. For example, one situation may convey warmth, another coldness, one may be formal and another informal, one may be about something else (transient or symbolic) and another as non-referential in that respect. Moreover, certain values might be assigned to a situation even though it is not possible to specify those values simply as the sum or average of the values associated with its discrete elements. The appearance of certain features may also give weight to gestures, acts, or utterances that otherwise have different weights or no specifiable weight at all. In all these cases, it is necessary to think of a particular utterance or bodily movement as part, or an instance, of something greater—for example, a practice.[3]

Perhaps the best way to think positively about the idea of a situation is, then, to shift from an emphasis on discrete actions, which are defined largely by their reason(s) and to some extent by the meanings that are attributed to their results, to the idea of a practice, which may be a sufficiently nonreductive notion to preserve the idea of a being in a situation and to distinguish it from the idea of a being among specific objects. For this, everything hinges on how a practice is shown to be a subsuming totality, possibly a structure, how agents know practices, and how a practice is connected to its enabling situations, general or specific. The discussion in Chapter 21 suggests that the idea of a practice, as described, fails to meet the challenge posed by the notion of a course of activity irreducible to what individuals think, intend, or undertake.

21

Practices, Situations, and Inter-subjectivity

Practices are often identified theoretically as institutional facts that are internal features of society distinguished particularly from arbitrary, momentary, statistically prevalent, or purely spontaneous activities or activities instigated by external facts. Examples often given of the latter are fads, riots, moral panics, reactions to surveillance, coercion, and/or deception, and a form of social movement that bears a relation to its society in some respects but that is classically said to be independent of the organizational principles of that society. Certainly, more is needed to connect practices thought of as top-down ordering principles to the idea of a situation, if the idea is to be relevant to a theory that links what people do to situated intentionality—and I have tried to show that it is impossible to do that on the assumption that the skin is a natural boundary of agency. However, for the moment, it is worth considering how a practice might appear without that qualification.

An institutional fact is usually thought of as a historically validated and relatively durable set of collectively meaningful expectations and/or obligations. Theories of such facts generally conceive of them holistically and as falling under the warrant of values that constitute "conditions of rational action." From the point of view of a system of such values, the sense of the term "value" in this formulation is somewhat different from ordinary usage in that institution-constituting values are identified with a logically limited number of historically articulated types of condition necessary for a collectivity to function as an adaptive, self-regulating system of action and, therefore, as a society. A logical limitation has to do with the identification of society as a form of life and an analysis of the latter in regard to two sets of necessary conditions. In the Parsonian scheme, these have to do with a system's relations with its environment (e.g., economy and polity) and the problems of maintaining system "identity" ("boundary maintenance") and the cooperative mechanisms of "integration" that provide for joint action. There are, of course, ambiguous cases, but these may pose problems of application rather than substance; their existence does not bear on the theoretical significance of identifying a practice as an institutional fact that has to do with the profound idea that sociality is an immanent feature of action necessary to its rationality.

The connection formed by the concept of a practice, between particular moments of agency (e.g., self-determined actions constrained by and committed to rules) and institutional facts, is helpful only if an institutional fact is conceived of in terms of a total institutional structure. In that case, it is the structure as a whole that makes rules "rules," allowing actions to be meaningful across all particular wills. A theory of action that incorporates the idea that a practice is an institutional fact depends on "society" referring to an entity composed of institutional facts and systematically functional relations among them. Such an entity cannot be the object of any person's experience and, therefore, cannot be said to be known to anyone in particular in the way we are said to be able to know such things as agency-independent objects of experience, abstract objects, or objects constituted linguistically. Society is conceived of as an autonomous form of intentionality that transcends particular wills.[1] It has its own dialectic and its own essential reflexivity. It is in this regard that social facts appear, as Durkheim (1966) said, to be "things" that resist every person's will and in that sense are "coercive." If the idea of a practice depends on the idea of an institution, by virtue of a necessary reference to rules, then it follows that something like "constitutive rules" define what it is to do something in a way that can be recognized by strangers who are also members (see Searle 1969, 33)[2] and that are not necessarily "regulative" (addressed to individual instances of conduct and not necessarily institutional facts derived from an institutional system). Rules that are institutional facts (and constitute a practice as an instance of such a fact) presuppose, then, a system in an environment of other systems that superintends the realization of particularly defined, generally significant fields of conduct—values in the sense discussed earlier.

The idea that most actions can be represented sociologically as elements or manifestations of a practice allows for a degree of regularity in social life independent of momentary exigencies and generally indifferent to the specific intentions of specific psychological individuals. In this respect, it does not require assuming that the skin is a natural boundary of agency. This depends on a logical connection between the rules constituting a specific practice (independent of situation) and an inclusive value identified with at least one societal institution and, through that, with society conceived of as an interactive system of institutional relations. Rawls refers to this as a "social structure" and thinks of it as the fundamental reality in regard to which a general theory of justice can be conceived.[3]

In certain respects, the philosophical concept of a practice loosely summarizes what sociological theory refers to as internally related, or "interpenetrating," roles and analyzes as essentially complementary in the type of durable and self-sustaining social arrangement identifiable as a group or society. But, as indicated previously, the distinction between constitutive and regulative rules seems misapplied in the case of institutional facts. It is only from the point of view of an individual member that certain rules, as a species of social fact, can be said to be regulative (and not merely demonstrative) or constitutive (aimed at constraining action or aimed at confirming the meaningfulness of what is done). The distinction appeals to the consciousness of individualized agents who are presumably trying to do things in situations for which regulation is a necessary feature, and trying to do them in recognizably meaningful ways. On the contrary, from the point of view of society, the rules governing institutional facts are constitutive in the sense of reflexive to values *and* demonstrative in the sense of self-confirming or reflexive to the wholeness of the system; and they perform those functions for an entity that has no psychology though it exhibits an intentionality or principle of motion all its own and appropriate to its environment. To the extent to which the original distinction is theoretically useful, the regulative function is part of the socialization of members. It has to do with the reliability of what might be called momentary performances *of* society, and is in this sense demonstrative, while the constitutive function has to do with the reflexivity of whatever is done to the conditions of its being meaningfully done, meaningful to anyone legitimately a member.

From this point of view, several things distinguish a practice from other social facts. First, the possibility of its being realized in particular situations is a constitutive feature of it, whether or not a particular intention is actually realized. This a priori possibility, independent of probability, may be what provides a practice with its extra-systemic aspect of obligation. Second, the only situations in which it can be *realized* are those that impose their own reasons on thought and action apart from reasons derived from the societally determined rules and content of the particular practice at issue. That is, given that a practice is an institutional fact, its rules and content cannot be sufficient to its realization. One can conclude that the constitutive feature of *possibly* being realized is qualified by another such feature, which is that the rules that define a practice cannot be sufficient to its fulfillment as an institutional fact. Without appropriate situations, there is no practice in the sense of a realizable routine that implements a value and is, in that respect, meaningful. Third, in regard to the immanence of the *possibility* of its being realized in particular *and* the *impossibility* of its being realized solely in terms of its own rules, a practice necessarily invokes society as a virtual totality that is both an immediate source of certain indispensable values and a basic value or good in itself.[4] A different way of saying this is that the idea of a rule-governed practice (where rules are conceived of as institutional facts) is intelligible only on condition of the idea of a social system.

In regard to the last point, practices can be considered institutional facts only in connection with two other ideas: (1) such facts are constitutive parts of a society, or parts or instances of constitutive parts, and (2) whatever can be thought of as a society must be an entity systematically composed of just such facts, and must be conceived of as a form of life that depends on what, on my reading of *The Social Contract*, Rousseau claimed to be a basic and irreducible fact—namely, that all instances of human intentionality are, as things stand, only knowable as such as reflexive to an indefinite and irreducible sociality. The surprising result, for this sort of theory, is that anything that can be called a practice has or is necessarily construed to have a distinctly extra-local and extra-systemic aspect of reference in which all objects engaged in the execution of the practice are inter-subjectively related to the conduct identified with it— and, therefore, are in that respect constitutive. That is, all referents that arise within a practice are both societally reflexive and reflexive to *agency-dependent* objectivity. In referring to such objectivities, a practice, in its being done, necessarily refers to itself; and that is what is most interesting about it since that seems incompatible with the idea of a practice as rule-governed in the sense intended by Rawls, among others.

Another way of saying this is that an instance of conduct is properly identified as an instance of a practice, which is also to say of practice in general, only on condition that it show itself to be (is for good reason interpretable as) organized by an irreducible purpose that is a constitutive value of the intentionality of all such instances (to the extent to which it is a necessary condition of society)—to a sense of obligation to others in general that all possible members must be held to have beyond what can be attributed to them as particular traits or desires, and that extends beyond the immediacy of a given situation to the universe of sociality shared with those recognizably societal others. This conclusion, which is a momentary result of considering the idea of a practice as an institutional fact in order to address certain limitations of the theory of action, returns us to our original analysis of sociality and to the idea of the dependence of each on all as a basic fact.[5]

The aim of this discussion is to provide another, and last, test of the positive notion of a situation—therefore, for a positive theory of action as the basis of a theory of the social. It defines social action in terms of the idea of a practice rather than as autonomous individualized behavior with reasons some of which involve taking account of others. This allows for a notion of a situation that is not fatally particularized in regard to what is being done by individuals in the presence of others or in regard to how others might be taken into account. If our sense of human beings is that they are essentially social, and if sociality cannot be reduced to what individuals do or take the form of a unitary instance of agency, then what people do cannot be represented in general by the individualistic notion of action. The idea of a practice seems to be a good candidate for the idea of an irreducible sociality since it embodies something crucial about what people do (namely, that doing is immanently social) and since it does not require that the skin be a natural boundary to agency or that agency be vested exclusively in individual persons.

When activity is thought of as organized by practices, the relationship between a practice and its situation appears to overcome at least some of the problems of a more individualistic notion of action for connecting what people do with what they must be taken to be doing if what they are doing is an instance of human affairs—by providing at the outset a social aspect to what is done. The idea of a practice momentarily appears to fill this need. My intention in discussing this possibility further is to show how this final defense of the positive notion of a situation, where individuated acts are acts for a practice-oriented situation, either leaves us without a notion of human affairs adequate to a theory of what people do together or provides one that contradicts some part of what is required for such a notion. My discussion focuses on what is entailed as "situation" by the idea of a practice, in order to see whether that might provide a way of building further on the idea that actions are immanently social. It should become clear that emphasis on practices also contributes to the separation of agency from the idea of the skin as a natural boundary, whatever problems it might otherwise have.

———

U nder this conception, everything properly referred to as a practice is fully part of what is properly referred to as a society. For what follows, a theoretically weak notion of society is adopted, one that expresses a popular use of the term as found in introductory sociology texts. For something to be a practice it must be an object of some degree of consensus about what is likely to be accomplished (or what has been or is being accomplished) jointly (among people) by certain gestures, expressions, or lines of action; and it must be meaningful within that consensus according to two criteria: (1) that the relevant behaviors are immediately seen as invoking a specific non-indexical purpose that can only be shared at large and that therefore requires cooperation if it is to be realized in a practice, and (2) that such a purpose can be perceived immediately as having to do with a value that transcends all immediate situations and their parties. From this point of view, a practice is an institutional fact for the weak conception of society based on a pre-theoretical idea of "consensus." It follows that practices and the institutional facts they are said to manifest are ultimately matters of convention rather than social function. Parenthetically, it seems in this regard that the "social" basis of convention is presumably different from the "social" basis of the order-constituting functional relations of practices that presumably carry the weight of consensus, and it is not clear how the difference can be theorized without undoing the conception of society as founded on agreement. Peter Berger and Thomas Luckmann's (1966) account of the "social construction of reality" assumes that the formation of institutions is essentially a process of trickling up from behavioral routines that gradually take on normative force as the bases of institutions and therefore society. To my knowledge, there have been no successful attempts to theorize the trickle-up process, and it ultimately rests on a mix of individualism and localism that, as we have seen, cannot provide for any idea of the social beyond isolated face-to-face encounters assumed to constitute, through their own mechanisms, more enduring and coherent social formations. In order to bring in a more inclusive idea of society, this notion of the formation of social reality is ultimately forced to bring in a mechanism at the top that works back against the very process by which the top, the institutional structure, was presumably constituted: despite itself, it becomes a theory of control disguised as a theory of individual and local freedom.

We have seen how the weak sense of society cannot avoid appealing to the very strong sense it was intended to challenge, one in which the structure ideally determines the individuals who, by virtue of their "socialization," comprise its membership. But the latter is not immune to a similar criticism. It invokes as its own contradiction the very process that Berger and Luckmann wished to take as the foundation of society. Each conception implies the other but is unable to include it in a theoretically plausible way. For the moment, I assume the weak sense, and what I take to be its most plausible implications, because it may still be more tempting to begin to theorize society from the point of view of self-conscious intending human beings rather than from the point of view of the social itself, despite the problems involved in realizing the former as a comprehensive theoretical program without contradicting its premises. This is the temptation that I have challenged in various ways throughout this book.

It is in this regard that reference to a situation makes a difference to the idea of a practice, at least that a practice cannot be reduced to a generalizable structure and that its behavioral features cannot be understood apart from the settings in which they have the sort of moral force that is implicit in the idea of an institutional fact (taken as a matter of convention).[6] Indeed, it is conceived of as a quintessentially situated activity because it can be realized only in connection with specific others or as a product of its situation. That we ordinarily do see a promise in expressions such as "I promise X" does not adversely affect this point (and, indeed, enables it), since what is at issue in the idea of a practice cannot merely be the form or structure of its expressions.

What is at issue is its meaning insofar as something can be an instance of a practice only if it is meaningfully received as such. This requires that it be constitutively situated since meaning in discursive language always has a situationally indexical aspect. One point is that the idea of a practice as normative precludes separating it from its instances. Therefore, to speak of a practice as justifiable apart from its instances may beg the question of whether the logic of instantiation is relevant to understanding the logic of the practice. An affirmative answer seems to confuse the instance of the practice with the practice as such, a confusion Rawls (1999b) hoped to dispel in his classical discussion of the relationship between practices and rules. Let us suppose for the moment that it is not liable to that confusion, and that the relation of a practice to its instances needs to be examined for the possibility that the distinction cannot be made radical enough to support the further distinction between rules and therefore types of justification. One possible conclusion is that for something (e.g., an expression, an act, or an utterance) to be considered an instance of a practice, it must instate something that started before it did and that will have ended sometime after it is done; and the difference between those two times can, from the perspective of the actor, vary in principle from virtual zero to virtual infinity. If so, then no definite behavior or expression can in itself instantiate a practice, though it can instantiate a sense of obligation; and a practice is, in principle, neither definable nor sufficiently indicated to account for consequences by any specifiable collection of specific behaviors or expressions. I believe that this is so both for the weak and the strong versions of "institutional fact," as convention or system function, though whether this is correct is not crucial to the argument.

Consider the hypothesis that to give an example of a practice is to narrate conditions under which specific gestures, utterances, and the like appear, as it were allegorically, as approximations of an ideal type. Those conditions are not conditions of the practice. They have to do with the situation in which the idea of a practice gives force to a certain interpretation; hence standards of justification are necessarily qualified by the facts of the given instance. But the practice itself cannot be taken to be an institutional fact without a theory or idea of a universe of institutions. Therefore, its justification goes beyond a canonical listing and comparing of reasons. To hold onto the idea, I might have to say that to justify a practice is not merely to give reasons in the usual sense (what it generally might accomplish, why anyone ought to approve of it, etc.), but to establish its fit to other, possibly more inclusive practices, ultimately to society as Rousseau's "most basic right" (see also Blum and McHugh 1984). In that case, justifying an action that instantiates a practice and justifying the practice itself are not necessarily distinct acts of justification.

To justify a practice according to the societal purpose or function of the rules that define it is occasionally thought to require momentary indifference to the instance or case, just as attempting to rationalize a given instance or case always requires an appeal to more than a single practice. At the least, it must be admitted that no practice is brought into play unequivocally by a single case and that no case is an unequivocal instance of a given practice. Rules that define a practice must, by the very conception of a rule, apply to more than one case; and since every case differs in moral respects from every other, no single case is exhaustively governed by the rules that are said to define any particular practice, even one that might be said to be its instance. At the same time, the practical validity of the rules requires that they allow for distinctions among different practices. So one might say that justifying the practice of judicially administered punishment, by appealing to the greater good of society at the *possible* expense of what is otherwise fair or morally appropriate in the specific case, is not the same as claiming that special features of the case make it irrelevant to deciding the validity of the practice as such. Rather, the justification itself should be understood as a matter of relative emphasis rather than a dogma—recognizing this is as merely one practice among and in connection with others such that the case must be thought of in terms of more than one set of rules. It is a corollary of this view that the justification of any practice in regard to the greater good includes a justification of not only the specific rules that define the practice but the meta-rules that fit it into a universe of practices that can be said to benefit society and that are, from the point of view of the individual, virtually limitless, unless they simply fail to conform to a rational standard.

This is how the classically utilitarian defense of torture in the aftermath of the destruction of the World Trade Center on September 11, 2001,[7] was able to satisfy even some humanists who oppose torture as a matter of principle—though I am not as confident as I would like to be in the following explanation (which is, in any case, a fairly common one). The defense claims an exception where a certain risk to society is unacceptable no matter how unlikely its occurrence and whatever risks might be involved in momentarily suspending one or another humanist principle. The exception draws a line between acceptable and unacceptable risks (that may or may not involve a calculus combining probability and qualitative aspects of possible loss) in a way that allows the moral question to be decided without further time- and energy-consuming discussion—where "being able to discuss further" is itself considered a matter of principle but one that is trumped by the exceptional circumstances of the case. In this respect, the defense of torture presents itself as a defense of humanism under conditions that justify a legitimate exception to a particular principle in the name of maintaining a principled state of normalcy in which the individual is the "ultimate claimant of moral discourse" such that without that idea moral discourse fails to be moral. From this point of view, those who, like me, would like to reject torture absolutely on humanist grounds betray humanism by failing to consider other equally important principles and therefore the set of principles that comprise a comprehensive humanism for which the idea of a possible exception is itself a principle in recognition of the further principle that every problematic case requires deliberation to determine in what respect it might present a principled need for an exception to at least one other principle. In other words, it would be a rare case that put no strain on a set of general principles whose own virtue lies in the generality of each principle and, therefore, on a high probability of conflict among them. Parenthetically, a more theoretically astute criticism might be less reliant on an attempt to limit what can be said on behalf of utilitarianism according to a distinction between cases and practices, instants and institutions, and then to offer a compromise based on the good sense of balancing the welfare of individuals with that of society (conceived of as "the many"). If, as argued previously, practice (systems of rules) and case (a momentary situation requiring application) are not as distinct as that argument requires, a criticism of torture, no less than its defense, might have to consider institutional facts on a different model from that of regular, justifiable, and recognized rule-governed performance—perhaps in regard to power, authority, and interests that motivate the use of power but have no necessary or "institutional" connection to the interest of the many or of society, or in terms of what is *distinctively human* about human life (which is where the problem of morality arises).

There are several points to this discussion. One is the defense of nondogmatic utilitarianism according to the distinction between a rational-legal institutionally determinate practice, such as judicial punishment, and a case in which priorities among principles may have momentarily to be settled according to what poses the problem of a possible exception. But the problems posed by torture are not germane to a conception of practice in coming to terms with what is distinctively human about human affairs, which is what is here at stake. The reason is not that such apparently nonpolitical practices are relatively free of power and particular will but that they can be conceived of only as intrinsically social and, therefore, cannot lend themselves to the sort of analysis that requires of each that it be taken as isolated in significant ways from all others and that it be possible to rely on a clear enough separation of justificatory standards for the practice and the instance to allow one to think of the latter as given its order by the former in the powerful way usually attributed to the effectiveness of rules in regard to conduct.

Finally, the notion of rules is, in this connection, and subject to what is argued in the next section, vague or self-defeating. In order to sustain the applicability of the concept of a practice, it is necessary to invoke an idea of a situation that is suited to the standard concept of action in a way that only hints at the possibility of bringing into play the idea of a course of activity. This further exacerbates the problems involved in referring to practices as a way of reconciling what people do among and with each other with why they do it—and doing so according to a concept (practice) that seems to lend itself to analysis more easily than the idea of a course of activity.

———

These considerations suggest that an emphasis on individuated expressions, gestures, or acts cannot be justified without an appeal to social settings including, in some cases, the possible justification of practices that such expressions, gestures, or acts may be taken to exemplify or instantiate. The problem for this argument is that such settings are treated as unitary particulars. In that case they can be identified relative to other such settings and must be taken to have their own more inclusive settings. This compromises the independence they must have if it is to be possible to connect instances of practices with conditions that uniquely invoke those practices. Moreover, if the justification of a practice requires reference to possible implementations or instances, therefore to expanded or alternative sets of rules, then no attempted justification can be valid without that reference, even if it is coherent in itself or otherwise seems plausible. In other words, absent the *deus ex machina* of convention or the state, there is no justification of a practice that is not also a justification of possible actions that might fall under it and, therefore, an acknowledgment of possible exceptions. But, while it seems sufficient to say that a practice without a qualifying justification cannot have the force of a practice, it is more accurate to say that it cannot *be* a practice. It is clear that something is not a practice, in the sense of a system of rules meant to be applied according to some value determination or generalizable consensus, if it cannot be justified—that is, if it lacks the element of value—and this element is meaningful as "value" only in light of possible instances and therefore possible exceptions. If what purports to justify a practice cannot justify variations, exceptions, interference among rules, and the like, whatever is thereby justified is not a practice.

For example, imagine a system of rules and a context in which that system can be recognized as imposing obligations on certain parties. The mere fact that it is recognized as such, and for reasons, does not constitute a sufficient justification unless such recognition includes reference to possible cases each of which might be governed by other principles as well or a yet more inclusive principle (or rule or set of rules), and therefore includes reference to those principles as well. That is, in recognizing something as a practice one is also, at the same time, recognizing possible applications such that the good of the practice cannot be independent of how its validity is to be considered in light of other principles or rules that might be inseparable from the cases projected as instances: the multiplicity of such practices in a given case raises questions about whether what appear to be rules can be understood or treated as rules, or whether what appear to be practices are sufficiently self-contained that "ideal typical" behavior of the sort projected by the idea that practices are independent can be validly described as such. Thus, the formal practice of judicial punishment is not well justified without reference to circumstances, mental states, equities, and the like, each of which invokes something like rules, that are bound to accompany critical instances of connecting judgments of guilt to final dispositions of the guilty. Without reference to possible cases, an attempt to justify punishment in the abstract is likely to be too general to make a significant difference in the concrete case or is not intelligible as a justification of the practice.

Moreover, if the setting is compromised in which instances are to be interpreted as instances of a practice, as it often is, it becomes difficult and perhaps impossible to decide whether what is going on is indeed an instance of a particular practice. The point is that hypothetical cases are not just ways of clarifying a practice; reference to them is part and parcel of justifying it. Justifying a practice means not only specifying general criteria that it satisfies but specifying in what sense it is indeed practical as a societally relevant institutional fact rather than something else. The problem is one of definition and not one of complexity. Yet it remains, as a practical matter, that we sometimes rely on the literal meaning and technical organization of an expression, taken by itself as if it could be understood apart from other expressions, when we assess its significance—as in the arrangements of words that constitute instances of a promise, assuming we are right to consider promising a practice in Rawls's sense. "As a practical matter" may have more to do with going on than with accomplishing a task or making explicit, repeatable sense. There is no question that the ordinary reliance on what might appear to an observer to be literal meaning or obvious form is of heuristic value for the observer/analyst, if the latter's point of view can be fit to the notion of "ordinary reliance." But ease or convenience should not dictate the course of analysis or its anticipated range of possible conclusions. Reliance on what is literal and/or obvious violates two principles of the analysis of discursive speech: that what is spoken may not be what is said, and that what is said discursively (therefore actually "said") is always in significant respects irreducibly ambiguous.[8]

The determination of what, in most instances of speaking together, constitutes a unit of meaning is itself an "ongoing accomplishment" and not just a matter of what is or is not independently real. There are, no doubt, occasions in which what constitutes a unit and its meaning are unproblematic. But it is doubtful that unitariness is generally unproblematic in discursive speech. Even if it were generally unproblematic, we would not be relieved of the critical obligation to see whether the assumptions about the unitariness of certain utterances or gestures or acts (such that they might be considered to form an instance of one practice or another) are valid. If unitariness is ordinarily problematic, then the use of static models to clarify the social significance of behaviors, including those that appear to indicate or be related to practices, is bound to be misleading, as is, I believe, fairly clear in regard to discursive speech (see, for example, Sacks 1974). This is especially so when an issue has arisen as to whether an utterance or gesture or activity constitutes the performance of a practice rather than, say, conveying information or expressing an attitude or a feeling; and it is here that analysis cannot do without phenomenology.[9]

That the literal meanings of the words and their sentences might be made clear for all momentarily practical purposes does not provide a basis for a general theory of what it is to instantiate a practice, say promising, and, then, what it is to justify holding the promisor to his or her promise. Reference to a situation does not merely make a difference in the force of an expression; it makes a difference in what it is in fact—where "in fact" has to do with the internal life of discursive communication. Another way of saying this is that referring to a situation makes a difference in whether gestures, expressions, and so forth are held to be distinct in a way that allows them to be considered as references to units of *experience* such that they can be units of the sort of *analysis* that hopes to enlighten experience; and it seems, so far, that the concept of a situation necessary to retain the sense of an internal relation of life and situation generally does not allow for such unalloyed unitary experiences or objects of analysis. Parenthetically, whatever privilege one might wish to give first-person testimony or memory, it too is theoretically problematic in ways that raise the same difficult questions.

We can, however, retain unitariness if we take "situation" to refer to facts that uniquely invoke the legitimacy of certain practices; and perhaps the term should be restricted to the contexts of acts that are already believed to instantiate practices. This is not just circular, since it says that practices must be identified prior to the situations in which they might be realized and that they pick out facts in that situation that are appropriate to deciding whether the putative practice is justifiable relative to the situation at hand. Regardless of what might be said in defense or criticism of this move, it seems to go beyond Rawls's restrictive definition of "practice" as an activity specified by a system of rules to a notion that includes the idea that a practice is accountable to specific circumstances that have to do with its obligatory aspect and with local determinants of order that might or might not be systematic. This does not mean that rules are irrelevant or that there are not institutional facts at work—just that neither illuminate the practice aspect of a practice. For example, for words to do things, they must be able to be done, and for rules to regularize behavior, they must carry the weight of an obligation; and that cannot be conceived of as given by an institutional structure. No matter how one tries to correct the concept in order to take account of the necessary element of situation, one arrives at the conclusion that a practice and its instances cannot easily be separated conceptually and that discursive speech cannot be understood as made up of or as significantly comprising practices (including doing things with words) in Rawls's sense of essentially institutional facts. In that case, many expressions that do not seem to have the structure or form of a performance may turn out in fact to be performances of something already taken for granted[10]—if one extends the idea of a structure of, say, an expression beyond the ideas that it is determined by the grammar of a particular set of words comprising the elements of the utterance: on the arguable assumptions that grammatical form is the natural form in which expressions have meaning, that the sentence is the natural unit for the analysis of meaning, and that the analysis of meaning refers primarily to an assessment of formal features of usage across significant situations—situations for which at least some practical obligations and possibly parts of all such obligations are ongoing accomplishments of an inter-subjective course of activity.[11]

At least the third assumption need not be rejected if the situation is to be taken into account. In that case "practice" will mean more than an institutional fact, and we will have to admit that it appeared to be such a fact not because of what it is but because, for historical reasons, its name invokes the idea of a specific set of rules, as it were idealistically. It follows that a practice defined in terms of rules that are institutional facts provides far less guidance than is desired for one's own actions and even less for understanding another's behavior; but, as with some applications of Weber's concept of the ideal type, it can provide an observer with reasons for judging behavior as if the ideal is a template of the good, and in this regard it can be conveniently appropriated not only to a critical disposition but to purposes that are ideological and authoritarian. The point is that the practice-instance distinction can be preserved, though only in a weak form, by incorporating the localizing effects of the situation into the definition. But this means, first, that neither can be rationalized without reference to the other and its rationalization and, second, that all rationalizations are provisional if not situational.

Consider the "I do" portion of the marriage service. On the one hand, it appears to answer a question, "Do you . . . ?" On the other hand, the capacity of the expression to *constitute* a promise depends on inflections, hesitations, and the like, all of which are social acts that make it a particular expression rather than, say, the emission of sounds or a different expression. It is not just that these are externalities. They are features of the expression and are part of the cross-personal course of a moral bond's being demonstrated (for example, marriage) by a completion of what the ideal requires. It is well known that the statement "I do," even in the context of the marriage ritual, and for the question to which the statement responds, is not unequivocally an instance of the performance of a promise with words. The performance that demonstrates or instantiates a moral bond is collective (beyond the immediate parties and their audience), and what *it* performs is a connection within the culture of the ritual such that "I do" is effectively part of a collective enunciation the content of which is a marriage and not a promise. What is actually uttered by the individual, "I do," remains ambiguous to the extent to which the ritual itself is situated ambiguously in its own context and is therefore not exactly "ritualistic." The words of promising may be deliberately ambiguous in precisely that regard for the sake of a marriage, an event of a collectivity, the ritual aspect of which is for its parties a necessarily ambiguous expression of the otherwise impossible relations of law, culture, and the intensity of an occasion.

Parenthetically, the apparent confluence of law, culture, and occasion must be seen as altogether exceptional and not, as it were, ethnographically key. Indeed, instances of the apparent coherence of institutional facts, as when different sorts of such facts seem to intersect, should be considered as ironical rather than directly indicative of a structure of practices and of social order. Such apparent intersections, apparent because of questions about the extensional properties of the referent of "institution," turn what might ordinarily be a far more casual activity into a semblance of systematic obligation—to the occasion *and* to the society. Taking that utterly seriously, say as a promise never to divorce, would probably be seen as untoward by members—assuming no enforcement of an official enactment or religious dogma, personal foibles of the parties, or the pressure of the desires of a plurality—something no authentic member would do, and would be misleading on the part of an observer if it became the principle of an ethnographic account that excluded irony. Sincerity is not necessarily free of irony, and ethnography requires acknowledging that as a permanent possibility in any "ritual."

There is a less radical version of the same point, that the language of a promise need not mean what "promise" means if it is considered independently of possible situations or instances. Consider, for example, someone saying "I promise to X," where X clearly refers to something to be done. As is well known, that does not by itself indicate an instance of promising. The speaker might be rehearsing a line in a play, uttering those sounds to herself, or responding to a situation in which that very assertion is intelligible as an instance of the practice of promising. Which is true may depend less on the motivation of the speaker and the literal meaning of the expression than on the situation that establishes the intelligibility and meaning of the utterance or its manifestation in the discourse of which it is part. Thus, for an expression truly to be a valid promise and something crucially justifiable as such, the X that is promised must be understood by all parties, and generally by an indefinite plurality of others, as something within the power of the ostensibly promising party, and the intention to promise must be clear, and not merely reasonably clear, to both speaker and listener and, probably, to other parties to the setting as well. It should be also noted, in passing, that the promise to do X, if it is a promise, is also a promise to de-situate the action or relationship promised and to ignore the inevitable challenges that de-situating brings into play. It is, of course, possible that the statement "I promise to X" is intended as a gesture of friendliness in which saying that one promises indicates affection but not an obligation actually to do X. Given these conditions, one must conclude that it is possible for a listener to be mistaken in what she understands to be the meaning of such an utterance. For an utterance to constitute an instance of the practice of promising, and therefore to carry the weight of a particular obligation, which is also the weight of promising to ignore all future situations that might raise doubt, it is not enough that it conform to the abstract standards of the performance of a formally authentic promise; it must also be independent within its setting, which relatively few such utterances can be, and it must actually be an instance of the practice—such that its justification, in its situation, and the justification of the practice are logically distinguishable even if they have to refer to each other.

Nevertheless, it is still fairly clear that no matter what the function of the utterance "I promise to X" might be, it carries a special weight (making irony possible) because it has the formal (therefore enforceable) features of an idealization of a practice of promising—just as the humorous force of a nasty joke may lie in some part of it that is normally taken as denigrating to its audience. That a particular sentence is formally denigrating may be part of what makes it work in the joke; but it does not follow that it expresses contempt toward its audience. The audience to a nasty joke may see itself as part of the joke's telling and not merely as potential recipients of a message, or its victims. In that case, it is no less detached from its referents than the teller, regardless of the teller's intention. The joke is not *on* the audience; otherwise it would not be a joke, which is typically *on* someone else (including one's self when that self, the attributed or "virtual" self, is not, in Goffman's [1963] ironical sense, one's "actual self").

This version of "situation" as whatever facts, taken together, make the intention of an act intelligible, as instantiating a type of act retains the metaphysical distinction between subject and object and, therefore, between speaker and both the facts that are conditions of intelligibility and the factual referent of what is, say, in the case of a promise, the promised object. It allows a further distinction between a constant form and a variable content, the first effectively independent of situation and the second dependent on it but in a way that is qualified by conditions under which standard meanings can be varied without a loss of sense. Note that this is burdened by a fundamental emphasis on meaning tied to the intentions of individual speakers. Thus, in "I promise to X," the form is clearly that of a promise, but it constitutes a promise in fact only if that status is conferred on it by its situation. It is not, however, a mere construct of its situation. It is a result of the interaction of a non-situated, "literal" or objective meaning with factors that modify it and allow for a tension between the standard meaning ("I promise to X" means I promise to X) and the variant (e.g., "I promise to X" means, in situation A, "This is what a promise looks like"). Here, the situation shifts the utterance from what it might be thought to accomplish in itself, which is an obligation, to a surrogate of another utterance. It is important to note that being a result in the sense just indicated goes beyond computation to a sense of situation that may or may not be capable of final rationalization, a sense of a situation as active *in itself.*

Does this mean that we should take as our starting point for the analysis of discursive speech the fact that certain words in a certain order may perform things other than the immediately intended effects, or that we should rather take as our starting point the fact that what words perform is often intelligible only within a discourse and the situation in which it is featured (where "situation" is conceived of as the "limit subjectivity")? It depends to some extent on what one believes is exceptional, and I believe that the first is the exceptional case, which explains why so few "promises" are kept or are even meant to be kept, or why there are so many exceptions to the appearance of promising in words that formulate a promise. Many apparent promises are not meant to be kept, and this is not because of the promisor's character flaws or a tacit reservation so much as what meaning is possible (or reasonable) in a situation that makes its own demands on speakers. This means that a promise might remain a promise though it is not meant to be kept in the mechanistic sense of "keeping" invoked in some discussions of the practice of promising. In other words, the moral content of promising may or may not consist of an obligation to do what the promise seems to say. If so, then what is its moral content? I suggest that it is tied to what it is to be involved in a course of activity, which is to say what is involved in the inter-subjectivity of discourse and collective life in general. If this is so, then the idea of a practice is less helpful than might have been expected in preserving the perspective of action by allowing that it is immanently social. Rather, it seems again to have brought us to the point of needing to shift from the idea of action to the idea of a course of activity and from the perspective of the ostensible individual to what makes that individual, and every ostensible instance of individuality, a moment.

L et us focus less on form and more on the variability of content, holding in abeyance further questions about the independence of form and the ideas of standard and literal meaning. We can see how indications of subjectivity begin to infiltrate the empiricist notion of a situation. The latter is fundamental both to the notion of practice discussed previously and to the standard concept of action for which "situation" stands for a factual basis of belief, for those conditions most essential to reasons. It is worth noticing in this regard that the idea of a situation, formally conceived of as a complex independent variable or set of independent variables, can also be understood less formally and perhaps more suitably by the idea of an *occasion*. The connotations of this term seem much closer to what is reflected in and constitutive of the course of an activity in which, for one reason or another, context cannot be ignored.

Goffman famously noted that the self-contextualizing aspect of an occasion raises two theoretical issues. First is the history of its parties: how is being "a party to an occasion" constituted, and by what sort of enabling work? This involves the immanent negativity of entrance and exit, that something is over and something else is not yet; and it involves a positive intention of each party to participate in an activity the course of which is, as far as the party's experience is concerned, relatively unpredictable, implicating an attitude of waiting. It also requires that the content of the occasion, therefore the meaning of at least some of its elements, is relatively open regardless of whatever prior conditions might appear to have been settled (see Goffman 1961b). Second is a sense of a right of reservation, based in part on the circumscribing and isolating aspects of occasions. This allows each party the moral possibility of showing that someone is mistaken about what is and is not proper under the circumstances—or allowing a party to withdraw from certain occasioned obligations based on extra-occasional, possibly "normal" or "standard," expectations tied to norms and roles.

It is crucial to the sense of an occasion as standing out from what is thought of as everyday life and its settings: it may be recognized in anticipation and appreciated in fact as exceptional or special. It is bracketed off from other activities that appear in that light to be subject to trans-situational norms or rules that only incidentally cohere in the forms of routines, practices, goal-oriented action, or institutional facts. Thus, registering at the desk of a hotel is what one does in order to be admitted to a room; washing dishes completes a meal; and meeting for lunch may be a way of fulfilling a schedule. We often call situations ordinary when they appear to impose a sense of orderliness that releases activity from the burdensome aspects of self-reflection, including the work of maintaining that very order, such that the reason for the activity itself is inessential to what is actually done. In contrast, an occasion turns its parties inward toward the situated aspect of its objects and therefore the inter-subjectivity of its relations. It does this in ways that dramatize the work involved in that reflexivity such that the activity itself is the essential feature of the occasion.

In this view, the activity of "going to work" is not occasional. One is entering the realm of necessity, where entering is not itself experienced as a course of activity but, instead, as nothing more dramatic than moving, being moved, from one's home to one's place of employment (disappearing from one setting and appearing in another). Like Rousseau's state of nature, acting within this realm of necessity (e.g., waiting for a subway) has no evaluative significance, though it is often accounted for, in anticipation or after the fact, according to standards; it expresses nothing in itself and shares no problem of maintaining conditions. That is, its reflexivity is not a matter of practice for individuals but a property of the occasion itself. This is despite the fact that one may at one time have chosen one's present job from among other opportunities. But the choice, what is taken to represent it as a choice, is logically, as well as chronologically and phenomenologically, prior to going to work and a matter of what might be called alienated reflection. It does not apply to the activity as such, and it is for the most part dictated by utilitarian or instrumental conditions set by the value-asserting (price-making) trans-situational market. Its main condition for ostensible individuals has to do with a utilitarian anticipation of a calculable result. This is quite different from what is involved in, say, going to the movies, where the anticipated result of seeing the film is only one condition of going, and perhaps a minor one. A more important condition has to do with the pleasure that accompanies occasioned inter-subjectivity, which is the pleasure of the course of the activity itself.[12] Given that, we can understand why it is necessary to characterize an occasion phenomenologically as unprecedented. We may weigh the advantages of one job over another, but we do not typically think of going to work as an occasion, only as a way of continuing the schedule-driven labors of a day.

Not all events we refer to as occasions are special in this sense of being unprecedented. But at least some are experienced as exceptional to what has immediately gone before and what might immediately follow. In this first sense of being special, an occasion constitutes a break from a particular kind of reflected past. Unlike breaks that renew one's determination or set the stage for something novel, it does not constitute a beginning. Nothing about it holds implications for further action beyond its moment as a course of activity. It stands apart from what it interrupts, and its corresponding pleasures are always somewhat guilty; and its value (what makes it incomparable, and therefore a negation) is determined by altogether different principles from the value it momentarily supplants, its comparability or uneasy complementarity with other activities or events. In this respect, an occasion is an aspect of a course of activity, and this is what is meant by the latter's setting. It is that aspect that allows us to see individuals as "parties to a setting." But it is a setting only in regard to the inter-subjectivity of what is being done, and not as conditions in the sense usually associated with what I have referred to as the positive version of situation. Second, the past it invokes does not appear as separable and externally connected events. Rather, that past appears to be all that now, in the retrospect of the break and its qualitative valorization as an occasion, is normally continuous across situations in ways that an occasion cannot be. In other words, the moment of the occasion is also the negative moment of a reflected ostensibly continuous past, therefore a past that, as a matter of the very logic of its own ostensible continuity, is capable of being interrupted and in fact is interrupted by every occasion and its course of activity. Relative to that commitment to temporal continuity, the occasion appears as the realm of freedom in opposition to what it interrupts, which appears as the realm of necessity.

But, as is becoming clear, this realm of freedom is determinately social because it is determinately inter-subjective. Its disruptiveness is, perhaps, one source of the pleasure of the occasion as a momentary whole—not merely that it is exceptional but that it interrupts something, declares itself, in a way that evokes the guilty pleasure of any negative exercise of freedom and, at the same moment, confirms that such a stance is always inter-subjective. What transpires at the moment of the occasion is a course of activity rather than an action or sequence of actions governed by prior conditions, superordinate forms of life (e.g., institutions), and the anticipation of measurable results. It is, therefore, a moment in which parties immediately experience life, being caught up in multiplicity, in contrast with what is only "life" in the technical, classificatory sense of the word. This is how the idea of a situation as occasion helps rationalize the relationship between justifying a practice and justifying an action that presumably falls under it. Situation and life are joined when what is situated about the latter is its moment as a course of activity, which is to say its occasion and, therefore, its inter-subjectivity.

To that extent, the sense of an occasion must be seen as qualifying the sense of an "institutional fact" as far as concerns our understanding of the circumstances under which an utterance or gesture qualifies as an instance of a rule-governed practice such as promising.[13] The term "situation" does not in itself, distinguished from the hermeneutics of the occasion, convey a sense of history or an appreciation of the moment. Nor does it suggest any reservation of a right to challenge an interpretation. In this regard, a situation can be said to invoke rules but not to create them. The meaning of what is done in a *situation* not thought of as an occasion draws almost exclusively on rules or other conditions that are effectively in place prior to activity, which is, then, inessential. To characterize the context of an activity as a situation in the standard sense is to attribute form to it independent of its being an aspect of a course of activity, something that is ongoing and not capable of repetition. It implies that the activities in question are necessarily subject to trans-situational meanings. Therefore, "situation" without the sense of "occasion" refers to something relatively permanent and dispositional about society. It does not suggest something exceptional, momentarily out of time. It rationalizes the relationship between justifying a practice and justifying an action that falls under it, but at the expense of showing how something is determined to be such an action and at the expense of accounting for how a practice might be justified without reference to its possible instances.

Since one connotation of "practice" is activity, it is still tempting to consider a course of activity as indicating nothing more than a practice. Therefore, it is necessary to consider what can be said further about practices when that connotation is not suspended. Specifically, it is still necessary to consider the possibility that the idea of a practice remains one way out of having to commit one's self to the entailments of inter-subjectivity and to the corresponding idea of a "limit subjectivity" that includes the subjective objectivity of agency-dependent objects, both of which suggest that situations, understood as occasions, are active and that individuals are not the focal point of the essential reflexivity of a course of activity.

To refer to something as a practice is to consider it as drawing the conditions of its justification from society at large, interpreted by "legislators" who represent society, regardless of the varied situations in which the referent might be instantiated as a practice. However, the subjects for whom such a justification might be valid cannot be citizens or members in the ordinary sense—since appreciating the justification expresses the attitude of one who legislates. If so, the question remains as to how the justificatory work of the legislator can justify what is or might be done by those who are supposed to enact the practice in particular situations to which it is presumably appropriate. To act in light of a practice is not to enact the practice, since that is, according to what has been said, either impossible or impractical. One might conclude that a practice (which is an object for the legislators) reconstitutes itself, in effect, as an object exclusively for an observer standing apart from whatever concrete obligations, constraints, and so forth are supposed to make a collection of rules a definite practice. Whatever makes rules intelligible as practice in the abstract, and therefore justifiable as such, does not have the same effect in the concrete and active sense of "a practice." Indeed, it is hard to conceive of how the issue of justification could arise for a practice beyond the confines of the legislator's quarters, unless all that is involved is the formal or technical question of how the rules fit together as rules. In other words, the justification of a practice independently of its applications arises only in connection with the question of how a set of prescriptions and proscriptions can form the detached formal entities called games; and it is not clear that citing games adequately exemplifies the sort of practice that most importantly includes punishing, promising, and so forth—where punishing and the like require both social validity beyond the act of legislating, and some reference to contexts of possible socially valid application.

To the extent to which the legislator attempts to connect a practice with its possible instances, she is no longer justifying the sort of thing that is composed of a coherent system of rules.[14] Apart from the question of how the need to justify practice in the abstract arises, a justification based on the distinction between a practice and the activities that presumably fall under it seems to assume the existence of a universe in which the rules could operate as a coherent practice without regard to the particularizing and often dissociating features of settings—for example, an absolutist's universe where there is only one setting in which all morally justifiable activity transpires or where only legislators are significant actors because only principles and the consistency of principles count. Even the legislator's need to justify a set of rules as a practice seems intelligible only according to the narrowest conception of legislative action possible—namely, as something done exclusively for and by legislators and justified exclusively among them (or in a legislative capacity regardless of role or office). Who else is in a position to evaluate the legitimacy of a justification of a practice independent of its concrete instances but those who are in principle indifferent to those instances? We might, then, ask how the results of deliberation under the veil of ignorance can be conveyed to those not parties to it or its conditions. It is not at all clear for whom a set of rules could be justified as a practice independent of possible cases or for whom such a justification might be valid. It is also not clear how the request for justification might arise in the first place, other than from a love of form and a willingness to disregard what is thereby excluded. It apparently cannot arise from within or in regard to any instance of application. It seems, then, to arise only within the activity of forming the system of rules, with emphasis on *system*.

Further, the identification of a practice and the identification of something as an instance of both practice in general and the "particular practice" in question are prior to the justification of either—that is, prior to justifying the very idea of a practice and then the particular practice such that one can decide whether an activity is an instance of it, and justifying the applicability of a particular practice in a given case and of decisions taken in that case. This priority is predicated on practices and activities having been clearly and distinctly defined and, accordingly, identified. It is a condition of the clarity of that identification, given the purpose of making the distinction in the first place, that the notions of practice and instant (or case) be pure enough for the distinction to hold; and it must hold when justifications are necessary in order to reconcile instances with practices. Yet it seems that the putative order of priority (practice and instance first and justifications second) is impossible on that condition. This is because those identifications are not ordinarily merely technical, and Rawls's statement about how he uses the term "practice" seems to suggest that they are. "I use the word 'practice' throughout as meaning any form of activity specified by a system of rules that defines offices, roles, moves, penalties, defense, and so on, and that gives the activity its structure. As examples one may think of games and rituals, trials and parliaments" (1999b, 20n). His examples and his reference to activity "specified by a system of rules" indicates that he intends more than a technical or exclusively theoretical meaning; and this is consistent throughout his 1955 essay, with its appeals to moral intuition and the idea of a type of authentic social action falling under a recognizable practice (1999b). Identifying a practice and its instances involves identifying such things as expectations and obligations, and both must be recognizable to persons other than the "legislators" whose momentary practice is presumably to justify a practice by interpreting an institutional order. If it is not recognizable by those not "in role" (or in office)—for example, by momentarily nonlegislating citizens—then it lacks the sort of social validity necessary for any applicability of a system of rules to social action; and, because social validity must be taken to depend on the courses of activity that instantiate "rules" as rules to abide by, specification is not enough for what is required by the idea of a justification. If the identification of a set of rules as a practice is possible only for those whose task is to justify it (or for anyone in that capacity), then its lack of social validity, indifference to its possible incorporation in courses of activity, is fatal to the aspiration for clarity and usefulness in designating it a practice, not to mention the attempt to capture the senses of expectation and obligation that must be presumed to adhere to an institutional fact. It might be argued that all that is meant in the discussion of justifications is that anyone involved in an activity that falls under a practice needs to distinguish between justifying the one and justifying the other. But the problem is not posed psychologically, and it remains theoretically material that justifying the one is radically different from justifying the other. As noted previously, the problem is the logical one of trying to understand how the two are linked. If their connection is only one of priority, we are left with the same problem: how can one be justified without appealing to the other. In that case, the rules and their system do not qualify as a practice and justification is irrelevant to the question of the relationship between a practice and the activities that fall under it. The examples Rawls offers appeal to just such a notion of validity, though the emphasis on a technical sense of a system of rules belies it.[15]

Rules justified in the abstract (across all possible applications such that no reference to a particular application or type of application is logically relevant) can be legitimate only in the realm of pure legislative discourse. They cannot thereby constitute a socially valid practice; and debates over utilitarian accounts of certain practices (e.g., punishing criminals) cannot be resolved by assuming either that such a pure realm exists or that if it does it has any bearing on what people do or think and on how cases, outside of the confines of institutions, are decidable. To constitute a practice, it seems that a set of rules must draw its intelligibility to actors other than "legislators" from features of their always self-particularizing and transforming situations. If so, it is incorrect to consider a practice as essentially an institutional fact (that operates across situations) rather than, say, as constraints created in situated courses of activities that establish varying degrees of regularity and obligation in what people do together.[16] While this may not be a problem for "judges," those who apply principles in their role in the order of authority (whether or not that fits the model of an institution), it is a fundamental problem for citizens in their immanent capacity of judging by attending to the settings to which they are parties—*and by being judicious in the course of their activity and not merely before or after it is done and appears in that light to have been a particular total action.*

The rules governing a practice in the abstract are not sufficient to provide a basis for the capacity to identify an instance of the practice; and this is to say more than just that there is a distinction to be made between rules justified as a practice and rules justified within an activity that are cognizant of the rules of the practice. It is to say that specifying a practice amounts to specifying a sign that invokes a concept (e.g., of obligation) but not a course of activity (e.g., a qualified obligation). An alternative would say that the sign of a practice is one in which the signifier operates solely among other signifiers to delineate an occasion in which its components can be reasonably interpreted according to what they comprise together (as a promise or as something else). We can say what a promise is as an abstract institutional (legislative) fact; but by virtue of that alone we cannot say what it is to promise. This alternative allows us to say that the very idea of a practice is more ambiguous than Rawls would have it since the notion of rules, on which it depends, is ambiguous in its explanatory status and in its justification when there is no situational qualification; and such a qualification involves a course of activity and not a fact or set of facts independent of such a course. Note that where there is such a qualification, rules are no longer "rules" in Rawls's sense and the necessity of qualification becomes a logically constitutive feature of the referent of the term. Then it appears that the word "practice" used in regard to clarifying what is involved in the difference between justifying a set of rules and justifying an application does not mean the same thing in both cases. The practice that consists of a set of rules is not the same sort of thing as a practice that is applied or constituted in the course of an activity cognizant of legislation.

I conclude that "situation" understood according to the logic of an occasion is not illuminated by the use of the term "practice," though the latter, conceived of as rules, requires just such a notion of situation, and this is so whether or not we maintain the requirement of an internal relationship between life and situation. If one were to return to the version of the idea of a situation that refers to objects taken one by one and as externally related, practices (that can only be understood as such according to a notion of the situations that bring them into play, for example, as interpretive devices) would be unaccountable in regard to the possibility of application or instantiation. If the logic of a pure rule-governed practice excludes or is not directly compatible with the possibility of application, then practice cannot be the sort of thing involved when a case refers to "higher rules." If that logic includes possible application, then it cannot be what Rawls says it is since the rules envisioned in the application are not the sort of rules that are said to make up a practice. It is not that rules (whether or not thought of as institutional facts) do not or might not exist; it is just that their significance is not illuminated by this idea of a practice when we think about the relationship between a practice (an institutional fact) and its instances or cases. If rules are not so illuminated, if what cases refer to (are cases of) are not even rules in the way the standard idea of a practice requires, then the significance of that idea is no longer clear. This does not mean that the notion of a practice as rules is empty; quite the contrary. It may very well illuminate the character and function of a certain mode of justification, though not the case as an instance of a practice.

The relationship that might otherwise be posited between situation and practice now appears to be purely formal. It does not lie, as might have been supposed, in the essential realizability of a practice (realization in instances), completing its idea as a normative concept. It is, rather, an abstraction from a point of view that is not conceivable *as* a point of view at either moment of the substantial referent of "practice"—neither at the moment one identifies specific rules and then identifies them as a totality that can regulate instances of application nor at the moment they are appealed to in order to rationalize a judgment or decision in a given case. Both practice and the idea of a situation as composed of conditions under which it is possible to identify something as an instance of a practice depend on the concept of a rule. This is, presumably, the same for both a practice and its ostensible instances. If what is meant by "rule" in regard to "practice" is not the same as what is meant by "rule" in regard to "cases," because the first has nothing explicitly to do with either action or courses of activity, then justified practices are less important than Rawls believed for the justifications appropriate to cases. This makes the discussion of practice and the situations in which a practice is imaginable irrelevant to understanding the very different sort of situation in which an instance might be justified when we must ask what it is an instance of.

One possible answer is that the momentary case itself projects or endorses the very higher rules that are said to constrain it and does not merely implement trans-situational rules already in place (see Bogen 1999; Coulter 1989). This implies that legitimation has a local aspect and is a feature of a course of activity. If so, we can see how the notion of an occasion is helpful. It indicates both that there is something regular about what parties are doing together (intelligible to others in general) and that this regularity is significantly produced in the course of the activities themselves, subject to external constraints such as power. *From this point of view, it is the momentary case that determines what constitutes the system of rules appealed to and not the system, such as it is, that determines the disposition of the case.* It does so at the point at which the question arises as to "what we are doing" or "what is being done," and it arises in the course of the activity itself, whether or not reference is made to abstract rules—obligations to which are not specifically imaginable. What we are left with, if that idea of a situation is to shed light on what is human about human affairs, is a notion of occasion that can neither support nor be supported by the idea of a practice—insofar as "occasion" refers not to a type of action or a typical series of separable acts but to an inter-subjective course of activity (a multiplicity) exceptional to both the past and possible futures of what is normally meant by "action." This leaves us with the provisional conclusion that a theoretically useful notion of a situation entails the idea of inter-subjectivity and a significant blurring of the distinction between subject and object. It is in that case, and so far only in that case, that we can understand the connection of situation and life as an internal relation of the internal relations that constitute the meaning of each term.

————

This returns us to the notion of agency-dependent reality as key to addressing the question "What is human about human affairs?" I have suggested that this has something to do with inter-subjectivity, which has to do with both subjects and objects and not just with individual subjectivities in the usual psychological or phenomenological sense. To go into this further requires a different sort of discourse and a different, less negative form of argument. If, as I believe, the social sciences and the humanities must be thought of together as human sciences or sciences of agency-dependence, then something needs to be said about what such an inquiry might look like. I have tried to describe some conditions of understanding sociality as a course of activity that transpires within a universe of agency-dependent objects. These are, I claim, the crucial ontological presuppositions of the human sciences taken together as a definite field. To complete the argument, it is necessary to say more about how individuation takes place and to establish an appropriate methodology and corresponding conceptions of knowledge and criticism consistent with the irreducibility of inter-subjectivity. I have hinted at a distinction between performance and participation that might provide the basis for theorizing the sort of knowledge that requires neither individuated knowers nor a separation of knowledge from what appears as its conditions. It is necessary, then, to reconsider what sort of truth can be claimed by the human sciences, in what respect such claims can be considered knowledge, and what this might mean for the more general concepts of reason and rationality and the concept of belief. If the human sciences study the universe of agency-dependent objects, and if that study is itself agency-dependent, what sort of knowledge can be credited to it and how does this fit into standard conceptions of what it is to know?

It is crucial to keep in mind that the notion of inter-subjectivity, derived from showing what is involved in considering what is human about human affairs, requires that relations be conceived of as internal, which makes the usual distinction between subject and object untenable. This shift entails the immanence of inter-subjectivity in favor of an ontology consonant with the sub-theoretical conception of the social that informs the human sciences when the question of their common object cannot be avoided. This involves the idea of a course of activity, a movement without horizon from within that falls between the formations of intentions on the part of ostensible individuals and the acts that presumably realize them. The perspective of *being within a course of activity* is, then, a minimal condition of establishing what knowledge can be for the human sciences. It follows that knowledge in the human sciences cannot be extracted from the course of activity in which what is knowable and known is bound to the activity itself. The question remains whether this qualifies as "knowledge" and how it stands in regard to the critical method that I refer to as *immanent reading. Again, the most important regulative point to keep in mind is that a valid theory must find itself in its object and its object in itself such that the tension between theory and theorizing is sustained and such that theorizing is an instance of the social as a course of activity.*

22

Criticism, Inter-subjectivity, and Collective Enunciation

The fields specializing in the knowledge of agency-dependent reality include, familiarly, history, anthropology, psychology, political economy, the humanities, and the fine arts. I have tried to show that they all rely on a conception of sociality as inter-subjective activity, where the "inter" is not meant to indicate separable subjects. It follows that each discipline must be considered to be essentially inter-disciplinary. Their distinctiveness depends on the aspect of sociality under which each is incorporated. An understanding of the integrity of each discipline depends, then, on a self-critical attitude that embraces sociality as its object. By this I mean a sociological attitude that is at once philosophical (attentive to the sub-theoretical aspect of its subject matter) and theoretical (concerned with and reflexive to the internality of relations brought to notice in the course of theorizing). It takes as its primary matter the knowledge-constituting aspect of human affairs in all respects *insofar as those affairs are essentially social*; and it takes as its secondary matter *whatever appears, as things stand, to manifest or indicate that dimension and, in that respect, to constitute a problem motivating the activity of theorizing.* A superficial reason for the claim that self-criticism is a necessary condition of such an attitude is the self-defeating aspect of the temptation to employ methods derived from sciences of agency-independent objectivity and therefore to rely on a corresponding epistemology incompatible with the study of agency-dependent objectivity. I try to show that this temptation is unavoidable within the course of theorizing and constitutes part of the critical tension intrinsic to its relation with the possibility of a product, a specific theory. It is unavoidable because of something about theorizing itself and not because of extra-theoretical tendencies to objectify, rationalize, or totalize. If so, then criticism must be thought of as a necessary feature of a course of activity and not something brought to it.

What follows is a speculative account of the relationship between the idea of criticism, including critical knowledge, and the idea of the essential sociality of human affairs—where sociality is understood in regard to the idea of a multiplicity, which assumes both inter-subjectivity and a course of activity in contrast with action as a particular event. The basic idea is that criticism is an immanent feature of such a course and the source of its transferable knowledge. Critical knowledge can then be identified with the movement of subjectivity within the universe of agency-dependent objectivity to the extent to which it is a moment of, reflexive to, a course of activity. It is then reasonable to say that critical knowledge is no more distinguishable from the course of action of which it is a moment than, for the activity of dancing, the dancer is from the dance. It displays itself as a *moment* of knowing insofar as it extrudes from, and thereby violates, the course of activity and is, in the same moment, embraced within what then appears to be another such course *for which* the first appears as a virtual totality. In regard to the latter, critical knowledge can be said to confront its object; in regard to the former, it is available as knowledge only from within and as an immanent feature of the tensions that motivate inter-subjectivity in the sense of constituting its momentum.

For this to be workable, the familiar idea of criticism as reasoned judgment in regard to a standard must be brought more thoroughly into line with the idea of what is human about human affairs. I have described this according to certain commitments—for example, to the internal relation of life and situation, inter-subjectivity and what that implies for the relation of subjectivity to the sort of objectivity that constitutes a situation, the notion of a course of activity in contrast with action, reflexivity, and the essential incompleteness of all ostensible individual instances of agency and all ostensible total and self-identical objects. The principle of this list is that each item presupposes an agency-dependent objectivity on which all the human sciences rely for their most general disciplinary claims and their relevance to our most comprehensive discourses on human affairs. The latter can be thought of as comprising a self-validating course of collective reflection. Reflection in this most general sense is qualified by limitations on doubt; and it involves interrogating, investigating, collecting, and other activities that reinforce, or otherwise make apparent, a sense of disciplinary integrity. Parenthetically, such activities are bound to display irony since each has little choice but to take itself as an object. This makes manifest a division of critical knowledge according to the distribution of the most general notions by which it is possible to regulate discourse across the various disciplines that address agency-dependent reality: thus the distinction between *criticism* and *critique.*

As things stand, these most general discourses involve ultimate, or primary, universes of reference. They include comprehensive reflection on the *good* (what is consistent with what is human about human affairs), the *true* (what is momentarily worthy of being a topic of sincere self-critical inquiry), the *beautiful* (the momentary realization, as in an attitude of waiting, of internal relations in a momentous but fleeting instance of a particularity in the course of passing), the *morally right* (the implication of inter-subjectivity that human beings are ends and not means), and the *politic* (the tension between a course of activity and its internally determined prospect of particularization). These discourses operate holistically across those disciplines that depend for their own integrity and the value of their claims, on being compatible with these and possibly other such ideas—though each comes to notice sub-theoretically. In that respect, each is qualified by the essential fact about human affairs, their constitution as irreducible inter-subjective courses of activity.

In regard to the relation of criticism to human affairs, my account depends on the following sub-theses: (1) a general idea of criticism underlies the most familiar definitions that connect it to judgment, and (2) the latter presuppose something more fundamental about human consciousness than that it is capable of deciding whether to apply a standard of comparison to a given, well-specified object or belief. *Given the discussion so far, the more fundamental presupposition is that criticism is immanent to subjectivity when the latter is understood as intrinsically social in the sense of inter-subjective and, therefore, as denoting a course of activity across bodies rather than an option for an individual actor. This is false unless agency is conceived of without the assumption that the skin is the natural boundary of its instances and unless we accept the idea that objects are agency-dependent and therefore also instances of life.*

"Criticism" is familiarly understood to refer to reasoned and informed evaluation that provides the possibility of rational comparison, though certain traditions identified with Marx's critique of political economy, the Frankfurt School, and some currents of post-structural theory define it differently. In its familiar sense, it involves comparing things according to a standard (or standards) or a model either invested with legitimacy derived primarily from the history of just such comparisons or reflective of possibly timeless ideals. The rationality of such evaluations depends on their being arrived at by independent (uncompromised) subjects for an indefinite audience of potential critics who are also sufficiently independent to appreciate the principle underlying a given comparison. From this point of view, criticism cannot be considered either a fundamental feature of or immanent to human life. While it is acknowledged that the critic is part of a historically specific society and is burdened by received categories and ways of classifying, drawing distinctions, and establishing analogies, these may be facts about the limitations of individual critics (who might learn to act otherwise) but they do not bear on the nature of criticism, which stands outside of the universe of objects it subjects to comparative judgment, in which case our understanding of its regulatory ideals allows us to evaluate its instances and, in doing so, to criticize the critic.

One result of the argument so far is that human affairs are conceived of as essentially and not accidentally or contingently social. They involve cooperation in all respects based on the inter-dependence of people who need not be acquainted, need not interact in ways identified with face-to-face encounters or mediated joint action, and need not "share a history" or specific circumstances other than the fact of an inter-dependence that constitutes and supersedes individuality (which is a condition of understanding human affairs historically). This is by no means deterministic; and it does not compromise the principle that "individuals are the ultimate moral claimants," if that proposition is taken as subordinate to what now seems to be the more precise and unavoidably universal proposition that "human life is the ultimate *referent* of moral discourse." This has to do with how instances of agency are instantiated in and constituted of the limitless and self-intensifying inter-dependencies that comprise society as the form of human life. For clarifying the nature of social reality, the dependence of each person on all constitutes an inter-subjective world of human affairs of which she is momentarily a feature. Therefore, it is rational to say that each constitutes and therefore deserves to be treated as a universe and that the gist of the categorical imperative—that humans are ends rather than means, hence connected to all possible ends as far as they are capable of being realized as such within a course of activity—is logically necessary to the very constitution of society.

From this point of view, persons cannot be considered as loci and origins of agency since, in their ordinary capacities, they are radically incomplete. This means that whatever they appear to do on their own or as discrete agents must be thought of as moments of participation *before* it can be understood as object-oriented, specifically intended, or expressive. What people do, what can be ascribed to them as their very own actions, are, first of all, moments of a course of activity—that is, instances of inter-subjectivity. They are not merely caused or otherwise influenced by specific facts related to specific forms or ideal types of cooperation. To that extent, one can conclude, *first*, that what they appear to do as persons taken one at a time is ostensible to the extent to which it transpires within the sociality of human affairs and, *second*, that it is theoretically reasonable to consider cooperation across a virtually infinite community of strangers as a form of life, hence as irreducible and, in a limited and no doubt problematical historical sense, "for-itself."

For criticism to be understood as related to what is human about human affairs, the latter must refer to an irreducible and nontrivial sociality. This goes beyond one well-known interpretation of the claim that the humanity of a being lies in its "being in a situation"—namely, that she is located *in* one setting or another. But a situation is not a collection of ostensible things and ostensible people that can first be examined as a collection and then the totality classified as either a situation or something else. It is social the moment it is thought of as a situation. Situations cannot, as things stand, be made ontologically intelligible as extra-human in their materiality (such that we can say that an instance of human life might not be situated or a situation might exist minus human beings). Being situated is a definitive feature of what it is to be human (to be an instance of the internal relations of life and situation, subjectivity): it is not a matter of location but of constitution. Still, one can and does speak of distinct situations as precisely what this conception says they are not. Is there an exception to the idea of situation as the limit subjectivity? Or can the two meanings be consistent? Clearly, consistency is preferred since the conception of a situation is internal to the conception of a "being in a situation." In order to appreciate the significance of the idea of a being in a situation, it is necessary to remember the logical distinction between a course of activity and its moments. For now, it is enough to say that what makes a situation an ostensible particular does not have to do with how its elements appear to be organized (according to one method of coding and analysis or another) or how they are taken to be the case by an independent agent.

It is a profound fact that all situations are, for the universe of agency-dependent objectivity, instances of the sort of inter-subjectivity we mean sub-theoretically to bring to notice when we speak of or otherwise indicate the social. As such, they can be intelligible only as moments of courses of activity and, therefore, as "ongoing accomplishments." One might say that their ostensible concreteness as particulars containing particulars is momentarily abstracted from what gives them value, just as playing the notes F, A-flat, and then B-flat refers to an abstracted moment of *Claire de Lune*'s being performed or catching the ball is an abstracted moment of a baseball game's being played or buying is an abstracted moment of the production and circulation of value. Playing notes is not an instance of music's being performed, and holding a ball is not being part of the game's being played, though both are moments of their courses of activity. What is uniquely social *is* the "being in a situation." Sociality is not merely one possible property among others of an otherwise independent "being" who happens to but might not be situated. If sociality were to be a contingent property of situations (to which actors then respond), it would be necessary to rethink the conclusions of the analysis of "situation" in Parts I and II of this book having to do with the social as a basic fact. Since those seem to follow from more fundamental considerations, the latter, too, would be put into jeopardy and with them the possibility of justifying the claim that the human sciences share a common object *as things stand*.

If sociality is a predicate, one might reasonably conclude that "cooperation" refers to something a person decides to do and then actually does by taking others, and not just their behavior, into account under conditions that encourage just such a qualified action over other possible options. For this conclusion to be true, cooperation would have to be defined independently of sociality; and there would be no need to refer either to inter-subjectivity or to agency-dependent objectivity, which implies that all objects pertaining to agency are to some decisive extent in common. There would be nothing distinctively human about it: it could as easily be predicated of a nonhuman device as of a person.

If one were then to consider what is distinctively human about human affairs, it would have nothing directly to do with life as being in a situation in which others are always acknowledged. Analysis could proceed indifferent to social life as the basic fact in the sense I have attributed to Rousseau, Nagel, and Strawson.

This would bring us back, regressively, to several ideas that I have tried to show cannot be sustained without omitting the social aspect of human affairs; naturally separable individuals, situations for which agency-dependent objects pose no theoretically significant problem, and a distinction between the individual who desires, wants, acts, and so forth, and the executive function (or agency) of that ostensibly self-same individual who executes the chosen act. These ideas leave little room for a suitably robust conception of a course of activity. Instead, they require a conception of what is done as a definite act, known only retrospectively or projectively, that realizes an individually concrete intention—and therefore an event that is or is not only successfully completed by an instance of agency for which the skin is a natural boundary, or completed with the help of others, or only under special circumstances that are theoretically inessential.

It is not clear what "cooperation" might mean if we reject the following propositions, *and, for reasons given so far, we must reject them as things stand*: (1) cooperation is nothing more than a type of action individuals are likely to perform under certain circumstances independently of their sociality, though not of the mere presence of others, (2) cooperation is nothing more than a statistical fact about "interaction" (possibly explainable by circumstances in common or the dispositions of the separate but convergent individuals), and (3) "rationality" is logically independent of "sociality" though its conditions include what can be anticipated about the behavior of others according to each actor's knowledge of their dispositions. If we reject those propositions for the reasons discussed previously, then "cooperation" refers not to what individuals do as separable agents but to a fundamental social fact that may be variously realized in one momentary form or another. In that case, more must be involved in cooperation, and the inter-dependence on which any conception of it must depend, than the simple statistical presence of socially motivated individuals within a population, presumably leading, only under special circumstances, to the "composition" of a "body politic"—that is, the sort of consensual society on which Rawls predicated his theory of justice, Nagel his analysis of altruistic reasons, Strawson his injunction about the irreducibility of the social aspect of life, and Davidson his holistic theory of knowledge. Parenthetically, it is well known that individual traits, no matter how distributed and no matter how intense their effects on motivation, cannot account for social facts of this sort without reference to sociality itself and that the problem of composing sociality out of separable individuals is insoluble without the artifacts of coercion, manipulation, or some other strictly external and independent fact.

If "situation," understood under the aspect of "occasion," directs us toward inter-subjectivity and away from a radically personalized distinction between subjectivity and objectivity, then we need to rethink the idea of the sort of cooperation that determines what it is to be human. Two things are clear. Cooperation, in general, cannot be explained either as a reason-based interaction of separable and distinct beings or as determined by traits of such individuals. If either is true, then cooperation does not exemplify the essential sociality of human affairs. Note that this discussion concerns whether "being in a situation" means "being social" such that there is an idea of critique that can illuminate what is human about human affairs. If cooperation is a realization of the basic fact, then it has the qualities of a course of activity, including the immanence of criticism.

To connect the idea of criticism to the idea of human affairs, as the momentary form taken by knowledge of those affairs, it must be possible to show that there is a credible meaning of "criticism" that points to the inter-subjectivity of human affairs and to the essential constitution of human beings as inter-subjective moments of courses of activity; and *it must be possible to show that criticism yields knowledge, though not what knowledge is taken to be in the sciences of agency-independent objects.* If human affairs and those for whom they are distinctively human are essentially social, then what is done is reflexive to, and therefore makes an ongoing difference within, a course of activity. If so, knowledge of human affairs from within has to do with the immanence of agency-dependence to the course of activity, and this yields momentary instantiations that are, among other things, simultaneously positive and negative, with neither distinct from the other.

Before attempting to clarify that connection, it is necessary to explain how something as apparently individualized as criticizing can be compatible with human affairs conceived of as essentially social, or how what is social allows for what appears to be individual and/or unique. On the conception of criticism as a particular type of action (e.g., evaluative) and sociality as contingent, criticism and human affairs are either opposed, or the first is exceptional to the second, which is then conceived of as not necessarily critical, or as essentially uncritical; or they are compatible in a way that, for the moment, seems inordinately difficult to specify. There is another possibility as well—namely, that each is a constitutive feature of the other, that the one cannot be thought without the other. In that case, neither term can be understood according to its standard definition (as evaluating and as acting jointly or in light of others), and conclusions drawn on the basis of those concepts must therefore be considered invalid. The following relies on this possibility. It allows us to consider what "cooperation" might mean if "being human" is equivalent to "being in a situation," and if the latter has to do with inter-subjectivity predicated on the idea of a universe of agency-dependent objectivity—which is a necessary condition of there being something distinctively human about human affairs and of that something being sociality as a course of activity.

23

Criticism and Human Affairs

We can begin by observing that the proposition that persons are essentially social beings does not imply that sociality is a distributed property of individuals or that it is exclusively a function of norms, rules, or principles of exchange. If it is conceived of as distributed or normative, then what people do might be social or it might not. Since it is inconceivable that there be something they do that is not at all social, we can conclude that everything done, every activity, is already socialized—before definite meanings are attached to behavior and before definite intentions are formed and/or decisions are made and actions undertaken. No factor having to do with human nature is required to explain that basic fact, say a propensity toward "pity" or an innate disposition toward empathy or "impartiality" (Nagel 1991). In fact, everything that has been introduced as an explanation turns out to assume what it claims to explain.

We have seen that one way every person can be thought of as social has to do with the fact that each takes others into account—or it has to do with how the activities of each are accountable in terms of the activities of others. While it is tempting to think of this as a hypothesis subject to evidence, it is generally thought to be necessary to the very meaning of "being human." In observing behavior we are always observing society. Yet Weber begins his theoretical writings on the relationship between action and situation apparently to the contrary. He defines "social action" by way of anticipating his account of social relations, corporate groups, authority, law, and the state: "Action is social in so far as, by virtue of the subjective meaning attached to it by the acting individual (or individuals), it takes account of the behaviour of others and is thereby oriented in its course" (1947, 88). Here, Weber begins with individuals and with the plausible but admittedly defeasible hypothesis that understanding living beings as human requires assuming that a tendency toward rationality is immanent to them. This means that whatever is done, no matter how apparently nonrational, exhibits tendencies toward efficiency and effectiveness according to values, desires, and beliefs. He thereby arrives at a conception of the social, one he could hardly have avoided, as a contingent property of action. There are, in other words, nonsocial actions, and "social action" means far more than that people respond to one another. In its strongest and most influential version, the definition says that it is a sufficient condition of an action's being social in a given situation that the actor take account of that other's behavior "in its course," in light of the subjective meaning she attaches or is attaching to what she is doing. She presumably does this by understanding what she is doing to be rationally responsive to her understanding of the intentional aspect of the other's behavior. In other words, for her to be rational in the presence of others, her reasons must be responsive to others' reasons and must have their own appropriate meanings, so that her action will be "oriented in its course." But an actor cannot discover the actual subjective state of another and, therefore, cannot predicate the meanings she assigns to her own behavior on the contents of the other's mind. Rather, she takes account of the actual behaviors of others by referring them to typical intentions appropriate to typical situations. The intentions are virtual. The possibility of identifying another's meanings and intentions in the course of assigning appropriate meanings to one's own action depends on "interpretation" according to "ideal types." These are presumably used by actors in taking account of the behavior of others and by scientists to understand actors, in particular their points of view as, hypothetically, instances of typical subjective states (given the nature of the situation and therefore limits on its possible definition by its parties).

In passing, it appears to Weber that the validity of a scientific interpretation depends to some extent on its convergence with the meanings actors assign to their own actions. Evidence (hence the opportunity to correct the application of an ideal type) is presumably provided by what the actor actually does over time in regard to particular others such that an interpretation can be corrected by what the scientist sees in that behavior. In any case, Weber believes that these are epistemologically legitimate bases for scientific observers to attribute intentional states to actors if the ways in which those actors account for the behavior of their others are to be understood as rational, and shareable, and if one is to avoid claiming that it is possible to read minds. It seems clear that action can only be rational by taking another's behavior into account if there is some sort of acknowledgment on the part of the actor that the behavior to be taken into account is intentional to begin with and that it is the behavior of an already significant other (one whose behavior is likely to be consequential beyond what she intends) and is, even beyond that, interpretable in a way that can become more accurate over the course of experience. No doubt many problems arise in regard to evaluating what the actor must already have grasped before attaching meaning to anything—which is to say the actor's own action and the "conduct" of the other. But I believe that they amount to the fact that Weber does not explicate a distinction on which he is nevertheless compelled to rely—namely, between meaningfulness and meaning, where the former has to do with those aspects or properties of an occurrence that suggest that it is a candidate for just the sort of interpretation he describes. Assuming that the instrumental rationality of the parties is insufficient, more is required if all this is to be explained, as well as accounting for how the actor can rely on the fact that the others are parties and not, say, bystanders. Weber is therefore unable to distinguish theoretically between the sociological *conditions* of "attaching" meanings (including the meaning of doing just that) and the putative *act* of "attaching" them. Yet the second is inconceivable without the first, as is clear from the assumptions he makes about language, in his notion of "ideal types," and about the prior sharing of meanings, hence sharing per se.

Consider the possibility that Weber's definition of "social action" is intended as well to clarify the meaning of the word "social." His discussion of "corporate" groups reinforces that possibility. At least it suggests that he has no further definition of "sociality" to offer than what one might infer from his analysis of social action. The most likely inference is that something more general about sociality underlies the possibility of an actor's being oriented. Taking this into account, the original definition might be reformulated as follows: *"social" refers theoretically to actions that take account of the behavior of others, subject to the condition that taking account is already accountable in some way and therefore at least presumptively social.* This version describes how "social" can qualify "action," but it implies something further that Weber neither conceptualizes nor discusses beyond distinguishing types of action (e.g., social, economic, political); nor, it should be added, does he define "action" in such a way that it can be conceived of as sometimes social and sometimes not. Ultimately, the quality of an action is determined by an intention, and the word "social" has no other meaning but the intention to take others rather than, say, monetary value, into account. This cannot have been what Weber meant to say since his notions of a "social relation" and a "corporate group" are predicated on but are by no means derived from the analysis of social action. Those concepts, among others, are necessary, in turn, for every other phenomenon he discusses and, it must be added, every recognizable instance of human association. In other words, his original definition is incomplete and only trivially informative as far as concerns extending and applying his sociology.

In that case, a great deal is still missing in the revised definition of "social action" that is necessary to our understanding of what is meant by "social." One missing element has to do with what makes an occurrence a candidate for an interpretative orientation aimed at appreciating intentionality and locating agency in one part of the occurrence (what then appears as the actor). In order not to beg the question, the explanation of the act of taking account, which, for Weber, constitutes the substance of the instance of social action, should not depend on a prior social character attributable to the occurrence (or its elements) since that is what "taking account" is supposed to explain. Yet it seems to depend on just such a character. For the occurrence or any part of it to provide for such a candidate object, one might expect it to have certain properties prior to those particular attributes that reveal distinct intentions capable of justifiable typification. Without going into greater detail, it seems that interpretable objects of any sort (to be interpretable) must be meaningful (have their place in social life) before the individual actor or observer considers them for their possible discrete and relatively fixed meanings, those presumably shared or able to be shared by actor and observer as well as the actor's other. In other words, sharing is presupposed by the very idea of an action's being social in the way Weber claims, and his definition does not take this into account. Sharing must be considered an instance of sociality. Therefore, the definition fails to encompass what can be meant by referring to action as social and therefore fails to clarify what is meant by "taking others into account." The idea of "internalized norms" or reference to a particular state of mind also will not solve the problem, since both preserve individualism in a way that defies reliable and informative uses of the term "social." *There seems, then, to be a social condition of an act's being taken as social—that is, taking the behavior of another into account—that is different from "taking into account" and that cannot be understood in individualistic terms. In short, the actor, no less than the observer, relies on a sense of something's being social before a specific meaning is attached to it if she is to try to interpret it as such, and if an act of individualized interpretation is sufficient to a sociological account of what people do in the presence of others. We can say, then, that the actor takes account of the behavior of others in the very fact of acknowledging that they need to be and should be taken into account (and only then assigns meaning), and that the observer identifies this in an actor by knowing in advance that she is an actor in the sense of one bearing intentionality (being already socially active).*

The problem is not merely that there is something about the actor (or the actor's other) that leads to the observer's judgment that there must be an as yet hidden property that accounts for how that actor (or her action) should be understood. This would reinforce the sort of individualism that creates the problem in the first place. Rather, there must be something about observation itself, by the observer and by the actor, that is already social and in that respect is a condition of knowing something (e.g., an other) as interpretable in a shareable way—assuming for the moment that "interpretation" describes what is going on when people do things in the presence of one another or jointly. It should be added, in that case, that there must be something about sociality itself that allows observation to be an instance of it without having to assume that observing is, as an instance of social action, merely a response to norms or the expression of a disposing mental state. For it will not solve the problem to suppose that sociality can be described adequately in static, organizational terms. That would reproduce the problem at a different level, requiring a further inquiry into the meaning of "sociality." If Weber were, in the first place, to have made the distinction between meaningfulness (the weight something bears that requires the accomplishment of meaning) and meaning (as something that can be "attached or attributed, or constitutionally objectifying), his definition of the social property of an action doubtless would have been somewhat different, perhaps a more developed version of the revision suggested previously. While it is not necessary to speculate further about this, one can at least agree that he would not have wanted to define an action as social by facts that themselves can be understood only as social, since that would beg the question he posed about social action and its significance as the object of a possible discipline—namely, sociology (and it would belie his well-known criticisms of functionalism).

It seems, then, that Weber presupposed certain undeniable social facts that cannot be defined in terms of an agent's taking account of particular others by attributing meanings to their particular behaviors, and that he means this presupposition to play a pre-theoretical role in his analyses of other phenomena. This seems clear from his references to sharing and language, both of which require that anything interpretable and/or accountable be recognized as socialized (including a *possible* instance of an "ideal type") before it becomes an object of a specific orientation. Parenthetically, if language is quintessentially social, it is presumably vested in a community; and because separable individuals are not that sort of totality and do not compose it one by one, their speaking together has to be explained by different principles from conventional psycholinguistic ones. A possibly misleading way of saying this is that language is social prior to its being subject to individualized use, and it is subject to individualized use only in forms different from the abstract communitarian form identified as language. In that case, the relationship between thought and language is not simply one in which the latter either realizes or determines the former, and meaning is not simply attached, like a string to a balloon, by one individual agent to her or another's behavior; nor can reference to "conventions," "agreements," or "human nature" solve the problem, since that fails to explain the "meaning" of a convention to the individual such that she can follow it as such.

It is unacceptable to consider a property of a community as distributed through a population of members. Therefore, it cannot be understood as internalized in the individual or realized individually in light of the individual's knowledge of the whole, say, as a rule within a system of rules governing use: or it can be understood that way if we are willing to return to the weak or poorly defined property Weber named "social." When individuals speak, they are not simply using whatever makes language "language": what makes language "language" has something to do with what makes a community "a community." They are doing something linguistic, but what they are doing must be thought of along the lines of participation in something the fullness of which is, in principle, inaccessible to the individual, something that some writers have tried to capture by the expression "collective enunciation," others by "discourse," and still others by "conversation."

Let us consider this along slightly different lines, beginning with Weber's original definition. What appears to be the behavior of an other is, from the point of view of the actor, a particular, an originary event, that is initially identified as belonging to that other—for the moment uniquely—in a way that distinguishes that other from yet others. This must already have appeared to the actor before he or she could have attached specific meaning to it in Weber's sense. Otherwise, identifying something as a relatively independent agent who has a specifiable intention (and is therefore capable of being noticed as a momentarily independent agent) is unaccountably intertwined with identifying and attributing his or her specific intention. Presumably, the intention attributed to an other must be (or approximate) the unique intention of that very other, and, for the moment of the attribution, which is also a moment of the sociality of action, it must not be the intention of anyone else. But we have seen that Weber's original definition is intelligible only if the attribution is predicated on a prior identification of the other exclusive of a specific meaning of a specific behavior; and that identification, such as it is, need not be the same sort of identification one means when speaking of a particular person in their particularity. But how can an intention be understood as belonging to someone if it is not yet an instance of meaningfulness, which is to say the *possibility* of having a meaning? It seems clear that the idea of an intention's "belonging to a particular other" cannot mean that it is held uniquely to the standard of a decisively individuated intention—which is required by Weber's definition of "social action." It may be attributed to the other but, like reasons in general, it resides first in the community, among people and not simply in each or many of them; therefore, it is unlikely to reside there in the logical form of a proposition.

We see again that something crucial is missing in his definition of "social action," and when it is added it may well change the definition in a radical way, in particular in a way that would belie Weber's emphasis on relatively fixed attachable meanings and absolutely individuated agency. The reason is that for something to belong to someone in this way prior to the assignment of a meaning to it, and be recognized as such, it must be pre-intentional (if concrete "intentions" are connected with meanings), just as the other significantly appears prior to the attachment of meaning to his or her behavior as distinctively human. Weber accepts the noncontroversial assumption that all meanings that can be part of social action, chosen and attached by the actor as the content of her orientation and as part of accounting for the behavior of an other, are shared and that this is an irreducible fact about them. Language, understood as a distinctively social phenomenon, always spoken in irreducibly social relations, is logically prior to the attachment of specific meanings in the course of an activity, say of interpretation.

I conclude that Weber is aware of a sociality logically prior to social action that his analysis of the concept of social action does not address, and that
meaningfulness, which is logically prior to meaning, is somehow derived from
it. In begging the questions posed by the distinction, he fails to show that his
theory of social action is either a theory of the social or an improvement in our
understanding of the sociological significance of the concept. It follows that
he also fails to show that his more general theory of action, which includes assumptions about rationality and a theoretically suggestive distinction between
types of rationality and the relations between them, is illuminated by the list
of predicates he supplies (social action, economic action, political action, etc.).
*In effect, without an adequate definition of sociality, his original definition sim-
ply states what is obvious and in need of explanation—namely, that persons are
somehow connected to others by virtue of whatever is being done.*

What appeared to be a theory turns out to be an expression of the problems
Weber has in considering several issues. Among these are (1) how or in what
sense individuation occurs as a pre-social fact so that one can legitimately begin with individuals in coming to terms with the social, (2) how it is possible for
an individuated agent to act rationally in light of the fact that she cannot know
what is in the mind of another and cannot independently validate her attributions, (3) how it is possible to have confidence in the validity of one's interpretation of another's reasons and how such confidence can be attached legitimately
to an analysis according to ideal types, (4) how, for scientific purposes, another's mind can be approximated by ideal types capable of providing a rational
basis for action (given the fact that ideal types are, after all, ideal), and (5) how
an actor who intends to take account of the behavior of another can come to believe that it is possible to attach a meaning to his or her own action in its course
consistent with the meaning of the other's behavior (a meaning the other would
presumably attach to his or her own behavior). The assumptions that Weber
made in order not to be disoriented by such issues include the following propositions: that the skin is a natural boundary of agency, that meanings are shared
in a way that allows for a reliable meeting of minds and a reliable interpretation
of the other, that methodological individualism should not preclude referring
to Durkheimian social facts for certain purposes (e.g., to explain language independently of speech), and that the paradigm for understanding action, and
by inference human affairs as far as they are social, is that of means-ends rationality (based on beliefs and desires and the calculation of likelihoods), with
"substantive" or "value rationality" dependent on what cannot, as far as Weber
is concerned, be rational—namely, politics (for his examples of ad hoc qualifications, see Weber 1947, 90, 97, 111–112, 120, 125, 133, 141).

In interpreting Weber along these lines, I have said that it is crucial to avoid
the convenient version that says that persons take others into account in
the same way they take account of nonhuman things, as factors, conditions,

reasons, and objects of variable kinds and degrees of interest. Apart from the fact that this threatens to reinstate an individualistic idealism, it requires that the meaning of a behavior can be fixed such that an attribution can be tested in the course of experience. For this to be possible, there must be something about a course of activity, for which meaning is an ongoing accomplishment, that makes it momentarily possible; and this is the best that can be said for it if my critique of the concept of action is correct. It also suggests that pre-social personal experiences are as distinct as the demand that they be given linguistic expression makes them appear to be. But it seems false to say that experience *consists* of discrete episodes and, therefore, false to claim that specific experiences can be picked out in order, say, to test what is presumably learned from them. *One can conclude, then, that learning in a socially valid participatory way does not generally occur in the ways in which psychology claims separable organisms learn; nor could it if what is "learned" has to do with being able to participate in a course of activity beyond just knowing "how" something is done.* Any attempt to formulate a rationalistic theory of action, in which what counts as far as the agent's others are concerned are the agent's beliefs about them, can succeed only by reinstating a host of assumptions that are at least highly questionable if not false—not to mention other problems of individualism having to do with the possibility of identifying sociality on the basis of individuated acts and of addressing the question "What is human about human affairs?" To attempt to modify such a theory in order to avoid those problems does not seem to be a satisfactory path to a solution; nor does deciding to consider the model of rationality on which it relies as merely normative (if one wishes to act intelligibly, make the most of one's chances, etc., this is how to act).

Nevertheless, one might suppose that the rationalist model can be salvaged as a rough but workable description of what people might be doing when they are not doing philosophy or writing novels. In that case, it is serviceable only as a clarification, from a certain point of view, of what appears to be going on in the doing of philosophy or the writing of novels, though it may appear to describe the sort of thing people do when they are not forming concepts, developing theories, or otherwise doing recognizably creative work. More ambitiously, the argument is that the model is generally descriptive of a certain kind of everyday life actor and, as such, there are several assumptions on which it relies. First, an agent, the proper subject of a theory of action, is and must be a psychological individual. Second, the action of an agent is social if and only if it involves taking others into account for some purpose. Third, taking another into account involves forming justifiable beliefs about certain facts, which require that there be the sorts of things about which there can be just such facts. Fourth, not being rational in this way is to be, in a sense, out of control, since the alternative is either to go with some flow or to select options as if picking at random or perhaps something else that has nothing to do with self-control, learning, accomplishing, adapting, and so forth. Putting aside previous criticisms of this position, it follows, loosely but plausibly, that taking account of people, and in that sense being social, is no different in principle from taking account of things. But this is apparently not true for highly reflective types of people such as intellectuals, or people in special situations that require more self-separating reflection than situations ordinarily require. It is, however, apparently true for people engaged in "ordinary affairs." In other words, it may well be that there is something about what is often referred to from that point of view as ordinary everyday life, perhaps its modernity, that is thought to commit actors tendentiously to be instrumentally rational. It is nevertheless acknowledged that this is realized only against a contingent background of exceptional noise generated by what are stipulated to be nonrational factors—which may have to do with emergent norms, the intensity of emotions, the charisma or attractiveness of certain parties, the fearful nature of certain events, or other conditions that qualify and can threaten to compromise the clarity of thought toward which everyday actors are said nevertheless to strive. These are neither parameters nor main sources of intentionality. They are conditions that may interfere with the conditions of rational action and, in that respect, may explain a certain amount of what is associated with "politics."

The picture that emerges is that people in their guise as "ordinary" are fundamentally instrumental in their orientations and therefore particularly open to instrumental possibilities in the ways a populist utilitarian might claim that they are: when possible, they give priority to goal-orientation and means-ends considerations over other possible structures of action. Their apparent capacity to adapt to their multifarious and alienating environments seems to support this point of view as does their apparent susceptibility to noisy factors and their de-rationalizing effects. Along these lines, one might thereby be tempted to hypothesize, first, that the tendency toward rationality would, in the world of everyday life, win out but for politics (or "tradition"), second, that politics is not as dominated by the imperatives of rational choice as might have been expected, and third, that everyday life, and possibly politics, can be described without any particular reference to creativity, generativity, self-reflection, and the like.

Even if one were willing to accept this as a working model of how we should think people ordinarily behave, what has been discussed so far suggests that it cannot be formulated in a way that addresses the problems we originally wanted theory to address—problems that have to do with what "social" can mean such that its meaning is consistent with what must be said about what is human about human affairs, and such that it can be consistent with the ontological presuppositions of the human sciences taken together, as inscribed in the history of philosophy and exemplified in the practices if not the reports of the various fields. Moreover, if, as I believe, its idea of everyday life is false and cannot account for the social aspect of behavior without assuming that very aspect and then distorting it, and in that regard accepts a view of it that belies the very possibility of sociality, the general model, which pits rationality against noise, is altogether misleading. Yet there seems another way of defending the idea that people are instrumentalists in everyday life without assuming that they are instrumentalists in all ways. This argument requires claiming that people live in two basic ways; one that requires self-oriented instrumental rationality and another that is governed by morality in the Kantian sense of seeing ends where under another orientation they see means (see Nagel 1991 for a particular version of this). These may occasionally interfere with one another, but they can be considered apart from one another for the purposes of analysis. We might say, then, that there is something about modern life, modernity, that compartmentalizes experience in such a way that respecting just such a division is compulsory of virtually everyone and can therefore be taken for granted as a condition of modern existence, which is the existence with which we need to be concerned.

Here, one version of the argument is that people are effectively dualists in everyday life, insofar as that involves balancing what pertains to the self, the governance of mind by the body, and what pertains to others, body governed by mind, and that any theory of social action must start with the assumption that the distinction is fundamental to the ordinary sense of what it is to be an agent, an effective participant in human affairs. In that case, it can be claimed that the practical reason that gives order to the activities of everyday life presupposes a strictly naturalistic attitude while such anti-instrumental aspects of life as celebrating, participating, playing, loving, being ethical, and enjoying presuppose a strictly nonnaturalistic attitude, at least toward others and possibly to certain objects or events. The argument continues by saying that the theory of social action is primarily concerned with either the one or the other, rationality or reasonableness, and allows for a process of balancing that seems to be an exception to both principles. The only thing that counts theoretically in everyday life insofar as it involves making choices are, first, situated objects regardless of type (human or nonhuman) though not regardless of the specific properties by which they can be incorporated rationally into a process of decision making, second, just such a process, and, third, situations that are, to use Allport's (1924) expression, "socially facilitating."

There is one way in which psychological idealism has been at least deferred when we say that persons are social inasmuch as they take others into account. This involves emphasizing the idea of an exchange-based intersubjectivity of person-to-person relations. However, this involves a change in the meaning of "taking . . . into account." If persons are inter-subjective with their ostensible others, then the way in which each, considered separately, takes account of those others involves more than merely believing that they are conditions of or factors in making decisions and attaching meaning accordingly. For that matter, it involves more than having the very notion of others in the usual sense of "subjects not one's self." Yet it is difficult to see how relations among persons can be anything but external in the interactionist model, though the criticism of psychological idealism requires that persons not be distinct except for the possibility of naming at any point in their collective activity. To preserve the criticism without falling into reductionism requires that interpersonal relations be internal and not external, therefore, in effect, cross-personal or supra-personal. In other words, "inter-subjectivity" can be clarified only under an acceptable notion of a sociality that is distinctively human. It is not possible to sustain idealizations of individual consciousness, personhood, experience, or action on the presupposition that relations are external.[1] In that case, the prefix "inter" is not quite adequate to the notion that underlies the use of the word "inter-subjectivity." It is, then, increasingly clear that taking others into account must be considered radically different from taking things into account if one is to understand what people do among people; and, correspondingly, taking things into account must be conceived of as radically different from what it is generally thought to mean.

A rough way to approach this that still retains something of the rationalist point of view is to say that a person taking account of another takes the point of view of that other, at least in some nontrivial part of what she thinks, feels, and does—possibly, as Mead (1962) claimed in a much discussed and still debated formulation, the point of view of another as an index and, as consciousness develops, a token of a "generalized other." This formulation is rough because it is far too simple and begs too many of the questions it is supposed to resolve. Moreover, like most simplifications of human affairs, it permits inferences that are either counterintuitive relative to what is sub-theoretical or intuitive only in the sense of being subject to as yet inadequately examined notions. Even so, this moves us beyond the Weberian idea that persons are social inasmuch as they take account of others.

We have seen that something other than interaction must be involved in the notion that human beings are essentially social, perhaps the capacity and/or disposition to adopt the point of view of another without the limitations of the idea that one can rationally generalize one's own experiences). But if this is to avoid psychological idealism, it must not be another version of the sort of interpretation that holds that what an other has done constitutes data from which it is possible rationally to induce an underlying rule, law, norm, or principle (a "deep" invariant property of the other) that allows the social actor who takes account of others to go beyond what is immediately present to what might occur in the immediate future—as if it is not problematic in the first place, and regardless of what else about this formulation is problematic, to assume that the actor can adopt or take another's point of view or frame of reference in the normal appropriative sense of "adopt" or "take." The points of view of parties cannot be taken for granted or assumed, any more than their mentality can be summarized as a "point of view," at least not if the expression "inter-subjectivity" is to have a meaning different from merely "paying attention to others" or "being responsive to them." *The very idea of a "point of view" places subjects at an absolute distance from one another, threatening the idea of inter-subjectivity, and therefore that of cooperation beyond particular tasks—if "point of view" is used theoretically to specify what it means to take account of others and, at the same time, to take account of "taking account" as a fact.*

Mikhail Bakhtin's (1981) analysis of the multiplicity of voices in the exemplary novels of Charles Dickens and Fyodor Dostoevsky may be helpful in clarifying the idea of inter-subjectivity, given his view that language is a social phenomenon before whatever else might be said about it. This is in contrast with claiming that taking others into account (and the idea of taking another's point of view) is a sufficiently adequate representation of the sociality of action. Bakhtin's essay "The Theory of the Novel" was, among other things, intended to develop a concept of the essential ambiguity of speech that has more general, extra-literary applications. To that end, he conceived of the modern novel as a dialogical text composed of a multiplicity of relatively unstratified voices, in which stratification is always problematically displayed. The notion of "dialogue," in contrast with "monologue," identifies the novel as a paradigm of multiplicity and takes ordinary discourse (in nonofficial situations, as spontaneous, and without reference to occasion) as the reality to which the paradigm most generally applies. This is clear from Bakhtin's theory of the compositional quality of the ordinariness of everyday life discussed in the first sections of *Rabelais and His World* (1968). The idea is that the activity of people taken together displays a degree of spontaneity, fluency, and momentum that cannot be adequately accounted for as expressing beliefs about facts, institutional or otherwise, or a prior positive commitment to a given form or a given content. These qualities presumably reflect the intrinsically motivating aspect of a multiplicity, therefore order(ing) without rules, conceivable only under such an aspect.

In the presence of differences among people, whenever difference is inescapable and where power and the possibility of arbitrary authority are at issue precisely because neither can abide difference, activity must be understood as incorporating the general fact of difference. It follows that whatever characteristics might be attributed to discourse, it will display *waiting* as one of its most prominent features and the momentum of the inter-subjective course of activity of which it can only be a moment. This incorporation of difference per se, the expectation of surprise, allows us to infer that to speak conversationally (with fluency and spontaneity) is, at each apparently singular instant, to be immanent to a collective enunciation and to be relatively indifferent to the concrete facts of specific differences, except for intrusive instances derived, for example, from principles of stratification that are incompatible with the idea of an "activity in its course." In other words, to speak as a moment of collectivity, more generally to be *of* such a moment, is, by the very sociality of speaking, to subvert any differentiation of status in regard, at least, to "voice" and "attitude." More prosaically, it is to participate in a moment of equal dependence, analogous to Rousseau's moment of the first convention. Difference, and not identity, is the substance of collectivity and therefore a fact of life for its momentary parties rather than a problem that either needs to be solved as such or that needs to be solved if the movement of collective unity ("community") is to be maintained. This is why Bakhtin (1968) refers to the basic manifestation of collective enunciation as "heteroglossia," a mixing of voices independent of individual agents where the fact of mixing is a condition of all meaningful vocalization. For parties to such settings, to speak meaningfully is to abide linguistically among others to a discourse. It is to recognize the essential incompleteness, hence reflexivity, of their discourse. Thus, each instance of speaking, each moment of enunciation, must be seen as invariably adopting or making room for possibly different "voices," and, thus, for the possibility of surprise. *Discourse is, then, permissive without permission being given.*

The same is true for a hypothetical external observer interested in reacquainting herself with the fact of collective enunciation: what becomes observationally knowable about a course of activity across ostensible individuals, what is displayed in whatever they do, is also *difference as such*; and this has the effect of transforming the sense of "across ostensible individuals" into the sense of an authentic collective, where "authentic" refers to the ongoing quality of the accomplishment. It is the hypothetical being, the observer, who "witnesses" projections and dissolutions of unity, therefore the course of activity beyond its moments. From the point of view of the nonparticipant, for whom human life is nevertheless essentially social, what appears is a texture of incomplete gestures in which the very fact of incompleteness supersedes every apparently individuated act. *Each such act displays an attitude of waiting, to the extent to which it participates in an intentionality it cannot govern, an immanent mobility that in one important respect attends all other mobilities and no motion in particular. The hypothetical observer is, then, forced to construct a reality that cannot be lived in order to testify to a living that cannot be constructed as such a reality.*

The observed "order" of waiting (beyond apparent instances of waiting as indicative of collective enunciation) appears, relative to theoretical expectations of unity, as a relative disorder in which participation appears to be motivated by temporary and local movements toward resolution. This is why I refer to that "order" as a multiplicity, differentiation that is self-animating, rather than, say, a structure, differentiation that is merely functional and formal but, as such, lacks, as Saussure (1986) said, vitality and therefore the possibility of realization. For this reason it is tempting to posit external motivational tendencies that are general enough in their putative force to allow for an implicit order across the observed field of display of the unending variety of gestures. But this posit, inferred from identifying what is being done with particular intentions, threatens to beg the question by bringing individuality in by the back door as a constitutive and not merely prior condition of the social—though it leaves open the question of how the individual moment of collective enunciation can become a moment. It does so by substituting the *deus ex machina* of the motivating mental state, or the self, in its account of that moment, for the embracing momentum of discursive speech itself, which, ironically, it assumes.

It is nevertheless tempting to posit individual intentions as motivating speech since there is no reason to doubt that individuals make utterances and are often held responsible for their manner or ultimate content. But the intention to utter, whatever form the utterance then takes, should not be thought of as an intention to encompass all that follows or could follow conversationally, since nothing has yet followed and the meaning of the utterance as part of a discourse has not yet been determined: *one can hardly intend as an individual what cannot be individually intended.* If someone were to venture so aggressive a move, it would not appear as part of a conversation so much as an intervention aimed at subverting or eliminating the very possibility of there being meaningful conversation. If we consider an utterance's occurring in the midst of such a discourse, it would be remiss to interpret it as an expression of a durable intention that could be realized as such only by somehow converting what is a social fact into a purely individualized one. If the conversion were to be complete, and conversation thereby brought to end, the meaning of what had been uttered in its midst could not be the same as its meaning independent of its being embodied in that or any situation.

This back door recovery of the compound idea of distinct and complete actions of individuals and comprehensive mental states seems to avoid the conceptual difficulties posed by the evident attitude of waiting. But the difficulties cannot be avoided without rejecting several propositions that I have tried to show are unavoidable by any responsive analysis of speech. First, speaking in an attitude of waiting is a constitutive feature of discursive speech. It makes speech recognizable as such. Second, this is so to the extent to which speech is conceived of as essentially, or first of all, social; and it cannot otherwise be conceived of without doing violence to the reliability with which the term presumably must be applied if analysis is to have any hope of success in providing a general, or generally usable, theory of speech that is also intuitively plausible. Finally, an account of speaking will fail to sustain a plausible sense of it, plausible for a possible speaker, and fail to establish generalizations that do not further distort the phenomenon, unless speech is conceived of as a course of activity and not a succession of discrete actions. In other words, to see why the back door recovery must fail, it is necessary to remember that the concept of an attitude of waiting is consistent with two related facts that are inconsistent with just such a recovery: the lack of distinctiveness of the gestures and the practical derivation, both for actors and observers, of their intelligibility from *their* participation in the gesturing and enunciating ensemble. Moreover, aside from denying the momentum inherent in a multiplicity that allows one to consider activity as participation in the first place, it requires rejecting an assumption about meaningfulness that is crucial to the notion of discursive speech—namely, that all utterances are, as instances of inter-subjective sociality, necessarily and intrinsically ambiguous. Meaning, as Derrida constantly reminds us, is always deferred.

Parenthetically, the fact that a nagging belief that ambiguity is not merely prevalent but systematic in ordinary communicative speech may be why so many philosophers of language have concluded that meaning cannot be complete in the individual statement—except under circumstances that ought to be treated as exceptional where the utterance can be taken as an isolated event or as an intervention in the sense described previously. If I am correct, it should also be admitted that meaning is not only incomplete (and therefore an ongoing accomplishment) but constantly being re-formed and therefore not properly interpreted as a complete and final intention at the moment of the utterance—as far as concerns the sociality in which meaning is an ongoing accomplishment. *This seems to me to support the more radical idea that the meaning of an utterance that appears in the form of a statement is also never completed (nor even approximately so) by a putative context of such statements (or possible statements), even one treated as a system. That would be to substitute one relatively fixed unit (the set of statements) for the other (the single utterance).*

That some philosophers of science consider a holistic interpretation of scientifically technical and systematically coherent propositions to be necessary to understanding the meaning of any subset of them, cannot constitute a paradigm of discursive speech in regard to its discursivity. The authors of scientific reports often attempt to fix meaning by the logical integrity of their particular text, or its participation in a larger integral text, and this is something that we cannot conceive of as what the activity of speaking is attempting to do: for if that were to be possible, discourse would be impossible. In passing, it must be remembered that the notion of discourse as a course of activity depends on the earlier discussion of the inter-subjectivity of the objectivity of agency-dependent objects. Otherwise, the idea of a course of activity easily degenerates into a standard notion of process, and with that into an unsustainable metaphysics of "process" that, correspondingly, reinstates the analytical priority of individual intentions and the lack of analytical significance of what transpires between intention and result or outcome (Rescher 1996).

In summary, the idea of the social cannot be represented as agents "taking others into account" even when doing so is said to rely on empathy, since this requires identifying activities apart from the conditions under which they are meaningful instances of discursive speech. Doing so begs the question of what it is to be social that seemed to require reference to both "taking others into account" and "taking the position or point of view of the other." The social must remain irreducible beyond its moments if the idea of the sociality of what people do among people is to be intelligible within the frame of reference of the human as a being in a situation—given that situations are essentially inter-subjective, or instances of multiplicity. In what follows, I continue to emphasize discursive speech, but it should be clear that, as things stand, the discussion is intended to apply to all instances of distinctively human activity.

24

Collective Enunciation

We can now say that the meaningfulness of discursive speech, of whatever is in the course of being uttered, is a feature of the general will. As far as "communication" is the issue, the general will is meaningfulness per se, which is *the becoming that is waited on* in every instance of uttering or gesturing. In this way, instances transpire in the attitude of waiting implicit in the sociality of life. Meaningfulness, in the moment of the general will that belongs to language, lies in the continuation of speaking—in the limitless circulation of a value for which there is no substitute and no standard of redemption—beyond whatever fleetingly appears as the vehicle of a particular meaning. As Rousseau showed, this is its strength and its vulnerability. The meaningfulness of an utterance does not lie in its intended use but on its discursive character. Something is a meaningful utterance insofar as it projects more opportunities for continuation than it can possibly command. In that sense, it anticipates and does not constitute agency and intentionality. The very being of "others in general," crucial to the idea of society, is constituted, brought to life, in the attitude of waiting that marks utterances as discursively meaningful and therefore as moments in the un-owned course of the activity of speaking.

An utterance that exemplifies discursive speech is, first of all, a venture in the continuation of a course of activity. It is, in this respect, consistent with how I interpret Rousseau's first convention, momentarily indifferent to particular, nameable others. If alienation has anything to do with this, it is not because of an opposition between individual and group. The meaning and significance of such an utterance cannot be theorized as an individual speaker's desire or accomplishment; and it cannot be understood as an instance of meaningful communication on the model of speaking and hearing as separable processes involving different but connected sorts of agency, as in Paul Grice's (1989) account of "conversation" in his discussion of "conversational implicature." Nor, in most cases, could it be such an accomplishment or an instance of such communication. This is because, as a moment of discursive speech, uttering is neither originary nor complete. It is not an act or a result of a decision. It is always passing through the hearing and speaking of "someones," which is how its meaningfulness is realized as an ongoing accomplishment. It is, then, not an action or the result of a "decision." Nor, it must be added, is it an instance of alienation, just the opposite.

For Russell (1974), "vagueness and imprecision" were defects of speech understood ideally as a series of monologues and turns and, correspondingly, on an implicit model of communication as an exchange of distinct messages aimed at a possible meeting of minds predicated on a prior meeting of minds (agreement about certain aspects of meaning that have to do with particular intentions). Such a model does not describe discourse, which is an irreducible course of activity that never succeeds in totalizing itself. Any attempt to individuate the utterance by "correcting" its discursive character (or modeling it accordingly) effectively negates its intelligibility: as if discursivity itself (sociality) undermines the activity of speaking. The immanent sociality of speaking makes something like communication inevitable. It depends on the irreducibility of discourse to particular durable forms and particular intentions. As we have seen, the temptation to reduce in either respect serves interests inhospitable to the sociality of which intentions and forms are merely moments. Thus, the idea of the social as a course of activity is necessary to the intelligibility of the idea of discursive speech.

This is in contrast with speech conceived of according to a logic of discrete and reproducible acts that realize intended meaning by virtue of the formal ordering of contents based on consensus about the limitations of their meaning, *and* based on a consensus that consensus itself provide such a standard—that the burden of proof is always on the statistically deviant. If speech is taken to be material in the sense of distinct and discrete actions capable of being extracted from their situation for interpretation or explanation, then the selection of that material must be interpreted and explained for its appropriateness to the choice of methods for analyzing it. This means that the linguistic material must already be both meaningful and intelligible.[1] An analysis of meaning that depends on an unstated theory of meaning does not resolve the problem presented to it by the facts we have been considering—namely, that instances of speech are always imbedded in discourse (*speech always within speaking*), that discourse is a reflexive course of activity in which each moment of speaking displays an attitude of waiting, and that meaning is not the sort of thing that can be attributed to abstracted acts, with or without appeal to equally abstracted contexts. Such facts are incompatible with formalist and statistical assumptions about the relationship between meaning and intelligibility and about discursive truth. One might conjecture, then, that intelligible speech understood as socially validating discourse constitutes itself as a multiplicity, not a plurality of utterances, no matter what else can be said about it and about formal criteria of a very different sort of intelligibility than what is appropriate to the idea of sociality as the human aspect of human affairs.

This relation of discursivity to the intelligibility of speech is not a matter of contingency, since what counts is continuation reflexive to itself. It is on the order of immanence and must be thought of that way, just as money is not something that intelligence adds to the exchange of commodities in order to rationalize it, or that people agree to try out, but something logically entailed by the very identification of something as a commodity (necessarily produced as something capable of being exchanged for any other such monetarized product). What is essential to speaking as an intelligible activity is not a matter of an individual utterer's calculated choice to fit into a specific event, to act according to the dictates of an occasion, or to address a collectivity (audience). Each is, of course, possible; but none is compatible with any course of activity except the activities defining and determining "choosing," "fitting in," and "addressing." There is, of course, a sense in which one does choose the occasion and settings of one's utterance and utters decisively. But, as a matter of method appropriate to discourse as a fact in its own right, as a course of activity, it is imperative that we consider at the outset the logical priority of setting over action, collective disposition or intentionality over particular will, and course of activity over action. Otherwise, we can easily drift toward reduction and reification, or reliance on paradigmatic simplifications that cannot be paradigms of social reality under the theoretical conditions necessary to exemplify it as distinctively human. It follows that the particular will asserts itself as a problem for the idea of intelligibility but not as a resource for determining meaning, or concrete occasion for further speaking, or a necessary condition of agency and therefore meaning in the sense of what is intended prior to what is uttered. Intelligibility, as an ongoing accomplishment, is not problematic for Bakhtin's (1968) conception of "heteroglossia." He uses this expression to substantiate the idea of collective enunciation as a multiplicity of multiplicities. It suggests that one can identify the form no less than the content of an ostensibly individual utterance only as internal to a discourse—in which case "identify" is problematic; but that poses a different sort of question.

One must respect, as one does a fact, that the utterance considered *as a unit of meaning* is never complete and that its incompleteness is a constitutive condition of its being *meaningful*. In that case, agency and meaning are ongoing accomplishments of internally self-diversifying voices in which every ostensible individual act is intrinsically ambiguous. One policy consistent with this line of speculation is that a pedagogically useful image of collective enunciation will correspond to the image of socially productive work—in a theoretical context in which the socialization of labor does not correspond to and is not tantamount to the socialization of individual laborers. It is interesting to note that conversational analysis occasionally uses "work" as a metaphor aimed at clarifying what is collective about discourse. In any case, the sort of multiplicity Bakhtin brings to notice is what about the everydayness of "everyday life" constitutes the "dialogism" by which he distinguishes "the novel" from monological speech and texts[2] and distinguishes the self-movement of the collectivity from all instances of "stratification" and finality. In passing, focusing on this is a minimal condition of addressing issues around meaning, truth, reference, and reflexivity, insofar as one attempts to illuminate what is human about discursive speech.

Russell's comment suggests, despite his apparent reluctance to consider it, that it is difficult to think of the intelligibility of an actual instance of speech without imagining its being implicit in some discourse and, therefore, as internal to a setting that is intelligible only in regard to the participation or constitution of utterers in the momentum of speaking, rather than by reference to their having access to it—as if the intelligibility of an instance of speaking depends on its adequacy as an objectively discrete message. Parenthetically, it should be noted that a great deal of philosophy since Russell has come close to acknowledging this. One thinks of the writings of W. V. Quine on conditions of translation and the problems they create for the idea of a possible meeting of minds (see Quine and Ullian 1970) and Grice (1989) on the significance of conversational discourse for any theory of meaning, though neither was able to establish an analysis appropriate to a course of activity, thus betraying the phenomenon they identify. To say that whatever is taken as an instance of intelligible speech is always a feature of a discourse suggests that the two are "compositionally connected" in the same way a modernist unsatisfied with the idea of "structure" might say that the elements of a still life or painted landscape are compositionally determined. A rough approximation of the sense of composition I have in mind is that something is compositionally coherent when it moves, through the internal relations of its voices, through a locally inexhaustible number of different courses of activity and their moments of activity-generating disruption.

It does not matter that a given utterance might, under certain circumstances, appear to initiate a discourse (as when someone poses a question followed by a discussion altogether constrained by the question). What comes first in discourse is, of course, rarely decidable, though there may be instances that are beyond dispute (or settled for "all practical purposes") and, for that reason, are selected as examples intended to clarify a general theory. It is not only that meanings are mixed—that indexical meanings, which are ephemeral, are conjoined with meanings that appear to be independent of their immediate setting and not ephemeral. Assuming the validity of the distinction, the conjunction itself limits the prospects of translation and interpretation, and it is impossible to fix, post hoc, the content of mixed expressions that operate as such only within a course of activity—in which content (reference, predication, etc.), considered as an overall *telos*, cannot be at issue without undoing what is discursive about the activity.

These are problems that make it impossible to rely, as findings, on extra- or post-discursive reports that assume the form of description. Moreover, the very momentum and reflexivity of a discourse defies attempts to simulate what "was happening such that participation was both spontaneous and committed." The character of the loose and shifting compositional motions among instances of discursive speech, which is its character for the hypothetical observer, has to do with the immanence of the social and, therefore, with the incessant anti-telic movement of expressions, gestures, postures, words, bodies, and things. From this point of view, intelligibility is not essentially a matter either of parties achieving literal interpretability (for the sake of being observed) or of their displaying a commitment to rules (in anticipation of simulation, translation, or modeling).

The idea of an extra-individual non-telic compositional aspect of speech in discourse may seem untoward from the point of view of research. But it derives from a generally agreed-on characterization of "discourse" in contrast with objectively comprehensible linguistic usage. This says that discourse constitutes an altogether mobile inter-subjective gestural field of "collective enunciation." It is only outside of it that utterances appear to be what they cannot be if they are moments of discourse—namely, discrete and integral entities analyzable as elements of a series or merely formally connected units. This is a matter more of analytical convenience than faithfulness to the object; and, like all such conveniences, there is a cost. It violates the idea of intelligibility *in* discourse to the extent to which it rejects one crucial aspect of discursive composition—that it negates in principle the particularity, unitariness, and translatability that analysis always affirms.

This is why I have argued that literal interpretation, context-conscious interpretation, and the sampling of ordinary and presumably repeatable usage cannot represent the intelligibility or social aspect of discursive speech and therefore cannot be about communication. All such options beg the question of the relations of utterance, intelligibility, and meaning. Instead, it is crucial to recognize that the very sense of the term "utterance" depends on its instances being moments of discourse, which irrevocably involves them in the anti-telic movements of collective enunciation. As such, discourse does not naturally decompose into separable elements that can then be retrieved and held up for inspection and comparison by observers and alienated speakers, according to the possibility of a meeting of minds. It is because of this that it is a mistake to characterize discursive utterances as discrete and unambiguous "speech acts," even relatively so. This is a point that I later return to in a somewhat different context. For now, as in all activity that can be said to be meaningful, to be laden with nonspecific sub-theoretical possibilities, to exhibit the tendency that early gestalt psychology referred to as *pregnanz*, discourse must be understood as dialogical through and through and within everything momentarily identified as a unit or moment or instance, including the "speech act" that only appears to be a motivated particular, and, as Bakhtin (1981) says, even the word itself. This multiplicity cannot be reduced to elementary units without a loss of intelligibility. Rather than "interaction among separable persons," it is this that best captures the meaning of "inter-subjectivity." It follows that analyzing an utterance or a gesture is reasonable, in the sense of true to the concept of its object, only if the analysis respects the irreducibility of the multiplicity of which it is a moment. In that case the utterance itself, the ostensible unit, must also be taken as a multiplicity, in which case "analysis" means something significantly different from what it is said to mean in accounts that rely on the reducibility of discourse to distinct actions and distinct parties and on the independent translatability of its moments (see Urmson 1956).

By "dialogue," Bakhtin might be understood to mean speaking divided by "turns" such that every utterance is predicated on another complete utterance and, therefore, that no utterance stands alone. This seems reasonable at first, but it is insufficient to the concept. To the extent to which "dialogue" describes speaking as a moment of discourse, it inevitably projects ambiguities that are bound to proliferate and, therefore, are rarely able to be resolved other than by having arrived at a point of "rest," momentarily and behind the backs of the parties. While this emphasis on ambiguity is essential to the idea of discourse as a course of activity, it is, as stated, not quite sufficient. Bakhtin's claim that the *word* itself is "dialogical" and his discussion of the "heteroglossia" implicit in the most fundamental sociality of which we can conceive suggest that he means more than that ambiguity invariably accompanies speaking with others—where this use of "ambiguity" has the sense of something "open to more than one interpretation in the context . . . in which it occurs" (Preminger and Brogan 1993, 40; Bakhtin 1968, 1981). Discursive speech, understood as dialogical, is intelligible only as a multiplicity of inter-subjective vocalizations each of which is a multiplicity. I refer to this, provisionally, as a "composition." Because it is, for Bakhtin, essentially dialogical, it is not intelligible in the way that a monologue is intelligible, assuming such a thing is conceivable as an instance of speaking; nor is the intelligibility attributable to a monologue capable of social validation in the same way that moments of dialogue are intelligible. Moreover, dialogical intelligibility has to do with something like participation, in Goffman's (1961a) sense of involvement or absorption in a course of activity, and not essentially with what is or could be in the minds of individual speakers.

Bakhtin means by "monologue" the projection of a singular, self-sustaining voice that exists as monological to the extent to which it excludes all other voices. It may envision a momentarily disengaged response or reaction on the part of idealized others, but its continuity belongs solely to the one who utters its sounds. What is heard always sounds complete, dead; as such, it only justifies celebration, commentary, or appreciation of the shell that appears to have simply emerged in its wholeness. To love such an object is to dismiss the relevance of how it might have come to be—as with those *connoisseurs* who love art with a passion that can exist only by despising artists and ignoring, as one might turn away from an unpleasant odor, what is involved in doing art, or dogmatists who idealize society as culture and tradition, as "civilization," but have nothing but contempt for it as a becoming, a human form of life. When monologue is taken as the privileged instance of communicative speech such that, in dialogue conceived of as turn taking, voices succeed one another as separate actions, each speaker will appear as a center of responsibility, ownership, and agency that brings about form, timing, content, and disposition.

Excluding other voices, each attempt at exclusion, amounts to a declaration in favor of the possibility of a single voice, therefore the desire for a private language that, in its futility, is all the more intensified. This cancels the collectivity of speaking together in favor of a fantastic inspired agency that, alone and as a matter of right, reaffirms individuality as the core of democracy—and at the same time and by the same gesture invalidates the democratic idea of "voice." Exclusion begins and ends by eliminating multiplicity, therefore sociality as such: it does not and is not intended to eliminate specific voices. But, because its intelligibility even to momentarily disengaged parties presupposes multiplicity, it is typically disguised as inclusive, as part of a generously or mercifully intended exchange or a series of monologues open to others but only in due time and in the proper form. This is how the unfulfillable desire embodied in monologic speech both undermines dialogue and appears to represent moves within dialogue by sanctioning the addition of voices on condition that each speak monologically and without any acknowledgment of the social reality on which their very quality as "voice" depends.

Monological communication is communication only in the sense of an exchange among radically detached ostensible subjects, which is to say "universal exchange" ("circulation") in which the particularity of each act can no longer be an issue. Since only one act occurs at a time, units of meaning are not dialogical and ambiguities are resolved or re-presented as an invitation. Whatever ambiguities appear in monological speech, strictly understood, seem contrived or the result of misunderstanding; or they are thought to be capable of elimination upon closer attention on the part of the audience to what is being or should be said. In this respect, speech act theory begins on the side of the monologue. If dialogue consists of alternating monologues, and is thereby deprived of the aspect of sociality, it cannot be what Bakhtin meant by identifying it as an expression of the essential sociality of discourse.[3]

Intelligibility of the sort required for a continuation of an essentially socialized communicative activity requires something more than a series of monologues. It requires that the activity of speaking display properties, including a degree of physicality, that incorporate others regardless of their ostensible differences. Bakhtin characterizes monologue disguised as dialogue as implicitly stratified and its audience subordinate to a series mistaken for collective enunciation—as one might once have asserted that bodily movements are inessential to and merely reinforce the spoken word the meaning of which is found within the intention of the speaker as the signified idea.[4] In that case, the origin of an instance of monologue can lie only within the individual speaker, whose speech invokes no sense of situation or occasion, though it does of "contingencies" or "conditions" and, therefore, no sense of a sociality that reveals itself in the attitude of waiting that marks the distinctively discursive quality of every instance of discursive speech. This mere semblance of dialogue projects monologue as a realm of necessity precisely where theory needs to acknowledge speaking as a realm of the freedom implicit in the general will and manifest as collective enunciation. What, then, counts as the meaning of what is spoken is independent of sociality, except in the trivial sense of being aimed at an audience whose reactions and responses might be anticipated. It is a performance within a scripted drama in contrast with the production of value by value, of significance to the course of activity in which it participates despite itself, even as a semblance of value.

Aside from the paradox implicit in the very idea of a monologue, it has two positive features. First, it highlights what is and what cannot be involved in the concept of a dialogue, and, second, it indicates a counter-dialogical tendency within discourse itself. This tendency to resolve difference, as the countertendency to enhance difference, reflects the fact that intelligibility as such is prior to the specific intelligibility of any instance of discursive speech, and the two tendencies are not quite compatible, for reasons discussed in the next section. For now, the idea of a dialogue, understood in reference to multiplicity, is crucial to the relationship of sociality to inter-subjectivity. That, in turn, is crucial to understanding what it is for an utterance to be meaningful and therefore to the very intelligibility, or social validity, of discourse. Still, while it is not difficult to understand why discourse must be thought of as a multiplicity, it is relatively difficult to show how it is that every given instance of discursively valid speech, intelligible speech, is a multiplicity in itself.

An abstract example might look something like the following, in which I dramatize the idea of "voice" in order to articulate the idea of a "multiplicity of voices." Imagine (consider oneself observing) someone describing an event, a situation, a place, or the activity of another. How that person's description is represented by its observer at first will affect how it is represented as an instance of dialogue. The voices are abstractions and the example is conjectural. The example shows that taking dialogue to be an instance of multiplicity (which is immanent to discourse) is different from taking it to be an instance of alternating monologues. It also shows how such a characterization might operate within the greater discourse of which it is a feature. The imagined or empirical description works for the observer only if it is intimately connected with other instances of speaking, gesturing, or otherwise indicating and expressing. Describing something as it is occurring, which relies on available descriptive terms, conveys information or, what amounts to the same thing, determines its value in the sense of the difference it makes, on condition that there are orienting gestures associated with the activity of describing.

This means that the intelligibility of the description to its observer depends, at first, on what might be called its legitimacy within a discourse, the latter being the source of legitimacy in the same way that something about society, the general will, is the source of what Foucault (2007, 2003, 2008) calls "governmentality": it depends on an invocation of one or another voice, gesture, or indication in regard to a setting of what might be called relations of accountability.[5] Moreover, it does not merely depend on an invocation of specific voices but necessarily of innumerable indefinite voices—as the "general will" implies that each member depends on innumerable others and not just on those immediately familiar or affectively connected to her. Such self-expansive relations are not typically coherent in the sense of a logical structure in the ways in which ethnologists once depicted "kinship" or social psychologists theorized "role structures" and sociologists the "functions of social conflict." These exemplify the most subtle versions in the literature of sociology of logically constructed ideal types to account for social action. In each case, it is assumed that activities organize themselves or are organized as practices, understood as systems of rules adequately modeled as logically integrated structures: the structures are self-integrating, presumably, because of an immanent tendency, possibly evolutionary, to perfect that very integration. It should be noted in passing that this strategy, at least as it appears in the later work of Parsons (see 1977), was designed as part of an effort to defend the notion of the relative autonomy of the social, a project that the present book endorses, though in quite different terms and with an altogether different argument and correspondingly different conclusions.

The relation of voice to discourse does not form a logically integrated structure and, therefore, cannot be coherent in the sense of "coherence" that attaches to the idea that a multiplicity of voices operates as a series of discrete turns or "exchanges." This does not, of course, preclude their being historical, if one means by "historical" the immanence of certain tensions in human affairs and not just what happens to such affairs over an externally determined course of time—that is, chronologically. They must be seen as bearing their own tendencies to change indefinitely in the very fact of their multiplicity. Those relations (e.g., of voice to discourse) are intelligible not if what counts are performances taken as events, one by one but only if they operate as multiplicities within the multiplicity of discourse.

I have argued that such ostensibly discrete performances must be taken to constitute a situation that lacks the features of the sort of situation that obtains in human affairs if we consider the latter in regard to what is human about them. So I have referred to "performances taken one by one" as only ostensibly what people are doing, and I have considered some negative consequences of taking what is ostensible as factual. One such consequence is that each "performance" is seen as a discrete event in a series. But this can be so only where the latter is conceptualized under the auspices of the idea of a system; and the reason why "system" becomes essential is that its concept is designed to provide for logo-centric tendencies, which is all that remains of the concept of human affairs after "performance" has been identified with strictly individuated acts. In other words, "system," in this regard, is designed to suggest what cannot otherwise be justified—namely, that absolute particulars can comprise something social.

Suppose that what is merely ostensible about human affairs in this sense (and the question remains "Ostensible to whom?") is considered adequate to understanding them in their own terms. In that case, there is little choice but to characterize putatively discrete performances in such a way that their meaningfulness, their relations with each other, can be accounted for only by assuming, tendentiously, the latency of an ideal model of integration. The assumption entails that the model be experienced as such by parties but only inexplicitly, as a latency, and as the simultaneity of the practices, as if they naturally function together, cohere, such that theory need only ratify that as a fact. I argue instead that the relations of voices and speaking to discourses are not typically coherent in the strict logical sense but that their coherence, in the sense of what makes them accountable, is of a different order of composition based on what is necessary to preserve the social quality of human affairs, and if that is to be connected with the idea of what is human about them. The multiplicity of utterances, gestures, and the like, which we have been forced to acknowledge as the essential feature of discourse, appears from the standpoint of the momentarily individuated observer as if it is a series of turns or exchanges among discrete performances; but this says more about individuated observation, which is monological and the perspective of a nonparticipant, than it says about the phenomenon itself, though such individuation may well be an as yet mysterious feature of the sort of discourse that it appears to reject.

Parties "know" the atemporal simultaneity of what appear to a hypothetical "one" who stands outside of the general will as merely elements of a more or less coherent series. For a point of view that can be attributed to them, the courses of activity constituting multiplicity must be theorized according to a situation that they collectively "intend" as such, though not in the sense of "intend" that suggests a motive to bring about an effect or complete a design. In this regard what they do is meaningful in respect of the multiplicity of which that doing is a feature. That is, if what a party is doing is intimately responsive to, a feature of, what is being done together, and if that is not because of the specificity of what the party is doing but because of its indeterminacy such that her activity must be seen under the aspect of the attitude of waiting, then the activity of which she is a moment must be one that not only tolerates ambiguity but is noticeably suited to its inevitability. It must be irreducibly dialogical or what amounts to the same thing, a multiplicity.

One way of clarifying this is to apply it to the idea of a conversation. From this point of view, each effective instance of speaking momentarily projects a historicity of collective enunciation—that is, its aspect of work or struggle. This projection supersedes and transforms what might otherwise be attributed to a speaker as she is speaking. The one speaking in the midst of dialogue cannot be considered the same sort of agency as one whose speech consists of distinct performances by an individuated actor who, in speaking, expresses herself according to what she needs or desires. As far as such an oddly monadic and self-fulfilling entity is concerned, the conversation appears to be an entity "held constant." It has no life of its own and must be considered, as it were, a "context" that the speaker might modify simply by issuing an utterance. Consequently, the idea of speaking intelligibly within discourse is fatally configured as interaction in which one distinct person takes account of others in the same way she takes account of things. A conversation is, then, conceived of as a result or product, not an instance of a life that constitutes forms of agency in what only appears to be a series of particular performances. As such, it is adequately described as an epiphenomenon and understood according to parties' mental states prior to speaking and the series of purely voluntary gestures that generate new conditions of speaking if the parties wish, for reasons still of their own, to continue, as well as interactively constituted "norms" such as rules of turn taking. Everything about this hinges on individuality. Nothing is left of the idea of immanent sociality, the idea that humans are fundamentally social beings, or the idea that we need to recognize something human about human affairs if we are to fulfill our obligations to the very notion of intelligibility without doing away altogether with the idea of "our."

Individualists are likely to leave to the side or neglect what seem, from their point of view, to be disturbing implications of attempting to theorize what is human about human affairs without compromising the idea of the human being as "a being in a situation." It is also said to be more convenient to rely on an idea of interactions between individual subjects than to work with the ideas of multiplicity, situation, a course of activity, and inter-subjectivity. The notion of the individual still seems as firmly embedded in theoretical discourse and writing as ever, despite cogent criticisms of the tendency even from within the analytic tradition. Still, one purpose of beginning theoretical work from the point of view of the immediacy of individuality is to preserve the autonomy of psychology and the related paradigms of those disciplines that have come to depend on it, or whose object is thought to be reducible to it. But the cost of maintaining the prospect of reduction is considerable. Without at least the prospect of an idea of the social as a basic fact, the theories of committed individualists are unlikely to be about what is human about human affairs, whatever else they might be about. Nor can an individualistic account be plausible, in a nonideological way, from a point of view attributable to those whose affairs are essentially social.[6]

Nevertheless, it has been argued that the perspective of the individual is an immediate feature of experience and therefore the most obvious point of departure for a theory that attempts to correspond to and illuminate experience. But if we take account of what has been discussed about the relationship between life and situation, and if it is true as things stand that humans are inter-subjective social beings before they are individuals, then individuality cannot be taken as a given or as an obvious starting point for understanding what is human about what they do. This is so even if one grants that experience is something individuals have *qua* their individuality: because, on the one hand, individual experience may not take a propositional form and, on the other, that individuals may have "experiences" at a primitive level (e.g., of sensation) does not imply that those are the sorts of experience that should be starting points for a theory of what is human about human affairs.

In passing, even to decide that thought depends on language is to agree that the thought at issue (certainly not all that could be called "thought") is essentially social. One reason is that those propositions capable of being thought in the usual sense of "thinking" cannot stand on their own, and such thought is rarely if ever complete without the discourse that makes propositions intelligible as such in relation to courses of activity.[7] Moreover, since the propositions that could be contents of thought cannot stand on their own, they are not propositions in a sense that draws on logic and linguistic theory to make a difference in debates over the fundamental nature of thought and meaning. In that case, the idea that thought depends on reliable, repeatable meanings and is therefore essentially propositional does not provide for a distinction between human and nonhuman entities and therefore cannot address questions that arise precisely in regard to the reasonableness of that distinction as things stand.

For theory, the third-party idea of the *experience* of a speaker, of one who is in the course of speaking, must be consistent with the following conditions of clarifying it as an idea about human affairs. First, we are, for good reasons, considering discursive speech; and the intelligibility of such speech, as always the speech of others, of someone that might be anyone, depends on its being internal to the course of activity I refer to as collective enunciation. That there is a course of activity involved in the individuated moment of the utterance is not a problem for this point of view, since that could be recognized as a meaningful act only if it is recognized as a feature of a course of activity that is extra-individual. In any case, what is meant by "discursive speech" is the activity of uttering that is "always already" a feature of a course of collective enunciation; and I try to show that we have little choice but to consider it this way if our aim is to arrive at an idea of the social that also makes room for the idea of individuated experience.

Second, the fact that the individual's experience in such a situation is, from the standpoint of the relation of meaningfulness to meaning, derived experience does not mean that there is no connection between an intention on the part of the speaker and what is uttered. There is no reason to deny that each momentarily identifiable utterance is accompanied by something like a prior intention of its being uttered at all. But that intention is not necessarily, or likely to be, the sort of intention that fits the third-party claim that the meaning of the utterance (within discourse) corresponds to a pre-discursive intention to issue the very words, gestures, sentences, and the like, that have been issued or to mean whatever they eventually come to mean. The idea of an intention that corresponds directly to a meaning attributable to an utterance is appropriate only for those utterances that can be taken as distinct acts apart from their implication in discursive speech and therefore as self-contained acts affected by whatever else is distinct and self-contained within equally distinct and self-contained contexts.

It must be granted that some sort of connection between intention and potentially meaningful utterance must be admitted if we are to use terms like "speech," "utterance," "speaking," and the like. My point is not that a momentarily individualized utterer (doing uttering) lacks an inclination to utter, since this would be absurd. It is that she must not be seen as "having" an intention tied to the meaning attributed to what is being said or was said in the only context that counts theoretically—namely, the discourse of which their speaking can only be merely a momentary feature. If this is stipulated as an instance of collective enunciation, an instance of a momentary concentration of sociality, no linguistic theory of meaning can yield an idea of the sort of meaningfulness that adheres in the course of that activity (and therefore in the course of any uttering and gesturing that can be considered discursive).

For the moment of individual experience, such as it is for a third party, the questions of meaningfulness and meaning arise only after uttering has begun or taken place, when what was being uttered appears as an instance of collective enunciation. An utterance can be seen as an instance of speaking (to and with) only when it manifests the attitude of waiting proper to a course of activity. It may well be that intentions having to do with being a party to activity accounts for why the momentary individual "begins to speak," and even an inkling of the eventual content of what will have been said. But such intentions need have nothing to do with a specific meaning or meanings of what is being (or what has been) uttered; and it is extremely unlikely within a discourse that they would have much to do with whatever meanings attach themselves to specific utterances, since what they mean in discourse has to do more with the supervening ongoing activity than with what might have been intended by a momentarily individual speaker. It is only within and for the course of activity that what is uttered acquires the meaningfulness and meaning that correspond to what theory for a third party needs to consider human about human life.

The alternative denies that an internal relation of life and situation is essential to accounting for what is human about speech. It is based on an individualistic theory of meaning and typically draws on examples from specialized technical deliberations, such as the sorts of problem solving and concept formation identified with the standard models of science and "formal reasoning," or on "ordinary language" made extraordinary by being abstracted from discourse. In contrast, theorizing "individual experience" as essentially social suggests a different field of examples, in which the utterers can be said to experience speaking—the momentary occupation of a voice, vocalizing—as simultaneous with *all* discursively available socially reflexive voices (vocalizations) and, correspondingly, as done in an attitude of waiting rather than, say, of controlling or completing meaning.

————

It should be clear by now why I believe that the alternative is unacceptable— that utterers experience their utterances as their own in the sense of being tokens of what they are intended to mean or to bring about as an effect, and as separable unitary elements of a series. It is unacceptable if we consider intelligible speech as dialogically discursive such that other voices are simultaneously involved in its course both as momentarily distinct and as instances of others in general. That is, "one's voice" always appears among voices, as a voice "someone" might occupy, and therefore as a moment of collective enunciation. A party to a conversation who attempts to preserve title to whatever she says would appear to other parties as at best odd and at worst destructive of the very possibility of conversation. What is at issue is not the psychology of the subject but the constitution of subjectivity and inter-subjectivity in the midst of a course of activity in which life and situation, speaking and being, are internally related and, consequently, *the line between subject and object can be drawn only within the perspective of subjectivity.* The commitment to this perspective, which is itself a moment of a course of activity beyond individuality, is founded in the necessity to consider what is human about human affairs as things stand.

25

Subjectivity and Objectivity

The objects of experience are intentional in the following sense: they are agency-dependent such that their dependency constitutes their objectivity. We can say, then, that their objectivity, as objects of possible apprehension, resides in the ongoing internal relation of life and situation and displays itself as momentary instantiations of inter-subjectivity. To speak of them in regard to their being *objects of experience* is to bring to notice the way in which the very idea of experience depends on their being "subjective objects" in the sense of being essentially inter-dependent (meaningful) and inter-subjective (belonging to a course of activity). It follows theoretically that the idea of "experience" does not require reference to distinct mental states of distinct individuals—though this does not mean that reference to mental states might not be otherwise meaningful. For a theory that takes seriously the idea of sociality, the *experience* of the inter-subjective momentary individual consists of the apprehension of something that also effectively apprehends an apprehensive subjectivity greater than the momentary individual (is reflexive to sociality). This progressively expansive mutuality implies that apprehending an object shows itself as the same attitude of waiting that classical social psychology attributes only to the perception of persons in contrast with the instrumental, consummatory, or collative attitudes that are said to correspond to the perception of agency-independent things. The same dialectic operates in the course of objects being apprehended *as* objects of experience, which is to say intentional, agency-dependent objects that may or may not be persons; and such a progressively self-expanding apprehension should be understood as essentially inter-subjective.

Given inter-subjectivity as a third-party (or theoretical) fact for which there is no first-party corrective, since there is no representable self-identical autonomous first party from the point of view of inter-subjectivity, it is possible to clarify the idea of a field of objects within the hypothetically limited purview of a momentary subject who can be said, in her apprehensiveness (attitude of waiting), to apprehend them, first as a field and then as momentarily distinct instances of meaning within that field. Inter-subjectivity does not merely qualify the apprehension of agency-dependent objects; it is what makes *meaningful* apprehension conceivable. This is why momentarily distinct objects are always apprehended within the tragic contradiction of essence and attributes that Hegel identified as that condition of "perception" that compensates momentarily for the unfulfilled promise of sense-certainty to provide a foundation for an unmediated experience of things. The contradiction yields an incessant oppositional movement between "presence" (essence) and "attribution" (or description). This movement, in which the object threatens always to be what it is not, is, ironically, the only objective referent that perception can ultimately claim for itself; and in that respect, it opens onto the realm "of the understanding" that knows only relations governed by laws. At the end of his chapter on perception, Hegel writes:

> The conceptual necessity of the experience through which consciousness discovers that the Thing is demolished by the very determinateness that constitutes its essence and its being-for-self, can be summarized as follows. The Thing is posited as being *for itself*, or as the absolute negation of all otherness, therefore as purely *self*-related negation; but the negation that is self-related is the suspension of *itself*; in other words, the Thing has its essential being in another Thing. (1977, 77; see also 76)

This movement can be characterized conveniently as a more volatile relationship than immediacy allows between the sense of the distinctness of a thing and the field in which that thing subsists and takes shape as the object it is becoming for the course of activity that constitutes its subject. The object as distinct always appears threatened and about to dissolve into indistinctness. Its distinctiveness is ostensible and, at most, a momentarily apparent unity of apprehension. Its status as an object of experience, for which the *apprehensiveness* of an attitude of waiting is necessary, depends on the labors of inter-subjectivity. Individual subjects, understood within the inter-subjectivity of which their incompleteness is a feature, are motivated to participate in the essential but futile labor of resolving the ambiguousness of the objects they share with all their others. This activity of resolving what cannot be resolved marks inter-subjectivity as the fullness of sociality as a course of activity. An object in its idealized form of an "in-itself," therefore as agency-independent, can never be objective in this respect when the "locus" of experience is a *course* of activity in which the experience "belongs" to an individual derivatively, and then only for the moment.

What, then, is the theoretical status of the thing in- and for-itself? What happens to the individual who presumably can know or apprehend such agency-independent things? Such a subject would have ways of representing the absolute clarity with which such things appear as distinct mental contents or ideas; and such things would appear to her as nonhuman and therefore meaningless. To know such meaningless things is to be independent not only of them but of all other knowers except those who represent these things in the same meaningless way, and therefore represent all things as meaningless, so that the very notion of distinct subjects disappears in a "position prior to the very possibility of meaning." This universe of uncontestable knowledge based on the fixity of things does not belong to any subject who can be identified as "human," though it might belong to a creature that is able to represent the totality of all possible human knowledge (and therefore stands for "the end of days"). A theory of mind, action, subjectivity, or consciousness that begins with hypothetical examples of relations between definite persons and definite nonpersons, objects that are essentially uncontestable, cannot, even if such cases can be found, provide a foundation for understanding human affairs: it cannot illuminate the activities of subjects in the presence, actual or virtual, of subjects. Parenthetically, the metaphysical notion of a shared object that can be the basis of a meeting of minds (a referent of an agreement or instance of communication) requires that it be fixed and inert in all salient respects. It assumes that anything short of that is vague and imprecise, thereby undermining both communication and the kind of social contract that is presumed to depend on a process of communication in which it is possible for parties to anticipate an actual meeting of reasonable minds. Consequently, a great deal of research in the social psychology and pragmatics of communication has been devoted to putative external influences that are said to regulate the communicative process, and to processes of feedback and mutual correction presumably aimed at reducing untoward vagueness and ambiguity in the face of what then appears as an obstacle—namely, sociality itself—to the attainment of *clarity in each mind about the other minds.*

The early literature of balance theory, influenced especially by Kurt Lewin, is notable for its attempts to show that ambiguity both reflects and destabilizes social relations (Festinger 1957; Brown 1965; Lewin 1935). But even there the direction of research is focused on the pragmatics of stabilizing sociality by reducing the ambiguousness of representation, something which, by the nature of the case, cannot succeed without transforming the course of activity and, thereby, introducing new ambiguities. There are, however, instances in which that strategy reveals its futility and the impossibility of maintaining intelligibility in a discourse predicated from the outset on the *telos* of final meeting of minds. One example that raises questions about some key assumptions implicit in the idea of a meeting of minds is the experiment by Blank (1980) mentioned previously. My interpretation of it is intended to illustrate the perspective of sociality as discussed so far.

Pairs of subjects looked through glasses at a design on a screen. They were instructed to discuss what they saw until they reached an agreement, at which time they were to state what they had come to agree was seen by both subjects. The subjects' glasses had different filters that projected the design as either protruding or receding. Yet they believed at the outset, and apparently throughout their conversation, that they were seeing the same object in the same orientation. As a result, each felt that the other's description was ambiguous and so acted rationally to achieve the meeting of minds required by their instructions. They reached apparent agreement after a succession of "exchanges" that consisted of a progressive series of discursive moves to higher and higher levels of abstraction.[1] Eventually, the ambiguity vanished and each subject became convinced that both were seeing the same object in a common orientation. In other words, there was an apparent meeting of minds based on making the difference obscure by virtue of a series of predicate changes that they saw as clarifying rather than redefining. Given the perspective of a meeting of minds, the progress of abstraction amounted to a process of effectively de-socializing communication such that only the result counted, which is, of course, what the subjects were instructed to do by way of completing their joint task.

It can be argued that this has nothing to do with the ambiguity of the object, and it is in any case unclear in what sense an object on its own can be ambiguous. The certainty of each subject about what he or she was seeing depended to some extent on the geometrical simplicity of the projected design and its lack of any obvious significance in other respects. Thus, for each individual, the object was simply what was seen and the ambiguity was a property of the other's attempt to describe what he or she saw. For each, the ambiguity of the other's account lay in its apparent looseness of fit to the object, requiring further "clarification." However, an object of individuated perception is not the sort of object essentially shared by persons in the course of coming to terms with one another—"essentially" if "in the course of" refers to an instance of human life. But even in regard to the ostensibly individual subjects, raising the level of abstraction must have involved more for each than merely overcoming apparent defects in the other's representation of the facts. Toward the end, each seemed to believe that she was getting closer to an objective description of what was projected on the screen, in such a way that the other could legitimately compare that stated description with what she also saw. This suggests that each became increasingly attentive to those features of the design that could be clearly stated and increasingly able to distinguish them from those features for which words might have been inadequate and, therefore, could be thought of, from the standpoint of sharing knowledge, as incidental or irrelevant.

It does not follow, however, that this was, for the individual parties, nothing more than a matter of connecting words with facts, as if perception is independent of language and the inter-subjectivity of discursive speech. I suggest that it is more plausible that their perceptions conformed to the selective functioning of their discourse, so that they experienced the object as shared along lines indicated by their descriptions. Whether or not they were actually seeing according to the prevailing description, it seems more than likely that their apprehension of the object as an object of experience was its socialized apprehension as a referential object of a collective enunciation that, in this case, consisted of the activity of increasing the level of abstraction at which the object could be sensibly described as "off the surface." Agreement was confirmed by the fact that each spoke as if her description progressively improved in accuracy (to an object independent of representation) so that both descriptions could be fairly compared; and each was confirmed by the fact that the increasing abstraction of the descriptions in the course of the conversation did not appear to them to reduce the ambiguity of what they said and heard until the very end. Rather, it seemed to decrease the difference between what each saw and what she reported so that the other could be confident that, as instructed, a meeting of minds and not merely words had taken place.

A theoretical distinction needs to be made between what the subjects believed they were seeing and what they took to be a process of settling possible differences between them in describing the object they were seeing. Yet, though the subjects may have been aware of the distinction, they were satisfied at the end that more was involved than reconciling descriptions and that, in a sense, the "meeting of minds" was a result of matching different descriptions to a self-same fact, though this is not sufficient to what is ordinarily intended by the phrase. Increasing the level of abstraction may have allowed the parties to describe what they saw as if their perception of the object had shifted in accordance with the imperatives of the conversation. One might say that they were dis-attending to some reportable features of the object (e.g., "it looks like it could hit my nose") that seemed crucial at first but as the conversation proceeded did not seem salient to what the design was as an object of collective regard, where "regard" has to do with the realization of an identification in discourse. On the one hand, one might say that in bringing the deferral of meaning to an end, they effectively canceled the course of activity, hence the subjectivity that they could have taken in its course for their "own."

On the other hand, for the individuals taken apart from the momentary subjectivities constituted within the discourse, the result was objective, given what they saw. In other words, from the point of view of observing the individuals taken one by one, their agreement composed a meeting of minds not about the objects they saw but about what could be said about those objects at the limits of reasonable description. But this interpretation works only for an observer for whom the discourse between the parties did not constitute an effective form of life—for which the resultant object was precisely the registerable object of experience available for each subject apart from the other. The subjects appeared satisfied that what they agreed on was not how to describe the design but the facts themselves. Certainly every ordinary description selects properties, just as perception is selective; so there is nothing odd about saying that a discourse, conceived of as a form of life, selects those momentary properties in reference to which parties can both claim to see the object according to those properties and, in fact, perceive the object or aspects of it according to them. It is only for the individuals taken apart from each other by the observer that the object of a meeting of minds appears as a severely reduced object, therefore that they do not agree in fact. It seems more appropriate to say, *if experience is the issue*, that the individuals' experiences as parties to a discourse were of an object that came to be described accurately in the course of their conversation: each subject can then be said to have apprehended the same object in a mode of participation that cannot be described adequately as a meeting of minds. It is in this sense that one can say that the design was the same object for both subjects within the inter-subjective sociality of their discourse, though not for each person taken alone, as if no conversation had taken place.

To that extent, what appears to have been a change in representation was a change in the agency-dependent object during the conversation. What the subjects agreed about was the one-dimensional reduction ("off the surface") of what had been perceived of, at first, in three dimensions. The object for each taken alone, prior to any conversation, might have been different from the object of the inter-subjective ensemble, but that is not relevant to the question of whether the final agreement represents a meeting of minds that remain distinct or a product of a conversation represented retrospectively as a constitutive object, a "true" referent of the conversation taken as a course of activity. Thus, at each inter-subjective moment, individual subjects were oriented as much or more to the object as shared as to the rather different object that preceded the course of activity. They can be said to have been oriented to that object of discourse only in the mode of being oriented to the activity in which such an object might figure. That is, they were parties subsumed by the course of an activity that neither controlled.

My point is not that the individuals did not, in some sense, "see" different things or things that had somewhat different properties than they reported. They did, but it is a trivial fact because "seeing," in the sense of registering data, is not what is at issue. It is that the object of their joint experience, the object constituted inter-subjectively and available to the subjects only as parties to their discourse, was actually constituted as an object, and not merely construed, in the course of their conversation, and neither prior nor subsequent to their apparent agreement about what they saw. Once the situation changed, once the "event" was over, that object as finally represented no longer existed. What can be held to be memorable about the encounter with the object is the course of activity in which enunciation and momentary objectification were increasingly socialized, yielding an object internal to that inter-subjectivity, and thereby constituted as a social thing. This could not have been an object of any single individual's attention; it commands a descriptive language suitable for an ideal object and an attitude of waiting appropriate to that object's situation. It also instigates a different sort of motivation from that instigated by objects that are independent and fixed. The former is predicated on the necessary dissolution of the object's ostensibly original distinctiveness and autonomy in the course of its being inter-subjectively intended, and therefore being an object of an experience that is also inter-subjective.

If what is private (independent) about knowledge has less to do with what is or can be public (dependent) about it than one might have thought, then what are called sharing, agreeing, communicating, and the like, cannot be modeled on the notion of a meeting of individually particular minds about individually particular things. Such object-oriented courses of activity are not about fixed and unambiguous things but, ironically, must be about the very sorts of active objectivity, what I refer to as subjective objects, otherwise thought to make a meeting of individual minds impossible. To the extent to which this refutes any notion of a sociality that excludes just such objects, it poses significant problems for theory that cannot be avoided.

I conclude that communication and agreement, as conceived of in the standard literature according to the idea of a possible meeting of minds, are impossible under conditions that must be admitted if we are to theorize what is human about human affairs. In that case, we are left not with Rousseau's "first convention" as that has been generally interpreted as an unprecedented instant of consensus, but with a notion of ongoing participation that is theoretically noteworthy in its emphasis on the social as a course of activity rather than an event or a state of affairs: in other words, participation in which the ostensible individual and ostensibly individuated acts are constituted momentarily within the activity of an ensemble is itself a moment of a course of activity. Key to this are the ideas of an attitude of waiting and inter-subjectivity, both of which are theoretically necessary if people and their objects are to be considered in the presence of objects and their people, and if it is intelligible to refer to theory's reflexivity to its own possibility (theorizing).

———

To enrich the idea of an experience that belongs to inter-subjectivity, we can begin again from the point of view of an ostensible individual for whom objects are ideally distinct. While this section considers the theoretical possibility of individuality, it should be kept in mind that the experience of participation is what is crucial. The experience *of* objects is derivative for individuals taken apart from their being social; and it is in this regard that I refer to them as ostensible individuals. It belongs to the ensemble and its constitutive course of activity. The distinctness of such objects can only be momentary and is limited by the inter-subjectivity in which they are featured. Because they are limited in this way, they take form relative to the experience of the ostensible individual as a field of tension. I have said that this field is characterized by a dialectics of vanishing, in which essence and properties give way to each other before either can become a clear and distinct idea of the object as such. This affects the apprehension of every possible agency-dependent object. But the apprehension of such an object and its moments by momentarily individuated subjects is different from what can be said, hypothetically, about the apprehension of independent objects by independent subjects. For one thing, the objects of such a field are grasped to some extent in their simultaneity and not one by one. Things that can be grasped one by one are not the sorts of things that are apprehended in their simultaneity. Objects of experience are, then, radically different from the independent objects posited by standard models of perception and cognition; and the very idea of an independent subject who processes information and makes decisions according to self-interest is predicated on those models, in particular on the independence they attribute to objects, for example, in the context of clarifying the role of beliefs in decision making.

The ostensible individual's experience of objects is also her experience of the objective field; and the imbeddedness of objects in that field, the fact that they are subjective objects because they are moments of inter-subjectivity, marks the experience as one of simultaneity rather than mere succession, of densities and flows and not merely of serial, logical, or architectonic order. It may seem reasonable to believe that at least some objects of experience can be referred to as an external reality that allows for agency-independent properties. But this turns out to be less a description of an object of experience than an attempt to fix something as if it is independent of experience—for example, by listing its physical properties and treating the list as a valid representation of the object as able to be experienced. These properties—color, size, monetary value, and so on—presumably attach themselves to any object, so that, no matter how lengthy the list, the objectivity of the object remains unspecified. In other words, such a description cannot yield the object that experience requires. Agency-dependence and agency-independence are not properties or aspects of objects but names of radically different objectivities. Indeed, a purely physical or otherwise agency-independent description yields the sense of an unattainable unity that cannot be thought of as belonging to experience, while a description according to the presence of the object in a field of tension among objects, and therefore according to its value within an object-oriented course of activity, and according to the inter-subjectivity that sustains that field, supports a sense of the provisional quality of its integrity and its value or significance. This quality manifests itself not in the absolute distinctness of the object of experience from all particular other objects but in its always ambiguous and therefore incomplete emergence and reemergence from the inter-subjectively objective field that threatens its integrity even as the work of that field in regard to its own tensions supplies the object with its momentary distinctness and particularity. In regard to the objective status of utterances thought of as features of discursive speech, these too appear as fleeting objects, momentary degenerations of a discourse, semblances of "events." Therefore, temporal and spatial dimensions cannot establish the relative location and status of the utterance as a particularity, but the para-spatial simultaneity that characterizes the field of which it must be part if it is itself to be an object of experience. This notion of simultaneity, when understood theoretically, reformulates the key concept of "location." Instead of the latter referring to a unique point at which space and time intersect, it now refers to the possibility of the object of experience being just such an object—namely, something of value, something that makes a difference and stands for the very possibility of making a difference. *That is, simultaneity provides a theoretical setting in which the very concept of value has value because it now speaks not only to a difference but to the sort of totalizing difference made by any object of experience to its field. In so doing, it allows us to speak about experience without sacrificing what, as things stand, is human about human affairs.*

To say that a party to a discourse grasps another's utterance as a distinct object seems to imply that this "grasping" is an "experience" of the uttered object as such. It does not imply an experience of certainty based on an inference from sense data, or an experience of an interpretation (the self-interpreting) of what is "perceived."[2] It seems that having an experience of such an object consists in grasping it as more than something distinct "in-itself," since its distinctness is not quite the same as its identity. Theoretically, what is immediate about this experience is that the object is grasped as reflexive to "being able to be apprehended": *that is how one knows it.* What the utterance "displays" is its dependency within a field such that it is always in the course of emerging and receding according to the activity that constitutes the field as a multiplicity; in that sense it is irreducibly inter-subjective. The utterance is, then, grasped in that momentariness and as a feature of the field as such, which is also to say as a feature of the course of activity. These related aspects of the utterance as an object of experience are not products of an additional act that organizes what is seen or heard; nor do they refer to a specific ownership of the utterance that points not merely to intentionality but to specific prior intentions behind the utterance thought of as a complete and fixed entity.

Perhaps the inter-subjectivity of the object is epiphenomenal or reference to it is nothing more than a rhetorical device that allows one to emphasize the "personal" in "personal experience." But this amounts to a denial of what is implicit in the idea of agency-dependent objectivity and therefore brings back a metaphysics of particulars and the contradictorily motivated pair, "self and actor," that caused so many problems for the standard model of action. In that case, what the object amounts to beyond its appearance as a mere particular, and therefore realizable only as the relatively fixed referent of propositions, is something *externally* connected with other such particulars (as part of a sequence, an argument, etc.). In this light, the perception of objects in terms of their relatedness appears to be relations among propositions. Objectivity is, in a sense, reduced to nomination; and knowing appears as a state of an impoverished self who merely nominates and is thereby one for whom only language and its users truly exist. But the language of nomination has nothing sub-theoretical about it, nothing that pertains to the incompleteness of all instances of nomination and the tension that is bound to generate as a feature of the activity of grasping something. It is not, then, the "language" intended by references to the world as "text." The latter embraces and works with and on a sub-theoretical concept of sociality that is allied with and not hostile to the idea of experience, unlike the notion of nominalization (particularization and realization exclusively in propositions). But, of course, it is allied with an idea of experience thought of as quite different from the idea that comes from reflecting on the individual's perception of an external reality that ends by the certainty of propositional argument and the loss of a sub-theoretical intuition about sociality that is nevertheless taken for granted.

It is also not enough to say that these aspects amount only to assumptions, since "assumptions" merely names the fact that I want to bring to notice— namely, that the reflexivity of the utterance, like that of all subjective objects, is as immediate a property (to experience) as the redness of an apple, regardless of the possibility of listing conditions that might disrupt that very immediacy. Therefore, one must say, in the interest of preserving the right of theory momentarily to posit a first-party point of view, that reflexivity is "displayed" by the object itself, as a subjective object, one proof of which is the attitude of waiting within gestures and utterances imbedded, as it were, in the course of activity. Again, the truth of this claim, indicated in the use of the word "fact," is not a matter of inference. It is a matter of what is necessarily true when we reflect on our essential sociality, if we are not to sacrifice the very idea of something human about human affairs and if our ideas about objects of experience are to be compatible with the notion of inter-subjectivity necessary to and implicit in the internal relation of life and situation. What the listening subject must be said to apprehend of the heard utterance, as such a subject, what must be at once the utterance's substance and its value, is just that reflexivity, whatever else might be involved; and this is so even before the question of literal meaning arises, therefore before one can legitimately decide whether an utterance is a "speech act." In other words, the experiencing subject must be taken to apprehend objects of experience, which are always agency-dependent, as meaningful before any particular meaning is momentarily accomplished in the course of their emergence and recession in the subjective field of which they are immediate features. Since meaningfulness precedes meaning, as its immanent condition, and since meaningfulness is reflexive to collective enunciation, the experiencing subject's initial apprehension of what theory wants to call an object of experience must itself be taken to transpire in a mode of inter-subjectivity to which that subject can in no sense be taken as transcendental.

The idea of an objective field from which momentarily specifiable objects must be said to emerge, recede, and reemerge in experience entails a subjectivity that cannot be individualized, and that is irreducibly and decisively social. In grasping the meaningfulness of the object, the ostensible individual, such as she is, in the midst of discourse and therefore as "someone," is, for theory, participating in a socializing course of activity, and therefore can no longer be thought of as *an* individual in the sense of being an independent agent capable of reflecting on herself as if another. Participation does not mediate this apprehension of the object; it is the immanent condition of its theoretical intelligibility. The apprehension must be thought of as a momentarily individuated work of inter-subjectivity whenever we need to think of experience and objects of experience in regard to what is human about human affairs—if we are to sustain the perspective of the internal relation of life and situation and the corresponding idea of the social. From this point of view, the category of utterances is not illuminated by what can be said about the subcategory of speech acts, if that means "rule-governed intentional behavior," where the rules are grammatical and the acts consist in and are intelligible as performances of the practices of stating, commanding, asking, promising, and the like, according to such rules (see Searle 1969, 16). The strong version of the theory of speech acts begins with the assertion that "all linguistic communication involves linguistic acts" (16). This obviously means more than the tautology that linguistic communication is linguistic communication. Among other things, it leaves open the possibility that not all acts in language are instances of linguistic communication. That is, there are linguistic acts that are not communicative, and this is true only if language is not fundamentally "discursive speech."

This is still not the most important latent element in Searle's assertion. He also invokes a conception of a linguistic event that involves more than what is comprehended formally by the term "language":

> The unit of linguistic communication is not, as has generally been supposed, the symbol, word or sentence, of even the token of the symbol, word or sentence, but rather the production or issuance of the symbol or word or sentence in the performance of the speech act. To take the token as a message is to take it as a produced or issued token. (1969, 16)

It seems crucial to understanding this last sentence that taking the token as "produced or issued" is an immediate taking, what I have been calling an "apprehension." A speech act is not merely literally interpretable words that comprise a sentence. It is an activity of producing, not merely performing, an instance of a practice that has effects, and the utterance must immediately be grasped by its hearer as just such a production, so that the distinction between the issuing of the utterance and its meaning now appears to be arbitrary (eventual). The latter cannot be separated from the former without undermining the possibility that what is spoken is apprehended as a "speech act," rather than, for example, a formally and semantically exemplary linguistic expression.

For Searle, it is sufficient to clarify this by saying that what makes something an instance of linguistic communication "is that the noise or mark was produced by a being or beings more or less like myself and produced with certain kinds of intentions" (1969, 16). Since a machine can produce a sentence that a person might treat as an instance of communication, more must be meant by "linguistic communication" than the exchange of messages or sentences or complete gestures; and it seems clear that an utterance, no matter how formally correct, cannot be a speech act unless it is apprehended as both produced and producing, and as bearing intentionality before specific intentions can be brought into play. For me to hear a communicative purpose in a sentence, to apprehend it as a speech act, is to assume a certain attitude that would not be assumed if the hearer believed that the origin of the sentence was a machine. It is also to take the utterance to be located elsewhere than in an individual speaker, to be "someone's" utterance; so that there is no question of inferring, as Searle seems to suggest, from the species of the speaker ("beings more or less like myself") to the intentionality of the noise or mark that he or she issues. Intentionality, in contrast with an intention, has to do with the fact that the utterance or gesture (like any agency-dependent object) is situated and not what the speaker who is the ostensible vehicle of its intelligibility wishes conveyed by what is uttered. To hear an utterance as intentional in this respect is to hear it as relatively independent of its ostensible speaker who is no longer necessary to its intelligibility—and therefore to hear it as a feature of a collective enunciation, no matter what credit is momentarily assigned to that ostensible speaker.

It seems to be an unadmitted latency in Searle's characterization of speech acts as "products" that the act is an instance of linguistic communication (indeed, both its theoretical and experiential unit) only if there is something about it that commands an attitude of waiting on the part of both speaker and hearer. This belies the possibility of the "act" being complete and self-sufficient, or being unitary in Searle's sense of the term. If Jane says "here is the dog," and I am the person to whom she addresses that assertion, or one who hears it simply as addressed, I do not then proceed to tell her that she has just specified the location of the dog ("here"): one does not make a statement in order to hear it in the mouth of another or in the expectation that the hearer will simply acknowledge it as having been said. To assert, question, or the like is to invoke an ongoing relationship within which alone the utterance can be apprehended immediately as an instance of communication, or, for that matter, a "speech act." But we are now well beyond the notion that a speech act is initiated by a specific prior intention to produce a specific meaning, since it is evident that intentionality is not reducible to the intentions of specific individuals and that the intentionality that identifies an utterance as communicative has to do with the course of collective enunciation of which every instance of discursive speech is a feature, in which "production" is a course of activity beyond individuality and in which "hearing" is the wrong word for registering what goes on when speaking is occurring.

Even if we grant the possibility, it would be rare for an utterance to be heard as the realization of what was actually intended by the person uttering it, though, from the point of view of the possibility, "we" may still be said to hear, react, or respond to some utterances as bearing specific intentions, and "we" may come to assign responsibility to an individual at some point in the course of participating in the discourse in which the utterance was issued and within which alone it might take on the immediate presence of "someone's" act, whether that person's or not. Parenthetically, hearing that transpires within a course of activity, is, by that very fact, socialized beyond what can be explained biologically or psychologically. For discursive speech, acts are moments of courses of activity and are, therefore, logically independent of specific persons with specific intentions. If one wishes to use the word "act," it is an act not because it can be designated by a reason-referring word but because it is a moment of a course of activity that transpires inter-subjectively among people, and, one must add, because such acts, unlike mere behavior, are not, insofar as they are distinctively human, essentially instances of following rules, or events. But that is also to say that the act is not complete in the sentence, or, indeed, in any form of a "unit of meaning" that can be ascribed to a specific utterance of a specific individual person who can be, as it were, rigidly designated. It is ostensibly complete as an act only in the course of being acknowledged as such by listeners also operating within the discourse and whose attitude of waiting, what makes them listeners, must also be held to be a feature of collective enunciation. We would not be willing to say that a listener is acknowledging a specific utterance as an act simply by repeating the words or analyzing their formal meaning and syntax, or even acknowledging that the sentence or phrase that was "heard" was a totality constituting what Searle wishes to think of as a specific and specifiable speech act.

It is not that the hearer assumes, as Searle seems to say, that an intention lies behind the utterance taken as a speech act. Rather, she hears it as a beckoning, not toward the ostensible speaker as if to her alone but toward the inter-subjective course of activity. In that respect, it is an instance of non-individualized desiring (of more speaking) that achieves only the momentum that makes it desire in general, rather than a specific need or want, when the activity of which the utterance is a feature is intensified and extended to the point at which its inter-subjectivity overwhelms any possibility of a final objectifying moment. At that point, each gesture is absorbed in the movement of the discourse within which questions such as "why are we doing this" or "what are we doing" do not arise. Even if we hold to Searle's language and the limits of his reductive metaphor of production, for someone to issue a "speech act" she must be held to have ventured something, not just to have performed it, therefore to have found venturing already possible before utterance-specific intentions. The reason is that an utterance can only be the performance of a speech act if parties (actual or virtual) other than its ostensible speaker and its ostensible listener acknowledge its intentionality independent of whatever might be imputed to that speaker as a prior specific intention (see Searle 1969, 22–26);[3] and this acknowledgment, in whatever form it might take, must be a feature of its "production" as an instance of communication. My point is that to make good on the notion of a speech act is to be led to the idea of collective enunciation and the idea of a course of activity for which acts in Searle's sense are moments and not what he initially defines speech acts to be—namely, events.

To the extent to which "language" is at least partially defined as a system of rules, speaking might be thought of as a approximate realization of rules. Searle uses the strong, and I believe misleading, expression "rule-governed" in his account of the intelligibility of speech. But it is not clear that the key to what he takes to constitute a speech *act*—that is, a certain intention—can be understood as rule-governed; and it will not do to say that the intention is not the act but the condition of the act, since, presumably, we can know that a group of words is an instance of linguistic communication only if we know or behave as if we know that the speaker intends her utterance as part of an ongoing discourse. If so, then whatever intention there is to utter a specific literally interpretable sentence is far less important than the intention to participate meaningfully, to be a party to a difference immanent to discourse. The fact that the utterance has its status as a feature of a discourse is a matter of what it is and whatever it will come to mean; and it is by no means clear that anything is gained theoretically by referring to this as "rule-governed."

Given this account, the claim that "it is always in principle possible for" a speaker to say exactly what she means seems gratuitous (Searle 1969, 18). If a speaker were to reiterate exactly what he or she meant when issuing the utterance, assuming that it is possible to do so meaningfully in the midst of an ongoing discourse, he or she would be annulling the communicative value of the utterance no less than its "original" meaning. One would then expect the speaker to be surprised if the other took what was said to have been complete and independent of that discourse and then behaved accordingly. The expected reaction to something that appears apart from discourse is either to ignore it, to give it only passing attention, or to treat it as a significant violation of the activity of collective enunciation, incompatible with what Searle elsewhere refers to as proper usage of "we." If there is no receivable sense of the possibility of reiterating what one "heard," then the utterance taken as a moment of discursive speech, of speaking, would be "heard" in the attitude of waiting appropriate to parties to a discourse. In that case, the utterance cannot be the sort of *act* Searle has in mind. It could be neither repeated nor brought to notice in its singularity without disrupting the very activity that makes it meaningful in the first place. *The attitude of waiting, that marks participation in a discourse, excludes the repetition of exactly what has been uttered and excludes acknowledging it as one would acknowledge the receipt of a thing or a mere datum.* This attitude corresponds to the nature of discourse: every moment is ambiguous and, because of this, every moment is self-motivating. In this sense, one might say that there is no end to the deferral of meaning implicit within a discourse; but the course of meaning being deferred is part of the self-expansive reflexivity of sociality. To recognize a discourse, then, is to see speaking as motivating itself; to participate in discourse is to be caught up in a certain momentum that is independent of individually specific motives or intentions. Since every instance of discursive speech responds to and is an instance of ambiguity, then it is an instance of socialized intentionality regardless of what desire or intention can be attributed to any ostensibly individual speaker. Instances of discursive speech, including utterances that engage other utterances and in that sense can be said to communicate, have properties that invoke further instances intelligible as such only in the course of an activity that constitutes a moment of collective enunciation. Each instance displays itself as a beckoning to others at large as well as a sense of being beckoned, indicating that more needs to be done if what has been uttered is to realize discursive value, therefore if it is to even approach the ideal of a speech act as an instance of "communication." This "more" entails work for which no one speaker can be specifically responsible.

Paradoxically, one can approach that theoretical ideal only by negating what the theory of speech acts also requires—namely, a characterization of each ostensible instance of speech as a particular, complete, unitary, individuated act. This paradox, in which the theoretical ideal is incompatible with what are identified as units of analysis, effectively affirms what Searle's version of the theory was intended to deny: the imbeddedness, the immanence, of the utterance in the only context for which the notion of communication is intelligible—namely, the collective enunciation that accounts for its meaningfulness before it can be said to have a specific meaning.[4] Suppose that a speech act can be known as such only by the intention that accompanies it in the course of speaking (and therefore must be understood as fully displaying intentionality in the ostensible individual's issuance of the utterance itself) and if its quality as an act (modified or not by a "context") cannot be separated from the sheer fact of its being issued. It follows that "the speech act or acts performed in the utterance of a sentence are in general a function of the meaning of the sentence" only if that meaning is prior, exclusively personal, and something repeatable in principle and intended to be performed as such (1969, 18). But that is not true if uttering is understood in connection with discourse, and therefore as immanent to a course of collective enunciation. A sentence certainly has meaning. It may or may not tempt hearers to interpret it, respond to it, or otherwise react. Considering it as an imposition or an invitation to react and possibly respond may be adequate to the idea of a discrete act for which other acts are merely "contextual," but it cannot give it or any utterance its force as an instance of "communication."

The speech act cannot, therefore, be taken as "in general a function of the meaning of the sentence." Instead, it is, *in general*, a function of what precedes, accompanies, and follows the issuing of the utterance, what appears as being done by other "someones," nonspecific others, regardless of whatever passes through the momentarily individuated mind of a given utterer at the moment she issues the more or less coherent sound that we refer to as an utterance.[5] That may or may not involve the attachment of a specific meaning to a sentence, phrase, and so forth, already uttered, but it necessarily involves some momentary presence of the utterance to the course of activity such that every party to "speaking" experiences each utterance not as a thing or event but as an invitation, a moment of communion rather than the mere issuing of information; and the readiness of every party is apparent in the attitude of waiting that necessarily characterizes parties to a discourse. It is trivial to say that propositional meaning counts in regard to the communicative force of discursive speech. It is true, but it is neither the most important fact about nor a necessary feature of the inter-subjectivity of communication. When communication is thought of as a socializing course of activity, collective enunciation, propositional content may be relevant to something but it is inessential to the course of activity. What is essential is social validity, the utterance's suitability to the reflexive inter-subjectivity of the activity. If the speech act is considered in general as "a function of the meaning of the sentence," then, according to Searle, "for every possible speech act there is a possible sentence or set of sentences the literal utterance of which in a particular context would constitute a performance of that speech act" (1969, 19). The important part of this claim seems to be that meaning and usage are necessarily related because every speech act is both an instance of usage and a meaning (actual or virtual, but in any case repeatable) that declares it to be the act it is in a context for which it could be an appropriate instance of whatever principle of continuity the act reinstates, for example, a practice. That is, the speech act is both act (say, an instance of a practice) and speech (say, an instance of communication). Searle conflates the two when he implies that the speech act is, by its nature, repeatable. But I believe that the more important point lies in his reference to context, if only because it is not clear what could be meant by "literal" outside of a context in which the literal "possible sentence" that shows propositional meaning is adequate to the interpretation of the ostensible utterance of the ostensible utterer.

If the priority of a meaning-constituting intention is to do something specific, the speech act is a complete and definite "product," confounding Searle's approach to the problem of theorizing discursive speech through the idea of communication. The introduction to *Speech Acts* suggests that this is indeed his project (1969, 3), making him vulnerable to this criticism: he holds that the fact that a given individual speaker "has" an intention at the moment of speaking that constitutes the intentionality of the utterance for a discourse and as an instance of discursive speech. That is, he seems to be claiming that the intention to issue the utterance corresponds to the meaning of the utterance within the ongoing discourse of which it can only be a moment and, possibly, that this meaning is essentially propositional in form.

From the perspective of *speaking*, in contrast with *speech*, an utterance is not merely a linguistic event but an instance of discursive communication. Then the constitution of a speech act as an important but relatively rare recognizable particular within a discourse must, like every other moment, be an ongoing accomplishment of the parties that transcends every ostensibly particular utterance. Similarly, Searle's distinction between "the effects in hearers that one means to produce" and the effects that are actually produced does not help (20), since it takes specifiable "effects" as the most important and reliable consequences of an utterance. On the contrary, for discursive speech, speech understood that way, it is not such effects that count most, or even that they count very much. Even if they count in some sense, which they certainly do, it cannot be specific effects on specific hearers that are important to the social validity or meaningfulness of the utterance. The very idea of "effects" in the study of human affairs suggests their independence from what produces them, something that is, at best, marginal to the ideas of discursive communication and courses of activity in general. But even if it were appropriate to speak of effects in regard to the idea of communication, it cannot be effects on hearers that count so much as "effects" within the discourse itself, the difference constituted as *value* by a speaking that transpires in the course of activity. The "effects" of the ostensible individual's utterances within a discourse are discovered, if at all, after the fact, and may or may not be interpretable as privately intended public effects. So, the standard idea of effects does not account either for utterances as instances of communication or for utterances as objects of experience, any more than the idea of a governing intention at the moment of the utterance helps us understand linguistic communication as discursive speech. The appeal to such an intention does little more than expand on the notion of a speech act as self-contained, a notion that, as we have seen, cannot sustain the concept of communication it is supposed to sustain. In other words, and in contrast with Searle's claims for it, his concept of a speech act is not compatible with a social conception of communication and can neither illuminate the idea of discursive speech nor help us understand what "speech" means in the expression "speech act."

With this in mind, we can return to the more general problem of how something can be understood as an object of experience such that one can, in regard to discursive speech, even discuss the idea of linguistic communication and, more generally, the idea of sociality. It appears impossible to evade the obligation to characterize the experienced utterance or act according to the inter-subjectivity that characterizes both the field of such objects and the objects in their volatile, ostensible, but passing particularity and therefore according to the simultaneity implicit in the notion of such a field and its ostensibly particular and definitely volatile subjective objects (see Martin 1990). As far as the experience of speaking intelligibly among others is concerned, we have seen why utterances taken as instances of discursive speech cannot be described validly in terms of formal properties, or as units, by their prospects of translation, and by assignments of propositional content. To that extent, they cannot be what speech act theory considers "acts." Similarly, acts, insofar as they are social, cannot be understood as such by reference to the mental states of individual agents—that is, by "their" reasons—and they cannot be identified under their social aspect apart from the course of activity of which they are moments. The value of a given instance of discursive speech, or any instance of sociality, has less to do with its relevance to an individual agent's mental state than with the difference it makes in the inclusive course of activity of collective enunciation or collective self-composition. This suggests that what is uttered or otherwise done by parties to a discursive setting does not bear the sort of necessity we associate with a product that yields certain evidence of its productive agency. What is done in the course of an activity cannot be understood as originating in a particular agent, as expressing a prior intention in the meaning it only *comes* momentarily to have, and as an instance of a complete and definite action in-itself.

Discursive speech is *meaningful* in two senses. First, to the extent to which it is discursive, it is issued and received in a manifest attitude of waiting. Second, it is, as we saw from Bakhtin's account of "voice," issued to others at large rather than to a particular other, regardless of the posture and apparent orientation of the utterance and its associated gestures—just as it is received by others at large. In other words, as in my translation and extension of Nagel's notion of a "timeless reason," it anticipates more to be done by "someone" but nothing in particular by anyone. An instance of discursive speech offers no guarantee on its own behalf, and indeed defies the possibility, that any specific other will respond to it or even that a final response of any specific other would be sufficient to some standard. It also offers no guarantee that the person who is the ostensible utterer will remember it as a personally engendered act to be measured against specific effects that match a prior intention. Both speaker and, more generally, doer must be thought of as finding themselves saying and doing just what is being said and done within the course of collective enunciation. But these implications of the lack of the sort of necessity that is said to arise from an individual's intention are not the only ones worth noting. There is no question that, on occasion, momentarily individuated parties to a situation may feel just such a necessity and that they may experience success or failure to the extent to which the effects of what they say correspond to an original intention. My point has been that this attitude violates the conditions of discursive speech and cannot be sustained discursively; and that the theory of the speech act is a theory of speech abstracted, as it were, from a universe of discourse that does not exist by the standards imposed as conditions of a "speech act." What speech act theory posits is a violation of speech as discourse and action as a course of activity.

It is an error to think of language as a coherent set of rules to which violations are merely exceptions, and it is an error to think of discursive speech as comprising acts that communicate by virtue of their independently assessable meanings and according to intentions that apparently set such acts in motion according to a logic of the exchange of meanings between discrete parties doing separable and repeatable types of action. The sense of the necessity of an utterance, what makes it appear to be a unit of analysis as well as real, lies in the fact that a certain moment in the course of speaking being done appears or is taken to be an effect of a prior intention and valuable in terms set by that intention. I have argued that this appearance is itself a moment of collective enunciation and that it is part of what might be thought of as a contradictory relationship between discourse as it *occurs* and discourse as it *is*. This is to say that momentary particularization or individuation appears as a disruption of a momentum that is bound, nevertheless, to override the force of any particularizing extrusion. But discursive speech, conceived of as a course of activity, does produce moments in which questions like "why are we doing this" or "what are we saying" arise, as it were individually though not as interpretable instances of personal self-reflection occasioned by a discourse abstracted from activity as a "linguistic event."

26

Summary, Reprise, and Transition

The first part of this book addresses the question "What is human about human affairs?" The answer justifies the claim that the human sciences form a single field insofar as they address a shared reality—namely, the sociality of human life. This requires showing that society, understood as in motion in the form of a course of activity, is the "basic fact," in the sense of being irreducible, irrepressible, and reflexive. I identify this with Rousseau's concept of a "first convention." It also requires distinguishing the language of agency from the language of individuality, a distinction I attribute to Marx and to certain currents of post-structuralism. My way of clarifying this is, first, to argue that standard models of sociality posit relatively fixed entities, normatively constrained processes, repeatable expressions of pre-social instances of intentionality, or unacceptably reduced forms of human association. In other words, models of organization, system, culture, exchange, overlapping intentions, and the like are either inconsistent with the idea of the social they are intended to affirm or unaccountably abstract. Virtually all such models depend on a sub-theoretical notion of the social as something altogether different from what they describe. This conclusion is reinforced by an interpretation of studies in the philosophy of action that, despite themselves, entail a latent conception of the social beyond interactions among intentionally oriented individuals. The conceptual problem of what "action" might mean when its social setting is taken into account is avoided in favor of individualistic solutions, in particular by adding a concept of the "self" intended to reduce a theoretically intolerable gap between reasons taken as causes and action taken as an undertaking that aims to satisfy a desire, need, purpose, and the like. Characterizations of the "gap" and the "self" rely on pre-theoretical intuitions more compatible with a radically different theory than the standard theory of action—for example, Nagel's account of "timeless reasons" in his explanation of altruism. Despite the evasion, it is possible to interpret Nagel's account as yielding intuitively acceptable prior notions of the social aspect of acting, perceiving, knowing, and doing, as long as "social" does not mean, as it does for Weber, simply taking account of the conduct of others.

That critique leads to an identification of the idea of the social as a course of activity among parties whose subjectivity is best understood as internal to it. This satisfies the requirement that the language of agency (in this case subjectivity) not be reduced to the language of individuality, with its assumption of external relations between intention and action and its characterization of "action" as a particular "event" originating in particular "persons" taken one by one. To clarify the identification of subjectivity with a course of activity requires rethinking several familiar distinctions. One is among situation, occasion, and context, each of which is subjected to the test of whether it is consistent with the idea of a course of activity. Another is between "subject" and "object" in favor of a notion of inter-subjectivity in which objects usually thought of as agency-independent "things," are no less subjective than the idealized independent agents of the sort that typically exhaust the meaning of "subject."

What makes the distinction difficult to defend is the necessity of accounting for agency-dependent knowledge when the standard used to distinguish knowledge from opinion, the determination of values, and expression is drawn from the natural sciences insofar as they are intended to account for agency-independent objectivity. In this regard, I try to show that an adequate conception of the social implies the notion of agency-dependent objectivity and, therefore, a different kind of knowledge, a different measure of truth, a conception of "practical reason" as essentially social, and a corresponding conception of what it is to know within a course of activity. For the latter, it is necessary, first, to reverse the priority given, in the theory of knowledge, to the agency-denying logic of "justification" over the radically different agency-reflexive logic of "discovery"; second, to criticize the distinction itself in regard to the sort of knowledge claims excluded by its principle; and, third, to show that justification leaves out the course of activity on which the sense of the object of discovery (e.g., a concept or theory) depends. Knowledge that is merely justified cannot be taught as possible: it cannot be shown to be the result of "coming to know" and is, therefore, incurably vague in the explication it offers of the knowledge it purports to represent.

Acknowledging that the objective domain of the human sciences is agency-dependent reality, and that this corresponds to what Rousseau referred to as the "basic idea" of the social when that refers to a course of activity, requires a further distinction between theorizing and theory, the former being the fundamental condition of the latter. If a theory is an instance of what is human about human affairs, it, like the "pre-theoretical" object it purports to *re-present*, is essentially social. This suggests that every theory must be judged by three criteria: it must find itself in its object and its object in itself; and, therefore, it must constantly submit itself, at all cost, to the unending work of theorizing. Like any course of activity, theorizing is reflexive to itself—that is, to its own activity. Consequently, anything that momentarily appears as a product, such as a particular theory, must be seen as disrupting the very activity that is the condition of its possibility as a product. It follows that every theory in the human sciences is, first of all, a self-contradictory *moment* of theorizing, a momentary, constitutionally incomplete, ostensible product that motivates, despite itself, a return to theorizing. This would be true of every instance of ostensible individuation (of speakers, objects of reference, utterances, listeners, etc.) in the course of activity of a discourse, or of anything else humanly being done. This emphasis on the reflexivity of what humans do by way of being human requires a discussion of what a number of contemporary writers have referred to as "collective enunciation."

The last part of this book looks at discourse in regard to the possibility of forming a conception of collective enunciation adequate to the idea of the social as the basic fact and which I refer to as "speaking" in contrast with "speech" (drawn from the standard concept of language) and "uttering" (in the sense of the deliberate issuing of a specific meaning). This leads to a critique of Searle's version of speech act theory and his conception of an "utterance" and to a tentative suggestion that a theory of discourse might serve as a paradigm of sociality as a course of activity and as the basic fact. In what follows, I briefly summarize what is involved in a conception of discourse as collective enunciation.

In discourse, the weight of necessity, the momentousness of the utterance or gesture, does not so much arise from a prior individual intention directly coordinate with meaning. It arises from the inter-subjectivity of discursive speech, which is the condition of its intelligibility and value, and the reason why speaking is spontaneous within the fluid motions of a course of activity. Parties to a setting apprehend the fact that apprehending is going on. Within that collective activity (agency as a social fact), agency-dependent objects, including sentient beings, are constituted as intrinsically volatile and subjective in and among themselves. The objective field of tension immediately implicates each party in the inter-subjectivity of which parties and their objects, objects and their parties, are features. In other words, the momentousness and value of an ostensibly distinct gesture or utterance depends on *its* participation as a moment of a course of activity and as an instance of collective enunciation or, more broadly, of sociality as the basic fact.

To the extent to which something transpires as a course of activity, or is a feature of a course of activity, its force, immediate and beyond, derives from the basic fact of sociality and not the idealized individuality referred to in most theories of mind and action. Value, force, momentousness, intelligibility, meaningfulness, and momentary meaning are constituted collectively, by which I mean within the course of activity of the enunciating virtual ensemble. Inter-subjectivity is profoundly indicated by the attitude of waiting that accompanies every meaningful expression and that displays the momentariness of individuality as in the course of *passing*. That this may appear to bring into play momentarily independent and nonambiguous instances of agency, objects, acts, or effects is consistent with this dialectic. It is one source of the self-motivating tension of any course of activity, what Rawls (1971) refers to as "striving." Once we focus on "speaking" as a realization of the social rather than, say, "speech" as a realization of "language" conceived of as a structure, there seems no other option but to theorize it as a course of activity, with all that implies.

It is now understandable why demands that ostensibly individual parties to a discourse account for specific utterances, or whatever else they appear to be doing according to prior intentions or anticipated effects, are not likely to be taken seriously within the course of activity, and may even be considered offensive. They are, in any case, likely to create confusion and a momentary dissolution of inter-subjectivity in the sense that the "we" invoked in such a demand is suddenly not "here" but "somewhere else." It is also understandable why parties can be expected to reject analyses that attribute effective responsibility to each of them for the value and meaning of "their" utterances and that treat each utterance as a relatively isolated, but not unqualified, complete speech act in a thing-like context of similar acts and things. Finally, it is understandable why parties might reject "translations" that purport to restate, in another form, the meanings of their utterances, as if the meaningfulness of an utterance can be fully appreciated outside of the activity in which meaning itself is an ongoing accomplishment. "Translation," as a variation of repetition, invalidates the sociality of uttering. It operates from a perspective that has little if anything to do with the discursive aspect of speech and the conditions of speaking—that is, with "speaking together." Such an intervention may be seen by a party—one being addressed as if she is not a party to a discourse but a distinct subject to what does not and cannot sustain particular subjectivities—to be merely irrelevant; but it might also be felt as insulting or otherwise disruptive, or as inviting dishonesty or speculation. Being separated from discourse and then asked, "Why did you say or do what you said or did?" imposes an obligation on the addressee to be other than the "social self" she was before the question was asked. It obliges her to speak from within the situation, however constituted, in which the question is asked about another situation in which the course of activity in itself cannot receive the question without dissolving itself, and in which her memory is constituted as such moment to moment. The question is intelligible only in its own situation, and the answer, no matter what it might be, cannot provide the information the questioner claims to desire. A theory based on such "subject reports" has lost its object and its truth as soon as it elicits those reports.

Inter-subjectivity must be understood as the irreducibly ongoing relational aspect of what is being done and said, doing and speaking. This does not preclude the possibility of something happening that can be treated as a complete act without disrupting the course of activity; but it allows for it on condition that more is taken into account than the ostensible individual can accomplish on her own account. To be social is, then, to be inter-subjective and involved in a universe of agency-dependent objects, such that it is knowledge of agency-independent reality that requires retheorizing; and it is in regard to this turning of the epistemological tables that the identification of social action with "taking others into account" needs to be understood and rejected. In attempting to clarify this, I have been operating to some extent within the very frame of reference to which I am objecting, in which persons are taken one by one and the idea of the social (as a multiplicity) always threatens to dissolve into the idea of a mere aggregate, what Rousseau called "the multitude." It seems to me that this framework has itself become a theoretical issue precisely because it fails to live up to its own conditions of making its phenomenon intelligible, which is what I set out to show. The notion of inter-subjectivity by itself cannot yield a full account of the social. It merely poses a problem for which the idea of an irreducible sociality that can only appear as such as a course of activity is one possible solution, and I believe that it is plausible and compelling as things stand.

Earlier, I discussed and criticized the idea that the sociality of social action consists in taking others into account in what one does. This idea, associated with Weber, works only if "others being taken into account" is a constitutive feature of anything we normally refer to as an instance of action. As such, it must qualify everything else that can be taken as a feature of action—for example, its ostensible purpose and rationality. That is to say that every instance of action is an instance of *social action*, but that taking others into account, the activity of doing so, is also an instance of *sociality*. In that case, if taking others into account is as social as doing something by taking them into account, then the meaning of "taking others into account" becomes an issue. But it is not the same sort of issue it once was if we take seriously the notion of inter-subjectivity and the concluding notion of objects imbued with subjectivity, which are necessary if speech is to be considered under the aspect of speaking and action considered as a course of activity.

I have argued that it is implicit in the points of view I have criticized that there is no such thing, in discursive speech or any other collective activity, as an "action" that is self-sufficient or complete or exclusively attributable to an individual person or individuated structure of intentionality. In that case, on the assumption that persons are social beings and not merely beings subject to influence, mediation, or cause, one might conclude that there are no such things as what philosophers call actions. If there are such things, their agents cannot be thought of as social beings according to the idea of the social as the basic fact. Whatever "action" refers to, it cannot be something that pertains to persons when they are not social beings or when "social" is defined either according to individual cognitions (and results of their application) or as the accidental or elective presence of others. I believe that the most compelling hypothesis, as things stand, is that persons are social beings in the sense I have attributed to Rousseau. Since this means more than that persons think "being together" under the warrant of the word "we" and the reductive hypothesis that they are singularly susceptible to events in their surroundings, "action" cannot mean what so much of the literature in the theory of action requires that it means.

If so, it is reasonable to continue exploring the implications of an inter-subjective sociality that reveals itself fundamentally to be a course of activity in which parties reveal themselves as such in an irrepressible "attitude of waiting." This is what makes it possible to imagine a common object of the human sciences, knowledge appropriate to that object, and a methodology that is immanent to sociality so understood. If the common object is what is distinctively human about human affairs, and if that is sociality understood as a course of activity in which the distinction between subjectivity and objectivity is subordinate to inter-subjectivity, and if that subordination has to do with the requirement that humans be considered through and through as abiding within a universe of agency-dependent objects, "subjective objects," and its momentary situations, then it is also necessary to take seriously the following hypothesis: *our knowledge of human affairs is itself a feature of participation and not something that can be extracted from those affairs and retain its identity as knowledge.* This is predicated on the idea that the human sciences share a common object, which is the sociality of the beings that are, in some sense, willing parties to courses of activity and, in that capacity, are instances of what is distinctively human about human life. This yields a second, tentative hypothesis about the possible moral and political implications of this inquiry: *the ultimate referent of moral discourse is not, as Gutmann said, the individual; it is the ongoing life of which every human is an instance, the social to which all are obligated and from which all derive their freedoms as human beings.*

Parenthetically, Rawls's description of the "desire" to be a just person reinforces the point, though not in the direction Rawls takes, given his commitment to a virtually absolute individualism. He says that this "is a desire to conduct oneself in a certain way above all else, a striving that contains within itself its own priority" (1971, 574). If this striving is constituted within a course of activity over which individuals, in principle, exercise no significant independent control, then the idea to which this leads is not the Kantian principle of personal autonomy but the idea of the social realizing itself and, in its course of self-realization, realizing individuality as participation and, by way of that, as the distinctively human form of life. To enable, sustain, and reinforce that life requires far more than emphasizing individual rights and duties, since those are conceivable, as Rousseau showed, only on the presupposition of the social as the basic fact. The first is inconceivable without the second, and the second must be thought of apart from the altogether too convenient notions of group membership, identity, and the ostensibly separable needs of persons taken one by one.

Acknowledgments

In the course of a conversation some years ago, Marie-Hélène Huet commented that "we do not have a language of cooperation." It was with this in mind that I began to write this book. My long association with Frank Rosengarten, my friend and cofounder of the journal *Socialism and Democracy*, enhanced my appreciation of the contribution of the humanities to our understanding of the social aspect of human affairs. My interest in this was originally stimulated by discussions with Frithjof Bergmann during my seven years at the University of Michigan. The most memorable of these, to me, focused on what was at stake morally and intellectually in what was then called "continental philosophy" and on the internal relationship between the humanities and the social sciences. I shared a somewhat different and competing interest in the philosophy of science with Harvey Wagner, my oldest friend. Our discussions often centered on what was most challenging to the social sciences and humanities in the "standard philosophical view" of science, prompting me to pay close attention to certain unstated assumptions about the social that seemed at first to be incompatible with that view and with analytic philosophy in general. I owe a debt to Michael Meyers for having helped me appreciate the difficulties involved in productively addressing the significance of words like "community" and "institution" and other social cognates in the philosophical literature. Conversations with Bertell Ollman and Paule Ollman, often for six hours at a time, helped me come to terms with the ideas of internal relations and the distinction between "justification" and "discovery." Paule's willingness to share with me her profound knowledge of Jean-Paul Sartre's work helped me through several difficult texts that play an important background role in this book. Marie-Hélène Huet and Jay Caplan read and criticized a draft of the sections on Jean-Jacques Rousseau and helped me negotiate the secondary literature and resolve differences among translations of Rousseau's work. They were particularly helpful in forcing me to defend my decision to treat *The Social Contract* as an autonomous text. Michael Raphael has been my technical assistant and provocateur for the past few years. His ability to do almost anything with a computer, his willingness to help at a moment's notice, and his patience made it possible, as a practical matter, for me to complete this book. Zachary Brown was supportive throughout the process, and I believe this book has benefited from his willingness to comment on my prose and to suggest different ways of stating the same idea.

Two people were most directly involved in the development of this book: Randy Martin and Marie-Annick Brown. Randy Martin's friendship and collaboration have deeply enriched me over the years. He read virtually every draft of this book and helped me see problems I had not seen before. His encouragement made it possible for me to complete what at times felt like an endless task. Finally, my discussions about art, literature, and politics with the artist Marie-Annick Brown over the course of our long association, and her willingness to share her thoughts, notes, and recordings about her works in progress, provided me with an opportunity to appreciate the experiential dimension no less than the theoretical significance of several concepts crucial to my account—what I refer to as "the course of activity": reflexivity, the subjective aspect of certain kinds of objects, and the inter-subjective aspect of thought.

Notes

1. The evidence for the claim that the elision is not only pervasive but systematic is overwhelming. It is clear not only in Strawson's account of the history of philosophical analysis but in other major studies, notably Urmson 1956, Dummett 1993, and Soames 2003.

2. Sartre's *Critique of Dialectical Reason* (1976) is perhaps the most notable exception. Taylor's work bears significantly on the problem of how the social might be represented in regard to problems otherwise addressed in the literature of analysis, though he does not quite get us to Strawson's radical view of sociality and adheres to the essentialist individualism associated with analysis (see Taylor 1985b, especially his introductory remarks and chapter 9). Ollman (2003) offers an approach to the difference between the logic of individuality and the logic of sociality that provides a somewhat different way of addressing some of the questions related to theory that I address in this book.

3. Much of Garfinkel's work on deliberative conversations and Erving Goffman's on "stigma" can be read as documenting the effects of anticipated discursive futility, especially the "work" of covering, extending, or otherwise muting it. From that point of view, discourse is seen not merely as communicative action but as activity oriented to the fact that communication cannot succeed in producing a meeting of minds when the grounds of communication cannot themselves be addressed. What makes this incurable is that communication, understood as an exchange between persons, seems to involve forms of speech that are incompatible with the notion of the social that alone provides for self-reflection in the midst of communication. I try to show that this conclusion depends on a theory of communication and not on what goes on or can be expected to go on between persons. In other words, the futility expected of parties to any topical discourse is an inference from premises that I hope to show are false, and a different sense of how people are among people yields a different understanding of discourse and what is essentially incomplete about it (compare Garfinkel 1967; Goffman 1963).

CHAPTER 1

1. We do not normally believe that the sum total of traits that might bear on one's ability to "associate" with others amounts to the holistically definable existential trait of "being social"; yet being social is still thought of as a necessary condition of being recognizably human. Donald Davidson's discussion of the necessary conditions of recognizing that another creature is thinking or has thoughts is a late expression of a theme that runs through much of his work on the relations among thought, speech, and action (2004b, 135–149). It is worthwhile comparing Davidson's fairly cautious discussion of "triangulation" (143, and with more detail in *Subjective, Intersubjective, Objective* [2001d]) with Martin Heidegger's (1968) discussion of the relations of object and thought.

2. Jacques Derrida's (1976, 165–195) account of Rousseau's essay on the origin of languages complicates the issue beyond my intentions, though it is important to understand the relations among Rousseau's concepts. In his account of inequality, Rousseau speaks of pity with a special rhetorical emphasis, as motivating prior to reflection, and places it among characteristics that do not distinguish humans from animals: whatever force it has for a theory of sociality, it is not relevant to the constitution of society—only to its possibility. At most, it explains what *The Social Contract* takes for granted—namely, that those "entering" society will be able to trust that others are doing so with the same vulnerability imposed by the alienation of "natural powers." It does not motivate people to associate; it merely makes possible the step from seeking protection to recognizing the general will, mediated by a first convention that has nothing to do with pity. This is how I interpret Rousseau's introduction of the "two principles anterior to reason, of which one interests us ardently in our well-being and our self-preservation, and the other inspires in us a natural repugnance to see any sensitive being perish or suffer, principally [but not exclusively] our fellow men. It is from the conjunction and combination that our mind is able to make of these two principles, without the necessity of introducing that of sociability, that all the rules of natural right appear to me to flow: rules which reason is later forced to re-establish upon other foundations when, by its successive developments, it has succeeded in stifling nature" (1964, 95–96). The construction of a concept of sociality in the one text is independent of what is said in the other text about pity. Nevertheless, the latter indicates a gap between what drives people together momentarily and what motivates their togetherness. See Derrida 1976, 141–195.

3. See Masters 1968 for an account of Rousseau's work as a coherent whole. I believe that the evidence typically cited is equivocal, including Rousseau's comments in his self-critical reflections. However, whatever position one takes on this should not bear on deciding how Rousseau constructs the notion of the social in *The Social Contract*.

4. I do not emphasize the rhetorical aspect of the text, though I do not ignore it, but rather focus on the place of Rousseau's version of the social contract in the history of social thought (de Man 1979, 246–277). The idea of the state of nature is most often discussed in reference to Thomas Hobbes. Durkheim notes that Rousseau recognized that the state of nature, "if not immoral, is, at least, *amoral*" (1933, 399). At the same time, he rejected the possibility of explaining the origin of society, the version of the problem he inherited from the interpreters of Rousseau. Thus, he speaks of "the progress of the division of labor" and not of its emergence out of a state of nature. His criticism of Herbert Spencer's rejection of the idea of a social contract follows the lines of Rousseau's account of why it is a necessary concept (see Durkheim 1933, chap. 7), and he concludes, as Rousseau did, that relations among diverse people depend on an underlying social constitution (215). Paul de Man's summary of the idea of the state of nature captures the

essence of the standard interpretation: it provides "an uncertain and precarious way of life," based on "natural independence," the "power to harm others," and the need to rely exclusively on "their individual strength" (1979, 276). Finally, John Rawls treats the idea of the state of nature from the point of view of Immanuel Kant, for whom it is "a purely hypothetical situation characterized so as to lead to a certain conception of justice" (Rawls 1971, 12). But even there the "original position of equality" is not the antithesis of society and therefore it can only clarify the principle of rationality on the basis of which "the principles of justice" can be "chosen behind a veil of ignorance" (12). There remains a question of how people can come to agree to consider the question of justice in the way Rawls has in mind unless there is some more fundamental equality identical with a sociality that allows individuals to suspend the suspicions they normally cannot do without. Rawls does not escape this problem. In this regard, Rousseau posed the essential problem of society—namely, that it presupposes something prior to social order.

5. The expression "primitive act of confederation" is used in the "Geneva Manuscript" (1978a, bk. 1, chap. 3, 164). I refer to this because it indicates the ambiguity of the expression "first convention"—an act of coming together (an event) and an agreement or "engagement" (a result that has the aspect of a performance). Rousseau seems to claim that the act of coming together is nothing more than the performance of the social contract.

6. We should conclude from the above, contrary to Talcott Parsons, that there can be no continuity of identity from the lack of articulation to articulation in theories of the evolution of societies (e.g., Parsons 1977). Therefore, variations in "degrees of articulation" cannot be understood as moves away from a pre-articulate condition. This is not to say that methods do not exist for constructing models of progressive articulation—if by articulation one does not mean the beginning of an approximation of an ideal. Melinda Cooper describes the development of such models in architecture and biology (2008, esp. chap. 4). What is relevant to sociology is the possible application of methods capable of reproducing "the various effects of force or strain in the morphogenesis of form, thus replacing a typology of essences with a grid of continuous morphological temptations" (118). What is under attack in the models is the presupposition of a "certain rigidity of space," and, therefore, the necessity to distinguish figure from ground or object and event from context (119). Recent work in biology "suggests that a truly ontogenetic theory or morphogenesis must move from the relatively restricted though nonmetric space of projective transformations to the continuous space of topology" (119). Certain attempts to form a concept of network may be open to such a program since it preserves the sort of information that standard analytical procedures eliminate and offers a way of clarifying what is meant in evolutionary sociology by the word "articulation" and the assumption that it emerges from the purest form of what Durkheim called "mechanical solidarity" (1933, 106).

7. This does not deny that such a creature might be able to tolerate its elision and even the consequences of doing so.

CHAPTER 2

1. The failure to consider the role of the unstated referent, society, poses problems for those theories of justice that emphasize the sufficiency of adversarial procedures to a minimally rational polity, or, as Stuart Hampshire (2000) puts it, processes that facilitate hearing all sides. Such processes are necessary to the sorts of deliberation that allow the losers in a debate to go along with the winners, the minority with the majority. But without a clear connection to the basic social fact, there will always be doubts about the

justice of any position, decision, or policy; and, therefore, the sense of doubt may over-power the sense of the rightness and necessity of the Law as such. Hampshire does not account very well for the refusal of those he refers to as absolutists ("monotheists") to ac-cept tolerance as a duty, given that differences among strongly held moral principles may lead to violence. He attributes this to their forgetting that they make many of their own decisions according to the rational principle of hearing all sides. It is sufficient, then, to remind them of that fact and what it entails. But it may be that the reason some people may remain suspicious of adversarial proceedings is that another crucial fact is excluded that diminishes the rationality of such proceedings. Hampshire observes that all socie-ties are morally divided, which poses the first problem a theory of justice must face: how to limit violence. He concludes that rational people ought to agree that it is necessary to guarantee that all sides will be heard. But without some reference to the social whole, the idea that the general interest can prevail is likely to be insufficient to support a com-mitment to procedural justice. If so, suspicion of existing adversarial proceedings might justify attempting to impose one's will on others on the grounds that each is trying to impose her will on all. See Nagel 1991 for an account of the prospects, limits, and para-doxes of equality and legitimacy, given his presuppositions of a permanent capitalism, the independent viability of democracy, the inability of large-scale centralized economic planning to sustain its society, and the lack of reasonable nonutopian alternatives to price-making money markets.

2. Rawls includes reference to "comprehensive doctrines" in his account of "the law of peoples" (1999a, 175) and comments on this in his short reflection on religion (Rawls and Nagel 2009, 261–269).

3. According to this, one might be legitimately dissatisfied with a judicial or legis-lative process because of the missing reason, regardless of whether all voices had been heard, a sense of injustice that Hampshire does not acknowledge as possible. But, how-ever a sense of justice arises, it does not follow that the violence anticipated when all voices are not heard is as likely as Hampshire says. That is only one possibility. The reap-pearance of the original conflict in a new register is often referred to as "cooptation," and it is a tactic in its own right but not one that belongs to the loser in the original dispute; rather it is one that belongs to the victors. In other words, the aftermath of an unjust resolution of a dispute is not the same as the situation prior to that resolution. This is why tyrants act under the cover of law, not to fool people into thinking that they actually received justice but to introduce a process that changes the conditions of conflict, regard-less of what other predicaments may follow (see Butler, Laclau, and Žižek 2000). My point is that hearing all voices may not produce a sense of a just process, but it changes things; and even when all individuated voices have been heard, the most important one, which is in principle not individuated, will not have been heard. There is, then, something of an injustice whether or not all individuated voices have been heard. Hampshire's theory of justice is in fact a theory of one type of injustice—namely, the injustice of not hearing all voices. But hearing them does not in itself provide justice. It follows that the condi-tions he outlines as necessary for the *institution* of hearing all voices should be thought of as part of the difference between justice and injustice. Does it follow that there are no grounds for saying that a given process is unjust? There are certainly grounds but only if the question of representation itself can legitimately be raised.

4. The Marxist critique of civil society has itself been criticized as tendentious (see Cohen and Arato 1995)—on the grounds that, while it may be true that the legal systems and civic norms of bourgeois society often disguise underlying conditions having to do with unquestioned power and practices of exclusion, this is by no means the whole story.

But the notion of "the whole story" itself presupposes a balance that cannot be rational-ized without risking the original critique. Whether or not Marx is correct, the claim is irrelevant to the critique of civil society offered here. It is not so much that power and exclusion are disguised. It is that no one can rationally address the question of whether civil society is or is not corrupt in this way as long as the very possibility of sociality, to which any reasonable test of agreement must find some way of referring, is ignored.

5. This is implicit in Rousseau's explication of his purpose: to show that "the social order is a sacred right which serves as a basis for all others" (1978b, 47). It constitutes "a form of association which defends and protects with all the common force the person and goods of each associate, and by means of which each, uniting with all, nevertheless obeys only himself, and remains as free as before. Such is the fundamental problem to which the social contract gives the solution" (47). The "act of association produces a moral and collective body, composed of as many members as there are voices in the assembly, and which receives from this same act its unity, its common *self* [*moi*], its life, and its will" (47).

6. Rousseau does not mean—when he says that his inquiry aims to discover a pos-sibility "within the civil order" and that he intends to consider "human beings as they are and laws as they might be"—that a different inquiry is possible, one that takes humans as they are not and that deals with a radically nonsocial condition (1978b, 47).

7. Rousseau says that "the social order is a sacred right which serves as the foun-dation for all others. This right comes not from nature; it must, therefore, have been founded on conventions," which he says is what is at stake in his inquiry. He then says "I must establish that which I have just advanced" (1978b, 47).

8. The allegory organized around the first-ness of the first convention should not be understood as part of a convenient fiction, as it is so often put. This would reduce it to a methodological device, and I am trying to show that its force is far greater than that. When he says, in regard to the "obligation of the small number to submit to the choice of the large," that "the law of the [majority rule] presupposes unanimity at least once" (1978b, 52), Rousseau cannot mean what the passage seems to say based on the expres-sion "at least once." Since a "law" of that sort, about how interests are to be disposed, can only manifest itself in all its instances, unanimity is presupposed in every instance. "At least once" can only refer to the "law" taken apart from its instances. What Rousseau is saying, then, is that an *originary* sense of unanimity characterizes each moment in which the issue is posed, which is every time there is a collective decision, and it does so as an expression of a commitment to an equality that manifests the general will. He is not say-ing that majority rule is necessary—only that if it is to operate, its principle must have the assent of all. All could agree to abide by the majority only under conditions of the first convention, which is to say equal membership rooted in inter-dependence.

9. I do not suggest that biological theories of animal behavior are adequate to what they purport to explain or that animals are not human-like or human in the moral sense advocated by some philosophers—only that the analogy breeds a biological approach to both human and nonhuman sociality, and this is what is mischievous.

10. If Strawson is correct in his claim that humans are social through and through, then the step he avoids is logically necessary—namely, that concern with solidarity is constant and not merely occasional (1992, 80–81). Garfinkel, perhaps more than any other ethnographer, has shown how—no matter how comfortable parties look in each other's company, no matter how involved they seem to be in what appears to be routine, fun, or a collective task requiring concentration—there is never a moment at which close observa-tion does not reveal precisely that sort of tension leading to the conversational "work" all parties engage in to reduce tension for the sake of going on (1967; see also Goffman 1963).

CHAPTER 3

1. See Stanley Fish's criticism of the assumption "that meanings can be specified independently of the activity of reading" (1976, 468). William Cain places this remark in the context of Fish's attempt to juggle the freedom of reading with the constraints of the text, but I believe he slights its importance to a different debate—namely, about whether reading is an activity or an action or event, and the warning against losing the activity of reading in the idealization of the book (1981, 80–87).

2. In Rousseau's treatise (1978, 137n28), Masters provides a possible response by Hobbes, beyond Rousseau's interpretation of the latter's concession that there is a "tacit acceptance" of majority rule as a concession to the first convention. Hobbes was concerned with the relationship between tacit acceptance and the formation of what we now call institutions, which may well require some other factor than the social contract to account for the formation of legitimate authority—namely, force of a certain sort and only that sort. Rousseau's move to the first convention by default and from there to recognizable society is missing crucial elements for it to be convincing but only if the narrative is the theory, and I claim that it is not and therefore cannot be read for its "plot."

3. See Nagel for how the autonomous continuous self looks under social conditions defined without any reference to sociality but "social units" (1970, 130). The problem is that each mention of a social unit (family, business, nation, etc.) requires an idea of what it is to be social, and each attempt to specify the idea of a continuing self without such an idea requires increasingly more tenuous qualifications on the notion of timeless reasons or restrictions on its applicability. Nagel's account of timeless reasons is undoubtedly significant, but what binds time is something he cannot specify or even consider—namely, the coherence of the human life that runs through time and transcends individuation. I hope to show that the coherence is not a product of memory alone but of continuing involvement in relations that cannot be fixed "social units"; nor can it belong to any individual or plurality.

4. See Derrida 1994, 27, on Heidegger in this regard.

5. Sociologists from Durkheim to Goffman have argued that a social fact is not many doing something, but that many do something is a result of a social fact. The problem has always been that to make this intelligible requires an independent definition of sociality that does not reduce it to individual actions taken one by one.

6. See Wollheim 1960, 104–122, for a critical discussion of the idea of "internal relations," and see Ollman 2003, 36–50, for a defense that seems to avoid some of the criticisms summarized by Wollheim.

7. Nagel says that altruism requires "a conception of oneself as simply a person among others all of whom are included in a single world," which is "a conception of oneself not merely as *I*, but as someone" (1970, 100). While he is certainly correct in saying that this does not require "a mystical identification of oneself with other persons" (99), it does require a sense of the social prior to a sense of self, at least if reasons are to be, as he says, objective. Similarly, with prudential reasons, he says that what is required is that the present be identified "as one time among others all of which are contained in a single life" (99). But since the singleness of a life must somehow be produced, or at least cannot be taken for granted, continuity, singleness, must be accounted for by reference to the universe of reasons that might apply in the present and future. That universe is what gives identification to a continuous life that then consists of an obligation to adhere to what that non-immanent continuity requires. One can hardly accept a theoretical solution to the rationality of prudence that assumes what it must explain—that is, the continuity of

the self. That there may be biological continuity is not to the point; it seems easier to say that continuous self-reference is a social fact than to say that it is simply obvious that various times "are contained in a single life" (99).

8. The last clause, "rather than yours," is problematic, given the discussion so far. The foundation of the concept of "someone" does not allow for a distinction between "theirs" and "yours."

CHAPTER 4

1. This is considered differently in Rousseau's essay on the origins of inequality, where insecurity is an effect of various causes of inequality instituted within a given society. In his account of the social contract, the question is not the effects of such a society but its most general preconditions (Rousseau 1964, 101–181).

2. Searle says, "The form that collective intentionality can take is simply 'we intend,' 'we are doing so-and-so,' and the like. In such cases, I intend only as part of our intending. The intentionality that exists in each individual head has the form 'we intend'" (1995, 26).

3. See Rawls 1971, 140, citing Rousseau 1974, bk. 2, chap. 4, par. 5.

4. See Durkheim's (1965, 66) critique of literal readings of Rousseau on the state of nature.

5. While Rousseau presents this argument in the "Geneva Manuscript" and hardly at all in *The Social Contract*, this is clearly the problem he hopes to solve. I claim that he solves it by doing away with the problem altogether. That is, individuals cannot *choose* society over nature because they cannot put themselves in a position to make such a choice, much less imagine the possibility of doing so.

6. A serviceable definition of "allegory" is "to compose a work so that its apparent sense refers to an 'other' sense. To interpret allegorically . . . is to explain a work as if there were an 'other' sense to which it referred" (Preminger and Brogan 1993, 31). While irony may attach to an allegorical composition, it does not attach to the "other" sense indicated, when it is understood not merely as a literary form but as a text intended to establish a final sense beyond which there is no other. This is consistent with "the aspiration of works to express the 'inexpressible'" (31). From this point of view, the force of an allegory, what makes the text *effectively* and not merely formally allegorical, lies in its capacity to leave its reader in a state of certainty beyond doubt—since the sense arrived at is one that could never have been put into question in the first place. It uniquely ratifies what must already have been known.

7. Literary scholars often say that allegory is difficult to identify. I rely on a specific sense of allegory as a narrative form of proof of Ludwig Wittgenstein's famous aphorism, "What we cannot speak about we must pass over in silence." This is preceded by "My propositions serve as elucidations in the following way: anyone who understands me eventually recognizes them as nonsensical, when he has used them—as steps—to climb up beyond them. (He must, so to speak, throw away the ladder after he has climbed up it.)" (1974, 74). Irony becomes an important feature of the proof, since recognition of ironical intent is necessary for the narrative to be read non-ironically as an allegory rather than, say, a description. An allegory is, from this point of view, a self-denying narrative that undermines its narrative form for the sake of a certainty that no narrative can otherwise deliver. While allegory understood this way may serve political purposes, it teaches us not to rely on conventional accounts of facts unfolding or evolving over time but on establishing conditions under which it would be at least uninteresting and at most unintelligible to suggest that what is held in need of an account may be other than

it seems to be. In this sense, all serious reading considers the possibility that its object is at least somewhat allegorical. I should add that this is not consistent with de Man's (1979) view of allegory as sustaining the perspective of temporality and, therefore, of history. It is not so much that allegory restores history by restoring temporality; it restores history by denying, negating, absolute time, the time of emergence and transition. It leaves the fruits of reason, as G.W.F. Hegel might have put it, in a position where it must account for the struggles that are endlessly internal to its idea, not record a chronology of "conflicts" in the sense of facts and events. In this version of the dialectical view of history, there is no emergence, evolution, and the rest. Whatever those are relevant to, they are not relevant to restoring the historical perspective as the perspective of possibility, or conditions of possibility.

8. John Lough (1980, 73) argues, to the contrary, that Rousseau's use of the term "social" was conventional and not intended to be theoretical, largely on the grounds that Rousseau was not writing in support of the standard ideas of a body politic (e.g., a contract between the king and his subjects). It is, of course, true that the word "social" does not come into play in the ways in which "the first convention," "association," "equality," "the body politic," and "the general will" do, yet it is important to keep in mind that the first convention, or social fact, inaugurates an equality among those who concede their powers to the whole and that this is a fundamental condition of all that follows. The text is not about specific historical societies so much as it is about the condition of any such arrangement—which is why Rousseau goes to pains to show that all political arrangements assume something analogous to an agreement or convention.

9. *The Rules* was originally published in France in 1895 and reissued in 1901. The first English translation of note is by Joseph Ward Swain, in 1915 (see Gilbert 1989, 243, for a discussion of the logic of *The Rules* and the idea of a "social fact"). A doctoral thesis at Columbia University, by Charles Elmer Gehlke (1915), apparently a student of Franklin H. Giddings, provides an early attempt to summarize Durkheim's sociological theory, with particular regard to the distinction between psychological and social facts. The first important theoretical summary of Durkheim in the United States appears in Parsons's *The Structure of Social Action* (1949), though the anthropology department at the University of Chicago became a virtual school of Durkheimian social science when Alfred R. Radcliffe-Brown joined the department in 1931 (for an account of Durkheim's influence on social science, see Nisbet 1965, 4).

CHAPTER 5

1. By "Marxism," I mean Marx's critique of the capitalist mode of production according to internal limitations that make it impossible for it to "reproduce" itself. By "post-structuralism," I mean the critique of the theory of the sign in regard to the contradictory relation of the signifier (what is uttered or written) and the signified (a concept that is the immediate referent of the signifier). If "meaning" requires a unit in the divided form of the sign, then what needs to be faced is the fact that the circulation of signifiers follows a course and has a temporality that cannot be attributed to the signified concept. A second level of this critique is the idea that something is left out of every formulation—that every signifier or formulation presents itself as "approximate" and, therefore, as insufficient to its object. Much of post-structuralism flows from this critique, to the extent to which it draws on Hegel's (1977) demonstration that an assertion can only guarantee certainty (therefore wholeness) at the expense of something excluded but necessarily taken for granted. This is what is meant by "critique" in Marx's "critique

of political economy." It allowed him to demonstrate that the conditions of rational action (exchange aimed at realizing an increase in value over costs) that capital takes as its own exclude precisely what is presupposed in the claim that such action is possible in its own terms. This is part of what Derrida (1994, 87) meant when he declared Marxism to be indispensable. De Man writes, "What we call ideology is precisely the confusion of linguistic with natural reality, of reference with phenomenalism. It follows that, more than any other mode of inquiry, including economics, the linguistics of literariness is a powerful and indispensable tool in the unmasking of ideological aberrations, as well as a determining factor in accounting for their occurrence. Those who reproach literary theory for being oblivious to social and historical (that is, ideological) reality are merely stating their fear at having their own ideological mystifications exposed by the tool they are trying to discredit. They are, in short, very poor readers of Marx's *German Ideology*" (1986, 11). My purpose is neither to defend post-structuralism nor to identify it with Marxism but to defend the claim that Marxism and post-structuralism are vitally connected and that ignoring this connection tends to reduce Marxism to a defense of a complete and consistent positive theory of an object of which it is not part.

2. Marx says that the estrangement of the worker "is manifested not only in the result but in the *act of production*—within the *producing activity* itself. How could the worker come to face the product of his activity as a stranger, were it not that in the very act of production he was estranging himself from himself? The product is after all but the summary of the activity of production. If then the product of labour is alienation, production itself must be active alienation, the alienation of activity, the activity of alienation. In the estrangement of the object of labour is merely summarized the estrangement, the alienation, in the activity of labour itself" (1975, 274; emphasis in original).

3. See Davidson's essay entitled "Actions, Reasons, and Causes," originally published in 1963 as "a reaction against a widely accepted doctrine that the explanation of an intentional action in terms of its motives or reasons could not relate reasons and actions as cause and effect" (2001a, xvi).

4. The political implications of this are discussed by Hardt and Negri (2000). If one conceives of a "system" that intensifies its application of power until there is no space unfilled by it, power can only turn back against itself. Power generalized beyond exception creates a total exception, which Hardt and Negri call "the multitude" and identify with the only responsive politics that remains sufficient to the task of social change under the circumstances defined as "Empire." In that case, the "politics" they identify against insufficient alternatives (e.g., parties) cannot be recognized theoretically, insofar as the terms of theory remain conventional. Therefore, they cannot be recognized as politics and can express their form of life only as a resistance that constitutes what Pierre Clastres (1977) referred to as "society against the state," meaning, I take it, the general will against the attempt to particularize all will. Marx's accounts of the "real subsumption" of labor (1990a, 1023, 1034–1038) and his account of the "collective worker" are the first systematic attempts to rethink power as an immanent feature of "societies in which the capitalist mode of production prevails" (Marx and Engels 1976, 464–465, 468–469, 483; see also vol. 3 of *Capital*, in which Marx briefly discusses "the contradiction of fictitious capital and the society of the producers" [1990c, 358], a contradiction that is the ultimately fateful one for the capitalist mode of production).

5. See Green and Shapiro 1994; for a general review, see Cook and Levi 1990, 1–16.

6. By "consociation," I mean something different from what Schutz refers to as the "we-relationship," which is idealized as purely interpersonal in his typology of levels of relationship: "In brief, consociates are mutually involved in one another's biography; they

are growing older together; they live, as we may call it, in a pure We-relationship" (1962, 16–17). What is most important about the way in which he derives his notion of consociation is the infusion of ostensibly particular relations with the universal fact of sociality. In this regard, the consociate relationship is one in which each party knows the other simultaneously as singular and as one of all—that is, at the center of two futile promises: to resolve all universals into a particular and to recognize at all moments the universal humanity of the one by virtue of its being merely one. This cannot be understood as a synthesis since each term depends on the other. What is important is the mobility of the senses of self and other as neither term can be realized before the other comes into play. Thus, the consociate relationship is one in which there is always a sense of prospective loss and never a sense of something or someone found. In passing, it is important to note that the Kantian no less than the Rousseauian in Derrida sees compassion as incapable of limiting itself.

7. I take this to mean the critique of "capital" from the point of view of the commodity as its unit of self-analysis. In this respect, Marx's critique attempts to constitute capital's best case in its own terms.

8. It is in that light that "class" has nothing to do with the sociological categories of inequality and access to markets. It specifies relations of the production and circulation of value according to the two main operations of capitalist production, the extraction of surplus value from human, or "variable," labor, and the deployment of surplus value relative to material production.

9. Such a duality is the only way mind can be conceived of when it is necessary to account for it by reference to conditions (or context) and where conditions must be accounted for by reference to further conditions under which they become specific conditions of mentality. It is these "further conditions" that can only be conceived of as intrinsic to commodity production in general, whatever else might be said about them, and more concretely, to the "price-making money market," the organization of labor along lines that makes it possible to extract the surplus that constitutes the uniqueness of capitalist wealth and that makes capitalist production possible, and the socialization of labor, which, under conditions of integrated production on a potentially unlimited scale, reaches beyond the immediate situations of "concrete" labor, hence the individual laborer.

10. While the design of Marx's argument is complex, there are fairly straightforward expressions of the notion of "subjectivity within agency." For example, toward the end of his discussion of "constant" and "variable" capital, Marx speaks of "the subjective factor of the labour-process, with labour-power in action" in a way that seems to identify it with the operation of labor as a social entity rather than with the individual laborer. So it might seem somewhat misleading to read, after this passage, the following: "While labour, because it is directed to a specific purpose, preserves and transfers to the product the value of the means of production, at the same time, throughout every instant it is in motion, it is creating an additional value, a new value" (1990a, 316). Several things can be said about why this is not a theory of the "labourer." First, the labor at issue is "labour-power in action," which is to say socialized labor. Second, the creation of a "new value" is not the work of an individual carrying out his or her specialty with its own "special object." It is the work of labor as such. The calculation appropriate to the new value is one that looks abstractly at the product as a whole and not the particular object of particular or concrete labor. It is in that regard that we can understand why by simply working the laborer creates the new value that is part of the product taken as the surplus available to the owner. Marx notes that labor-power is one mode "of existence which the value of the original capital assumed when it lost its monetary form and was transformed into

the various factors of the labour-process" (317). Finally, "the same elements of capital which, from the point of view of the labour-process, can be distinguished respectively as the objective and subjective factors, as means of production and labour-power, can be distinguished, from the point of view of the valorization process, as constant and variable capital" (317). For a useful analysis and summary of Marx's method in distinguishing, say, "points of view," see Ollman 1993, especially part 2. This is the most comprehensive, though controversial, treatment of Marx's method I know of and it provides an important and compelling version of "dialectics."

11. Thus, it would be inappropriate to sample "labor" by "sampling" a "population."

12. In using the terms "mode" and "form," Marx allows for the possibility that a theory of agency will find different instances in regard to different modes of production, and, of course, different dualities. There is no need to appeal to a mechanistic base-superstructure type of argument to make this case, and, indeed, reference to "modes" of production is designed at least to leave that issue open.

13. Davidson translates the conclusion of his argument about knowledge, that "knowledge of other minds is thus basic to all thought," into "thus, the acquisition of knowledge is not based on a progression from the subjective to the objective; it emerges holistically, and is interpersonal from the start" (2004b, 18). The problem is made even more manifest in his essay in the same volume, "What Thought Requires" (2004c, 143), where "sharing" is not theorized but, it is clear, cannot be taken for granted.

14. This is in the context of a discussion of the "prisoner's dilemma," and it has to do with the attempt, which Max Black thinks is futile, to reconcile "rationality" and "sociality," or, as Rousseau put it, "utility" and "justice," in such situations.

CHAPTER 6

1. On one interpretation of reductionism, if the problem is prediction, and prediction aims at individuals and statistical changes in categories of individuals, then it seems true, as Laird Addis (1975) seems to say, that sociology is impossible except as a stop-gap. Moreover, if the idea of the social has to do with what people do rather than with what they are, and with entities that are merely the accumulation of individual responses based on psychological laws having to do with the effects of the presence of others, then there are no such things as societies. Finally, if we wish to predict and to do so according to facts and reasonable inference based on something like laws, then it is possible to declare that other ways of thinking about the problem of defining social science may be interesting but they are not part of acquiring knowledge. Thus, Addis says, with a hint of sarcasm, "having analyzed the issue [of explanatory reductionism] as we have, we are in a position to see clearly that little except the cold, scientific fact itself seems logically to ride on the answer—not whether our social responses are different from our nonsocial ones, not whether we are basically driven by instincts or not, not whether our loves and hates and commitments determine our behavior in large measure, and certainly not, as we have already argued, whether society is something more than the properties and relations of individual persons" (66–67). For a discussion of the normativity of theories of action based on the idea of rational choice, see Davidson 2004a.

2. Said refers to sociology as an "ideology and policy" science, which, therefore, had little choice but to attempt to immunize itself against the sort of criticism that was beginning to make its presence felt as "literary theory" (1979, 15).

3. Bertell Ollman (2003) characterizes these as abstractions, a notion central to his account of "dialectical method." He introduces it as follows: "In thinking about

any subject, we focus on only some of its qualities and relations. Much that could be included—that may in fact be included in another person's view or thought and may on another occasion be included in our own—is left out. The mental activity involved in establishing such boundaries, whether conscious or unconscious—though it is usually an amalgam of both—is the process of abstraction" (60).

4. I use "historicism" in the sense of a concern with context and with the very idea of a context and not in Karl Popper's sense of a "prophetic" historiographical attitude or trope (Montrose 1992, 392–418; Veeser 1989; Popper 1957).

5. I refer here to Weber's discussion of the coordination of deliberate action across a plurality of individuals. Parsons saw Weber's idea of a tendency toward rationalization over the long run as the formulation of a "law," given a level of analysis appropriate to the social as a system of action and given mediations of various sorts. Parsons writes: "This conception of a law of increasing rationality as a fundamental generalization about systems of action is, of course, not original. It is the most fundamental generalization that emerges from Weber's work" (1949, 752). It is, perhaps, in that regard that the following should be interpreted: "Roughly, for Weber, bureaucracy plays the part that the class struggle played for Marx and competition for [Werner] Sombart" (509); and for Weber, "what characterizes capitalistic acquisition is rather its 'rationality'" (505).

6. Early references in "industrial sociology" to "spontaneous involvement" made room for the use of "informal organization," as did studies of the role of interaction in the social order of a group (see, for example, Blau and Meyer 1987, chap. 3). Sociologists often refer in this regard to the Bank Wiring Observation Room, reported in Roethlisberger, Dickson, and Wright 1946, 379.

7. As already discussed, models are bound to raise doubts about the category of "familiarity." Morris R. Cohen (1956, 97–98) hinted at some such notion in his discussion of metaphors in science. Along somewhat related lines, Black's statement that "every metaphor is the tip of a submerged model" may be inverted to read that "every model imposes a universe in which the metaphor it supports is not metaphorical but referential." If the way a metaphor works is by keying in an alternative universe in which it is a description, it is likely to appear, relative to the universe for which it is metaphorical, as entailing what cannot be entailed (see Black 1990a, 62). I suggest that the model of rational organization operates in just that way—by juxtaposing two universes, one in which the social life of humans is portrayed as law-like behavior and the other in which it is not conceivably so. The first is populated by various realizations of a higher order, with people as operatives who manifest the local imperatives of that order; the second is composed of people among people. The juxtaposition is accomplished by the inapplicability of the model of rational organization without introducing it as metaphorical to the second, familiar, universe. In that case, we read it and find ourselves challenged to think of what life would be like if the model were "the basic fact."

8. I rely on a distinction between totality and totalization, where "totality" means "a being which, while radically distinct from the sum of its parts, is present in its entirety, in one form or another, in each of these parts, and which relates to itself either through its relation to one or more of its parts or through its relation to the relations between all or some of them" (Sartre 1976, 45). Parsons's (1951) concept of the social system is an example, as is what I am calling "a theory." Such a thing exemplifies the idea of "the inert": "the synthetic unity which produced its appearance of totality is not an activity, but only the vestige of a past action" (Sartre 1976, 45). What holds it together is external to it, and it must therefore be thought of as passive and, "in fact, eroded by infinite divisibility." Sartre speaks, then, of "present action" that makes objects "seem like totalities

by resuscitating, in some way, the *praxis* which attempted to totalize their inertia" (45). In this regard, "the *totality* . . . is only a regulative principle of the totalisation," which is a course of activity in contrast with a product or regulative principle (46). The "movement of totalisation" in which is established "the intelligibility of dialectical Reason," is toward a multiplicity increasingly self-differentiating as a multiplicity of multiplicities, something on the order of a unifying movement that creates conditions of disunification (46). For Sartre, the "negation of the negation becomes an affirmation" only within "the framework of totalisation" (46). But since every determinative moment negates other moments, excludes them, the affirmative occurs as a movement toward a more differentiated multiplicity that remains "superficially" unified. He concludes, "Thus, it is only within a developing unification (which has already defined the limits of its field) that a determination can be said to be a negation and that the negation of a negation is necessarily an affirmation" (47).

9. It is not just that a concept requires other concepts; but that a concept takes form as an instance of the course of theorizing and cannot be extracted from it without effectively distinguishing between theory and the life it is purported to be about. When "life" is the issue, such a distinction is fatal to the claim that the theory is about an instance of life. This poses a problem—namely, how to reconcile the holistic notion of a concept (as dependent on all the other concepts within its universe of reference) with the notion of a concept consistent with the idea of life: such a concept must, in other words, show itself to be part of the life it re-presents.

10. W. B. Gallie's essay "Essentially Contested Concepts" seems too narrow in what he claims fits the category (1968, 157–191). If theoretical concepts are thought of as momentary expressions of a course of activity that cannot legitimately be divorced from the meaning (including the sense) of that expression (which must depend on their "expressing"), then all concepts in the human sciences are essentially contested, which is why the Kuhnian idea of "paradigm" is too static a notion to apply to the social sciences and humanities. That is, concepts are essentially contested when they are taken to be conceived, or to be conceptions, which is to say when they are acknowledged in what is written in the name of theorizing to be reflexive to the contests of which they must be moments if it is to be sensible to say that they are "conceived." Otherwise, they are not essentially contested, with the consequence, fatal to the human sciences, of the hypostatization of "theory" and the corresponding projection of "debates" among propositionally instated "theories." There is, of course, another way of interpreting "essentially contested" that offers a yet more radical conclusion—namely, that certain concepts lose their usefulness when they are taken as not essentially contested. But this seems to assign essentially contested concepts to the field of use or application of a theory that is more or less well-formed and to beg the question of whether "contest" is a necessary feature of certain or any concepts. That is, as Gallie suggests, a given concept might be essentially contested if it engages competing values. But this is to trivialize the intuition that underlay his use of "essentially," and the very possibility of there being a "given concept" is incongruent with the notion that concepts erupt, as it were, within a contest that they inevitably express. It may be true that we must speak of the "givenness" of a concept in order to examine the moment at which the hypostatization of "theory" poses problems for theorizing, given the difficulty writing poses for expressing the internality of the relationship between a course of activity and the products of such a course. But these are minimized to the extent to which every concept is approached as *essentially reflexive* to the course of activity, hence contest, of which it can only be a moment. While there are doubtless many issues that need to be resolved if this argument is to be fairly represented, the basic idea seems

sound. There is one question that seems potentially more explosive than others I can think of: how is it possible to speak of concepts without concepts? While I do not believe that this poses as many difficulties as might initially appear, it does suggest a certain tension between the sort of philosophy that engages theory after it is an ostensible fact and as if "ostensible" does not count, and the sort of philosophy that attempts to contain within the sense of the concept (to retain its sense) the course of activity in which it fit-fully makes its appearance. Hegel's phenomenology is written with that in mind, as he indicates in the preface to *Phenomenology of Spirit*, where he speaks of the need to rec-ognize that "the real issue is not exhausted by stating it as an aim, but by carrying it out, nor is the result the actual whole, but rather the result together with the process through which it came about" (1977, 2).

11. The "as if" is mischievous. Given that one is in the midst of activity, the proper-ties of the activity itself, including momentary points of reference, are not explicitly taken into account. To participate in a course of theoretical activity is, then, not to act "as if" the concepts, such as they are, have lives of their own but to act in ways that are intel-ligible only if they have such a life.

12. It is tempting to equate the sub-theoretical with the real and the theoretical with the virtual, as in Goffman's (1963) ironical characterization of the dilemmas of "social identity." But because of the irony, the analogy does not work. The sub-theoretical is not real in the sense of real in itself, versus the theoretical, which is virtual in the sense of merely constructed. The former is what the latter is obliged to comprehend, and I de-scribe how theory arises out of theorizing in such a way that the obligation cannot easily be met, if it can be met at all.

CHAPTER 7

1. "In the previous modes of certainty what is true for consciousness is something other than itself. But the Notion of this truth vanishes in the experience of it" (Hegel 1977, 104). "Self-consciousness exists in and for itself when, and by the fact that, it so exists for another; that is, it exists only in being acknowledged. . . . Now this movement of self-consciousness in relation to another self-consciousness has in this way been rep-resented as the action of *one* self-consciousness, but this action of the one has the double significance of being both its own action and the action of the other as well. For the other is equally independent and self-contained, and there is nothing in it of which it is not itself the origin" (111–112). These remarkable passages are part of Hegel's account of what happens when self-consciousness finds itself among what had appeared to be things and are now objects taken as forms of life. In other words, self-consciousness intrinsically involves the sense of objects as subjects.

2. Since concepts must be thought of as active within the activity in which they are inserted, we can speak of their involvement with the object presumably re-presented. There is no idealization of the concept, since a concept is always a feature of an activity and is never settled unless activity is displaced by its ostensible product. Nor is it suffi-ciently settled within a course of activity since it is the nature of such a thing that what-ever appears settled about it is only ostensibly so. In other words, the only way a concept can be said to be settled is if theory is abstracted from the activity that makes it possible as an ostensible product. In that case, the concept is understood as an inert part of some-thing inert and its consolidation is no longer a feature of the struggle that is immanent to the course of activity that engages the life of the concept. It is of interest that the language of "theory" and "concept" is analogous to the language of machine-like systems, defined

in terms of things in external relations with other things. F. H. Bradley's notion of the "sensible" or "felt whole" need not be thought of as something different from other sorts of thing, since, arguably, all objects of consciousness have that aspect to them—and, therefore, so do all objects, which are what I refer to as "agency-dependent" in the remainder of this book (see Bradley 1962, 313, 314). Bradley's notion of "internal relations" remains crucial to understanding such objects, to the extent to which his theory is read as a meta-physics of a universe that they uniquely comprise, and not as metaphysics in the traditional sense of the word. In this regard, he says: "There is but one Reality, and its being consists in experience" (1951, 403; see also, Bradley 1962, 267n). Bradley distinguishes those fields for which mechanistic notions are sufficient from those that have no choice but to reject them. It is in this sense that I understand his comment that "the ideal of spirit, we may say, is directly opposite to mechanism" (1951, 441).

3. This refers to "action" according to the standard definition described by Hugh McCann: "In general, human actions constitute a class of events, in which a subject (the agent) brings about some change or changes" (1995, 6). That actions are events makes them particulars in contrast with what I call a course of activity. McCann reserves the word "activity" for change brought about by "an ongoing process," by which he seems to mean an event looked at under the aspect of time and governed by something like a total intention. This is not what I mean by "a course of activity," at least because if there are particular events involved, they must be thought of as abstractions from such a course. Either an activity is, according to the standard notion, a series of events or it is an event under the aspect of time. If it is the latter, it refers to a particular that happens to transpire over time but otherwise is no different from one that is located at a moment and a specific locale. If it is the former, it merely names a set of particulars under the aspect of their constituting a series. In neither case it is a concept coordinate with the concept of action. "Course of activity" is a concept thus far defined negatively to distinguish it from "action." In following chapters, I attempt to approach a positive definition and to substantiate it by using it to clarify certain conceptions associated with the ideas of subjectivity and inter-subjectivity. For now, if a course of activity is to be thought of as a particular and as an event, it is from a position altogether outside of and unconnected to it, and it would have to be shown that such a position is possible and, if possible, that it grasps what people do in a way that is consistent with what is distinctively human about human affairs. The problem is to develop notions that allow for something like an internal point of view, and for such a point of view, a course of activity cannot be analyzed either as comprising events or as an event looked at under the aspect of temporality.

CHAPTER 8

1. This often appears as an attempt "not to leave the field open to the skeptic" (Davidson 2001d, xiii). Typically, however, it involves declarations of first principles.

2. Fritz Heider provides a classical instance in his work on "person perception," in which his concept of the social has to do with mutual presence (1958, 1). Citing Egon Brunswik, he says "that the objects of social and nonsocial perception are similar in regard to their formal characteristics as well as in regard to the processes by which they are perceived, is in general a valid framework for discussion" (21). By "social perception," he means "the perception of another person" (21).

3. This position is identified with Parsons's accounts of "social action" and "the social system" (1949, 1951). At the very least, it aims to defer reference to the psychological individual, as understood by psychoanalysis and much of what is written in the

philosophy of action. Goffman provides examples of this in situations that Heider describes as "interpersonal" (Goffman 1959, 1961b, 1963).

4. Nagel, for example, distinguishes between two positions, or "standpoints," that characterize each person's moral orientation, the impersonal and the personal (1991, chap. 2).

5. This example is taken from Shwayder 1965, 129. See also Goffman 1961b.

6. This notion of ideology does not rely on the derivation, logical or otherwise, of a proposition from premises that are beyond question, though that might not be precluded, or on the claim that ideologies operate as a whole such that a decision about a single proposition must engage the structure of which it is part, or on the notion that "ideology" refers to a message that is essentially interested but is presented as disinterested.

7. The historicist might argue that all that is needed is a sufficient reason to criticize the proposition, not a reason beyond all reasonable doubt, given that the consequences of such criticism for the sense of the integrity of the disciplinary literature are bound to be severe.

8. Searle says that consciousness is a biological fact that is, nevertheless, irreducible. But this does not require a causal model in the accounts he cites and proposes. One might argue that a conception of consciousness as transpiring across bodies is more in keeping with Strawson's observation (1992) and with the complex literature on consciousness from various disciplines than the attempt either to show how reasons can operate as causes, how selves intervene in just such an operation, or that what we recognize as "states" of mind are directly but complexly rooted in biological facts. To get to this point, Searle would have to revise his view of what sociology is, how social facts operate, and the relationship between what appear to be individuated facts (having, for example, to do with emotion, thought, deliberation, etc.) and the priority Strawson would like philosophy to give to sociality. I have not found in the modern American philosophical literature any attempt to examine and understand the conditions of a social science as a science of agency-dependent objectivity without treating social facts as merely mediating individually accountable action. I have mentioned Gilbert's analysis (1989) of the ordinary and extraordinary uses of certain social terms, but the problem of exactly what world sociology studies is not featured in her account, though, at the end of her book, she hints at a way of approaching that issue. Some of the work associated with "new historicism" and post-structuralist philosophy and literary analysis, and earlier work in phenomenology, are promising in this regard. When we compare what exists in American philosophy today about sociology with earlier systematic accounts of the ontological presuppositions and epistemology of psychology and economics, the absence of a systematic literature is evident and, given what appears to be at least tacit agreement with Strawson's observation, odd.

9. See Philip Kitcher's (2001) account of qualifications of the purist idea of science and his attempt to incorporate criticisms of that idea within a sociologically oriented philosophical account of the relationship between scientific practice and philosophical analysis of the terms by which science is distinguished from other sorts of discipline.

10. Habermas's (1971) account of "knowledge and human interests" attempts to show that the stipulation of something as agency-dependent depends on the prior formation of a collective will based on a yet prior critique of "distorted communication." That is, a positive science is justified only in the context of a collective will that can be understood as a general will rather than a collection of wills. This is because he identifies positive science as expressing an interest in control and what is considered a proper subject of control as expressing an interest in social solidarity supported by a science of praxis (see

also Kitcher 2001 for a different discussion with a similar conclusion). Another way of saying this is that when an object or objective realm is identified as agency-independent, the value of the science will have something to do with how that identification fits into the reasonable constitution of a collective will, what Kitcher calls "society."

11. I address only a simple but common view of knowledge represented by a standard way of defining it as "justified true belief" and a standard distinction, occasionally taken to exhaust the range of theories, between rationalism and empiricism. A distinction among three types of knowledge is equally standard: acquaintance knowledge, ability knowledge, and propositional knowledge, the latter being most important in the contemporary literature (see, for example, A. C. Grayling's introduction to the section on epistemology in *Philosophy 1: A Guide through the Subject* [1998] and Scott Sturgeon's account of theories of knowledge in that section). My account is less directed at philosophy than at a view of science that, to be sure, appears in some philosophical texts but is often encountered in discussions with scientists and in popular books and articles. My interest is how the standard model and its ideal of reliability applied to the social sciences and to the humanities creates a politics in which what is apparently most important is to establish what knowledge is definitely not. My purpose is to examine the workings of a distinction commonly made between knowledge that, with or without limitations, is provided by science, and intellectual work loosely thought of as falling on the side of values and value-determination (what Weber referred to as "substantive rationality") provided by the arts and the humanities, with the social sciences lying somewhere between or divided between what of them is scientific and what of them is ideological. The distinction is analogous to that between reason and judgment. I do not intend to deny that something like scientific method is used and is useful as an adjunct way of approaching certain aspects of "texts" and claims in many endeavors that are not motivated either by instrumental considerations or pure epistemic interest. This seems true in historical studies though it by no means defines historical methodology, and it is true when certain questions arise in, say, the arts and literary studies.

12. One might argue that good research addresses questions that merely arise from practices. This is what Lazarsfeld and his colleagues (1967) seem to claim. Given their idea of research as profession, "the relation between the sociologist and the client" is less important than the weight they give that model in evaluating disciplinary development (xxii). Yet "experts will sometimes reach swift agreement on the significance of new work; often time is required before an idea is recognized. But overall it certainly makes sense to talk of the gradual extension of basic knowledge. *Yet it is the ensuing knowledge that is basic and not the research or the purpose for which it was originally undertaken*" (xxiv; emphasis added).

13. I read Dorothy Emmet as representing a moderate version of historicism. On the one hand, she writes that it is "a common starting-point for both sociology and ethics" that "people need to live in social relationships with each other, not only for survival but if they are to carry out any of the characteristically human enterprises" (1975, 33). On the other, she seems to distinguish between social and nonsocial environments (125) and wishes to keep open the option of "detachment" and a certain tension between "persons and personae" (chap. 8). Her ambivalence is indicated in the question she asks: "But in actual fact can we identify the pure subject in action apart from the social and institutional support represented by the notion of the human person?" (178). Without pressing the point, it seems that she wants to say that humans are essentially social but that whether they are in any particular situation is at least subject to question. She comes close to recasting the theory of action along the lines of the essential sociality of the actor,

but stops short, perhaps out of respect for the possibility that the theoretical outlook, which requires the essentialist position, is itself subject to question. It is important to keep in mind that the intention here is to consider what is required of theory, not what we purport to know, a priori, about the subject matter. A different version of historicist moderation may be found in Ruben 1985, which is concerned with the possibility that "social properties" are not reducible and that social entities can be properly said to exist. I refer to this as moderate because, though its plausibility ultimately rests on the intuition that human beings are essentially social, it deliberately begs the question in order, I believe, to conserve the level of analysis at which society can be said to be real. In any case, D. H. Ruben is circumspect about this, restricting his critique to the claim, identified with "methodological materialism," that psychological facts provide an adequate reductive account of social facts (171). This version of moderated historicism is designed to show that it is reasonable to suppose that there is a level of sociological analysis sufficient to a type of fact, social, that cannot be understood at any other level (e.g., psychological) without risking the very idea of the social. Human beings, seen from the vantage point of social facts, are essentially social, if that vantage point can be sustained. However, this does not mean that they are not social when seen from, say, the vantage point of psychological facts. If we were to think of humans as psychological (purely so, at the outset), it would be impossible to move to their being social since to do so presupposes that we already see them as social. Thus, social psychology, in some of its versions, says that what seems independently social is really an expression of what is in the minds of gathered individuals—if they believe they are together in a way that authorizes the use of the word "we," then they are social. But from the point of view of the critique of individualism, it is important to move, as Goffman and Garfinkel attempted to do in most of their work, not from the individual outward (since there is no "outward" if we begin with the individual) but from the outside inward. He meant by this that it is only after we exhaust social explanation in any given case that we can decide whether what is left over belongs to the individual properly speaking. In this respect, he also represents what I call the moderate historicist position.

CHAPTER 9

1. Weber's discussion of rational legal authority, and rational organization in general, presupposes that substantive considerations are radically external to instrumental and formal rationality and can appear in the latter contexts only as disruptive factors. It is in this regard that the problem of representation takes on another guise in Weber's account, which either qualifies or undermines rational organization.

2. The taking of an entity as human and then designing a simulation is arbitrary in the sense that it cannot be accounted for by a science that relies on simulations. In other words, every simulation suffers from the lack of a cogent account of how it preserves what it simulates so that it can finally be applied to that reality. There is no account of the difference between a simulation and what it simulates that does not make the simulation theoretically irrelevant.

3. This critique assumes that humans know each other as social. To say, as Jerry Fodor does, that the idea of "epistemic unboundedness" is incoherent may be true, but the issue can be addressed only if it refers us from the start to the social reality of what we are used to taking as mental and pre-social or extra-social (1983, 121–129).

4. Neither side of the debate provides a sense of what it is to criticize, which is part of the problem they share in being unable to specify what is human about human affairs

such that, if the answer is "sociality," the proposition that humans are essentially social can be put into question—if "putting into question" is what is meant by criticism.

5. In this way, "definitions of the situation" are said to be neither arbitrary nor symptomatic of the dynamics of the individual's psychology, but reflections of shared frames of reference, the normative force of reference groups, or, in some cases, imitation. Again we see the assumption of a transcendent situation that points to an irreducible sociality, without the theoretical apparatus or critical discussion that could make that clear.

6. This assumes that the meaning of a word, from the standpoint of the discourses in which it operates, is qualified by the history of that meaning as an "ongoing accomplishment." When I use the term "chair," as in "May I bring the chair closer?" the meaning of the word cannot be determined apart from the difference the answer makes to the question and, prior to that, the difference anticipated in asking the question. Thus, John may say, "Please leave the chair where it is, since we have just finished decorating the room. I'll get you another." Or he may say, "Of course, anywhere that you find comfortable." In the one instance, "chair" is an object that has a certain shape and color and therefore can be designated by pointing, but it is also, as just the object it is, imbued with a history consisting of the force of ambiguity associated with the chair as a property of a room design and the chair as an object of pure utility. All objects are ambiguous to some degree and possible sources of ambivalence; and at least some of that ambivalence derives from the social significance they have, and their meaning cannot be divorced from that condition of meaning. The reason is that under that condition, meaning is undecided until the die is cast. Yet the question "May I bring the chair closer?" occurs prior to the casting of the die. That this is a matter of the logic of meaning is evident when we realize that in asking the question of my host, I am, in effect, anticipating the possibility of a negative answer and therefore of different substances to which the word "chair" refers. It is important to keep in mind that this assumes that we are talking about meaning *in the midst of discourse and not as a property of words extracted from discourse.*

7. Searle's concept of "human institutions" as "a structure of constitutive rules" is derived from the interactive model that underlies his theory of speech acts. To that extent, it too is inadequate to what I take to be the minimal situation of speech (1995, chap. 6).

CHAPTER 10

1. While the conceptual status of "society" has recently come into question, the focus has largely been on the effects of globalization on the idea of limited totalities rather than on the idea of the social itself. See Albrow and King 1990; Kuper 1992; and Urry 2000. See also Inglis and Robertson 2004, in which the authors discuss the possibility of a "post-societal sociology," where "society" refers to "a particular, bounded, primarily self-sufficient entity" (167). The debate has in no small way been influenced by Hardt and Negri (2000).

2. Davidson wrote, "We all have knowledge of our own minds, knowledge of the contents of other minds, and knowledge of the shared environment" (2001b, xiii). While this seems to use "knowledge" in a systematically misleading way, since the term cannot have the same meaning in those three domains, what is most important about it here is Davidson's dependence on an unexamined notion of the social.

3. Georg Simmel alludes to this in the following comment: "Everything present in the individuals (who are the immediate concrete data of all historical reality) in the form of drive, interest, purpose, inclination, psychic state, movement—everything that is

present in them in such a way as to engender or mediate effects upon others or to receive such effects, I designate as the *content*, as the material, as it were, of sociation" (quoted in Schutz 1967, 4; emphasis in original; see also Simmel and Wolff 1950).

4. For Alfred Schutz, our world "is from the outset an intersubjective world of culture. It is intersubjective because we live in it as men among other men, bound to them through common influence and work, understanding others and being understood by them." (1967, 10; see also Habermas 1984, esp. 50). A strong interpretation of this would exclude identifying inter-subjectivity with interpersonal interaction or with taking account of others.

5. Sartre has examined the relationship between "need" and "the living totality": "need is a link of *univocal immanence* with surrounding materiality insofar as the organism *tries to sustain itself* with it; it is already totalising, and doubly so, for it is nothing other than the living totality, manifesting itself as a totality and revealing the material environment, to infinity, as the total field of possibilities of satisfaction" (1976, 80). Similar claims can be found in Schutz's (1970) and Kurt Lewin's (1936) classical accounts of the invariant and transformative properties of the "space" in which actors are connected to objects.

6. It is often inferred from Marx's discussion of the "fetishism" of commodities that relations among things can "capture" subjectivity, in effect constituting it. This is an upshot of the critique of "commodification." But it assumes that the account of fetishism analyzes the social psychological implications of commodity production and universal exchange. Whether such an analysis is possible, that is not Marx's point. In his account, it appears as a logical extension of universal exchange as a possible universe that the subjectivity of that universe is fetishistic, taking objects as all the life and all the society there is. Marx demonstrates throughout *Capital* that he does not believe that exchange "captures" consciousness in this way, and, indeed, given the contradictory character of capitalist production, it could not. Rather, the section on the fetishism is designed to show that it would be ludicrous to adopt the position that the economy of capital can constitute an authentic society and that the extension of its logic produces an absurdity (1990a, chap. 1).

7. Mary Douglas (1986) discusses one way in which the irreducibility of the social can be expressed. She nevertheless concludes that the problem is solved by a notion of "sharing" in the context of institutions understood in part as communities. I try to show that an emphasis on normativity is inadequate to the task.

8. For an example of a reductive approach to "the logic of society" that attempts to reach beyond the normal limits of "descriptive individualism," see Addis 1975. For an antireductionist position aimed at avoiding the version of social realism associated with Émile Durkheim, see Ruben 1985. The conceptions of person and identity derived from models of interpersonal interaction do not require reference to bodily identity and its necessity or sufficiency to personal identity. The issue I discuss does not have to do with "personal identity" in the sense of someone being conscious of his or her own separateness. Nor need those conceptions depend on whether the concept of a person is logically primitive, since it remains necessary to ask what a person is under theoretical conditions that require "person" to refer to a primitive concept, and necessary to consider the conditions under which certainty of personhood is not in doubt or under which it is inconvenient to reject it as referring to such a concept. If "person" is no more ambiguous than arguments about its logical status seem to suppose, there would be no fields of sociology, social psychology, or the humanities. It may be, however, that certain philosophical positions may be impossible without the concept of a person being logically primitive and/ or without bodily identity being necessary or sufficient to personal identity (and identity

being necessary to a reasonable discussion of human affairs). One of my purposes is to show that the human sciences cannot be bound to models constrained by those positions and still deal with what is human about human affairs. Donald Gustafson (1964) provides a useful survey of those positions.

9. This supposes that, given that the idea of the social is intrinsically unproblematic, historical and comparative sociological study are sufficient bases on which to develop theories of human affairs.

10. Several writers have addressed the problem directly, most notably Garfinkel 1967, Goffman 1963, and Blum and McHugh 1984. See also Martin 1990. Literary theoretical texts regularly deal with issues around discourse, vocalization, performance, testimony, textualization, and other indexes of irreducibly collective courses of activity. I consider de Man's essay *The Resistance to Theory* (1986) to be in one respect about the character of human experience insofar as it is intrinsically collective and only extrinsically affected by attempts to individualize it. Derrida's *Politics of Friendship* (1997) addresses it most directly and in a way that has important consequences for politics and for ideas about democracy. See also Deleuze and Guattari 1987 and, from a different point of view, Gilbert 1989 and Ruben 1985. The Marxian literature poses many of its questions in ways that require at least some conceptualization, as in Marx's account of the socialization of production as a "society of producers." However, the writers identified by Perry Anderson (1976) as comprising "Western Marxism"—from Lukács to Adorno and Horkheimer and, later, Habermas—provide one of the most substantial continuing discussions available in the Marxist literature. In passing, the literature on civil society has more to do with the idea of the civil than that of the social, and studies of new social movements have neglected, for the most part, what it is about these movements that is social in a theoretically significant way.

11. Unlike most claims, if it cannot be guaranteed that something is trivial, then the claim that it is trivial is false. If there is any room for doubt at all, then it is clear that what is claimed to be trivial is not trivial, unless being in the midst of doubt can be trivial. Because it is false, it provides no reason to be indifferent to what was said to be trivial. There may, of course, be other, possibly good reasons for indifference, but they are not a proper part of the present discussion.

12. May Brodbeck describes what remains programmatic in the philosophy of the social sciences. Having noted that "the problem is to give an analysis of the relation between individual action and social events that will adequately account for how they impinge on one another" (1968, 239), she defines a social fact: "A social fact is a fact expressed by a sentence containing terms that are used collectively for human groups and institutions. Groups have characteristics that individuals do not. . . . No one denies that there are such facts. The issue concerns not their existence, but the proper analysis of the collective terms used to talk about them. . . . Are collective terms definable in terms of individual behavior? These are requests for a *description* of social events, properties, or entities that will enable us to know what we are talking about when we use collective terms" (239–240). Normally, this is sufficient to describe a philosophical project, but there are difficulties with it that seem to derive from the phenomenon to be described so that we can "know what we are talking about when we use collective terms." First, it is hard to imagine a description of social life that does not use collective terms and for which that use is not basic to the description. While the use of such terms is itself a social fact that can be described only in its collective aspect, this is not the most important problem raised by Brodbeck. The first point is far more important. But it is also the case that there is a certain ambiguity preserved in the way collective terms are normally used,

including in social science, and this may well be due less to lapses in clarity of meaning or proper use than to the fact that there is something about the phenomenon that does not allow talk about it to be fixed and still remain talk about *it*. This may be less a problem than it appears, since it is not unreasonable to analyze texts, as Brodbeck is recommending, though it might at least be problematic to assume that the analysis produces the sort of results that allows one to distinguish between description and attribution and to assume that the terms extracted from the texts, when clarified, still apply to the phenomena to which they were originally said to apply. In other words, philosophers of the social sciences cannot take refuge in the type of project appropriate for ideas about nonsocial phenomena, which is to clarify language, if the basic phenomena are not capable of being fixed in a way that allows for the sufficiency of that project to an improvement of those sciences. This is why the most interesting contributions by philosophers of the social sciences are either about theories that try to fix the phenomena despite the fact that the theoreticians often admit that there is something resistant about it, or about language as part of the course of activity that constitutes social phenomena. In the first case, philosophy pursues its own traditional project. A good example is Black's (1976) edited collection of critical responses to Parsons's theories of action and the social system. The second case has to do with philosophies that are not easily accepted by analysts trained in the Anglo-American tradition and that are often identified with "literary theory" and "post-structuralism." What I believe these all have in common that is not easily acknowledged in the Anglo-American philosophical tradition is that they do not separate language from activity and description from ascription or the application of words; nor do they assume that the ambiguities of language about collectivities are not rooted in the social world itself. There are no doubt many difficulties with this position, but they are fewer and less distorting than those with positions that exclude it. No one can deny that it is crucial to study linguistic usage in the social sciences, but it is not yet clear how to establish a connection between that study and the phenomenon at issue.

CHAPTER 11

1. That a proposition is incorrigible has primarily to do with its position in an argument or a body of discourse. By "virtual truth," I mean that, regardless of whether it is incorrigible in the sense described, it is reasonably taken to be true in two respects: it is felt to be certain, and its content justifies rejecting doubt. It is the case that the virtual truth of a proposition and its incorrigibility within an argument typically go hand in hand, but not necessarily so. As a result, we can examine the conditions of virtual truth without having to consider the role the proposition has in an argument or a discourse. It seems to me that the overlap is crucial in the present case. In that regard, I consider the incorrigibility of the proposition to be a reinforcing agent for its virtual truth, though the reverse is not the case.

2. The ideas of "fictional truth," metaphor, allegory, and tropes in general are typically discussed independently of the problem of truth, though there is some agreement among scholars that the certainties attached to them are not arbitrary and are subject to processes of reasoning, albeit not necessarily those identified with science as things stand (see Riffaterre 1990). Thus, in arriving at the idea of "fictional truth," the plausibility of a representation may be sufficient to support a sense that it is true; but how plausibility is arrived at remains a problem. In regard to metaphor, there is always a surplus of meaning. Yet a number of arguments have been made that "true" is not an inappropriate predicate of a metaphorical statement. Nelson Goodman, for one, points out that a

sentence can be false when taken literally and true "when taken metaphorically, as in the case of 'the Joint is jumping' or 'the lake is a sapphire'" (1979, 175). In holding that a sentence can be true when taken metaphorically (not that "the truth of the sentence is metaphorical" [175]), Goodman seems to be defending the possibility of a true statement for which there are no definite procedures for showing how it might be false and no definite criteria for settling the issue, even momentarily. I do not see any good reason to disagree, but it seems to me that this allows that the sense that something is true may be no less legitimate than its being justified, even for those committed to a strict definition of truth. When we realize that to speak in a "natural language" is to rely on a sense that many such statements are true, it is not enough to say merely that what is relied on is incorrigible. There is a sense of truth indicated both by the capacity to speak or act with certainty and by the willingness to defend the proposition relied on. To discredit that sense is to discredit almost everything we say and do. To claim that certain philosophical problems derive from how we use language or from language itself is not inconsistent with this point since there are many instances of thought and action in science and daily life that require certain propositions, ideas, and so forth that are beyond question but not beyond discussion. In regard to metaphor and the problems it raises for translation and interpretation, it must also be the case that what we want to understand by our theories of action cannot be understood without recognizing that there are truth-like claims that are not irrational but that cannot be submitted to the criteria associated with rationality in the usual sense. With Davidson (1979), we may not want to use the term "truth" in evaluating metaphorical sentences, but that in no way changes the problematic nature of the distinction between sentences for which the strict notion of truth applies and those for which it apparently does not. It is not enough to say that the issue of truth does not arise for metaphorical sentences, as Davidson does. The whole range of language for which that issue does not arise may be precisely the range of greatest interest, philosophically and "scientifically." If so, no theory of that domain will be adequate that does not go through a kind of historical-like reconstruction of the possibility of degrees of certainty, types of reasoning, and the like. Until the life of that language is fully appreciated, no theory of metaphor (therefore of what is allegedly not metaphorical) can be clearly relevant to the study of language.

3. See Levi 1983, esp. chap. 1; Doppelt 1983; Davidson 1999; and Putnam 1992, esp. chap. 5. For the social sciences, see Ruben 1985. An early discussion that remains relevant is Pears 1957.

4. See Elgin 1983 for a discussion of "metaphorical truth" that opposes Davidson's (1975) denial that sentences that are metaphorical can be true. For the distinction between "the truth of the sentence is metaphorical" and "the sentence taken metaphorically is true," see Davidson 1979; see also Goodman 1979, 175n. Davidson notes that while metaphors do not have meaning, they can be understood: "Understanding a metaphor is as much a creative endeavor as making a metaphor, and as little guided by rules" (1979, 29). In doing so, he denies that it has "cognitive content in additional to the literal" (30). Black, arguing against Davidson, notes that to agree with Davidson's position it is necessary to believe that the speaker of a metaphorical statement is not affirming, is not serious, and says nothing, that the intention to speak metaphorically amounts to denying that what is said should be taken literally, and that speaking or writing metaphorically cannot fail or succeed (Black 1979, 181–186).

5. One reason for attempting to make explicit what might seem latent or inexplicable about activity is to allow that human beings are essentially rational in a certain way, which, as Weber (1947, 92–93) noted, does not include being rational in some other way.

The privileged rationality involves being able to characterize an action in terms of reasons that have directly to do with what the action appears to do (its aim), which is to say
being able to rationalize what could not have been rationalized in advance. This seems to
be what Davidson has in mind when he says, "Whenever someone does something for a
reason . . . , he can be characterized as (a) having some sort of pro attitude toward actions
of a certain kind, and (b) believing (or knowing, perceiving, noticing, remembering) that
his action is of that kind" (2001d, 3–4). Schutz's (1967) attempt to develop a concept of
"social rationality" makes a prima facie case for the possibility that there are other ways
of showing human beings to be essentially rational. What seems at stake in Davidson's
essay is not whether actions are caused, though that is how he introduces it, but whether
actions can be active in the sense of comprising a course of activity and, at the same time,
be made explicit in the ways he believes are required. This question presupposes that an
action is not adequately described as an event and therefore the issue of causation is moot
until this is decided.

CHAPTER 12

1. Searle's (1995) strategy for thinking about social life relies on extremely Spartan
representations, in contrast with what is implicit in Strawson's comment. These are quite
different ways of clarifying the idea of the social, and, as with all such moves, they imply
more than their proponents may have wished. I believe that it is best to lean to the side
of the strategy of enrichment, given the poverty of our theoretical language concerning
the social.

2. Derrida's (1988) response to Searle's criticism of his 1972 essay, "Signature Event
Context," seems to agree, at least as far as language is concerned. For example, he says
that "if one admits that writing (and the mark in general) *must be able* to function in the
absence of the sender, the receiver, the context of production, etc., that implies that this
power, this *being able*, this *possibility* is *always* inscribed, hence *necessarily* inscribed *as
possibility* in the functioning of the functional structure of the mark" (48; emphasis in
original).

3. If this is a methodological question, then she is left with a "bare subjective 'I'"
and an obligation to at least account for it, which she does as a "limiting concept," no
less so than the "behaviouristic notion of the incumbent of a role and function" (Emmet
1975, 178). In other words, there is no way of connecting persons to their personae when
what they do is separated in principle from "conditions" of their doing it and when those
conditions include what theory might well consider constitutive features of action. The
methodological solution seems slippery at best, since it requires at least some attention
to the problem of distinguishing the limiting concepts from those we need positively.
Philosophers rarely dispute the point that action cannot be separated from orientation,
but there is a line of thinking that requires a distinction between action and relations.
From this, someone studying what people do together might reasonably claim that the
theoretical problems have something to do with attempting to align theory with what is
only alleged to be common usage. The lesson learned is not merely that we should study
human activity as actors see it in their relations with other actors, though that is certainly
of value. A greater lesson is that theory has work to do that cannot be done in the terms
of a discourse given with the received object of study. In regard to ends, Charles Taylor
says that an action is defined by its end, and both are different from any distinct result
(1964, 28–32); nor is goal-directed action all the action there is. However, he proceeds as
if the lack of a theoretical language adequate to his point is not likely to interfere with

evaluations of the analysis. What is significant here is not the importance of analyses of action for philosophy but how those analyses might be relevant to the human sciences. Thus, the theoretical issue posed by the fact that action and aim cannot be separated without undoing each concept is one that can hardly be avoided by disciplines concerned with what is human about human affairs. It is not just a matter of what can be stated. It may turn out that such disciplines prove of no particular use, or that they might be shown merely to have smuggled in an individualistic morality under the guise of universalism, but until either (or something else) happens, it seems worth addressing the theoretical problem as best one can. Some philosophers of justice have made claims that bear on this. Sandel speaks of "more or less enduring attachments and commitments which taken together partly define the person I am" (1998, 179). Again, while this hedges bets, there is at least the suggestion that it is worth considering the theoretical entailments of how a person is defined by where she is and activities in which she is, deliberately or not, implicated.

4. Compare this with George Herbert Mead's (1962) "generalized other" conceived of as a repository of rules that arises in the course of experience first as an individual fact and then, through the mediation of symbols, as a social fact. But the idea of rules requires a step beyond experience and, in effect, assumes that what is projected from generalized expectations is, in a sense, already there. In other words, to go beyond one's expectations to the sense of a norm is not to invent the norm but to acknowledge one that is already in operation. Otherwise, it would be wrong to say that the rule-governed aspect of any type of action arises from the generalization of expectations. It can arise for the individual only if it is already a social fact for that individual. But it can be such a social fact only if it precedes individually held expectations—not just logically but empirically. Indeed, such expectations can be referred to only as expectations, and therefore activating, if something transforms experience into a probability that serves as a condition of the rationality of an instance of action. The very term "expectation," used in a general account of human action, supposes a basis for predicting that is not implicit in individual experience.

5. There is no implication here that those we call animals to distinguish them from humans cannot have been misclassified. The category of "animal," like that of "machine," is intended to articulate an exclusion—namely, "human," something radically different from "nature," itself an idealization.

6. I assume that it is insufficient to say that the difference is that humans represent their surroundings in a unique way or that what is involved is the capacity of human beings to form an idea that corresponds to "we" (see Searle 1995, esp. 26; Gilbert 1989, esp. chap. 7).

7. Though his aim is altogether different from what I am proposing, Alexander Rosenberg claims, controversially, that a species (e.g., *Homo sapiens*) is "a spatio-temporally restricted particular, though scattered, object" (1985, 40). If we accept that, then it remains to ascertain the "natural kinds into which human behavior and its determinants fall" (40). That is, in considering what "kind predicate pertains to human life," we need to avoid essentialism and the assumption that life, like species, changes (42). Rosenberg's problem has to do with how a social science can be framed in such a way that it is possible to issue improvable generalizations about causes and effects. But his critique of relying on "the sort of artificial gerrymandered kinds" (42) (e.g., species) applies to our problem as well—which is to decide what conception of human life, of life in that sense, allows us to say that it is exemplified by all who are recognized as human beings. If we can do that, and if the reasons for accepting such a conception and the results of using it are sufficiently compelling to overcome the problems otherwise instated by this apparent

teleology, then we are in effect undertaking to examine human affairs as exemplifications of life. The most compelling reason for this would be that otherwise we are unable to account for the questions we persistently ask about just such a thing and to account for the persistence of disciplines that operate on the premise that human life is a "natural kind" in the required sense for the substantiation of knowledge claims. Rosenberg says at one point that "for purposes of a social science with nomological potential we must surrender this conception of ourselves as agents" (45). He then adds, in parentheses, "For all other purposes, of course, we may continue to employ it" (45). However, those "other purposes" are also purposes for choosing a social science with nomological potential and are not merely related to evaluation, emotion, and self-satisfaction. That is, we "surrender this conception of ourselves as agents" at the cost of being able to conceive of ourselves as choosing to develop a social science according to certain criteria and, it must be added, as bearing the burden of a host of questions that effectively constitute the history of philosophy. In other words, as things stand, we cannot do away with the concept of life that is approximated by reference to agency, and we cannot allow that concept to inhabit discourses that have no knowledge potential. Therefore, we need to think of the knowledge potential of the human sciences, including the social sciences, in terms radically different from what Rosenberg has in mind when he refers to "improvable generalizations." This, I believe, does more to explain why the naturalist model can see the social sciences only as having failed—since they are not the sort of science that can succeed according to that criterion—than the idea that they are burdened by flawed "typological commitments" based on "*false* beliefs about the natural kinds into which human behavior and its determinants fall" (40; emphasis in original). The flaw is not based on such beliefs; it is based on a failure to clarify what it is about human affairs that makes them a "natural kind"—that is, something that is not merely made up of individual parts but that "manifests itself" as the coherence of those very affairs and that constitutes a proper object of the human sciences given the questions they have still to address.

Bernard Williams offers a different interpretation from Rosenberg of the idea of human affairs when he says that "it is an ethological fact that human beings live under culture (a fact represented in the ancient doctrine that their nature is to live by convention)" (1973, 14). He concludes that "humanity" is, "of course, a name not merely for a species but for a quality, and it may be that the deepest contemporary reasons for distrusting a humanistic account of the human sciences are associated with a distrust of that quality" (22). What such an account might consist of remains to be seen.

8. One cost of this attempt is the elimination of "crowds" from the category of the political, which limits the problem of mobilization, hence political action, to processes difficult to dissociate from official notions of politics. For a discussion of the political aspect of the "crowd" and the political dimension of its classification, see Brown and Goldin 1973.

9. Compare Mancur Olson's *The Logic of Collective Action* (1971), which provides an underdetermined notion of collective action, with Neil Smelser's (1963) overdetermined notion of collective behavior. Subsequent developments in the study of social movements drew on Olson's conception as part of attempting to show a greater degree of rationality than Smelser could accommodate. For the decentering aspects of membership and identity, see Hampshire's (2000) discussion of the localizing effects of socialization. Hampshire identifies the decentering aspects but does not address the problem of its effects on the meaning of membership and identity.

10. Foucault (2008) accounts for neoliberalism as a self-generalizing form of life. David Harvey (2005a) describes neoliberalism as a class-hegemonic practice and ideol-

ogy. Randy Martin (2002) discusses risk assignment as neoliberalism's organizing principle. Liam Murphy and Thomas Nagel (2002) provide a comprehensive account of the complexities of the relationship between tax policy and justice, though they accept, apparently somewhat reluctantly, the constraints of neoliberalism discussed by Martin, Harvey, and Foucault; and their attempt to distance themselves from anything that might be associated with the history of socialism allows for too easy a negative reflection on what can be learned from the history of planned, semi-planned, or command economies. I believe that they were right to avoid that question, given the focus of their argument and the limits within which rational argument against the myth of "pretax income" can play a role in policy making. Nevertheless, the question of how a capitalist system allocates rights legitimately raises the more basic question of whether the principle of allocation can be made rational in regard to the relationship between justice and two inter-dependent concerns: the maintenance or reproduction of society and the maintenance or reproduction of its mode of production.

11. Complexity and the possibilities of communication presumably qualify "taking something into account." For Weber, every interpretation of conduct depends on a prior purpose that the interpretation aims to enlighten. The problem is that it seems unlikely that one can imagine such an aim that does not presuppose a prior characterization of the act as taking account of others who are not merely things. "Taking account" seems to be an act itself, which is a problem for Weber. In any case, it is not a unified category. This suggests that it makes obscure what needs to be clarified—namely, the nature of the "others" the taking account of which makes a behavior "social." Nevertheless, the emphasis on the observer's purpose, and therefore on her point of view, remains important. Weber's idea of "taking account" refers not to others but to their conduct. But it seems clear that taking account of the *conduct* of others is possible only if the latter is, through and through, the conduct of *others*. Accountable behavior, behavior that can be taken into account, cannot be separated from an attribution of intentionality; and this requires that behavior be taken to be an extension of an intentionality that is logically prior and yet not clearly connected to any specific purpose (of the observer or the one taking account of the conduct of others. In this regard, Weber says that "in 'action' is included all human behaviour when and in so far as the acting individual attaches a subjective meaning to it. . . . Action is social in so far as, by virtue of the subjective meaning attached to it by the acting individual (or individuals), it takes account of the behaviour of others and is thereby oriented in its course" (1964, 88). Parsons's interpretation of Weber seems, on similar grounds, to generalize beyond the reference to the "behavior of others" (1949, 636, 715–719).

12. I cannot wholly agree with the idea that we attribute to others what we find in ourselves, since it is not clear enough what is meant in this context by "attribute" and "find," and I am not sure what motivates this attribution, and, presumably, it must be motivated unless it is just what such organisms do. In any case, this use of "others" presupposes what it is supposed to explain—namely, that others are intentional others. Nagel discusses this in connection with the problem of solipsism (1970, 104–107). Even though I believe that Nagel is more committed to the idea that we know others by what we know of ourselves than he seems to be, his account is subtle and compelling and may well lead in a different direction: "What is it to accept the same judgment about another person that one accepts about oneself in acknowledging a reason to act, or in reaching a conclusion about what one should do?" He goes on: "To apply the judgment in the same sense to others, one must first be able to apply it to oneself conceived as merely one person among others." But is it possible not to do so? If the answer is no, then it is not clear

how to rationalize "to apply," "be able to apply," and "conceived." These are not trivial questions, since Nagel's version of individualism lies in his assumption that what individuals seem to do (e.g., make judgments) seem to originate in them: "The only personal residue, therefore, which is not included in the system of impersonal beliefs to which I am committed by a personal judgment, is the basic personal premise itself, the premise which locates me in the world which has been impersonally described" (103).

13. This is not necessarily a problem for theories that deny that agency, intentionality, and all that fills out and substantiates what Williams calls a certain "quality" of being human need to be considered in theories of mind and action (see, for example, Churchland 1988). In this regard, Hampshire comments that "we have this interesting view of true empiricism as being the doctrine that we can reconstruct natural creatures, and to reconstruct is to understand. It is not to have a map of a possible reconstruction but an actual reconstruction that is most enlightening about the nature of understanding" (1959, 256). Fred Dretske anticipates criticisms of his statement of a theory of action that "simplifies" the problem in terms of fairly "primitive" beliefs, reasons, and desires: "But though, given this narrow focus, the complaint is entirely reasonable, it is not, I think, a reasonable *criticism* of what has so far been done. To reject or ignore this model because it is too simple is like rejecting Copernican astronomy because it doesn't account for the return of Haley's comet" (1988, 138; emphasis in original). I believe that Dretske begs the question. The argument against simplicity is not an argument against simplicity as such but an argument that denies the validity of what only appears to be a simplification of something complex. If that is correct, then adding complexity later cannot do the trick. I suggest that many apparent simplifications are really models of something altogether different from what is typically claimed to be their referent, which is what people do by way of being human.

14. Not to mention risking what Cohen long ago summarized as "the fatal weakness of the neo-Hegelian idealistic doctrines based on such concepts as *the self, the good*, etc." (1956, 205; emphasis in original).

CHAPTER 13

1. While it may or may not be true that it is a "prejudice that the concept of action itself is by itself sufficient to mark the domain of the essential human virtues," Hampshire is certainly right in suggesting that more is involved in what is human about human affairs than what the theory of action refers to as "action." But it does not follow that the latter is sufficient to allow that "more" to be delineated as independent of it. Moreover, Hampshire allows for a distinction between "thoughts and feelings" and "actions" and the idea that the former are expressed in action and sufficiently accounted for as such (1959, 92). But he allows the formal notion of action to determine how he thinks of human affairs as such, and this is the problem I address. In any case, if one agrees that action is not "itself sufficient to mark the domain of the essential human virtues"—with the qualification that the latter are to be thought of as human affairs—it does not follow that human affairs are not intrinsically active. If they are, then this should not only raise doubt about the adequacy of a theory of action to the question of what is human about human affairs but to raise doubt about the relevance of the concept of action, as we find it, to anything that has to do with human affairs in their distinctively human aspect. Again, Hampshire introduces a notion of a self to enrich the idea of a "whole person" who sometimes acts and sometimes feels and thinks. This notion, while of value in some contexts, begs the question of the constitution of that sort of personhood such that it may

include such diverse potentials as feeling, thinking, and acting (or such that these might be thought of without such a notion). Hampshire nevertheless indicates the possibility of a strong enough sense of "sociality" to support a very different account of human affairs than one that relies on the distinction between personhood and action (20–21).

2. Searle lists three gaps "between the 'causes' of the action in the form of beliefs and desires and the 'effect' in the form of action" (2001, 13). One is a gap between reasons and decision. The second is between decision and action, and the third is between "the initiation of the action and its continuation to completion" (14–15). He says, in regard to the third, "even once you have started you cannot let the causes operate by themselves; you have to make a continuous voluntary effort to keep going with the action or activity to its completion" (15).

3. Lawrence Lombard offers a "theory about events construed as concrete particulars" (1986, vii) in which events are changes in the properties of objects, therefore changes in entities that might or might not change. Otherwise objects are events: at least this is so in regard to agency-dependent objects. This is rather a different concept from the notion of an event as something that happens at the intersection of courses of activity or at the point at which structure meets its fundamental condition that Derrida calls "the play of structure." In other words, Lombard's conception is not relevant to a phenomenology of action and is relevant to theories of action that are not phenomenological and that exclude phenomenological considerations. As will later appear, the notion of an event, relative to understanding affairs as human, must be coordinated with the notion of a course of activity and not with the notion of action, events, and so on, as concrete particulars. What, then, are concrete particulars for such an understanding? My answer is that they must be thought of as moments, and the important question becomes "moments of what?"

4. Searle begins his "summary of the argument for the existence of an irreducible, non-Humean self" by stating that its existence is necessary if we are to speak coherently of responsibility, blame, approval, and so forth (2001, 90–91). It goes almost without saying, first, that such a self may be a necessary condition of those evaluations but it is certainly far from sufficient and, second, that they are terms of such ambiguity and controversy that Searle's argument can only be presented as a plausible conclusion that probably could not survive the examples needed to clarify it.

5. His notion of the self raises doubts not only about the concept of action but also about the philosophical project around action as the realization of intention and about the program outlined by Searle: "It is impossible to understand rational action if you do not understand what an intentional action is in the first place, and it is impossible to understand reasons for action if you do not understand how humans can create commitments and other meaningful entities and thereby create reasons. But it is impossible to understand these notions without first having some understanding of intentionality in general" (2001, 34). If one begins at the first part of this program, as Searle did in his earliest work, one is unlikely to move easily to understanding rational action as he later defines it. If, however, one begins with the most general conditions, understanding intentionality and how people can create commitments, and so forth, then it is doubtful that one will get to the notion of rational action executed by an individual actor as a realization of her intention according to the standard criteria of rationality. When Searle brings the self into this, it seems too late. What I think Searle's programmatic statement actually amounts to is a warning that if one attends to the most general conditions of understanding the rationality of action, one may have to sacrifice the idea of action as something that originates as such within individuals and the idea that intentionality

belongs to individuals in their being as organisms. Searle avoids these possibilities in his attempts to address some problems in the social sciences, but once one appreciates what he has brought together as a philosophical program, one sees how the last parts of it do not easily accommodate the first parts and how difficult it would be to join the individualistic aspect of the program with what requires an understanding of the extra-individual dimensions of commitments and reasons.

6. Goffman (1963) uses "social identity" to refer to typifications based on categories and the significance typically attached to whatever might be singled out as a categorical attribute. While persons usually try to avoid all such attributions, Goffman is primarily interested in those that are either discrediting or discreditable and how attribution sets in motion processes that he ultimately calls "political." Social identity is, as he sees it, not an entity in the same way as what is called "ego-identity." It is always a moment of a collective process already under way when the person to whom attributions are or might be made, one who comes under scrutiny for one reason or another, comes to notice as a possible topic. Goffman notes that one part of the politics of identity involves trying to avoid coming to notice and therefore collaborating in bringing another to notice as "other" to the setting. He also does not claim that one's social identity, the social identity that is the result of a collective process, is merely linguistic or mental. It is a feature of such a process or course of activity and can be theorized only by theorizing the latter.

7. It can be argued, as Searle seems to have, that the fact that the self is tied to a mortal body means that the condition and fate of this body should override most other reasons for an act, say smoking cigarettes. At best, this cannot be taken for granted as far as any theory of action is concerned; and it is not at all clear how reasons tied to the possibility of death are connected to rationality in the same way as reasons having to do with getting what one wants. If Searle is actually introducing the self in order to take account of our finitude, on the assumption that biological death is always an overriding concern in decisions, when death in the future from some cause is a matter of probability, there needs to be an analysis of all that is involved, and I suspect that doing such an analysis will do as much damage to the theory of action as not doing it.

CHAPTER 14

1. In regard to the normative element in thought, Davidson writes, "The crucial point isn't that norms enter in the one case and not in the other, but that they enter in a special and additional way in the study of mental phenomena. Whatever is studied, the norms of the observer will be involved. But when what is studied is the mental, then the norms of the thing observed also enter. When thought takes thought as subject matter, the observer can identify what he is studying only by finding it rational—that is, in accord with his own standards of rationality. The astronomer and physicist are under no compulsion to find black holes or quarks to be rational entities" (2004a, 98, 91).

2. Williams (1973) considers limitations on the relation of memory to identity in his essay "Personal Identity and Individuation." R. S. Downie discusses issues involving the limitations of the definition of a "person" as "a human being who is capable of exercising rational choice," in which case, as he points out, it is possible to be a human being and not a person (1971, 131). John Locke's view that "person" consists in "same consciousness" remains a part of philosophy, though there is a tendency to limit the identity of a person to physical continuity, and the sense of "physical" in this regard is far from settled. See Shoemaker and Swinburne 1984, 574–575. The issue of identity and the question associated with that—"Is this the same person?"—have given rise to a considerable literature.

Solutions may be adequate to some but not all purposes. The problem has to do with the conception of person coordinate with conceptions of self, situation, and time in regard to the theory of action, and that is where distinctions are relied on that give rise to the issues discussed here. Robert Nozick's discussion of "personal functions" exemplifies at least some of the difficulties, when he speaks of "a person" as a location of functions—"because principles of behavior have a personal (or an intellectual) function"—as some sort of defining agent that also integrates its "life over time" and gives it "more coherence," and as an entity served by those functions. He goes on to say that "these personal functions of principles concern one's life or identity as a whole, or at least extended parts of it" (1993, 12–14). Douglas (1986) summarizes E. E. Evans-Pritchard's account of collective memory and argues for a theory that goes beyond the idea that social facts influence individual memory to say that collective memory is in no sense instantiated in individualized consciousnesses. Her account of Evans-Pritchard's study of the Nuer is intended to provide evidence for this claim.

3. I consider how McCann poses the problem, not how he attempts to solve it. He says that "a satisfying account of the unity of agency does become available, however, if we accept temporally extended actions, since these have more tolerant identity conditions" (1998, 4). My problem with this is that once we accept temporal extension, we have removed ourselves from immediate concrete situations. These two, "temporal extension" and "immediate concrete situation," are not points along a dimension and therefore cannot be compared in the way McCann seems to suggest. Once we have accepted the temporal extension, we are no longer within the domain covered by the theories of action to which he directs his critique. It is worth adding that the problem is one of theory and not one having to do with "self-referentiality." I argue that the concept of self-referentiality begs the question posed by the reflexivity of action, which has to do with what appears, is displayed, in the course of activity as grounds, and this may or may not turn out to be "self." I try to show why the general case involves sociality, beyond even an impersonal or nonpersonal self. I do not deny that activity must be reflexive; just the reverse, since I am claiming that the problems associated with reflexivity do not in general involve the self.

4. A concept operates within a logically organized conceptual field for which it has value in the sense of making a general difference. It is in this sense that I understand Christopher Peacocke's statement that "concepts are constituents of complete contents which are evaluable as true or as false" (2000, 335).

5. One might argue that the theory of action explains not what is to be expected but what is unlikely in a concrete situation, given minimal assumptions about the rational disposition and knowledge of the actor. Thus, where situations are complete and apparent, the actor is unlikely to act in ways that are inconsistent with the corresponding beliefs unless other factors, such as habits or influence, intervene. In that sense, the theory makes room for a theory of the self by establishing what might be called situational parameters within which such a self might be active. This assumes that situations can be identified independently of selves, and to defend such an assumption would be difficult. Again, one saves the theory of action in this regard only if one limits the idea of a self to what follows from objective circumstances, the "objectivity" of which is unaccountable. In any case, the theory of action thought of as an attempt to establish subjectivity (the actor as decision maker) as a reflection of the objective situation ends by being a theory of the situation and nothing more.

6. Jennifer Hornsby reviews several views of how causation operates for a theory of action, with special emphasis on the work of Roderick Chisholm and Georg Henrik von Wright (Hornsby 1980, esp. chap. 7; see also Chisholm 1976, 199–212; von Wright 1971).

Hornsby's position is summarized by Dretske as identifying "actions (and thereby, by implication, behavior) not with the overt movements in which behavior typically culminates, but with the internal *causes* of these movements" (1988, 16; emphasis in original). Dretske rejects this on the grounds that it is implausible to allow for the possibility of someone causing something before it happened (17). His argument is that it is wrong to argue that behavior is located either "after it begins or before it ends" on the grounds that it should not be identified with either effect or cause (17), but rather with "a *process*" that begins with the cause and ends with the effect. The behavior is what goes on in the course of moving from the one to the other. "This avoids the paradoxes of both extreme views by making behavior begin where it should begin (with those efferent activities that bring about bodily movement) and end where it should end (with those external events or conditions that the behavior requires for its occurrence). A person's moving his arm is then a piece of behavior that begins with those internal events producing arm movements and ends with the arm movements they produce. If we are talking about a more 'extended' piece of behavior (a pitcher's striking out a batter, for instance), the behavior begins, once again, with those internal events producing arm movement. The behavior ends, though, not with the arm's movement, but with the batter's missing his third swing at the ball" (17–18). The perspective of sociality does not require that behavior "ends" in this way or that it is sufficient to describe its internal causes, since what counts as action (and therefore, as Dretske says, behavior) is from the outset conceived of as social in the fullest sense, yet to be clarified. Therefore, questions about causation, however "causation" is defined, will refer to different facts from those referred to where the skin is taken as a natural boundary and the individual person is the site of the most important causes of what can only be effects coming from that same person. Dretske's discussion of "representational systems" comes too late to move beyond the individualist ontology substantiated by his summary of the theory of action (138). The complexity of such systems is essentially confined to the individual, and the degree of complexity required may not be compatible with the spontaneity with which actions take place in normal contexts. In any case, this is taken up in later parts of this book. See also McCann's (1998) discussion of these issues.

7. I rely on one notion of complexity, though the word may still be inadequate to what I want to say: by the complexity of something studied in the human sciences, I mean (1) that the activity of theorizing it is imputable to its object, and (2) that the object is essentially reflexive and therefore cannot be realized by a cross-sectional analysis or a type of model for which action as an event rather than a course of activity is the crucial concept. See Jay 1986 for an account of autobiographical literature that provides a far more complex and compelling idea of the self than one finds in prevailing philosophical theories of agency and action, that defies, by its very nature, designation, memory, a clear sense of identity, reduction to a source of reasons, and causal analysis.

8. While this allows for changes that are ongoing processes, called an "activity," the emphasis is primarily on actions more easily classified as particular "events." As such, they are unified in one way or another, have a beginning and an end, can be identified more than once or in contrast with something else, and often can be evaluated as to their responsiveness to conditions. "Concrete actions" are "time-bound: each belongs to a single behavioral episode, and other instantiations of the same act-type count as distinct events" (McCann 1995, 6). While there are many ontological issues around the concept of action, it is enough for the purpose at hand to focus on this standard conception. Actions are, then, concrete particulars that are explained by reasons that can be attributed to concretely particular agents, where a reason combines an attitude toward an outcome

and "a belief to the effect that the outcome may be achieved by performing the action in question" (1995, 7). Many theories of action specialize in deliberative action and thus may be said to overlap decision theory. Even when deliberation is not in evidence, whenever options are present it is tempting to analyze the relationship between situation and act on the analogy to deliberation. I argue that all these theoretical features of action are placed in jeopardy by the introduction of the self, either because the theory now becomes trivial (if "self" is merely a construct) or because it has no legitimate points of reference outside of itself (if "self" is a concept).

9. For a defense of dualism in this regard, see Foster 1991. John Cottingham's more general comments are appropriate to rethinking the consequences of the attempt to complete the theory of action by adding something incompatible with its conception: "Yet to acknowledge the vital role of inherited tradition for productive philosophical inquiry is immediately to confront the problem of how that tradition is generated. Again, more than perhaps any other subject, philosophy has a tendency to canonize, or to demonize, the great figures of its past. Of these two opposite tendencies, over-reverential hagiography is a lesser danger (at least in the Anglophone philosophical world) than the kind of polemicism that wildly caricatures famous dead philosophers in order to dismember their supposed doctrines. The fate of Descartes in the twentieth century is a spectacular example of this latter process, so much so that the label 'Cartesian' has become in many quarters almost a term of abuse, designating all the confusions and errors from which today's philosophical champions claim to protect us; an obscurantist immaterialism in the philosophy of mind; a suspect foundationalism in epistemology; an incoherent subjectivism in the theory of meaning; a blinkered apriorism in the philosophy of science" (1998, xiii–xiv). Implicit in this is that current philosophy, too, is more indebted to those now rejected than it can admit, which is one premise of this book.

10. For a history of this, see Jay 1986, esp. 33–34, 104, 107–108, 112, 117, 156, 159, 174.

CHAPTER 15

1. Searle (2001, 84, 87) treats statements in the theory of action as essentially eliding reference to the self.

2. Cottingham comments in this regard, "Cartesian ideas dominated the scientific and philosophical thinking of Europe for a long time to come. The writings of the philosophical giants of the early modern period, Spinoza, Malebranche and Leibniz, on the Continent, and Locke, Berkeley and Hume, in the British Isles, all, in different ways, bear the unmistakable imprint of Descartes' thought concerning the structure of human knowledge, the nature of the mind and the relationship between mind and matter. It is impossible to examine the arguments and conceptual apparatus of any of the canonical philosophers of the late seventeenth and early eighteenth century without seeing the irresistible aptness of the traditional accolade which is so often bestowed on Descartes: he is, indubitably, the true 'father of modern philosophy'" (1998, xxxvii).

3. Searle attempts to give formal status to his notion of a self when he summarizes his account: "There is an x such that x = self S, and there is a y such that y = action token A, and there is some z such that z = reason R, and x performed y and in the performance of y, x acted on z" (2001, 87). But this merely says that an account without mention of an explicit self either takes the self for granted or is wrong. The fact that the word can be used in a formal proposition tells us nothing about its theoretical status. Indeed, that status can be established only within the theory that is indicated by the proposition. So far, all that Searle has shown is that S stands outside of the brackets that surround the

theoretically formed concepts of action, reason, and performance. The x that equals self S is the actor that completes the grammatical requirements of speaking of action. The self is supposed to give a certain substance to that x. In other words, it is better to say that Searle's introduction of the notion of a self is neither innocent (of what it imports) nor theoretical; nor is it a postulation, though Searle says that "in order to account for rational agency, we must postulate a self that combines the capacities of rationality and agency" and that subsists over time (94–95). The term names a "construct" in the sense that it deliberately challenges any theoretical restrictions that might be imposed by a concept. It is open to association, in particular, to associations that are restricted only by the history of philosophy itself, and it gathers these into a dangerous but apparently unavoidable bundle of possible implications and entailments difficult to reconcile with the meta-theoretical conditions of the theory to which it is somehow added. I do not take this to be a flaw of Searle's "notion," rather a strength: because, in reopening these ages-old questions he is also reopening the question of how Descartes, among others, is to be read and understood, and because introducing the self, with all the attendant risks, begins to weaken the hold the theory of action has on the study of what human beings do by way of being human. That is, by suggesting that the theory cannot make good on the claim that the individual is the central figure in the drama of action, it not only opens the way for a self but also opens the way for a very different notion of the social than we get when we begin with an individualistic ontology, as the theory does with or without the addition of the self.

4. Lombard argues that events are concrete particulars. While he does not consider the connection between events and actions, he intends to provide for it in regard to the ideas that events are "the changes that objects undergo when they change" (1986, viii) and that "a criterion of identity must play an important role in any theory about the nature of the entities that there are" (viii–ix). On the one hand, to say that an action is an event is to say that it involves change in some definite state of affairs. On the other hand, this is limited by Lombard's main point, that "events are changes that objects undergo when they change non-relationally" (238). One difference between this and what I later argue is that it precludes the possibility of an event that is identical with the action of a collectivity or ensemble (238). The example Lombard uses is that two people greeting each other is not an event, as is each instance of greeting. So, there can be "pluralities of events" but, apparently, no event that is a plurality (239). Thus, his view of events can only be extended to referents of "social" in a reductionist way, as if groups and collections of people are the same sorts of thing, though he restricts himself to horses in a field as an example of a plurality. Some of his statements lend themselves to this characterization—for example, that "the state of the world does not change; things change, thereby creating a new state for the world to be in" (241). The concept of a thing, on which this relies, is attributed to common sense, which seems to say that a thing is a potential object of a justifiable belief (6–7). I have no objection to a theory of events predicated on things of this sort, but I do not think that it reflects the ways in which we ordinarily operate or even think under the aspect of ordinariness. Of course, the "we" is a problem here. It is better to say that most descriptions of ordinary affairs (e.g., under the auspices of conversation analysis, studies of discourse and culture, and "collective behavior" in the broad sense of the term) do not show people acting as if things are that clear, as if the changes are so evident, or as if events cannot be assigned to what Lombard tendentiously calls "pluralities"—"tendentiously" because it is difficult to avoid the tautology of finding against pluralities by deciding that they cannot sustain and define an event. That is, if one is already committed to reductionism, then the theory is weakened by its inability

to surprise us with that hypothesis, and it cannot do so because it begins with a view that it is evident that the world (for which the idea of an event is appropriate) is made up of concrete particulars that are not pluralities. It seems to me that the most important question is "Are the things Lombard takes as elements of the sort he says they are (warranted by 'common sense')?" If not, what accounts both for the thing-likeness that seems to be crucial in certain instances of reference and for something quite different from thing-likeness that can be noticed in other instances of speaking and, perhaps, thinking? A reliance on conversational language, or discourse, yields a rather different picture of the universe in which "event," "plurality," "action," and the like are commonly subjects of sentences and extended units of meaning, from language taken apart from the circulation of signs in the sorts of discourse in which subjects can be said to "lose themselves." Lombard considers arguments having to do with the problem of identifying "basic kinds of things" (18), all of which make assumptions about observation and perspective that I believe are no less problematic than, say, how to delineate something clearly and distinctly. An interesting by-product of his discussion has to do with whether the perception of an event involves comparing two states of an entity or involves apprehending the event as the indefiniteness of any entity (that could change). Hegel's attempt to show that perception comes to involve just such a replacement of things by sheer movement from properties to essence to properties, and so forth, and Sartre's attempt to show how loss can be part of the very apprehension of a thing are well-developed instances of a different understanding of "common sense" and the idea of "ordinary" speaking and thinking.

5. Other philosophers have reinforced this predicament, if only inadvertently. See Davidson's essay "What Is Present to the Mind?" For now, it seems to me that claiming that "having a thought" does not require "a special psychological relation to the object used to identify the state of mind," when that object is objective only in a context in which minds are being compared, raises questions about whether it is necessary to conceive of agency as vested in a concretely particular person (2001d, 61, chap. 4). In other words, by challenging the idea that states of mind depend on objects with which one can be acquainted, one can then ask whether what we mean by "a state of mind" might be independent of the concrete individuals to whom they are likely to be attributed, as far as theory is concerned. If so, then it should be possible to evaluate the obstacles to accepting such a view that become important in preserving individualism because the original view of the individually vested mind is no longer necessary. In passing, Rawls's progressive elaboration and correction of his theory of justice may partly reflect the difficulties involved in adhering to an individualistic ontology at all cost. Samuel Freeman refers in this regard to Rawls's "emphasis on individuals and individual rights, rather than groups to group rights, that is central to liberalism" (2007, 91; see also 79).

6. Davidson says that "an action . . . must be intentional under some description, but an action is intentional only if it is caused by mental factors such as beliefs and desires" (2001d, 216).

7. One reason I believe that Davidson has unduly restrained himself in his appeal to the social dimension of thought (and action) is his citation of R. G. Collingwood: "The child's discovery of itself as a person is also its discovery of itself as a member of a world of persons . . . ; and since the discovery of myself as a person is also the discovery of other persons around me, it is the discovery of speakers and hearers other than myself" (Collingwood 1958, 248). Prior to this passage, Collingwood says that "consciousness does not begin as a mere self-consciousness, establishing in each one of us the idea of himself, as a person or centre of experience, and then proceed by some process, whether of 'projection' or of argument by analogy, to construct or infer other persons. Each one

of us is a finite being, surrounded by others of the same kind; and the consciousness of our own existence is also the consciousness of the existence of these others" (248). To be "a member of a world of persons" cannot mean simply being subject to norms or knowing through the "triangulation" of two points of view (or points of view conceived of as enumerable), either for Collingwood or for Davidson. The tenor of Davidson's conclusion also supports the point. He says that "our propositional knowledge has its basis not in the impersonal but in the interpersonal" (2001d, 219). He continues, "Thus, when we look at the natural world we share with others, we do not lose contact with ourselves, but rather acknowledge membership in a society of minds. If I did not know what others think, I would have no thoughts of my own" (219–220). This passage is remarkable not only for the solution it offers as to how self-knowledge, our knowledge of the external world, and our knowledge of other minds might be reconciled but for its suggestion that once we look closely at what can be meant by "sharing," "a world of persons," "member," "community," and the like, neither norms nor points of view are sufficient to account for what we do and how what we do can be said to be intentional. Rather, we have situated activity and cognition in that very same irreducible universe. Having done so, our work has just begun. It is not that his answer to the question of how the three sorts of knowledge fit together is a satisfactory one, given the way in which the problem is posed; it is that his answer undermines the ontology on which the problem depends and, therefore, the theories of mind and action predicated on it.

8. Searle has argued against reducing mind to an epiphenomenon of the brain and identifying cognition with computation (1994, chap. 9). It is worth noting that evaluating and learning are, in this formulation, not instances of action in the action-theoretical sense; and if they are not, then it has to be made clear how to define "action" such that they are not instances of it.

9. It should be evident that stating reasons is an instance of social action no matter how it is defined and that the requirement to do so is almost always imposed such that the imposition and response are also socially implicated if not determined. Searle here confuses justification with coming to act in a way that might or might not be subject to demands for justification.

10. Consider the early discussions in Pears 1957 and Rescher's defense of the idea of a philosophy of process and of "philosophy in process": "Most of the major philosophical movements of the twentieth century have (from a variety of very different perspectives) insisted upon the inappropriateness of metaphysics. . . . One after another, the avant garde movements of twentieth-century philosophy have abandoned the problems of traditional metaphysics as reflecting the outmoded concerns and conceptions of a bygone era. However, process philosophy firmly sets itself against all of this negativism. It yields to no one in point of appreciating the fruits of scientific and cultural studies. But it sees in them not a substitute for traditional philosophizing but rather a source of grist for philosophy's mill. Against the current of the age, process philosophy does not see science or logic or language theory or artificial intelligence as providing replacements for philosophy as traditionally conceived, but regards all of these enterprises as enriching the agenda of issues and as furnishing materials for productive philosophy" (1996, 166). Mary Warnock's comment is of particular interest: "There are no criteria by which one may test a given statement to see whether it is metaphysical or not. Absolutely any statement could be metaphysical—and any argument could, equally, be a metaphysical argument. The test is what the argument is being used for or what the statement means in its context. And if we can't apply any ready-made test to statements to separate the metaphysical from the non-metaphysical, it follows that we shall have to consider every

statement on its merits. There will be no ready-made refutations either" (quoted in Pears 1957, 152–153). She later moderates the tone of her remarks by attempting to distinguish between "metaphysical system-making" and "broadening our horizons" (159). The point she is making is not that we need to return to an older theory of being but that we need to recognize and, perhaps continuously, reengage the questions that gave rise to it and still give rise to its temptation.

CHAPTER 16

1. This criticism suggests that philosophers have overestimated the extent to which "the ideals which have inspired our society have been utilitarian ideals" (Iris Murdock, quoted in Pears 1957, 114). It is fair to say that those ideals have inspired modern philosophy, but there are many reasons to question whether they are incorporated in everyday life, whether they are acceptable in the social contexts of daily life, and whether they are coherent as ideals from the point of view of social life. Note that the provocative phrase "oriented in its course" has not, with few exceptions, been discussed by sociologists.

2. For a discussion of one version of "process," see Rescher 1996, in which he says that "process metaphysics as a general line of approach holds that physical existence is at bottom processual" (2) and places it in opposition to substantialism, a distinction that I criticize.

3. Weber refers to the need not only to account causally for behavior in terms of its intentions and effects but to account as well for what he refers to as "its course" (1947, 88), and to "what a person is doing when he tries to achieve certain ends," though this is not, to my knowledge, discussed in his theoretical writings. This may be why it is tempting to interpret Weber's notion of a course of activity as a succession of actions integrated by an overall aim and, perhaps, subordinate to an overall plan. He eliminates the possibility of such a discussion when he consigns states of mind that might be thought of as intrinsic to the meaning of an action to the category of deviance and when he fails to engage the question of how "substantive rationality" is realized, thereby allowing him to proceed to a concept of rational action that is informed but not constituted by the determination of value. The radical separation of value from action is a serious flaw in Weber's general sociology, and it has been revised with more or less critical results by Parsons, whose notion of the "system of action" includes value determination as a component of the act, and Garfinkel, who, among others, has attempted to demonstrate that no action can be divorced from the ongoing determination of values, which is to say that value determination is an immanent and therefore fundamentally unsettling feature of all action (Garfinkel 1967; Parsons 1951; Goffman 1963; Latour 2005).

4. One might say, however, that persons can learn both the humanity of others and a "generalized other," and that this requires only a theory of how the results of this learning play themselves out (as well as its conditions). But such a theory is not open to the problems addressed by this book, and it assumes what is most important not to assume— about personhood, agency, taking account, orientation, and so forth—and it envisions the social as a condition and not a constitutive feature of agency.

5. The defense of rational choice theory by Donald Green and Ian Shapiro (1994) admits that the model has been overextended, admitting, in effect, that it is, in that extension, a figure of speech. For the idea of "folk psychology," see Churchland 1988, 44–45.

6. Alfred Mele (1987) poses two questions. First, are there actions that are "akratic or incontinent" in the sense of being "*free, intentional* action contrary to the agent's *better judgment*"? Second, can "the notion of akratic action" be clarified in such a way that

it is possible to answer the first question? He does not mean that the agent of such an action intends to act in such a way, though the agent may intend to do just what he or she did (4–5, emphasis in original). What he eventually calls "motivated irrational behavior" can be, as he says, useful in "our understanding of *rational behavior*," but it may also indicate, as I argue later, something about participation that defies characterizing the rationality of the individual's behavior, such as it is, according to the characterization of it as "action." Weakness of the will is featured in many other texts. See, for example, Davidson 2001c, 200–205; McCann 1998, chap. 11; Charlton 1988, chap. 7; Searle 2001, chap. 7. Searle argues that the referent of "weakness of the will" is common enough that it makes little sense to doubt it: "I think the basic mistake . . . is to misconstrue the relationships between the antecedents of an action and the performance of the action" (220). If Searle is correct, then the logic of an "action performed" is not the same as the logic of an "action to be performed." It seems to follow that the situation of the former is not the same as the situation of the latter, and I rely on this observation in my account of what I later call "the course of activity." The problem is not to find a way to join the two but to recognize that they are really separate theoretical objects requiring different explanatory principles. The "action performed" is essentially social, while the activity of determining what action to be performed is social though the mental state of readiness is mental in the individual sense. But being ready to perform an action does not mean that the action performed is the action one was ready to perform. If the moment of performance is sufficiently "social" to be thought of as participatory, then an account of the action must begin with its being a moment of something ongoing and inclusive, and this is what is missing in every philosophical account of action of which I am aware.

7. Jon Elster summarizes why rational-choice explanations may fail, beyond the fact that a situation may "not allow a unique behavioral prediction from the hypothesis that agents behave rationally." Following Weber, he goes on to say that "we should not forget that it sometimes fails simply because people act irrationally. They yield to wishful thinking, in the sense of letting their desires determine their beliefs. . . . Or they succumb to weakness of will, in the sense of acting for the sake of a desire which they themselves value less highly than the remaining set of desires. Finally, their intentions and beliefs may be subject to various inconsistencies that are also incompatible with rational choice" (1994, 320; see also Elster 1983, 55–68, 241–243). It is worth noting at this point that the idea of "bounded rationality" seeks to preserve the presumption of rationality rather than, as with some of the followers of Schutz, to rethink the concept according to the social conditions that both define human conduct and create the limits of its being rational.

8. For a discussion of the problem, see Chang 1997, and Raz 1997, 110–128. "Most of the argument of this essay was designed to show that the fact that a person wants something is no reason for that person to perform the action that is most likely to facilitate the satisfaction of the want" (Raz 1997, 126).

9. For an account of the problems of rational choice theory from within that perspective, see Green and Shapiro 1994; Cook and Levi 1990; and Schmidtz 1995.

10. There is considerable movement within the philosophical literature on the intersection of the theory of mind and the theory of action away from cognitive rationalism, individualism, and natural science paradigms, but little movement toward a different understanding of sociality than depends on the notion of society as an entity (see Ruben 1985; and see various contributions to Chang's *Incommensurability, Incomparability, and Practical Reason* [1997]; see also Martin and McIntyre 1994). Holism, historicism, organicism, and skepticism are among the unacceptable risks thought to be imposed by breaking with cognitivism and naturalism in theorizing sociality.

11. Parsons discusses the relationship between the nontraditionalist notion of "economic rationality" and the idea of a social system: "The postulate of rationality, however, occupies a somewhat curious status in the theory of action. It is a clear implication of the theory of action on both the personality and the social system levels, that 'rational action' is a type which presupposes a certain mode of the *organization* of all the elements of action. It is something which is possible within the limits imposed by value-orientation patterns and by the situation, and by a certain mode of integration of motivational elements. On the personality level, that is, rational action is a type which exists within certain limits of the organization of personality. On the social system level, correspondingly, there is scope for rational adjustments within certain limits imposed by the institutionalized role-system" (1951, 549).

12. Parsons's analysis of the interactive aspect of medical practice begins to approach these issues. See 1951, chap. 10, esp. 474–479.

13. Allport's (1924) original reference to "social facilitation" was intended to allow for the possibility of an impersonal sociality, though it was still dependent on the idea of present others.

14. For a controversial survey and critique of the reception of "French theory" in the United States that at least introduces the topic, see Cusset 2008.

CHAPTER 17

1. Ollman's discussion of "internal relations" attempts to demystify the notion associated with F. H. Bradley and criticized by G. E. Moore. See Soames 2003, 94–101; Wollheim 1960.

2. Derrida's disclaimer is against simplistic, mechanistic, and teleological interpretations of the idea of dialectics and not toward the version that emphasizes the self-transforming movement of the desire to complete and the impossibility of completion (1994; but see 47, 75, 93).

3. I do not endorse the idea of two realities. Rather, I am concerned with questions about the idea of agency-dependent reality, or the idea of our knowledge of an agency-dependent world.

4. I understand Putnam (2002) to be saying that the rejection of knowledge claims about values (e.g., in ethics) depends on an unsustainable assumption that science is value-free and on a failure to reckon with the fact that it has proven impossible to show that at least some values are not objective. A defense of science, and any factual claim as an instance of knowledge, requires a defense of the values by which every such move is informed. Such a defense applies as well to other sorts of value, suggesting that it is reasonable to think of at least some values as objective. It seems to follow that even if the human sciences rely on values this does not invalidate their claims to provide knowledge. My own position is somewhat different, though I am sympathetic with Putnam's argument in its context. I argue that the fact/value distinction is not relevant to the human sciences or to deciding whether their claims are, in general, true.

5. Michael Riffaterre (1990) argues that truth in fiction lies in the plausibility of fictional depictions—the test being whether what is depicted might have been like that, which is to say possible in a stipulated universe containing conditions of its possibility. This is insufficient to warrant using the word "knowledge" for the result, say, of reading a novel. If he is correct, then the test of plausibility lies outside of the text: its truth is a function of the reader's willingness to impute something to the text beyond what is written. I do not object to the claim that the capacity to judge the plausibility of a depiction is

part of what a reader brings to the text, but the question is what the text provides that can be called knowledge no matter how it is received as such, and the answer cannot simply involve reference and referring (see Iser 1993, 22–25, 308–311nn1–2). But this has something to do with what I have referred to as the course of activity that we call "reading" in contrast with a positive understanding of the idea of a "text." I only hint in this book at how this might be described and understood.

CHAPTER 18

1. For discussions of some of the issues involved in determining the scientific status of the social sciences, see Martin and McIntyre 1994. See also Latour 2005.

2. Rescher (1998) seems to connect the concept to the idea of difficulty. Given that reality is, for us, endless, and given that one is invariably confronted with the "profusion and variety" of its elements (xvi) and increased "elaborateness of their organizational and operational make-up" (1) for which resources can never be sufficient, there is a need for "complexity management." Our resources are finite, which "points to the ever more urgent role of choice-guiding personal values and priorities in an increasingly complex operating environment" (xvi). But this cannot just be a matter, as Rescher seems to believe, of "bounded rationality," since that assumes a sphere of deliberation free enough from the complexity of circumstances that decision makers can at least estimate the distance of their own procedures from the ideal, and this seems inconsistent with his depiction of the pervasiveness of escalating complexity. It may be a matter of rationality itself. It is not enough to say that we need to focus on devices for managing complexity—for example, by returning to what Weber called "substantive rationalization." This is because complexity is depicted in the first instance as beyond management. We need to ask what the word stands for in the present state of human knowledge, what problem is created by the apparent unmanageability of variety, profuseness, and elaborateness of organization. What is the problem Rescher names "complexity" if that problem cannot be the one he says it is without denying what he says about it? I believe that he has attempted to make the search for knowledge heroic by a quasi-narrative in which his hero is confronted by a universe in which no amount of knowledge will be adequate to anticipate predicaments, in which decisions need to be made without looking back and without assuming that it is possible to satisfy the desire to reduce costs or "collateral damage." Clearly, decisions about values that are arbitrary are not adequate to the problem he identifies; but complexity precludes that those decisions be rational in any but the least consequential sense of the term. Therefore, the appeal for complexity management amounts to an appeal to a kind of indifference (in which one might claim values absolutely in order to avoid having to consider the possibility of their being poor ones), much as CEOs are prized in certain industries for the quality of never looking back, for their willingness to face any unanticipated predicament without regard to the associated damage that accompanies their decisions and without regard to the "obvious fact" that the only way to settle value questions under the conditions Rescher describes is by fiat, and, presumably, fiat requires that mix of indifference and force identified with power rather than authority, particular will rather than society, competition rather than cooperation, disposition rather than justice.

3. For critical comments on Fritz Machlup's use of the term "complexity," see Martin and McIntyre's (1994) introduction to part 1 of their edited book. Durkheim (1966) attempted to develop rough indices of what he thought of as several dimensions of societal complexity, depending, for example, on such factors as density and degree of

concentration. This was designed to allow for historical comparisons among societies, which he considered necessary for evaluating the "normalcy" or "pathology" of certain social facts. While it is possible to read into Durkheim's account of social facts the same sorts of consideration of what constitutes a scientifically definable object that one finds in Saussure's (1986) discussion of the idea of a "system," the concept, such as it is, is insufficiently formed to give the notion of a social fact as clear a theoretical status as would be necessary to consider complexity a variable applicable to all social entities.

4. Durkheim writes, "To make an inventory of all the characteristics belonging to an individual is an impossible task. Every individual is an infinity, and infinity cannot be exhausted" (1966, 79). Durkheim accepts the need to manage this complexity, but there seems little doubt that he is thinking of forms of life, individual and social.

5. For Parsons (1951), a social system is a structure of intentionality not identifiable with individuals as agents. One reason why Durkheim did not develop such a notion, and therefore identify society with collective intentionality in Parsons's sense, may be that he was uncomfortable with the implication that the development of society in its environment and the problem of maintaining its identity or internal integrity is as amenable to the operations of normal institutional processes as Parsons believed. There are passages in his works that seem consistent with this interpretation—namely, when he speaks of the *progress* of the division of labor as always accompanied by a degree of social conflict, suggesting a different dynamic to social structure from the one that describes the functional integration of a system of social action (intentionality) at the level of analysis of society (Durkheim 1933).

6. One such assumption has to do with beliefs about the basis for differentiating among disciplines. It is often said that comprehensive knowledge classically required the integration of thought across all its disciplines; modern consciousness tends to locate knowledge in relatively few fields. This devolution by specialization, whatever its philosophical warrant, has a history, and that history leaves traces within each specialty. For an example of a history of the scientific reception of the theory of evolution that incorporates both internal and external aspects of the scientific enterprise, see Desmond 1989.

7. Lazarsfeld elsewhere provides an optimistic account of sociology (1973). He is less than optimistic about theory, as can be seen from the following: "A fairly clear-cut notion of theory has developed from the practices of the natural sciences. First, a number of basic concepts are established. To some of them measurements are related; others are constructs, the validity of which is left undecided at the beginning. Operations between these basic units are then defined, permitting the derivation of new conclusions. Finally, these can be tested against concrete observations. In their most highly developed form, such theories are likely to have two further characteristics. One is that the operations and derivations are usually given in mathematical form; the other is a 'reductionist' tendency. . . . No one believes that this kind of theory exists at the moment in sociology or that it is likely to develop in the near future" (36).

Since 1970, a number of texts have been written in and about sociological theory that draw, usually uneasily, on other resources than the philosophy to which Lazarsfeld refers. See, for example, Sica 1998. See Latour 2005 on the development of "science studies" as an empirically based program that reinforces optimism about the possibility of representing social reality. See also Blum and McHugh 1984.

8. While this problem has been on the minds of sociologists for more than three generations, the debate gained force with the publication of Winch's *The Idea of a Social Science* in 1958 and the controversy that followed (Wilson 1970). More recently, critical ethnography has reengaged the issue, though often on the broader plane of the

philosophy of science influenced to a great extent by the Frankfurt School and by the debates surrounding the reception of Kuhn's *The Structure of Scientific Revolutions* in 1962.

9. While Soames's (2003) history of analytic philosophy seems to me to be designed to avoid the conclusions I draw, I believe that it supports this claim.

CHAPTER 19

1. Ollman (2003) provides one of the few discussions of the idea of internal relations, with special attention to the problem of contextualizing activity and observation. Parsons used the idea of "interpenetration" to avoid certain dangers implicit in an organicist interpretation of society, perhaps in regard to Weber's claims that in reality types are mixed, but theory requires that they be conceived of as independent. This leaves open whether their being mixed is a theoretical fact, and if so might it not be a *logical* property of systems. His idea of a system points to an external relation of situation and life (system based on exchanges among its parts, each of which has the system as its environment) disguised as an internal one. Still, Parsons's account of the relations among subsystems seems, despite itself, to suggest that identifying "life" with "system" requires far more than is possible given the standard ideas with which he had to work: the coordination of specialized functions identified with "pure types"; variables that exhaustively describe the possibilities of organization, where the idea of a boundary is nonproblematic; and members as former pre-social beings (1951). In that respect, Parsons may have carried the idea of a system as far as possible, given that it is not preceded by an account of what is human about human life and that it is committed to a particularistic conception of action.

2. I do not agree with Davidson's criticism of "Putnam's claim that 'meanings ain't in the head.'" "The argument assumes that if a state or event is identified (perhaps necessarily, if it is a mental state or event) by reference to things outside of the body, then the state or event itself must be partly outside the body, or at least not identical with any event in the body. This is simply a mistake. . . . Mental states are characterized in part by their relations to events and objects outside of the person, but this does not show that mental states are states of anything more than the person, nor that they are not identical with physical states" (Davidson 2001c, 48). That is, Davidson's point is relevant when individuality provides the initial frame of reference of analysis, not when we begin with the idea of the social, and I do not believe that beginning with individuality is required as a result of any available critique of beginning with the social. This is evident in one of his summary points: "The fact that states of mind, including what is meant by a speaker, are identified by causal relations with external objects and events is essential to the possibility of communication, and it makes one mind accessible in principle to another; but this public and interactive aspect of the mind has no tendency to diminish the importance of first person authority" (52).

3. The capacity to be surprised, which is crucial to what social psychologists refer to as "person perception," derives from this incessant activity; and it is the recognition of this capacity that distinguishes the perception of human life (e.g., persons) from the perception of things. "Totalizing" has to do with the tendency of any activity to exceed itself (the conditions of its subjectivity), which is to say that to be perceivable as human activity is to be surprisingly more than can be described. We need to say that activity is totalizing when we try to account for our distinction between life and things.

4. McCann defines action as follows: "In general, human actions constitute a class of events, in which a subject (the agent) brings about some change or changes. . . . When the change brought about is an ongoing process . . . , the behavior is called an *activity*. . . . Since actions are events, the question of their ontology is in part a matter of the general

ontology of change" (1995, 6). He writes later that "actions are explained by invoking the agent's reasons for performing them" (7). See also McCann 1998, 1–13.

5. The general notion of action I describe is explicit in Davidson's 1963 essay, "Action, Reasons, and Causes" (2001a).

6. I assume that it is well established that one cannot clarify the idea of a passionate reasoner by separating the two and attributing distinctive traits to each. Passionate reason cannot be reason without passion; nor can it be illustrated or supplemented by examples of or reference to such "reason." The same can be said for passion, which cannot be illuminated for this purpose by a theory of emotions that, at the outset, distinguishes emotion from reason. I should add that the claim that separating the two "for purposes of analysis" is reasonable only if the separation does not reflect a pre-analytical intention (e.g., to analyze each and see if they can then be put together rather than analyze each in light of what can be said about the other where their interpenetration is taken as a condition of analysis and not just something to explain based on it). But this would be somewhat different from what Soames (2003), for one, identifies as "analysis."

7. It is reasonable to say that specifying need only go far enough to fit what is specified into a conceptual field, but that treats specification as independent of the field, and the human sciences are not able, as things stand, to make that sort of argument in a convincing way. I take it that this has something to do with the nature of their object.

8. See, for example, Searle 1994, esp. 2–3, and see Nagel's (1995) reflection on these solutions.

9. One point of using "totalization" is to mark a distinction from "totality," which cannot represent human life as life, though it can represent what might be imagined, something taken as a distinct product, or something momentarily de-animated, say, by the imposition of "the realm of necessity," as in the application of force. Sartre's definition of "totality" is helpful in reminding us of the importance of the distinction and the logical demands it makes on theory. He writes, "A totality is defined as a being which, while radically distinct from the sum of its parts, is present in its entirety, in one form or another, in each of these parts, and which relates to itself either through its relation to one or more of its parts or through its relation to the relations between all or some of them. If this reality is created (a painting or a symphony are examples, if one takes integration to an extreme), it can exist only in the imaginary . . . , that is to say, as the correlative of an act of imagination. The ontological status to which it lays claim by its very definition is that of the in-itself, the inert. The synthetic unity which produced its appearance of totality is not an activity, but only the vestige of a past action. . . . Through its being-in-exteriority, the inertia of the in-itself gnaws away at this appearance of unity; the passive totality is, in fact, eroded by infinite divisibility. Thus, as the active power of holding together its parts, the totality is only the correlative of an act of imagination. . . . In the case of practical objects—machines, tools, consumer goods, etc.—our present action makes them seem like totalities by resuscitating, in some way, the praxis which attempted to totalize their inertia" (1976, 45–47). Thus, if human life refers to a being in a situation, as Sartre typically characterizes it, then the perspective from which it is recognizable as such is that of "activity," which I discuss as a course of activity. But to sustain this perspective, and that is always the problem, is precisely to see its moments of apparent finality, which is to say totality, as imaginary, and as moments inasmuch as the very attempt to sustain totality activates, in the imagination, the movement of what appears in that conception as parts. Moreover, the incessant movement of which even the perspective of totality must remain aware can be thought of only as a movement within the object, hence the object as active rather than passive or inert.

10. Randy Martin (1990) has provided an example of what it is to see subjectivity vested in a situation in his analysis of a particular dance from initial conception to realization as a performance.

11. Ernest Sosa defines the word as "a state of affairs or 'way things are,'" though he is interested in declarative sentences, in which case condition is "most commonly referred to in relation to something that implies or is implied by it" (1995, 149). For the purpose at hand, it is his initial proposition that is important. It illustrates the problems involved in using the word in accounting for phenomena where that use invokes at least a minimal metaphysics of context.

12. Peter McHugh (1968) comes close to acknowledging that the priority of "situation" is almost impossible to make theoretically intelligible.

13. This assumes that we understand that "subject" and "object" are now points of emphasis in the discussion—emphasis on what appear as either a detached object or a detachable subject when both appearances of detachability are moments of the internal relation of subject and object. The exchangeability of subject and object means that the analytic terms appropriate for the one are, under certain conditions of analysis, appropriate for the other. A simple example can help. When phenomenologists speak of the object as "beckoning," they are using a word closely associated with terms like "intention," "reason," and "action." It would be a mistake to see this as a metaphor, where one sense of a term momentarily substitutes for another or where multiple senses are brought to bear on something that otherwise might be described in a more limited way. This is not to attribute human qualities to things but to recognize that the perception of certain objects, what I have called "situated objects," is, in fact and immediately, to see them as imbued with human qualities. Nor is this a mistake, since it is unavoidable that situated objects would be seen as situated *ab initio*.

14. This is where we rejoin Gutmann's claim that individuals are the ultimate referents of moral discourse, which is my interpretation of their being "ultimate claimants." This cannot be accepted unless the problem of otherness is resolved as a philosophical and not merely practical matter, and this requires recognizing that the distinction between subjects and objects cannot provide a basis for the moral argument and yet it is assumed to do so. In that case the claim would include "individuals," and the idea that they are ends and not means, but not with respect to their being "ultimate" in the sense of their being self-identical individuals. I claim that it is the moral status of life that yields a notion of individuality in Gutmann's sense such that the individual is an ultimate claimant and referent in the sense that individuality is a manifestation of what is human about human life.

15. It would be inappropriate to say that we should start with distinct objects because they immediately appear to be the case. Nothing discussed so far suggests that objects are not real, and it is possible to establish the abstraction, the object momentarily taken as distinct, only by showing what it is that abstracting in this way disrupts. It follows that one must never forget that the desire to support the abstraction of distinctness cannot replace the obligation to submit every abstraction, designation, reference, and description to theoretical work. If one begins with the abstraction, one is unlikely to find a way back to what made the abstraction necessary and possible.

CHAPTER 20

1. From this point of view, situation is to action as object is to object, with subjectivity something on the order of an intervening variable. One problem that allows for such

an idea of subjectivity is, if Searle is correct, that reasons are insufficient to account for action, and since reasons are causes, it must be concluded that there is an essential gap between the one and the other that should not exist if reasons are causes. This gap allows for a notion of subjectivity that intervenes, in effect adding something to reasons that cannot be understood in strictly objectivist terms. The important thing is that subjectivity and objectivity are externally related, as are situation and action. The status of subjectivity appears to be, then, that of an added cause that, perhaps, and then somehow, operates across the range of existing causes or reasons. I probably have not done justice to Searle's idea, but my point is only that this way of thinking about situations, actions, and minds, whether or not it is fair to attribute it to him, appeals to the logic of external relations regardless of what qualifications are then made to accommodate a notion of subjectivity that is not immediately counterintuitive (see Searle 2001).

Hornsby cautions that "a claim about particular actions" is often "confused with a claim about kinds of action": "The confusion arises from a pervasive misunderstanding of the phrases we employ when we begin to talk about action in a general way, and speak of 'doing something' or 'performing an action'" (1980, 1). This is partly a problem of how to teach the idea of action in general, since examples are likely to be helpful and, if she is correct, as likely to be confusing. Dretske takes issue with Hornsby's identification of actions (and thereby, by implication, behavior) "not with the overt movements in which behavior typically culminates, but with the internal *causes* of these movements. . . . This view, unlike the identification of behavior with overt movement, is, on the face of it, implausible" (1988, 16–17; emphasis in original). But it is precisely the distinction between action and behavior that is at issue, and this is so despite the fact that one and the same description may indicate instances of both. When we use the term "action" in a way that distinguishes it from behavior, the "it" so distinguished is no longer a bodily movement but an instance of a type of agency. The problem arises for Hornsby when she tries to retain a positive view of an action as the expression of a mind. It is not so much that she has mistakenly identified actions with "the internal *causes* of" bodily movements as that she has tried to retain the externality of the relationship between mind and movement: "To describe an event as a perception (a perceiving of something) is to describe it in terms of its causes: to describe an event as an action is to describe it in terms of its effects" (1980, 111). Whether my action is a bodily movement, as in Dretske's account, or something in my head, as Hornsby claims, it is determined by conditions of rationality, and it typically expresses those conditions, which include reasons operating as causes.

2. It is in this sense that we can understand why action must be thought of as behavior in the sense of bodily movements rather than something inseparable from subjectivity—whether or not one means that action is essentially an "internal" event, as Hornsby sees it, though her notion of "actions seen as revelations of the human mind" remains ambiguous (1980, 1). It is a correlate of my discussion that the notion of differences among agents is one source of ambiguity in the discussion of action and that this has to do with the fact that "action" presupposes "course of activity" in such a way that it is not possible to exclude the subjectivity of objects; hence, subject and object may not be different in the ways in which they are typically said to be, and, consequently, the subject of "an action" may not, and in many if not most cases in which sociality is a crucial aspect of situation, be a psychological individual. In that case, the account of an act will look different from accounts in terms of distinct individual agents.

3. In a far more rigorously restricted context than this, and in regard to declarative sentences, Michael Dummett distinguishes two features of meaning: "the *assertoric content* of the sentence" from its "*ingredient sense*." The former has to do with "how the

hearer takes things to be if he accepts the assertion [of a declarative sentence] as correct."
The latter has to do with the "contribution that sentence makes to the assertoric content
of a more complex sentence of which it is a subsentence, and this is not in general determined by its own assertoric content" (2004, 32; emphasis in original). I do not mean to
suggest that Dummett's account of meaning opens the door to a holistic theory of action,
only that the idea of "ingredient sense" suggests that communication, as far as it involves
meaning, may require a collective effort at establishing meaning since the meaning of
any particular sentence may depend in significant part on other sentences the meaning
of which is known to someone else.

CHAPTER 21

1. Ruben uses "practice" as a synonym for "custom" in the context of a discussion
of rules (1985, 117), which places it on the side of routines rather than what I mean by a
"course of activity." It also suggests a virtual mechanical sense of the obligation one has
to a custom, and, whether or not this makes anthropological sense it does not capture
the sense of "practice." (See Rawls 1999b for the definition of "practice" as an "institutional fact.") One point of the discussion of practices is that any talk of such a thing is
talk about society, or some entity that can be defined in terms of institutional facts at the
same level of conception at which the practice at issue comes to notice. A corollary is that
no instance of a practice and no aspect of what is said to be a practice can be understood
outside of its full mediation by society. This is, in effect, an analytical fact, or is plausible
in the same way: no instance of whatever is taken to be a practice is not an instance of
society, given that society is conceived of as comprising institutional facts (including
practices) in a systematic (mutually mediating) relationship with one another. To claim
anything about a practice, even to characterize it logically, is only intelligible beyond its
stated definition when the systematically enabling concept of society is reasonably explicit in a way that accounts for its being just such a concept. It would be false, of course,
to claim that a society is composed of nothing but practices or that practices are the only
kinds of institutional facts—though some symbolic interactionists and phenomenologists have come close to just such a claim (see, for example, Berger and Luckmann 1966).
In regard to the idea of "institution," I have listed characteristics of the concept as it appears in sociological theory. Certainly Parsons held such an idea, and his definition of
a social system as the interpenetration of institutions (which are, for analysis, "parts" of
such a system) is the only attempt I know of to establish a concept competent to a general theory that has demonstrated its generality regardless of what one can say about its
predictive quality. There is, however, a nontheoretical, possibly heuristic use of the term,
deriving from one of its standard dictionary definitions—namely, to indicate a setting
up or something set up—and it is also said to mean any arrangement that outlasts its
originators. I am concerned only with the most developed concept, since the question
I address has to do with the most general thing that can be said about what is human
about human affairs as things stand. I take it that this is something like what Rawls had
in mind when he defines "the basic structure of society" as "the arrangement of major
social institutions into one scheme of cooperation" (1971, 54), and defines "institution"
as an "abstract object" that allows one to conceive of it as more or less "realized," and as
"a public system of rules which defines offices and positions with their rights and duties,
powers and immunities, and the like" (55). It is as realized that Rawls seems to mean that
it exists at "a certain time and place." But it seems clear that, thinking of justice in general
as well as in particular, as he suggests we do, requires that the realization be a realization

of the form of a system and not merely something set up regardless of how it is sustained and made visible or as if there is no need in a theory of justice to support the idea that a system is somehow sustained as a totality.

2. Rawls cites Searle's definition in his account of institutions (1971, 54–55).

3. Ruben discusses the differences between activities that are and those that are not necessarily rule-governed. I believe that his account of "relations" is not incompatible with my suggestion that the idea of a social relation does not entail relations among specifiable (or possibly specifiable) persons and that it entails something on the order of a system (1985, 116–117). "Justice," conceived of in terms of system theory, may be thought of as referring to the value of reciprocity, which has to do with the integrative functions of the society as what Parsons calls "conditions of rational action." It is a value in the different sense of being a historically determined or arbitrary standard only in regard to particular wills, which register it as "fairness."

4. From the point of view of methodology, to say that it invokes society is to say that any interpretation of something as a practice, and then the practice-related activities as such, is justified only on condition of evidence of such an invocation. Otherwise, the activity is not intelligible as a practice in the sense of an instance of an "institutional fact."

5. It is interesting to speculate on the possibility that social beings, conceived as equal in Rousseau's sense of equally dependent on all others, are analogous to early Wittgenstein's "metaphysical simples" (1974, 6–7). Theory cannot avoid implicating sociality as things stand and in this specific sense. Whatever problem this creates, it requires that no theory be considered complete relative to its sub-theoretical object and that the object (the social) be understood as intrinsically resistant to completion. I have argued that a concept that satisfies these conditions is a "course of activity." I do not mean that there is a logical connection between Rousseau's concept of the social contract and Wittgenstein's notion of the indifference of simples to one another or that the problems he was addressing were related to the ones discussed here—only that sociology thought of in this way, and according to Rousseau's demonstration that the nonsocial cannot be thought, requires reference to entities that are, for theory, perfectly equal such that the general will is undivided, thereby providing a basis for a theory of society. The difficulties this poses, not unlike the difficulties summarized by Scott Soames in his account of Wittgenstein's early ideas (2003), do not so much vitiate the theory as reveal its limitations and suggest the need to rethink certain basic conceptions according to what might be entailed by the sub-theoretical object as things stand.

6. The moral force of a practice, taken as an institutional fact but not necessarily as an institution, lies to some extent in the fact that its obligatory aspect does not have to do with utility and does have to do with human association, which G. E. Moore thought of as a fundamental good and not merely a means to an end. So, in engaging in a practice, one is immediately involved with others. That involvement is morally confirmed by the terms of the performance, and the undertaking itself cannot be explained as an attempt to increase or maintain pleasure, to decrease or prevent an increase of pain, or to maintain self-respect or increase the respect in which one is held by others.

7. The reasons I oppose torture should become increasingly clear from my account of the human aspect of life. I believe that these reasons are sufficient to invalidate both an uncompromising and a more nuanced utilitarian defense of torture after 9/11—if I am correct in emending Gutmann's declaration about the moral status of individuals on the grounds that she supposes a pre-social individual external to the courses of activity in which individuality finds its conditions of possibility. In my emendation, the individual may be the ultimate moral claimant in moral discourse but not the ultimate object of that

discourse. In that case, what is moral is not the claimant or the act of claiming, but what is claimed, so that, on my emendation, the individual claimant claims only in the name of what is human about human life, and not for herself as if a single deserving soul. This suggests that the only claim that can be about the particular individual has to do with her suffering, which, as Nagel argued, provides a reason for all possible actors to respond. This is certainly an important condition of moral discourse, but an equally important condition is the idea that life, which is intrinsically social, is the ultimate object (or subject) of moral discourse in contrast with the pre-social individual, who is a participant in the works of agency but not their origin or the foundation of their realization as courses of activity.

8. This is an inevitable feature of discursive speech. But even if one were to disagree, it must be admitted that in the course of participating in a discourse it is rarely possible to tell when and if the ambiguity of any particular expression has been effectively reduced. That discourse proceeds across the particularity and ambiguity of its constituent expressions is an interesting fact and not a defect that needs to be corrected. One thing that this explains is why attempts to analyze ordinary speech by reducing it to a set of utterly clear propositions does not work when introduced into discourse itself. It cannot in general yield discursively valid expressions—only isolated expressions for which the analysis stands as a demonstration of the impossibility of such expressions for discourse, hence for ordinary usage.

9. It is common in sociology, after Weber, to say that the rationality of goal-oriented acts presupposes a prior solution to the "value question"—as in saying that it is possible to rationalize an act (to direct it toward greater efficiency and/or effectiveness) only when the practice of which it is an instance is instantiated. The priority is not logical but chronological, at least in Weber's (1947) account. But it matters whether we see an act as value-laden, as a matter of practice or something that looks, as it were judicially, only to the past; and the Weberian formulation envisions the necessity of the latter in light of the completion of a value or a practice. At some point, he claims, values must cease to operate and the action should be seen as nothing more than oriented by a goal to a future of the attainment of that very goal. For Weber, as for Rawls, given that a practice is instantiated, the justification of it plays no role in the action that instantiates it. Garfinkel's (1967) contribution to classical theory arguably lies in his demonstration that ordering principles (practices, values, etc.) are always implicated in reasons and justifications for action in process, and that those principles are themselves ongoing accomplishments of action in its course.

10. For example, merely undertaking an activity that another wishes done may create (simply by beginning) the sense of an obligation on the order of a promise though it lacks the formal properties of the institutional fact. While this may be because of "tacit" rules, that seems to stretch, and thereby undermine, the meaning of "rule." Similarly, identifying a game such as chess with the rules that govern the moves of pieces and determine the end of the game would be insufficient to understand what it is to play chess according to rules, which is why some early chess programs, notably at Carnegie Tech in the 1950s, were designed to make use of heuristics, which had to do with strategic possibilities and the pragmatics of the immediate situation of play. The practice of playing chess is limited by but cannot be identified solely with the official rules of play.

11. The term "usage" is not adequate to the idea of "discursive speech"; nor was it originally intended to be so. It points to something like consistency across situations, and this allows for a concept of rules that is similarly independent of situation.

12. This pleasure is not the pleasure of doing something but the pleasure of doing something inter-subjectively.

13. Searle used the expression "institutional fact" to refer to certain "facts dependent on human agreement" (1995, 2). But unless "institutional" adds something to "human agreement," nothing is gained by this move. Later, he defines "institutional facts" as a "subclass of social facts," and declares that these are "facts involving human institutions" (26). A "social fact" is, for him, "any fact involving collective intentionality," and by "collective intentionality," he means "intentionality that exists in each individual" having "the form 'we intend'" (26). His examples of institutions, including language, indicate something far more substantial than what that definition requires and more substantial than can easily be described by reference to rules (see 27, 31–51). It is, of course, true that the "rules of chess create the very possibility of playing chess" and "are *constitutive* of chess in the sense that playing chess is constituted in part by acting in accord with the rules" (28; emphasis in original). But it is also true that for someone learning to play chess, playing the game is more clearly defined by "trapping the king"—that is, by its end or purpose—than by the rules that regulate the movements of the pieces. At the same time, the fact that playing is fun, that there is pleasure in the activity itself, may not be extraneous to what is meant by "chess" to someone who expects, hopes, plans "to play" it. Those rules may define what the word "chess" literally means, but they do not define its meaning to players who already know the rules. Thus, Searle's way of describing chess describes it for someone who either does not play and therefore needs a literal definition that distinguishes the one game from others, or someone who plays well and therefore thinks of the meaning of "chess" (among players) according to other criteria. So, while it is a rule of chess that the game ends when a king is in check and no further move is possible for any of his pieces, and it is clear that this is not arbitrary, or a matter of whim, it is not at all clear that the things a nonplayer would call conventional are, for players, merely arbitrary. It is true that a player may not consider the relative size of king and pawn to be necessary, but it is also true that a player would consider elements of strategy to constitute the game insofar as it is something to do and not merely to know about, and the player may well consider it as a certain type of fun as well. In Searle's discussion of institutions (chap. 2), he considers three elements of an account of "institutional facts." The first is "the imposition of function on entities that do not have that function prior to the imposition," the second is "collective intentionality," and the third is the "distinction between constitutive and regulative rules" (29). Without going into detail, several questions arise in this regard. For one, from whose perspective is it possible to speak of functions in this way? If the ethnologist's, then there is a problem of the relationship between this way of accounting for institutions and the "social facts" as they exist for the individuals who make up the "social." For another, Searle's account of collective intentionality begs most of the questions that bring that notion to mind in the first place. Finally, the distinction between constitutive and regulative rules is clear from one perspective and not from others. How does one account for that perspective, and how is it possible for that to yield an account of institutional facts as those transpire in a social context in which people form intentions together?

14. To say that such a system contains a special set of rules designed to handle the problem of application seems ad hoc, since if such a set existed, it would not appear to be part of what makes the rules coherent and would seem to suggest that the total system, including the set, cannot meet the criteria of a practice justifiable as such. It also does not help to say that utilitarianism builds in the idea that a utilitarian argument about the greater good is not appropriate to individual cases when it leads to conclusions that are intuitively unacceptable—as in justifying the punishment of an innocent person in the interest of the greatest number. This attempts to correct utilitarianism by appealing to utilitarians. It is true that most instances of the "practice" of punishing for breaches

of the law make just this claim, but that only puts further in jeopardy the very notion of practice as an account of what is principled about punishing. That there are constitutional principles, or other legal or moral or social restrictions on the conduct of a case, does not imply that these need to be understood as constituting a practice justifiable in its own right, and I do not believe the history of constitutional law is easily interpreted that way. However, there is no need to throw rules out with the idea of a practice. All that one needs to throw out are the connected distinctions between types of rule and justifications. In that case, one may well attempt to show that in any instance of decision making rules may get more attention than possible applications, or the reverse; but this does not mean that we are dealing with the sort of coherence Rawls attributes to practices as systems of rules. It is, of course, true that judges insist on consistency of the law over time and on the relevance of that to the greater good. But this does not require that laws be considered as composing a system abstracted from contexts of possible application. Nor, as already indicated, do we benefit in the analysis of practices and their activities from using examples from the law, since the question of social validity involves more than the legitimacy of official actions. It has to do more with citizenship than with offices, though the former may be vitally connected to the latter.

15. When Rawls (1999b) says that he uses "practice" technically, he must also mean that his usage corresponds to both ordinary usage and the sense of a practice that ordinary discourse conveys. Otherwise, his term could not refer to something that has social or normative force. Therefore, his conception of practice is not only technical; it is a conception of something that is technical in a different sense for those to whom the term and its special obligations might have more than a passing interest.

16. Nothing in this implies that situations are independent of their contexts—only that the standard idea of a practice leaves unclear the connection between the regularities in actions that are situated and those that are somehow trans-situational.

CHAPTER 23

1. The point is not that idealization per se is fatal but that an idealization that does away with the notion of the nonidealistically essentially social character of persons poses more than a simple problem. If so, then it is constructively criticized by showing that another conception, which is only possibly idealist, accounts for what the first does and does not deny what no account should deny. Given that, it remains to be seen whether the risk of yet another idealization leads to the same sorts of problem as what it replaces, and whether it advances the project of understanding human life without denying its essentially social aspect.

CHAPTER 24

1. The issue of intelligibility arises in regard to the possibility of speaking coherently and not in regard to the capacity of interpreting what is spoken according to rules derived from linguistics or otherwise organized as a system of translation—from possibly misleading to clear and decisive expressions, for example. See Urmson's (1956) version of how this distinction arises in the history of analytical philosophy. It is alluded to in Strawson's (1992) account of the logic of analysis. See also Dummett 1993.

2. Monological speech cannot, on this account, be understood as discursive, and its way of being intelligible radically differs from the intelligibility that, given the distinction, must be attributed to the latter.

3. Consider the effects of bans on satire, as in England in 1599 and Brazil during the 1970s. In each case, the intention was to disrupt the fluency of discourse such that it is recomposed as a series of definite utterances. Humor notoriously projects multiplicity—as in the permission to laugh offered by a joke (Sacks 1974), the juxtaposition of contradictory narratives provoking the sense of a "punch line" (Koestler 1964), and layers of possible application that cannot but reference one another (Freud 1963). In the case of political satire, it is not only that authority may be under attack but that the fluency of discourse is annulled such that only explicitly accountable utterances are permitted. Monologue is, from this point of view, totalitarian, though it is not for this reason alone to be denied. Within discourse, monologue may emerge not as a fact but as a project; in this respect its constant possibility is a feature of the self-generative aspects of dialogue. To say that dialogue operates against the possibility of monologue, presumably in the interest of preserving intelligibility in the sense of social validity, is not to say that the force of monologue is only negative. As a danger dialogue poses to itself, it is a subversion of what might need momentarily to be disrupted.

4. Habermas's (1970) early Rousseauian characterization of the "ideal speech situation" points to the gestural moment in which speaking projects the equality of speaker and hearer, and therefore becomes intrinsically critical of all that defies that moment of the social contract in which each person realizes his or her dependence on all others and, simultaneously, realizes human freedom in inter-dependence.

5. The fact that something is accountable does not mean that it can or should be accounted for: parties to a discourse are, as Garfinkel (1967) says, uninterested in accounts though their utterances are accountable. What is then meant by accountability is that parties would consider it untoward to ask, "What are we doing?" or "Why don't we do something else?" "Accountability" implies that borders are taken to be closed, and speech continues without fear of interruption, as if only the discourse counts. This is "as if" in the sense that fear or its lack is not a topic but the way that activity actually takes place, what it displays such that no further comment is required. Parties' activities are visibly geared to maintaining the integrity of the discourse, the inter-dependence of voices, though no one need or could consider explicitly the problem of maintaining that order. The word "maintaining," when used in the context of human affairs, means acting in such a way that certain questions do not arise, and this is possible only if no questions arise about acting in that way.

6. The extent to which this is a problem is clear in Searle's discussion of "collective intentionality" (1995, esp. 1–29). He argues against reducing collective intentionality to individual intentionality on the grounds that it is false to claim that "because all intentionality exists in the heads of individual human beings, the form of that intentionality can make reference only to the individuals in whose heads it exists" (25). So, he concludes, "the form that my collective intentionality can take is simply 'we intend,' 'we are doing so-and-so,' and the like. In such cases I intend only as part of our intending. The intentionality that exists in each individual head has the form 'we intend'" (25–26). The social in this formulation amounts to mental contents of individuals, and people thinking "we." Instead of reducing collective intentionality to individual intentionality, Searle reduces it to a linguistic element in the mental states of individuals. The social refers, then, to a turn of phrase, and because of this, his examples are often implausible. For example, he finds it perfectly acceptable to speak of money as a substance about which there is agreement among users as to the appropriate use of its tokens. None of this can be very satisfactory to anyone committed to the idea that there is something more to the idea of the social than the appearance of the word "we" in the heads of individuals and to

a notion of money (and other such "social institutions") that goes far beyond the exclusive contractual characterization of it as a normatively governed instrument of exchange. In other words, Searle has not been able to reach the point that he wants to reach in his book—at a clarification of the reportable reality of the social—and this seems to be a result of his being entrenched in the perspective of the individual as the starting point of social theory and his belief that it is obvious that all that can be referred to as instances of agency lie in the minds of individuals, the concept of which is decidedly not problematic.

7. For Dummett, it is a mistake to make "the philosophy of thought part of the philosophy of mind" inasmuch as "philosophy is not concerned with what *enables* us to speak as we do, but with what it is for our utterances to have the meanings that they have, and nothing that happens in the brain can explain that" (1993, 187–188; emphasis in original). Yet, if mind is not identified with or reducible to brain, it may be relevant to accounting for meaningfulness and the meaning of utterances; but I claim that mind, understood in regard to that, need not be and should not be considered a property of individuals. Dummett also denies that the philosophy of language should be regarded as part of the philosophy of action (188). He admits that "talking is one mode of doing something; that's undoubtedly correct." But, he adds, "it gets you nowhere. The *only* sense I see in it is something we have already talked about, namely that a linguistic utterance is made with some intention or some motive; hence all those considerations that hold generally within the philosophy of action apply. They belong, however, to the background. It is essential to describe language as a conscious activity of rational creatures" but the latter is not "specific to language" and, therefore, presumably not specific to thought conceived of, at least in part, linguistically (188). Thus, he concludes that "the specific features of language are not explicable in the framework of the general philosophy of action" (188). Dummett's review of these ways of assessing the "status of the philosophy of language" in analytical philosophy leaves him supporting the position that, by and large, philosophical questions are "questions in the philosophy of language." It seems to me, however, that if utterances are not units in the sense of things having specifiable meanings that are themselves propositions traceable to the intentions involved in a given utterance, the situation is quite different from Dummett's account. It is necessary to uncouple the idea of an utterance and the idea of an intention, since whatever mental state accompanies uttering, it need not be the intention to issue something that has a particular meaning relative to the course of considering whatever the utterance is about, and is somehow isomorphic with the utterance as such. Indeed, it not only "need not be" but probably is not and in any case should not be assumed to be where the issue is discursive speech.

CHAPTER 25

1. To say that the object is oriented away from the surface is more abstract than to say that it protrudes or recedes, since the former can include either option.

2. Mediation by a process of inference diminishes the object by shifting from the experience of it to the experience of the process of inference. To say that the experience of the object (utterance) is also an experience of the structure that sustains it seems better; but what is lost is the dependence on the utterance by the one who apprehends it, and is therefore *already waiting*, and the sense, implicit in waiting, of every possible utterance as agency-dependent (such that, in the course of waiting, the apprehending subject is object-dependent). Finally, the interpretation of an utterance also impoverishes both the object (now fixed by virtue of its apparent interpretability) and the subject who apprehends it (interpretation only fixes the interpreting subject).

3. Certainly one would not be registering the experience of having uttered something to another as "I just performed a speech act." Nor would the hearer's response be an appropriate one if he or she said, "I thought I heard a speech act."

4. In this regard, Searle says that "speaking a language is performing speech acts," that "all linguistic communication involves linguistic acts. The unit of linguistic communication is not . . . the symbol, word or sentence, or even the token of the symbol, word or sentence, but rather the production or issuance of the symbol or word or sentence in the performance of the speech act" (1969, 16). He continues, "If my conception of language is correct, a theory of language is part of a theory of action, simply because speaking is a rule-governed form of behavior. Now, being rule-governed, it has formal features which admit of independent study" but only in the context of actual application (17). He concludes that "since every meaningful sentence in virtue of its meaning can be used to perform a particular speech act (or range of speech acts) and since every possible speech act can in principle be given an exact formulation in a sentence or sentences (assuming an appropriate context of utterance), the study of the meanings of sentences and the study of speech acts are not two independent studies but one study from two different points of view" (18).

5. An older literature on communication deals with the order of presentation as if each utterance is influenced by what precedes it (see Hovland, Janis, and Kelley 1953). A. Paul Hare reviews this literature in the context of "interpersonal relations in the small group" (1964, 217–271), where he attempts to show how structural effects on individuals derive from features of their groups. He refers to the effects of norms on cognitive presentations (judgment, conformity, decision, etc.). In discussing "the initial phase of the social act" (230), Hare says that "this includes a description of the individual's perceptions of himself and others, and the part these perceptions play in the imagined interaction between self and others through which the individual pretests his behavior" (230). He provides a fairly detailed description of how the course of activity is governed by minute interactions clearly below the threshold of reportable consciousness. Later, he discusses communication according to the concept of a "communication network" (247). It is fairly clear from his description that the term "network" is used to preserve the essentially individual cognitive model standard to social psychology at the time. Thus, "expectations" are the key element in understanding the effects of structure. Yet the ways in which structure, norms, networks, and the like are described do not easily fit this notion of a directive state within persons. That is, if persons' specific intentions merely explain the fact that they are participating (that they enter an interaction) and not the content of what they do or the meaning attributable to it, then those terms substitute for what I call a course of activity. In other words, the studies Hare reviews may lend themselves to an alternative interpretation according to the idea of a collective course of activity and its condition of inter-subjectivity. For various reasons, the tendency in social psychology was to try and fit the findings to a model that depends on individual cognition, with its assumptions of persistent psychologically internal directive states and intentions prior to action. We can see the same elision of sociality in the recourse taken to notions of background expectancies or things "taken for granted" (Garfinkel 1972, 3).

References

The works in this list that are not explicitly cited in the book were consulted for general information and have informed the author's analysis.

Addis, Laird. 1975. *The Logic of Society: A Philosophical Study*. Minneapolis: University of Minnesota Press.

Adorno, Theodor W. 1976. *The Positivist Dispute in German Sociology*. London: Heinemann.

Agamben, Giorgio. 2005. *State of Exception*. Chicago: University of Chicago Press.

Albrow, Martin, and Elizabeth King. 1990. *Globalization, Knowledge, and Society: Readings from International Sociology*. London: Sage.

Allport, Floyd Henry. 1924. *Social Psychology*. Boston: Houghton Mifflin.

Anderson, Perry. 1976. *Considerations on Western Marxism*. London: New Left Books.

Babbitt, Irving. 1928. *Rousseau and Romanticism*. Boston: Houghton Mifflin.

Bakhtin, Mikhail Mikhaïlovich. 1968. *Rabelais and His World*. Translated by H. Iswolsky. Cambridge, MA: MIT Press.

———. 1981. *The Dialogic Imagination: Four Essays*. Translated by C. Emerson and M. Holquist. Austin: University of Texas Press.

Berger, Peter L., and Thomas Luckmann. 1966. *The Social Construction of Reality: A Treatise in the Sociology of Knowledge*. Garden City, NY: Doubleday.

Bhabha, Homi. 1994. *The Location of Culture*. London: Routledge.

Black, Max. 1976. *The Social Theories of Talcott Parsons: A Critical Examination*. Carbondale: Southern Illinois University Press.

———. 1979. "Afterthoughts on Metaphor." In *On Metaphor*, edited by Sheldon Sacks, 181–192. Chicago: University of Chicago Press.

———. 1990a. *Perplexities: Rational Choice, the Prisoner's Dilemma, Metaphor, Poetic Ambiguity, and Other Puzzles*. Ithaca, NY: Cornell University Press.

———. 1990b. "Some Puzzles about Meaning." In *Perplexities*, 13–29. Ithaca, NY: Cornell University Press.

Blank, Arthur E. 1980. "Rules of Order, or So to Speak." Ph.D. diss. City University of New York.

Blau, Peter Michael, and Marshall W. Meyer. 1987. *Bureaucracy in Modern Society*. New York: McGraw-Hill.

Bloor, David. 1991. *Knowledge and Social Imagery*. 2nd ed. Chicago: University of Chicago Press.

Blum, Alan, and Peter McHugh. 1984. *Self-Reflection in the Arts and Sciences*. Atlantic Highlands, NJ: Humanities Press.

Bogen, David. 1999. *Order without Rules: Critical Theory and the Logic of Conversation*. Albany: State University of New York Press.

Bourdieu, Pierre. 1969. "Intellectual Field and Creative Project." *Social Science Information* 8 (2): 89–119.

———. 1993. *The Field of Cultural Production: Essays on Art and Literature*. Cambridge, UK: Polity Press.

Bradley, F. H. 1951. *Appearance and Reality*. Oxford: Oxford University Press.

———. 1962. *Essays on Truth and Reality*. Oxford: Oxford University Press.

Brodbeck, May. 1968. *Readings in the Philosophy of the Social Sciences*. New York: Macmillan.

Brooks, Peter. 1984. *Reading for the Plot: Design and Intention in Narrative*. Oxford: Clarendon Press.

Brown, Michael E. 2009. *The Historiography of Communism*. Philadelphia: Temple University Press.

Brown, Michael E., and Amy Goldin. 1973. *Collective Behavior: A Review and Reinterpretation of the Literature*. Pacific Palisades, CA: Goodyear.

Brown, Michael E., and Randy Martin. 1991. "Rethinking the Crisis of Socialism." *Socialism and Democracy* 7 (3): 9–56.

Brown, Roger. 1965. *Social Psychology*. New York: Free Press.

Burawoy, Michael. 2005. "2004 ASA Presidential Address: For Public Sociology." *American Sociological Review* 70 (1): 4–28.

Butler, Judith. 1990. *Gender Trouble: Feminism and the Subversion of Identity*. New York: Routledge.

———. 1995. "Subjection, Resistance, Resignification: Between Freud and Foucault." In *The Identity in Question*, edited by John Rajchman, 229–250. London: Routledge.

———. 1997. *The Psychic Life of Power: Theories in Subjection*. Stanford, CA: Stanford University Press.

———. 2000. "Competing Universalities." In *Contingency, Hegemony, Universality: Contemporary Dialogues on the Left*, edited by Judith Butler, Ernesto Laclau, and Slavoj Žižek, 136–181. London: Verso.

———. 2004. "Jacques Derrida." *London Review of Books* 26 (21): 32.

Butler, Judith, Ernesto Laclau, and Slavoj Žižek. 2000. *Contingency, Hegemony, Universality: Contemporary Dialogues on the Left*. London: Verso.

Cain, William E. 1981. "Constraints and Politics in the Literary Theory of Stanley Fish." In *Theories of Reading, Looking, and Listening*, edited by Harry Raphael Garvin and Steven Mailloux, 75–87. Lewisburg, PA: Bucknell University Press.

Cassirer, Ernst. 1957. *The Phenomenology of Knowledge*. Vol. 3 of *The Philosophy of Symbolic Forms*. New Haven, CT: Yale University Press.

———. 1963. *The Question of Jean-Jacques Rousseau*. Bloomington: Indiana University Press.

———. 1971. *The Logic of the Humanities*. New Haven, CT: Yale University Press.

Castoriadis, Cornelius. 1987. *The Imaginary Institution of Society*. Cambridge, MA: MIT Press.

Chang, Ruth. 1997. *Incommensurability, Incomparability, and Practical Reason*. Cambridge, MA: Harvard University Press.

Charlton, William. 1988. *Weakness of Will*. Oxford: Blackwell.

Chisholm, Roderick. 1976. *The Agent as Cause*. Dort: D. Reidel.

Churchland, Paul M. 1988. *Matter and Consciousness: A Contemporary Introduction to the Philosophy of Mind*. Cambridge, MA: MIT Press.

Clastres, Pierre. 1977. *Society Against the State: The Leader as Servant and the Humane Uses of Power Among the Indians of the Americas*. Translated by Robert Hurley and Abe Stein. New York: Urizen Books.

Cohen, Jean L. 1985. "Strategy or Identity: New Theoretical Paradigms and Contemporary Social Movements." *Social Research* 52 (4): 663–716.

Cohen, Jean L., and Andrew Arato. 1995. *Civil Society and Political Theory*. Cambridge, MA: MIT Press.

Cohen, Morris Raphael. 1956. *A Preface to Logic*. Cleveland: Meridian Books.

Cole, Stephen. 1980. *The Sociological Method: An Introduction to the Science of Sociology*. Chicago: Rand McNally.

Collingwood, Robin George. 1958. *The Principles of Art*. Oxford: Clarendon Press.

Cook, Karen S., and Margaret Levi. 1990. *The Limits of Rationality*. Chicago: University of Chicago Press.

Cooley, Charles Horton. 1962. *Social Organization: A Study of the Larger Mind*. New York: Schocken.

Cooper, Melinda. 2008. *Life as Surplus: Biotechnology and Capitalism in the Neoliberal Era*. Seattle: University of Washington Press.

Coser, Lewis A. 1956. *The Functions of Social Conflict*. Glencoe, IL: Free Press.

Cottingham, John. 1998. "General Introduction." In *Descartes' Meditations: Background Source Materials*, edited by Roger Ariew, John Cottingham, and Tom Sorell, xiii–xviii. Cambridge: Cambridge University Press.

Coulter, Jeff. 1989. *Mind in Action*. Atlantic Highlands, NJ: Humanities Press International.

Cusset, François. 2008. *French Theory: How Foucault, Derrida, Deleuze, and Co. Transformed the Intellectual Life of the United States*. Minneapolis: University of Minnesota Press.

Davidson, Donald. 1975. "Semantics for Natural Languages." In *The Logic of Grammar*, edited by Donald Davidson and Gilbert Harman, 18–24. Encino, CA: Dickenson.

———. 1979. "What Metaphors Mean." In *On Metaphor*, edited by Sheldon Sacks, 29–45. Chicago: University of Chicago Press.

———. 1999. "The Folly of Trying to Define Truth." In *Truth*, edited by Simon Blackburn and Keith Simmons, 308–322. New York: Oxford University Press.

———. 2001a. "Action, Reasons, and Causes." In *Essays on Actions and Events*, 3–20. Oxford: Oxford University Press.

———. 2001b. *Essays on Actions and Events*. Oxford: Oxford University Press.

———. 2001c. "The Myth of the Subjective." In *Subjective, Intersubjective, Objective*, 39–52. Oxford: Oxford University Press.

———. 2001d. *Subjective, Intersubjective, Objective*. Oxford: Oxford University Press.

———. 2001e. "Three Varieties of Knowledge." In *Subjective, Intersubjective, Objective*, 205–220. Oxford: Oxford University Press.

———. 2004a. "The Problem of Objectivity." In *Problems of Rationality*, 3–18. Oxford: Oxford University Press.

——. 2004b. *Problems of Rationality*. Oxford: Oxford University Press.

——. 2004c. "What Thought Requires." In *Problems of Rationality*, 135–150. Oxford: Oxford University Press.

Dawkins, Richard. 2006. *The God Delusion*. Boston: Houghton Mifflin.

Dehaene, Stanislas. 2009. *Reading in the Brain: The Science and Evolution of a Human Invention*. New York: Viking.

De Man, Paul. 1979. *Allegories of Reading: Figural Language in Rousseau, Nietzsche, Rilke, and Proust*. New Haven, CT: Yale University Press.

——. 1986. *The Resistance to Theory*. Minneapolis: University of Minnesota Press.

Deleuze, Gilles. 2005. *Pure Immanence: Essays on a Life*. Translated by Anne Boyman and John Rajchman. New York: Zone Books.

Deleuze, Gilles, and Félix Guattari. 1987. *A Thousand Plateaus: Capitalism and Schizophrenia*. Translated by Brian Massumi. Minneapolis: University of Minnesota Press.

——. 1994. *What Is Philosophy?* Translated by Hugh Tomlinson and Graham Burchell. New York: Columbia University Press.

Derrida, Jacques. 1976. *Of Grammatology*. Translated by Gayatri Chakravorty Spivak. Baltimore: Johns Hopkins University Press.

——. 1978a. "Structure, Sign and Play in the Discourse of the Human Sciences." In *Writing and Difference*, 278–294. Translated by Alan Bass. Chicago: University of Chicago Press.

——. 1978b. *Writing and Difference*. Translated by Alan Bass. Chicago: University of Chicago Press.

——. 1988. *Limited Inc*. Translated by Samuel Weber. Evanston, IL: Northwestern University Press.

——. 1994. *Specters of Marx: The State of the Debt, the Work of Mourning, and the New International*. Translated by Peggy Kamuf. New York: Routledge.

——. 1997. *Politics of Friendship*. Translated by George Collins. London: Verso.

Desmond, Adrian J. 1989. *The Politics of Evolution: Morphology, Medicine, and Reform in Radical London*. Chicago: University of Chicago Press.

Doppelt, Gerald. 1983. "Relativism and Recent Pragmatic Conceptions of Scientific Rationality." In *Scientific Explanation and Understanding: Essays on Reasoning and Rationality in Science*, edited by Nicholas Rescher, 106–142. Lanham, MD: University Press of America.

Douglas, Mary. 1986. *How Institutions Think*. New York: Syracuse University Press.

Downie, R. S. 1971. *Roles and Values*. London: Methuen.

Dretske, Fred I. 1988. *Explaining Behavior: Reasons in a World of Causes*. Cambridge, MA: MIT Press.

Dummett, Michael A. E. 1993. *Origins of Analytical Philosophy*. Cambridge, MA: Harvard University Press.

——. 2004. *Truth and the Past*. New York: Columbia University Press.

Durkheim, Émile. 1933. *The Division of Labor in Society*. New York: Macmillan.

——. 1961. *Moral Education: A Study in the Theory and Application of the Sociology of Education*. Translated by Everett K. Wilson and Herman Schnurer. Glencoe: Free Press.

——. 1964. *The Division of Labor in Society*. Translated by George Simpson. New York: Free Press.

——. 1965. *Montesquieu and Rousseau: Forerunners of Sociology*. Translated by Ralph Manheim. Ann Arbor: University of Michigan Press.

———. 1966. *The Rules of Sociological Method*. Translated by Steven Lukes. New York: Free Press.

———. 1982. *The Rules of Sociological Method*. Translated by Sarah A. Solovay and John H. Mueller. New York: Free Press.

Elgin, Catherine Z. 1983. *With Reference to Reference*. Indianapolis: Hackett.

Elster, Jon. 1983. *Explaining Technical Change: A Case Study in the Philosophy of Science*. Cambridge: Cambridge University Press.

———. 1994. "The Nature and Scope of Rational-Choice Explanations." In *Readings in the Philosophy of Social Science*, edited by Michael Martin and Lee C. McIntyre, 311–322. Cambridge, MA: MIT Press.

Emmet, Dorothy Mary. 1975. *Rules, Roles, and Relations*. Boston: Beacon Press.

Faris, Robert E. L., ed. 1964. *Handbook of Modern Sociology*. Chicago: Rand McNally.

Fay, Brian, and J. Donald Moon. 1994. "What Would an Adequate Philosophy of Social Science Look Like?" In *Readings in the Philosophy of Social Science*, edited by Michael Martin and Lee C. McIntyre, 21–36. Cambridge, MA: MIT Press.

Festinger, Leon. 1957. *A Theory of Cognitive Dissonance*. Stanford, CA: Stanford University Press.

Fish, Stanley E. 1976. "Interpreting the 'Variorum.'" *Critical Inquiry* 2 (3): 465–485.

Fodor, Jerry A. 1983. *The Modularity of Mind: An Essay on Faculty Psychology*. Cambridge, MA: MIT Press.

Foster, John. 1991. *The Immaterial Self: A Defense of the Cartesian Dualist Conception of the Mind*. New York: Routledge.

Foucault, Michel. 1965. *Madness and Civilization: A History of Insanity in the Age of Reason*. Translated by Richard Howard. New York: Pantheon Books.

———. 1994. *The Order of Things: An Archaeology of the Human Sciences*. New York: Vintage Books.

———. 2003. *Society Must Be Defended: Lectures at the Collège de France, 1975–76*. Translated by David Macey. New York: Picador.

———. 2007. *Security, Territory, Population: Lectures at the Collège de France, 1977–78*. Translated by Graham Burchell. New York: Palgrave Macmillan.

———. 2008. *The Birth of Biopolitics: Lectures at the Collège de France, 1978–79*. Translated by Graham Burchell. New York: Palgrave Macmillan.

Freeman, Samuel Richard. 2007. *Rawls*. London: Routledge.

Freud, Sigmund. 1963. *Jokes and Their Relation to the Unconscious*. New York: Norton.

Gallie, W. B. 1968. *Philosophy and the Historical Understanding*. New York: Schocken Books.

Gans, Herbert J. 1989. "Sociology in America: The Discipline and the Public American Sociological Association, 1988 Presidential Address." *American Sociological Review* 54 (1): 1–16.

Garfinkel, Harold. 1967. *Studies in Ethnomethodology*. Engelwood Cliffs, NJ: Prentice-Hall.

———. 1972. "Studies of the Routine Grounds of Everyday Activities." In *Studies in Social Interaction*, edited by David Sudnow, 1–30. New York: Free Press.

———. 2002. *Ethnomethodology's Program: Working Out Durkeim's Aphorism*. Edited by Anne Warfield Rawls. Lanham, MD: Rowman and Littlefield.

Gehlke, Charles Elmer. 1915. "Émile Durkheim's Contributions to Sociological Theory." Ph.D. diss. in *Sociology*. New York: Columbia University.

Gilbert, Margaret. 1989. *On Social Facts*. London: Routledge.

Goffman, Erving. 1959. *The Presentation of Self in Everyday Life*. Garden City, NY: Doubleday.

———. 1961a. *Asylums: Essays on the Social Situation of Mental Patients and Other Inmates*. Garden City, NY: Anchor Books.

———. 1961b. *Encounters: Two Studies in the Sociology of Interaction*. Indianapolis: Bobbs-Merrill.

———. 1963. *Stigma: Notes on the Management of Spoiled Identity*. New York: Simon and Schuster.

———. 1983. "The Interaction Order: American Sociological Association, 1982 Presidential Address." *American Sociological Review* 48 (1): 1–17.

Goodman, Nelson. 1979. "Afterthoughts on Metaphor." In *On Metaphor*, edited by Sheldon Sacks, 175–180. Chicago: University of Chicago Press.

Gordon, Scott. 1991. *The History and Philosophy of Social Science*. London: Routledge.

Grayling, A. C. 1998. *Philosophy 1: A Guide through the Subject*. Oxford: Oxford University Press.

Green, Donald P., and Ian Shapiro. 1994. *Pathologies of Rational Choice Theory: A Critique of Applications in Political Science*. New Haven, CT: Yale University Press.

Grice, H. Paul. 1989. "Logic and Conversation." In *Studies in the Way of Words*, 22–40. Cambridge, MA: Harvard University Press.

Grünbaum, Adolf. 2001. "The Poverty of Theistic Cosmology." In *Philosophy of Physics and Psychology: Essays in Honor of Adolf Grünbaum*, edited by A. Jokik, 159–234. Amherst: Prometheus Books.

Gustafson, Donald F. 1964. *Essays in Philosophical Psychology*. Garden City, NY: Anchor Books.

Gutmann, Amy, ed. 1992. *Multiculturalism: Examining the Politics of Recognition*. Princeton, NJ: Princeton University Press.

———. 2003. *Identity in Democracy*. Princeton, NJ: Princeton University Press.

Habermas, Jürgen. 1970. "Toward a Theory of Communicative Competence." In *Recent Sociology*, vol. 2, edited by Hans Dreitzel, 114–150. New York: Macmillan.

———. 1971. *Knowledge and Human Interests*. Boston: Beacon Press.

———. 1984. *The Theory of Communicative Action*. Boston: Beacon Press.

———. 1987. *The Philosophical Discourse of Modernity: Twelve Lectures*. Translated by Frederick Lawrence. Cambridge, MA: MIT Press.

Hampshire, Stuart. 1959. *Thought and Action*. London: Chatto and Windus.

———. 2000. *Justice Is Conflict*. Princeton, NJ: Princeton University Press.

Hardt, Michael, and Antonio Negri. 2000. *Empire*. Cambridge, MA: Harvard University Press.

———. 2004. *Multitude: War and Democracy in the Age of Empire*. New York: Penguin Press.

Hare, Alexander Paul. 1964. "Interpersonal Relations in the Small Group." In *Handbook of Modern Sociology*, edited by Robert E. L. Faris, 217–271. Chicago: Rand McNally.

Harney, Stefano. 1996. *Nationalism and Identity: Culture and the Imagination in a Caribbean Diaspora*. Atlantic Highlands, NJ: Zed Books.

Harvey, David. 1990. *The Condition of Postmodernity: An Enquiry into the Origins of Cultural Change*. Oxford: Blackwell.

———. 2005a. *A Brief History of Neoliberalism*. Oxford: Oxford University Press.

———. 2005b. *The New Imperialism*. Oxford: Oxford University Press.

Harvey, S., M. Hobson, D. Kelley, and Samuel B. Taylor, eds. 1980. *Reappraisals of Rousseau*. Manchester: Manchester University Press.

Hebb, D. O. 1949. *The Organization of Behavior*. New York: Wiley.

Hegel, Georg Wilhelm Friedrich. 1977. *Phenomenology of Spirit*. Translated by A. V. Miller. Oxford: Clarendon Press.

Heidegger, Martin. 1968. *What Is Called Thinking?* Translated by Fred D. Wieck and J. Glenn Gray. New York: Harper and Row.

———. 1975. *Poetry, Language, Thought*. Translated by Albert Hofstadter. New York: Perennial.

———. 2008. *Towards the Definition of Philosophy*. Translated by Ted Sadler. London: Athlone Press.

Heider, Fritz. 1958. *The Psychology of Interpersonal Relations*. New York: Wiley.

Horkheimer, Max, and Theodor W. Adorno. 1972. *Dialectic of Enlightenment*. New York: Herder and Herder.

Hornsby, Jennifer. 1980. *Actions*. London: Routledge and Kegan Paul.

Horowitz, Asher. 1987. *Rousseau, Nature, and History*. Toronto: University Press of Toronto.

Hovland, Carl Iver, Irving L. Janis, and Harold H. Kelley. 1953. *Communication and Persuasion; Psychological Studies of Opinion Change*. New Haven, CT: Yale University Press.

Huet, Marie-Hélène. 1993. *Monstrous Imagination*. Cambridge, MA: Harvard University Press.

Hulliung, Mark. 1994. *The Autocritique of Enlightenment: Rousseau and the Philosophes*. Cambridge, MA: Harvard University Press.

Hume, David. 1985. *Essays: Moral, Political, and Literary*. Edited by E. F. Miller, T. H. Green, and T. H. Grose. Indianapolis: Liberty Fund.

Inglis, David, and Roland Robertson. 2004. "Beyond the Gates of the Polis." *Journal of Classical Sociology* 4 (2): 165–189.

Iser, Wolfgang. 1993. *The Fictive and the Imaginary: Charting Literary Anthropology*. Baltimore: Johns Hopkins University Press.

Jameson, Fredric. 1992. *Postmodernism, or, The Cultural Logic of Late Capitalism*. Durham, NC: Duke University Press.

Jay, Paul. 1986. *Being in the Text: Self-Representation from Wordsworth to Roland Barthes*. Ithaca, NY: Cornell University Press.

Juris, Jeffrey S. 2008. *Networking Futures: The Movements Against Corporate Globalization*. Durham, NC: Duke University Press.

Kahneman, Daniel. 2011. *Thinking, Fast and Slow*. New York: Farrar, Straus and Giroux.

Keen, Suzanne. 2007. *Empathy and the Novel*. Oxford: Oxford University Press.

Kitcher, Philip. 2001. *Science, Truth, and Democracy*. Oxford: Oxford University Press.

Koestler, Arthur. 1964. *The Act of Creation*. New York: Macmillan.

Kuhn, Thomas S. (1962) 1970. *The Structure of Scientific Revolutions*. 2nd. ed. Chicago: University of Chicago Press.

Kuper, Adam. 1992. *Conceptualizing Society*. London; New York: Routledge.

Laclau, Ernesto, and Chantal Mouffe. 1985. *Hegemony and Socialist Strategy: Towards a Radical Democratic Politics*. London: Verso.

Lamont, Michèle. 2009. *How Professors Think: Inside the Curious World of Academic Judgment*. Cambridge, MA: Harvard University Press.

Lanser, Susan S. 1993. "Plot." In *The New Princeton Encyclopedia of Poetry and Poetics*, edited by Alex Preminger and T.V.F. Brogan, 916–918. Princeton, NJ: Princeton University Press.

Latour, Bruno. 1987. *Science in Action*. Cambridge, MA: Harvard University Press.

———. 2005. *Reassembling the Social: An Introduction to Actor-Network-Theory*. Oxford: Oxford University Press.

Lazarsfeld, Paul Felix. 1973. *Main Trends in Sociology*. New York: Harper and Row.

Lazarsfeld, Paul Felix, William Hamilton Sewell, and Harold L. Wilensky, eds.1967. *The Uses of Sociology*. New York: Basic Books.

Le Bon, Gustave. 1952. *The Crowd: A Study of the Popular Mind*. London: Ernest Benn.

Levi, Isaac. 1983. *The Enterprise of Knowledge: An Essay on Knowledge, Credal Probability, and Chance*. Cambridge, MA: MIT Press.

Lewin, Kurt. 1935. *A Dynamic Theory of Personality: Selected Papers*. New York: McGraw-Hill.

———. 1936. *Principles of Topological Psychology*. New York: McGraw-Hill.

Lombard, Lawrence Brian. 1986. *Events: A Metaphysical Study*. London: Routledge and Kegan Paul.

Lough, John. 1980. "The Encyclopédie and the Contrat Social." In *Reappraisals of Rousseau*, edited by S. Harvey, M. Hobson, D. Kelley, and Samuel B. Taylor, 61–74. Manchester: Manchester University Press.

Machlup, Fritz. 1994. "Are the Social Sciences Really Inferior?" In *Readings in the Philosophy of Social Science*, edited by Michael Martin and Lee C. McIntyre, 5–19. Cambridge, MA: MIT Press.

March, James G., and Herbert A. Simon. 1958. *Organizations*. New York: Wiley.

Martin, Michael, and Lee C. McIntyre. 1994. *Readings in the Philosophy of Social Science*. Cambridge, MA: MIT Press.

Martin, Randy. 1990. *Performance as Political Act: The Embodied Self*. New York: Bergin and Garvey.

———. 2002. *Financialization of Daily Life*. Philadelphia: Temple University Press.

Marx, Karl. 1967a. *Capital: A Critique of Political Economy*. Vol. 1. New York: International.

———. 1967b. *Capital: A Critique of Political Economy*. Vol. 2. New York: International.

———. 1967c. *Capital: A Critique of Political Economy*. Vol. 3. New York: International.

———. 1975. *Economic and Philosophic Manuscripts of 1844*. New York: International.

———. 1978. "Theses on Feuerbach." In *The Marx-Engels Reader*, edited by Robert Tucker, 143–145. New York: Norton.

———. 1979. *The Eighteenth Brumaire of Louis Bonaparte*. In *The Collected Works of Karl Marx and Friedrich Engels*, vol. 11, 99–197. New York: International.

———. 1990a. *Capital: A Critique of Political Economy*. Vol. 1. Translated by Ben Fowkes. New York: Penguin Books.

———. 1990b. *Capital: A Critique of Political Economy*. Vol. 2. Translated by David Fernbach. New York: Penguin Books.

———. 1990c. *Capital: A Critique of Political Economy*. Vol. 3. Translated by David Fernbach. New York: Penguin Books.

Marx, Karl, and Friedrich Engels. 1976. *The German Ideology*. Vol. 5 of *The Collected Works of Karl Marx and Friedrich Engels*. New York: International.

Masters, Roger D. 1968. *The Political Philosophy of Rousseau*. Princeton, NJ: Princeton University Press.

McCann, Hugh J. 1995. "Action." In *The Cambridge Dictionary of Philosophy*, edited by Robert Audi, 6–7. Cambridge: Cambridge University Press.

———. 1998. *The Works of Agency: On Human Action, Will, and Freedom*. Ithaca, NY: Cornell University Press.

McHugh, Peter. 1968. *Defining the Situation: The Organization of Meaning in Social Interaction*. Indianapolis: Bobbs-Merrill.

Mead, George H. 1962. *Mind, Self and Society*. Edited by Charles Morris. Chicago: University of Chicago Press.

Mele, Alfred R. 1987. *Irrationality: An Essay on Akrasia, Self-Deception, and Self-Control*. New York: Oxford University Press.

Merton, Robert K. 1957. *Social Theory and Social Structure*. Glencoe, IL: Free Press.

Milgram, Stanley. 1975. *Obedience to Authority: An Experimental View*. New York: HarperPerennial.

Mills, C. Wright. 1959. *The Sociological Imagination*. New York: Oxford University Press.

Montrose, Louis. 1992. "New Historicism." In *Redrawing the Boundaries: The Transformation of English and American Literary Studies*, edited by Stephen Greenblatt and Giles Gunn, 392–418. New York: Modern Language Association.

Morrison, Kristie. 1994. "The Self." In *A Companion to the Philosophy of Mind*, edited by Samuel Guttenplan, 550–558. Oxford: Blackwell.

Müller-Doohm, Stefan. 2005. *Adorno: A Biography*. Cambridge, UK: Polity Press.

Murphy, Liam B., and Thomas Nagel. 2002. *The Myth of Ownership: Taxes and Justice*. Oxford: Oxford University Press.

Nagel, Thomas. 1970. *The Possibility of Altruism*. Princeton, NJ: Princeton University Press.

———. 1991. *Equality and Partiality*. New York: Oxford University Press.

———. 1995. *Other Minds*. New York: Oxford University Press.

Nisbet, Robert A. 1965. *Émile Durkheim*. Englewood Cliffs, NJ: Prentice-Hall.

———. 1994. "Society." In *The Blackwell Dictionary of Twentieth-Century Social Thought*, edited by William Outhwaite and Tom Bottomore, 626–628. Oxford: Blackwell.

Nozick, Robert. 1993. *The Nature of Rationality*. Princeton, NJ: Princeton University Press.

Ollman, Bertell. 1993. *Dialectical Investigations*. New York: Routledge.

———. 2003. *Dance of the Dialectic: Steps in Marx's Method*. Urbana: University of Illinois Press.

Olson, Mancur. 1971. *The Logic of Collective Action*. Cambridge, MA: Harvard University Press.

Parsons, Talcott. 1949. *The Structure of Social Action*. Glencoe, IL: Free Press.

———. 1951. *The Social System*. Glencoe, IL: Free Press.

———. 1954. *Essays in Sociological Theory*. Glencoe, IL: Free Press.

———. 1968. "The Academic System: A Sociologist's View." *Public Interest* 13 (Fall): 173–197.

———. 1977. *The Evolution of Societies*. Englewood Cliff, NJ: Prentice-Hall.

Peacocke, Christopher. 2000. "Précis of *A Study of Concepts*." In *Concepts*, edited by Eric Margolis and Stephen Laurence, 335–338. Cambridge, MA: MIT Press.

Pears, David, ed. 1957. *The Nature of Metaphysics*. London: Macmillan.

Perry, John. 1994. "Intentionality." In *A Companion to the Philosophy of Mind*, edited by Samuel Guttenplan, 379–395. Oxford: Blackwell.

Popper, Karl R. 1957. *The Poverty of Historicism*. New York: Basic Books.

Preminger, Alex, and T.V.F. Brogan, eds. 1993. *The New Princeton Encyclopedia of Poetry and Poetics*. Princeton, NJ: Princeton University Press.

Putnam, Hilary. 1992. *Renewing Philosophy*. Cambridge, MA: Harvard University Press.

———. 2002. *The Collapse of the Fact/Value Dichotomy and Other Essays*. Cambridge, MA: Harvard University Press.

Quine, W. V., and J. S. Ullian. 1970. *The Web of Belief.* New York: Random House.

Raffman, Diana. 1993. *Language, Music, and Mind.* Cambridge, MA: MIT Press.

Ramsey, Paul. 1993. "Society and Poetry." In *The New Princeton Encyclopedia of Poetry and Poetics*, edited by Alex Preminger and T.V.F. Brogan, 1160–1164. Princeton, NJ: Princeton University Press.

Rawls, Anne Warfield, ed. 2002. "Editor's Introduction." In *Ethnomethodology's Program: Working Out Durkeim's Aphorism*, by Harold Garfinkel, 1–64. Lanham, MD: Rowman and Littlefield.

Rawls, John. 1971. *A Theory of Justice.* Cambridge, MA: Belknap Press of Harvard University Press.

———. 1996. *Political Liberalism.* New York: Columbia University Press.

———. 1999a. *The Law of Peoples.* Cambridge, MA: Harvard University Press.

———. 1999b. "Two Concepts of Rules." In *Collected Papers*, edited by Samuel Richard Freeman, 20–46. Cambridge, MA: Harvard University Press.

———. 2007. *Lectures on the History of Political Philosophy.* Edited by Samuel Richard Freeman. Cambridge, MA: Harvard University Press.

Rawls, John, and Samuel Richard Freeman. 1999. *Collected Papers.* Cambridge, MA: Harvard University Press.

Rawls, John, and Thomas Nagel. 2009. *A Brief Inquiry into the Meaning of Sin and Faith: With "On My Religion."* Cambridge, MA: Harvard University Press.

Raz, Joseph. 1997. "Incommensurability and Agency." In *Incommensurability, Incomparability, and Practical Reason*, edited by Ruth Chang, 110–128. Cambridge, MA: Harvard University Press.

Rescher, Nicholas. 1996. *Process Metaphysics: An Introduction to Process Philosophy.* Albany: State University of New York Press.

———. 1998. *Complexity: A Philosophical Overview.* New Brunswick, NJ: Transaction.

Riffaterre, Michael. 1990. *Fictional Truth.* Baltimore: Johns Hopkins University Press.

Roethlisberger, F. J., W. J. Dickson, and Harold A. Wright. 1946. *Management and the Worker: An Account of a Research Program Conducted by the Western Electric Company, Hawthorne Works, Chicago.* Cambridge, MA: Harvard University Press.

Rosenberg, Alexander. 1985. "Human Science and Biological Science: Defects and Prospects." In *Reason and Rationality in Natural Science: A Group of Essays*, edited by Nicholas Rescher, 37–51. Lanham, MD: University Press of America.

Ross, Dorothy. 1991. *The Origins of American Social Science.* Cambridge: Cambridge University Press.

Rousseau, Jean-Jacques. 1964. *The First and Second Discourses.* Translated by Roger D. Masters and Judith R. Masters. New York: St. Martin's Press.

———. 1974. *The Social Contract; or, Principles of Political Right.* Translated by Charles M. Sherover. New York: New American Library.

———. 1978a. "Geneva Manuscript." In *On the Social Contract, with Geneva Manuscript and Political Economy*, translated by Judith R. Masters, edited by Roger D. Masters, 157–208. New York: St. Martin's Press.

———. 1978b. *The Social Contract.* In *On the Social Contract, with Geneva Manuscript and Political Economy*, translated by Judith R. Masters, edited by Roger D. Masters, 41–156. New York: St. Martin's Press.

———. 1992. *Du Contrat Social.* Paris: GK-Flammarion.

———. 1997. *The Discourses and Other Early Political Writings.* Translated and edited by Victor Gourevitch. Cambridge: Cambridge University Press.

Ruben, D. H. 1985. *Metaphysics of the Social World.* London: Routledge and Kegan Paul.

Russell, Bertrand. 1974. Introduction to *Tractatus Logico-Philosophicus*, by Ludwig Wittgenstein, ix–xxii. Atlantic Highlands, NJ: Humanities Press.

Sacks, Harvey. 1974. "An Analysis of the Course of a Joke's Telling in Conversation." In *Explorations in the Ethnography of Speaking*, edited by Richard Bauman and Joel Sherzer, 337–353. Cambridge: Cambridge University Press.

Said, Edward W. 1979. "Zionism from the Standpoint of Its Victims." *Social Text* (1): 7–58.

Sandel, Michael J. 1998. *Liberalism and the Limits of Justice*. 2nd ed. Cambridge: Cambridge University Press.

Sartre, Jean-Paul. 1947. *"No Exit" and "The Flies."* Translated by Stuart Gilbert. New York: A. A. Knopf.

———. 1963. *Saint Genet, Actor and Martyr*. New York: New American Library.

———. 1976. *Critique of Dialectical Reason*. Atlantic Highlands, NJ: Humanities Press.

———. 1988. *"What Is Literature?" and Other Essays*. Cambridge, MA: Harvard University Press.

———. 1992. *Truth and Existence*. Chicago: University of Chicago Press.

Saussure, Ferdinand de. 1986. *Course in General Linguistics*. Edited by Charles Bally and Albert Seshehaye. Translated by Roy Harris. La Salle, IL: Open Court.

Schmidtz, David. 1995. *Rational Choice and Moral Agency*. Princeton, NJ: Princeton University Press.

Schutz, Alfred. 1962. "Common-sense and Scientific Interpretation of Human Action." In *The Problem of Social Reality*. Vol. 1 of *Collected Papers*, edited by Maurice Natanson, 3–47. The Hague: Martinus Nijhoff.

———. 1967. *The Phenomenology of the Social World*. Translated by G. Walsh. Evanston, IL: Northwestern University Press.

———. 1970. *Reflections on the Problem of Relevance*. Edited by Richard Zaner. New Haven, CT: Yale University Press.

Searle, John. 1969. *Speech Acts: An Essay in the Philosophy of Language*. London: Cambridge University Press.

———. 1971. "What Is a Speech Act?" In *Philosophy of Language*, edited by John R. Searle, 39–53. Oxford: Oxford University Press.

———. 1984. *Minds, Brains, and Science*. Cambridge, MA: Harvard University Press.

———. 1994. *The Rediscovery of the Mind*. Cambridge, MA: MIT Press.

———. 1995. *The Construction of Social Reality*. New York: Free Press.

———. 2001. *Rationality in Action*. Cambridge, MA: MIT Press.

Searle, John R., Daniel Clement Dennett, and David John Chalmers. 1997. *The Mystery of Consciousness*. New York: New York Review of Books.

Sen, Amartya. 2002. *Rationality and Freedom*. Cambridge, MA: Harvard University Press.

Sheehan, James J. 1991. "Coda." In *The Boundaries of Humanity*, edited by Stephan Sosna and Morton Sosna, 259–265. Berkeley: University of California Press.

Sherover, Charles M., ed. 1974. Preface to *The Social Contract; or, Principles of Political Right*, by Jean-Jacques Rousseau. New York: New American Library.

Shoemaker, Sidney, and Richard Swinburne. 1984. *Personal Identity*. Oxford: Blackwell.

Shwayder, D. S. 1965. *The Stratification of Behaviour: A System of Definitions Propounded and Defended*. New York: Humanities Press.

Sica, Alan, ed. 1998. *What Is Social Theory?* Cambridge, MA: Blackwell.

Simmel, Georg, and Kurt H. Wolff. 1950. *The Sociology of Georg Simmel*. Glencoe, IL: Free Press.

Simon, Herbert. 1990. *Reason in Human Affairs*. Stanford, CA: Stanford University Press.

Smelser, Neil J. 1963. *Theory of Collective Behavior*. New York: Free Press of Glencoe.

Soames, Scott. 2003. *Philosophical Analysis in the Twentieth Century*. Princeton, NJ: Princeton University Press.

Sokal, Alan D., and J. Bricmont. 1998. *Fashionable Nonsense: Postmodern Intellectuals' Abuse of Science*. New York: Picador USA.

Sontag, Susan. 2003. *Regarding the Pain of Others*. New York: Picador.

Sosa, Ernest. 1995. "Condition." In *The Cambridge Dictionary of Philosophy*, edited by Robert Audi, 149. Cambridge: University of Cambridge Press.

Spivak, Gayatri Chakravorty. 1987. *In Other Worlds: Essays in Cultural Politics*. New York: Methuen.

Spurlin, Paul Merrill. 1969. *Rousseau in America, 1760–1809*. University: University of Alabama Press.

Starobinski, Jean. 1988. *Jean-Jacques Rousseau: Transparency and Obstruction*. Chicago: University of Chicago Press.

Stiglitz, Joseph E. 2010. *Freefall: America, Free Markets, and the Sinking of the World Economy*. New York: Norton.

Strawson, P. F. 1992. *Analysis and Metaphysics: An Introduction to Philosophy*. Oxford: Oxford University Press.

Sturgeon, Scott. 1988. "Maximalism and Mental Processes." *Philosophical Studies* 53 (2): 309–314.

Sudnow, David. 1961. *Passing On*. Englewood Cliffs, NJ: Prentice-Hall.

Sukhov, Michael J. 2007. "Political Activism and Deferred Agency." Ph. D. diss. in *Sociology*. New York: City University of New York.

Taylor, Charles. 1964. *The Explanation of Behavior*. London: Routledge and Kegan Paul.

———. 1985a. *Interpretation and the Sciences of Man*. Cambridge: Cambridge University Press.

———. 1985b. *Language and Human Nature*. Cambridge: Cambridge University Press.

Tucker, Robert C., ed. 1978. *The Marx-Engels Reader*. New York: Norton.

Turner, Ralph. 1964. "Collective Behavior." In *Handbook of Modern Sociology*, edited by R.E.L. Faris, 382–425. Chicago: Rand McNally.

Urmson, J. O. 1956. *Philosophical Analysis: Its Development between the Two World Wars*. Oxford: Clarendon Press.

Urry, John. 2000. *Sociology Beyond Societies: Mobilities for the Twenty-First Century*. London: Routledge.

Veeser, H. Aram. 1989. *The New Historicism*. New York: Routledge.

Von Wright, Georg Henrik. 1971. *Explanation and Understanding*. London: Routledge and Kegan Paul.

Weber, Max. 1947. *The Theory of Social and Economic Organization*. Glencoe, IL: Free Press.

West, David. 1995. "The Contribution of Continental Philosophy." In *A Companion to Contemporary Political Philosophy*, edited by Robert E. Goodin and Philip Pettit, 39–71. Oxford: Blackwell.

Williams, Bernard. 1973. *Problems of the Self*. Cambridge, MA: Cambridge University Press.

Williams, Raymond. 1977. *Marxism and Literature*. Oxford: Oxford University Press.

Wilson, Brian, ed. 1970. *Rationality*. Oxford: Blackwell.

Winch, Peter. (1958) 1990. *The Idea of a Social Science and Its Relation to Philosophy*. London: Routledge.

Wittgenstein, Ludwig. 1974. *Tractatus Logico-Philosophicus.* Translated by D. F. Pears and B. F. McGuinness. Atlantic Highlands, NJ: Humanities Press.

Wollheim, Richard. 1960. *F.H. Bradley.* Harmondsworth, UK: Penguin.

Yeats, William Butler. (1927) 1996. "Among School Children." In *The Collected Poems of W. B. Yeats.* New York: Simon and Schuster.

Žižek, Slavoj. 2001. *Did Somebody Say Totalitarianism?* London: Verso.

Index

Ability knowledge, 457n11
Absolutism, 371
Abstract labor, 125, 165
Acceptable and unacceptable risks, 359
Acquaintance knowledge, 457n11
Act: defined, 218, 229; as socially reflexive, 76
Acting social versus being social, 38
Action(s), 8, 63, 206, 227; versus activity, 253;
agency in, 258; as alternative to course of
activity, 241; as automatic executive operation, 328; based on a self, 239, 242–243,
246; as behavior with reasons, 72, 239, 336;
bounded by a situation, 239; changing in its
course, 230; as class of events, 239; concept
of agency in, 240; confusion in language
describing, 484–485n1; contexts of, 112;
and "course of activity," 11, 38, 68, 300, 331,
385; criticism of, 243–244; as elements of a
practice, 353; Emmet on, 210–212; as event,
8, 38; excluding the self, 250; external conditions and agency in, 332; as function of its
situation, 234; and intentionality, 212, 227,
246, 329; as labor undertaken, 184; location
of, 331; McCann on, 248, 482–483n4; mediated by beliefs and desires, 38; and mental
state, 330; Nagel sustaining standard theory
of, 63; ontology of, 243, 258–259, 262–263;
as a particular, 95; performed versus to
be performed, 477–478n6; possibility of
combining, 239; rationalist model of, 391;
relationship between mind and, 212; as

rule-directed, 211; as social, 384; sub-theoretical sense of, 247; theoretical problems
with, 256, 421; utilitarian model of, 333–334;
what is human about, 329. See also Theories
of action
Active subjectivity ("ego"), 183
Activity: versus action, 253; of going to work,
368; organized by practices, 356; and practice, 372; reproducing its own principle, 18;
resistant to objectification and reduction,
258; self-transformation of, 331; subjectivity
and objectivity in, 253
Actor-Network-Theory, 111
Actor(s): as agent, 220, 274; as calculating devices, 273; conceptions and representations
of, 219–220; distinguishing existence from
undertaking, 263; hidden properties of, 387;
in last person scenario, 272; motivational
states of, 256; as preset mechanism, 328;
providing motivational value to, 276; and
situation, 271; taking account of others, 275–
279; and temporality, 242, 256; as transcendent across situations, 256–257
Addis, Laird, 451n1, 460–461n8
Administration, 295–296
Adorno, Theodor, 122
Affairs, human affairs as, 12
Agency, 112, 240, 247; and action, 66, 112, 184,
210, 329; and actor, 220; agents as situated
beings, 351; and altruism, 68, 73; in ball
being kicked in a game, 153; continuing

Agency (*continued*)
  beyond act, 184; as feature of its situation,
  253; formless, 105; ideas associated with, 56;
  and individuality, 64, 103; McCann on, 240,
  332; objects implicating, 299; organizational
  model and, 124; political theories of, 38; in
  primitive animals, 272; properties of, 329; as
  property of being human, 273; questions of
  meaning of, 116; realizing, 184–185; recognizing, in others, 185; reconciling self with,
  253; as reflexive throughout course of action, 229; requiring a conscious actor, 256;
  rethinking, 247; skin as natural boundary
  of, 63–64, 293; and sociality, 25, 110, 167;
  studying reality independent of, 320; subjectivity within, 109; trans-situational, 226;
  validity of, as concept, 334
Agency-dependent objects, 8, 18, 433; action
  and, 334; and act of being observed, 347;
  and "apprehension of their object," 338; and
  attitude of waiting, 340; and contradiction
  in human sciences, 119, 334, 421; definitions of, 323, 336; as events, 469n3; in human sciences, 320, 323–324, 375, 377–378,
  456n8; implied by the social, 433, 434–436;
  and inter-subjectivity, 300, 375, 383, 414,
  418, 420–421; and language, 321; may or
  may not be persons, 413; money as, 322; no
  complete knowledge of, 332; not a property,
  337; persons must be, 437; and reliability of
  observation, 318; "situation" and, 323, 341,
  346; subjective objectivity of, 370; and sub-
  theoretical region of being, 146; utterances
  and gestures as, 424
Agency-independent objects, 8, 328, 334; human sciences and, 157, 163, 298–299, 313; as
  life of a concept, 141; as objects of experience, 413–415, 420; observation of, 316–318;
  sciences engaged with, 319–320, 377, 383,
  456–457n10; "situation" and, 323; as things,
  not beings, 183
Agreement: in Blank experiment, 415–419; and
  communication, 419; as meeting of minds,
  59; versus sharing, 147; society founded on,
  356
Akratic action, 477–478n6
Alertness, 230
Allport, Floyd H., 97, 393, 479n13
"Alter," 183, 276, 279
Altruism: and agency, 73; and choice, 72; extended theories on, 69; and individualism,
  67–69; manifesting social in regard to itself,
  69; Nagel on, 57, 62–64, 68–71, 236, 242,

247, 282, 336, 446–447n7; no gap between
  perception of need and action in, 62–63; and
  parties to courses of activity, 68; requiring
  personal motivation, 72; and social action,
  66; subject and object interchangeable in, 63;
  by a third party, 67
Ambiguity: inevitability of, 12; in social rela-
  tions, 415; in speaking, 404; in theorizing,
  131
Analytic philosophy, 482n9
Anderson, Perry, 461n10
Animate subject versus inert objects, 188–190
Anticipation, 124, 230
Anti-discursive other, 326–327
Aporias, 10–11
Apprehension: and apprehensive subjectivity,
  413–414; grasping as, 421; of a speech act,
  423. *See also* Attitude of waiting
Approval and the self, 265
Art: connoisseurs of, 405; as other, 103–104;
  and sense of world, 336
Assertoric content, 485–486n3
Associated self, 86–87
Association, 282
"As things stand," 9, 16, 113, 174, 303
Attitude of waiting, 297; and altruism, 74; collective enunciation and, 396, 399; complexity and, 274; as cooperative by nature, 340;
  in discursive speech, 16, 173, 424, 426; and
  "finding of ourselves," 94; in interpreting
  contradictory statements, 119; inward focus
  of, 340–341; not a choice or option, 345;
  participation as, 112; and shifts in perspective, 274; situated objects and, 340; theorizing operating in an, 143; toward others in
  general, 294
Attributable and self-asserted identities, 325
Authority and power/force, 25, 35, 50
Axiomatization, de facto, 288

Bakhtin, Mikhail: on dialogue and monologue,
  11, 404–406; on discourse, 404; on "heteroglossia," 396, 401–402, 404; *Rabelais and His
  World*, 395; "The Theory of the Novel," 395
Balance theory, 415
Ball games, 153, 381
Basic fact of sociality, 33, 76; altruism and, 68;
  best level for approaching, 79–80; as falsifiable, 53; historic and anti-historic responses
  to, 154–155; in history and experience, 50;
  if explicit, 43–44; and individualism, 409;
  as instantaneous, inerrant knowledge, 52,
  54; as necessary to rationality of decisions,

46; no imaginable alternative to, 47; not a justified belief, 90; only confirming evidence for, 473; refusing to acknowledge, 100, 105; Rousseau's statements on, 36, 53–54; as true for all practical purposes, 48; as true for historicists and anti-historicists, 165; utilitarianism and, 57–58; and valid expression of equality, 59; Weber and, 270. *See also* Social, the

Beautiful, the, 379

Behaviorism, 214

"Being in a situation," 347, 351; "being human" as equivalent to, 175, 383; positive model and, 333; resistance and, 325; Sartre on, 75, 483n9; and situated objects, 336; and what is human about human affairs, 380–383, 398, 409

Being *of* society, 60

Being together: and doing together, 16; and equality of dependence, 16; and sociality as contingent, 48–49

Belief/believing: as a function of language, 29–30; immediate sense of, 73; progressing to sense of obligation, 40–42, 73–74

Benefit of the doubt, 119

Berger, Peter, 356–357

Bhabha, Homi, 105

Bias, 39, 117, 314–319

Bio-power, 105

Black, Max: on metaphorical statements, 452n7, 463n4; and paradigm case, 128; on reconciling rationality and sociality, 451n14; response of, to Parsons, 461–462n12

Blame and the self, 265

Blank, Arthur E., 416–419

Body as machinery, 330

Boundaries, 99, 291, 353

Bounded rationality, 316, 478n7, 480n2

Bradley, F. H., 454–455n2

Brodbeck, May, 461–462n12

Brunswik, Egon, 455n2

Cabinetmaking, 182

Cain, William, 446n1

Capital, 109; Marx's critique of, 25, 101, 108–110, 217; "real subsumption" of labor by, 106

Carroll, Lewis, 126

Cartesian thought, 473n9, 473n2

Cassirer, Ernst, 287

Castoriadis, Cornelius, 114

Categorical collections, 30

Causal picture, 122, 249

Certainty, sharing of, 74

Chair as object with history, 459n6

Chess, 489n13

Circulation, 217; of fictitious capital, 110, 217; of money or meaning, 322; of needs, 68; of signs/signifiers, 9–10, 448–449n1, 474–475n4; as universal exchange, 105; of value, 381, 399, 450n8

Citizenship, 46, 88

Civilization(s): as arbitrary entity, 164; as authoritarian value, 166; as human form of life, 405; war of, 94

Civil processes, 215

Civil unrest, study of, 203

Claims of need and merit, 166

Cohen, Morris R., 452n7, 468n14

Collateral damage, 93

Collective behavior: contrasted with collective action, 215; deemed institutionally deviant, 98, 198, 203, 296, 466n9; and equality, 59–60; in exchange model, 216; and intentionality, 491–492n6; organizational model of, 124–125

Collective enunciation, 389, 399; conversation and, 395, 409; discourse and, 403, 430–431, 434–437; and experience of speaking, 410–412, 425, 427–428; as "heteroglossia," 396, 401; "I do" as, 364; and intentionality, 424; listeners and, 425; and meaningfulness, 422, 427, 430; monologue mistaken for, 405–406; and "off the surface" objects, 417; and reflexivity, 422, 434; as socializing course of activity, 428, 430; and socially productive work, 401; and speaking conversationally, 395; and utterances engaging utterances, 427; and value of discursive speech, 430; violations of, 426; waiting and, 396

Collective laborers, 109

Collective reflection, 322, 378

Collective terms, 461–462n12

Collingwood, R. G., 475–476n7

Coming to terms, 198

Commitment: as actively passive, 144; facilitating self-criticism, 145; relying on connection, not reasons, 41; sudden recovery of, 140; within theorizing, 128–130, 132, 141–142

Common, the, 186

Communication: and agreement, 419; distorted, 456–457n10; linguistic, 423–426, 429, 493n4; and meetings of minds, 441n3; as network, 493n5; and order of presentation, 493n5; possibilities of, 467n11, 482n2; speech and, 321, 427–429

Community: and norms, 260; realizing itself, 295; versus society, 1; weak conception of, 204

Complexity in social sciences, 302, 472n7; accessing progress, 306–307, 310; addressing defects arising from, 313–314; and attitude of waiting, 274; and choice of research topics, 311–312; distinguishing nature and culture, 304; as an epistemological problem, 305; historiography, 304–305, 309; human affairs and theorizing, 303; and immaturity issue, 318–319; methodological remedy for, 313; normalizing remedy for, 313; and objective conditions of knowledge, 308; observer and observed issue, 314–318; and predictive power, 305–306; as progressively disunifying differentiation, 305; relativism in evaluating, 308; Rescher and, 480n2; research situation and, 311–312; and validity, 308–309, 311, 312–313

Composition, 402, 404

"Comprehensive doctrines," 117

Concept, life of the, 132–133, 135–136, 141

Concept of circulation, 217

Concepts of democracy and of society independent, 3

Concern for self, 27–28

Concrete, social as, 67

Concrete labor, 125, 165

Concretely situated action: decisions, 233; problems with standard idea of, 240–242, 257; relation of, to self/actor, 238–239, 248, 257; as time-bound, 472–473n8

Conditions: of change, 271; of rational action, 352; of trust and mutuality in discourse, 36–37

Confidence in findings, 314–318

Conjuncture, 83–84

Connoisseurs of art, 405

Consciousness: across bodies, 456n8; as conscious of itself, 91; general structure of, 230; impersonal aspect of, 63; as irreducible and ultimate, 287; Marx and, 460n6; Searle on, 155–156; in sociology, 111; and statements as substantiating a universe of reference, 121

Consensus in practice, 356

Conservative political discourse, 93–94

Consociation, 107, 449–450n6

Constitutively situated beings, 50

Constitutive rules, 353–354

Content of thought (objectivity), 316

Contingency, 123, 149, 249–250, 279, 336, 401

Contradiction(s): and experience of solidarity, 39; of fictitious capital and producers, 449n4; of intelligible and valid sentences,

119; motivation and, 25; between "presence" and "attribution," 414; response to, 150, 175, 190; of "sense certainty," 295; of skin as natural boundary and activity across bodies, 150–152; between sociality and self-sufficient subject continuity, 56; of theory within course of theorizing, 136–137, 300–301; tragic, 15, 85, 103, 132, 161, 414

"Convention" in *Social Contract. See* First convention (Rousseau)

Conversational discourse, 344, 409–412

Conversational implicature, 400

Cooley, C. H., 107

Cooper, Melinda, 443n6

Cooperation, 381–383

Corporate form, 296

Corporate groups, 147

Cottingham, John, 473n9, 473n2

Course(s) of activity, 17–18; agency-dependent reality and, 323–324; cessation of, 77; communication as, 25; in contrast to action, 293, 327; critical knowledge and, 378; encounters between, 337; linguistic communities as, 121; mind and, 330; negation of, 165; not an event, 8; not a particular, 96; object-oriented, 419; occasion as aspect of, 368–369; orientation implying, 270; parts of sociality as, 291; as practice, 370; as process, 398; and promising, 366–367; resistance as normal expression of, 18; situated objects within, 335, 339; sociality as, 18, 42, 50, 293, 297; sociality theorizing as, 166; speech as, 13–14, 425; subjectivity from within, 334–335; and subject/object distinction, 288; and timeless reasons, 68; Weber and, 270; and within/without distinction, 17–18

Critical historiography, 116

Critical knowledge, 378

Critical literary studies and social theory, 122

Critical self-reflection. *See* Self-critical reflection

Criticism, 379; and agency-dependent knowledge, 323; versus critique, 378; and human affairs, 383, 384; and knowledge, 8; legitimacy of, 379; not a type of action, 301; proper use and timing of, 243–245

Critique: of capital (Marx), 101, 108–110, 217; versus criticism, 378; of the human sciences, 288, 303, 318–319; of materialism (Marx), 101–102, 181–182; of Nagel, 433; of political economy (Marx), 140; of Searle, 434. *See also* Social contract narrative of Rousseau

Critique of Dialectical Reason (Sartre), 1

Cross-sectional analysis, 116

Crowds, 466n8

Cultural studies, 116
Culture as opposed to nature, 8, 117
"Culturological," humanities as, 298–299
Custom, 287

Davidson, Donald, 105, 111, 177–178, 329; on
   agency and rational action, 329; on Collingwood, 475–476n7; on mental states, 482n2;
   and metaphorical sentences, 462–463n2,
   463n4; on normative element in thought,
   470n1; on person as physical object that
   learns, 237; on philosophies of action, 105;
   on propositional thought requiring communication, 260, 271; and rationalization, 463–
   464n5; on society of minds, 475–476n7; and
   theory presupposing social, 111; triangulation concept of, 177–178, 442n1; use of term
   "knowledge," 459n2; "What Is Present to
   the Mind?," 475n5
Dawkins, Richard, 156
Death: and friendship, 108; of a loved one, 107
Debate. *See* Dispute/debate
Decision(s): decisiveness without consensus,
   16; justness of, 42; theories of the firm, 216
Deliberation, 328
De Man, Paul: on allegory, 447–448n7; on ideology, 448–449n1; *The Resistance to Theory*,
   134, 461n10; on state of nature, 442–443n4
Democracy: effect of Rousseau on, 96; as possible only within society, 3
Dependence: of each on all, 60; as suggesting
   contingency, 336
Derrida, Jacques, 106–108, 125, 397; on death
   of a loved one, 107–108; on dialectics, 479n2;
   on Marxism, 448–449n1; on meaning as
   always deferred, 397; on "play of structure,"
   125, 469n3; *Politics of Friendship*, 461n10; on
   problems of modernity, 106; response of, to
   Searle, 464n2; on Rousseau, 442n2
De-situating, 365
Dialectics: as issue in humanities, 116; and
   production of theory, 291–292; Sartre on,
   290; of vanishing, 419–420
Dialogue versus monologue, 395, 402, 404
Dickens, Charles, 395
Difficulty, 480n2
Discipline(s): authentic knowledge of, 312;
   versus development of knowledge, 312; and
   naturalist philosophy, 311; recent projects
   within, 215–217; social sciences and identity
   as, 311; as "what its practitioners do," 164.
   See also Human sciences; Social sciences
Discourse/discursive speech, 8, 366, 410, 425;
   as collective enunciation, 434–436; as col-

lective phenomenon, 15; and desire for finality, 13; discursive other, 326–327; elision of
   social grounds of, 14; endlessness of, 13, 17,
   43–44, 46; external ordering function to,
   14; and general will, 399; making designations rigid, 325; meaningfulness of, 430;
   method of modeling, 15–16; as moments of
   courses of activity, 425; operating within,
   9; permissiveness of, 396; political, 325; and
   possibility of futility, 14; premature closure
   in, 44; presupposing subjectivity, 323; as
   property of group self, 326; pursuing its own
   possibility, 322; Russell and, 320–321; silence
   of social during, 39–40; speech in contrast
   to language, 13; as subjectivity, 16; and
   theorizing, 291; voice and, 406–407. *See also*
   Ultimate referent of moral discourse
Discovery: versus justification, 165–166; of
   meaning, 321
Disposition, 28
Dispute/debate: beliefs and obligations within,
   40–43; fact of sociality prior to, 37; and im-
   manence of the social, 39–40; individualism
   raising inexpressible doubts, 39–40; losers
   accepting legitimacy of result, 40, 43; ques-
   tions of trust within, 44; separating content
   from sincerity/trustworthiness of parties, 36
Distributed sensibility, 77–79
Distributive justice, 171
Division and self-generation, 327–328
Dogmatism, 405
Doing together and being together, 16
Dostoevsky, Fyodor, 395
Doubt. *See* Insecurity/doubt
Douglas, Mary, 204, 460n7, 470–471n2
Downie, R. S., 470–471n2
Dretske, Fred, 468n13, 471–472n6, 484–485n1
Dualism in everyday life, 393
Dummett, Michael, 485–486n3, 492n7
Durkheim, Émile: on every individual as an
   infinity, 303, 481n4; on moral basis of law,
   172; on "organic" and "mechanical" solidari-
   ties, 294, 443n6; on rules of sociological
   method, 97, 307; on social facts, 8, 49, 111,
   353, 446n5, 480–481n3; on societal complexity, 480–481n3; on society as autonomous form of life, 287; on state of nature,
   442–443n4

Each: choosing/working for all, 79, 84; depend-
   ing on all, 60, 94, 96; as a "singularity," 94
Economics, 298. *See also* Capital
Ego, 183, 276, 278–279
Elderly, acts of deference to, 197

Elision(s), 5, 441n1; of concept of social, 10, 15, 43, 205–206; do not qualify sociality concept, 198

Elster, Jon, 478n7

Emergent norms in discourse, 14

Emmet, Dorothy Mary: on characteristic actions of people, 260; as moderate historicist, 457–458n13; on pure and autonomous self, 236; on the social, 209–212, 464–465n3

Empathy, 82, 384, 398

Empirical research: emphasis on, 312; weaknesses in, 289. *See also* Human sciences; Social sciences

Empirical truth, evolution in direction of, 317

Enacted knowledge, 60–61

Endlessness of discourse, 13, 17, 43–44, 46

Enlightenment and the "body politic," 106

Epistemic unboundedness, 458n3

Equality: of dependence, 16, 60; only recalled collectively, 59; Rousseau's use of, 58; sense of, versus belief in, 60

Essential differentiation, 324

Essentiality, 174

Evans-Pritchard, E. E., 470–471n2

Everyday life, 109, 392–393

Evidence, interpretation of, 385

Evolution of knowledge, 317

Exchange model(s): commercial, 216; and concept of circulation, 217; concept of social in, 127; of discourse, 16, 37, 114

Exclusionism, 94, 139–140, 173

Exigency and momentum, 145–146

Experience: objects of, 413–414, 420, 429; of the social, 39; of a speaker, 410–412; and subjectivity, 334, 337, 391; units of, 362

Expression versus idea, 116

"Face-to-face interaction," 295

Fact: personal and social, 211; versus value, 297

Families of nameable entities, 287

Feuerbach, Ludwig, 101–102, 181–182

"Fictional truth," 462–463n2

Finality, desire in discourse for, 13

Findings, acceptance of, 314

First convention (Rousseau), 31–32; and basic fact of sociality, 432; benefits/value derived from, 87–88, 120; conditions leading up to, 55, 81; as course of activity, 399, 419; dissatisfaction leading to, 56; explaining continued association after, 83, 87; literal interpretation of, 27–28, 55, 86–89; as moment of unanimity, 56; Rousseau's descriptions of, 53–54; as social fact(s), 448n8. *See also* Social contract narrative of Rousseau

Fish, Stanley, 446n1

Fixity of things, 415

Fodor, Jerry, 458n3

Folk psychology, 214, 274, 318

Football, agency in a game of, 153

Forces, balance of, 281

Foster, John, 473n9

Foucault, Michel: on governmentality, 54, 407; on madness and art, 103–105, 336; on neoliberalism, 466–467n10

Frames of reference, 119, 153, 165, 261

Freedom: adversarial conceptions of, 94; defining, 104; law expressing, 86; and particular wills, 92; providing security while retaining, 80, 81; as recognizably human, 91; and rule of law, 24

Freud, Sigmund, 279, 304

Friendship, 116

Funded research, emphasis on, 311

"Gain," Rousseau's use of, 88

Gallie, W. B., 453–454n10

Game-related satisfaction, 46

Games, 153, 370, 372, 381

Gap(s) between reasons and undertakings, 225–226, 231–232; accumulation of, 248; filled by self, 234, 246, 255, 261, 267, 432–433; metaphors and, 254; and rethinking of action and agency, 251; in theory of action, 259, 350

Garfinkel, Harold: and accountability, 491n5; on conversational "work," 445n10; on discourse, 441n3; on living and doing together, 11, 195; and moving from outside inward, 457–458n13; and ongoing accomplishments, 253, 274; and value determination, 477n3

Gehlke, Charles Elmer, 448n9

Generalization of expectations, 211

Generalized other, 282, 394, 465n4

General will, 47; confusion over, 23; as immanent feature of society, 85–86; individuals and, 106; indivisibility of, 16, 339; maintaining the, 84; as meaningfulness, 399; not defined by number or ratio, 16; and relation to particularity, 85; waiting as expression of, 340

"Geneva Manuscript," 80, 443n5, 447n5

The German Ideology (Marx and Engels), 102

Gilbert, Margaret, 111, 456n8

Goffman, Erving, 455–456n3; axiomatic propositions advanced by, 175–176; on dilemmas of social identity, 454n12; on discursively determined subjectification, 325; on moments and persons, 235; and moving from outside inward, 457–458n13; on participation in speech, 404; on self-contextualizing of occasion, 367; on social identity, 231; on sociality as self-reflective entity, 326; on spoiled identity, 326; on "stigma," 441n3; and "tension management," 325; use of term "social identity," 470n6

"Going beyond," 331

Going to the movies, 368

Goodman, Nelson, 462–463n2

Gordon, Scott, 117

Government, proper sphere of, 46

Governmentality, 54, 407

"Grasping" an utterance, 421

Grayling, A. C., 457n11

Greater versus immediate situation, 253

Green, Donald, 477n5

Greetings, instances of, 474–475n4

Grice, Paul, 400, 402

Grief, 108

Group identity, 327

Grünbaum, Adolf, 156

Gustafson, Donald, 460–461n8

Gutmann, Amy: *Identity in Democracy*, 1, 3, 190; on identity politics, 106; on individuals as ultimate referents, 484n14

Habermas, Jürgen, 92, 106, 456–457n10, 491n4

Hampshire, Stuart: on concept of action, 227, 468–469n1; on dialogue as negative thinking, 167; on empiricism, 468n13; on language, 224–225; on localizing effects of socialization, 466n9; and theory of justice, 42, 43, 83, 172–173, 443–444n1, 444n3

Hardt, Michael, 105, 449n4

Hare, A. Paul, 493n5

Harvey, David, 466–467n10

Having in common, 60

Hearing requiring listening, 172

Hegel, Georg Wilhelm Friedrich: on assertion and certainty, 448–449n1; on perception, 295, 414; on reason and its history, 12, 301, 447–448n7

Heidegger, Martin, 132, 182, 442n1

Heider, Fritz, 455n2

"Heteroglossia," 396, 401, 404

Heuristic value, 167

Historicism and anti-historicism, 8; choosing between, 166–173; and critique of where things stand, 174–179; and exceptions to the social, 170; and limits in social theories, 127; moderated historicism, 160–162, 457–458n13; and totalizing claims, 122–123, 148, 158–160

History: as immanent to human affairs, 113; relying on and denying, 139

Hobbes, Thomas, 28, 34, 48, 442–443n4, 446n2

Hornsby, Jennifer, 264, 471–472n6, 484–485n1

Human affairs: addressing human aspects of, 257–258; "as things stand," 113; and coming to know, 314; as courses of activity, 8; as essentially social, 173, 380; and history, 113; as immanently social, 9, 288; nonsocial instances of, 168–169; and objectivity, 315–318; practice as instance of, 356; referent of propositions about, 10; and relations among objects, 8; and standard logic of belief, 10; as tension-preserving, 301. *See also* "What is human about human affairs"

Humanities: concepts of truth in, 118; as dealing with agency-dependent realities, 297; intersection of, with social sciences, 117, 299

Humans: as agents, not things, 183; and being human, 383; being social as necessary condition of being, 442n1; born free, 78; changing terms of life, 331; depending on countless unknowable others, 294; mode of life of, 102; moral equality of, 172, 174; as "natural kind," 329; no laws possible about, 181; properties of being, 273, 329–330; as social before all else, 4–5, 7, 38, 52, 86; traits of, as individual, not collective, 97. *See also* Basic fact of sociality; Human affairs

Human sciences, 4; and agency-dependent reality, 323; beginning with people living together, 7; clarifying common object in, 4, 17, 18; discourse in, 291; distinguished from natural sciences, 117, 122; failing when avoiding questions, 297; impression of no essential unity within, 117; as knowledge-constituting disciplines, 305; object of, as dialectic, 293; as products of theorizing, 127–128; reexamining sociality and historicity, 89; relying on untheorized criteria, 289; as science, 298; shared reality of sociality, 432; as single field, 2, 89; sociological attitude in, 377; status of theory in, 6; synthesizing disciplines and, 319; theoretical controversy in, 8. *See also* Social sciences

Hypostatization, 138, 140, 141–142

Idealism, 101, 393–394

Ideal of universal exchange, 217

The Idea of a Social Science (Winch), 481–482n8

Idea versus expression, 116

Identity: attributable and self-asserted, 325; as fixed, 242; identifying with others presocially, 28; and identity politics, 106, 190;

Identity (*continued*)
    individuality of, 325; personal, 460–461n8;
    social identity, 231; spoiled, 326
Identity in Democracy (Gutmann), 1
Ideology, 8, 154–155, 456n6
Ignorance: and attitude of waiting, 274; nam-
    ing our, 267
Imagination and language, 30
Imagining the absence of imagination, 29
Immanence: criticism as immanent to subjec-
    tivity, 9, 379; how to read references to, 116;
    of law, 35; of politics, 54; of sociality, 4, 8,
    116; of work, 330–331
Immanent reading, 204, 376
Immature sciences, 163, 318–319
Immediate certainty, feeling of, 61
Immediate versus greater situation, 253
Incorrigibility, 199, 205, 462n1
Independent identities, 337–338, 348
Independent individuals, 4
Independent observation, 315–318
Indifference to others, 28, 79
Individualism: as authoritarian value, 166;
    as default model for failure, 218; as default
    position in social science, 287; and indepen-
    dence of mind, 248; versus sociality, 38–42,
    49–50, 207; and society, 106; and "taking
    into account," 387, 391; and views of dis-
    course, 409–412
Individuality, 8; emergent moments of, 82;
    language of, 2; logical conditions of moral,
    4; Marx on, 103; as moment of collective
    reflexivity, 322; as ostensible, 18; presuppo-
    sition of, in human sciences, 103–105; prior to
    sociality, 61, 250
Individual(s): immanence of sociality to, 4;
    independence of, 4; as an infinity, 97; as last,
    not first, referent, 7; as locus, 261; ostensible,
    419–420, 422–423; as system resources, 98;
    as ultimate moral claimants/referents, 1, 3–
    4, 7, 38
Inequality, limits on, 207
Information: Goffman's use of term, 325–326;
    information exchange model, 16
Inglis, David, 459n1
Ingredient sense, 485–486n3
In-itself-ness, 414–415
Insecurity/doubt: breakdown of rule of law as,
    85–86; in Rousseau's narrative, 77, 81–83;
    in society versus in nature, 81; as unable to
    explain society, 77, 86
Institution, 204–205, 486–487n1
"Institutional action," 216

Institutional fact(s): apparent coherence of, 364;
    constitutive and regulative rules and, 353,
    354; defined, 352; and practice, 353, 358, 363
Institutionalization of meaning, 321
Institutional order of society, 296
Institutional politics, 215
Instrumentalists, people as, 393
Intellectual work, 457n11
Intelligibility: and logic in human sciences,
    119; meaning of, 116, 118
Intentionality, 11, 184–185; and actions, 248,
    330; as applying uniquely to persons, 237,
    287; Emmet and, 210; interpreting, 385; and
    mental causes of action, 227; and natural-
    ism, 313; and objects of experience, 413; and
    "ongoing accomplishments," 229; as prop-
    erty of agency, 186; of reciprocal effect, 186;
    Sartre and, 209; skin as natural boundary to,
    220, 234, 337, 352; and taken-for-granted ac-
    tions, 197; in utterances, 397, 424
Interaction, 147, 282
Interchangeability of subject and object, 338
Inter-dependence: as external, 185; and inten-
    tional reciprocity, 186; meaning and impli-
    cations of, 185–188; sub-theoretical ideas of,
    61
Interdisciplines, 319
Internal relations, 144
Interpersonal behavior, 185, 190–191
Interpretation, 387; and self-contradiction, 116
Inter-subjectivity, 8, 184, 380; ambiguity of
    term, 185; and attitude of waiting, 340; dia-
    logue and, 406; exchange-based, 393–394;
    experience of, 346–347, 413–414, 419–422;
    as fact separately and together, 342; as folk
    psychology, 349–350; human sciences rely-
    ing on, 377; of life and situation, 324; Schutz
    on, 460n4
Intuition, reliance on, 7, 213
"Iron cage," 164
Irony, 41–42, 90–91; impossibility of, in social
    contract, 54, 90–91

Jay, Paul, 472n7
"John," eating with, 343–347
Jokes, 365, 491n3
Justice: as conflict, 83; emphasis of, on indi-
    viduality, 206; and game-defined solutions,
    45; judges and, 373; and judging just deci-
    sions, 42; and judicial punishment, 361; and
    neoliberalism, 217; Rawls's social structure
    and, 353; as right, 47, 166; Rousseau on rec-
    onciling, with utility, 35, 47, 50; under rule

of law, 96; as society itself, 58; within system theory, 487n3

Justification versus discovery, 165–166

Kafka, Franz, 126

Kahneman, Daniel, 38

Kant, Immanuel, 442–443n4

Kicking a football, 153

Kitcher, Philip, 157, 173, 456n9, 456–457n10

Knowledge: criticism and, 8; enacted, 60–61; expressive, value-related, 118; and knowable reality, 157; meaning of, 159–160; private and public aspects of, 419; "social stock of," 120; as special province of science, 319; types of, 457n11; understanding versus causal explanation, 122

Knowledge-constituting science of human affairs, 117, 298

Kuhn, Thomas, 310, 481–482n8

Labor: as "labor power," 110; "real subsumption" of, by capital, 106

Language: acquired in social context, 208; believing as a function of, 29–30; Bertrand Russell's notion of, 320–322; field-restricted, 118; imagining negation of society without, 29–30; of individuality and of agency in action, 2; inevitably failed representation of, 121–122; and intentions as motivating speech, 397; and interpretation, 388–389; and inter-subjectivity, 8; language-constituting rules, 158–159; linguistic communities, 120–121; logical contradiction in field-restrictive, 118; Marx on, 102–103; meaning as a function of, 320; as rule-governed, 426, 430; of scientific reports, 398; speaking and, 13, 121–122; vagueness of, 320, 398. See also Speech/speaking; Utterance(s)

Last person scenario, 272

Latour, Bruno, 254, 481n7

"Law of peoples," 56

Law prior to or immanent to society, 35

Lazarsfeld, Paul Felix, 310, 312, 457n12, 481n7

Learned sociality, 78

Learning, 391

Le Bon, Gustave, 104

Legislators representing society, 370–371

Lewin, Kurt, 415, 460n5

Life: as creating surplus of itself, 328; as essentially differentiated, 324; incessant totalizing activity of, 327; instances of, 329; as irreducibly generative, 331; irrepressibility of, 324; quality of, 249

"Life of the concept," 132, 137–138, 142, 144, 146, 165

Limits of theories, discerning, 127, 128

Limit subjectivity: and agency-dependent objects, 370; defined, 331–332; situation and, 335, 366, 381

Linguistic acts, 423

Linguistic communication, 423–424. See also Language

Literary theory, 116, 461–462n12

Location, 421; of an action, 331; of agency, 245, 316; of meaning, 193; of representation, 215; of thought, 260, 316

Locke, John, 470–471n2

Logic and intelligibility, 119

Logic of justification, 301

Lombard, Lawrence, 469n3, 474–475n4

Loss of veritable universe, 107–108

Lough, John, 448n8

Loyalty as authoritarian value, 166

Luckmann, Thomas, 356–357

Machlup, Fritz, 480–481n3

Madness and art as others, 103–104

Madness and Civilization (Foucault), 103, 336

Manifestations of sociality, 113

"Manifold relations," 187

Market: access to, 450n8; conditions set by, 368; marketplace of ideas, 317; Marx on labor power and the, 110; price-making money market, 216–217, 443–444n1, 450n9; scarcity and market-driven competition, 296

Marketplace of ideas, 317

Marriage ritual as practice, 364

Martin, Randy, 466–467n10, 484n10

Marx, Karl, 25; on alienation, 109; on concrete versus abstract labor, 125, 165; critique of capital, 101, 108–110, 217; critique of materialism, 101–102, 181–182; critique of political economy, 140; on "fetishism" of commodities, 460n6; and ideal of universal exchange, 217; on "manifold relations," 187; on social forces of production, 108–109, 461n10; on "species being," 102; "Theses on Feuerbach," 101–102, 108, 181–182

Masters, Roger, 80–81, 446n2

Materialism: absolutist, 157; Marx's critique of, 101–102, 181–182; and philosophy, 158; and scientific worldview in social science, 155–158

McCann, Hugh J.: on agency as mysterious phenomenon, 332; on agency in action theory, 239–240, 258; definition of human

McCann, Hugh J. (*continued*)
actions, 248, 455n3, 482–483n4; on temporally extended actions, 471n3
McHugh, Peter, 484n12
Mead, George Herbert, 233, 282, 394, 465n4
Meaning: as always deferred, 397; conditions and acts of attaching, 386; as continuous or strictly situated, 9; discovery and institutionalization of, 321; location of, 193; and meaningless things, 415; units of, in speech, 401, 405
Meaningfulness: of apprehension, 414; of discursive speech, 399, 411, 430; versus meaning, 388; in metaphor, 147; in sociology, 10
Mechanical solidarity, 294
Mechanism, sense of, 273
"Mediators," 254
Meeting of minds: agreement as, 59; based on fixed, inert object, 415; Blank experiment on, 415–419; as currency exchange, 322; as function of language, 320–321; impossibility of, 13; irony in, 41–42; modeling discussion on, 39, 59
Mele, Alfred, 477–478n6
Membership versus individuality, 153–154, 215
Memory: of move from nature erased, 82; persons operating largely through, 238; and "veil of ignorance," 44–46
Mental composition, 256–257
"Mentality," 109
Mental "system 2," 38
Metaphor(s): action as, 254, 273, 334; and competing propositions, 120–121; concepts as, 129, 146–148; confusion of, with subject/object exchangeability, 484n13; and discursive language, 116; and discursive sense as a field, 339; of materialist sociology, 158; models as, 452n7; as models for projects, 126; originary subjects as, 278; production as, 425; and projects, 126; in science, 452n7; self as, 254; social action as, 147, 273; substitution by, 126; surplus of meaning in, 462–463n2; theory as, 147–148; of timeliness, 246; truth and, 203, 462–463n2, 463n4; of war, 93; work as, 327, 402
"Metaphysical simples," 487n5
Methodological materialism, 457–458n13
Methodological option in social sciences, 313
Metonymic organizing principle, 273
"Me" versus "I," 233
Mind, 8; and mental composition, 256–257; mind-body problem, 330; relationship between action and, 212; as social and not

skin-bound, 213–214; subordination of self to, 233
Minimum wage, 110
Models: from agency-independent nature, 298; as constituting novel reality, 115; of exchange, 127; as formal and pure by nature, 114; limitations of, 115–116; as metaphors for projects, 126; of organization, 127; of rational action in topical discourse, 45; requirements for valid, 114–115; of social life, 112; units of analysis in, 114
Modernity, problem of, 106
Modern nations, 46
Momentariness, 341–342, 354
Momentous community of strangers, 295
Moments and their persons, 235
Momentum and exigency, 145–146
Money compared to speech, 322, 401
Monologue versus dialogue, 395, 405–406
Moore, G. E., 487n6
Moral discourse: human life as ultimate referent of, 3, 380, 437, 487–488n7; individuals as ultimate referents of, 1, 3, 7, 38, 206, 359, 484n14; moral content of promising, 366; and notion of a self, 265; and notion of the social, 265–266; as supra-disciplinary, 3
Morally right, the, 379
Motivation, 327; for irrational behavior, 477–478n6; motivational psychology, 215; of speech, 397
Multiplicity: discourse as a, 406–407; humans as a, 324; perspective of, 324, 325, 327, 331; power as reflexive, 106; speech/speaking as, 401
"Multitude," 45, 79, 100, 105, 214, 449n4
Murdock, Iris, 477n1
Murphy, Liam, 466–467n10
Music, playing, 381
Mutuality, 62, 166

Nagel, Thomas, 446n3; on altruism, 57, 62–64, 68–71, 236, 242, 247, 282, 336, 446–447n7; on ends and means, 393; on human activity and association, 85; on neoliberalism, 466–467n10; and self as closing gap between reasons and actions, 225; and social units, 446n3; on solipsism, 467–468n12; on standpoints, 456n4; on "structure" outside of individuality, 65; on timeless reasons, 57, 62, 65, 433
Nasty jokes, relation of audience to, 365
Nation: confusing society with, 89, 99; and exclusionist patriotic appeals, 94

Naturalistic perspective, 298; humanities and, 313–314, 319–320; objectivity within, 317–319; social sciences and, 313–315, 319–320

Natural language, statements in, 462–463n2. *See also* Language

Natural sciences, 298

Natural sciences model for human studies, 163, 165–166, 298; consequences of use of, 151–152; and differences in agency, 297; immature sciences, 163, 298, 318–319; and impact of observer biases, 117; knowledge-constituting fields, 156, 165–166; and observer and observed issue, 314–318. *See also* Complexity in social sciences

Nature. *See* State of nature

Need: expression of, as creating obligation, 69; subjectivity and, 188–189; and timeless reason to act, 63

Negation of society, imagining, 29–32

Negative thinking and theorizing, 167

Negri, Antonio, 105, 449n4

Neoliberalism, 115, 216–217, 296, 466–467n10

Networks model, 114

Nisbet, Robert, 1

Nomination and objectivity, 421–422

Nonhumans, 29, 33, 48, 214, 272, 275

"Non-Humean self," 259, 261

Noninstitutional politics, 215

Nonreductive sociology, 158

Non-rigid signifiers, 9

Normalization, 198, 313

Normativity, 274

Norm of justification, 139, 141, 143–144

Noticeability, 326

Nozick, Robert, 333, 470–471n2

Objectivity: in activity, 253; agency and, 77; content of thought as, 316; and human affairs, 315–318; meaning of, 18; and nomination, 421–422; objective conditions of knowledge, 308; and reliability of observations, 117–118, 299; of situated objects, 337–340; subjective objectivity of agency-dependent objects, 370; subjectivity versus, 8, 299–300, 288, 334–336

Object(s): as affecting versus effecting subjects, 189; of experience, 413–414, 421; as having no specifically referential value, 19; of orientation, 188; physical properties of, 420; relations among, 8; versus subject, 8

Obligation: belief progressing to sense of, 40–42; feeling of, as social, 70–71; finding an, 70–71; to interpret meaning, 272

Observations: observer and observed issue, 314–318; reliability of, 299; unbiased, 117

Occasions, 367–370, 375

Ollman, Bertell: and internal relations, 479n1, 482n1; on logic of individuality and of sociality, 441n2; on mental activity, 451–452n3; on social as human, 290–291

Olson, Mancur, 466n9

"Ongoing accomplishments," 253, 274

Ontology, 16

Oppositional division, 324

Order: as authoritarian value, 166; of discovery and of justification, 17, 138–139, 141; of presentation and of justification, 2; of waiting, 396

"Ordinary affairs," 392

Organic solidarity, 172, 294

Organizational model(s): of action, 123–124; concept of social in, 127

Orientation, 270

"Original position" of selfless impartiality, 58–59

Ostensibility, 408; of individuality, 18, 65, 75; and products of theorizing, 136

Others: "alter," 183–184, 188; inter-subjectivity and, 393–394; as irresistible action-salient facts, 218, 271; and last person scenario, 272; as nonhuman, 271; an other among others in general, 294; pain of, 78–79; presence of distinct, 348; as properties of agent's situation, 238

Pain of others, 78–79

"Paradigm case," 128

Paradox(es), 10, 47, 197–198

Parsons, Talcott: and collective intentionality, 481n5; and conditions of rational action, 487n3; and economic rationality, 479n11; and interpenetration and institutions, 177, 486–487n1; on 1960s student movement, 98; on social action and social system, 455–456n3; on socialization of children, 99; and system of action, 477n3, 482n1; system theory of, 97, 352–353

Particular will(s): in absence of sociality, 44; and domination, 106, 152; and fairness, 487n3; finding basic principle of unity, 35; inequality and, 26, 43, 207; and intelligibility, 401; limiting powers of, 207; momentary suspension of, 171; and notions of freedom, 92; relative strengths of, 282; Rousseau's conception of, 82; rules and, 353; situations and, 332–333; society transcending, 353;

Particular will(s) (*continued*)
　　subjectivity of, 332; tension of, with general
　　will, 88, 96, 106; and utility, 166
Party to an occasion, 367
Passage from nature to society, 26
Passionate reason, 483n6
Patriotism, appeals to, 94
Peacocke, Christopher, 471n4
Pears, David, 476–477n10
Pedagogy, 158, 221
Perception: product of, 337; versus "sense" and
　　"understanding," 324; and sense-certainty, 414
Performances in discourse, 407–409
"Personal advantage," Rousseau on, 82
Personal identity, 460–461n8
Personality as resource, 97
Persons: as instrumentalists, 393; operating
　　largely through memory, 238; people among
　　people, 164; personhood (agency) versus
　　person (agent), 213; as possessing but mor-
　　ally inert, 237; possessing selves, 236–238;
　　as universes, 380; uses of term, 460–461n8,
　　470–471n2. *See also* Identity
"Perspective of the social," 205
Phenomenology, 13; of action, 469n3, 484n13;
　　"as things stand," 113; and going to work,
　　368; Hegel's, 453–454n10; of practices,
　　486–487n1; and ramifications of Rousseau's
　　demonstration, 27, 84, 93–94; of vanishing
　　objectivity/subjectivity, 341–342
Philosophy: of action, 58, 164; analytic, 482n9;
　　ignoring concept-users as social beings, 5;
　　inadequate to ostensible objects, 57; natural-
　　istic, 311; of process and in process, 476–
　　477n10; and ramifications of Rousseau's
　　demonstration, 93; of science, 317; of social
　　sciences, 461–462n12
Pity, 27–28, 83
"Play of structure," 125
Point of view, 394–395
Politic, the, 379
Politics: and absolutist materialism, 157; dis-
　　course and, 56–57, 93–95; and distortion of
　　science, 156; excluding reference to society
　　of equals, 44–45; and failures of process or
　　representation, 43; as immanent to human
　　affairs, 54; institutional and noninstitu-
　　tional, 215; as irrational collective behavior,
　　296; and justice, 38; and ordinary affairs,
　　392; and play of power, 104–105; and reason,
　　98, 104; and social facts, 38, 42, 88
Politics of Friendship (Derrida), 461n10
Popper, Karl, 452n4
Positive science, 456–457n10

Positivism, 97
Post-capitalist democracy, transition to, 106
Postmodernity, Foucault and, 105
Post-societal sociology, 459n1
Post-structuralism, 432, 456n8, 461–462n12;
　　and critique of human sciences, 288; and
　　critique of the theory of the sign, 101, 163,
　　448–449n1; and definition of "criticism,"
　　379; and immanence of sociality, 108; and
　　Rousseau, 112, 432; in sociology, 281
Power: versus authority, 35, 50, 96; of custom,
　　287; as reflexive multiplicity, 106
"Practical ensemble," 113, 187
Practicality, 48
Practice(s): distinguishing from other social
　　facts, 354; general and particular, 371; of
　　"I do" in marriage service, 364; versus in-
　　stance, 363–364; and instances of conduct,
　　355; as institutional fact, 352, 355–356, 363;
　　as interpenetrating roles, 353–354; as irre-
　　ducible sociality, 355; justification of a, 358–
　　361, 370–373; as object of consensus, 356;
　　promising as a, 362; reconstituting itself as
　　an object, 370; relation of, to its instances,
　　357–358; and rules, 357, 363, 371–374; scien-
　　tific, 157; situation and, 356–357; and weak
　　notion of society, 356
"Practico-inert," 281
Pragmatics, 198, 201, 415
Pre-deliberative confidence in speaking, 46
Pregnanz, 403
Premature closure in discourse, 44
Premise of human history, first, 103
Pre-philosophical discourse, 4
Presence versus attribution, 414
Pre-social: agentic self as, 223–224; first con-
　　vention as, 85; individuality, 77, 103, 229;
　　individuals acquiring social knowledge, 60,
　　390; individuals engaging in social action,
　　223–224; individuals imagining social knowl-
　　edge, 88, 90, 93; instances of intentionality,
　　432; newcomers and infants, 98–99; personal
　　experiences, 391; sense of obligation, 70; state
　　of being, 28, 31, 78, 85
Pre-theoretical notions, 4, 254, 293; of consen-
　　sus, 356; defined, 6, 254; of essential sociality,
　　213, 279, 433; intuitions, 241, 247, 432; of
　　nonhumans, 220; of self, 254, 264; of self and
　　agency, 241; of situation, 332, 341; of struc-
　　ture of action, 260; versus sub-theoretical
　　notions, 247, 293
Prevalence and social facts, 49
"Price-making money market," 216–217
Primary groups, 107, 282

Primitivism, 318

Private ownership and forces of production, 108–109

Procedural justice, 45

Production: and human affairs, 103; social forces of, 108–109; "society of producers," 106, 109–110; of speech, 424; of theory, 291

Progressive democratic polity, 37

Progressive imperatives, 166

Project, sociality as an ongoing, 198

Promising as a practice, 362–367

Properties of being human, 273, 329–330

Propositions: as contents of thought, 410; intelligibility of, 119–120; propositional knowledge, 457n11

Psychology, 298, 393–394, 409

Pure reason and reflection, 104

Putnam, Hilary, 297–298, 479n4, 482n2

Quality of life, 249

Quasi-concepts, 217–218

"Queen of Hearts" (Carroll), 126

Quine, W. V., 402

Rabelais and His World (Bakhtin), 395

Radical physicalism, 330

Radical utilitarianism, 51

Ramsey, Paul, 1

Rationality: accompanied by irrational reaction, 318; in action, 225, 231–232, 234, 479n11; conditions of, 171; defined by actor, 329; degrees of, 169–170; meaning of, 253; models and, 125–126, 216; rational agency model, 114; rational choice theory, 478n7; requirements of, 274; in social sciences, 274; symbolic aspect of, 333

Rationalization of commerce, 217

Rational organization, 124, 458n1

Rawls, John: on "comprehensive doctrines," 117, 157; on "desire" to be a just person, 437; on essentially institutional facts, 363; on "law of peoples," 56; on "original position," 44, 296; and practice, 178, 353, 355, 362–363, 489–490n14, 490n15; on practices and rules, 357, 373–374; on reasoning and norm of reciprocity, 122; and Rousseau, 170–171; on "social structure," 353; on state of nature, 442–443n4; and use of term "institution," 486–487n1; and use of term "practice," 371–372; and "veil of ignorance," 79

Reaction, 184

Reading: and confidence of audience in text, 314; and imagining negation of language, 29; immanent, 204, 376; in the mood of writing, 108, 291–292; and passive readers, 244–245; and a "text," 479–480n5. See also Social contract narrative of Rousseau

Realism, 157

Realm of freedom, occasion as, 369

"Realm of necessity," leaving, 77

Reasonableness over rationality, 319

Reason(s): for action, rational and nonrational, 269; versus causes, 38; critical versus positive, 320; fear that reason is in peril, 158; immediacy of, 247; privately held, 267; reasoning across difference, 95

Referents of moral discourse, individuals as, 1–2

Reflection: and immanence of work, 330; and modernity, 106; as object to itself, 138; unified objects of, 257

Reflexive course of activity, 58

Reflexive endlessness of topical discourse, 13, 17

Reflexivity, 327; displayed by object itself, 422; how to read references to, 116; and immanence of work to life, 330; and individuation, 295; substituting for self-reflection, 287–288

Regressive denial, 107

Regularities and social fact, 49

Regulative rules, 353–354

Relation(s): of accountability, 407; among people, 189–190; between people and things, 189–190; between subject and object, 338; units of analysis as, 114

Relativism, sociology and, 111

Reliability of communication, 15

Religious sentiment and sociality, 101–102, 181

Repetition and self-generation, 327–328

Re-presenting/representing: action, 220; ambiguities, 405; by historicists, 122; human affairs, 115, 238, 433; of life as lifeless, 143; of object as concept, 133, 135–136, 138; of purported reality, 140, 169, 238, 333, 433–434; the social, 45; social organization, 122; theoretical location of, 215

Reproducibility, 216

Republican ideal of social contract, 34, 35, 50

Rescher, Nicholas, 305, 476–477n10, 477n2, 480n2

Research: and exclusionary rule, 198; ironical, 203; meaning of "research process," 199–201; versus theory, 198

Reservation, right of, 367

Resistance to theory, 18, 126, 134, 140, 143, 325

The Resistance to Theory (de Man), 461n10

Responsibility and the self, 265

Responsiveness, 121

Riffaterre, Michael, 479–480n5

Right of reservation, 367

Rigid designation, 325–326

Robertson, Roland, 459n1

Rosenberg, Alexander, 181, 465–466n7

Rousseau, Jean-Jacques: on human intentionality, 355; and meaningfulness, 399; and modernism/postmodernism, 112–113; on society as not merely a collection of individuals, 214. *See also Social Contract* (Rousseau); Social contract narrative of Rousseau

Ruben, D. H., 457–458n13, 460n8, 486–487n1, 487n3

Rule(s): constitutive versus regulative, 353–354; defining a practice, 358; and generalization, 211; as institutional facts, 353; language-constituting, 158–159; of observation and inference, 159; and practices, 357, 363, 371–373; rule-governed practices model, 114, 211, 354–355, 423; rule of law and social contract, 24

The Rules of Sociological Method (Durkheim), 97, 307

Rumsfeld, Donald, 79

Russell, Bertrand, 320–322, 400, 402

Sacred right, 47

Said, Edward, 122

Sandel, Michael J., 464–465n3

Sartre, Jean-Paul, 1; on "being in a situation," 75; on the dialectic, 290; on history, 209; on humans as a "multiplicity," 324; on humans as consitutively situated, 50; on Nazis in Paris, 105; on "need" and "the living totality," 460n5; on negation of the negation, 452–453n8; on permanent actuality of human relation, 209; on "practical ensembles," 113, 187; on the "practico-inert," 281; on "totality," 483n9

Satire, bans on, 491n3

Saussure, Ferdinand de, 13, 396, 480–481n3

Scarcity and market-driven competition, 296

Schick, Frederic, 111

Schutz, Alfred, 460nn4–5; on inter-subjectivity, 460n4; and social rationality, 463–464n5, 478n7; on space connecting actors and objects, 460n5; on structure of relevance, 218; on understanding, 122; on "we-relationship," 449–450n6

Science: normalcy of a, 310; restricting and regulating work of, 173; "science studies," 156–157, 481n7

Searle, John, 111; on collective intentionality, 489n13; on consciousness, 155–156, 456n8; on effect of mortality on self, 470n7; on gaps between reasons and actions, 225–226, 242, 255, 469n2, 484–485n1; on institutional facts, 489n13; on intentionality, 469–470n5, 491–492n6; on "irreducible notion of the self," 255; on mind and brain, 476n8; on "non-Humean self," 259, 265–267, 469n4; on playing chess, 489n13; on rationality and agency, 473–474n3; and "rationality in action," 13, 265, 469–470n5; on "scientific" conception of world, 155; on self, 228, 230, 239, 256; on speech, 177, 423–429, 493n4; on student smoker, 249–250; on weakness of the will, 477–478n6

Secondary associations, 282

Second Discourse (Rousseau), 27–28

Secular sociology, drive to establish, 117

Self: as abstract presence, 236; actions based on, 239, 242–243, 246; and actor, 421; of the actor, 223–224, 260; agentic, 64, 158, 224–225; allowing for moral considerations, 255; alternatives to, 234–235, 263; blame and the, 265; combining with theory of action, 226–227; concern for, 27–28; as continuing and stable presence, 230; doing versus being social, 223–224; as emitting activity, 263; and gap between reasons and undertaking, 231, 236; and intentionality, 230, 255, 265; as marker and reminder, 229, 242; as meaningful, 239; and mind, 233, 255; as motivated from within, 226; needs of, as "someone's," 71; operating theoretically, 259; opposition between society and, 61–62; as pedagogical, 221–222, 255–256; as possessed but morally active, 263; as possessed by a person, 236–238; as pre-theoretical, 254; as reserved for actor, 262; as rhetorical, not conceptual, 248, 250, 255; Searle on, 266–268; as separate from what is personal, 67; as storehouse of past and future reasons, 235; structure of the, 231; and sub-theoretical intuition, 255; superordinate, 236–237; as sustaining context of reasons, 230; taking account of others, 226; tying to biological longevity, 226; value of reference to, 241–242. *See also* Agency

Self-abstraction, 128

Self-concepts, 56

Self-conscious criticism, 8

Self-correcting marketplace of ideas, 317

Self-critical reflection: as applying uniquely to persons, 287; and historicism, 148, 172; and priority of life, 134, 137–139; theory without, 166; unavoidable and immediate, 130

Self-differentiation, 325

Self-generation, 327

Self-knowledge and knowledge of others, 24

Self-referring endlessness of topical discourse, 13

Self-reflection: as course of activity, 58; Goffman on, 326; Habermas on, 106; instantiation of a model as, 115; and modernity, 106. *See also* Self-critical reflection

Sense: of action, sub-theoretical, 247; of versus belief in equality, 60; of believing, 73; and certainty, 295; of versus fact of, 237; ingredient, 485–486n3; meaning of, 116; versus "perception" and "understanding," 324; of the social, 193; of society, 293; of truth, 203; of truth of a statement, 201–203; weak sense of society, 356–357; of world, 336

September 11, 2001, attacks, 359

"Shameful defects," 325

Shapiro, Ian, 477n5

Shared identity, 277

"Shared meaning," 184

"Shared representations," social facts as, 212–213

Sheehan, James J., 182

Shwayder, D. S., 239

Sign(s): critique of the theory of the, 101, 163, 448–449n1; indicating termination of theorizing, 127; of a practice, 373; self as discursively mobile sign, 242; as unit of meaning, 116

Simmel, Georg, 459–460n3

Simon, Herbert, 316

Simulations, 458n2

Situated agency, 248; and self, 253, 351

Situated objects, 335–336; as active, 337; humans as, 166, 220–221; as momentary, 350; objectivity of, 337–340; subjectivity of, 336

Situated others as things, 270–271

Situation(s), 331; action as function of, 234; and actor, 271; and agency-dependent or agency-independent reality, 323–324, 332; assigning values to, 351; and communication, 332; constant form and variable content, 366; and context, 216; of eating with "John," 343–347; evaluation of, and decision to act, 260; as fundamental to idea of agency, 248; general theory of, 234–236; immediate versus greater, 253; as internally related to life, 332, 343, 350; invoking but not creating rules, 369; joined with life, 369; as limit subjectivity of course of activity, 335, 381; and momentariness, 342; "negotiating" a, 243; and occasion, 367–370; as ongoing

accomplishments, 381; ordinary, 367; and person-specific mental state, 349; positive sense of, 343–351, 369; and practice, 351, 356–357, 373; promising as, 331, 364–366; rethinking concept of, 251, 252, 266; as self-identical across subjects, 349; separated from will, 333–334; situated agency, 248, 253, 351; socially facilitating, 393; subjective aspect to, 252; total life and total situation, 238; and tragedy, 341; transcendental aspect of, 176–178

Skepticism, 315

Skin as natural boundary, 150; to agency, 152, 293, 329, 353, 356; contradicting activity across bodies, 151–152, 346–347; in a football game, 153; to intentionality, 220, 234, 337, 352; of mind and agency, 215; and personal identity, 190

Smelser, Neil, 466n9

Soames, Scott, 482n9, 483n6

Sociability, basis for, 28, 442n2

Social, the, 23–24, 190; acting versus being social, 38; as axiomatic in human sciences discourse, 287; and collective experience, 123; as a course of activity, 42, 400, 433; difficulty in identifying, 183; and doing versus being, 223; Emmet on theoretical status of, 209–210; essential incompleteness of, 15; exceptions to, 170; historicist and anti-historicist meanings of, 167; humans as essentially social, 32; as ideal of orderliness, 205; immanence of, to human affairs, 116; as incorrigible, 205; as inherently ambiguous, 11; as instance of "organization," 164; inter-dependence and, 187; as irreducible, sub-conceptual, 39; knowing oneself as social, 57; as latent idea, 193–194; as modifier of terms, 69; need for interdisciplinary agreement on, 5; need to clarify meaning of, 23–24; as object of theory, 6, 183–195; as obvious, 194; ontology of, 258; perspective of, 205; as quality of "agency," 213; sense of, 193; taken for granted historiographically, 304; as theoretically primitive, 190, 205; universality of, 294. *See also* Basic fact of sociality

Social action: altruism and, 66; as course of activity, 271; as "oriented in its course," 146; and self, 232; and "taking others into account," 184, 218–219, 229, 241, 262, 269, 349; unavoidably metaphorical in use, 147; Weber on, 146–147, 218, 270

Social beings acting badly, 76

Social construction of reality, 356

Social Contract (Rousseau), 27; Durkheim on, 96–97; and "Geneva Manuscript," 80, 443n5, 447n5; Parsons on, 97–99

Social contract narrative of Rousseau: as allegory, 28, 34, 47, 77, 87, 91–94; as answering need to defend society, 36; and appeal to experience, 48; arguing against human nature and force, 47; attempting literal reading of, 27, 35–36, 51, 55, 81–84, 88–90; basic concept of, 25–27; chronological method of, 35–36; "clauses" of, 86–87; considered as an essay, 25; contract as ontological condition, 94; contract not "formally pronounced," 87; as default position, 35; as demonstration, 51, 92–94; effect of, on readers, 31–32, 55–56, 79, 84; and equality, 58, 339; five conditions for truth of, 88, 89–90, 171; and human intentionality, 355; as implying loss of memory, 82–83; and impossibility of imagining life outside society, 172; and juridical concept of contract, 34; language communities and, 121; Masters on, 80–81; motivational tendencies seen in, 81; narrative as essential part of, 34; as neither true nor fictional, 34; as presentation of theory, 52–53; proper approach to reading, 89, 91–92; as providing immediate sense of truth of the social, 79; and radical distinction between society and state of nature, 25–26; readers of, unable to imagine negation, 28–29, 107; reconciling justice and utility, 35; seen as totalitarian or Romantic, 96; and society as founded on equality among people, 28; and society as perpetual state of emergency, 89; statement of problem answered by, 80; as "useful fiction," 31, 33–34

"Social facilitation," 97

Social fact(s), 38, 178–179; agency as, 434; and agency-dependent objectivity, 456n8; ambiguity as, 319; Brodbeck on, 461–462n12; as coercive things, 353; continuous self-reference as, 447–448n7; cooperation as, 382; deference as, 197; as distinguished from nonsocial facts, 178–179; distinguishing practice from other, 354; Durkheim on, 8, 49, 111, 353, 446n5, 480–481n3; as external to what people do, 176; first convention as, 448n8; Goffman on, 446n5; intentionality as, 297, 397; irreducible, 103; knowledge of, 280–281; language as, 321, 390; politics and, 38, 42, 88; predicates applying to, 169; prevalence and, 49; versus psychological facts, 448n9, 457–458n13; regularities and, 49; rules as, 354; as "shared representations,"

212–213; in social sciences, 315; as subset of institutional facts, 489n13; and symbols, 465n4; theory as, 105; thing-like, 8; Weber on, 388; Winch on, 281. *See also* Basic fact of sociality

Social identity, 231

Sociality/society, 8, 25, 30; as an activity, 25; always moving beyond, 11; attempting to imagine negation of, 29; as autonomous form of life, 287; as basic and irresistible, 47; cannot be explained by insecurity, 77; cannot perceive nature from within, 27; can only be indicated, 292; cessation of course of activity as other to, 77; versus collective life of nonhumans, 214; versus community, 1; as community of volunteers, 35; conceivable only as in flux, 197; confusion of, with aggregate or nation, 89; as contingent, 48–49, 172–173, 186; as course of activity, 186; defining, 289; difficulties of theorizing, 163–164; as discursive resource in sociology, 114; distinguished from other groups, 164, 191; as distributed sensibility, 77–79; equality at base of, 28, 44, 56–57; existence and value of, 33–35; as having no determinate form, 95; historiography of, 281–283; as human kind of freedom, 47; as immanent, 61; as immediate sense shared by all, 52; versus individualism, 38–39; and individuality, 250; as interpersonal behavior/interaction, 190; as irreducible, 42; as irresistible, 47; and justification, 74; knowledge of, 61; law prior to or immanent to, 35; momentary performances of, 354; as necessary association of equals, 77; necessity of distributive justice to, 171; necessity to defend idea of, 36–37; as negation of its negation, 77, 95; as negation of nature, 31, 95; not distributed or normative, 384; as an ongoing project, 198; as only workable point of view, 8; passage from nature to, 26; as pervasive, 191–194, 197; as predicate, 381; as preserved by reading the whole in each of the parts, 290; primitive forms of, 31; as prior, 2, 37, 57, 78; "reasonableness" over "rationality" in, 95; reduction of, to analytical units, 289; as reflexive without prospect of completion, 13; seldom formulated as concept, 2; as self-reflective entity, 326; as shared object in human sciences, 2; "sharing" as expressing, 60; of speaking, 400; versus state, 1; as sub-theoretical basic fact, 31; as taken for granted, 197, 205; trivializing of, 191–194, 199–201, 205–206; as ultimate referent of discourse, 44; as uniquely shared object of human sciences, 288; use of terms, 25; as virtual, 12. *See also* Basic fact of sociality

Socialization, 189; of members, 354

Socially facilitating situations, 393

Socially valid ideology, 139

Social movement, study of, 203

Social organization, 204; formal and informal aspects of, 124, 127; re-presenting/representing, 122

Social perception, 455n2

Social psychology, 123, 281, 415, 457–458n13

Social sciences, 302; Brodbeck on philosophy of, 461–462n12; effect of Rousseau on, 96; as insufficiently mature, 298; and naturalism or humanities, 313–314, 319; and quantitative and qualitative methodologies, 122; as relying on received notions, 295; scope of application for, 151–152; socially alienated discourse within, 151–152; social psychology, 123, 415, 457–458n13; as trying to encompass conflicting perspectives, 152–153; use of "person" within, 153. *See also* Complexity in social sciences; Human sciences; Sociology

"Social stock of knowledge," 120

Social structure, 353

Social system as source of control, 97

Society. *See* Sociality/society

"Society" (Nisbet), 1

"Society and Poetry" (Ramsey), 1

"Society of producers," 106, 109–110

Sociology: contracted empirical research in, 310; Lazarsfeld on, 481n7; meaningfulness in, 10; as regulating social terms, 9; and relativism, 111; as a "scandal," 122; and subjectivity, 112; Weber on, 215, 270. *See also* Social sciences

Sokal, Alan, 158

Solidarity, 37, 39–41, 44

"Someone": and discursive speech, 430; as universal category, 62–66, 68–71, 76

Sontag, Susan, 78

Sosa, Ernest, 484n11

Sovereignty, 46

Species, humans as, 465–466n7

Speech/speaking, 397; acts of, 425–427; as altruistic, 74; ambiguity in, 398; as continuation of sociality, 321–322, 428; in contrast with language, 13, 321; conversational, 173; and "conversational implicature," 400; "fixing," 321; and group identity, 326; as having its own momentum, 14; intelligibility and meaning in, 400–404; as multiplicity, not

plurality, of utterances, 401; for oneself, 177; as rule-governed, 426; and units of linguistic communication, 423. *See also* Language; Utterance(s)

Spencer, Herbert, 442–443n4

Spivak, Gayatri, 105

Spoiled identity, 326–327

"Spontaneous contribution," 124

State and society, 1, 104

"State" of being, 93

State of nature: imagining a, 33–34, 172; as inconceivable, 48, 85–86; move from, erased from memory, 82; as negation of society, 36, 55; no threat of return to, 84; not negation/other of society, 27, 77, 86; as opposed to culture, 117; passage from, to civil state, 26; "primitive act of confederation" leading out of, 26; radical distinction between society and, 25–26; social beings not yearning for, 86; society no protection against, 93

Strawson, P. F.: on actors as social beings, 332; on philosophical tradition, 5; on priority of the social, 250; on the social, 208–209; on society/sociality as immanent, 53, 61, 66, 183, 445n10; on thought and action, 247

Structural constraints, 187–188

Structure model, 114, 260

"Structure of relevance," 218

Student movement of 1960s, 98

Sturgeon, Scott, 457n11

Subjectivity, 18; agency and, 186–187; of animate subject versus inert objects, 188–190; apprehensive, 413; constant change in, 252–253; within course of theorizing, 128–129, 133–135, 140–142; critical self-reflection and, 135; encountering another subjectivity, 337–338; as essential to but not within a theory, 116; how to identify, 212; and idealism, 101; imposed on objects, 189; inauthentic, 142; as irreducible to individual mentalities, 323; as lives dependent on lives, 145; modeling, 126; versus objectivity, 8, 299–300, 288, 334–336; and objects of experience, 413; orders of justification and discovery in, 138; with otherness, 294; prior to interpersonal connection, 186; pure, 210; questions of meaning of, 116, 118; revalued as "hard science," 134; Sartre and, 210; as separate from activity, 142; and situated objects, 336; across situations, 333; social aspect to, 252; in sociology, 112; without subject(s), 7, 19; validity of concept of, 334; volatility of, 333

"Substantive rationality," 269, 390, 457n11, 480n2

Sub-theoretical, the, 69; moving from, to explication, 7; versus pre-theoretical, 293; sub-theoretical objectivity, 140, 137, 294

Sub-theoretical sense of sociality, 4; as always latent, 6; American attempts to clarify, 295; as indeterminate, ultimate referent, 6–7; as test of human sciences theories, 293; and validity of agency and subjectivity, 333–334; weakness of models depending on, 432

Suddenness, 72, 73–75, 140, 345

Superordinate self, 235–236

Superstition, 318

"Supreme head," 164

Surprise, 345, 482n3

"Sweetness" of commerce, 217

Synthesizing fields, 319

System/system theory, 114; and basic fact of sociality, 100; collective behavior in, 98; membership and agency in, 97; pre-socialized individuals in, 98; and social contract, 97–98; "social" in, 204–205; strain in, 98–99; theorizing as part of, 131

"Taking account" of others, 218–219, 223–224, 229, 241, 349; being human as, 384; and individualism, 387; nonhuman others, 271, 275–277; and self reserved for actor, 262; and situation, 243; taking account of one, 273; taking another's point of view, 394–395; Weber on, 270

"Taking for granted," 197–198

Taking turns, rules and exceptions for, 196–197

Tautologies, 198

Taylor, Charles, 441n2, 464–465n3

Temporality, reconciling, 116

Tension, field of, 419

"Tension management," 325

Textuality, aspects of, 116

Text versus context, 116

Theories of action (alternatives to standard model): agency in, 247; altruism in, 67–69; comparing with alternatives, 244–245; and concept of the self, 224–232, 250; distinguishing subject from object, 334; distinguishing theory from heuristics, 240–242; Emmet and, 210–212, 457–458n13; extended, 235, 238; intentionalist, 215; and inter-subjectivity, 184; logic of, 255; may be no problem to solve, 267; and Parsons, 97; philosophies of, 58; positive theory, 355–356; reformation of, 259; theory of conditions, 221; and theory of mind, 478n10; utilitarian model, 333–334; validity of, 334

Theories of action (standard model), 256, 273; actors in, 272; altruism and, 65, 336, 433; audience for, 222; clarifying conditions of, 258–259; essential sociality depending on, 264; and focus on "behavior with a reason," 72; as general to universe of agents, 66; individualistic perspective of, 72, 232; initiating in, 346; intuition as sub-theoretical to, 264; Nagel on, 63; problems with, 234, 244–246, 256, 257, 332; as requiring external conditions/agency distinction, 332; self in, 221; subjectivity and objectivity in, 253; worth of, 274

Theorizing, 300; ambiguity in, 131–132; ambivalence in, 132–133; as being lost in the object, 128; beyond commitment to resistance, 140; commitment within, 128–130, 132, 141–142; as a course of activity, 132, 135, 141, 143; criticism and, 243; dedicated indifference to, 200; at discipline level, 199, 203, 206; and discourse, 291; as discovering a lost world, 131–132; as discovering its object, 140–142; dissolution of, 134; and historicism, 130; on human activity separate from sociality, 257; "intending itself," 142; justice, 207; and "life of the concept," 132, 135–136, 141; negative thinking as necessary feature of, 167; post-theoretical aspect, 128–129, 132, 135; product of, as merely ostensible, 142; rejection of, 199, 202–203; re-turning, 144–145; role of readers in, 244–245; self-confrontation in, 141, 142–143; of sociality, difficulties in, 163–164; suspension of concepts during and after, 129–130; and text as object for audience, 245; trying to find itself, 141; the unknown and unknowable in, 130, 135, 138, 141

Theory in contrast to theorizing, 131–138; and boundaries, 291–292; and course of activity and its negation, 165–166; and dialectics, 292–294; and propositions versus course of activity, 60; rejecting theorizing not same as rejecting theory, 198; theorizing as fundamental condition of theory, 433–434; theory as momentary outcome of theorizing, 245

"The Theory of the Novel" (Bakhtin), 395

Theory/theories: cannot teach or be taught, 301; challenges to, 158; comparing of, by shared object, 225; as crucial to constitution of knowledge, 163; excluding contradictory ideas from, 150; inevitable self-rejection of, 142–143; as instance of its own object, 172; literary cast to, 147–148; as metaphor, 147–148;

nature of, 116; not an order of knowledge, 139; as product of course of theorizing, 127, 136; publication of a, 134; of rational choice, 105–109; research versus, 198; of self and action, combining, 226–227; of theory, 300; as transcendent accomplishment, 142–143. *See also* Theories of action (alternatives to standard model); Theories of action (standard model); Theory in contrast to theorizing

Thing-like social facts, 8

Thought and language, 410

Timeless reason(s) for acting, 62–70; as abstract, 67; course of activity as expression of, 68; as essentially social, 64; and evidence of subjectivity transcending situations, 64; and justification, 73; Nagel and, 57, 64–65, 246; pain as, 79; for responsiveness, 121; and timeless response tendency, 65

Topical discourse: endlessness of, 13, 17; model of rational action in, 45; overcoming incompleteness of, 14–15

Torture, defense of, 359–360, 487–488n7

Totalizing, 482n3; as activity of life, 327; tendency of, in theorizing, 127; "totalization" versus "totality," 483n9; totalizing attribution, 326; totalizing claims, 122–123; totalizing language, 121; and truth of claims, 155

Transactional theory, 215

Trickling up formation of institutions, 356–357

Triviality, 461n11

Truthfulness as lack of further question, 118

"Truth" in regard to human sciences, 299; based on value yielded/received, 120–121; and contradiction, 118; establishing truth for practical purposes, 117–118; as internal to disciplines, 120; meaning of, 116; as opposed to natural sciences, 165; plausibility/"sense" as sufficient for, 119, 202; as post hoc property, 120; speaking and, 121–122; standard criteria for, 202

Turner, Ralph, 14

"Type concepts," 269, 324–325, 363

Ultimate referent of moral discourse: human life itself as, 3, 380, 437; individual person as, 1–4, 7, 38, 206, 265, 484n14; sociality as, 44, 173

Unavoidable questions, 7

Understanding: knowledge through, 122; versus "sense" and "perception," 324

Unified objects of reflection, 257

Unitariness, 362–363

Universalizing act of identification, 170–171

Utilitarianism: and basic fact of sociality, 57–58; and defense of torture, 359–360; and ordinary affairs, 392

Utility and justice: interest and right and, 47; means and ends and, 24; and principle of law, 90; Rousseau's reconciling of, 35, 94

Utility as value, 166

Utterance(s): of discursive speech, 399–401, 411–412, 420–421; effects of, 428–429; grasping of, 421; as instances of discursive communication, 428; never completed, 398; social validity of, 428; as speech acts, 422, 424, 429. *See also* Language; Speech/speaking

"Validity" in regard to human sciences, 299; validating norms, 139

"Value rationality," 269, 390

Value(s): concept of, 421; versus fact/truth, 151, 297, 479n4; immanence of, 275; institution-constituting, 352–353; motivational, 276; and "substantive rationality," 269, 390, 457n11, 480n2

Vanishing, dialectics of, 419–420

"Veil of ignorance," 44–46, 59, 67, 79

"View from nowhere," 205

"Virtual" and "actual" identities, 325

Virtually undertaking self, 225

"Virtual truth," 462n1

Vitality, principle of, 266

"Voice," 116, 166, 405–408, 412, 430

Waiting subjectivity, 341. *See also* Attitude of waiting

"War against terror," 93

War and basic fact of sociality, 100

War metaphors, 93

Warnock, Mary, 476–477n10

"War of civilizations," 94

"The way things stand," 9, 16, 113, 174, 303

Weak sense of society, 356–357

"We" as taken for granted, 78

Weber, Max: actor must be an agent in theory of, 272; on behavior and "its course," 477n3; on "corporate" form, 164, 296; and definition of "social," 386–387; on "imperative coordination," 164; and "law" of progressive rationalization, 125; on others as not distinctively human, 219; problems for, 390; on rational organization, 458n1; on social action, 146–147, 218, 270, 384–389; on sociology and social action, 215, 270; on "substantive rationality," 269, 275, 390, 457n11, 480n2; and "taking account," 387, 467n11;

Weber, Max (*continued*)
    and "type concepts," 269–270, 363, 482n1;
    on validity of scientific interpretations, 385;
    and "value question," 488n9
We-relationship, 449–450n6
"What interest demands," 47
"What is human about human affairs," 8, 17,
    102–103, 432; action theory on, 212–213, 274;
    and asking questions, 282–283; discourse
    and, 17, 409; in human sciences models, 114;
    as irreducible and nontrivial sociality, 380;
    as irrelevant, 299; lack of independence in,
    318; language appropriate to, 119; metaphors
    and symbols on, 121; and need for research,
313–314; negative answers to, 117; sociality
    and individuality in, 253; theorizing and,
    141, 142, 163
"What right permits," 47
Whitehead, Alfred North, 177
Williams, Bernard, 465–466n7, 468n13, 470–
    471n2
Winch, Peter, 280–281, 481–482n8
"Within" in relation to experience, 334
Wittgenstein, Ludwig, 447–448n7, 487n5
Work: as immanent to sociality, 330–331; in-
    ternal subject/object relation as, 338

Yeats, William Butler, 182

Michael E. Brown is Professor in the Department of Sociology and Anthropology at Northeastern University and former Professor of Sociology at Queens College and the Graduate School of the City University of New York. He is the author of *The Historiography of Communism* (Temple), *Collective Behavior,* and *The Production of Society* as well as coeditor of *New Studies in the Politics and Culture of U.S. Communism.*